The SAGE
Handbook of

Mentoring
and Coaching in
Education

The SAGE
Handbook of

Mentoring
and Coaching in
Education

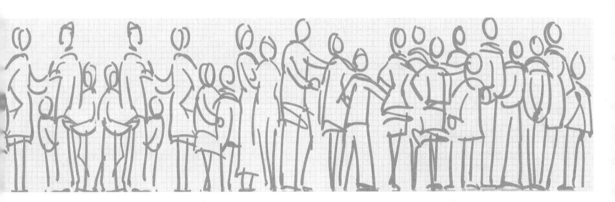

Edited by
Sarah J. Fletcher
and Carol A. Mullen

Los Angeles • London • New Delhi • Singapore • Washington DC

SAGE Publications Ltd
1 Oliver's Yard
55 City Road
London EC1Y 1SP

SAGE Publications Inc.
2455 Teller Road
Thousand Oaks, California 91320

SAGE Publications India Pvt Ltd
B 1/I 1 Mohan Cooperative Industrial Area
Mathura Road
New Delhi 110 044

SAGE Publications Asia-Pacific Pte Ltd
33 Pekin Street #02-01
Far East Square
Singapore 048763

Library of Congress Control Number: 2011924968

British Library Cataloguing in Publication data

A catalogue record for this book is available from the British Library

ISBN 978-0-85702-753-5

Typeset by Cenveo Publisher Services, Bangalore, India
Printed in India at Replika Press Pvt Ltd
Printed on paper from sustainable resources

Contents

About the Editors

Sarah J. Fletcher is Editor in Chief for the *International Journal for Mentoring and Coaching in Education.* She founded a Special Interest Group for Mentoring and Coaching for the British Educational Research Association and she runs on-line outreach lists promoting discussion about Mentoring and Coaching and Teacher Research. Her website at http://www.TeacherResearch.net chronicles her work as an international research mentor for teachers in diverse educational contexts.

Combining her passion for web-based te to enable teachers to elicit, represent and t their learning, Sarah has presented and research at leading international educational research conferen years. This has earned her a feature in the Gallery for the Carneg for the Advancement of Teaching and Learning as well as the of recognition for Teacher Learning by the Teacher Learni in the UK.

Enabling research between colleagues in universities and teachers in schools, in Japan and in the UK, represents enactment of her belief in integrating mentoring, coaching and action research. Now running her own consultancy company, Sarah was previously a senior lecturer for mentoring and coaching and prior to that she was trained as one of the first school-based mentors for initial teacher training.

[handwritten note: www. teacher research . net • journal article.]

Carol A. Mullen (PhD, The Ontario Institute for Studies in Education of the University of Toronto, 1994) is Professor and Chair, Educational Leadership and Cultural Foundations Department, at The University of North Carolina at Greensboro, North Carolina, USA. Since 2007, she has been serving in this administrative scholarly leadership capacity. She specializes in mentoring, diversity, and innovations in learning and professional development within the leadership field across higher education and K-12 settings, and she mentors new professionals and collaborates with scholars and practitioners. She teaches doctoral courses of her own design in scholarly writing and discourse, as well as dissertation proposal preparation and professional development. She was editor of the *Mentoring & Tutoring: Partnership in Learning* journal (Routledge/Taylor & Francis) from 2003–2011 [includes volume/issue *19*(1)]. Her authorships encompass more than 200 refereed journal articles and book chapters, 14 special issues of journals, and 14 previous books. Edited books include *The Handbook of Leadership and Professional Learning Communities* (2009) and *The Handbook of Formal Mentoring in Higher Education* (2008). Authored books include *Curriculum Leadership Development: A Guide for Aspiring School Leaders* (2007) and *Write to the Top! How to Become a Prolific Academic* (with W. B. Johnson, 2007). Among her numerous awards for research, teaching, and service, she received the American Educational Research (AERA) Award for her co-edited book *Breaking the Circle of One* from Division K's "Teaching and Teacher Education"; the President's Award for Faculty Excellence and the Women's Leadership Award, both from the University of South Florida (USF), Tampa, Florida; and the Florida Association for Supervision and Curriculum Development's Excellence in Teaching and Research Award. In 1997, she founded AERA's Special Interest Group Mentoring Mentorship and Mentoring Practices, serving as its first chair. In 1999, she established the Mentoring for Academic Writing program for AERA's Division C, "Learning and Instruction" and coordinated this initiative, which also thrives. She then founded USF's New Faculty Mentoring Program for which she was the Faculty Mentoring Director. Dr. Mullen serves as President of the National Council of Professors of Educational Administration (NCPEA) (http://www.emich.edu/ncpeaprofessors/) in 2012–2013. Her department and school are institutional members of both the NCPEA and the University Council for Educational Administration (UCEA).

Notes on Contributors

Tadashi Asada is Professor of Human Sciences at Waseda University, Tokyo, Japan. His academic field spans Educational Technology, Educational Psychology and Pedagogy (Teacher Education, Self-Concept, Lesson Study, Action Research and Mentoring). He regularly presents his research at international research conferences including BERA and ECER. His research largely focuses on mentoring for teachers' ITE and CPD, particularly with regard to the practice of 'kounai ken', the main form of on-going teachers' professional development in Japan. He has been collaboratively researching mentoring in schools in Japan and in the UK with Sarah J. Fletcher since 1999.

Natalia Buckler, PhD, is Principal Research Manager for the Centre for the Use of Research & Evidence in Education, UK. She has worked on projects sponsored by the National College, the Training and Development Agency, the Paul Hamlyn Foundation, and the Qualifications and Curriculum Development Agency. She is a former language teacher whose work was with children and adults and her professional experience includes teacher training and programme design. Her doctorate is from the Hertzen Pedagogical University in Russia.

Suzanne Burley is the Academic Leader for Teacher Education and Professional Learning at London Metropolitan University and has oversight and strategic leadership for all initial teacher training and teacher professional learning and development. Suzanne has worked extensively in the area of initial teacher training running the PGCE English with media/drama course and managing the secondary initial teacher-training programme at the University. She was also Academic Leader for Continuing Professional Development within Education for 3 years. She taught English, media and drama in London secondary schools for 18 years and has first-hand experience of the ways in which education in London has developed and changed over the last thirty years.

Sonya Clark, MA, is a training coordinator for the Department of Communications at Alabama State University (ASU) in the US and co-coordinator of the Department's internship programme. Clark has a master's degree in management and human resources management. She is currently a doctoral student in the Educational Leadership, Policy and Law programme at ASU.

Philippa Cordingley, MA, is founder and Chief Executive of the Centre for the Use of Research & Evidence in Education (CUREE), UK. As adviser to the Department for Education and national government agencies, she developed national support programmes to promote research and evidence-informed practice. She led CUREE team projects that fostered development of the evidence-based National Framework for Mentoring and Coaching. Other projects include generating innovative practical resources for engaging practitioners in research. She is founder of and professional adviser to the National Teacher Research Panel, and she serves on national steering groups for research projects.

Gary M. Crow, PhD, is Professor and Department Chair of Educational Leadership and Policy Studies at Indiana University, Bloomington, Indiana, USA. His research interests include school leadership and school reform, leadership development, and professional identities. His most recent book is *The Principalship: New Roles in a Professional Learning Community* (with L. Joseph Matthews) (2009). He co-edited the *International Handbook on the Preparation and Development of School Leaders* (2008) and *Handbook of Research on the Education of School Leaders* (2009). He is former president of the University Council for Educational Administration.

Dannielle Joy Davis, PhD, Associate Professor of Educational Leadership, Policy, and Law at Alabama State University, USA, earned a doctorate at The University of Illinois at Urbana–Champaign in educational policy. Her interdisciplinary, K-20 research examines organizational policy and practice, including marginalization in education. She has done research in Ghana, South Africa, and other countries. She has published over 20 journal articles and book chapters. In addition to holding writing workshops for faculty, she leads a Write on Site group.

Helga Dorner, PhD, holds a doctorate in educational science and is currently Instructor at the Center for Teaching and Learning at the Central European University, Budapest, Hungary. She joined validation teams of the European Union-funded research and development projects eTwinning, Calibrating eLearning in Schools project, and Knowledge Practices Laboratory project. She researches issues of mentoring and social learning in online environments and professional development. She consults with educational organizations, publishes articles, and presents at conferences.

Michael Gasper was a teacher for 27 years, 17 as a Head, in a range of schools covering children aged 4–13 before moving into Early Years and Multi-Agency research. Joining the Centre for Research in Early Childhood (CREC) in 1998, he co-ordinating the team led by Prof Chris Pascal and Prof Tony Bertram evaluating the the DfES Early Excellence Centre programme between 1999 and 2004, where his interest in mentoring for leaders crystallised. An Early Years consultant since 2006 he has also worked in teams delivering the National Professional Qualification in Integrated Centre Leadership (NPQICL) as a mentor, facilitator and assessor for CREC and SERCO provider teams with the Universities of Warwick, Worcester, Wolverhampton and Birmingham City University. Gasper believes passionately in the value and importance of mentoring and coaching for leaders in early years, particularly of multi-agency settings.

Susan Groundwater-Smith is an Honorary Professor in the Faculty of Education and Social Work at the University of Sydney where she convenes the Practitioner Research Special Interest Group. A significant part of the group's work is the establishment and ongoing maintenance of the Coalition of Knowledge Building Schools <ckbschools.org/Coalition_Home.html> a hybrid network of schools including both privileged independent schools and those facing the most challenging circumstances. The Coalition has been operational for over a decade, with practitioners making an important contribution to both the professional and academic literature. Over a number of years she has been involved in similar communities with a commitment to teacher agency, professional learning and engagement with action research. She is also Adjunct Professor of Education at the Utrecht University of Applied Sciences where she works with likeminded academics with a particular emphasis upon investigating student learning outside the classroom; specifically in Museums.

Catherine Hansman, EdD, is Professor and Director of graduate programmes in Adult Learning and Development at Cleveland State University, Ohio, USA. She is a Cyril O. Houle Emerging Scholar in Adult and Continuing Education Scholarship recipient and, in 2005, was awarded a Distinguished Faculty Award for Research by her University. She is former chair of the Commission of Professors of Adult Education and President of the American Association for Adult and Continuing Education. Her research encompasses learning in adulthood, mentoring, communities of practice, low-income adult learners and diversity issues. Her research interests are reflected in the two books she has edited, *Understanding and Negotiating the Political Landscape of Adult Education* (with Peggy Sissel), and *Critical Perspectives on Mentoring: Trends and Issues*, in book chapters published in numerous books, and in her articles published in various journals, such as *Adult Education Quarterly, Adult Learning, Journal of Adult Basic Education, Community College Review,* and the *Journal of Excellence on College Teaching*.

Andrew Hargreaves, PhD, is the Thomas More Brennan Chair in Education at Boston College, Massachusetts, USA. He founded and was co-director of the

International Centre for Educational Change at The Ontario Institute for Studies in Education of the University of Toronto, Canada. Previously, he taught primary school and lectured in English universities, including Oxford. His *Changing Teachers, Changing Times* (1994) and *Teaching in the Knowledge Society* (2003) received outstanding book awards from the American Educational Research Association, the American Libraries Association, and the American Association of Colleges for Teacher Education. His research interests include the emotions of teaching and leading, educational change, and the sustainability of change and leadership in education.

Sandra Harris, PhD, is Professor and Director of the Center for Doctoral Studies in Educational Leadership at Lamar University, Texas, USA, where she teaches about social justice and qualitative research. Formerly, she served as a teacher, principal, and superintendent in public and private schools. She has authored or co-authored 15 books, including *Examining What We Do to Improve Our Schools: Eight Steps from Analysis to Action* (2009), and over 100 academic articles. She researches issues of doctoral study, administrator preparation, and school environments. She is one of two recipients of the 2011 National Council of Professors of Educational Administration's Living Legends award.

Andrew J. Hobson, PhD, is Research Professor in Education at Sheffield Hallam University, UK. His main research interests relate to the experiences of and support for beginning teachers. He has led several research studies in these and other areas, including the large-scale 'Becoming a Teacher' project (2003–2009) and the 'Modes of Mentoring and Coaching' study (2010–2012). Recent publications include: Hobson *et al.* (2009) *Navigating Initial Teacher Training: Becoming a Teacher* (Routledge); Hobson (2009) 'On being bottom of the pecking order: beginner teachers' perceptions and experiences of support' (*Teacher Development*); Hobson *et al.* (2009) 'Who withdraws from initial teacher preparation and why?' (*Educational Research*).

Juanita Johnson-Bailey, EdD, holds the Josiah Meigs Distinguished Teaching Professorship. She is Director of the Institute for Women's Studies and a professor in the Department of Lifelong Education, Administration, and Policy at The University of Georgia, USA. Her book *Sistahs in College: Making a Way out of No Way* (2001) received the Phillip E. Frandson Award for Literature in Continuing Higher Education and the Sadie T. Mossell Alexander Award for Outstanding Scholarship in Black Women's Studies. She is co-editor of *Flat-Footed Truths: Telling Black Women's Lives* (1998) and *The Handbook of Race in Adult Education* (2010).

Joellen Killion, MA, is the Deputy Executive Director of Learning Forward, formerly the National Staff Development Council. Joellen's work focuses on improving professional learning for all educators. She is a frequent contributor to the *JSD* and *Teachers Teaching Teachers*, Learning Forward's premier magazine and newsletter for teacher leaders and coaches. Joellen has extensive experience in professional development. At Learning Forward, she has led a number of initiatives related to examining the link between professional development and student learning. She has extensive experience in planning, design, implementation and evaluation of professional development both at the school and system level. She is the author of a number of books related to coaching and professional development.

Po-yuk Ko, PhD, is Director of the Centre for Learning Study and Assistant Professor in the School Partnership and Field Experience Office, Hong Kong Institute of Education, Hong Kong. She has authored or co-authored 7 books and over 20 journal articles. Her research interests encompass learning study, teacher professional development, mentoring, and Chinese language education. She has led large-scale projects involving over 200 local schools that support teachers in developing mentoring skills, improving student learning, and using action research.

Frances Kochan, PhD, is Wayne T. Smith Distinguished Professor at Auburn University, Alabama, USA, where she was education Dean. Her research interests are collaboration across individual, organizational, and cross-system levels, with focus on mentoring, leadership, and culture. She has published over 60 articles and book chapters, edited 10 special issues, and co-edited a book series on mentoring. She has been on the executive boards of the Holmes Partnership, the International Mentoring Association, and the University Council for Educational Administration where she served as President.

David Leat is the Executive Director of the Research Centre for Learning and Teaching (CfLaT) at Newcastle University and Professor of Curriculum Innovation. His research interests include teaching thinking, enquiry based curriculum, coaching and professional learning. He is the series editor for the 'Thinking Through …' books, which include editions for many secondary subjects and the award winning 'Thinking Through School'.

John Chi-kin Lee, PhD, is Vice President (Academic) and Professor of Curriculum and Instruction at the Hong Kong Institute of Education, Hong Kong. Formerly, he served as education Dean and a professor at the Chinese University of Hong Kong. He has co-authored and co-edited over 20 books and chapters and over 150 journal articles. In editorial support capacities, he has done work for such premier journals as *Mentoring & Tutoring: Partnership in Learning, Teachers and Teaching,* and *Educational Research and Evaluation.*

Mun-ling Lo, PhD, is Adjunct Professor at the Hong Kong Institute of Education where she was Director of Field Experience and Head of the Department of Curriculum and Instruction. Her pioneering work has contributed to teachers' professional development in over 200 primary and secondary schools in Hong Kong. A founding member of the World Association of Lesson Studies, she was elected its first president. Her research interests cover mentoring, school–university partnership, professional development, and curriculum evaluation.

Rachel Lofthouse is Head of Teacher Learning and Development (Education) in the School of Education, Communication and Language Sciences (ECLS) at Newcastle University. She is the degree programmes director for both the M.Ed in Practitioner Enquiry and the Masters in Teaching and Learning, and course leader for PGCE Geography. Her research interests include professional learning, practitioner enquiry and innovative pedagogies.

Joanne Moles is Co-Director of a Master's programme in mentoring and has considerable experience lecturing in Physical Education, Teacher Education and Mentoring with the University of Limerick. She acts as an external referral examiner for teaching practice. Her reasons for involvement in mentoring reflect commitment to education and a concern to position it in a way which is concerned for all individuals. She recognises the challenge of heightening awareness in mentor teachers as a powerful influence on young lives. She values the development of teachers as genuine professionals who can defend their practice both philosophically and empirically." to "Her research interests focus on teachers' perceptions allied to a commitment to professionalism.

Janet Oti PhD, is the MA PCET Pathway Leader and Module Leader for the MA Mentoring module at the University of Wales Newport. She has over 24 years of teaching experience and lectures across the school of education spectrum from undergraduate to post graduate programmes, including ITT (PCET) and supervision of MPhil and PhD students. She gained her PhD in Education from Cardiff University which examined a specific policy and practice and the conflicts of power and control, including the effects of change management etc. Mentoring and its importance in the FE/PCET sector is a main research interest.

Norbert Pachler is Professor of Education at the Institute of Education, University of London. His areas of academic interest and expertise include foreign language education, new technologies in teaching and learning (with a particular emphasis on mobile learning, e-learning and technology-assisted language learning) as well as teacher education and development. He has led on, and contributed to various research projects, teaches on Masters programmes and supervises a number of research students. He has published widely and has extensive expertise as journal editor. Since 2007 he is the convenor of the London Mobile Learning Group (http://www.londonmobilelearning.net), an international, interdisciplinary group of researchers from the fields of cultural and media studies, sociology, (social) semiotics, pedagogy, educational technology, work-based learning and learning design. He is also an experienced external examiner across teacher education, Masters and doctoral level provision.

Joseph T. Pascarelli, EdD, is Professor Emeritus at the University of Portland, Oregon, USA. He is former President of the International Mentoring Association and former co-chair of the American Education Research Association's Special Interest Group Mentoring Mentorship and Mentoring Practices. His specializations embrace leadership, mentoring and organizational development in K-12, higher education and human service sectors. He has consulted in the USA and different countries. Presently, he is establishing a global research agenda on mentoring and co-editing a series titled *Global Perspectives on Mentoring*.

Cathy Pomphrey was a languages teacher for twenty years in London secondary schools before transferring to London Metropolitan University. She has extensive experience of providing teacher education at all levels, including the design and delivery of programmes for mentors and coaches.

Cathy has researched and published in the fields of languages and language awareness as well as teacher education and has presented papers at national and international conferences in these areas. She now works as an education consultant specialising in teacher education and languages education.

Hal Portner, MEd, received a Masters in Education from The University of Michigan, Ann Arbor, USA and a CAGS from The University of Connecticut. He is a former public school teacher, administrator, and member of the Connecticut State Department of Education. He helped develop the Connecticut State Department of Education's teacher mentoring initiative and coordinated the State's Institute for Teaching and Learning and partnered with school districts to deliver programmes for teachers. He developed and facilitates "Mentoring and Professional Development," one of the core online interactive education courses offered by Western New England University leading to a MEd degree in Curriculum and Instruction. He has authored over 50 articles and books including *Mentoring New Teachers* (3rd edition, 2008), *Being Mentored: A Guide for Protégés* (2002), *Teacher Induction and Mentoring: The State of the Art and Beyond* (2005), and *Workshops that Really Work* (2006).

Mary H. Portner earned a BA from Smith College, Massachusetts, USA. After 25 years as a graphic designer, she enrolled in the Springfield (MA) College Graduate School, and is currently pursuing a Masters in Education. She works as an education consultant and presents workshops. She has taught for Americorps and Springfield's inner-city public schools, coordinated classes for the Massachusetts Comprehensive Assessment System, and taught and administered in an early college high school programmes for low-income students. She has also taught high school English.

Kara Provost, PhD, is Professor of Academic Enrichment and Coordinator of the First Year Honors Program at Curry College, USA. She earned a master's degree and doctorate in English from The University of Minnesota, specializing in American poetry, Native American and African American literature, and composition studies. At Curry, she teaches composition and interdisciplinary Honors seminars. She has published widely in literary magazines. *Nests*, her first book of poetry, was followed by a collection published in 2011.

Maureen Rajuan, PhD, is a teacher trainer in the English Department of Achva Academic College of Education in Israel and English as a Foreign Language teacher at Hebrew University, Jerusalem. Her doctorate is from Eindhoven Technical University, The Netherlands. She published a book titled *Student Teachers' Perceptions of Learning to Teach as a Basis for Supervision of the Mentoring Relationship* (2008). Previously, she was a high school English teacher and counselor. She translates manuscripts in Hebrew and researches teacher and peace education.

Jean Rath, PhD, has worked in a variety of post-compulsory education settings including community education and universities in the UK, New Zealand and Australia. She is the Manager Researcher Development at the University of New South Wales, an Honorary Research Associate at the University of Oxford's Learning Institute and Deputy Editor for the International Journal of Mentoring and Coaching in Education. Her research interests include evaluation of academic development programmes, use of creative texts to investigate culture and the self-in-process, participatory research practices, and reflective practice as a professional development process. She is involved with several research projects focussing on academic identity, academic practice and the experiences of doctoral students, research staff and new academics.

Ana Redondo is Senior Lecturer in Education and Subject Leader of a Secondary PGCE in Modern Languages at the University of Bedfordshire with significant experience in Teacher Education and CPD across Primary and Secondary education and in working with secondary languages teachers in partnership schools. Before that she taught at the Institute of Education, University of London.

Prior to moving into HE, she led the learning of languages from a senior position in the secondary phase and headed several Modern Languages departments.

She has co-edited *Teaching foreign languages in the Secondary School: a practical guide* (London: Routledge, 2007) as well as a Special Issue of *Support for Learning*, the *British Journal of Learning Support* on 'Inclusive approaches to teaching foreign languages' (NASEN, 2005). Her scholarly interests are in the fields of the global dimension in education, international citizenship and developing appropriate pedagogies in technology-enhanced contexts.

Christopher Rhodes, PhD, worked in schools and colleges for 14 years prior to taking up a post in higher education. He was previously the Director of Postgraduate Studies in the School of Education at the University of Wolverhampton and currently holds the post of Senior Lecturer in Educational Leadership in the School of Education at the University of Birmingham, UK. He has a long standing interest in the professional learning of staff and in the development of leaders in particular. His research and writing have included a strong focus on mentoring and coaching as mechanisms to promote this learning. His recent work has been associated with exploring staff succession management in schools.

Richard J. Reddick, EdD, is Assistant Professor in Educational Administration at The University of Texas at Austin, Texas, USA. His research focuses on the mentoring and community engagement of Black faculty members. He was a K-12 teacher and student affairs administrator at several colleges. A former editor of the *Harvard Educational Review* and current editorial board member of the *Journal of Student Affairs Research and Practice*, Dr. Reddick's co-authored and co-edited books include *Legacies of Brown: Multiracial Equity in American Education* (Harvard Education Press, 2005) and *A New Look at Black Families* (6th ed., 2010).

Dale H. Schunk, PhD, is Professor in the School of Education at The University of North Carolina at Greensboro, North Carolina, USA. He was the School's Dean from 2001 to 2010 and was a long-standing department chair at Purdue University. He is an educational psychologist who researches the effects of social and instructional variables on cognition, learning, self-regulation and motivation. Among other books, he has authored *Learning Theories: An Educational Perspective* and co-authored *Motivation in Education: Theory Research and Applications*. He co-edited, with Barry Zimmerman, the *Handbook of Self-regulation of Learning and Performance* (2011).

Geraldine Mooney Simmie lectures in education at the University of Limerick. She is Course Director of a Master's programme on mentoring in education and She has an academic leadership role in developing the school placement experience for student teachers and is Co-Director of a structured PhD programme in education. Her recent research commitment has been to number of European

Comenius projects over the last few years including CROSSNET and GIMMS http://www.gimms.eu/. Geraldine's research interests lie in the fields of comparative education, curriculum as cultural and political text and the continuing education of teachers. Her doctoral study is a comparative study of upper secondary science and mathematics education between the Kingdom of Norway and the Republic of Ireland.

Jane Skelton, received her doctor in Curriculum and Instruction from Boston College, Chestnut Hill, Massachusetts. Her research integrated critical discourse analysis in the examination of micropolitics and literacy coaching as a school reform strategy. She is currently working as a district curriculum director in Malden, Massachusetts.

Pete Sorensen is a Lecturer in the School of Education, University of Nottingham. Pete taught at secondary level in England for many years, working as a mentor from early on in his career and moving on to senior management roles with an emphasis on teacher education and professional development. He has also lectured in science education at the University of Cape Coast, Ghana and Canterbury Christ Church University, England. At Nottingham he has taken on leadership roles on the flexible PGCE course and in partnership and mentor development. His research and publications have involved national and international collaborations in the field of teacher education, with an emphasis on collaborative practices, paired and multiple school practical placements and alternative routes into teaching.

Jenepher Lennox Terrion, PhD, is Associate Professor in the Department of Communication at the University of Ottawa in Ottawa, Canada. She studies the impact of peer mentoring, leadership development, family support, and training programs, and social capital. She has published in *Mentoring & Tutoring: Partnership in Learning, Studies in Higher Education, Journal of College Student Retention,* and *Journal of Management Development.* She serves on the editorial board of the *International Journal of Evidence Based Coaching and Mentoring.*

Sylvia Yee Fan Tang, PhD, is Assistant Professor in the Department of Education Policy and Leadership, Hong Kong Institute of Education, Hong Kong. She researches teacher education and development, and mentoring and the internationalization of higher education. She has published over 20 journal articles and book chapters, and contributed to the *International Handbook on Teacher Education Worldwide: Issues and Challenges for Teacher Profession* (2010).

Carl Towler has worked as a research associate and a teaching fellow within the Research Centre for Learning and Teaching at Newcastle University since 2008.

He completed a Master's degree in Education Research at Newcastle University in 2008 and has specialised in the analysis of video and sound recordings of learning related talk. Prior to joining the university he taught for 8 years and was Primary Strategy consultant for 3 years.

Shelley Tracey coordinates a teacher education programme for adult literacy and numeracy practitioners at Queen's University Belfast. Shelley has a special interest in engaging literacy and numeracy tutors in practitioner research to develop their professional identities and contribute to knowledge in an under-researched area. Her practice also focuses on developing the role of poetry in adult literacy learning.

Paul Watling has worked in the field of Community Development and Children's Services for over 25 years initially as a youth and community development worker in local government and also in the voluntary sector. He has managed multi-disciplinary teams in Birmingham and the West Midlands and led wave2 Sure Start Local Programme from delivery plan to designation as a children's centre. After completing the NPQICL pilot programme in 2005 and an MA in Leadership in 2007 at Pen Green he took the opportunity to become a freelance trainer and facilitator in children's services nationally working mainly with Children's Centre Teams.

Ken Young, PhD, received his doctorate in educational psychology from Baylor University, Texas. Currently, he is an Assistant Professor in the Center for Doctoral Studies in Educational Leadership at Lamar University, Texas, USA, where he teaches courses in adult educational theory, qualitative research, and quantitative research. Dr. Young's research and interests incorporate adult learning theory, ethics, cognitive epidemiology, and research methodology.

Michelle D. Young, PhD, is Executive Director of the University Council for Educational Administration and Associate Professor of Educational Leadership at The University of Texas at Austin, Texas, USA. Her scholarship focuses on how school leaders and policies can ensure equitable and quality experiences for all students and professionals. She received the William J. Davis award for the most outstanding article published in *Educational Administration Quarterly*. Her work has also appeared in journals such as *Review of Educational Research, Educational Researcher, American Educational Research Journal, Journal of School Leadership*, and *Journal of Educational Administration*. She co-edited the *Handbook of Research on the Education of School Leaders* (2009).

Editorial Advisors

Editors' Introduction

The SAGE Handbook of Mentoring and Coaching in Education is a leading source of theories and practical applications about mentoring and coaching. We offer readers an authoritative, engaging and useful text that maps state-of-the-art learning for discussion, critical engagement and application. As co-editors, we express our gratitude to our distinguished contributors who have described innovative research and promising practices they have personally initiated as well as experienced, reflected on and assessed. We would also thank SAGE for their support in managing this project for publication of our *Handbook*.

The terms 'mentoring' and 'coaching' are frequently used interchangeably in education contexts. Just as distinctions among different kinds of mentoring have emerged, so distinctions among different kinds of coaching are beginning to evolve. We have sought to represent convergences between mentoring and coaching practice as well as divergences in meaning where their use leads to agreement and overlap.

The knowledge base of mentoring in education has grown considerably in the last two decades on both sides of the Atlantic. The knowledge base of coaching in education is less well developed, largely because coaching has only come to the fore in education in the past decade, although it has a far longer history, like mentoring. Coaching has tended to focus upon the skills end of the learning continuum and its true potential as an open-ended learning activity is only now being realised. Gilbert Ryle (1949) has reminded us that 'good practice precedes the theory of it', and so it is with coaching, which is becoming widely practiced but is, as yet, undertheorised and underresearched. Nevertheless, research into coaching is underway in educational contexts and we have taken on the challenge of reporting salient coaching research alongside substantial research pathways into mentoring.

These chapters respond to the rapidly growing interest, which traverses both national and international research on schools, higher education and other educational contexts and disciplines within education. We aim to widen the conversational circle about mentoring and coaching theory and practice from our diverse work locations that span the globe. This *Handbook* offers the essential reference point for educators and those involved in educational provision. Chapters aim to provide readers with a unifying, cohesive picture of the past, the current and the perceived future era of mentoring and coaching.

Academics, internationally, are realising the potential of mentoring and coaching and developing research capacity among institutions' own teaching staff as well as in partnership with teachers working in schools. This interest is reflected by ongoing support for the British Educational Research Association's (BERA) Special Interest Group (SIG) for Mentoring and Coaching and the American Educational Research Association's (AERA) Mentorship and Mentoring Practices SIG. These SIGs, founded and coordinated by the co-editors of this *Handbook*, have grown robust and 'gone global' with sessions and e-seminars focused on mentoring and coaching across professions and national borders.

We are committed as contributors, editors and editorial advisers to present the evidence base and alternative worldviews in which concepts of both are untangled and substantiated. Importantly, educational capacity for learning institutions and relationships is facilitated through those we know to be 'scholar practitioners' who experience breakthrough ideas that are both theorised and enacted. We recognise that mentoring and coaching theory are not simple or uniform concepts but complex educational ideas that inevitably change because of their contextual dependency, philosophical rootedness and political idiosyncrasies. We also recognise that mentoring and coaching call for human agency activism that transforms institutions, relationships and individuals and that necessitate the collaborative work of change agents, educational professionals like our readers and ourselves.

Chapters in our *Handbook* focus on mentoring and coaching outline perspectives that have an international appeal, a provocative meaning and an immediate utility. As contributors, we all focus on mentoring and coaching for *learning*. We are aiming to move debate towards a worldview of interventionist education aimed at such crucial initiatives as professional support for all educators and students and social inclusion of all students and adults. All contributors were invited to respond to these editor-generated guidelines for shaping their content and writer's perspectives:

1 Provide contextual definitions of educational mentoring and coaching for education and give an explanation of why the form of professional learning that the contributor is writing about matters.

2 Explain the framework or theory the contributor is using to study, explain, or enact, mentoring or coaching for education.
3 Describe the role of policy or legislation on the mentoring or coaching context being explained.
4 Set out the effect on learning of the mentoring or coaching process/program/situation being described and identify the sources consulted for any claims made about the effects.
5 Describe practical application(s) that best demonstrate the topic, as in the processes or programs, which support the contributor's ideas and the broader frameworks of professional development, accountability, or other that serve or impede efforts.
6 Possibly use a metaphor or image to illustrate the author's concept, message, or topic of mentoring or coaching in educational terms.

We hope our readers will use this *Handbook* to add substance and clarity to their own mentoring and coaching work and to any new initiatives, including furthering construct developments and assessment practices. We have presented democratising challenges in these pages, with the goal of inspiring all of us to work towards promoting the success of all students, schools and professionals as part of our vision of an enriched global learning community. At the reader's fingertips are educational ideas, practices and tips that they can use to make a difference in educational terms. The contributions to this *Handbook* show how mentoring and coaching can be effective as a series of organisational and interpersonal relationships which connect with the values and attitudes, understandings and skills that characterise educational practice as *learning*.

REFERENCES

Rhyle, G. (1949) *The Concept of Mind*, New University of Chicago Press.

Overviews of Mentoring and Coaching

Mentoring: An Overview

Carol A. Mullen

CONCEPTIONS OF MENTORING THEORY

Mentoring is typically thought of as a personal, long-term professional relationship that deepens over time, with a ripple effect (Varney, 2009). Mentors' industry on behalf of their protégés produces a 'multiplying investment' in people's lives and communities (Moerer-Urdahl and Creswell, 2004). From this perspective, mentoring is, metaphorically speaking, an investment in the younger generation. When viewed alternatively as a developmental relationship that is sustained and valued for humanistic reasons, the root metaphor of mentoring changes to a journey. Mentoring as a journey encompasses both or all parties – implied is the notion that learning is open-ended, creative, and uncertain, and as well as subject to unknowns. While ways of understanding relationships vary depending on epistemological outlook, belief systems, and more, the idea I wish to foster is that mentorships are developmental, intentional, and generative. From this perspective, mentors foster critically supportive, nurturing relationships that actively promote learning, socialization, and identity transformation within their work environments, organizations, and professions (Johnson, 2006; Mullen, 2011a).

Theorized to involve more than the transfer of skills within dyadic (one-to-one) relationships, mentoring theories emphasize these value-laden ideas:

- an educational process engaging individuals and groups in reciprocal learning, networking, and sponsoring (Tharp and Gallimore, 1995/1988);

- a systemic reform strategy that builds capacity in formal and informal ways to provide assistance and support socialization (Crow and Matthews, 1998);
- a social justice perspective on mentor–mentee identity transformation with respect to cultural differences (Tillman, 2001; Young and Brooks, 2008); and
- a discovery tool for investigating sociocultural elements of international and diverse contexts (Kochan and Pascarelli, 2004).

Theoretically, mentoring encompasses different phases (Kram, 1985/1988; see also Chapter 6) and functions (Rose, 2003), and it has traditional and alternative meanings. Mentoring theory is an educational idea that is inevitably changing, situated, and partial because of its contextual dependency, philosophical rootedness, and political idiosyncrasies. As captured by the worldviews postulated in *The SAGE Handbook of Mentoring and Coaching in Education*, mentoring incorporates particular skills, values, and understandings, culturally based concepts, school contexts, adult and higher education contexts, inclusion, and research issues (see Sections 2 through 7). However, the points of view I express herein do not speak as a kind of general truth for the contributors to this text. Our mentoring experiences and backgrounds are differently situated and, as will become clear to readers, our lenses for viewing mentoring are pluralistic in that these do not amount to a single breakthrough idea or even consensual understanding of the educational process. As contexts framing this chapter, in addition to the, primarily North American, mentoring literature and chapters in this book, I have drawn upon research and experiences across public schools and universities in the United States.

Mentoring phases

Mentoring relationship phases are addressed in Chapter 6, which describes the operationalization of initiation, cultivation, separation, and redefinition.

Mentoring functions

Two major functions of healthy developmental relationships are psychosocial and career. Regardless of discipline and perspective, these functions are considered pivotal to any academic mentoring relationship or program. The career function has had more prominence because of the description of 'sponsorship, exposure and visibility, coaching, protection, and challenging work assignments', as well as professional ethics (Johnson, 2006) that become activated when mentees network and seek employment (Young et al., 2004).

The need for mentors to contribute to the psychosocial development of their protégés has been a more gradual unfolding, with recent attention on learners who are female, culturally ethnic, and nontraditional in other ways (Mullen, 2008; Tillman, 2001; Young and Brooks, 2008). Psychosocial functions incorporate role modelling, social acceptance, and counselling; the psychosocial dimension of mentoring is enacted when mentors actively listen, provide advice, and encourage development (Nora and Crisp, 2008). Psychosocial mentoring includes such benefits as friendship and emotional support, enhanced self-esteem, and confidence (Darwin, 2000; Hansman, 2003; Young et al., 2004). However, psychologists have proposed that the friendship element of educational relationships is a thorny issue due to the ethical dilemmas that mentoring can elicit (e.g., Johnson, 2006).

ORIGINS AND OF MENTORING THEORY AND ITS DISTINCTIVENESS

In the 1980s, Kram (1985/1988) established mentoring as a workplace model and it has since proliferated in such forms as social psychology, learning theory, adult theory, organizational development, leadership theory, and systems thinking. Mentorship historically involves training youth or adults in skills building and knowledge acquisition (Merriam, 1983), provoking the metaphor of mentoring as training. Technical mentoring involves the transfer of skills within authoritative and apprenticeship contexts whereas alternative mentoring questions hierarchical learning and favors new forms of socialization (Darwin, 2000; Hansman, 2003).

I believe that mentoring and peer coaching are often mistakenly interchanged even though some researchers have argued that they are similar because they share commonalities. Coaching, like mentoring, can be difficult to define, largely because these practices are multifaceted, ambiguous, and contextually driven (Gallucci, Van Lare, Yoon, and Boatright, 2010). Briefly, peer coaching, like mentoring, has been construed as a nonjudgmental and nonevaluative approach to professional development. While some theorists think of coaching as a type of mentoring, others see the exact reverse – that is, mentoring as a type of coaching. Coaching is informed by a unique set of principles and practices embedded within learning and instructional contexts (see Chapter 2). As another muddled entanglement, mentoring and induction concepts tend not to be distinguished, most notably at refined levels. Frequently, in fact, researchers and practitioners see mentoring (and coaching) as elements of induction theories and programs. Effective site-based induction programs are content-based initiatives in which new teachers are 'mentored' within a 'highly organized and comprehensive staff development process' (Wong, 2004: 107). However, more needs to be known on the theory and empirical levels about the role of 'instructional coaching', for example, especially given that it dovetails with a proliferation of district-wide reforms (Gallucci et al., 2010).

Mentoring is theory steeped and it is probably more developmentally based than coaching. Cornerstone tenets of mentoring are lifelong, humanistic learning, and reflection upon learning as well as social self-reflection by the engaged mentoring parties. *Humanistic mentoring*, which is integral to voluntary mentoring, focuses on 'care and nurturance' of the protégé over the duration of a long-term relationship (Varney, 2009: 128). Whether traditional or progressive, the learning relationship is sustained, although the character of it changes in the separation and redefinition phases once the relationship has been success-fully cultivated. The mentoring relationship is also intrinsically focused, with feedback geared toward deepened understandings and sensitive practices reflected within the learning process that includes uses of constructive criticism in writing and communicating. In its alternative forms, mentoring is a developmental human project that promotes identity growth, extending beyond pre-set goals, planned activity, and one-way learning. From this perspective, protégé and mentor alike are adult learners engaged in new learning, relearning, and unlearning in chang-ing organizational contexts that demand a new view of educational and other occupational careers not as hierarchical and static but as fragmented and in flux (Allen and Eby, 2007). They benefit from reciprocal learning, activism, and agency that change how they work with others and how they interface with their organizations to model new ways of interacting, learning, leading, and policy-making (Mullen and Tuten, 2010).

TRADITIONAL MENTORING THEORY

Traditional mentoring theory encompasses skills-based, goals-oriented learning passed down through generations. Professionals tend to carry out this work one-to-one in exclusive learning arrangements. Veteran teachers and school princi-pals, for example, mentor by nurturing, advising, befriending, and instructing, and they serve as advocates, advisors, and promoters. Accordingly, seasoned practitioners shape how novice personnel (e.g., newly qualified teachers) learn through professional development as part of a larger structure informed by school improvement and student achievement goals (Portner, 2008).

Traditional and alternative theories alike describe, to varying degrees, the principles governing the mentoring gestalt of places and people. Synergistic leadership (defined later) can be adapted to this broader framework of mentoring (see Mullen, 2011b, for a fuller discussion). Each theory is itself a philosophical framework for explaining human interaction, organizational structure, and cul-tural change. The alternative models identified (e.g., collaborative co-mentoring) share fundamental principles and core values that promote a view of mentoring as greater than the sum of its parts. The spectrum of traditional and alternative theories of mentoring is influential in the interpersonal arenas of learning, social-ization, and professional development, as well as the organizational functions of leadership, management, and preparation. Adult learning (e.g., lifelong learning) and feminist principles underscore some of these models (Hansman, 2003; see also Chapter 24), as do systems and instrumental thinking (Lick, 1999).

Mandated mentoring theory and US government policy

Mandated mentoring is at the extreme end of the prescribed spectrum of teaching and learning where the metaphor of mentoring as mandated prevails

(Mullen, 2011c). Mentoring newly qualified teachers is a reform strategy that US state agencies are prescribing. On the one hand, newly qualified teacher mentoring is a technical, evaluative activity rather than a high-quality professional development experience. On the other hand, policy expectations for mentoring help ensure that new teachers, most importantly, receive the support and assistance they often badly need. In fact, for many teacher mentors, policy demands frame professional development and set in place top-down expectations for school relations, including the work of experienced teachers with their new colleagues (Britton, Paine, Pimm, and Raizen, 2003). When policy is prescriptive about expectations for promoting teacher retention, for example, mentors tend to focus on classroom management strategies that address emotional barriers and curriculum knowledge deficits; when concern is about achievement, mentoring is typically utilized as a means for cultivating instruction and student learning (Portner, 2008).

Given the current policy climate, mandated mentoring has been given credence (Mullen, 2011c). This oxymoronic concept is associated with possibilities because it necessitates staff development for and by public school teachers, giving professional collegial learning importance and visibility. Mentoring along these lines can help schools to satisfy requirements related to induction and certification, teacher retention and performance standards, all while assisting novice teachers in their adjustment to a school's culture. While such mentoring seemingly reflects a higher commitment to new teachers, it introduces inescapable pitfalls. One such problem is the expectation of assigned mentors and protégés to heavily document their learning activity using prescribed templates that shape the direction of the mentoring work and interfere with progress. Importantly, mandated mentoring can complement voluntary mentoring but they should not be confused. Contrasting with voluntary mentoring, then, *mandated mentoring* is an educational reform initiative that compartmentalizes in mechanistic ways the goals and outcomes of mentoring, as well as the relational work of veteran teachers and novice teachers (see Chapter 20).

Voluntary as well as mandated mentoring build the productive capacity of people and organizations, but voluntary mentoring, transpired through informal, spontaneous, as well as creative communication, can enhance the development of the whole person (Varney, 2009). Required mentoring, formalized through program initiatives, is geared toward the systemic reform goals of school improvement and student achievement. It *requires* teachers to mentor and be mentored, and protégés are expected to make documented gains that may feel impersonal and evaluative. This kind of mentoring occurs when teachers are forced to commit to a relationship that is otherwise presumed voluntary, nonevaluative, and humanistic. In contrast, *humanistic mentoring* focuses on nurturing the mentee as a whole person within voluntary relationships (Varney, 2009: 128).

While the heightened expectations that accompany mandated mentoring could enhance veteran teachers' performance and improve organizational efforts, the voluntary spirit and integrity of mentoring can be jeopardized. To what extent voluntary mentoring relationships can be successfully formalized (in reality, regulated) depends on many variables. The personal connection between mentors and mentees is not replicable, and, moreover, organizations typically treat mentoring as an 'add-on' responsibility. This approach contradicts the sustainability goals of a mandated mentoring agenda.

The purposes and uses of mentoring have greatly shifted in the current policy context. Mandated mentoring and voluntary mentoring each have merits and valuable goals and, where thoughtfully facilitated, can even be implemented simultaneously. Conceptions of mentoring as a voluntary professional service have changed since American legislators launched accountability requirements for the supervision of new public school teachers. Policy initiatives focus on teacher induction as a primary solution to teacher attrition and quality deficits, citing the responsibility of veteran teachers in assisting newly qualified teachers to adapt to student diversity and other school climate issues (Feiman-Nemser, 1996; Portner, 2008). Since the 1980s, policies have spearheaded mentoring goals aimed at closing the achievement gaps of ethnic and socioeconomic *student groups* and making equitable resource distribution for low-performing schools (Luebchow, 2009).

Because intentional mentoring can positively affect retention and satisfaction with the profession, it is being harnessed as a resource to help meet state accountability goals. Governmental reform policies require mentoring programs for satisfying such goals through pay for performance and other compensatory incentives. However, the master teacher is not envisioned as someone who understands complexities of learning and who inspires growth in novice teachers (Wong, 2004); rather, some state governments cast the role of mentor as an instructional technician with specific credentials for fulfilling coaching and evaluative functions. *Mentor* is, to the states, a public school expert who has 'demonstrated mastery of the critical competencies for a job role' and the protégé is someone who possesses the required certifications and who is assisted by the expert to develop 'mastery of specific educational competencies' (North Carolina State Board of Education, 2009: para. 28).

State directives for public school systems require master teachers to success-fully mentor new inductees, teach low-performing students, and when feasible move to high-needs schools to provide critical support. Congress has set the bar, mandating that districts redistribute teachers and increase the salaries of those teaching in disadvantaged schools. Master teachers who are National Board certified are urged to instruct in high-need schools, with carrot-like incentives ranging from salary increases to better working conditions (National Board for Professional Teaching Standards [NBPTS], 2009).

The adaptation of mentoring as a mandated policy mechanism can turn mentoring into a mere achievement measure for schools for purposes related only to school improvement, accreditation, and testing. Changes in laws have established the role of systems thinking for schools and 'outside–in' accountability for student achievement goals. Mentoring is infused with leading, teaching, and supervising, and notably teacher evaluation (Mullen, 2005). Note the trend in this direction over time: the Carnegie Forum on Education and the Economy (1986) endorsed a view of classroom teachers as change agents and mentors supporting student achievement. The Carnegie Report led to the establishment of the NBPTS, which has infused mentoring expectations into the National Board process. National Board certified teachers are thus required to use their expertise in mentoring other teachers to become accomplished educators.

Former US President George Bush's No Child Left Behind Act of 2001 brought issues of mentoring – specifically professional development and collaboration among administrators, teachers, and parents – squarely into line with standardized testing and stronger accountability (US Department of Education, 2002). This program requires a highly qualified teacher in every classroom across America. Implying a direct correlation between student test scores and teaching quality, measures of teacher effectiveness and high-stakes testing have since flourished. The accountability context deflates opportunities for teacher growth and meaningful learning. Teacher mentors are expected to fulfill previously supervisory functions and are charged with such bureaucratic mandates as standardizing the curriculum and controlling teacher behavior within high-pressure testing environments. Rewards and sanctions are linked to student scores, school grade, and reputation.

Because mentoring summons notions of civic virtue and goodness, it is useful as a political tool. Rhetorically exploited, mentoring concepts (e.g., 'mentor teacher') have been co-opted and aligned with national standards. As one effect, policymaking has advanced technical mentoring in a contemporary guise; goals and processes of management have been resurrected as a source of empowerment. Within education, technical mentoring systems and processes have magnetic appeal, making it easier for mentoring to be mandated, not just formalized.

Mentoring sometimes has to be formalized, even mandated, or it simply will not occur. As documented, voluntary mentoring involves greater commitment and risk because the promised assistance does not always occur (Blake-Beard, 2001) and formal mentoring has yielded numerous benefits that include support for new professionals (Mullen, 2008). Thus, school teams formalize mentoring at the building level through programs, learning communities, and other avenues, in effect collaboratively deciding upon their performance expectations of veteran and novice staff members. Because some research has established that mentors and mentees prefer that mentoring processes be as informal (hence 'natural') as possible (Noe, 1988), leaders have been encouraged to build mentoring programs alongside those who will inherit them. While pitfalls can occur with both types of mentoring – required and voluntary – each has also been effectively fostered as well as combined.

Mandatory mentoring takes formal mentoring to another level, though, in that it is required by governmental policy. Because it is in an early stage of evolution, it remains to be seen whether mandated mentoring is a viable solution to teacher attrition, low student achievement, and negative school culture. What we do know is that mentoring in effective voluntary-required configurations can compensate for situations bereft of teacher bonding and collegiality, and replete with low morale and satisfaction (Varney, 2009).

No schoolwide mentoring process is free of concerns, regardless of the type(s) of mentoring that is adopted. Human dynamics complicate mentoring situations, rendering them unpredictable, and so any mentoring process will have blemishes. As Fullan (1999: 3) cautioned, dynamics can be 'designed and stimulated in the right direction but can never be controlled'. School teams that use mentoring theory to make educational policy potent for their context might find it particularly useful to experiment by creatively combining mandated mentoring elements and voluntary mentoring elements to tap into the benefits of each. By doing so, they may benefit from new networks that renew their learning community.

ALTERNATIVE MENTORING THEORIES AND PRACTICES

Alternative mentoring theory expands upon and even resists traditional mentoring theory, which is the underlying worldview of systems and policies that treat mentoring as a commodity to be traded and exchanged within a market economy (e.g., schools). While alternative mentoring theories in their plurality are budding in the educational literature, traditional mentoring theories remain dominant in the discourse. Mentoring change theorist Darwin (2000) argues that awareness of alternative mentoring is important for redressing this imbalance and transforming educational cultures. Alternative mentoring theories include collaborative mentoring (co-mentoring), mosaic mentoring, multiple-level co-mentoring, and synergistic leadership. To the contrary, technical (or functionalist) mentoring exemplifies traditional mentoring theory, assuming pervasive forms, such as apprenticeships, that perpetuate closed systems. Alternative and traditional mentoring concepts are ideologically disparate but overlap in theory and practice.

The historical and originating antecedents of mentoring have set the stage for the countercultural thrust of alternative conceptions. Alternative mentoring theorists critique traditional mentoring relationships and systems as developmentally limited and exclusive of diverse populations. Traditional mentoring theories are construed as having an underlying masculinist perspective that noncritically assumes the mentoring birthright of an entrenched power class (e.g., White males); normative ideologies perpetuate moral authority in areas that govern sexuality, religion, and citizenship. As a means of enabling social and intellectual capital along these lines, traditional mentoring sustains a biased class structure, facilitating only the psychosocial and career benefits of mentoring for some groups by some groups (Darwin, 2000). Critics have exposed paternalism, dependency, privilege, and exclusion in mentoring contexts. Alternative theories present a breakaway mindset from defunct hierarchical systems, disempowering relationships, and exploitative arrangements.

Democratic theorists wrestle with new worldviews that celebrate radical humanist conceptions of relationships and systems. These epistemologies underscore (1) collaborative and cross-cultural learning partnerships that are egalitarian and less role-defined, and (2) transformed learning organizations that model interdependence, inclusiveness, and openness (Hansman, 2003; Johnson-Bailey and Cervero, 2004).

Unlike functionalist mentoring approaches, alternative mentoring awakens theories and practices of empowerment that are critical about and mindful of uses and abuses of power, and that are steeped in nonauthoritative dynamics, progressive learning, and open solutions. Organizing principles are used to foster holistic development, cultural engagement, and institutional change. Mentoring as an equalizing force requires a commitment to ethical agendas involving power, virtue, and circumstance (Hansman, 2003). Intentional mentoring promotes critical care and fosters satisfying but challenging learning environments (Galbraith, 2003). While an ethic of care is associated with interdependence and interpersonal nurturance in educational relationships, 'critical care' is activist oriented, and dedicated to fostering diverse social spaces of learning (Antrop-González and De Jesús, 2006). Alternative learning contexts span mentoring networks, formal mentoring programs, professional learning communities, coalitions, alliances, cross-cultural mentoring, inquiry/writing groups, peer coaching, professional and political activism, staff development, and e-mentoring and virtual learning (Mullen, 2005). Through such conduits, mentors remedy archaic notions of education, support quality in student learning, mobilize underrepresented groups, transform closed systems, and problem solve within organizations that they are aiming to change.

Ideologies of alternative mentoring are value laden, promoting the values of collaboration, co-mentorship, democratic learning, humanistic mentoring, and shared leadership. Democratic learning can be formal or informal, with the team helping all members develop the desired knowledge and/or skills. Members participate in the democratization of learning through team building, setting such goals as identifying and resolving conflict. Teams and leaders facilitate shared leadership and collaborative decision making in ways that function democratically or autocratically (Mullen, 2005).

Institutional leaders who mentor in nontraditional ways strive to make a difference and concurrently learn from others (e.g., co-mentorship). They mentor beyond the demands of their position, seeking to educate mentees outside the supervisory or advisory context. In fact, psychologists describe mentorship as a superordinate function 'above and beyond' teaching and instruction. Alternative mentors take risks, experiment with ideas, exert influence, and confront adverse forces within workplaces and society. Mentors who are transparent provide feedback and elicit it, and seek understanding of the influence of their ideas on others while actively improving themselves. Moreover, the social justice advocates among them confront barriers that constrict access or learning for disenfranchised groups (Darwin, 2000), and they integrate a diversity of ideas and people in their mentoring and leadership (Irby, Brown, Duffy, and Trautman, 2002; Johnson-Bailey and Cervero, 2004).

Collaborative mentoring theory

Also known as *relationship co-mentoring*, collaborative mentoring is a proactive force that unites individuals or groups in a reciprocal, developmental relationship situated within a dynamic context for learning. This theory is founded upon feminist postmodern values that, when effectively operationalized, bring women and minorities into educational networks (Bona, Rinehart, and Volbrecht, 1995). A goal is to mobilize social equality among individuals of various statuses and ability levels, enabling productive synergy and solidarity (Kochan and Trimble, 2000; Mullen and Tuten, 2010).

Collaborative mentoring is key to the viability of think tanks, such as mentoring mosaics and cross-cultural mentorships in which vision, commitment, discipline, and synergy all play a role (Johnson-Bailey and Cervero, 2002). Co-mentoring theory is also evident within dyadic mentoring relationships, engaging adult learners through power sharing, turn taking, co-leading, dialogue, constructive feedback, collegiality, transparency, and authentic learning. When learning is reciprocal, mentors and mentees function as adult educators and learners (Galbraith, 2003). More powerfully, as partners in learning they overcome cognitive distancing, shedding the power-laden stigma of 'mentor' and 'mentee' (Mullen, 2005). Because co-mentors have deep personal and professional influence, their microcosmic actions can change their institutional cultures for the better.

Mentoring mosaic theory

A significant alternative conception of mentoring is Kram's (1985/1988) 'relationship constellation,' also known as mentoring mosaic (Tharp and Gallimore, 1995/1988). Even though network mentoring was articulated more than 25 years ago, it is only more recently affecting educational studies. The mentoring mosaic theory posits that members' shared interests and respective strengths activate peer interaction. Members who are primary mentors (e.g., recognized instructional leaders) and secondary mentors interchange roles as mentors and mentees, sponsoring the learning of all through a synergistic, flexible structure. This network is indispensable for cultivating peer mentors, compensating for the dissatisfactions of traditional mentoring and facilitating team projects

(Mullen, 2005). Indeed, if mentoring is defined more as communal learning than individualistic activity, then teams that extend to professional (and virtual) learning communities engage in nurturing, advising, befriending, and instructing. Within such energizing networks, distinctions between 'mentor' and 'mentee' blur as subject specialists, counselors, protectors, advocates, and more emerge. The camaraderie, interdependence, identity development, and ownership that this model supports underscore the value of how learning and mastery are achieved (process), not just what is learned (product) (Galbraith, 2003).

Multiple-level co-mentoring theory

Multiple-level co-mentoring theory underscores facilitating co-mentoring at various levels of an organization via school-based focus teams, study groups, and leadership (Lick, 1999). Serious research and inquiry aimed at reform initiates a mentoring process that is not limited to classrooms or certain groups. Social cultural systems must be deliberately reinvented and teacher resistance confronted through self-directed, authentic engagement.

Collaborative mentoring is essential to a climate of interdependence, commitment, and empowerment, as well as participative leadership. Principals, teachers, and staff decide what changes are necessary, and they spearhead and monitor them. Systems thinking, change management, instrumental methods, and co-mentoring techniques are all embedded functions. Entire systems are the target of change and outsiders (e.g., school boards) may sponsor or initiate the reforms. Stakeholder buy-in and planned transitions accentuate ownership of the change process. Design scripts adapted from change management theorists (e.g., Peter Senge) guide this mentoring theory's implementation.

Synergistic leadership theory

Synergistic leadership theory, while not identified as a mentoring theory typology per se, can be interpreted as such – it offers a holistic alternative to traditional mentoring. This theory is framed around feminist, postmodern interpretations of public schooling and administrator preparation. Male-based theories often do not accommodate 'feminine' values and approaches, such as collaborative relationships and diversity (Ardovini, Trautman, Brown, and Irby, 2010). The changing reality is that most individuals in university-based leadership preparation programs are female (and increasingly culturally diverse). Synergistic leadership theory promotes the integration of four factors: 'leadership behavior, organizational structure, external forces, and attitudes, beliefs, and values' (Irby et al., 2002: 312). Arguably, synergistic leadership enhances collaborative and multiple-level mentoring through an overarching but situated view of 'the feminist organization' in which leadership, decision making, and power are shared experiences for all cultures.

CRITIQUES OF MENTORING THEORIES

Alternative mentoring theories do not simply present mentoring in an entirely new form. In fact, some are predicated upon technical approaches to mentoring, such as the apprenticeship model, while mandated mentoring models influence others. Postmodernist theory gives space to co-existences and continuities in educational discourse, as well as contradictions that 'force' creativity in learning, teaching, and leading (English, 2003; Irby et al., 2002). This is not to imply that assumptions guiding administrative management and leadership theories, including mentoring theories, should fester undetected. Given that co-mentoring theory was birthed as a feminist critique of traditional mentoring, it is a catalyst for changing traditional practices, hierarchical systems, and homogeneous cultures (Bona et al., 1995). For example, while the conception of mentor as above and separate from follower is outdated, it has a foothold in modern-day notions of mentor expertise and apprenticeship.

Political ideologies inform most alternative mentoring theories. As postmodern feminists have argued, because career advancement is a protected 'investment', mentors 'represent dominant cultural values' (Hansman, 2003: 103). Hence, intentional and reflective alternative mentors seek to diversify school systems by critically analyzing the replication of organizational values and generating creative solutions that open up access, expand learning options, and generate new knowledge. In contrast, mentors guided by 'technical rationality' act in ways commensurate with knowledge founded upon untested faith and inherited norms (English, 2003). From a postmodern perspective, multiple-level mentoring reforms resemble a management makeover for schools dependent upon overloaded personnel. While envisioned democratically as change agents, practitioners can be subjected to doing even more labor without compensation. A school's transformation can occur, then, at a serious cost to an organization's wellbeing. Alternative theorists are not ideological purists but rather borrowers of different frameworks. As another example, collaborative mentors who initiate the apprenticeship of nontraditional individuals enact a double helix of shared power and systems thinking. Perhaps mentoring today is less about co-mentoring than a kind of process model for enacting collaborative (and systems) concepts (Cannon, 2003).

Technical mentoring perpetuates a 'foundational epistemology' (English, 2003) that circumvents 'why' and 'what if' questions, sociocultural and political influences, and the regulatory control inherent in it (Mullen, 2005). While ideologically restrictive, technical mentoring is useful for support within practical apprenticeships and skills-building contexts. Human interaction, positive engagement, and fair treatment can be upheld in this context. Hence, one should not assume that technical mentoring has no educational value or that it cannot coincide with robust forms of mentoring. On the other hand, critics (e.g., Darwin, 2000; Freire, 1997; Hansman, 2003) believe that the power and authority, and the efficiency and competitive values implicit in technical mentoring, undermine the capacity for democratic mentoring at human and organizational levels, and so should not be tolerated.

POLICY AND INTERNATIONAL IMPLICATIONS OF MENTORING THEORY

On the education policy front, mandatory mentoring is an oxymoron signaling a hidden curriculum where teachers are *required* to mentor and make documented gains (Mullen, 2005). While the mentoring of new practitioners is vital to their success, the US, the UK, and some other countries are increasingly mandating some version of school-based and district-wide mentoring (Mullen, 2011c; see also Chapter 20). Such trends are most likely an outgrowth of evidence-based educational policy that set expectations for teaching practice that bypass complex social roles and particular contexts with instrumental goals that turn the education profession into a metric-driven 'technological enterprise' (Biesta, 2007). Consequently, new teacher mentoring resembles more of a technical, evaluative activity than a process for fostering professional collaboration.

This is not to say that evidence-based practice cannot be successfully tailored to educational contexts – new mentoring as well as coaching interventions and applications can be designed to have a positive effect (see Chapter 26). Perhaps this is one reason why prescribed mentoring in public schools at the individual and collective teacher level has seemingly had mixed reactions, with some teachers receptive or noncritical and others citing unresolved tensions and barriers to change (Hutinger and Mullen, 2007). From a critical theory perspective, schools are objects of change-based mentoring that strips away the voluntary nature of this act. Governmental authorities want to reduce teacher attrition; this is not an issue *per se*. Rather, wholesale, top-down accountability expectations may be confounding the very integrity associated with mentoring. To what extent mentoring relationships, which are personal, contextual, and cultural in nature, can be formalized (in reality, regulated and codified) depends on many variables that are confounded by dynamics involving uniqueness at the individual and contextual level. Hence, mentoring practice does not always reach its ideals – moreover, organizations typically treat it as an 'add-on' responsibility rather than a professional calling for which educators should be recognized.

Arguably, then, the adaptation of mentoring as a policy mechanism has rendered this educational learning process an accountability-driven achievement measure for schools. Changes in US law have mechanized mentoring across the platforms of leading, teaching, and supervising, and especially teacher evaluation. Because mentoring summons notions of civic virtue and goodness, it is useful as a political tool. Rhetorically exploited, mentoring concepts related to professional learning and lifelong growth for teachers (e.g., 'instructional mentorship') are part of the national leadership standards. As one effect, policies advance technical forms of mentoring in a contemporary guise as best practice. Goals of management (e.g., 'accountability safeguards') have been resurrected as a source of empowerment (e.g., 'cross-cultural mentoring'). Within education, technical mentoring processes and systems are in wide use; these need to be interrogated and modernized.

Studies of mentoring in an international context that more fully attend to diversity and cultural issues are vital. These initiate new understandings of non-American cultures, disenfranchised populations, aboriginal cultures, and feminine leadership. For example, Schlosberg, Irby, Brown, and Yang (2010) investigated a private school in an impoverished part of Mexico whose leaders were committed to serving at-risk students. Results underscored the importance of leaders developing a balanced leadership style as they facilitate change in difficult circumstances. MacCallum and Beltman's (2003) study of aboriginal youth culture in Australia produced insight into the cultural integration of mentoring partners in linguistically enriched mentoring programs. Research that has a global education orientation, albeit resembling a roughly fitted cobbled walkway at this time, makes possible knowledge discovery of cultural contexts and commonalties and differences across them (Kochan and Pascarelli, 2004). This body of research is at an early but promising stage of development, as can be seen from chapters in this book that are informed by and situated within various educational and cultural contexts across countries (e.g., Chapters 12, 20, 21, and 26). Publishing trends suggest that we will see much more study of education on an international scale whilst innovations in mentoring will keep springing up faster than research can keep pace.

PARTING WORDS

Journeying forward as an international research community with this book as one of many touchstones, we are each called upon to tap into our dreams of a better world that are implicit in our productive critiques. Mentoring as a higher calling incites imaginative and democratic civic participation in the global arena for which mentor-activists hold responsibility and stewardship to their constituents.

As educators grapple with mentoring theory, innovate using its desirable tenets, and report outcomes, they may see growth that is more desirable and dynamic. Practitioners can benefit from translating educational ideas in their daily practice through intentional, multifaceted mentoring interventions. Mentoring that is centered in shared principles and practices that are internally generated create the conditions not only for innovation to be possible but also for a desirable education. Mentoring that stimulates democratic civic participation builds capacity beyond the microcosmic, grassroots level to form bridges that bring together different peoples, places, and countries.

ACKNOWLEDGEMENTS

This chapter incorporates content from two of the author's previous publications (Mullen, 2011b, 2011c, the citations of which follow).

REFERENCES

Allen, T. D., and Eby, L. T. (Eds.). (2007). *The Blackwell Handbook of Mentoring: A Multiple Perspectives Approach*. Malden, MA: Blackwell.

Antrop-González, R., & De Jesús, A. (2006). Toward a theory of *critical care* in urban small school reform: Examining structures and pedagogies of caring in two Latino community based schools. *International Journal of Qualitative Studies in Education, 19*(4), 409–433.

Ardovini, J., Trautman, H. D., Brown, G., & Irby, B. (2010). Including female leadership experiences and behaviors: A qualitative validation of synergistic leadership theory. *International Leadership Journal, 2*(3/4), 22–52.

Biesta, G. (2007). Why 'what works' won't work: Evidence-based practice and the democratic deficit in educational research. *Educational Theory, 57*(1), 1–22.

Blake-Beard, S. D. (2001). Taking a hard look at formal mentoring programs: A consideration of potential challenges facing women. *Journal of Management Development, 20*(4), 331–345.

Bona, M. J., Rinehart, J., & Volbrecht, R. M. (1995). Show me how to do like you: Co-mentoring as feminist pedagogy. *Feminist Teacher, 9*(3), 116–124.

Britton, E., Paine, L., Pimm, D., & Raizen, S. (Eds.). (2003). *Comprehensive Teacher Induction: Systems for Early Career Learning*. Norwell, MA: Kluwer.

Cannon, D. A. (2003). *Mentoring: A Study of Processes and Relationships in a Collaborative Curriculum Reform Research Project*. Unpublished dissertation, The Ohio State University, Columbus, Ohio.

Carnegie Forum on Education and the Economy. (1986). *A Nation Prepared: Teachers for the 21st Century*. New York: Carnegie Corporation. ERIC Document NO. ED 268120.

Crow, G. M., & Matthews, L. J. (1998). *Finding One's Way: How Mentoring can Lead to Dynamic Leadership*. Thousand Oaks, CA: Corwin.

Darwin, A. (2000). Critical reflections on mentoring in work settings. *Adult Education Quarterly, 50*(3), 197–211.

English, F. W. (2003). *The Postmodern Challenge to the Theory and Practice of Educational Administration*. Springfield, IL: Charles C. Thomas Publisher.

Feiman-Nemser, S. (1996, July). Teacher mentoring: A critical review. *Peer resources: The primary source for peer, mentor, and coach resources*, 1–3. Retrieved February 7, 2011, from http://www.islandnet.com/~rcarr/teachermentors.html

Freire, P., with Fraser, J. W., Macedo, D., McKinnon, T., & Stokes, W. T. (Eds.). (1997). *Mentoring the Mentor: A Critical Dialogue with Paulo Freire*. New York: Peter Lang.

Fullan, M. (1999). *Change Forces: The Sequel*. London: Falmer.

Galbraith, M. W. (2003). The adult education professor as mentor: A means to enhance teaching and learning. *Perspectives: The New York Journal of Adult Learning, 1*(1), 9–20.

Gallucci, C., Van Lare, M. D., Yoon, I. H., & Boatright, B. (2010). Instructional coaching: Building theory about the role and organizational support for professional learning. *American Educational Research Association, 47*(4), 919–963.

Hansman, C. A. (2003). Power and learning in mentoring relationships. In R. Cervero, B. Courtenay, & M. Hixson (Eds.), *Global Perspectives: Volume III* (pp. 102–122). Athens, GA: University of Georgia.

Hutinger, J. L., & Mullen, C. A. (2007). Supporting teacher leadership: Mixed perceptions of mandated faculty study groups. In S. Donahoo and R. C. Hunter (Eds.), *Teaching Leaders to Lead Teachers: Educational Administration in the Era of Constant Crisis, 10* (pp. 261–283). Oxford, UK: Elsevier.

Irby, B. J., Brown, G., Duffy J. A., & Trautman, D. (2002). The synergistic leadership theory. *Journal of Educational Administration, 40*(4), 304–322.

Johnson, W. B. (2006). *On Being a Mentor: A Guide for Higher Education Faculty.* Mahwah, NJ: Erlbaum.

Johnson-Bailey, J., & Cervero, R. M. (2004). Mentoring in black and white: the intricacies of cross-cultural mentoring. *Mentoring and Tutoring: Partnership in Learning, 12*(1), 7–21.

Kochan, F. K., & Pascarelli, J. T. (Eds.). (2004). *Global Perspectives on Mentoring: Transforming Contexts, Communities, and Cultures.* Greenwich, CT: Information Age.

Kochan, F. K., & Trimble, S. B. (2000). From mentoring to co-mentoring: Establishing collaborative relationships. *Theory Into Practice, 39*(1), 20–28.

Kram, K. E. (1985/1988). *Mentoring at Work: Developmental Relationships in Organizational Life.* Lanham, MD: University Press of America.

Lick, D. W. (1999). Multiple level comentoring: Moving toward a learning organization. In C. A. Mullen, & D. W. Lick (Eds.), *New Directions in Mentoring: Creating a Culture of Synergy* (pp. 202–212). London, England: Falmer.

Luebchow, L. (2009, June). *Equitable Resources in Low Income Schools,* 1–20. (New America Foundation, Education Policy Program.) Retrieved February 8, 2011, from http://www.newamerica.net/files/Equitable_Resources_in_Low_Income_ Schools.pdf

MacCallum, J., & Beltman, S. (2005). Bridges and barriers in Australia's youth mentoring programs. In F. Kochan, & J. Pascarelli (Eds.), *Global Perspective on Mentoring: Transforming Contexts, Communities, and Cultures* (pp. 73–103). Greenwich, CT: Information Age.

Merriam, S. B. (1983). Mentors and protégés: A critical review of the literature. *Adult Education Quarterly, 33,* 161–173.

Moerer-Urdahl, T., & Creswell, J. (2004). Using transcendental phenomenology to explore the 'ripple effect' in a leadership mentorship program. *International Journal of Qualitative Methods, 3*(2), 1–28.

Mullen, C. A. (2005). *The Mentorship Primer.* New York: Peter Lang.

Mullen, C. A. (Ed.). (2008). *The Handbook of Formal Mentoring in Higher Education: A Case Study Approach.* Norwood, MA: Christopher-Gordon.

Mullen, C. A., & Tuten, E. M. (2010). Doctoral cohort mentoring: Interdependence, collaborative learning, and cultural change. *Scholar-Practitioner Quarterly, 4*(1), 11–32.

Mullen, C. A. (2011a). Facilitating self-regulated learning using mentoring approaches with doctoral students. In B. Zimmerman and D. H. Schunk (Eds.), *Handbook of Self-regulation of Learning and Performance.* New York: Routledge.

Mullen, C. A. (2011b). Mentoring theories for educational practitioners. In B. Irby, G. Brown, & R. Lara-Alecio (Eds.), *Handbook of Educational Theories.* Greenwich, CT: Information Age.

Mullen, C. A. (2011c). New teacher mandated mentoring, a policy direction of states. *Kappa Delta Pi Record, 47*(2), 63–67.

National Board for Professional Teaching Standards. (2009). *Making Best Practice Everyday Practice in Schools,* 1–4. Retrieved February 7, 2011, from www.nbpts.org

Noe, R. A. (1988). An investigation of the determinants of successful assigned mentoring relationships. *Personnel Psychology, 41,* 457–479.

Nora, A., & Crisp, G. (2008). Mentoring students: Conceptualizing and validating the multi-dimensions of a support system. *Journal of College Student Retention, 9,* 337–356.

North Carolina State Board of Education. (2009). *Glossary of Terms.* Retrieved February 7, 2011, from http://www.ncpublicschools.org/curriculum/lbc/08lbcglossary

Portner, H. (2008). *Mentoring new teachers* (3rd ed.). Thousand Oaks, CA: Corwin.

Rose, G. L. (2003). Enhancement of mentor selection using the Ideal Mentor Scale. *Research in Higher Education, 44*(4), 473–494.

Schlosberg, T., Irby, B., Brown, G., & Yang, L. (2010). A case study of Mexican educational leaders viewed through the lens of the synergistic leadership theory. *International Journal of Educational Leadership, 5*(1), 1–18 (part 1); 1–14 (part 2).

Tillman, L. C. (2001). Mentoring African American faculty in predominantly White institutions. *Research in Higher Education, 42*(3), 295–325.

Tharp, R. G., & Gallimore, R. G. (1995/1988). *Rousing Minds to Life: Teaching, Learning, and Schooling in Social Context.* New York: Cambridge University Press.

US Department of Education. (2002, January 8). *No Child Left Behind Act of 2001.* Washington, DC: Office of Elementary and Secondary Education. Retrieved February 7, 2011, from http://www.ed.gov/policy/elsec/leg/esea02/107-110.pdf

Varney, J. (2009). Humanistic mentoring: Nurturing the person within. *Kappa Delta Pi Record, 45*(3), 127–131.

Wong, H. K. (2004). Producing educational leaders through induction programs. *Kappa Delta Pi Record,* 106–111.

Young, M. D., & Brooks, J. (2008). Supporting graduate students of color. *Educational Administration Quarterly, 44*(3), 391–423.

Coaching: An Overview

Sarah J. Fletcher

INTRODUCTION

Where the education world's attention was transfixed on mentoring between 1995 and 2005, it has dramatically shifted towards coaching since then. As a relatively recent initiative in education practice, coaching is perceived as being nearer to the practical than the theoretical end of the mentoring continuum and remains scantly researched. Such research as there is, tends to be exploratory. A somewhat parallel situation can be observed in the research archives about mentoring. This is because, in part, mentor and coach practitioners do not tend to research their own practice. There are notable exceptions (Fletcher, 2000), but the research has largely been undertaken by non-practitioners, although in coaching Tolhurst (2006) is a noteworthy exception. A further reason why coaching remains under-researched at the present time is that few universities have, as yet, become involved in coach preparation to the same extent as they have been in mentor development. There are some signs of change (Silver, Lochmill, Copland and Tripps, 2009).

The teacher who authored the National College for School Leadership (NCSL) Report in 2003, set out the professional values, as he perceived them, which relate to leadership coaching, while citations and extracts in the report predominantly draw on coaching literature and are mainly from business. Lofthouse and colleagues' CfBT study (Lofthouse, Leat, Towler, Hall and Cummings, 2010), on the other hand, does focus on educational sources and offers us a definition of coaching, thoughtfully distinguished from mentoring:

> Coaching is usually focused on professional dialogue designed to aid the coachee in developing specific skills to enhance their teaching repertoire. For teachers, it often supports

experimentation with new classroom strategies and coaches are not normally in positions of line management in relationship to their coachee. The focus of the coaching is usually selected by the coachee and the process provides opportunities for reflection and problem solving for both coach and coachee. (2010: 8)

In overt contrast to mentoring, the report points out that '[c]oaching tends to have its roots in psychotherapy and counseling'. As in mentoring, 'establishment of trust is paramount'. Tensions can arise unless 'confidentiality is assured.' (ibid. 10). This study also points out some of the potential problems implicit in embedding coaching in a school improvement culture. It warns that 'coaching in the school target-generating and monitoring procedures … may deter participants from exploiting some of the potential to share and tackle personal concerns and queries relating to practice that coaching can offer' (ibid. 10). Drawing on interviews with coaches, this report identifies coaching's applications:

- sharing classroom practice with a colleague;
- judging the quality of practice and seeking or giving feedback;
- supporting induction or career transition;
- working toward a school or department development priority;
- supporting a professional development course or Masters level study and
- working towards a performance management target (ibid. 14).

Confusion appears to arise over the relative purposes of mentoring and coaching. 'Mentoring', according to the National Framework for Mentoring and Coaching (CUREE, 2005), supports induction and career transition, while 'coaching' is said to lead to knowledge creation. CfBT research indicates that it rarely has done. In the US, Cornett and Knight (2008) observed that enquiries they reviewed into coaching did not meet 'the standards of rigorous research'. It is ironic, given how widely it is practiced as a form professional development, that its value is gauged by anecdotal data. There is no academic journal specifically for coaching in education, while the Mentoring and Coaching Special Interest Group, established in 2004 for the British Educational Research Association, provides welcome opportunities for discussion.

DEFINITIONS OF COACHING

The use of coaching to support teachers improving their practice has, according to Rhodes and Beneike (2002), been explored in Dutch schools. He refers to the research by Veenman (1995) and Veenman, De Laat and Staring (1998), who have studied the impacts of skills training in coaching 'on the efficacy of school counselors, primary schoolteachers and school principals as coaches of teachers' (Rhodes, 2002: 298). Pertinently, Veenman, Denessen, Gerrits and Kenter (2010) have recently evaluated the benefits of coaching for cooperating teachers. Rhodes further suggests that coaching and mentoring within the corporate business learning environment might well 'be pertinent to draw upon … to explore coaching, mentoring and peer networking relationships' (ibid. 300). One of the many difficulties of drawing upon business related practice is that the distinctions between mentoring and coaching are not necessarily the same as they are education and the aims differ. Furthermore, while Brockbank and McGill (2006), use 'mentoring' and 'coaching' (more or less) interchangeably, in the National Framework for Mentoring and Coaching, for example, devised by CUREE in 2005, distinctions between mentoring and coaching in schools are emphasised. The National Framework for England is the same framework as that proposed by Carnell, MacDonald and Askew (2006) for higher education coaching schemes. While stating that mentoring and coaching are similar 'structured sustained processes', the National Framework distinguishes between them. In higher education, where coaching and mentoring also overlap, they can substantially differ and Wisker, Exley, Antoniou and Ridley (2008: 21) distinguishes between mentoring, coaching, supervising and personal tutoring activities occurring in higher education: 'Coaching is a structured one-to-one learning relationship between coach and coachee aimed at developing competence and improving performance in the coachee.'

COACHING IN EDUCATIONAL CONTEXTS

Because there is a dearth of coaching publications authored by writers from education, writers from *business* tending to dominate the field. Brockbank and McGill (2006) is a popular example where authors from a business background are now writing for an education context. Such research into coaching as exists tends therefore to draw upon business-oriented literature rather than on educational research, specific to education.

While it is my opinion that educators should read coaching books that are authored by business and sports coaches, they also need to gain an insight into accumulated knowledge from experts in the education field. There are informative business texts: Crane's *The Heart of Coaching* (2009) for example, which argues for a new understanding about leadership that is beyond coercion.

On the other hand, it seems hardly surprising that practitioners of coaching and mentoring continue to merge definitions of their crafts when the European Mentoring and Coaching Council (EMCC) considers mentoring and coaching to be so close in meaning that there is no discernible difference between them (Hay, 2008). There might well be, however, discernible differences between mentoring and coaching in the context of schools as well as in further and in higher education.

Ask most educators to identify who has substantially changed the theory and practice of education in the past 100 years and Schön (1987) is probably on their list. Donald Schön's ideas have shaped initial teacher education and continual professional development (CPD) programmes and many educators would claim their practice embodies his ideas.

Few realise, however, the value he placed upon coaching and, in *Educating the Reflective Practitioner*, Schön stresses the importance of flexibility and context in its practice. Using recording dialogue between coach and student, the approaches he identifies (Joint Experimentation, Follow me! and Hall of Mirrors) call for different forms of improvisation, and also offer different orders of difficulty, as well as being appropriate for very different contextual conditions. Educators may also benefit from reviewing Schön's (1988) observations on coaching, which he portrays as a kind of dialogue.

> In joint experimentation, the coach's skill comes first to bear in the task of helping a student formulate the qualities she wants to achieve and then, by demonstration on description, explain different ways of producing them ... the coach can show her what is necessary according to the laws of the phenomena with which she is dealing ... the coach works at creating a process of collaborative inquiry. (ibid. 296)

Here we can see a forerunner of models of coaching that are integrated with action research, such as Robertson's (2009), since Shön explains that 'coach and student, when they do their jobs well, function not only as practitioners but also as researchers.' His 'Hall of Mirrors, can be created only ... when coaching resembles the interpersonal practice to be learned, when students recreate in interaction with coach or peers the patterns of their practice world' (Schön, 1988: 297). In Schön's writing, we might also perceive a precursor to Bloom and colleagues' *Blended Coaching* (Bloom, Castagna, Moir and Warren, 2005), since he does not favour one coaching model above another: '[A] coach may shift ... adapting herself to the needs and difficulties of each student before her.'

Similarly, Knight's model of 'Instructional coaching' (2007) is similar to Schön's (1988) ideas in 'Coaching reflective teaching', but what stands out in Schön's models is that the teacher-as-coach 'helps the kid connect his spontaneous understandings or know-how to the privileged knowledge of the school' (1988: 22). The coach is not helping the student to set goals by which his or her achievement will be assessed. The goal is the creation of *new* knowledge and this is the inspiration for and the educational intent for the KNOW model which is introduced later on in this chapter. Whereas the National Framework talks about using coaching to assimilate new knowledge into practice (i.e., knowledge from research), Schön's idea is that coaching *between* the schoolteacher and the school student *creates* knowledge. If Schön is correct, then coaches *should* research their practice with a view to testing his hypothesis that knowledge is created.

THE DEVELOPMENT OF COACHING IN EDUCATION

When Showers and Joyce wrote about the evolution of peer coaching in 1996, they looked back to their seminal research in 1980 to gauge how the practice of coaching had developed. In their early work, they tested the hypothesis that 'regular (weekly) seminars would enable teachers to practice and implement the content they were learning. The seminars or coaching sessions focused on class-room implementation and the analysis of teaching, especially students' responses' (1981: 1). In 1996, they revisited their own recommendations for peer coaching among small groups of teachers in school (not pairs). Insisting that peer coaching is neither an end in itself nor by itself a school improvement initiative, it must operate in a context of training, initiative and general school improvement. Coaching is not a tacked-on extra but has to be integrated into the very fabric of any school, properly organised and enabled in a culture that can support it as just one approach among many for school improvement. Showers and Joyce detail their history of peer coaching in their 1996 paper, which reveals a different model from that Lofthouse et al. (2010) observed in schools. Joyce and Showers envis-aged teachers sharing teaching, planning together and pooling their experiences, not a few minutes watching one another teach, asking 'How do you think that went?', exploring what happened, yet avoiding posing any challenges.

While coaching is being offered in many schools, globally one has yet to see research (beyond self-reported anecdotes) that substantively confirms that coach-ing *does* assist students' learning. According to Joyce and Showers, by sharing in teaching, planning and pooling experiences, teachers can practice their newly acquired skills and new strategies more appropriately than their counterparts who work alone to expand their teaching repertoires. What is very interesting, how-ever, is that these expert educator-researchers 'found it necessary and important to omit verbal feedback as a coaching component'. It is not clear why, precisely, but it seems that by omitting feedback the emphasis on 'performance' diminished while the overall positive impact of peer coaching sessions remained unchanged. The authors explain that

> numerous staff development practices are called 'coaching'; 'technical coaching'; 'collegial coaching'; 'challenge coaching', 'team coaching'; 'cognitive coaching' and also to the vari-ous uses of peer coaching to refer to traditional supervisory modes of pre-conference/obser-vation/post-conference. They emphasise that 'none of the models mentioned above should be confused with or used for evaluation of teachers' and 'coaching is not the appropriate mechanism for gauging performance'.
>
> (Showers and Joyce, 1996: 2–3)

In a similar vein, with coaching as a core enabling rather than evaluative process, the Teacher Learning Academy (TLA) in England, currently offers four Stages of Recognition for teacher learning and, reportedly, tens of thousands of teachers have successfully submitted research accounts of their work as educators for TLA verification. As core tenets of the scheme, coaching and mentoring offer opportunities for progress review and evaluation. Coaching in the TLA's process focuses on SMART (Specific, Measurable, Achievable, Realistic and Time-based) goals. The scheme has been very successful according to an evaluation report published by the National Foundation for Educational Research (NfER) (Lord, Lamont, Harland et al. 2009), not least because of its coaching and its mentoring components. One-to-one professional development works well as professional development. In my experience in presenting success-fully for TLA Stage 4 Recognition, mentoring integrated with Appreciative Inquiry (Fletcher, 2009) was more motivational than a problem-solving approach.

EVOLVING MODELS IN SPORTS COACHING EDUCATION

Sports coaching has been practiced for some two hundred years now but similarly remains under-researched and indications of success remain largely anecdotal. Lyle (2002) recounts how coaching activities developed from the sport of boxing in the early 1800s, thence through to the early coaches for team sports in public schools. Coaching was restricted to enthusiastic (young) teachers introduced to the game while at university. Lyle's writing (2002) is intended to contribute to the academic development of coaching and to the study of sports coaching that has penetrated higher education. 'There is a three-way relationship between athlete coaching and performance but a dearth of literature and research linking the coach and performance outcomes' (2002: 23). 'There are no overarching theories that will unifying theories about sports coaching … the field has been conceived of as too diffuse in purpose and practice to encourage this' (ibid. 29). Sports coaching has retained its (strong) similarity to sports teaching although coaching is concerned more with improving performance of a sportsperson competent in their sport rather than 'teaching' sports-related skills.

According to Jones (2006), coaching remains an ill-defined and under-theorised field (2006: 1) where 'coaching, like teaching, is an inherently non routine, problematic and complex endeavour; a great deal of untapped, tacit knowledge … exists in athletes and coaches … coaching is an activity primarily based on social interaction and power' (ibid. 2). Coaching apparently rests on eliciting and managing situated learning (Lave and Wenger, 1991) as indeed does coaching within other disciplines including education. Jones argues that teaching and the pedagogical theory that informs it 'has tended to lie outside traditional conceptualisations of coaching' (1991: 6). He further suggests that 'instruction and facilitation figure in the practice of top level coaches and a pedagogic role (is) an important role in the make-up of coaches' personas' (ibid. 7).

Usefully, Cross and Lyle (2002) distinguish between *participation* coaching and *performance* coaching. 'Participation coaching' best describes contexts in which the principal goal is not competition success. The performers are thus less intensively engaged in the process and may be concerned more with improve-ments in order to enjoy participation and its immediate satisfactions. The empha-sis is on participation (i.e., taking part) rather than preparation. The coaching process is not implemented to systematically controlled plan, and the quality of the interpersonal relationship between athlete and coach may be emphasised beyond other goals (2003: 11). A parallel may be drawn between the state of coaching in sports and education. While coaching is widespread and its value not disputed in raising achievement, 'little research has explored the conceptual development of the coaching process and treated the coaching process as a problematic aspect of the research (ibid. 13). As in education contexts, there is restricted critical engagement. Where a core debate in sports coaching is between what constitutes teaching and what coaching, in business it focuses upon counselling, coaching and mentoring. The debate is reflected in an MA programme at Oxford Brookes Business School, which draws upon psychotherapeutic models of practice. Understanding the role of emotions is essential in coaching and 'Emotional Coaching' (Hromek, 2007) is crucial as educators set about enabling young people from troubled backgrounds to cope. Coaches certainly need to understand emotions.

THE DYNAMICS OF EDUCATIONAL RELATIONSHIPS

Exploring an overview of coaching, as I am attempting to do here, across education, sports and business I visualise a pattern something like that depicted in Figure 2.1. While each of the four aspects is distinct, there is a possibility of cross-fertilisation between them. Mentoring sits alongside coaching; once thought of as a subset of mentoring in education, many educators would now regard mentoring and coaching as equal in their relevance to developing educational practices. Training and counselling skills underpin good practice in mentoring and in coaching, and coaching often draws on training (instructional coaching) while mentoring draws on counselling (understanding the emotional

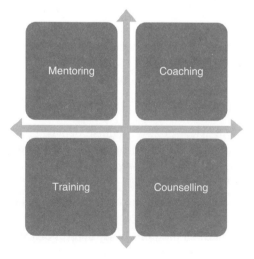

Figure 2.1

responses of a mentee are crucial to good practice). The arrows indicate that learning can emanate from any, but not necessarily all, combinations of mentoring and coaching, training and counselling. Context will determine the effective combination and learning will be 'situated' in its context. This perspective reflects research by Lave and Wenger (1991) on situated learning.

The longer-term learning support strategies that peer learning relationships can offer are sometimes squeezed out in the race to deliver a performance-focused agenda. This situation is likely to be aggravated where a 'performance' approach to coaching is borrowed from noneducation contexts without regard to subtle differences therein.

COACHING IN A BUSINESS CONTEXT

This chapter does not attempt to engage critically with coaching in business since Cox, Bachkirova and Clutterbuck (2010) accomplish that purpose admirably. Instead, it draws attention to a model originating in business, Whitmore's GROW model (2002), which is now in use in education contexts. While popular in schools, its outcomes-based focus might *impede* learning.

Somehow we need to find a model of coaching that can integrate mentoring as well as training and counselling. We need to re-examine the aims of education as a process of learning rather than getting hooked into an outcomes-focused agenda. Before we can move on to explore new models of coaching for education, we need to examine models that are in use in schools. Tolhurst (2006) suggests the LEAP model for coaching leaders but there is apparently no substantial research into it. GROW is a (migrated) business model and this is recommended reading for students researching coaching.

The acronym GROW stands for:

Goal setting
Reality check
Options available
Wrap up (what will the client do?)

Whitmore adds his own cautionary note about

> the hunger for coaches [which] has resulted in hastily and inadequately trained so-called coaches failing to meet the expectations of those they are coaching. In too many cases they have not fully understood the performance-related, psychological principles on which coaching is based. Without this understanding they may go through the motions of coaching, or use the behaviours associated with coaching but fail to achieve the intended results.
>
> (Whitmore, 2002)

Whitmore further emphasises the value of mastering self-coaching and this is an area where research is urgently needed, since it may be useful for educators to implement.

While GROW is widely valued as a useful means for motivating teams and achieving goals, one has to ask how applicable it is to use in the current global economic crisis. It can empower a leadership elite, and it can increase organisational motivation, but as a model for enabling education, which is a process and not a series of problem-solving steps, it needs to be used judiciously. GROW as a process is not far detached from an action research cycle; set a goal for improvement, consider one's reality and options that are available and set about aiming to achieve as an act of (conscious) willpower. The main problem with GROW is how novice coaches use it as a step by step process which, like an overly managed action research cycle, leads to frustration and boredom.

A second drawback of the GROW model's use, though not necessarily of the original intention for the model, which was designed to be fluid and flexible, is that the goal identified at the start of the process is likely to shift and is often replaced by another as reflection occurs. Becoming stuck in seeking a goal at the start point of a learning process could inhibit motivation and free-thinking through which creativity emerges.

It must be stressed that the drawback in GROW often originates in how it is utilised rather than in the model. Used judiciously in education GROW can be a valuable tool.

THE ART OF *QUESTIONING* IN COACHING

Questioning plays a more central role in coaching than in mentoring since the coach seeks to draw learning from the coachee, rather than passing on existing knowledge. O'Connor and Lages (2007) emphasise its importance where they state:

> Knowing how to ask questions is the first core skill of coaching ... Questions guide (clients') attention and test the coach's hypotheses about the situation. All models of coaching agree on this and NLP (Neuro Linguistic Programmed) coaching and ontological coaching deal with the linguistic aspect of questions in depth. (2007: 164)

De Haan (2008) goes further and recommends what, how and who types of questions for coaching. Various techniques for using questions to develop coaching conversation are also explored by Parsloe and Leedham (2009). Sections about 'Observant listening' and 'Feedback for adult learners' are applicable for educational coaching and coach education practices.

While some authors stress the usefulness of questioning, McLeod (2004) highlights the value of silence: 'The real work of coaching is done in the coachees' episodes of thinking and feeling in which the coach plays no part other than silent witness' (2004: 9).

Many authors are convinced that effective practice in coaching lies in conversation, a point developed by Cheliotes and Reilly (2010) who explain that ineffective coach–coachee conversations often result when people engage in four unproductive patterns of listening; judgement or criticism; autobiographical listening (the need that a coach can easily succumb to, in interceding about his/ her own experiences); inquisitive listening (inquisitiveness about irrelevancies); and solutions listening (not listening to what is said but thinking only about offering solutions). 'Coach-like' leaders communicate through their conversations that they see themselves as partners (2010: 15). Additionally, conversations can draw out creative learning and can sustain a democratic growth of knowledge. At the same time as enabling the coachee to improve their practice, the coach is making sense of their own practice by analysing the teaching and learning of their coachee ... Not only does this feedback impact on the coach's own performance, but it enables him/her to make judgements about how best to support teachers (Street and Temperley, 2005: 89). By developing coaching as collaborative enquiry the teaching profession could construct its own knowledge base. As Hiebert, Gallimore and Stigker (2002) emphasise, the need in education is for long-term, school-based, collaborative professional development. Peer coaching may offer just such a pathway.

The report produced for the TDA/NfER by Lord, Atkinson and Mitchell in 2008, examined the role of 'mentoring and coaching for professionals' across England. It examined empirical and practice-based evidence but omitted several key studies. A comprehensive, rigorously researched evidence base is an urgent priority for coaching in educational contexts.

SCHOOL-BASED APPLICATIONS OF COACHING MODELS

Bloom et al. (2005) emphasise the importance of *blended coaching* in leadership but note, 'Coaching is all the rage, yet it enjoys no common definition and little research has been done on its efficacy' (2005: 3). The authors usefully outline several approaches:

- Facilitative: building on the coachee's existing skills, interpretations and beliefs and helps the coachee construct new skills, knowledge, interpretations and beliefs that will form the basis for future actions (ibid. 60).
- Instructional: the coach shares his or her experience and craft wisdom with the coachee by using traditional teaching strategies. These may include modelling, providing resources and direct instruction (ibid. 68).
- Collaborative: this strategy falls between the core strategies of instruction and facilitation because the coach is constantly in both modes (ibid. 75).
- Consultative: the coach-as-consultant possesses resources or expertise that will benefit the coachee and his/her school (ibid. 80).
- Transformational: 'we gain new knowledge, skills or ways of acting in incremental steps. As we experience success with these new ways of doing things, we begin to change our way of thinking. As our new knowledge becomes integral to who we are ... we are transformed' (ibid. 85).

Instructional coaching is becoming very popular in US schools. Developed at the University of Kansas, its impact has been researched by Knight and Cornett (2008).

They have concluded that instructional coaching will encourage teachers to adopt new teaching practicesand increase the likelihood that teachers will use the practices with a higher degree of quality inside the classroom, when compared with teachers who do not receive coaching support following professional development. There is much to commend the instructional coaching model. It aims to encourage dialogue and partnership between the instructional coach and classroom teacher. The coach is trained within a specially designed programme at the University of Kansas who claim their seven step induction model for introducing their own instructional coaching model into schools is robust:

- The coach enrols the teacher by conducting a one to one interview with each teacher prior to his or her experience of professional learning.
- The coach engages in collaborative planning with the teacher.
- The coach models the lesson.
- The teacher and coach meet to discuss what the coach while teaching.
- The coach observes the lesson being taught by the teacher.
- The teacher and coach discuss the teacher's lesson.
- The coach provides support until the teacher is fluent and habitual in their use of the new teaching model.

Questions that arise about the viability and desirability of the instructional coach model relate to funding, time and quality of coaching. The instructional coaching model is labour intensive and the coaches are funded. In a current strained economic climate globally, educators consider whether sufficient time and money are available.

Perhaps the more pertinent question is: 'Can the education community afford *not* to research the practice of coaching which is already so widespread in institutions?' As educators we need to know the impact of coaching on student learning and understand how using video to record coaching in the classroom can impact on student learning.

Cornett and Knight (2008) have researched instructional coaching but there is, as yet, no validation external to the university where the Instructional Coaching model originated. This is not to undervalue their research but offer a rationale for more of it. Their investigation into coaching across more than 200 publications 'describing some form of research relevant to coaching' has already identified four main approaches:

- peer coaching;
- cognitive coaching;
- literacy coaching; and
- instructional coaching.

Peer coaching is more an *organisational* structure through which coaching takes place in the UK. Teacher coaches are not generally trained or funded for input and this may explain why their dialogical interactions can lack depth (Lofthouse et al., 2010). Literacy coaching is a contextual application rather than a model.

Hull's research in cognitive coaching (in Cornett and Knight, 2008) concluded that while examination achievement scores for the students whose teachers received cognitive coaching and nonverbal classroom management training was larger than that of matched control group teachers, findings did not represent statistically significant differences. Study of instructional coaching revealed that it is indeed an effective professional development for teachers but 'it is unknown whether particular components of the instructional coaching model are more effective than others (2008: 15). Clearly, further research is needed to inform its practice.

Knight (2007) identifies a theoretical underpinning for several coaching books being used in schools (2007: 16), including those relating to leadership coaching: Bloom et al. (2005), and Killion and Harrison (2006). He does not specifically mention coaching manuals devised by practitioners and the surge in such publication occurred after this overview was researched. Toolkits devised for schools, like Allison and Harbour (2009), contain training and support material. Resources created by CUREE for mentoring and for coaching in schools are comprehensive and attractive and external investigation into their impact and effectiveness (over time) in schools in England is to be welcomed.

Costa and Garmston's *Coaching; A Foundation for Renaissance Schools* (2002), draws on cognitive coaching and like Kise's *Differentiated Coaching; a framework for helping teachers change* (2006), it appears valuable as it explains some of the challenges that are involved in coaching adult learners. Once again, research into their effectiveness, over time, in a range of school contexts is needed. Kise usefully notes that one coaching model does not suit all and like Kise, Silver et al. (2009) point out that '[d]ifferent coaching models exist and each model may require training that prepares coaches for service in different contexts' (2009: 230). The research agenda beckons.

The reception of coaching in schools has not been universally welcoming. Hargreaves and Dawe (2002) point to opposition in some US schools where it was seen as 'imposed and contrived collegiality'. Unlike true collegiality where trust develops over time and through shared experience, dialogue coaching provided by an external agency can be inappropriate and may be viewed as an intrusion. When linked to performance management mechanisms, coaching has become decidedly unpopular. With confidentiality and a non-judgemental approach as underlying principles this is hardly surprising. One wonders if the meaning of performance in coaching literature has been hijacked as a means for education institutions to check up on their teachers. This echoes the point made earlier by Showers and Joyce (1996) regarding evaluation.

COACHING FOR LEADERSHIP IN EDUCATION

Examining a burgeoning literature relating to coaching for leadership, some educators may ponder about a need for coaching for followers too. Too many leaders, each with their own goals may be as problematic as too few. While a rousing call for RESULTS is endorsed by Kee, Deering, Harris and Shuster (2010), in a model based upon cognitive coaching principles, some educators may tire at the business hyped style of the text which exhorts them to **R**esolve (to change results); **E**stablish (goal clarity); **S**eek (integrity); **U**nveil (multiple pathways); **L**everage; **T**ake (action) to **S**eize (success). They may prefer Robertson's erudite and reflective observation that 'within the framework of leadership coaching, action research involves several steps. These include identification of a need or vision and the related goal setting; gathering data, developing an initial action plan; implementing action; reconnaissance on that action; modification of the action plan and then further agreed action' (Robertson, 2009: 60). The coach's role in Robertson's approach involves monitoring the clarity of the leader's goals, evaluating the degree of change during intervention; assisting with evaluation through reflective interviews with staff and, observing an executive team meeting. Robertson endorses the GROW model.

Day's research (2001) provides valuable contextualisation for literature on coaching for leadership where he highlights 'conceptual confusion between leader and leadership development' (2001: 581). The latter confers competitive advantage to organisations especially in business contexts whereas leader development is a crucial aspect of an educator's role. Recognising those who have potential to be inspiring and visionary leaders at an early stage and offering coaching to enable them to develop is recognised as one of the critical factors in leader development. A McKinsey report, (2010), produced for the National College, stresses the importance of attracting and selecting those with the 'right' qualities as leaders to ensure the leadership capacity of an educational establishment. Early experiences of leadership, being identified as a potential leader and having opportunities to take on leadership are crucial factors in 'growing leadership'. Developing talent is, according to the report, more important than increasing the attractiveness of leadership positions. Coaching enables building a shared vision, sense of purpose and generativity whereby school principals who have been coached are able to identify and coach aspiring leaders in their institutions.

INTRODUCING THE KNOW MODEL OF COACHING FOR EDUCATION

The model outlined in Figure 2.2 offers parameters rather than a lock step process linked to predetermined goals. It can be combined with already popular coaching models in education such as GROW and Instructional Coaching and is designed to remind educators about the purposes of education as a whole: creating knowledge, building networks within and between societies and mobilising learners to deploy wisdom in making decisions.

Education is a process, not an end product with clearly managed goals. Its goal is the capacity to create knowledge, use knowledge to build learning networks and to use networks such as the Web to elicit, represent and disseminate

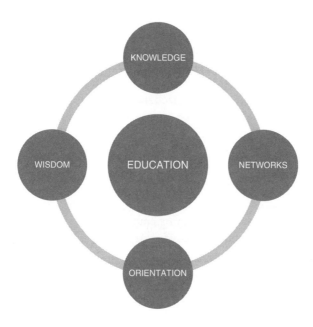

Figure 2.2

knowledge. Seeking short-term goals is a part of learning to learn and create knowledge but if learning is not networked and orientated, learning loses focus and purpose. Wisdom is the sought-after outcome of education, knowing how to learn and use learning is its aim.

Knowledge

'Knowledge is power', so said Francis Bacon in 1597. Having power to make choices, to take responsibility and develop talent is crucial in education.

Networks

The brain appears to be a vastly interconnected network and is much like the Internet. Learning to exercise the brain improves how we learn. Using the Internet can enable knowledge to be accessed, shared and critiqued and aids creation of 'new' knowledge.

Orientation

The Spanish translation for 'to mentor' is 'orientar'. Mentoring is an ingredient of coaching and vice versa. To orientate indicates finding direction, finding bearings within a mass of information that otherwise can confuse and distract the learner.

Wisdom

Wisdom enables the learned to use their knowledge for the benefit of humanity.

CONCLUSION

Until now, sustained and rigorous research into coaching in education contexts has been very limited. From being regarded as a minor subset of mentoring, coaching is increasingly seen as the transformational relationship to enhance all aspects and all sectors of education. However, it is crucial not to be swept up in an evangelical rush to proclaim coaching as the solution to every ill in educational practice. Coaching is neither a quick fix nor a cheaper, shorter-term version of mentoring. Coaches need opportunities for sustained professional development and should be encouraged to research their own coaching. Bearing in mind Schön's models (1988), a focus on enabling students' learning and reflective practice by educators would provide a sturdy basis for developing suitable models for education. Unquestioning acceptance of popular business-based coaching models is misguided and educators may need to re-examine the aims of education in order to recognise parameters for models appropriate for education contexts where competition is not the main motivational driver. Learning from business and sports models of coaching, incorporating strategies such as contracting and defining goals is likely to be useful to develop new concepts for coaching, like KNOW, for education. Whichever models of coaching are adapted from other professional contexts or which are developed specifically for education use, there is a need for research to provide us with an evidence base from which better practice, that promotes learning by students and educators, can evolve.

REFERENCES

Allison, S. and Harbour, M. (2009) *The Coaching Toolkit*, SAGE, London.

Bloom, G., Castagna, C., Moir, E. and Warren, B. (2005) *Blended Coaching; Skills and Strategies to Support Principal Development*, Corwin Press, Thousand Oaks, CA.

Brockbank, A. and McGill, I. (2006) *Facilitating Reflective Learning Through Mentoring & Coaching*, KoganPage, London.

Carnell, E., MacDonald, J. and Askew, S. (2006) *Coaching and Mentoring in Higher Education; A Learning-centred Approach*, Institute of Education, University of London.

Cheliotes, L. G. and Reilly, M.C. (2010) *Coaching Conversations; Transforming Your School One Conversation at a Time*, Corwin Press, Thousand Oaks, CA.

Cornett, J. and Knight, J. (2008) *Research on Coaching*, pp. 192–216, accessed at http://www.instructionalcoach.org/research.html on 23 February 2010.

Costa, A. and Garmston, R. (2002) *Coaching; A Foundation for Renaissance Schools*, Christopher-Gordon Publishers, MA.

Cox, E., Bachkirova, T. and Clutterbuck, D. (2010) The Complete Handbook of Coaching, SAGE Publications, London.

Crane, T. G. (2009) *The Heart of Coaching; Using Transformational Coaching to Create a High Performance Coaching Culture*, 3rd edition, FTA Press, San Diego.

Cross, N. and Lyle, J. (2002) *The Coaching Process*, 3rd edition, Butterworth/Heinemann, Edinburgh

CUREE, (2005) National Framework for Mentoring and Coaching, accessible at http://www.curee-paccts.com/files/publication/1219925968/National-framework-for-mentoring-and-coaching.pdf

Day, D. (2001) 'Leadership Development: A Review in Context', *Leadership Quarterly*, 11(4), 581–613.

De Haan, E. (2008) *Relational Coaching*, John Wiley and Sons, Chichester.

Fletcher, S. (2000) *Mentoring in School: A Handbook of Good Practice*, RoutledgeFalmer, London.

Fletcher, S. (2009) The Mentor of Bath's Published Resource for Teachers-as-Learners, accessed 3 June 2011 at http://www.cfkeep.org/html/snapshot.php?id=52570385348583

Hargreaves, A. and Dawe, R. (2002) 'Paths of professional development: Contrived collegiality, collaborative culture and the case of peer coaching', *Teaching and Teacher Education*, 6, 227–241.

Hay, J. (2008) *Reflective Practice and Supervision for Coaches*, 2nd edition, The Open University Press, Maidenhead.

Hiebert, J., Gallimore, R. and Stigker, J. (2002) 'A knowledge base for the teaching profession; What would it look like and how could we get one?' *Educational Researcher*, 31(5), 3–15.

Hromek, R. (2007) *Emotional Coaching*, SAGE, London.

Jones, R. (ed.) (2006) *The Sports Coach as Educator; Re-conceptualising Sports Coaching*, Routledge, London.

Joyce, B., and Showers, B. (1980) 'Improving in-service training: The messages of Research', *Educational Leadership*, 37(5), 379–385.

Kee, K., Dearing, V., Harris, E. and Shuster, F. (2010) *Results Coaching*, Corwin Press, Thousand Oaks, CA.

Killion, J. and Harrison, C. (2006) *Taking the Lead; New Roles for Teachers and School-based Coaches*, National Staff Development Council, Oxford, OH, USA.

Kise, J. (2006) *Differentiated Coaching; A Framework for Helping Teachers Change*, Corwin Press, Thousand Oaks, CA.

Knight, J. (2007) *Instructional Coaching; A Partnership approach to Improving instruction*, Corwin Press, Thousand Oaks, CA.

Knight, J. and Cornett, J. (2008) *Studying the Impact of Instructional Coaching*, University of Kansas, Centre for Research on Learning, Lawrence, KA.

Lave, J. and Wenger, E. (1991) *Situated Learning*, Cambridge University Press, New York, NY.

Lofthouse, R., Leat, D., Towler, C., Hall, E. and Cummings, C. (2010) *Improving Coaching: Evolution not Revolution*, National College for Leadership in Schools and Children's Services, Nottingham.

Lord, P., Lamont, E., Harland, J. et al. (2009) *Evaluation of the GTC's Teacher Learning Academy (TLA): Impacts on Teachers, Pupils and Schools*, report for the National Foundation for Educational Research (NfER), accessible at http://www.nfer.ac.uk/nfer/research/projects/evaluation-teacher-learning-academy/evaluation-teacher-learning-academy_home.cfm

Lord, P., Atkinson, M. and Mitchell, M. (2008) *Mentoring and Coaching for Professionals; A Study of the Research Evidence*, TDA/NfER, UK.

Lyle, J. (2002) *Sports Coaching Concepts; A Framework for Coaches' Behaviour*, Routledge, London.

McLeod, A. (2004) *Performance Coaching*, 2nd edition, Crown House Publishing, Carmarthen, Wales.

McKinsey (2010) 'Capturing the Leadership Premium', accessed 3 March 2010 at www.mckinsey.com/clientservice/Social.../schoolleadership_final.ashx

National College for School Leadership (2003) *One to One Leadership; Coaching in Schools*, NCSL, Nottingham.

O'Connor, J. and Lages, A. (2007) *How Coaching Works*, A & C Black Publishers, London.

Parsloe, E. and Leedham, M. (2009) *Coaching and Mentoring; Practical Conversations to Improve Learning*, 2nd edition, KoganPage, London.

Rhodes, C. and Beneike, S. (2002) 'Coaching, mentoring and peer-networking; challenges for the management of teacher professional development in schools', *Professional Development in Education*, 28(2), 297–310.

Robertson, J. (2009) *Coaching Educational Leadership*, SAGE, London.

Schön, D. (1987) *Educating the Reflective Practitioner*, Jossey-Bass, CA.

Schön, D. (1988) 'Coaching reflective teaching', in Grimmett, P., and Erickson, G. *Reflection in Teacher Education*, Teachers College Press, New York, NY.

Showers, B. and Joyce, B. (1996) 'The evolution of peer coaching', *Educational Leadership*, 53, 12–17.

Silver, M., Lochmiller, C., Copland, M. and Tripps, A.-M. (2009) 'Supporting new school leaders; findings from a university-based leadership coaching program for new administrators', *Mentoring and Tutoring Journal*, 17(3), 215–232.

Street, H. and Temperley, J. (eds) (2005) *Improving Schools through Collaborative Inquiry*, Continuum Press, London.

Tolhurst, J. (2006) *Coaching for Schools; a practical guide to building leadership capacity*, Pearson Education, Harlow.

Veenman, S., Denessen, E., Gerrits, J. and Kenter, J. (2010) 'Evaluation of a Coaching Programme for Cooperating Teachers', *Education Studies*, 27(3), 317–340.

Veenman, S., De Laat, H., and Staring, C. (1998) 'Evaluation of a coaching programme for mentors of beginning teachers', *Journal of In-service Education*, 24(3), 411–431.

Veenman, S. (1995) The Training of Coaching Skills; an implementation study, *Educational Studies*, 21, 415–431.

Whitmore, J. (2002) *Coaching for Performance*, 3rd edition, Nicholas Brealey Publishing, London.

Wisker, G., Exley, K., Antoniou, M. and Ridley, P. (2008) *Working One-to-one With Students*, Routledge, London.

Skills, Values and Understandings

Improving Coaching by and for School Teachers

David Leat, Rachel Lofthouse
and Carl Towler

INTRODUCTION

We believe that coaching that is most productive of professional learning entails an interpersonal communication process that involves externalisation and internalisation processes. Externalisation allows practitioners to articulate their thoughts and principles for examination and elaboration, and requires trust and a personal relationship which transcends any organisational role. Such a relationship permits dialogue which, as Sidorkin (1999) argues passionately, is the site for our humanity. Internalisation allows a dialogic process, a pattern of voices, to become a self-regulative, metacognitive process, that we might term 'inner voice'. Coaching does not require friendship but it needs to pay attention to the close intertwining of our cognitive and emotional systems, and indeed how action is linked to both, in the pursuit of experimentation. However, there is a diversity of understandings and models of coaching. Garmston (1987) identified three different forms of coaching:

- *Technical coaching* focuses on teachers learning specific new skills.
- *Collegial coaching* uses reflection and professional dialogue between teachers to both improve practice and to challenge the organisational norms and structures if they are perceived as an impediment.
- *Challenge coaching* is a hybrid of the other two models targeting specific and persistent problems in instructional design and delivery that need attention, which implies a failing on the part of the teacher.

Denton and Hasbrouck (2009) provide a fuller elaboration of coaching types based on empirical studies in the US. These typologies clearly highlight variation of purpose in coaching and expose different principles and ideologies. We believe that all can be justified in context, but what is important is that advocates can justify the chosen approach in their context, and explain it to others. We have taught a masters module on teacher coaching for more than a decade, and have researched the topic for nearly as long. Our reading of the context in the UK leads us to privilege a model similar to collegial coaching, because, as we will argue, teachers often work in a culture in which their professional identity is compromised by overbearing managerialism.

In this chapter, we will draw upon our teaching experience and two research projects. The first project was unfunded and involved interviews with coaching pairs to explore the experiential benefits of coaching and difficulties encountered, which are summarised in the next section. The second, the 'Improving Coaching' project was funded and involved 15 interviews with teachers, coaching coordinators and senior leaders in schools, as well as notes from field meetings, an online survey and analysis of 29 coaching transcripts (Lofthouse, Leat and Towler, 2010). The coaches were all serving teachers, coaching in their own schools and had received training from a variety of sources, some commercial and some from their local authority, usually only comprising one or two days. Their roles in their schools were also quite varied, from classroom teacher to subject leader, senior leader and specialist coach. In nearly all cases the coaches had been coached themselves either as part of their training or before being trained (which in many cases provided motivation to be trained). The 14 schools in this project were drawn from four contrasting localities in England. A core aim of this second project was working in partnership with teachers and schools to develop approaches for improving coaching. It is these co-developed approaches which are the focus of the chapter.

THE BENEFITS OF COACHING FOR TEACHERS

Some of the particular advantages that teachers recount in relation to coaching are worth rehearsing (Leat and Lofthouse, 2006). First, coaching does seem to be *enjoyed* by many participants. As this is not a word associated too frequently with professional learning, and it is consistent in our data, it is noteworthy. This pleasure comes from the chance to have time to reflect upon, and explore through dialogue, teaching and resultant learning in their classrooms. Some teachers felt that it was the first time since their initial training that they have thought deeply about their teaching. The enthusiasm is captured well by this teacher:

> It's bringing back some of the fun into our teaching. There is time for professional dialogue and you cannot overestimate the importance of that … Everyone is so excited by our coaching.

The coaching dialogue provided a space for them to step outside the intensity of everyday planning and teaching tasks and it gave them license to think of themselves as learners again. The second benefit described by many comes from the interrogation of small episodes, which can help explain the course of whole lessons. For example:

> I have really enjoyed looking at those small incidents that just flash past in lessons … we have been able to slow them down, replay them, really understand what is happening. You can't do that for a whole lesson but … you learn so much from small bits of lessons.

In our masters teaching we have been strong advocates of using video of lessons in coaching. Being filmed does raise anxiety levels as it is not a cultural norm in teacher professionalism. This is partly because of the fear of being confronted by an image of oneself and partly because of concerns about surveillance and safeguarding. If teachers can overcome the emotional sting then video becomes an invaluable tool (Hennessy and Deaney, 2009). Video does not catch everything and it is not completely unbiased, but more than any other method of lesson observation it captures the unique ecological wholeness of a lesson. The effectiveness of video as a learning tool often surprised:

> Video was a surprise … It was far more useful tool than I ever thought it would be to me.

As a final case for the use of video, many teachers commented on the way that it enabled them to see the lesson and their teaching from 'alternative perspectives'. It is hard to get inside the heads of pupils, but video can at least allow teachers to view lessons from the back of the room:

> Way back I was really against being videoed. I showed the video to pupils and it was really revolutionary for pupils' behaviour. I saw that when we were doing speaking and listening that I did all the speaking and they did all the listening. Next time I put on a slide and said get on with it and I stood back. It really changed my role. … Video helps you crystallise and revisit and helps you focus in on what individuals and groups did.

THE PROBLEMS ENCOUNTERED IN COACHING

While the dominant response to coaching of teachers we have encountered was overwhelmingly positive, a number of recurring problems surfaced. These are important markers for the development of coaching, as they indicate pinch points in our educational structures and cultures. First, many teachers lament the lack of time that is made available for coaching. They need time to meet before and after 'focus' lessons and many found themselves fitting coaching into non-contact time such as lunchtimes, before or after school. Even where a school had provided some time to support coaching, perhaps perversely, some teachers felt guilt.

The second major issue was how to find a focus for coaching and sometimes a coaching partner. Teachers are accustomed to being given broad solutions for issues that policy demands that they consider – differentiation, emotional literacy, challenge – whether they perceive them as an issue or not. While these are important, there is a danger that they may be so far removed from a teacher's current practice that they cannot be incorporated into their work without radical, and often unrealistic, changes. Change requires detailed work in beliefs and action, and a lack of focus can become an irritation:

> It was quite difficult initially – the focus was too wide. When we came back (for a new term) we focused down on making connections.

Finally, we draw attention to a facet of teacher accountability systems in England, known as *performance management,* which is currently the fulcrum of professional development in schools. The process of performance management involves an annual review, classroom observation and professional development target setting. Sadly, for most, it is not experienced as a developmental process. Generally, teachers make the point that coaching needs to be divorced from performance management, as one is based on trust and development and the other substantially on power relationships and accountability. Several interviewees were adamant that if teachers saw coaching as part of performance management and monitoring they would be less likely to enter a coaching partnership. When observers visit classrooms they are often perceived as 'hostile witnesses'. Most educational systems are very top down and centralised. This assumes that the higher up the pecking order you are, the more you know and the greater expertise you have. This is a mistaken assumption, as much pedagogical expertise resides in the teaching workforce. For collegial coaching to work well strenuous efforts have to be made to negate power and to establish relationships based on trust.

This account of some the raw edges of coaching has some resonance with the findings in the 'State of the Nation' (Pedder, Storey and Opfer, 2008), an official report on continuing professional development (CPD) in England which shows that most teachers' experience of CPD is not collaborative or informed by research. It tends to involve passive forms of learning, is not sustained or embedded and the outcomes are fragmented. On experiencing coaching, which has the power to excite personal perceptions, concerns and successes, comparisons are made which result in coaching being reported in glowing terms.

THE NEED FOR IMPROVEMENT?

We have deliberately started with a strong empirical basis to this chapter, reflecting our evidence of many teachers' experiences of coaching. To reprise, when teachers are free to examine and discuss their teaching, especially aided by video recordings, they enjoy the immersion in dialogue, the development of relationships and the exploration of meaning in relation to their classrooms. They are, however, cautious about coaching as they perceive that rarely will it be sufficiently resourced and are anxious about power relationships and account-ability regimes invading the process. This gives some bearing on the need for improvement. Perspectives from the broader literature on coaching and profes-sional learning allows the building of a more precise picture of how coaching could assume greater significance in schools and colleges.

The first perspective shines a light on the importance of school cultures which in turn reflect the status of teacher professionalism. In 1990, Andy Hargreaves and Ruth Dawe drew attention to one of the most troublesome relationships affecting teacher coaching – the exercise of managerial power. They drew a com-parison between collaborative cultures and contrived collegiality. They focused on specialist or technical coaching, which had been particularly popularised by the work of Joyce and Showers (1988), which provided evidence that teacher coaching was the most effective form of professional development in terms of impact on student outcomes. For Hargreaves and Dawe contrived collegiality results from administrative direction to implement curricula and pedagogy designed by others – it is a top-down managerial approach. Collaborative cul-tures, on the contrary, are derived from more equal power relationships which generate trust and more open and reflective stances. Such cultures provide energy for curriculum and professional development.

Subsequently Hargreaves (2000) has described teacher professionalism as developing through four historical phases in many countries: the pre-professional age, the age of the autonomous professional, the age of the collegial professional and the fourth age which he characterises as post-professional or post-modern. The third age, the collegial, he argues was marked by the waning of the authority of external expertise associated with off-site training and teachers turning to each other to solve practice problems. This age coincides with the emergence of socio-cultural theories of learning, in which learning is regarded as situated and is epitomised by Wenger's (1998) concept of community of practice. The post-modern age which, it is suggested, emerged around the turn of the present century, is one of uncertainty. Globalisation and the spread of new digital technologies, accompanied by neo-liberal market ideology have seen a de-professionalisation of teachers. This has resulted in teachers being held increasingly accountable for the outcomes of their work, as measured by stan-dardised tests. In addition in some countries there has been a closer control over curriculum, attendant teaching materials and even methods of teaching. It is argued (Ballet, Kelchtermans and Loughran, 2006) that in this managerial milieu teachers' creativity is eroded and professional learning is increasingly directed in line with external agendas. Merson (2000) sees this shift of power as adversely affecting collegial relationships and relaxation. Time is squeezed and the space for dialogue is diminished. Eleanore Hargreaves (2010), in a study of mentoring/coaching amongst administrative and academic staff in a higher education insti-tute, highlights how coaching can reverse some of the effects of intensification. The research indicates the importance of positive personal relationships in the 'learning conversations', which encouraged the participants to see themselves as more powerful and less hemmed in, to express their feelings, construct new identities and co-construct new practice knowledge. In their wider group meetings, they appreciated getting to know each other and hearing each other's work experiences and interpretations. Much of this Hargreaves attributes to the non-hierarchical relationship.

An alternative frame for professionalism is provided by the Aristotlean concept of phronesis, which encapsulates the process of wise practical reasoning. Critically, what guides practical reasoning is morality, so that action might deliver change which enhances the quality of life. Phronesis is not merely a skill but involves the ability to reflect upon and determine appropriate ends. It is acquired through experience, but aided by deliberation with others, in the sifting of meaning, causes, possibilities and consequences. This communal deliberation secures multiple interpretations and frees us from reliance on the insularity of individual perception and belief. Such deliberation, as Eisner (2002) stresses, needs a language. It cannot be taught and the reasoning is context sensitive and immune from universal objective rules or theories. Instead genuine knowledge is unique to context, which reflects a counterbalance to imposed centralised standards. For Elliott (2006), phronesis is educational inquiry, a form of practitioner research that uses what he calls common sense theorising in that there is a degree of rationality and metacognitive choice that can be deployed. In keeping with the rejection of universal truths guiding action, phronesis demands that sense making is dynamic as we construct and reconstruct our values through successive judgements (where possible collaboratively). Coaching fits this epistemological stance.

More broadly and pragmatically there is evidence from coaching studies that, as one might expect, front-loaded coaching training with no chance for analysing practice, reflection or feedback often fails to translate into idealised practice. In the Netherlands, Bergen, Engelen and Derksen (2000) used content analysis of tape-recorded coaching sessions to investigate what was 'going on' in coaching conversations. Their analysis showed that coaches spent an inordinate amount of time clarifying their interpretation of what they had observed and what the teacher had intended. The coaches thus dominated the conversation more than intended. Where coaches made suggestions for improvement, many of these were not followed up. The coaches also varied enormously in terms of the role that they played (companionship, feedback, analysis, adaptation and support). In England, in the context of professional development for school leadership coaching ('Leading from the Middle'), Simkins, Coldwell, Caillau, Finlayson and Morgan (2006) found evidence that, after relatively cursory training, senior leaders acting as coaches were not sufficiently skilled or committed, and that many lapsed into a more general mentoring role. Typically this involved checking that their charges were making the progress expected of the course. This reflects the recurring ambiguity in coaching practice between managerial and development outcomes. Some coached teachers felt that their coaches did not understand the significance of the commitment required.

So, on the basis of this evidence, improvement in coaching would require action on the following fronts:

- Work on school structures that provide the resources and support for coaching partnerships.
- Resolution of contradictions in institutional cultures, which lead to confusions in the understandings of purposes related to coaching. Culture comprises a set of informal expectations and values which shape how people think, feel and act in schools.
- Practice development by communities of school coaches, guided by a metacognitive awareness of that practice and developing consciousness of appropriate ends for that practice.

COACHING DIMENSIONS – AN ANALYTICAL LANGUAGE FOR PRACTICE DEVELOPMENT

One of our assumptions in the 'Improving Coaching' project, taking inspiration from Eisner and other proponents of phronesis, was the importance of a pragmatic analytical language through which to relate means and ends for coaching practitioners. The evolution of the dimensions of the analytical language associated with coaching took some time. The dimensions were suggested from a wide variety of sources including a range of theoretical perspectives, transcripts and many discussions with project teachers about their experiences. The dimensions have been through three rounds of discussion with the teachers, the first when the ideas were introduced (based on our analysis of the teachers' coaching transcripts), the second when, in workshop formats, they were applied to a coaching transcript, and lastly in a focus group meeting of teachers in northeast England. The dimensions have served two purposes. First, they allowed us to analyse coaching practice as manifested in the transcripts and feed the data back to teachers. Second, they offered the building blocks of an emerging language for teachers to investigate their coaching practice. A short rationale for each of the dimensions follows.

Initiation

The initiation dimension marks whether it is the coach or the coached teacher who starts an episode in the coaching transcript. This is usually, but not exclusively done through a question.

The justification for this dimension rests on the importance of choice and power. Prompted by the I–R–F (Initiation, Response, Feedback) pattern identified in discourse analysis (Sinclair and Coulthard, 1992), we homed in on initiation as a key indicator in coaching, as it implies power. The person who instigates an episode has power because they select the particular focus, can control the dialogue and keep the coached person in a response mode. It is interesting to analyse therefore which party initiates in the coaching session.

Example of a coach initiating: Just putting instructions on the board, is that something you'd normally do?

Stimulus

Stimulus refers to whether observation/notes, video clip or artefact are used to provide focus or concrete manifestation in initiating a coaching episode.

> *Example of video being used:* (Coach) I've got a clip here, I spotted aspects where you might go on to change and develop that. If that was set up slightly different it might have improved and learning become subsequent. Shall we watch it?

Tone

Tone refers to the character and degree of evaluation; often stated directly but also commonly inferred. The five point coding scale ranged from very negative to very positive with a mid-point of neutral tone, which implies no evaluation.

A critical human characteristic is our need to have a positive self concept. Evidence suggests that people have many subtle ways to protect themselves against feedback that challenges that self concept. Negative feedback from a line manager, for example, can lead a teacher to denigrate the source of the evidence, which allows it to be discounted. There is a need to avoid an overly negative tone of judgement. Conversely the work of Dweck (2000) on student self theories would suggest that lavish praise should be used sparingly. Such considerations would suggest that coaches need to tread a careful path, being neither substantially positive nor negative.

> *Example of very positive tone:* (Coach) Well I've done that lesson, but I've never had the two hours that you did and it was fantastic to watch
>
> *Example of negative tone:* (Coached teacher) The only thing   that has worked so far is saying 'answer these five questions: if they're not done, you're not going anywhere', and that's not really what you want to be doing.

Scale

Scale provides an indication of the level of generality or specificity in the coaching episode. The categories are not related to strict measures of time. 1 = critical moment, 2 = lesson episode, 3 = whole lesson, 4 = theme (related to pupils, the subject, teaching and/or learning, or the teacher), 5 = issues related to schools, education or society.

Scale relates to the degree of the particular as opposed to the degree of the general. In research on planning (Hayes-Roth and Hayes-Roth, 1979) it is evident that the thinking behind the successful planning of tasks does not proceed from a master plan to meticulous implementation. Instead good planning veers levels, from a metalevel overview to the fine detail of small tasks and levels in-between. One level informs the others in an iterative fashion. At a very pragmatic level, transfer of thinking is associated with some degree of generalisation, and therefore if a coaching conversation only explores particulars there is some doubt about whether it will support internalisation and transfer.

> *Example (A coach teacher focusing on scale 2, a lesson episode and then progressing to a general point):* I expected them to look at the mark scheme … I thought it was obvious, there is the mark scheme, there are the answers to the questions … And I think that's maybe indicative of kids (moving to the general), maybe they just need to do it more and more and more so they don't just rely on me.

Time orientation

The time category refers to whether the conversation refers backwards to the lesson planning or the lesson, forwards to future lessons, or 'sideways' thus being non-time specific.

In a complete coaching cycle one might expect that the process would analyse lesson planning, lesson events and look forward to future teaching.

> *Example 1 (Coached teacher looking forwards):* The aspect I want you to look at really is the homework. Mainly because in the past it's been quite a hard thing for me to get out of the children
> *Example 2 (Coached teacher reflecting on lesson events):* I've got some of the characters, Mark (name changed), for example, he was a little bit of a pest for me, I must say.

Interaction function

Interaction function was the most challenging dimension as there was the need to reflect a wide array of processes between the partners. Asking a question or giving a clarification, explanation or justification, were some of the more obvious categories. We were also interested in whether coaches challenged their partners and what response this drew; for example, registering dissonance (Tillema, 1997), acceptance or resistance. Another key issue was whether coaches made suggestions, whether new ideas were sparked and whether generalisations were made, all of which suggest a certain level of creativity. The full list of interaction categories is: Question, Evaluation, Summary, Acceptance, Challenge, Context, Generalisation, Clarification, New Idea, Justification, Explanation, Continuity, Dissonance, Defence and Suggestion.

> *Example:* (Proactive coach making suggestions) Get the students to put their aprons on and wash their hands, so get all that done first and then get them lined up, because (switching to explanation) after that if they hadn't put their aprons on, you then have to send them off to do that.

> *Coached teacher (asking a question):* Once we've done the starter, we've got recipe cards haven't we? Shall we put those on the table straight away?

Co-construction

A final dimension evolved near the end of the project as we considered progression in coaching, as we had identified episodes when some coaching conversations 'took off' as partners tuned into each other's thinking. It is marked by a number of 'turns' which are characteristically short and where the coach and coached teacher are collaboratively developing an idea, building on the successive contributions of their partner.

COACHES' REPERTOIRE

We provide a brief outline of the analysis of the 29 coaching transcripts as a bearing for teachers' reflections on improving their coaching practice (given later). The majority of interaction in coaching sessions is explaining/justifying, clarifying and evaluating episodes in the lessons. Notably, challenge by coaches was unusual (only 6 per cent of post-lesson interactions) and this seemed to be a style issue. Those coaches that did utilise challenge used it as part of their routine practice, while many others did not challenge at all. Thirty-eight per cent of all challenges were generated by one coach and 17 per cent by another. Very few coaching segments referred to the thinking behind the planning of the lesson, thus rarely were teachers' assumptions and beliefs exposed. There were relatively few extreme positive or negative comments or tones. Most of the extremely negative comments come from the coached teacher where they were particularly unhappy with an aspect of the lesson. Less than 1 per cent of coaches' interactions expressed dissonance, while the figure for coached teachers was 3 per cent. Many coaching sessions contained no dissonance. This is not necessarily a weakness, but dissonance is a sign of shifting thoughts and beliefs. There was a variable amount of moving from the particular to the general, but where this happens the generalisations are generally at the craft level. These, in other circumstances, have been termed 'situated generalisations', sifting out what seems to work with these students in this particular school, rather than referring to broader pedagogical principles. The most important focus in terms of scale concerned themes (scale 4), followed by episodes (scale 2) and then whole lessons (scale 3), but the differences are small. Episodes tended to focus on lesson 'parts', such as starters, or whole activities or in a few cases transitions between activities. There was very little consideration and unpacking of critical moments (scale 1).

In Figures 3.1 and 3.2 we present graphical representations of the frequency of the interaction features of two coaches and their partners. The differences are very marked, with Angela having a wide repertoire of types of interaction, including challenge, clarification (of what she meant) and suggestions, which in turn prompted a wide array of responses, although explanation does dominate. Miriam on the other hand predominantly asks questions and provokes evaluation, clarification and explanation in return. Angela and Miriam have different beliefs about coaching: Miriam believes that coaches should in no sense solve their partner's problems as the solutions reside within them, while Angela believes in a more dialogic co-constructive approach.

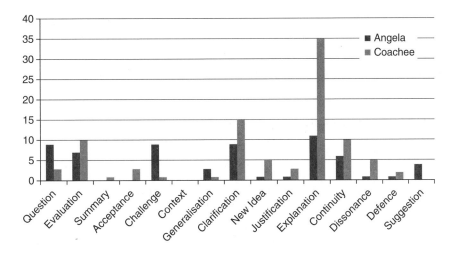

Figure 3.1 Frequency with which each interaction function is employed by 'Angela' and her partner

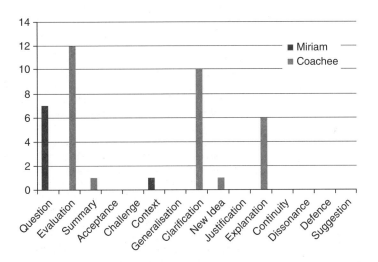

Figure 3.2 Frequency with which each interaction function is employed by 'Miriam' and her partner

FOUR LEVELS OF COACHING PRACTICE

While the dimensions provided a language for more deliberative analysis of practice, both by the coaches and researchers, there was also a need for a model to indicate coaching development. From discussions with teaching groups, coaching literature (e.g., Costa and Garmston, 1994) and analysis of transcripts it was evident that there were some key features in the progression of coaching practice.

These focused on a depth of reflection, criticality and the ability to co-construct and thus solve problems. From these starting points we devised a model of four levels of coaching development (see Table 3.1), which was shaped and refined through consultation with and feedback from teachers in the project.

Table 3.1   Four levels of coaching development

Level	*Description of overall coaching conversation*
Level 1: Emergent coaching	The coach asks questions which lead the coachee to give an account of features of the lesson by drawing on recall and anecdotal evidence. The coaching conversation is focused on individual aspects of teaching, the classroom environment or pupils' learning experiences. The coach and coachee tend not to integrate these aspects and the conversation is thus largely descriptive. The lesson being discussed tends not to be considered in relation to wider contexts of policy, pedagogical frameworks, educational theory or the coachee's professional development or learning. However some comparison may be drawn with the coachee's past experiences.
Level 2: Deliberative coaching	The coach asks questions which prompt the coachee to consider the impact of their teaching on pupils' learning. The coachee describes the decisions they made before and during the lesson and considers how the pupils responded. The coaching conversation draws out some links between aspects of teaching, the classroom environment, the pupils' experiences and learning outcomes. These may be discussed through reference to the coachee's previous experiences, and may lead to specific problems or issues being discussed. The coach and coachee might begin to consider the lesson in relation to the wider contexts of policy, pedagogical frameworks, educational theory or the coachee's professional development or learning.
Level 3: Strategic coaching	During the coaching conversation the coach and coachee discuss teaching, the classroom environment and pupils' learning using evidence gathered during the lesson. There is a significant focus on learners' progress. The coach asks questions which prompt the coachee to begin to problem-solve, hypothesise and reflect on the significance of their actions or beliefs. This leads the coach and coachee to 'step back' from the specific lesson. Through appropriate questioning the coach begins to challenge the coachee's assumptions about teaching and learning. This may lead them to engage with the wider contexts of educational policy, pedagogical frameworks and the coachee's own professional learning or development.
Level 4: Co-constructive/ self-regulating coaching	The coaching conversation allows both the coach and coachee to make connections between evidence from the coachee's practice, and the wider contexts of educational policy and pedagogical frameworks. There is significant focus on enhancing learning opportunities. The coach and coachee use the discussion to critically review their understanding of the relationships between the teaching, the classroom environment and pupils' learning experiences and progress. The questions that they ask each other allow them to successfully explore their own understandings. Through reflecting on, and responding to, each others' contributions they identify alternative pedagogic approaches. This leads to exploratory talk related to opportunities for professional learning and development and the ways in which they might analyse the impact of this on pupils' progress.

TEACHERS' ACCOUNTS OF PRACTICE DEVELOPMENT

In the project meetings there was a mixed response to the dimensions, broadly positive but with some general reservations and some specific points of concern. The two dimensions that were most readily embraced were tone and scale. The teachers were attuned to the importance of tone as they had in previous meetings commented on how important feelings and trust are between coach and partner. In the anonymised coaching transcript used in the project meetings, they soon picked up on the pattern of the coach adopting a mediating tone, by, for example, balancing a negative evaluation by their partner with a positive contribution. There was a general agreement that most coaching should be substantially neutral in tone (the middle three categories) and that the extremes would be notable and interesting. Scale was seen as very important by a few and worthy of consideration by most, in terms of understanding their own practice. One coach commented that it was very important to do that '4 stuff – the principle bit, it allows you to talk more deeply and you hope that this might stay with them in other lessons' (in the scale dimension, '4' refers to theme). Another commented that she had not realised it before but she could see why it was important. It was comments such as the following that proved persuasive to others:

> I have watched my DVD and even from memory I can think I was mainly 2, did I do enough 4, watch that 5 does not become whingeing and you need the video for 1 because you miss the 1s, they are easily missed. … Actually I can almost 'see' the colours (which refer to the time orientations).

Interaction categories proved more taxing. We were aware in developing the categories that there were likely to be too many to be quickly internalised by teachers. Challenge and suggestion were seen as critical interactions, even though many admitted to shying away from challenge. There was some discussion of how one should deal with coaching partners who have little convergence in their analysis with the coach. It was a minority of coaches who spoke about the importance of suggestions but generally they persuaded the majority that coaching is a collective activity and it is through engaging with planning that one can build trust and change norms. One coach explained that he offered suggestions but in no way insisted on them being followed and this helped to position him as a co-planner. Other teachers were less sure and saw suggestions as developing dependency, reinforcing the habit among some young teachers of wanting an answer to problems. One young teacher caused some consternation by explaining that he would get in a lot of self criticism before the coach would start as a form of self-defence, as it had been his experience during his initial teacher training and first year of teaching that mentors were inclined to be critical and 'picky'.

The online survey, to which there were 23 responses, provided another indication of the extent to which teachers were able to recognise and work with the dimensions in analysing coaching practice. For example, 52 per cent of the respondents stated, at the end of the second year of the project, that they had already worked successfully to improve their use of stimulus (such as video, observation and pupil work) to prompt thinking during coaching. Fifty seven per cent stated that they were consciously managing their tone of voice during the conversation, and thirty three per cent said they were working to improve this. Eighty-one per cent had been working to improve the balance between the coach and coachee initiating the lines of discussion and also in managing the scale of discussion (critical incident etc.). There were detailed comments on the use of video from seven respondents (82.6 per cent of the respondents reported using video to record lessons), all of whom made somewhat similar points about the value of being able to examine and reflect on the detail of events, which in several cases had not been noticed in the heat of the moment.

Although the survey is based on self report, which has attendant questions marks over validity, the evidence from the meetings was considerable in showing that teacher coaches do not need much support and encouragement to enter into analysis and debate about their practice. Although there were many differences in viewpoints, and indeed surprises, this always felt healthy as there were some rapid shifts in viewpoints and some sense of emergent cultural norms. We should be clear however that there remained some marked differences in opinion as befits a dialogic space. In our teaching programme and dissertation supervision, teachers are readily turning to the dimensions and levels model as methods for analysing and reflecting on practice, but not uncritically. An interview extract from a coaching co-ordinator captures the power of a new vocabulary:

> When you are talking about the dimensions, when they were introduced to me it changed the way I thought about coaching.

CONCLUSION

Although Basil Bernstein's (1996) concepts of classification and framing were developed to explain the disadvantage of working class pupils in the school system, their application to the context of teacher learning brings insight to changing power relationships and professional identity in schools. Classification refers to the strength of the boundaries between subject domains. Framing refers to the regulation rules governing communication, and ultimately to the selection, organisation, pacing and timing of the knowledge to be transmitted to students. Strong framing reflects teacher control of the object of study, whereas weak framing offers some freedom to the learner. Framing encompasses a regulative discourse concerning the expectations of conduct, character and manner in learning settings – essentially who can speak to whom about what with what licence or authority. We might regard them as the rules of engagement. Bernstein regarded framing as the locus of pedagogical change. It is important to remember that there is a pedagogy of teacher learning and the increasing expectations and managerialism inflicted on schools has materially changed teachers' working conditions, notably in the opportunities for dialogue and rich professional relationships. The discourse of performativity is pervasive. We would argue that if teachers are given sufficient time, space and analytical frameworks, such as the coaching dimensions (with their imperfections), they can begin to throw off some of the shackles that impede their professional growth. It is through strong professional relationships, founded in trust and respect, and in which dialogue is possible, that practical wisdom, or phronesis, can emerge. At present in many countries, national policies translated into managerial imperatives insert strong boundaries not only between subjects, but also between subject teachers. Furthermore school cultures and policies strongly influence the rules of engagement, or framing of the professional discourse between teachers. It does not have to be this way – there is opportunity for a more informed professionalism.

REFERENCES

Ballet, K., Kelchtermans, G. and Loughran, J. (2006) Beyond intensification towards a scholarship of practice: analysing changes in teachers' work lives, *Teachers and Teaching: Theory and Practice*, 12(2), 209–229.

Bergen, T., Engelen, A. and Derksen, K. (2000) What is going on during the coaching conference between coach and teacher? Paper presented at the American Educational Research Association, New Orleans, April 24–28, 2000.

Bernstein, B. (1996) *Pedagogy, Symbolic Control and Identity*, London: Taylor & Francis.

Costa, A. L. and Garmston, R. L. (1994) *Cognitive Coaching: A Foundation for Renaissance Schools*, Norwood, MS: Christopher-Gordon Publishers.

Denton, C. and Hasbrouck, J. (2009) A description of instructional coaching and its relationship to consultation, *Journal of Educational and Psychological Consultation*, 19(2), 150–175.

Dweck, C. (2000) *Self-Theories: Their Role in Motivation, Personality, and Development*, Philadelphia, PA: Psychology Press.

Eisner, E. (2002) From episteme to phronesis to artistry in the study and improvement of teaching, *Teaching and Teacher Education*, 18, 375–385.

Elliott, J. (2006) Educational research as a form of democratic rationality, *Journal of Philosophy of Education*, 40(2), 169–185.

Garmston, R. (1987) How Adminstrators Support Peer Coaching. *Educational Leadership*, 44(5), 18–26.

Hargreaves, A. (2000) Four ages of professionalism and professional learning. *Teachers and Teaching*, 6(2), 151–182.

Hargreaves, A. and Dawe, R. (1990) Paths of professional development: contrived collegiality, collaborative culture, and the case of peer coaching, *Teaching and Teacher Education*, 6, 227–241.

Hargreaves, E. (2010) Knowledge construction and personal relationship: insights about a UK university mentoring and coaching service, *Mentoring and Tutoring: Partnership in Learning*, 18(2), 107–120.

Hayes-Roth, B. and Hayes-Roth, F. (1979) A cognitive model of planning. *Cognitive Science*, 3, 275–310.

Hennessy, S. and Deaney, R. (2009) The impact of collaborative video analysis by practitioners and researchers upon pedagogical thinking and practice: a follow-up study, *Teachers and Teaching*, 15(5), 617–638.

Joyce, B. and Showers, B. (1988) *Student Achievement Through Staff Development*, New York: Longman.

Leat, D. and Lofthouse, R. (2006) Coaching for geography teachers, *Teaching Geography*, 31, 132–134.

Lofthouse, R., Leat, D. and Towler, C. (2010) *Coaching for Teaching and Learning: A Practical Guide for Schools*, Reading: CfBT Educational Trust.

Merson, M. (2000) Teachers and the myth of modernisation, *British Journal of Educational Studies*, 48(2), 155–169.

Pedder, D., Storey, A. and Opfer, V. D. (2008) *Schools and Continuing Professional Development (CPD) – State of the Nation research project*, report commissioned by the Training and Development Agency for Schools, Cambridge University and the Open University, London: Training and Development Agency.

Sidorkin, A. S. (1999) *Beyond Discourse: Education, the Self, and Dialogue*. New York: SUNY Press.

Simkins,T., Coldwell, M., Caillau, I., Finlayson, H. and Morgan, A. (2006) Coaching as an in-school leadership development strategy: experiences from Leading from the Middle. *Journal of In-Service Education*, 32, 321–340.

Sinclair, J. and Coulthard, M. (1992) Towards an analysis of discourse, in M. Coulthard (Ed.) *Advances in Spoken Discourse Analysis*, pp. 1–34. London: Routledge.

Tillema, H. (1997) Promoting conceptual changing learning to teach, *Asian Pacific Journal of Teacher Education*, 25(1), 7–16.

Wenger, E. (1998) *Communities of Practice: learnings, meanings and identity*, Cambridge: Cambridge University Press.

Fostering Face-to-face Mentoring and Coaching

Andrew J. Hobson

INTRODUCTION

This chapter considers means of fostering mentoring and coaching in the broadest sense by outlining the optimum conditions for their effective or successful use as suggested by research evidence. Such conditions may operate at various levels: *macro* – through national or regional policy; *meso* – via organisations; and *micro* – in individual mentor–mentee dyads. The matter under consideration is a significant one in an international context in which, in recent decades, mentoring and coaching have come to play an increasingly prominent part, at not inconsiderable expense, in supporting the professional development of teachers and those in a range of other professions. Yet while the potential gains of mentoring and coaching are substantial, if an appropriate enabling environment within which they are carried out is not established then the various gains are unlikely to be realised and may even be outweighed by associated drawbacks and costs.

In this chapter these issues are discussed in the context of school-based mentoring and coaching provided as key elements of support for beginning teachers[1], and the arguments presented draw on the international research literature in this field. That said, many of the arguments may apply to mentoring and coaching carried out in other settings.

Before proceeding to the main body of the chapter, namely a consideration of the conditions for effective mentoring and coaching, a context for this discussion is provided in the form of an overview of the benefits that can and do result from these conditions being created. Such benefits can and do fall by the wayside where an optimum enabling environment is not created. First, I would like to set out my understanding of the key concepts and the limits of the analysis which follows.

While the terms 'mentoring' and 'coaching' tend to mean different things to different people and are sometimes used interchangeably, most authorities on the subject see mentoring as the broader of the two concepts (Clutterbuck, 1992; Kram, 1985; Malderez and Bodoczky, 1999), an interpretation shared by this author. For the purposes of this chapter, mentoring is taken to refer to the one-to-one support of a novice or less experienced practitioner (the mentee) by a more experienced practitioner (the mentor), designed primarily to assist the development of the mentee's expertise and to facilitate their induction into the culture of the profession (in this case, teaching) and the specific local context (here, the school or college). Coaching is seen as one amongst a number of potential roles that mentors can play, and one which relates to attempts to support an individual's development of one or more job-specific skills and capabilities (Hopkins-Thompson, 2000). For Malderez and Bodoczky (1999), coaching forms part of what they describe as the *educator* role of the mentor, through which the mentor seeks to create appropriate opportunities for the mentee's professional learning. Other roles that mentors may adopt include those of *model* (to inspire and to demonstrate), *acculturator* (to help induct the mentee into the particular professional culture), *sponsor* (to 'open doors' and introduce the mentee to the 'right people') and *provider of psychological support* (to provide the mentee with a safe place to release emotions or 'let off steam') (ibid.).

Given the understanding and interpretation of mentoring and coaching set out above, in what follows I mostly use the term mentoring, as the broader of the two concepts which potentially incorporates coaching. It also follows from the working definition of mentoring as 'one-to-one support by a more experienced practitioner' that this chapter does not deal with the ideas and practices of 'group mentoring' (Mitchell, 1999) or 'peer mentoring' (Cornu, 2005). The chapter focuses on the practice of mentoring as a formal arrangement, in which people are specifically designated to perform the role, sometimes within the context of a mentoring scheme. This should not be taken to suggest, however, that the under-researched area of informal mentoring, in which colleagues provide support for others' professional development outside of formal arrangements, is not vitally important for the learning and well-being of many beginner teachers (Tracey, Homer, Mitchell, Malderez, Hobson, Ashby and Pell, 2008).

THE POTENTIAL BENEFITS AND COSTS OF MENTORING

Research has shown that the potential positive outcomes of mentoring are substantial; indeed some studies suggest that mentoring may be the single most effective method of supporting the professional development of beginning teachers (Franke and Dahlgren, 1996; Hobson, 2002; Marable and Raimondi, 2007;

Su, 1992). It has been found, for example, that mentors can play an important role in the socialisation of novice teachers, helping them adapt to the norms, standards and expectations associated with teaching in general and with specific schools (Edwards, 1998; Feiman Nemser and Parker, 1992). Beginner teacher mentoring has also been associated with a range of other benefits including reduced feelings of isolation, increased confidence and self-esteem, and improved self-reflection and problem-solving capacities (McIntyre and Hagger, 1996), in addition to improved classroom and behaviour management skills (Lindgren, 2005; Malderez, Hobson, Tracey and Kerr, 2007). Related to some of the findings reported above, a growing body of evidence also suggests that teachers who are mentored are less likely to quit teaching (Ingersoll and Kralik, 2004; Johnson, Berg and Donaldson, 2005; Smith and Ingersoll, 2004).

While the primary intended beneficiaries of mentoring and coaching are mentees, a wealth of research evidence shows that mentoring can also have a positive impact on the professional and personal development of the mentors themselves. As well as deriving satisfaction and pride from undertaking the mentor role, notably through witnessing their mentees' progress and noticing evidence of their own impact on mentees' professional development (Beck and Kosnik, 2000; Hagger and McIntyre, 2006), research shows that through encountering 'new ideas' and 'new perspectives' (Abell, Dillon, Hopkins, McInerney and O'Brien, 1995; Simpson, Hastings and Hill, 2007) mentors can enhance their own knowledge and skill in a range of areas including teaching styles and strategies, communication skills and the use of information and communication technology (Davies, Brady, Rodger and Wall, 1999; Lopez-Real and Kwan, 2005; Moor, Halsey, Jones, Martin, Stott, Brown and Harland, 2005). Studies have also found that, as a result of their engagement in mentoring, mentors can become more confident in their teaching and enjoy improved relationships with pupils and colleagues (Bodoczky and Malderez, 1997; Davies et al., 1999), as well as enhanced recognition in the professional community (Wright and Bottery, 1997). In turn, mentoring can lead to a consolidation of mentors' teacher identity and professional status, and an increase in their self-worth (Bodoczky and Malderez, 1997; Templeton, 2003), in addition to an enhanced commitment to teaching or re-engagement with the profession (Hobson, Malderez, Tracey, Homer, Mitchell, Biddulph et al., 2007; Moor et al., 2005).

If the numerous potential benefits of mentoring for mentors and mentees set out above (and others[2]) are realised, there are likely to be resultant gains for those teachers' pupils/students and schools, as well as the broader educational and social systems within which they are situated. Unfortunately, however, in practice such gains are not always realised, and in some cases mentoring can even have a negative impact (Colley, 2002; Sundli, 2007). A number of studies have suggested, for example, that mentoring has resulted in the promotion and reproduction of conventional norms and practices (Feiman Nemser, Parker and Zeichner, 1993), which renders beginner teachers unlikely to develop or consolidate their knowledge and use of progressive and learner-centred approaches.

Research has suggested that in some cases the work of mentors has been harmful to beginning teachers' self-esteem, created anxiety and stress, and contributed to decisions to withdraw from initial teacher preparation or leave the profession (Beck and Kosnick, 2000; Hobson, Giannakaki and Chambers, 2009b; Lee and Feng, 2007; Maguire, 2001). Some research has shown that mentors themselves experience increased and sometimes unmanageable workloads (Robinson and Robinson, 1999; Simpson et al., 2007), while other studies (e.g., Tauer, 1998) have found little evidence of mentors growing professionally from the experience. Furthermore, some mentors have reported feeling nervous, insecure, threatened and even inadequate at the prospect of having their lessons observed by mentees or through their mentees bringing new ideas (Bullough, 2005; Orland, 2001).

It is clear from the foregoing analysis that '[m]ere access to a mentor does not ensure that mentees become better teachers' (Roehrig, Bohn, Turner and Pressley, 2008: 685), and nor is mere participation in mentoring sufficient to produce the various benefits for mentees, mentors and educational systems outlined previously. I now turn to the main focus of this chapter – to paint a picture of the optimum enabling environment for effective or successful mentoring.

CREATING AN ENABLING ENVIRONMENT: THE CONDITIONS FOR EFFECTIVE MENTORING

As suggested earlier, the extent to which mentoring is able to maximize its potential benefits and avoid or minimize the kinds of drawbacks and costs outlined above is determined largely by the extent to which a variety of 'conditions for effective mentoring' exist or can be created. These relate to:

1   mentees' openness to being mentored;
2   contextual support for mentoring;
3   mentor selection and pairing;
4   mentoring strategies employed; and
5   mentor preparation and support.

Each area is considered, in turn, in the following sections.

Mentees' openness to being mentored

Some research suggests that successful mentoring depends to a significant degree on the 'readiness' of the mentee to be mentored and on associated characteristics such as openness, willingness to learn and change, and preparedness to operate outside of their comfort zone (Little, 1990; Schmidt, 2008; Valencic Zuljan and Vogrinc, 2007). This is perhaps an especially poignant issue in relation to the 'high stakes' initial preparation and induction (or probation) of beginning teachers. As Edwards and Ogden (1998) found in relation to the initial preparation of primary school teacher candidates in England, many come into schools with ready-made 'identity projects' that they seek to enact, whereby they are primarily concerned with presenting an appearance of competent performance to mentors and others. Roehrig et al. (2008) thus found that there was a relationship between beginner teachers' progress or effectiveness in class and the extent to which they were 'accepting of, or open to, the mentoring they received' (2008: 697), with some of their 'less effective' participants demonstrating 'defensiveness' while those judged to be relatively effective were more proactive in seeking assistance and more open to critique. These authors quote one of the mentors in their study, who was critical of a mentee for 'resenting' the available mentor support:

> At least come open minded. [My mentee] didn't act like she wanted to be at the meetings – what you get out of it is what you put in.
>
> (Roehrig et al., 2008: 684)

The authors conclude from this mentor's account that '[i]t is clear ... that the attitudes of the beginning teacher mentee are important to the outcomes of a mentoring relationship" (ibid.). However, while this is undoubtedly the case, and assuming that the mentor's account provides an accurate representation of the mentee's approach to being mentored, what is less clear is what might have been the cause of such an attitude or whether an appropriate enabling environment was in place to encourage an alternative one.

Whilst on the surface the mentee's 'willingness' to be mentored may be something over which mentors and others appear to have little control, and though research studies on this issue are not commonplace, it seems likely that a mentee's openness to mentoring will be influenced to at least some extent by each of the conditions for effective mentoring discussed below, namely the context within which the mentoring takes place, the characteristics and suitability of the mentor to whom they are allocated, and the training and preparation received and strategies employed by that mentor. I thus return to this issue periodically in the discussion that follows.

Mentor selection and pairing

Research suggests that variation in the success with which mentoring is employed is related, in part, to the ways mentors are selected or appointed on the one hand and paired with mentees on the other. First, mentors should be models of good professional practice (Foster, 1999) who possess excellent subject knowledge (Abell et al., 1995) and are both willing to 'make their work public' and able to make explicit the factors underlying their classroom practices (Simpson et al., 2007). They should be trustworthy, approachable, supportive, empathetic, positive, non-judgemental and good listeners (Abell et al., 1995). It is also important that mentors want to do the job and are committed to the work of mentoring (Lindgren, 2005; Wildman, Magliaro, Niles and Niles, 1992).

Second, mentoring tends to be more successful, other things being equal, where the dyad does not merely represent a 'marriage of convenience' but where care is taken to try to ensure an appropriate matching of mentor and mentee

(Schmidt, 2008; Wang, 2001). It is important that mentor and mentee are comfortable working together, while some studies suggest that it is beneficial for the mentoring relationship if they get along both personally as well as professionally (Abell et al., 1995). Research has also found that mentoring tends to be *more* successful where decisions about mentor–mentee pairings take account of mentees' strengths and limitations and where mentors teach the same subject specialism as their mentees (Hobson et al., 2007; Johnson, 2004; Smith and Ingersoll, 2004). Mentoring tends to be *less* effective where the mentor is the mentee's head or deputy head teacher, partly because more senior colleagues may be less able to consistently find sufficient time for mentoring, and partly because mentees can be inhibited and less likely to admit to any difficulties where their mentors have a more exalted status within the school (Hobson et al., 2007; Oberski, Ford, Higgins and Fisher, 1999). Unfortunately, research findings are inconclusive on the question of whether mentors and mentees should be paired on the basis of similar or contrasting pedagogical beliefs (Jonson, 2002).

Finally, it is important that mechanisms exist which enable both mentees and mentors to initiate the establishment of an alternative pairing should they feel that the relationship is not (or is no longer) productive (Association for Supervision and Curriculum Development, 1999).

We have seen that a number of considerations relating to mentor selection and pairing can potentially impact on the mentee's openness to being mentored. So too can various aspects of the broader context within which mentoring is carried out.

Contextual support for mentoring

The success or otherwise of mentoring is influenced by a range of contextual factors. The most consistent finding in this area is that mentoring tends to be more effective where mentors are provided with a sufficient amount of release or non-contact time to help them prepare for and undertake the mentoring role (Lee and Feng, 2007; Robinson and Robinson, 1999), and where timetabling allows mentors and mentees to meet together during the school day (Bullough, 2005). Second, mentoring is more likely to be successful where it takes place within schools characterised by collegial and learning cultures and which value 'learning teachers' (Edwards, 1998; Lee and Feng, 2007), and where both mentors and mentees have access to support outside of the mentoring relationship, such as from other teachers in the school or from external networks of peers (Whisnant, Elliott and Pynchon, 2005).

Some research (e.g., Evans and Abbott, 1997; Simpson et al., 2007) has suggested that, other things being equal, mentors will be more committed to the role and thus more likely to be effective where there exists an appropriate financial reward or recognition, or where being a mentor 'contributes to teachers' status or prestige' (Lee and Feng, 2007: 252). Other studies have argued that mentoring will tend to be more effective where it is carried out in contexts relatively free from excessive emphases on externally determined goals and agendas such as prescriptive criteria for teaching practices, notably those which emphasise teacher performance as 'curriculum delivery' (Edwards, 1998; Yusko and Feiman-Nemser, 2008).

Finally, a number of studies (e.g., Heilbronn, Jones, Bubb and Totterdell, 2002; Hobson, 2009; Williams and Prestage, 2002) have suggested that mentoring will have a greater potential for success where the mentor is not charged with the responsibility for assessing as well as providing various kinds of 'instruction-related' and 'psychological' support (Gold, 1996) for the mentee. Mentees in Abell et al.'s (1995) study indicated that they 'wanted their mentors to first and foremost be that person with whom they could talk about anything' while the mentors 'believed that if they had assumed an evaluative stance, then interns would have felt powerless in the relationship and failed to develop the mutual trust and respect that seemed necessary for risk-free learning to occur' (1995: 186). However, the research evidence on this issue is inconclusive. Adey (1997) argues that there need be no conflict between the role of the mentor as supporter/friend and assessor, provided the relationship with the trainee has been well established at the outset, while the student teachers in Foster's (1999) study were reported to be comfortable with their mentors' role in formative assessment and believed that with good mentors, the tension between the support and assessment role was not an issue.

Mentor preparation and support

Since even excellent school teachers may not be effective facilitators of adult learning (Yusko and Feiman-Nemser, 2008), it would seem highly desirable for all mentors to receive initial preparation and continued support for their work as mentors. Indeed, while the evidence base on this subject is currently underdeveloped, a number of studies have concluded that mentors are more likely to employ effective mentoring strategies where they have undertaken mentor training (Crasborn, 2008; Valencic Zuljan and Vogrinc, 2007), some research has linked mentor training and development to improvements in teaching and learning (Strong, 2009), and some has attributed evidence of poor mentoring practice, at least in part, to a lack of appropriate training (Feiman-Nemser and Parker, 1992). It has also been found that effective preparation and support can help to alleviate some of the drawbacks of mentoring, such as those relating to workload (Moor et al., 2005).

Academics working in this area have argued that, amongst other things, mentor training should help mentors to understand the importance and potential benefits of discussing pedagogical issues with mentees (Lindgren, 2005), and should seek to help mentors develop their interpersonal skills (Rippon and Martin, 2006) as well as their ability to stimulate mentees to reflect on their actions (Crasborn et al., 2008; Dunne and Bennett, 1997).

Bullough (2005) argues that mentor preparation should go beyond training for skill development, that there should be provision for ongoing (post-training) support for mentors, and that mentor preparation and support should incorporate methods of assisting individuals to develop their identities as mentors. He suggests that this could be achieved through mentors' involvement, along with university-based teacher-educators, in seminars 'organized around the practice of mentoring' (2005: 153). These could operate as 'affinity groups', facilitate the development of a shared discourse for mentoring, enhance mentors' skill development through conversations about mentoring practice and pedagogy, and help to overcome mentor isolation. Other studies have suggested that similar benefits might accrue from mentors' participation in collaborative inquiry groups. Graham (1997) describes a collaborative inquiry scheme developed as part of an initial teacher preparation programme in the US, in which mentors and their student teachers act as co-inquirers into aspects of their practice, and mentors and other teacher educators form part of a broader network. She shows how the scheme has been effective in a number of ways, including overcoming mentor isolation and improving the mentoring of student teachers, through enabling mentors to discuss issues of concern with their peers and draw on the collective expertise of mentors and teacher educators.

Unfortunately, research suggests that, at present, the quality of mentor preparation programmes is variable, with some giving relatively greater emphasis to administrative aspects of the role than to methods of developing mentors' ability to facilitate mentees' professional learning (Abell et al., 1995). In addition, many mentor training programmes are not compulsory and are poorly attended (Feiman Nemser and Parker, 1992), and we should not ignore the possibility that those mentors who do attend the available courses are not those who are most in need of training and support. Finally, while most mentors at least have the opportunity for some kind of initial training, those who are provided with meaningful opportunities for ongoing support may be in the minority.

Mentoring strategies

Research has identified a number of common approaches or strategies that have been successfully employed by mentors operating in a variety of contexts. The most effective mentors are those who provide their mentees with emotional and psychological support, helping them feel welcome, accepted and included (Hascher, Cocard and Moser, 2004; Rippon and Martin, 2006), who make time for and have regular meetings with mentees (Harrison, Dymoke and Pell, 2006; Johnson et al., 2005), who encourage and support mentees' critical interrogation of their own and others' practice (Harrison et al., 2006; Smith and Ingersoll, 2004), and who provide mentees with an appropriate degree of challenge on the one hand and autonomy on the other (Rajuan, Douwe and Verloop, 2007; Valencic Zuljan and Vogrinc, 2007). In addition, mentors of beginner teachers might profitably encourage these to focus less on their 'performance' as teachers and more on how their students learn (Furlong, 2000), while helping them to notice the positive impact of their work on particular students (Hobson, Malderez, Tracey, Homer, Ashby, Mitchell et al., 2009c).

Research also suggests that one of the most valuable specific mentoring strategies is lesson observation – both of and by the mentee – with subsequent discussion between the observer and the observed (Heilbronn et al., 2002; Hobson, 2002). Mentors' observation of mentees' teaching tends to be most valued where it is preceded by a meeting to agree the objectives of the observation, and followed by another, conducted in a sensitive manner, which provides an opportunity for constructive dialogue including exploration of the perceived strengths and limitations of the mentee's teaching and the development of ideas for potentially overcoming any perceived limitations (Martin and Rippon, 2003; Schmidt, 2008). Some studies (Burn, 1997; Roth and Tobin, 2002; Tomlinson, 1995) have suggested that engaging in collaborative teaching with their mentees, incorporating shared planning, team-teaching and joint reflection, is another highly powerful potential strategy at mentors' disposal, though research conducted in this area remains somewhat thin on the ground.

While a number of mentoring strategies have been shown to be effective across different contexts, it is clear that, like teaching, mentoring is most successful where it is personalised and adapted to the needs of the individual mentee. Mentors should thus seek to ensure that the strategies employed to support mentees' learning take sufficient account of their learning styles, are responsive to their concerns and appropriate to their current stage of development (Lindgren, 2005; Valencic Zuljan and Vogrinc, 2007). Various studies suggest that at an early stage in the relationship, mentors should encourage mentees to identify and interrogate critically their conceptions of teaching, learning to teach and being mentored (Edwards, 1998; Rajuan et al., 2007). Such conceptions can sometimes present barriers to learning and development (Sugrue, 1996; Wubbels, 1992) and their identification and potential modification can reduce mentees' concern to present an appearance of competence to mentors (Edwards and Ogden, 1998) and enhance their openness to mentoring more generally. In addition, mentors should meet with their mentees early on in the relationship, to clarify or seek agreement on the mentee's individual goals and the objectives of the mentoring experience, and should periodically revisit and review these (Lindgren, 2005; Stanulis and Weaver, 1998). It follows from all this that a successful mentoring relationship is a dynamic one, which changes over time as the experience, expertise and needs of the mentee develop and as the relationship itself naturally matures.

In practice, much mentoring takes place which does not meet these standards. For example, some mentors are not sufficiently 'available' for their mentees and fail to provide adequate support for their emotional and psychological wellbeing (Hobson, 2002; Oberski et al., 1999), while some mentees are insufficiently challenged or not granted enough autonomy (Dunne and Bennett, 1997). In addition, some mentors appear to see their role primarily in terms of the provision of safe sites for trial and error learning by their mentee (Edwards, 1997), and in doing so devote too little attention to pedagogical issues, the promotion of reflective practice and an examination of the principles behind the practice (Franke and

Dahlgren, 1996; Lindgren, 2005). Again, much of this may be explained by the absence of one or more 'enabling factors'. For example, the first issue (unavailability) could be chiefly accounted for by mentors' institutions failing to release them from other responsibilities to enable them to find time to prepare for and undertake the mentoring role; and this in turn could be explained by a lack of financial support for mentoring at policy level. The second and third issues could be explained by a lack of appropriate mentor preparation. And all three issues could be part-caused – and the mentoring potentially doomed to failure at the outset – by a flawed process of mentor selection and pairing.

CONCLUSION: THE CENTRALITY OF THE RELATIONSHIP

There remains scope for new and in-progress research studies to enlighten us further on how to foster effective mentoring. For example, research might fruitfully uncover which particular mentoring strategies are most likely to promote each of the potential benefits of mentoring discussed previously. And as suggested earlier, more valuable work might be carried out to investigate the nature and impact of informal mentoring, of collaborative teaching by mentors and mentees, and of different approaches to mentor preparation and training.

As shown in the chapter, however, a wealth of studies conducted since the early to mid 1990s have already told us a great deal about fostering mentoring for beginner teachers (and others). Research has demonstrated, above all, that mentoring has the potential to bring about substantial benefits for the professional and personal development of both mentees and mentors. It has also shown that the mere allocation of a mentor or establishment of a mentor–mentee pairing is not normally sufficient for these to be realised. It is clear that some instances of unsuccessful mentoring may be explained, in part, by mentees' unwillingness or lack of openness to be mentored, or by individual mentors' failure to provide appropriate kinds of support. Yet in many cases these may be explained or exacerbated by a failure at policy and/or institutional levels to create the kind of enabling environment in which mentoring is most likely to flourish.

I would like to finish by suggesting that, while being conscious of the vast number of considerations which can impact on the potential effectiveness or success of mentoring, we try not to forget that mentoring is first and foremost a relationship. As such, mentoring may flourish or fail in the nature and substance of the interaction between the two individuals involved, and in the extent to which the two colleagues are comfortable with and trust each other. This point was brought home strongly through my experience of talking to many beginning teachers and mentors (and analysing data from many others) for the 'Becoming a Teacher' (BaT) project, a large-scale, longitudinal study of the initial preparation, induction and early professional development of teachers in England, conducted between 2003 and 2009 (Hobson et al., 2009c). Whilst *all* trainee and newly qualified teachers (NQTs) in England are allocated a formal mentor, the BaT research showed that, more than simply having a mentor, it is the *quality of the mentoring relationship* which has a pivotal impact on various aspects of beginner teachers' experiences. For instance, NQTs' ratings of their relationship with their mentor proved the strongest single predictor of their ratings of the overall support for their professional development – the more highly NQTs rated their relationship with their mentor the higher their overall rating of the support provided. In addition, NQTs who gave higher ratings of their relationship with their mentor were more likely to report that they had been recommended to pass their induction (and thus judged to have met the national standards) by the end of their first year in post. And in a context in which schools are not obliged to provide school-based mentors 'post-induction', those second, third and fourth year teachers who *did* have a post-induction mentor were not only significantly more likely to give a higher rating of the support they received but also reported higher levels of enjoyment of teaching than those who did not have a mentor.

All of this, together with the outcomes of other research (e.g., Oberski et al., 1999), and Roehrig et al.'s (2008) finding that the 'less effective' beginner teachers in their study encountered difficulties in 'connecting with their mentors' (2008: 697), underscores the importance of:

1   attempting to ensure that those selected to act as mentors to their colleagues possess the appropriate personal characteristics as well as appropriate degrees of professional knowledge, skill and experience;
2   taking care to try to ensure an appropriate mentor–mentee pairing; and
3   ensuring that there is contingency provision to 're-pair' mentors and mentees where any given relationship proves fatally unproductive.

In addition, the evidence presented here makes a case for providing all mentors and mentees with training and development opportunities to enhance their capacities for building and sustaining productive working relationships. In seeking to forge such relationships with beginning teachers, potentially successful mentors will acknowledge that, like mentoring itself, learning to teach is highly emotional labour characterised by 'delightful highs and distressing lows' (Bullough, 2009: 34), frequently associated with feelings of hope, excitement, enjoyment, satisfaction and reward on the one hand, and those of vulnerability, fear, frustration, humiliation and despair on the other (Bullough, 2009; Hobson et al., 2009c). Mentors must ensure that they take mentees' emotional wellbeing very seriously as part of the broader remit for supporting their professional learning.

ACKNOWLEDGEMENTS

I am grateful to Pat Ashby and Angi Malderez for their insightful comments on a draft version of this chapter.

NOTES

1 In this chapter, I use the terms 'beginning' and 'beginner' teacher interchangeably to refer to those undertaking programmes of initial teacher preparation or in their first 3 years as qualified teachers.

2 A more comprehensive account of the potential benefits of mentoring beginning teachers is provided in Hobson et al. (2009a).

REFERENCES

Abell, S. K., Dillon, D. R., Hopkins, C. J., McInerney, W. D. and O'Brien, D. G. (1995) 'Somebody to count on': Mentor/intern relationships in a beginning teacher internship program. *Teaching and Teacher Education*, 11(2), 173–188.

Adey, K. (1997) First impressions do count: Mentoring student teachers. *Teacher Development*, 1(1), 123–133.

Association for Supervision and Curriculum Development (1999) *Mentoring to Improve Schools*. Alexandria, VA: ASDC.

Beck, C. and Kosnick, C. (2000) Associate teachers in pre-service education: clarifying and enhancing their role. *Journal of Education for Teaching*, 26(3), 207–224.

Bodoczky, C., and Malderez, A. (1997) The INSET impact of a mentoring course. In D. Hayes (Ed.), *In-Service Teacher Development: International Perspectives*. Hemel Hempstead: Prentice Hall, pp. 50–59.

Bullough, R. V., Jr. (2005) Being and becoming a mentor: school-based teacher educators and teacher educator identity. *Teaching and Teacher Education*, 21, 143–155.

Bullough, R. V., Jr. (2009) Seeking eudaimonia: The emotions in learning to teach and to mentor. In P. Schutz and M. Zembylas (Eds.), *Teacher Emotion Research: The Impact on Teachers' Lives*. New York: Springer, pp. 33–53.

Burn, K. (1997) Learning to teach: The value of collaborative teaching. In D. McIntyre (Ed.) *Teacher Education Research in a New Context: The Oxford Internship Scheme*. London: Paul Chapman Publishing, pp. 145–161.

Clutterbuck, D. (1992) *Mentoring*. Henley: Henley Distance Learning.

Colley, H. (2002) A 'rough guide' to the history of mentoring from a Marxist feminist perspective. *Journal of Education for Teaching*, 28(3), 257–273.

Cornu, R. L. (2005) Peer mentoring: engaging pre-service teachers in mentoring one another. *Mentoring & Tutoring: Partnership in Learning*, 13(3), 355–366.

Crasborn, F., Hennisson, P., Brouwer, N., Korthagen, F. and Bergen, T. (2008) Promoting versatility in mentor teachers' use of supervisory skills. *Teaching and Teacher Education*, 24, 499–514.

Davies, M. A., Brady, M., Rodger, E. and Wall, P. (1999) Mentors and school-based partnership: Ingredients for professional growth. *Action in Teacher Education*, 21(1), 85–96.

Dunne, E. and Bennett, N. (1997) Mentoring processes in school-based training. *British Educational Research Journal*, 23, 225–238.

Edwards, A. (1997) Guests bearing gifts: the position of student teachers in primary classrooms. *British Educational Research Journal*, 23(1), 27–37.

Edwards, A. (1998) Mentoring student teachers in primary schools: assisting student teachers to become learners. *European Journal of Teacher Education*, 21(1), 47–62.

Edwards, A. and Ogden, L. (1998) 'Mentoring as protecting the performance of student teachers', Annual Meeting of the American Educational Research Association (AERA), San Diego.

Evans, L. and Abbott, I. (1997) Developing as mentors in school-based teacher training. *Teacher Development*, 1(1), 135–148.

Feiman Nemser, S. and Parker, M. B. (1992) *Mentoring in Context: A Comparison of Two U.S. Programs for Beginning Teachers*. Michigan State University: National Centre for Research on Teacher Learning (NCRTL). Available at: http://ncrtl.msu.edu/http/sreports/spring92.pdf

Feiman Nemser, S., Parker, M. B. and Zeichner, K. (1993) Are mentor teachers teacher educators? In D. McIntyre, H. Hagger, and M. Wilkin (Eds), *Mentoring: Perspectives on School-based Teacher Education*. London: Kogan Page, pp. 147–165.

Foster, R. (1999) School-based initial teacher training in England and France: trainee teachers' perspectives compared. *Mentoring and Tutoring: Partnership in Learning*, 7(2), 131–143.

Franke, A. and Dahlgren, L. O. (1996) Conceptions of mentoring: An empirical study of conceptions of mentoring during the school-based teacher education. *Teaching and Teacher Education*, 12(6), 627–641.

Furlong, J. (2000) School mentors and university tutors: Lessons from the English experiment. *Theory into Practice*, 39(1), 12–19.

Gold, Y. (1996) Beginner teacher support: Attrition, mentoring and induction. In J. Sikula, T. J. Buttery and E. Guyton (Eds), *Handbook of Research on Teacher Education*. New York: Macmillan, pp. 548–594.

Graham, P. (1997) Tensions in the mentor teacher-student teacher relationship: Creating productive sites for learning within a high school English teacher education program. *Teaching and Teacher Education*, 13(5), 513–527.

Hagger, H. and McIntyre, D. (2006) *Learning Teaching from Teachers: Realising the Potential of School-based Teacher Education*. Maidenhead: Open University Press.

Harrison, J., Dymoke, S. and Pell, T. (2006) Mentoring beginning teachers in secondary schools: An analysis of practice. *Teaching and Teacher Education*, 22, 1055–1067.

Hascher, T., Cocard, Y. and Moser, P. (2004) Forget about theory – practice is all? Student teachers' learning in practicum. *Teachers and Teaching: Theory and Practice*, 10(6), 623–637.

Heilbronn, R., Jones, C., Bubb, S. and Totterdell, M. (2002) School-based induction tutors – a challenging role. *School Leadership and Management*, 22(4), 371–388.

Hobson, A. J. (2002) Student teachers' perceptions of school-based mentoring in initial teacher training (ITT). *Mentoring and Tutoring*, 10(1), 5–20.

Hobson, A. J. (2009) On being bottom of the pecking order: beginner teachers' perceptions and experiences of support. *Teacher Development*, 13(4), 299–320.

Hobson, A. J., Ashby, P. Malderez, A, and Tomlinson, P. D. (2009a) Mentoring beginning teachers: what we know and what we don't. *Teaching and Teacher Education*, 25(1), 207–216.

Hobson, A. J., Giannakaki, M. and Chambers, G. N. (2009b) Who withdraws from initial teacher preparation programmes and why? *Educational Research*, 51(3), 321–340.

Hobson, A. J., Malderez, A., Tracey, L., Homer, M. S., Ashby, P., Mitchell, N., McIntyre, J., Cooper, D., Roper, T., Chambers, G. N. and Tomlinson, P. D. (2009c) *Becoming a Teacher: Teachers' Experiences of Initial Teacher Training, Induction and Early Professional Development. Final Report*. Research Report DCSF-RR115. Available from: http://www.dcsf.gov.uk/research/data/uploadfiles/DCSF-RR115.pdf

Hobson, A. J., Malderez, A., Tracey, L., Homer, M., Mitchell, N., Biddulph, M., Giannakaki, M. S., Rose, A., Pell, R. G., Roper, T., Chambers, G. N. and Tomlinson, P. D. (2007) *Newly qualified teachers' experiences of their first year of teaching: Findings from phase III of the becoming a teacher project*. Nottingham: Department for Children, Schools and Families (DCSF).

Hopkins-Thompson, P. A. (2000) Colleagues helping colleagues: mentoring and coaching. *NASSP Bulletin*, 84, 617, 29–36.

Ingersoll, R. and Kralik, J. (2004) *The Impact of Mentoring on Teacher Retention: What the Research Says*. Denver, CO: Education Commission of the States. Available at: http://www.ecs.org/clearinghouse/50/36/5036.htm

Johnson, S. (2004) *Finders and Keepers*. San Francisco: Wiley.

Johnson, S., Berg, J. and Donaldson, M. (2005) *Who stays in teaching and why; A review of the literature on teacher retention*. The Project on the Next Generation of Teachers: Harvard Graduate School of Education.

Jonson, K. (2002) *Being an Effective Mentor.* Thousand Oaks: Corwin.

Kram, K. (1985) *Mentoring at Work: Developmental Relationships in Organizational Life.* Glenview, IL: Scott Foresman.

Lee, J.C. and Feng, S. (2007) Mentoring support and the professional development of beginning teachers: a Chinese perspective. *Mentoring and Tutoring: Partnership in Learning,* 15(3), 243–263.

Lindgren, U. (2005) Experiences of beginning teachers in a school-based mentoring programme Sweden. *Educational Studies,* 31 (3), 251–263.

Little, J. W. (1990) The mentor phenomenon and the social organization of teaching. In C.B. Cazden (Ed.), *Review of research in education* (Vol. 16, pp. 297–351). Washington, DC: American Educational Research Association.

Lopez-Real, F. and Kwan, T. (2005) Mentors' perceptions of their own professional development during mentoring. *Journal of Education for Teaching,* 31(1), 15–24.

Maguire, M. (2001) Bullying and the post-graduate secondary school trainee: an English case study. *Journal of Education for Teaching,* 27(1), 95–109.

Malderez, A. and Bodoczky, C. (1999) *Mentor Courses: A Resource Book for Trainer-trainers.* Cambridge: CUP.

Malderez, A., Hobson, A.J., Tracey, L. and Kerr, K. (2007) Becoming a student teacher: core features of the experience. *European Journal of Teacher Education,* 30(3), 225–248.

Marable, M., and Raimondi, S. (2007) Teachers' perceptions of what was most (and least) supportive during their first year of teaching. *Mentoring and Tutoring: Partnership in Learning,* 15(1), 25–37.

Martin, M. and Rippon, J. (2003) Teacher Induction: personal intelligence and the mentoring relationship. *Journal of In-Service Education,* 29(1), 141–162.

McIntyre, D. and Hagger, H. (1996) *Mentors in Schools: Developing the Profession of Teaching.* London: David Fulton.

Mitchell, H. J. (1999) Group Mentoring: does it work? *Mentoring and Tutoring: Partnership in Learning,* 7(2), 113–120.

Moor, H., Halsey, K., Jones, M., Martin, K., Stott, A., Brown, C. and Harland, J. (2005) *Professional Development for Teachers Early in their Careers: An Evaluation of the Early Professional Development Pilot Scheme.* Nottingham: Department for Education and Skills.

Oberski, I., Ford, K., Higgins, S. and Fisher, P. (1999) The importance of relationships in teacher education. *Journal of Education for Teaching,* 25(2), 135–150.

Orland, L. (2001) Reading a mentoring situation: one aspect of learning to mentor. *Teaching and Teacher Education,* 17, 75–88.

Rajuan, M., Douwe, B. and Verloop, N. (2007) The role of the cooperating teacher: bridging the gap between the expectations of cooperating teachers and student teachers. *Mentoring and Tutoring: Partnership in Learning,* 15(3), 223–242.

Rippon, J. H. and Martin, M. (2006) What makes a good induction supporter? *Teaching and Teacher Education,* 22, 84–99.

Robinson, I. and Robinson, J. (1999) Learning to live with inconsistency in student entitlement and partnership provision. *Mentoring and Tutoring: Partnership in Learning,* 7, 223–239.

Roehrig, A. D., Bohn, C. M., Turner, J. E. and Pressley, M. (2008) Mentoring beginning primary teachers for exemplary teaching practices. *Teaching and Teacher Education,* 24, 684–702.

Roth, W-M. and Tobin, K. (2002) *At the Elbow of Another: Learning to Teach by Coteaching.* New York: Peter Lang Publishing.

Schmidt, M. (2008) Mentoring and being mentored: the story of a novice music teacher's success. *Teaching and Teacher Education,* 24, 635–648.

Simpson, T., Hastings, W. and Hill, B. (2007) 'I knew that she was watching me': the professional benefits of mentoring. *Teachers and Teaching: Theory and Practice,* 13(5), 481–498.

Smith, T. and Ingersoll, R. (2004) What are the effects of induction and mentoring on beginning teacher turnover? *American Educational Research Journal,* 41(3), 681–714.

Stanulis, R. N. and Weaver, D. (1998) Teacher as mentor, teacher as learner. *The Teacher Educator*, 34(2), 134–143.

Strong, M. (2009) *Effective Teacher Induction and Mentoring. Assessing the Evidence.* New York: Teachers College Press.

Su, J. Z. X. (1992) Sources of influence in preservice teacher socialization. *Journal of Education for Teaching*, 18(3), 239–258.

Sugrue, C. (1996) Student teachers' lay theories: Implications for professional development. In I. F. Goodson and A. Hargreaves (Eds), *Teachers' Professional Lives.* Washington DC: Falmer Press, pp. 154–177.

Sundli, L. (2007) Mentoring – A new mantra for education? *Teaching and Teacher Education*, 23, 201–214.

Tauer, S. M. (1998) The mentor-protégé relationship and its impact on the experienced teacher. *Teaching and Teacher Education*, 14(2), 205–218.

Templeton, L. (2003) Into the fray on the very first day: lessons from an unconventional mentor. *Mentoring and Tutoring*, 11(2), 163–175.

Tomlinson, P. D. (1995) *Understanding Mentoring: Reflective Strategies for School-based Teacher Preparation.* Buckingham: Oxford University Press.

Tracey L., Homer, M., Mitchell, N., Malderez, A., Hobson, A. J., Ashby, P. and Pell., G. (2008) *Teachers' Experiences of their Second Year in Post: Findings from Phase IV of the Becoming a Teacher project.* Nottingham: Department for Children, Schools and Families (DCSF).

Valencic Zuljan, M. and Vogrinc, J. (2007) A mentor's aid in developing the competences of teacher trainees. *Educational Studies*, 27(3), 317–340.

Wang, J. (2001) Contexts of mentoring and opportunities for learning to teach: A comparative study of mentoring practice. *Teaching and Teacher Education*, 17(1), 51–73.

Whisnant, E., Elliott, K. and Pynchon, S. (2005) A review of literature on beginning teacher induction. Prepared for the Centre for Strengthening the Teaching Profession, July 2005.

Wildman, T. M., Magliaro, S. G., Niles, R. A. and Niles, J. A. (1992) Teacher mentoring: an analysis of roles, activities, and conditions. *Journal of Teacher Education*, 43, 205–213.

Williams, A. and Prestage, S. (2002) The induction tutor: mentor, manager or both? *Mentoring and Tutoring: Partnership in Learning*, 1, 35–45.

Wright, N. and Bottery, M. (1997) Perceptions of professionalism by the mentors of student teachers. *Journal of Education for Teaching*, 23(3), 235–252.

Wubbels, T. (1992) Taking account of student teachers' preconceptions. *Teaching and Teacher Education*, 8(2), 137–149.

Yusko, B. and Feiman Nemser, S. (2008) Embracing Contraries: Combining Assistance and Assessment in New Teacher Induction. *Teachers College Record*, 110(7), 1–12.

Fostering the Use of Web-based Technology in Mentoring and Coaching

Sarah J. Fletcher

INTRODUCTION

In this chapter we explore the relatively recent impact of using web-based technology to assist the processes of mentoring and coaching. Through the eyes of one research mentor working with teachers in schools, we look at how its potential is realised for evoking, representing and disseminating their knowledge and that of the mentor too.

The very mention of web-based technology can still send a shiver of apprehension tingling through an educator's spine, even though there are mobile phones everywhere, sales of computers continue to soar and roads and pavements are excavated as mile upon mile of fibre-optic cable is installed. The surge in technological growth is very recent but nonetheless dramatic in educational terms. Harasim (2000) heralds the shift to online education as a new paradigm in new paradigm in learning yet reminds us that

> Remarkable as it may seem, (given the exponential rate of adoption) e-mail communication and computer referencing began less than three decades ago. (p. 42).

> Exploring this new paradigm, according to the author, has resulted in new modes of educational delivery; new learning domains; new principles of learning and new learning processes and outcomes, new educational roles and entities. It is the 'convergence of the computer network revolution and profound social and economic changes, she says, that has led to a transformation of education at all levels'. (p. 59)

Modern universities, according to Ryan, Scott, Freeman and Patel (2000), are 'seeking to become global, virtual institutions, while others are using the Internet as part of a mixed economy combining traditional modes of delivery with on-line teaching' (2000: 7). With the erosion of certainty of a job for life, mentoring, particularly e-mentoring, offers support in making rapid changes that such life shifts demand, but what does online learning require of mentors and mentees? French, Hale, Johnson and Farr (1999) suggest five major skills are proving amenable to coaching and mentoring: interpersonal relationships through electronic networking; harvesting the Internet for instructional resources; assessment of websites; integrating the web in teaching through self-directed modules; and utilizing collaborative conferencing systems (1999: 9). Thus, potential mentors and coaches might need to be skilled in each of these areas, a proposal that endorses my view (Fletcher, 2000) that mentors need mentors (and coaches) to prepare and sustain them.

One of the most respected proponents of technology use in education is Curtis Bonk. His R2D2 model of 'Read, Reflect; Display and Do' offers purpose and a direction for web-based technology use. Bonk (2009) makes no apologies for frequently strong and conflicting emotions using new technology can evoke: Frustrated; Challenged; Excited; Passionate; Overwhelmed; Opportunities; Waiting. How is web technology impacting upon classroom teachers? Some shun it, some embrace it with excitement and some will come round to using it through a supported exploration by mentoring and coaching; indeed Denton, Davis, Smith, Strader, Clark and Wang (2006) have written about how the Technology Mentor Fellowship Program has improved teacher Internet use for continual professional development (CPD).

EMBEDDING WEB-BASED TECHNOLOGY IN TEACHERS' RESEARCH

The Mentoring with Action Research and Coaching MA modules I designed in 2005 for teachers' CPD required them to use the web in order to gain a pass. After initial reticence they were soon emailing excitedly as they saw their knowledge displayed. The MA module and web-based templates from teachers at Bitterne Park School are documented via the homepage at http://www.TeacherResearch.net. Not all teachers were won over to web use as an integral part of MA study. Some left the programme while others went on proudly to present their web-based research to colleagues at the British Educational Research Association and National Teacher Research Panel Conferences.

I wish, in retrospect, that I had read Salmon's five-stage framework and e-tivities (2002) before I worked at this school. I would have appreciated more fully the key role of online socialisation in the online learning process. Instead, I rather viewed it as a distraction from the real task. Insight into providing blended learning such as Jolliffe and colleagues' *The Online Learning Handbook*

(Jolliffe, Ritter and Stevens, 2001) and Macdonald's *Blended Learning and Online Tutoring* (2006) would have been useful too:

> There are two approaches for supporting students to develop as e-investigators. One is to offer generic study skills advice and the second is to embed the practice of e-investigation within course assessment so that the process is closely related to the course concepts being studied. (2006: 133)

As it was, I used the Internet largely intuitively, without a research base, and I consequently missed out on exploiting some of the potential of web-based technology to enable me to research mentor and coach teachers. As Bierema and Merriam said in 2002:

> Overall the literature thus far on electronic mentoring reflects only the most tentative forays into this potentially rich media. Further, as is true of nearly all of the work on entry, there is a wide range of behaviours and activities being labelled a mentoring. Much still needs to be done in identifying those aspects of this electronic medium limit as well as foster a genuine mentoring relationship. (2002: 215)

SOCIAL NETWORKING AS AN EDUCATIONAL TOOL

When using web-based technology, many respond enthusiastically to new opportunities for mentoring and coaching but clear definitions of e-activity remain elusive. In their presentation for the International Mentoring Association, Single and Muller, (1999), proposed that 'E-mentoring is a merger of mentoring with electronic communication and has been termed tele-mentoring, cyber mentoring or virtual mentoring … and add electronic mentoring provides opportunities for mentoring prohibited by face to face mentoring programs'. A decade later there are many websites (www.horsesmouth.co.uk is one example), offering social networking for informal mentoring. Arguably, Twitter and Facebook offer informal mentoring too. So much has changed dramatically in a relatively short time. In 1978, Burton and Sealy Brown heralded computer-based learning. Few could have foreseen changes which have taken place since then, although what they wrote remains relevant:

> The pedagogical motivation underlying much of coaching research can be characterised as guided discovery learning. It assumes a *constructivist* position, in which the student can distract his new knowledge from his existing knowledge … A subtle requirement of this theory is that the coach does not interfere too much. If the coach immediately points out the student's parents, there is a real danger that the student will never develop the necessary skills for examining his own behaviour and looking for the causes of his own mistakes. There are two major but related problems that must be solved by a computer coach; when to interact with students' problem solving activity and what to say once it has been interrupted. (1978: 2)

Twenty-five years on, Bierema and Merriam (2002) proposed a new definition and a conceptual framework for e-mentoring, as a 'computer mediated, beneficial relationship between mentor and a protege which provides learning, advising, encouraging, promoting and modelling', and claimed 'that it is often boundary less, egalitarian and qualitatively different from traditional face-to-face mentoring' (2002: 214).

POTENTIAL DRAWBACKS IN E-MENTORING

In contrast, Shrestha, May, Edirisingha, Burke and Linsey (2009) discussed commonality between face-to-face and e-mentoring, proposing that e-mentoring impacts 'differently' on mentors and mentees, and explained some of the implications for the selection and training of mentors. They found that

> while e- mentoring may be more accessible for those for whom time and geographical distance obstacles to participation, it can act as a barrier to participation in a mentoring scheme through making it less accessible to those unfamiliar with computers and the Internet technology. To be effective in this new medium requires skills other than those of a good 'face-to-face' mentor. The implementation of e-mentoring schemes should include a thorough training of mentors in the use of ICT and an audit of mentees' ICT familiarity if it is to live up to the extra stations of this increasingly popular form of educational and professional development support. (2009: 123)

In 2007, Lamar pointed to the lack of research into e-mentoring. She claims there are no theoretical e-mentoring models in the literature and posits Moore's Theory of Transactional Distance for researching synchronous and asynchronous mentoring.

Kasprisin, Single, Single, Ferrier and Muller (2008) point to major constraints of face-to-face mentoring being time and geography as well as increasing costs for the use of facilities, printed materials and transportation. They detail applications of e-mentoring in education and claim the main benefit of e-mentoring is asynchronous communication. Contrary to traditional models where emphasis is on mandated training for mentors, they advise mandated training for protégé and voluntary training for mentors (2008: 171). E-mentoring, they point out, enables flexibility and the potential for a choice of mentors from which a protégé might choose but protégé commitment is essential. Yaw explains that 'e-mentoring is so new it has not yet evolved to a point where it is possible to critically evaluate its effectiveness' (2007: 1). Nevertheless there is research, not least my own study.

USING TECHNOLOGY TO BUILD RESEARCH CAPACITY AMONG TEACHERS

As educators, we need to understand better how mentoring supports both building research capacity among teachers and more effective approaches to e-mentoring and e-coaching in order to relieve pressure on the shortage of research mentors available for teachers. Understanding my own mentoring seemed key to being able to help educators to research their work. My resources are a pilot study where I have embedded autobiography into web-based technology as a means of modelling how teachers might research their practice.

Raising one teacher's awareness of his or her own practice as a basis for improving it is undoubtedly a worthy outcome. Raising one teacher's awareness in a way which can be disseminated as a model for others to engage with critically and to learn from is also worthwhile. Web-based technology enables such dissemination. But this is a process of dissemination that creates problematic issues. How might we know that one teacher's account of his/her own practice is valid? If teachers construct their own reality as they communicate their practice, how can the 'Other' know this is an accurate representation of what has occurred? This, to my mind, is where the true value of web-based technology can come into play. Using video footage of what has occurred in a lesson and offering the teacher, the students and observers opportunities to critically engage is not a foolproof means way of discovering the truth of a situation. But on balance, a video is likely to enable the 'Other' to gain insights into what has occurred as well as being able to witness realities constructed by teachers and students involved.

ENCOURAGING CRITICAL ENGAGEMENT

Using multimedia embedded in web-based technology offers the potential for more rounded depictions of events than de-contextualised text-only accounts written by a teacher. Little (2001) discusses the problems associated with the de-contextualised accounts of practice by teachers and concluded that, while not ideal,

> [t]o describe these classroom accounts as brief, condensed and disembodied is not to suggest that they are meaningless of unimportant. Making sense of one another's stories, speculations, explanations, comments, jokes, complaints and observations – treating them as 'situationally meaningful' and adequate for some purpose – is a central and constitutive feature of teachers' collective practice, (2001: 34)

Taber (2007) observes that opening up accounts of practice to feedback from colleagues and mentors enables feedback to be 'tied to specific issues that have been identified as the focus for development in trainee-mentor sessions' (2007: 154). Crucially, he suggests that the observer who engages critically with what he/she sees needs to be properly briefed beforehand.

Web-based technology has a role to play here to by offering suitably situated insights into critical engagement with teachers' practice. If videos showing critical feedback and reflection can be embedded in webpages alongside videos of teaching in classroom teaching this could be one way forward. Peer coaching colleagues need to understand that in their conversations they hold a major responsibility for improving not just what happens in one classroom, but also how professional the practice of teaching *per se* is at a given point in time and space. Viewing feedback in coaching as a responsibility to the profession of teaching and not just 'to the teacher in the next door classroom' raises the profile of teachers' research as learning so it take its (rightful) place alongside other forms of academic enquiry. As a profession we need to move beyond a 'I know it's not proper research' stage (Clayton, O'Brien, Campbell, Qualter and Varga-Atkins, 2009) so that teachers' research into others' practice is valued as professional development by everyone in education.

WHAT KIND OF TEACHER RESEARCH AND WHAT KIND OF TECHNOLOGY?

We need to consider the kinds of research teachers might usefully undertake with support from mentors and coaches and the technology that best enables teachers to elicit, represent and disseminate their knowledge and understandings. Focusing on why teachers should undertake research, Loughran (2003) summarises concisely:

> Teacher-researchers bring to bear their expert knowledge and understanding of practice in their research of their practice. Teacher-researchers are then at the forefront of the challenge associated with better understanding the daily concerns and implications of practice that classroom teachers face.

There is a misunderstanding that teacher research is identical to action research. Teachers might opt for action research as an approach to enquiry but equally they might opt for ethnography, for example. Coaching and mentoring to support teacher research appear to, in my own experience, align better with small-scale self study action research than ethnography.

RAISING ISSUES IN USING WEB-BASED TECHNOLOGY

What kinds of web-based technology are we considering when we talk about fostering the use of web-based technology in mentoring? Internet, e-mentoring and e-coaching, using video mail, telephone mentoring/coaching, video conferencing, using web-based templates to elicit, represent and disseminate teachers' learning? What about online discussion lists like the one I run as outreach activities for the Mentoring and Coaching Special Interest Group I convene for the British Educational Research Association at http://www.JISCmail.ac.uk/MENTORING-COACHING? What about blogs? What about intranets between schools to enable their collaborative mentoring?

What might it mean in terms of ethics? Prosser, Clark and Wiles (2008) are already talking about visual research ethics being at a crossroads. Focusing on visual representations of what occurs in classrooms globally will alter prior ethical standpoints in co-mentoring that occurred within a shared context, a shared culture. How will ethical guidelines be drawn up for sharing multimedia representation of teachers' practice inter-culturally?

Development of web-based technology opens up whole new areas for consideration, raising questions about cultural norms and taboos. One needs to progress mindfully. The same web-based technology that opens up possibilities for online research can close down understandings unless handled with sensitivity in intercultural awareness.

E-MENTORING AND E-COACHING: A LACK OF AWARENESS

The National Strategies Report published on 27 August 2010 in England highlighted a lack of awareness among teacher educators of the National Framework for Mentoring and Coaching. Opportunities for co-coaching in initial teacher training and in CPD are being missed because educators do not yet understand what they might be able to do as co-coaches. Equally then, educators are likely to miss the exciting opportunities for co-mentoring that web-based technology offers. We need to educate these educators! Mentoring and coaching can provide the support educators need to develop skills for using web-based technology and aside from that web-based mentoring and coaching can supplement mentoring and coaching relationships where they are in short supply. Using asynchronous learning networks we can augment and improve mentoring and coaching provision for educators, complementing face to face availability as required. According to Carol Twigg, cited in Swan and Shea (2005):

> the biggest obstacle to innovation in is thinking that things can or should be done in traditional ways. Trying to make online education 'as good' as traditional education … often encourages us to make it the same as traditional education. When, in fact, online education has the potential to support significant paradigm changes in teaching and learning. (2005: 253)

LEARNING FROM SUCCESSFUL PRACTICE

Clarke (2004) has identified several characteristics of successful online learners, and one could reasonably expect successful online mentors and coaches to share similar mindsets. Successful e-mentors and e-coaches will need to be confident when operating in non-formal settings; have a positive attitude to their work; be self motivated to succeed; have an ability to collaborate and co-operate with others and also be competent and confident users of web-based technology. Mentors and coaches working online will need to adapt to a potential lack of visual cues but as Garrison and Vaughan (2008) report in their account of the emergence of mentoring distance learners:

> while there was great concern in the early research that the lack of visual cues and body language would seriously inhibit the effect of asynchronous text communication … it became clear that participants could communicate a wide range of socio-emotional messages. (2008: 20)

Other findings in their research have encouraging implications for using web-based technology in mentoring and coaching:

> Community is not defined by physical presence. Network supported and facilitated communities have the great advantage of being accessible anywhere and at any time. (ibid. 27)

> Face to face seminars created more new ideas but online conferences produced more important, justified and linked ideas. (ibid. 36)

> It would seem that having the opportunity to reflect before contributing to the discourse adds an important critical dimension. The online environment also has the distinct advantage of a permanent record that students can use to reflect upon. (ibid. 37)

Obviously, much of the success of online mentoring and coaching, whether it relies on email or embedding video as a means to communicate, will rest on the user friendliness of any web-based technology chosen.

POTENTIAL PITFALLS IN MENTORING WITH WEB-BASED TECHNOLOGY

Neville, Adam and McCormack (2003) stress the need for careful planning in implementing e-mentoring programmes but also point to the persuasiveness of offering up web-based technology for mentoring as a 'just in time' solution. When the mentor is ready, he or she is more likely to embrace technology use, especially where it demonstrably solves otherwise intractable problems such as shortages of time and funding for mentoring provision that are likely to continue to plague the teaching profession. Weller (2007) suggests one reason that web-based technology has aroused more polarised opinions than the earlier technologies including video cassettes, CD-ROMs and television is that these were vehicles for communication of content. The web enables dialogue as well as the communication of content. It is the dialogue perspective that arouses fear. Dialogue cannot be controlled in the same way as content-only communication. In mentoring and coaching, the flow of interaction through dialogue is likely to benefit from using web-based technology. However, die-hard mentors accustomed to working face to face only may well feel uncomfortable, initially at least, when working online.

FOSTERING MY OWN USE OF WEB-BASED TECHNOLOGY

In 2002, I took part in an International Conference for Teacher Research in Baton Rouge near New Orleans. From that time, the nature of the research mentoring and coaching that I provide for teachers changed as I worked increasingly online. This is all down to what I saw when a group of seven classroom teachers explained how they were using web-based technology to enable them to represent and share their ideas.

They were talking about KEEP (i.e., Knowledge, Exchange, Exhibition and Presentation) web-based templates, developed by the Knowledge Media Lab for the Carnegie Foundation for the Advancement of Teaching. My own experience of using KEEP to develop resources for mentoring and coaching comprises the case study later in this chapter. Incidentally, the KEEP Toolkit Template system was adopted by MERLOT (Multimedia Educational Resource for Learning and Online Teaching) on 16 October 2009) and so the original KEEP Toolkit template functionality, accessible at http://www.cfkeep.org, has been replaced by the access at http://www.merlot.org.

My own web-based resources have been designed to enable teachers to create online portfolios in a way not dissimilar to that of Roney and Davies (2007) who discuss the use of the TaskStream web-tool for e-coaching teachers for professional development.

In all, I mentored and coached some 75 practising teachers to access thousands of pounds for research via the DfES Best Practice Research Scholarship (BPRS) Scheme, working face to face when time allowed and in an online capacity when my time was limited. In 2003, after the announcement that the scheme was to close, the DfES commissioned an evaluation, which was undertaken by Furlong, Salisbury and Coombs. Top of the list of factors influencing the quality and impact of the BPRS projects was mentoring and authors discovered that 80 out of the 98 BPRS mentors were employed in universities. They found that teachers often sought out several mentors to assist them in designing the research project and offer research training. Mentors sometimes went well beyond their brief, offering up pastoral care and detailed tutoring as well as research training.

Furlong et al. observed that 'mentoring is therefore vitally important part of the BPRS scheme; and all of the scholars revisit it made active use of their mentors'. They also pointed out that there was considerable inconsistency in mentoring practice and that many teachers would have benefited from some access to formal research training and guidance in research design. With these findings in mind, I began to design my online resources. Using multimedia I created research mentoring webpages to supplement (and where necessary replace) face-to-face research mentoring for schoolteachers.

In 2009, my presentation on using web-based technology for research mentoring for teachers was awarded the highest level of recognition for teacher learning by the TLA (Teacher Learning Academy). This enabled me to bring together the many webpages that I had created using various KEEP Toolkit templates since I began using them in 2005 (accessible at http://www.TeacherResearch.net) The first thing I learnt was that I could use the KEEP template as a holding ground for resources. I realised I could add comments to sections on the webpage as and when I wanted and I did not have think linearly as I do when writing a paper. I could work at my own rate on any subsection of any webpage, adding video, audio, text and colour as I went along. This flexibility, together with the kinaesthetic satisfaction of moving text and images when I felt I needed to, was particularly motivating for me. I added subheadings to sections – some before I wrote them and others later on – deciding on the subtitle when I had had a chance to reflect. Being able to present a 'clean' copy without alterations suited my learning style too. I used paper and pencil to jot down ideas when a computer was not available but as soon as I could access my KEEP dashboard I added the comments to my pages. I was also learning that I could 'stitch' pages so that it was possible to access other pages from a menu in the page I was working on. This means that I could provide links to layers of text and multimedia as my ideas developed and were added.

What is the most suitable kind of web-based technology to assist teachers through mentoring and coaching to elicit, represent and share their learning? Clearly, it must be possible to share files and any system chosen needs to be secure, accessible and cost-free. There are numerous webpage construction templates on the web that offer these attributes. Ideally, it needs to be specifically designed for use in educational settings, but nothing, in my view, came close to the sophistication KEEP offered. If I was to assist teachers to develop what Winter (1997) terms 'methodological inventiveness', I needed flexibility with user-friendliness to help scaffold teacher enquiries. If I was to assist teachers to recognise and evidence their own professional multiplicity of self in action I needed a web-based system that encompassed appeal to the senses – sight and hearing – in a dynamic way that could help me to enable teachers to construct their own realities online rather than reifying the knowledge in a page of static text.

I decided that my use of the KEEP medium would be the message – I would show how my self-study could be recorded using KEEP templates as a model for teachers researching their own educational practice. As my ideas develop I have recorded the questions I asked myself as well as the responses I gave to my own questions – in other words I was not only creating a narrative, I was creating a resource that showed how a narrative could be represented and simultaneously showing how I was eliciting my own learning – I think this would be almost impossible with two-dimensional text. The capacity to add colour injected additional motivation for me as I was intrigued to see how my learning would develop online as I explored my own creativity in depth.

Aware my audience might be in Japan, I was keen to include examples of mentoring relevant to educators there as well as photographs and images I guessed would appeal. One of the aspects of a TLA presentation is the need to explain the so-called learning breakthroughs one makes as one recounts one's learning 'journey'. Some of this, I felt, should remain confidential and I appreciated being able to decide by the click of a switch which items would have open access and which would not. I could send the URL of webpages I had created but did not want to be globally available to friends and mentors. I did not have to reveal all of my thinking to everyone viewing my work. Deciding what could and could not be shared online reminded me of a responsibility to act ethically. My work was potentially to be disseminated to a very wide audience. I found that I could add a hyperlink to previous webpages I had created such as the ones I created in various schools but again I was mindful of ethical responsibilities as some of my photographs were of pupils and I needed to check I had permissions to display them. Aware that photographs can be lifted more easily from webpages than pages of text in hard copy, I selected images and any video clips with close attention.

Initially, whatever I chose to portray was biased and claims I made were not open to verification except where I shared them with my various mentors for this project. Rather than have one mentor, I chose a selection. Among others, I opted for a teacher researcher, a researcher in a university, a teacher research consultant and I also asked the originator of the TLA Stage 4 scheme to be my mentor – was I being true to what she envisaged when she designed the scheme? I contacted my mentors by email and by telephone, sending them Microsoft Word documents and links to my emerging webpages. I do not recall ever asking how to portray an aspect of my learning journey but I did ask for feedback about how well I was communicating my learning and adjusted as they responded, clarifying and amplifying as I went along. I asked how more contentious areas came across in my narrative and checked I was meeting Stage 4 requirements.

The three-column webpage template worked better for me, rather than a broader one column (or two). I perceive this was because I could simultaneously add notes about past, present and projected events. I could also manage the colour and balance of shape across three columns and being a keen photographer helped me with designing the space and layout, and the blanks as well as populated areas of my various webpages. I settled on adding a large photograph at the top of most pages above my three columns as a kind of statement and mood setter. I chose the typeface carefully to complement the layout and tried to write in roughly symmetrical patterns – something I would not consider when writing a hard copy paper. I feel it emerges that I was much more creative when working online with multimedia than writing text. Consequently, I felt more exhilarated creating a paper online than writing a hard copy. I knew I could delete and move round representations of my learning as I went along. This was a far more dynamic process that enabled me to represent my learning about research mentoring than I had found before. With the text, image and layout available in front of me I did not have to rely on memory to recall where I had written a section. Proofreading proved more difficult than in a Microsoft Word document and for some reason cutting and pasting text from a Word document was problematic. This feature has been improved with the move to MERLOT. Checking spelling has also improved now, I understand!

THE IMPACT OF WEB-BASED TECHNOLOGY ON MY MENTORING

So much then, for eliciting and representing ideas on research mentoring for teacher researchers using web-based technology. How did the use of web-based technology influence how I could mentor and coach teacher researchers? In the first place I found that teachers were more ready to have a go at using web-based technology if I could show them step by step how I was using it and help them to learn from my mistakes. Showing them how to access a KEEP template, then giving them one with writing in already to alter, to add colour to and rephrase worked well. Giving teachers a blank webpage, saying 'Set out your ideas about mentoring and research' did not appeal to them. Providing a safe environment for getting accustomed to working online and then inviting them to create their own webpages was a highly successful strategy. I was astonished by the sheer sophistication of the teachers' webpages and worries about having enough time just dissolved as they became engrossed in playing online. Feedback from me when they sent me through the URL for pages they were using to represent their research was crucial. I could work asynchronously which was a boon.

I created webpages for my Stage 4 presentation and these can be accessed from the homepage of my website at http://www.TeacherResearch.net. Some teachers do still encounter difficulty accessing pages because schools block websites. Slow broadband speeds can be a curse! More than once a presentation of my webpages on mentoring has wavered because I was unable to show various video clips properly. I took advice from an information and communication technology (ICT) teacher and created separate pages for fast and slow broadband speeds. This has enabled me to communicate similar content about research mentoring for use with high and low speed provision. When I first developed v-mail using video clips embedded in web-based templates that played when the webpage was accessed I was told that only the very top of the video clip image was visible with slow broadband. Audio played whatever the speed, thus accessibility via the web can be problematic.

I summarised my impressions of the impact of the mentoring and coaching provided by 'significant others' for me along my learning journey as I have developed my web-based resources to enable mentoring and coaching researchers for TLA presentation.

Each of my mentors brought different, yet complementary, strengths to our working relationship. Some I had worked with in face-to-face contexts and some I had never met. I did not find that using email de-personalised our relationship. In fact, I saw my mentor as I worked with him and her online, picturing them interacting from a photograph they had sent me. That was important – putting a face to the comments.

Likewise, being thousands of miles from my e-mentors was not in itself problematic except perhaps for a time lag when we needed to work synchronously. I felt enabled to interact (whether it was synchronously or asynchronously) and the advantage of asynchronous communication was having anopportunity to reflect on as well as in action. So when I mentored I experienced an ongoing presence especially where my mentor questioned me. Having a mentor who completely understood what I was trying to aim for – the TLA Stage 4 award (because she had helped to create this) – was an enormous help, as was her reminder of key deadlines. It was useful to have free questions and challenges. To be expected to come up with answers was useful but I also needed a mentor who knew the system and one who could open up opportunities for me too.

If my mentors struggled to use my resources, this provided me with useful insights into how my target audience might react and supportively enabled me to rehearse my interactions with teacher researchers using web-based technology. I had opportunities to amend and adjust my resources before they went live. Getting my feedback from a wide variety of end users and especially users who had no specific relationship with me (on my JISCmail list) provided me with an additional source of helpful feedback.

WEB-BASED TECHNOLOGY: A MIXED BLESSING; A RESEARCH AGENDA

As I have discussed elsewhere (Fletcher 2005, 2006), web-based technology complements face-to-face mentoring and coaching practice. How much it could replace is uncertain because long-term studies of web-based-only relationships have yet to be undertaken. While there is some research into online mentoring, there appears to be less with regard to online coaching, perhaps because that has been more prevalent in business than in the education of practising teachers. Socialisation is one vital step in online communications where the mentee and mentor can visualise one another's reactions online and gain insights into how comments are being initiated and received. The ability to work asynchronously aids reflection but where immediate feedback would be useful technology cannot always deliver – it can be unreliable. Mentors and their mentees need to have time to 'get to know one another' online before interactions (particularly where a mentee has problems) are underway. We need to look beyond traditional ways of working with web-based technology in mentoring and coaching in education contexts. We need to be creative and innovative. Using web-based technology will open up ways of working, ways we have not yet imagined. As a community of educators, we need to embrace such changes but we also need to be careful and not lose the essence of existing good practice either.

> The Internet and associated technologies make this an exciting time to be involved in education. It is also a frightening and worrying prospect because many of the important values embodied in the education system might be weakened.
>
> (Weller, 2002: 33)

Web-based technology is transforming my mentoring and coaching in ways that I would never have dreamed possible when I became one of the first school-based mentors in the UK. It is, however, a mixed blessing. The hours of frustration when an email is lost, the risks of misinterpretation in email communication, plagiarism that can result from sharing research into mentoring and coaching online, and threats to confidentiality by hacking are all realities but despite of all these possible problems, opportunities to share in mentoring and coaching relationships present themselves, all because of the web.

REFERENCES

Aggarwal, A. (2003) *Web-Based Education; Learning from Experience*, Information Science Publishing, Hershey.

Bierema, L. and Merriam, S. (2002) E-mentoring: Using computer mediated communication to enhance the mentoring process, *Innovative Higher Education*, 26(3), 211–225.

Bonk, C. J. (2009) *The World is Open: How Web Technology is Revolutionizing Education*, Jossey-Bass, San Francisco.

Burton, R. and Brown, J. S. (1978) *An Investigation into Computer Coaching for Informal Learning Activities*. Research report supported in part by the Advanced Research Projects Agency, Air Force, Lowry AFB/Technical Training, Denver.

Clarke, A. (2004)s *E-Learning Skills*, Palgrave Study Guides, Basingstoke.

Clayton, S., O'Brien, M., Campbell, A., Qualter, A. and Varga-Atkins, T. (2009) 'I know it's not proper research, but…' how professionals' understandings of research can frustrate its potential for CPD, *Educational Action Research*, 16(1), 73–84.

Denton, J., Davis, T., Smith, B., Strader, A., Clark, F. and Wang, L. (2006) Technology Mentor Fellowship Program; A technology integration professional development model for classroom teachers, *National Forum of Teacher Education Journal*, Vol. 16 (3), accessed on 23 March 2011 at http://www.nationalforum.com/Electronic%20Journal%20Volumes/Denton,%20Jon%20Technology%20Mentor%20Fellowship%20Program.pdf

Fletcher, S. J. (2000) *Mentoring in Schools; A Handbook of Good Practice*, Kogan Page, London.

Fletcher, S. J. (2005) Research mentoring; The missing link, in Bodone, F. (Ed.), *What Difference Does Research Make and for Whom?*, Peter Lang, New York.

Fletcher, S. J. (2006) Technology enabled action research in mentoring teacher researchers, *Reflecting Education Journal*, 2(1), 50–71.

French, D., Hale, C., Johnson. C. and Farr, G. (1999) *Internet Based Learning*, Kogan Page, London.

Garrison, R. and Vaughan, N. D. (2008) *Blended Learning in Higher Education*, JossyBass, San Francisco.

Harasim, L. (2000) Shift happens; online education as a new paradigm in learning, *Internet and Higher Education*, 3, 41–61.

Jolliffe, A., Ritter, J. and Stevens, D. (2001) *The Online Learning Handbook*, Kogan Page, London.

Kasprisin, C., Single, P., Single, R., Ferrier, J. and Muller, C. (2008) Improved Mentor Satisfaction: emphasising protégé training for adult-age mentoring dyads, *Mentoring & Tutoring, Partnership in Learning*, 16(2), 163–174.

Lamar, P. (2007) E-mentoring interaction models. Paper presented at the International Research Conference in the Americas of the Academy of Human Resource Development, Indianapolis, 28 February–4 March 2007.

Little, W. J. (2001) Inside teacher community: representations of classroom practice. Paper presented as an invited address at the bi-annual conference of the International Study Association on Teachers and Teaching, Faro, Portugal, 21–25 September 2001.

Loughran, J. (2003) 'Exploring the nature of teacher research', in Clarke, A. and Erickson, G. (Eds), *Teacher Inquiry: Living the research in everyday practice*, RoutledgeFalmer, London.

Macdonald, J. (2006) *Blended Learning and Online Tutoring*, Gower Press, Aldershot.

National Strategies Report (2010) *Mentoring and Coaching in Initial Teacher Education: review and development*, accessed on 5 June 2011 at http://www.dcsf.gov.uk

Neville, K., Adam, F. and McCormack, C. (2003) A web-based platform to mentor distance learners, in Aggarwal, A. (Ed.), *Web-Based Education: Learning from Experience*, IRM Press, Hershey.

Prosser, J., Clark, A. and Wiles, R. (2008) Visual Research Ethics at the Crossroads, in *Realities*, accessed on 10 October 2010 at http://www.manchester.ac.uk/realities

Roney, K. and Davies, M. A. (2007) Coaching and mentoring on the Internet highway, *Innovate*, Vol. 3 (5), accessed on 12 October 2010 at http://www.innovateonline.info

Ryan, S., Scott, B., Freeman, H. and Patel, D. (2000) *The Virtual University: The Internet and Resource-based Learning*, Kogan Page, London.

Salmon, G. (2002) *E-tivities; The Key to Active Online Learning*, Kogan Page, London.

Shrestha, C., May, S., Edirisingha, P. Burke, L. and Linsey, T. (2009) From face-to-face mentoring to e-mentoring; does the 'e' add any value for mentors? *International Journal for Teaching and Learning in Higher Education*, 20(2), 116–124.

Single, P. B. and Muller, C. (1999) Electronic mentoring; Issues to advance research and practice. Paper presented at the annual meeting of the International Mentoring Association, Atlanta, 15–17 April 1999.

Swan, K. and Shea, P. (2005) The development of virtual learning communities, in Hiltz, S. and Goldman, R. (Eds), *Learning Together Online; Research on Asynchronous Learning Networks*, Lawrence Erlbaum Publishers, London.

Taber, S. (2007) *Classroom-based Research and Evidence-Based Practice; A Guide for Teachers*, SAGE Publications, London.

Weller, M. (2002) *Delivering Learning on the Net*, Kogan Page, London.

Weller, M. (2007) *Virtual Learning Environments*, Routledge, London.

Winter, R. (1997) Action research, universities and 'theory'. Paper presented to the annual conference of the Collaborative Action Research Network Conference, London, 17th –19th October 1997.

Yaw, D. (2007) E-mentoring in virtual education. Presentation at Indianan State University, accessed on 23 October 2010 at http://www.scribd.com/doc/31592367/E-Mentoring-in-Virtual-Education

Operationalizing Phases of Mentoring Relationships

Carol A. Mullen and Dale H. Schunk

INTRODUCTION

Effective mentoring unfolds as a learning process over time. Four distinct phases of mentoring inform developmental mentoring relationships: initiation, cultivation, separation, and redefinition (Kram, 1985/1988). (See Figure 6.1 for the mentoring phases.)

For each phase discussed, we draw on the mentoring and psychology literature, including chapters from this book, *The SAGE Handbook of Mentoring and Coaching in Education*. We also searched for ways to enliven each phase by

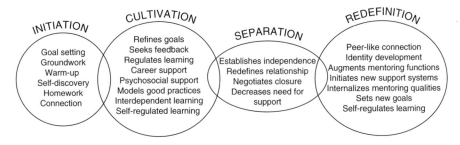

Figure 6.1 Mentoring relationship phases from the protégé's perspective (Mullen and Schunk, 2011)

trying to capture some sense of what effective mentoring in education looks like in doctoral programs, with degrees of applicability to other contexts.

Although mentoring researchers consider the lexical definitions of the four phases in Kathy Kram's model to be adequate, more operational detail is needed. How would someone know or be able to discern what phase (e.g., initiation, cultivation) a protégé is involved in, based on observing this individual in action? If these phases could be described qualitatively and defined behaviorally, they would provide a tangible platform for investigating related variables. Because research has supported the validity of these mentoring phases as characteristic of effective mentoring (Bouquillon, Sosik, and Lee, 2005; Chao, 1997), we endeavor here to put 'a face' on the phases at a more practical level. Although we are eager to spark ideas for mentors, we write with the doctoral protégé in mind, hoping to facilitate skills, values, and understandings. This focus shifts the image of the mentoring relationship as conveyed in some of the literature, placing emphasis on the protégé's role as adult learner rather than received beneficiary. In this vein, we encourage protégés to develop opportunity contexts for enabling their work as conscientious lifelong learners. As Ko, Lo, and Lee (Chapter 20) attest, it is essential that protégés, not just mentors, understand how to take advantage of and benefit from the mentoring process. And, we call upon mentors to diversify mentoring in academia through means such as creating culturally diverse support networks.

INITIATION PHASE OF MENTORING

Launching the initiation phase

Even before initiating a mentoring relationship, would-be protégés prepare by doing what one mentoring dyad (i.e., group of two) has aptly termed 'groundwork' (Kochan and Trimble, 2000). Such protégés ask, what are my strengths and weaknesses? What are my learning goals? Who can help facilitate my goals and cultivate learning relative to my interests? What expertise, skills, and qualities am I seeking in a mentor?

The learner who is striving for acceptance as a protégé asks initial questions like these that serve the threefold purpose of

1 getting to know oneself better as a learner relative to desirable and expected competencies;
2 becoming informed about the background, experience, and expertise of potential mentors in one's field or program; and
3 identifying experts and more advanced peers who might serve as mentors in an area of interest.

Protégés elicit suggestions for mentors from colleagues and experts. They often rely on established reputation and recommendations for making an initial identification. More protégés would benefit from reading about potential mentors to create an informed picture for themselves. They can also observe potential mentors in action, actually interviewing them, and complete a self-appraisal. Self-appraisals can prove informative, laying the groundwork for self-development (Kochan and Trimble, 2000; Mullen, 2005). Behavioral and attitudinal data can give a snapshot of one's strengths and weaknesses. Protégés can create targets for learning so that self-improvement can more readily take place.

In psychology, the use of self-appraisal instruments is common. Excluding those designed for mental health purposes, they can serve as a diagnostic tool for mentoring purposes. Inventories can roughly classify these using Kram's (1985/1988) primary mentoring functions: career and psychosocial. Protégés can learn more about themselves with regard to coping styles, behaviors, and attitudes (psychosocial function of mentoring), and dominant drives, interests, and goals (career function of mentoring).[1]

The protégé featured in Kochan and Trimble's (2000) informal mentoring account took some of the steps listed. Based on information gained from a self-appraisal, she decided that she wanted to become more assertive (e.g., vocal) in groups, so she intentionally set in motion the rest of her learning with this target in mind. She interviewed potential mentors before choosing a confident, successful female leader who mirrored her career trajectory. Negotiating entry into an informal network of mentors and peers can occur like this too, although it may be more involved. In this case, the mentor or group may interview the interested party to explore personality fit and possible membership (Mullen, 2005).

To identify mentors who fit with their career or life trajectory, protégés could benefit from knowing how culture influences mentoring in their own setting (Johnson, 2007). Kochan and Pascarelli's (Chapter 12) report of the literature they examined suggest differences between career-oriented mentoring in the United States and developmental tutoring in Europe. They also note how, in Asia, seniority and social class are closely linked to leadership power, whereas in American culture power is more associated with position, experience, and/or expertise, all of which can impact mentoring experiences. Although generalizations of cultures and countries are 'slippery' for reasons that include variability across contexts and people, protégés can still benefit from pondering macro ideas that may assist with their own decision making. By doing so, they become more attuned to understanding the very types of mentoring relationships – such as dyadic or communal – they are likely to initiate and experience at different times.

Just as protégés build social capacity by having some knowledge of their mentor's context, mentors help foster mentoring relationships in their early phases. Mentors build social capital by being culturally informed of similarities and differences across cultures, and by being sensitive to cultural influences within their own academic communities. Other areas of cultural fit also matter to the initiation process, including what Hansman (Chapter 24), Kochan and Pascarelli (Chapter 12), and Ragins and Kram (2007) all refer to as power-distance. High power-distance signals more top-down, authoritative relationships that command role respect and independence, and low power-distance are conducive to communal or collaborative as well as interdependent and co-mentoring relationships. Students and scholars of color have had to generate networks of their own in order to navigate predominately White institutions (PWIs), which communicate high power-distance. Normative structures are seen as problems where they advantage majority, middle-class student populations and operate in nuanced, even elusive, ways (Reddick and Young, Chapter 27). The type of social capital that is invaluable is, for example, paid assistantships with the most qualified and dutiful of mentors and invitations to join inner academic circles.

Protégés build social capital by seeking guidance and advice early on in their programs and throughout. They make connections not only through meetings with potential mentors but also through making informal contact, such as during events that include orientations, conferences, and seminars. They become knowledgeable about the possibilities for creating the conditions for their own learning. The mentoring literature, including chapters in this book, has ideas about how mentors and protégés have creatively worked together, met special needs, and affirmed individual and cultural differences (e.g., Davis, Provost, and Clark, Chapter 29; Mullen, 2005, 2008). Protégés can participate in learning communities that serve as a resource for intentionally attracting, promoting, and graduating students from all walks of life.

Becoming immersed in the initiation phase

During the *initiation* phase, reported by the workplace literature to take 6 to 12 months (Kram, 1985/1988), mentor and protégé begin interactions, testing first impressions. However, this phase probably takes far less time in educational circles. Students who have full-time jobs, for example, rely on compressed timeframes for academic progress in their programs. Reddick and Young (Chapter 27) acknowledge that mentoring relationships can take as little as a few months in academic contexts, a reality that summons forth questions about the value being placed on healthy, productive mentor–protégé relationships where enriched opportunity contexts may be unavailable or denied to some protégés. Typically, during initiation, protégé behavior is directed at capturing the mentor's imagination by establishing a patch of common ground. Mentoring strategies for persons of color seeking supportive, bonding relationships are documented in this chapter and Chapters 27 and 29.

'Development-seeking behaviors' characterize this phase of the mentoring relationship (Higgins, Chandler, and Kram, 2007: 354). Such protégé behaviors include information seeking, advice seeking, counseling, and feedback. These focus on the development of skills, knowledge, learning, and career development in such areas as sponsorship, protection, and visibility. One can see a protégé at work as s/he seeks information, advice, counseling, feedback, and so forth from potential mentors. Questions asked in the initiating phase reflect one's priorities, goals, and needs and they are of an orienting nature. They also vary depending on the protégé's context, personality, and background in mentoring. Mentors select protégés who show potential and competence as high performers, known as the 'rising-star effect' (Ragins and Kram, 2007: 7). Because it is generally thought that similarity breeds bonding, which is likely the antithesis of 'race-conscious practice' (see Reddick and Young, Chapter 27), protégés whose culture, ethnicity, citizenship, language, identity, or other differs from the norm will need to be vigilant about finding creative ways to compensate for a White-majority bias.

A major goal is for protégés who initiate mentoring relationships to exhibit behaviors and dispositions that reveal their competent and capable qualities and learning potential. With the mentor, they share who they are relative to their learning goals and knowledge of the expert and program based on such indicators as reputation *and* accomplishments. As they interact more, they learn first-hand about the mentor's personal style, work habits, and thinking process. This relationship phase can vary significantly in length, although it would not be unusual for protégés to think of it as a single contact or encounter. In contrast, mentors may more readily identify with what Kochan and Trimble (2000) refer to as the 'warm-up' phase of getting to know one another. During this time, relational possibilities and practicalities are mulled over for some time. These include potential benefits and challenges associated with the relationship and the time commitment involved both in the immediate and distant future. Zachary (2002) has described this warm-up phase as 'preparing' whereby mentors assess the protégé's skills, needs, and potential, and weigh potential benefits to the mentor.

In this phase, the relationship can be informal (voluntary and spontaneous), meaning that the mentoring parties have agreed to work together. Or, the relationship can be formal (structured and planned), meaning that they have been brought together by a third party (e.g., department chair) or matched through a structured mentoring program (e.g., the US Barbara Jackson Scholars network, which forges links between doctoral students of color and a national network of mentors). Higher education relationships tend to be voluntary, except where temporary advisements or formal matches with mentors are made. This distinction informs the developmental context of mentoring relationships from beginning to end (Allen and Eby, 2007). The relationship is also initiated differently depending on whether it is a mentoring pair or an alternative arrangement, such as a support group that facilitates constructivist learning. Mentoring relationships, whether informal or formal, dyadic or group-based, incorporate goal setting, career advice, psychosocial support, academic or practical knowledge, and social modeling (Kram, 1985/1988).

Protégés have much to weigh as they enter this phase, knowing that their mentor will likely be serving as a voluntary support. Learners can certainly gain from being aware of desirable protégé attitudes, behaviors, and actions. Protégés' levels of initiation should be high, not low, during mentoring. High initiation is evidenced by frequent enactment of development-seeking behaviors; alternatively, low initiation means that such behaviors are being enacted infrequently (Higgins et al., 2007). The idea is to have frequent contact with the (potential) mentor, otherwise one will be struggling to accomplish too much in too few work sessions. Stress can result in poor-quality, rushed work and relationship strain. In contrast, routines promote mutual benefit, developmental learning, constructive feedback, expected progress, and satisfaction. Protégés should not feel (or be made to feel) they are intruding on the potential mentor's time, thus hindering their initiation and development-seeking behaviors. Being under-assertive or too assertive is not a plus. Working with mentors to create a rhythm for the relationship, protégés bring forward the best of their personality characteristics (e.g., optimism, empathy, open-mindedness). Good planning coupled with a respectful demeanor and openness to constructive criticism exhibited early on attracts mentors (Kochan and Trimble, 2000). Being overly demanding, needy, poorly organized, unreliable, or too sensitive tends not to be attractors. Because theorists cite extraversion (sociability, high energy, positive emotions) as a desirable quality in protégés, this is worth knowing. However, positive mentoring still occurs where protégés are more introverted than mentors or vice versa, meaning that complementary personality fits can also work (Ragins and Kram, 2007).

The initiation phase can take forms that stretch beyond the traditional apprenticeship. As a highly structured system, mentoring embeds different structures, rewards, and capital ranging from the social to the human. Mentoring relationships facilitate different mentoring functions (i.e., career and psychological) that mentoring parties operationalize through their behaviors as protégés progress through the sequence of phases. A further complexity that Crow describes (see Chapter 15) is that this expansion of types of mentoring from dyadic mentoring to alternative arrangements has produced dynamic, proliferating features of mentoring relationships. Protégés may have more than one mentor, may engage in reciprocal mentoring, may be immersed in e-mentoring, and may have as a primary identity affiliation a high-energy network rather than a single expert (Kochan and Pascarelli, 2003).

Some researchers think that mentoring should be formalized – not left to chance – or at least have built-in structural elements. Under-represented members of groups (e.g., cultural ethnic minorities) can have greater assurance of being included in learning contexts. Formal mentoring encompasses planning, mentor selection, matching, preparation, and evaluation, and sometimes even a contract, which outlines expected roles and responsibilities. A 'mentoring creed' – a social contract that guided an informal doctoral writing group – describes the values and behaviors conducive to high-quality, interdependent work (Mullen, 2007, 2008).

Protégés who participate in formalized dyadic arrangements should know that while benefits commonly encompass learning, coaching, career planning, and psychosocial support, problems have included mentor–protégé mismatches, scheduling difficulties, and geographic distance (Eby and Lockwood, 2004). Mentoring parties will need to work especially hard in the initiation phase to be well matched, or else seek a different pairing. Because expectations can be unmet by protégés and because mentors tend to accept protégés who are similar to themselves, under-represented individuals across academic settings are thought to benefit from formal mentoring. So, more researchers have been recognizing the value of programs that incorporate the participation of females and minorities professionals in relational learning and career building (e.g., Mullen, 2008). Further, Johnson-Bailey (Chapter 10) argues for the preparation of faculty members in the mentoring of protégés whose culture, gender, or something else is different from their own. Faculty preparation for this mentoring role and four phases calls for more emphasis on being culturally responsive within increasing diverse academic contexts that benefit from cultural knowledge and diversity. Mentors who are expansive and inclusive in their choice of protégés, and who are informed about cultural differences, have higher social capital. Once initiated, mentoring across difference connects people whose identity differs from one another, thereby enriching programs.

CULTIVATION PHASE OF MENTORING

Mentoring relationships that have been effectively initiated enter the cultivation phase. Cultivation is estimated to last two to five years (Kram, 1985/1988), although this varies depending on many variables that include one's context or program, motivation, goals, progress, norms, and personality (Reddick and Young, Chapter 27). Zachary (2000) has aptly concluded that this phase is the longest one and that it presents the greatest challenge, requiring the most need for mentor support. Zachary's description of cultivation includes what she terms 'negotiating' and 'enabling.' Since the former involves coming to agreement about goals and a structure for the relationship and its content, it overlaps with the initiation phase, especially where the initial phase is long. (Where the initiation phase is short, the negotiating process is fulfilled during it.) The enabling phase is the cultivation phase: Here, characterizing behaviors include participating in open conversations, affirming cultural differences, asking probing questions, and receiving feedback perceived as thoughtful, timely, and constructive (Zachary, 2000). The mentoring party builds on and refines the learning goals already set and facilitates the protégé's sense of self-efficacy for attaining them (Schunk, 2001). While working on tasks, protégés regulate their success by observing their mentor in action and by monitoring progress, believing they can accomplish goals by maintaining focus, keeping commitments, working diligently, and sustaining motivation, as well as adopting new and better learning strategies. Protégés also seek out constructive feedback (e.g., corrective, progress) at increasingly advanced and sophisticated levels. Thus, protégés engaged in relationships that mature to this phase have internalized self-regulated learning. Mentoring functions are provided through career development, psychosocial support, and social modeling. It is in this phase that such functions peak.

Our reader should ideally be able to observe a protégé and know that he or she is in the cultivation phase but not in all cases, as mentoring does not follow a reductionistic or simplified recipe. As one complication, while a mentor may consider the informal mentoring relationship to be in the 'getting to know you' (initiation) phase where a full commitment is being contemplated, the protégé may assume that a commitment has already been made, so how is an observer to know for sure? The protégé may not know the decision-making style of the mentor or subtleties of academia, for whom a fit may occur more gradually. Hence, it is helpful for mentors to have awareness of the mentoring phases and how these get played out in real time with actual people and contexts so that they can attune others to the learning process itself.

Observationally and behaviorally speaking, one can see the mentoring pair hard at work negotiating and forging the relationship. Conversation is focused in this direction, with attention on developing a 'road map' for the work (Zachary, 2000), which is vigorously extended or deepened during cultivation. Regular communication, closeness, productivity, dynamic interchanges, adjustment, and feedback are to some degree observable actions. These can be summed up as frequency of contact and monitoring of progress – two crucial components of effective mentoring practice (Young and Harris, Chapter 22) – nurtured by trust, acceptance, transparency, skills building, and routines. Importantly, as Crow (Chapter 15) has noted, mentoring relationships do not just fulfill these psycho-social and career functions. Intensity makes the difference. The extent to which mentoring relationships are passionately committed to a shared purpose helps determine the level of cultivation, the quality of the relationship, and the kind of work that gets accomplished.

Hansman's snapshot of a healthy, productive mentoring relationship from the perspective of a female minority protégé is informative (see Chapter 24). During what we interpret as the cultivation phase with her dissertation supervisor, she was mentored through activities of an increasingly complex nature that spanned skills building (e.g., receiving feedback on writing drafts) and cultural knowl-edge (e.g., gaining inside knowledge about academe). Protégés in the cultivation phase receive feedback of greater specificity. Effective mentoring develops their knowledge and skills in such crucial areas as critical thinking, writing, and presentation.

Beyond eliciting feedback from mentors, protégés enable their own learning by developing strategies for responding effectively. For example, they might bring to their work sessions – whether these are face-to-face or electronic – not only the revised work in the expected writing format (e.g., dissertation chapter), but the feedback they were given and their response to each major point. The idea is to show, as authors do of manuscripts revised for review with editors and pub-lishers, what changes were acted upon and how. Protégés may find it helpful to 'diagram' the actual changes addressed. Here, the protégé can be observed at work cultivating his or her own learning by using meta-level strategies for orga-nizing feedback and for bringing transparency to the revising process. Some writ-ers track their changes in Word programs and use the same document to make comments for readers (known as callouts recorded as bubbled comments in the file's margins). Protégés can also use this feature as progress notes for showing the process of their thinking. The use of such strategies can activate a metacognitive level of writing, synthesis, and analysis. The idea is to avoid encountering the same types of problems or changes from mentors on subsequent drafts.

Here is an example of how a mentor might give feedback: The dissertation supervisor signals a problem – the protégé's non-analytical style of writing suggests that he is too close to his study population. The protégé's description of his data results is thought by the mentor to reflect a surface treatment of participants' (digitally recorded) statements, bereft of an interpretive or a critical treatment. Among the numerous examples cited are the sentences: 'Wanda loves teaching and enjoys student interaction,' and 'Tamson moved to Toronto because of her desire to experience an urban multicultural school district.' Numerous other examples in the writing also convey that the protégé is donning a participant's 'hat', not a researcher's 'hat'. The textual effect is one of mimicking the stories of and claims made by participants as though these are somehow self-evident. A critical self-reflective process of engagement, in this case, translates into an academic struggle with the data collected, presented, and, ultimately, rendered. The dissertation writer will shoulder the responsibility of transforming the text so that the 'story' told by the researcher reflects a meaningful pattern of information. The mentor continues in this scenario, indicating the need for intellectually probing the data presented through such means as depth of analysis, supporting evidence, and use of argument and artistry in the write up.

In this scenario, the mentor helps the protégé to demonstrate higher order thinking by making meaning of the data. As an instance, the dissertation writer might perform an in-depth analysis that brings forward possible motivations of teachers for moving to a new country to teach full time. Illustrating this point about a probing analysis, the mentor discourses with the protégé to draw out analyses and perhaps to repeat back what the protégé is saying or what is being heard. The protégé has been taking notes and exhibits comprehension, suggesting that he has internalized the constructive criticism that will enable him to tackle the problem at hand – that is, the surface treatment of participants' words for which creativity combined with self-corrective monitoring is needed. Because he understands, he makes fewer of the same types of errors on ensuing drafts. Progress becomes discernible. In contrast, protégés who lack the metacognitive ability for understanding the feedback received, or who are defensive about their draft writing or who have low motivation for making progress, have difficulty meeting goals.

While the norm is for students to address feedback in an original Word file without keeping a separate log of what was actually done and how, this submerges the revision process. Protégés who take good notes during sessions and who follow up with a summary are using writing strategies that propel comprehension and good communication. Using such writing systems makes explicit the use of feedback, enabling deeper ideas to form and better questions to emerge. A detailed writing plan contains major goals and specific goals, as well as timelines for work productivity. We refer to this type of meta-process as managing upward, in effect metaphorically placing protégés in the 'driver's seat' of their own learning.

At the group level, the cultivation phase of doctoral learning occurs in ways that are similar to and different from mentoring dyads. In a peer cohort that functioned for seven years, members communicated their changes in documents based on the feedback from mentors *and* peers, and they learned to give constructive feedback as a group on dissertation proposals and chapters (Mullen and Tuten, 2010). They reported that participation in an intensive writing group improved their motivation to write and finish their doctorate. To quote participants, 'The group "keeps my feet to the fire", which makes my dissertation much more attainable to me' (Mullen, 2005: 79). As Young and Harris attest, adult learners who are internally motivated especially benefit from being involved in the decision making that governs their own learning from planning to assessment (see Chapter 22). Although it is not the responsibility of mentors or mentoring relationships to hold protégés accountable for their progress and success, the reality seems to be that protégés who are extrinsically motivated need prodding (e.g., reminders) during the cultivation phase. Within a support network, a shift occurs in that the members assume responsibility for each other and, on a higher note, for the success of the group itself (Mullen, 2005).

During cultivation, whether within groups or networks, interpersonal bonds strengthen. Positive affect is also evident without trading off rigor, honesty, and risk-taking. The climate for learning should be experienced as safe and supportive, as well as professional and ethical, and a synergistic connection is forged. In this phase, goals set during the initiation phase are developed and refined, and even, in some cases, attained. Greater familiarity with each other is evidenced as the mentoring parties draw on a store of knowledge in their communications. The protégé feels more comfortable opening up and experimenting with creative thinking and problem solving. Mentoring support for the protégé does not just occur through interactions but through work that occurs 'behind the scenes' as mentors tap into talent pools to nominate their protégés for opportunities aligned with that person's interests (Dougherty and Dreher, 2007: 87).

As a balance, like the exemplary protégé described by Kochan and Trimble (2000), protégés are tasked with being especially vigilant of the mentor's time when they feel relaxed. Sticking to the allotted time for work sessions communicates respect for busy schedules, not just good planning. Checking in even while in session to reflect on progress and time for additional questions or clarification shows mindfulness. Not asking the most important questions toward the end of sessions is also a sign of good planning. While protégés should not feel (or be made to feel) they are burdening the mentor, they nurture the relationship by monitoring their own actions and demeanor.

In the cultivation phase where co-mentoring and co-learning are underway, mutual development emerges. Instead of one-sided development that benefits only (or mostly) the protégé, dynamics can take the form of a 'complementary cross-fertilization of needs, knowledge, and practice' (Ragins and Kram, 2007: x). In such hybrid mentoring relationships, the mentor and protégé coach and learn from each other, and both make personal and professional gains.

SEPARATION PHASE OF MENTORING

The separation phase is a natural part of mentoring relationships. After a sustained cultivation period in which goals are met, the protégé typically seeks autonomy and independence or outgrows the need for the relationship. Dynamics like these signal an end in sight. Unfortunately, 'separation' has a negative connotation, especially since 'mentoring as marriage' is a popular belief system reflected in the literature and conversationally, but separation in marriages is a precursor to divorce or abandonment. However, in mentoring theory and practice, separation is an inevitable outcome that follows from an intense learning experience, even one of mutual benefit.

As many know, this phase can get played out as a positive or a negative experience or as more of a blended reality, and it can be prematurely assisted or prolonged. Realistically, the way this phase unfolds determines how the individuals involved redefine their relationship. During this time, the mentor and protégé's personality characteristics become tested. Emotions such as grief, loss, sense of abandonment may escalate, on the one hand, or sense of appreciation and feelings of loyalty and identification, one the other hand. The parties face bringing their mentoring to closure and making the decision to end or renegotiate the relationship. This can be an emotionally challenging and even draining time, which may be why separation is considered the most neglected mentoring phase (Zachary, 2000).

Protégés who are self-confident about their ability to function autonomously are more likely to enter a positive separation (and redefinition) phase. Mentors who are supportive of their protégé's independence and affirming of a peer relationship will likely experience this phase in a similar way (Ragins and Kram, 2007). The separation phase is intended to be short but well managed, especially as mentors have a role to play in assisting protégés to redefine their identity. Formal mentoring relationships may have lingering problems because they tend towards premature or abrupt closure more than informal relationships.

The separation phase benefits from the use of productive conversational strategies for transitioning the mentoring relationship through which the intensity of learning will greatly lessen so that a new dawn of development can emerge. A simple goodbye on the part of either party is to be avoided. Instead, as Zachary (2000) attests, the mentor works with the protégé to make this new phase of their relationship work. They can evaluate the learning that occurred, acknowledge progress, express appreciation, and celebrate achievement. Mullen (2005, 2007, 2008) has shown how such strategies have worked and how co-mentoring protégés can benefit from not only cultivating more junior peers through such means as academic networking but also reflecting on the results. Faculty mentors who initiate opportunity contexts for development at this level assist protégés with the lifelong work of personal identity transformation for which development as mentors, collaborators, and role models may be vital.

In the separation phase, the needs of the protégé or the mentoring party have changed. Just as the protégé's independence increases, the mentor's efforts decrease. The psychosocial and career functions the mentor provides are intended to slow down and become even more targeted. Along with intensity, contact greatly lessens and the protégé's questions have a different focus. Typically career-directed, the goal is to secure a particular type of work such as an assistant professor or promotion within a current employment context. In addition, the mentor provides targeted help by, for example, coaching along the lines of reinforcing that applications must respond to position announcements in ways that are specific, not generic. All such changes reflect the importance of emerging as a new being in the world. In a positive mentoring relationship, the mentor's letting go is not to be confused with lack of commitment or abandonment. A natural closure to the relationship occurs because the protégé's program has ended, for example, or because something has caused an imbalance within the relationship. Relationships can end for psychological or physical reasons, with physicality being a major reason. One sees this occur when a student graduates and physically leaves the university or when the mentor departs by moving or retiring (Ragins and Kram, 2007).

This phase of the relationship can be delicate and misunderstandings can arise, so mentors pay close attention to the interpersonal dynamics. Many of us know mentoring parties that disbanded where the mentor or protégé wanted to terminate the relationship and not see the other again. Issues include relational misfit, disrespect or mistreatment, lack of appreciation, high dependency, mismanagement of the learning, over-association, inappropriate behavior, and ethical misconduct (Johnson, 2007). The need for separation can result, then, from negative factors including perceived problems with the relationship, lack of stability or other dysfunctional elements, or feeling dissatisfied.

Mentoring relationships do not need to disband if there is a strong psychological bond, in which case the relationship is redefined and continues in some form. Separation functions differently in synergistic, peer-like pairings whereby learning is mutual and benefits are reciprocal; such relationships are poised for a new chapter to be written about the relationship and the protégé's identity.

The classic goal in the separation phase is twofold: protégés separate from their mentors and redefine themselves by continuing to develop their identity. Mentors will typically find that after their protégé has graduated, which establishes a natural separation for dyads, they are called upon as a key agent in career promotion by providing letters of support, introducing their protégé to networks, and so forth. Commitment, stability, and modeling continue in this phase where visibility, promotion, and sponsorship may be crucial to the protégé's career and satisfaction.

Cultures of individualism and collectivism permeate this phase. Where individualism is the cultural norm, whether at the macro level of institutions or micro level of people, mentors and protégés are more apt to part ways. Mentors have exhibited a particular work style that does not match a protégé's. For example, a male mentor's emphasis on technical skill building and competition through such means as careerism (e.g., advancement) may not fit a female protégé's desire for collaborative and relational engagement, including counseling (Johnson, 2007). Kitayama (2002) has critiqued research that makes generalizations about cultures, providing the example of Americans being depicted as more individualistic than other cultures. She views cultural generalizations as indefensible where serious limitations are evident in the research methodology (such as the use of self-report to assess attitudinal measures). Mentoring in the separation phase could benefit from meaningful cultural information.

REDEFINITION PHASE OF MENTORING

At this point, the protégé has separated entirely from the mentor or has entered into a new type of relationship. In the redefinition phase, a positive mentoring experience may have peer-like dimensions, characterized by mutual support and informal contact (Chao, 1997). Some mentors may take this a notch higher, seeing this not only as the outcome of good mentoring but also as a major initiating goal where friendship is a psychosocial function to be fulfilled. Academics in this phase can be seen presenting together at conferences, co-authoring, or contributing to one another's ideas.

Freire (1997) warned that protégés should not emulate their mentors or bypass transforming their identity, implying that the separate and redefinition phases of mentoring must be actualized. Through this learning, protégés will be challenged to engage in deeper, lifelong questions about who they are and what they are becoming. Despite having an obvious mentoring imprint, they will not want to be 'branded' a mini version of the mentor. Protégés who have offset followership maximize their identity development through such means as testing out new ideas beyond the scope of what they have been taught. For example, we know a graduate (now a full professor) whose doctoral preparation by a well-known scholar–mentor in cultural minority language acquisition became the basis of her identity as global peace activist researching schools struggling for survival within war zones. Self-actualizing protégés have also branched out from the primary mentoring relationship through relational work with support networks, professional memberships, and productive peers (Mullen and Tuten, 2010). Of course, augmented ways of learning are even more valuable if initiated earlier, during the cultivation phase. Some academic employers are dismissive of protégés who overly identify with their mentors. Protégés of this type may excessively quote their mentors, only know their body of work, or lack a vision of their own. Strings that are tight signal dependency and even infantilization in extreme situations.

Nonetheless, the reality is that protégés who have successfully entered the redefinition phase are a work in progress. They will be testing their wings in a changing educational profession that is subject to transitions, unknowns, and insecurity for which they must prove themselves adaptive, creative, and persevering. A fundamental part of their identity is strong ties with networks, associations, and other groups, so they need to assess not only what affiliations they can join but also what role they can play. They can also gain from learning what additional experience, expertise, or credentialing through coaching or self-learning they may need in research, practice, or teaching. Graduates should not hesitate to broaden and diversify what they have to offer their profession in such targeted areas as clinical experience and research methodology.

Developing the identity of a professional whose work is self-directed and whose expertise is sought after is a different kind of goal necessitating being highly self-regulated. Intrinsically motivated people work beyond structured program goals towards mastery, a major 'source of achievement' that McGregor identified as occurring 'over the long haul' (1960: 48). The most successful graduates, to continue his line of thinking, 'often aren't directly pursuing conventional notions of success. They're working hard and persisting through difficulties because of their internal desire to control their lives, learn about their world, and accomplish something that endures' (ibid. 48). Doctoral protégés who are on a journey of self-development and mastery have moved from the initiation to the redefinition phase, experiencing a shift from social regulation, to guided self-regulation, to increased self-regulation through development of these capacities and skills (Mullen and Tuten, 2010). Protégés with high metacognitive ability develop personal mastery that extends their competence beyond merely emulating or patterning their thoughts and behaviors after their mentors and other role models (Schunk, 2003).

In this phase of learning, protégés seize multiple opportunities, continually negotiating the boundaries of who they are as they refine their goals, manage their transitions, and construct their careers, perhaps more intensively and strategically than some of their mentors who may have experienced more definitive career paths as educators within hierarchically organized organizations (Allen and Eby, 2007). Students and graduates who pursue a range of options for making meaning of their profession foster their identity, success and satisfaction – they manage the stress of temporary assignments, workplace disruptions, career transitions, and economic hardships. Protégés who mindfully select from a whole host of personality characteristics, behaviors, and commitments integrate compelling attractors, such as a heightened relational awareness, a steadfast writing habit, and an activist professional outlook within their shifting core self. They also stay abreast of a changing profession that national and international trends in accountability, standardization, digitization, restructuring, inclusiveness, and more are heavily influencing. More than ever, the direction they take in work and life necessitates being flexibly responsive and improvisational, interdependent and imaginative. Like their mentors, protégés extraordinaire will leave their own imprints that contain the traces of many others.

CONCLUSION

Would-be protégés can be faced with the need for a mentoring relationship and not know how to effectively initiate it, cultivate it, ease its separation, or redefine it. Understanding the mentoring phases can better enable their learning, satisfaction, and success over time through productive, meaningful relations with mentors and peers.

NOTE

1 We refrain from recommending any instruments as these are context-dependent; also, some Internet-accessible software tools carry corporate sponsorship and require payment. Thus, discerning experts can be consulted.

REFERENCES

Allen, T. D., & Eby, L. T. (Eds.) (2007). *The Blackwell Handbook of Mentoring: A Multiple Perspectives Approach*. Malden, MA: Blackwell.

Bouquillon, E. A., Sosik, J. J., & Lee, D. (2005). 'It's only a phase': Examining trust, identification and mentoring functions received across the mentoring phases. *Mentoring and Tutoring: Partnership in Learning, 13*(2), 239–258.

Chao, G. T. (1997). Mentoring phases and outcomes. *Journal of Vocational Behavior, 51*, 15–28.

Dougherty, T. W., & Dreher, G. F. (2007). Mentoring and career outcomes. In B. R. Ragins & K. E. Kram (Eds.), *Handbook of Mentoring at Work: Theory, Research, and Practice* (pp. 51–93). Los Angeles: SAGE.

Eby, L. T., & Lockwood, A. (2004). Protégés' and mentors' reactions to participating in formal mentoring programs: A qualitative investigation. *Journal of Vocational Behavior, 67*(3), 441–458.

Freire, P. (Ed.) (1997). *Mentoring the Mentor: A Critical Dialogue with Paulo Freire*. New York: Peter Lang.

Higgins, M. C., Chandler, D. E., & Kram, K. E. (2007). Developmental initiation and developmental networks. In B. R. Ragins & K. E. Kram (Eds.), *Handbook of Mentoring at Work: Theory, Research, and Practice* (pp. 349–372). Los Angeles: SAGE.

Johnson, W. B. (2007). *On Being a Mentor: A Guide for Higher Education Faculty*. Mahwah, NJ: Erlbaum.

Kitayama, S. (2002). Culture and basic psychological processes – toward a system view of culture: Comment on Oyserman et al. *Psychological Bulletin, 128*(1), 89–96.

Kochan, F. K., & Pascarelli, J. T. (Eds.) (2003). *Global Perspectives on Mentoring: Transforming contexts, Communities, and Cultures*. Greenwich, CT: Information Age.

Kochan, F. K., & Trimble, S. B. (2000). From mentoring to co-mentoring: Establishing collaborative relationships. *Theory Into Practice, 39*(1), 20–28.

Kram, K. E. (1985/1988). *Mentoring at Work: Developmental Relationships in Organizational Life*. Glenview, IL: Scott, Foresman & Company.

McGregor, D. (1960). *The Human Side of Enterprise*. New York: McGraw-Hill.

Mullen, C. A. (2005). *Fire and Ice: Igniting and Channeling Passion in New Qualitative Researchers*. New York: Peter Lang.

Mullen, C. A. (2007). Confessions of a doctoral supervisor: Valuing interdependence rooted in a mentoring creed. In C. A. Mullen, T. Creighton, F. L. Dembowski, & S. Harris (Eds.), *The Handbook of*

Doctoral Programs in Educational Leadership: Issues and Challenges (pp. 148–160). Miami, AZ: NCPEA Press.

Mullen, C. A. (Ed.) (2008). *The Handbook of Formal Mentoring in Higher Education: A Case Study Approach.* Norwood, MA: Christopher-Gordon.

Mullen, C. A., & Tuten, E. M. (2010). Doctoral cohort mentoring: Interdependence, collaborative learning, and cultural change. *Scholar–Practitioner Quarterly, 4,* 11–32.

Ragins, B. R., & Kram, K. E. (Eds.) (2007). *Handbook of Mentoring at Work: Theory, Research, and Practice.* Los Angeles: SAGE.

Schunk, D. H. (2001). Social cognitive theory and self-regulated learning. In B. J. Zimmerman & D. H. Schunk (Eds.), *Self-regulated Learning and Academic Achievement: Theoretical Perspectives* (2nd ed.) (pp. 125–151). Mahwah, NJ: Erlbaum.

Schunk, D. H. (2003). Self-efficacy for reading and writing: Influence of modeling, goal setting, and self-evaluation. *Reading & Writing Quarterly, 19,* 159–172.

Zachary, L. J. (2000). *The Mentor's Guide: Facilitating Effective Learning Relationships.* Thousand Oaks, CA: Jossey-Bass.

Culturally Based Concepts

Educating the Critically Reflective Mentor

Geraldine Mooney Simmie and
Joanne Moles

INTRODUCTION

Mentoring relationships of learning in teacher education have become more wide-spread in the last decade and are no longer adequately defined by novice–expert conceptions (Mullen, 2005; Wang and Odell, 2007). This chapter considers a meta-analysis of ten masters studies of mentoring in continuing teacher education conducted in the Republic of Ireland. The authors provide a theoretical frame-work for mentoring as a comparative analytical lens for this study. They draw on theory from Bernstein (1990, 2000); Darling-Hammond and Bransford (2005); Lingard, Hayes, Mills and Christie (2003); and Noddings (2003b, 2007). Each masters study is positioned with regard to its stance on critical thinking, profes-sional agency and inquiry within its cultural context. The paradoxes within which teachers work are well described by various contemporary writers (Ball, 2009; Gerwirtz and Cribb, 2009; Giroux, 2009; Hoban, 2005). It is clear that to balance a desire to promote creativity and critical thinking within a system that measures outcomes in competency terms requires enormous skill and perhaps some self-delusion. Findings suggest several constraints operating with regard to educating the critically reflective mentor especially with regard to engagement with a vari-ety of critical discourses on education and research. This chapter raises substan-tive issues for the international academic research community, policymakers along with the teaching team. It concludes with suggested research proposals for the mentoring construct in a rapidly changing and challenging society.

EDUCATING THE CRITICALLY REFLECTIVE MENTOR

Researchers and policymakers, both in Ireland and internationally, regard teaching within a continuum and recognise the need for teachers to become lifelong learners and professionals throughout their career (Darling-Hammond and Bransford, 2005). This requires teachers to use a reflective and inquiry-oriented stance to their teaching for the development of individual learners and promoting the school as a learning community. Mentoring is often proposed as an ideal way to advance professional learning (Hargreaves and Fullan, 2000; Maynard and Furlong, 1995; Wang and Odell, 2007). It is viewed as a way of teachers supporting teachers across the career span from initial teacher education through the phases of induction and in-career development.

Developments in the recent past in the Republic of Ireland have seen teaching as a profession advocated and advanced by the Teaching Council, a statutory self-regulating body, who have implemented a code of professional conduct and are currently engaged in a consultative process for the development of a policy paper on teaching as a continuum (Teaching Council, 2007, 2011). In addition to these developments a national induction programme for newly qualified teachers has, after a decade as a pilot project, become national policy (Killeavy and Murphy, 2006). This induction is offered to newly qualified teachers by experienced mentor teachers, on a voluntary basis, not at the school site but in the evening at regional education centres.

The paradoxes within which teachers work are well described by various contemporary writers (Ball, 2009; Gerwirtz and Cribb, 2009; Giroux, 2009; Hoban 2005). It is clear that to balance a desire to promote creativity within a system that measures outcomes in competency terms requires enormous skill and perhaps some self-delusion. Similarly, the marrying of critical thought within an examination driven curriculum where right answers are recognised as the route to success, may well be an unrealistic demand on the teaching force. Despite some progress on developing the teacher's role as a professional, there has been an increasing body of evidence pointing toward the limited capacity of schools in Ireland to lead learning using an evidence-based lens (McNamara and O'Hara, 2006; Sexton, 2007).

This lack of an inquiry stance at the school site has implications for mentoring. If school cultures resist the mentor teacher who is willing to question the status quo, then mentoring will merely serve as a way of socialising student teachers and newly qualified teachers into existing traditional inherited practices. We are concerned with how mentoring can develop as a professional practice and, in turn, support teaching as a professional practice? The way we informed our research was to set up a masters course as a three-year part-time academic study at the University of Limerick to bring an evidence-informed, research and scholarship lens to mentoring. This study of mentoring provided a pathway of accreditation with graduate Certificate, graduate Diploma and Masters qualifications. The first year of the study is supported financially by the Department of

Education and Skills and offers students, including teachers, tutors and other education personnel, an opportunity to gain a Masters qualification resulting in a small remuneration paid in annual salary. The study attracts teachers who have become mentors in their schools, or who wish to become mentors, and want to inquire into their practices and broaden their perspective of the mentoring.

Studies of mentoring in the Nordic countries show that experienced teachers, without the teacher educator acting as critical friend, use mentoring and reflective practice at the school site in traditional ways that do little to integrate theory and research with practice and push the boundaries of learning forward (Ottesen, 2007; Sundli, 2007). By inviting mentor teachers in our study to look at alternatives and view their practices through a variety of lenses we were aware that we were threatening the basis of their professional self-confidence, as they are reproducing their experiences in ways that are tacitly approved and affirmed by colleagues, pupils, parents and school management.

THEORETICAL FRAMEWORK

We define mentoring as a complex intellectual, social and emotional construct with the capacity for professional support, learning and professional knowledge generation within the context in which it is practised and within broader societal norms and values. This coincides with our view of teaching as an intellectual activity, a moral and ethical activity and a humanistic activity. Our theoretical framework for mentoring emerged over a four-year period of collaboration, philosophical inquiry and cognitive dissonance as we progressed our understanding through critically interacting with each other and with mentor teachers around their academic studies (Mooney Simmie and Moles, 2011). The theoretical basis for the work continues to evolve on an ongoing basis. This framework places professional caring, professional agency and critical thinking at the heart of a model which is culturally responsive (Bernstein, 2000; Darling-Hammond and Bransford, 2005; Lingard et al., 2003; Noddings, 2003a and 2003b). Cain (2009) posits that, given the idiosyncratic nature of mentoring, mentors need to use research to inform and underpin their practice, to understand a variety of perspectives and interrogate their practice using 'an evidence informed lens' (2009: 63). We now reconsider mentoring through the sub-headings of *critical thinker*, *professional carer* and *professional agent* within the contemporary *cultural context*.

MENTOR TEACHER AS CRITICAL THINKER

Educating the reflective practitioner inside a community of practice is perceived as important for professionals working within a professional practice (Schön 1983, 1987). Different scaffolds and approaches have been advocated for this process. Brookfield (1995) argues for self-inquiry, inquiry with significant others and inquiry using the comparative lens of the literature. In this way the mentor teacher researcher is required to look within and beyond the confines of their own immediate experience. Mentor teachers, as mentor researchers in this academic study, were invited to develop their capacity for critical thinking through self-reflection, reflection with a critical friend and engagement with their tutors and the research literature. Dewey (1933) reminds us of the inherent challenge involved in developing this type of critical disposition:

> One can think reflectively only when one is willing to endure suspense and to undergo the trouble of searching. To many people both suspense of judgement and intellectual search are disagreeable; they want to get them ended as soon as possible. They cultivate the over-positive and dogmatic habit of mind, or feel perhaps that a condition of doubt will be regarded as evidence of mental inferiority. (1933: 176)

MENTOR TEACHER AS PROFESSIONAL CARER

The moral and ethical aspects of teaching and professional caring are expounded in Noddings' (2003a and 2003b, 2007) theory of care. Giving professional support in the form of empathy, listening and emotional support is a well-recognised role of the mentor teacher (Fletcher, 1998, 2000). Increased reflexive knowledge of self, with regard to beliefs and philosophical values, is defended as a core aspect of personal development for mentor teachers. However, the concept of the mentor teacher as a caring professional does not easily coincide with the anecdotal view of the traditional teacher in Ireland, where transmission models of teaching and compliance with regard to right answers appear as the twin aims for success (Lynch and Lodge, 2002).

MENTOR TEACHER AS PROFESSIONAL AGENT

Teachers and mentor teachers have the opportunity as professional agents to advocate for a more equal society through interrupting the cycle that retains education as a privilege for some rather than an opportunity for all (Lynch, 1999). A study by Lynch and Lodge (2002) shows the high level of discrimination in terms of race, religion and gender that happens on a daily basis in Irish schools, classrooms and staff rooms. Their research raises concerns about the isolation of teachers by some colleagues who may have, within the hierarchy of the school system, found unequal levels of acceptance with their school management:

> Some of those who documented unfair or unequal treatment by their school principal focused on a sense of being excluded from a powerful or influential group because they were not personally close to management, or because they held alternative opinions on educational or school matters. Individual teachers perceived that opportunities for promotion were tied to membership of groups that were either friendly with management, or were believed to hold the same political or philosophical values.
>
> (Lynch and Lodge, 2002: 169)

MENTOR TEACHER WITHIN A CHALLENGING CONTEMPORARY CULTURAL CONTEXT

Freire (1970/1993) argued that transmission models of teaching were based on *a banking concept of knowledge* which, within the mentor–mentee relationship, places the experienced teacher as expert knower and the pre-service student teacher or newly qualified teacher as a novice lacking in knowledge. He also argued that the teacher–student contradiction remains at the heart of the learning dilemma:

> In the banking concept of education, knowledge is a gift bestowed by those who consider themselves knowledgeable upon those whom they consider to know nothing. Projecting an absolute ignorance onto others, a characteristic of the ideology of oppression, negates education and knowledge as processes of inquiry ... (whereas) Education must begin with the solution of the teacher-student contradiction, by reconciling the poles of the contradiction so that both are simultaneously teachers and students.
>
> (Friere, 1970/1993: 53)

The Republic of Ireland is currently dealing with an actual banking crisis as well as a banking conception of knowledge crisis. Society is being forced to realign itself and find a better way for teachers to become professionals in a context where success in schooling has traditionally been measured by right answers in examinations. A society where teachers are flexible and have the intellectual capital for professional knowledge generation as well as the social and emotional capital for professional support and agency is more consistent with education as a genuine quest for learning. Mentor teachers in this study described a school system that was running at a pace that left little space or time for dialogue. O'Connor stated that the lack of 'time in our frenetic schedules in schools leaves little time for planning and co-operation ... because of our preoccupation with an exam-driven system, there is little time left for dialogue on learning' (2009: 68).

Drudy and Lynch (1993) identified three dominant ideologies in Irish educational discourse. The first of these, consensualism describes how 'society is viewed as an undifferentiated whole' (1993: 49). The second of these ideologies is essentialism which is a view of people as having a given set of abilities which determine success and levels of success. Standardised testing lends weight to the idea that achievement is finite and measurable. The third ideology identified in Ireland is called 'meritocratic individualism'. This reflects the idea that ability and effort combine to produce success and that individuals have success in their own hands.

In contemporary Ireland, some of the underlying assumptions are being challenged by changes in the personnel in classrooms as well as some of the long held truths being questioned. The scandals about authority figures' mistreatment of children have shaken long-held hierarchies. Non-national children, whose views on the role of schools are different from the Irish perceptions, serve to challenge teachers' ideological positions.

THE SETTING FOR THE ACADEMIC STUDY

Each post-graduate mentor engaged in a journey over the three-year period that involved learning to critique the literature, to position themselves as researchers and conduct a research study into their own chosen aspect of mentoring. Supports and scaffolds provided by the teaching team during this period included full-day seminars on campus, reflective writing assignments at the site of their professional practice and an annual meeting with national policymakers. Caring by the university team was demonstrated in a number of ways including paying special attention to assisting students to relieve the stresses of daily school life through physical exercise. The mentors were invited to become involved in gentle stretching exercises every time they came to campus and visited the dance studio for creative movement sessions at residential weekends and summer schools. Opportunities to know oneself were provided both physically and in less formal situations where individual contributions were valued.

METHODOLOGY

This study involves a meta-analysis of findings from the first cohort of ten masters theses (Paul, 2005: 36). Four studies focused on mentoring in their own schools (Bernard, 2009; Clarke, 2009; Fallon, 2009; O'Connor, 2009). Two of these studies, one at primary level and one at post-primary level, focused on offering mentoring support for pre-service and newly qualified teachers (Bernard, 2009; Clarke, 2009). The other two studies developed approaches to increasing awareness of mentoring as caring, collaborative and inquiry-oriented. Another study focused on mentoring for student teachers through a university partnership (Scannell, 2009). The remaining five studies focused on external perspectives. Ferris (2009) explored a comparative perspective with policymakers in Ireland and Australia. Lonergan (2010) considered models of mentoring in two different schools. McManus (2009) researched the perspectives of students in the academic study. O'Brien (2009) explored subject mentoring for newly qualified teachers at their voluntary subject association. Kavanagh (2009) interrogated the perspectives of mentors within her region and their implications for professional practice.

Our aim in the meta-analysis of these studies was to raise questions which would facilitate ongoing improvement of the study offered, enrich the mentoring debate in the literature with regard to professional learning and education and present national policymakers with research evidence. We also aimed to find greater clarity with regard to our future research and development trajectory.

Preliminary examination of the mentors' theses showed that mentor teachers in the study regarded the concept of the caring mentor as largely unproblematic. They were concerned with the willingness of mentor teachers to give back to the profession through extending themselves for the development of other teachers, such as the student teacher or the newly qualified teacher. We decided that this aspect of the study was largely inconclusive and required additional comprehensive research data going forward.

Revisiting our theoretical framework, taking the focus of the students' research studies into account, yielded four questions which were used to underpin the analysis:

1   What contextual factors supported or constrained reform-minded mentoring?
2   What evidence is there to suggest that mentor teachers developed a critical discourse with regard to research?
3   What evidence is there to suggest that mentor teachers developed a critical discourse of education and mentoring?
4   What evidence is there to suggest that mentor teachers developed their capacities for professional agency?

FINDINGS

The findings that emerged from this meta-analysis assisted the authors in positioning the studies, helped identify gaps between theory, research and practice and gave deeper insights into improvements required into the future. Evidence from the studies with regard to each of the four questions, *contextual factors*, *becoming a researcher*, *critical thinking* and *professional agency* are now considered in turn.

Cultural context

These ten masters theses were geographically based in an all-Ireland focus, north, south, east and west were included. The studies were inclusive of all school types and while the majority were from the post-primary sector one study examined the primary sector. Bernard's (2009) study found that primary teachers were supportive of her attempts to extend the mentoring team inside her school to include some established teachers in co-planning and observation for an improved whole school focus:

> Experienced teachers made themselves and their classes available for observations session for N.Q.T.'s (newly qualified teachers). Teachers in same class groupings became involved in organised planning both for long and short term plans and shared resources with each other. Teachers with specific expertise, for example, in provision of special needs or English as an additional language (EAL), shared their knowledge in planned workshops. (2009: 65)

Scannell (2009) was involved in mentoring student teachers in her post-primary school. She explored the need for a more structured school–university partnership in this regard. Assessment and mentoring of teaching practice for student teachers continues to remain in the Republic of Ireland as the sole responsibility of the university and higher education institutions. Scannell (2009) noted the possible benefits, in her literature review, of promoting improved partnership approaches for recreating the profession. Her study observed that teachers were 'less willing or comfortable to allow classroom observation, team teaching, joint lesson planning and discussion' (2009: 63). She also observed that lecturers at the university appeared to have 'very little (teaching) experience in second level classrooms' (ibid. 52). Overcoming this apparent dissonance between school and university required the development of trust and finding a new way forward:

> Bernstein (1990) comments, what matters is how we respond to one another, whether we are prepared to respect each other as potentially legitimate, or whether we resort to our own prejudicial standpoints and refuse to entertain the idea that other ways of knowing might be as legitimate as our own. (ibid. 59)

Fallon's (2009) study involved raising awareness in her school of the opportunity mentoring could provide to improve collaboration among teachers. Progress to date was regarded as 'slow and haphazard' (2009: III) with an obligation on all key stakeholders and school management to make the time available for teacher–teacher dialogue during the school day (ibid. 2). Many fears were raised about the possible threats that this new type of collaboration might present to teachers who continue working in isolation (ibid. 66). O'Connor (2009) questioned the value-system of a cultural context that makes no formal provision for dialogue with regard to teaching and learning:

> Have we in the second-level system become overly focused on a system that is strongly pastoral, that of year head and class tutor to the detriment of a structure that focuses on teaching and learning? Why are management in second-level schools not engaging with their teaching staff around teaching and learning? (2009: 12)

O'Brien's (2009) study focused on the development of a broader partnership model for the continuing professional learning of subject teachers through mentoring relationships of learning. She argued that teachers have no contractual obligations currently to become involved in mentoring and induction. Mentoring was being conducted as a 'grace and favour' system that could easily be withdrawn given a change in the circumstance of teachers (2009: 6). McManus (2009) found the issue of fear expressed as a cultural constraint by teachers 'where staff members are fearful or insecure they can be very closed to ideas around collaboration and sharing' (2009: 50). This aspect of fear also surfaced in the comparative study between two different schools by Lonergan (2010) who stated that there 'are real fears surrounding change and uncertainty for teachers. By not accounting for these in planning personal and professional development the needs of certain teachers are being left unmet' (2010: 82). Kavanagh's (2009) study argued that mentoring had the potential to reculture schools and 'could significantly impact professional development and practice. Where a supportive school culture was seen as necessary for mentoring programmes to be successful, mentors also believed that mentoring could promote collaborative cultures' (2009: 67).

This latter stance was the preferred approach taken by policymakers in Ireland and Australia interviewed by Ferris (2009) where she found 'overwhelming agreement among policymakers and educationalists that collegial practices enhance teaching and learning. However, all recognise that a culture change is needed and that mentoring can lead that change'(2009: 95). Contextual factors that supported mentoring appeared to be the positive way this construct was largely perceived. However cultural constraints abound. Taking the fears and concerns of teachers into account in the change process appears to be of central importance in supporting reform-minded mentoring. Findings indicate the need for further research data about the practices of schools in this regard. This needs to be supplemented with qualitative data about the perceptions of policy-makers, school owners and managers.

Becoming a researcher

A cursory examination of the Masters' theses indicates that the concerns of these thesis-writing teachers are consistent with 'what is' as opposed to 'why it is'. With the exception of two studies, one who opted for a mixed-methods research design and another who opted for an interpretivist paradigm, all other research studies were typically contained within the 'action research' paradigm:

> Action research is a form of self-reflective enquiry undertaken by participants in social (including educational) situations in order to improve the rationality and justice of (a) their own social or educational practices, (b) their understanding of these practices, and (c) the situations in which the practices are carried out.
>
> (Kemmis, 2007b: 168)

Mentor teachers' use of action research to interrogate practices demonstrates three common characteristics within these theses. First, the mentor teachers are keen to place the work being done in a situation where they feel safe and potentially in control. Second, their concerns with meeting the criteria of the university's assessment procedures and research ethics committee ensure that the level of risk taking is low. The third common characteristic is that none of the students questioned the dominant discourses within their schools. There is apparently a tacit acceptance of what constitutes education and there is little evidence of a willingness to interrogate the underpinning rationale associated with Irish education, nor to compare their understandings with other pedagogical or curriculum discourses.

The net effect of these factors is that the theses are an indication of a rather safe and unchallenging approach toward educational research evidenced by a group of motivated teachers who are investigating mentoring in a variety of settings including their own practices. These teachers want to be successful within the system as they perceive it currently. Because they were exposed to systematic inquiry about education and mentoring within theoretical frames through which they could analyse their own teaching and mentoring and the contexts in which they worked (both micro and macro) it is significant that their summative assessment is consistently couched in careful respect for the education establishment.

Both of the present authors question the value of a narrow type of action research as an unproblematic practitioner research stance. The field of practitioner research has become increasingly important with the growing recognition of the intellectual and professional judgment demands of professional practice. Kemmis (2007a: 12) in his foreword to a collection of action research studies notes the tensions that exist between university and higher education institute researchers and the perspectives of teachers. He asserts that action research can position teachers as 'co-actors and co-producers of knowledge' and affirm their professional agency (ibid. 15). However we have witnessed action research used in a more ambiguous way to control the choice of research topic by practitioners, confining them to examining their own practices only, and keeping them firmly inside the walls of their own immediate workspace without sufficient research study of their broader contextual landscapes. This narrower view is not always advanced and more recent studies by Rönnerman, Furu and Salo (2008) show broader perspectives. What is clearly needed is a broadening of the research debate between ourselves and our students, and the trialling of a variety of different approaches to scaffolding students' journeys in becoming mentor teacher researchers.

Critical thinking

Mentor teachers became engaged in questioning teachers' mindset and perspectives with regard to developing reform-minded mentoring:

> There is no doubt that teachers have a comfort zone which is their own classroom. Are teachers open to engaging in critical debate particularly about their own teaching? I think we are not yet ready as a profession to open our own teaching to scrutiny especially to our own colleagues.
>
> (O'Connor, 2009: 69)

Lonergan (2010) noted that there needed to be a 'change in the mind-set of some teachers' with regard to mentoring for it to contribute to a culture of professional learning (2010: 68). Clarke (2009) offered an induction programme for newly qualified teachers in her post-primary school through weekly meetings, support of colleagues and the compilation of a booklet of information. Mentoring was primarily used for the socialisation of teachers into the existing school culture with little sense that it was perceived as an active agent for change and learning:

> New teachers fit into school and are encouraged to be part of school life. Things run smoothly when everyone knows what they should do. All this helps with the integration of new staff and this ensures that new teachers get to know the culture of the school quickly. It gives a sense of working as a community with one another. As one teacher points out, 'well organised and confident teachers lead to a calm atmosphere and happy students.' All this creates a sense of belonging and support.
>
> (Clarke 2009: 53)

PROFESSIONAL AGENCY

Development of the professional agency of students in this academic study was facilitated through an annual policymakers' conference. During this conference students' held centre-stage and debated their viewpoints with regard to mentoring and what they perceived as key requirements in terms of future national policy on continuing teacher education. Overall students appeared more willing to critique national policy while remaining more careful and circumspect with regard to their immediate school environments. Their critique of national policy focused on models of mentoring that would open access for all teachers to collaborate with other teachers, especially with regard to dialogue on teaching and learning and the creation of the school as a community of learners.

Lonergan proposed the 'introduction of legislation making teacher professional development obligatory, as a prerequisite to ongoing registration with the Teaching Council of Ireland' (2010: 72). Bernard (2009) suggested that mentoring should be extended inside schools to include all established teachers. Ferris called for a model of mentoring that 'deprivatises practice' and develops a community of practice (2009: 104). McManus recommended the designation of a 'mentor school' for schools with a proactive focus on mentoring for leading learning (2009: 76).

The overall finding threading through these studies was that schools and teachers left to their own devices would not have the capacity to engage with the kind of sustainable change required for a reflective, inquiry-oriented approach to mentoring and continuing teacher professional learning and development:

> If the Teaching Council is serious about the importance of the reflective teacher and the core values of collegiality and collaboration, they will need to put in place a public space for dialogue in schools to drive this educational discourse. Schools left to their own devices will not have the energy or motivation to enact and develop new pedagogical and leadership practices in professional development across the continuum.
>
> (O'Connor, 2009: 68)

CONCLUSION

This study reviewed the masters theses on mentoring in teacher education to elicit a deeper understanding of the positioning of the studies, the possible gaps between these and the authors' theoretical framework, and the implications of these for the international academic community, policymakers and the teaching team. The analysis explored various aspects of the framework within these studies, including critical thinking, professional agency and the cultural contextual factors that enhance or constrict a collaborative, caring, inquiry-oriented type of mentoring. It considered the extent to which mentor teachers were developing a critical discourse on becoming researchers and suggested possible directions for our research and development synergies into the future.

Mentor teachers used action research not only to frame their research questions but to become involved in some type of social, political or practical action. Models of mentoring most acceptable to schools in the Republic of Ireland, based on these studies, could largely be described as humanistic models, where advice-giving, support and developing a sense of belonging far outweighed the conception of mentoring as inquiry-oriented and critically reflective (Wang and Odell, 2007).

Rather than having research students working independently, with looking at his or her own practice, a better approach may be to have students working in study circles and clusters examining a central question through different lenses. The theoretical lenses provided for these students include a structural approach looking at the sociology of the curriculum, primarily drawing on theory provided by Bernstein (1990, 2000). Pedagogy is interrogated within the framework of productive pedagogy from Queensland, Lingard et al. (2003). Nodding's (2003b, 2007) care theory provides a compelling rationale for regarding teaching as a caring profession. It is feasible that data could be gathered and analysed which would describe a more detailed picture of what is happening in schools in Ireland. Quantitative data could indicate the changed social mix in schools as well as indicating how subject choices are distributed. Variables such as gender, social class, religion, family size and so on could be correlated with other measures such as examination success or type of school attended. The more introspective research associated with inductive reasoning provides insights into the complex nature of schools. The clustering of students would allow for a more considered approach to the research questions where theory can be tested and new theory can be evolving by systematically examining mentor teachers' practices.

We believe since the start of the study that we need to facilitate students' ability to analyse by providing tools that are defensible in the most rigorous terms and which are accessible to teachers, providing theory which abuts with their experiences in schools. The theory we present also fits into the analysis of mentoring that we embrace. This theory promotes inquiry and is reform-minded. The role of a mentor within our thinking is as a teacher who is informed by theory and whose practice draws on evidence rather than relying on. We reject the narrow outcomes-based approach to education which involves reductionism to provide numerical data for a cause-and-effect style of rational analysis. Our desire to embrace complexity requires a more sophisticated analysis of the role of education and the teacher's contribution to the process. Our metaphor for mentoring involves a blend between understanding teaching as an intellectual activity through viewing the 'nature of teacher work in a critical and potentially transformative way', as argued by Giroux (1988: xxxii), and the teacher as professional agent and carer with 'an uneasy social conscience' posited by Noddings (2003b: 261). By involving ourselves and our students in this complex analysis we are aware that we are accepting the more difficult choice of how to construct, present and assess postgraduate education:

> Seeing mentoring as a way of preparing teachers to become effective change agents who are committed to making a difference in the lives of young people and are skilled at the pedagogical partnership developments that make success with students possible. Mentoring in this way becomes not just a way of supporting individual teachers but also a device to help build strong professional cultures of teaching in our schools, dedicated to improving teaching, learning and caring.
>
> (Hargreaves and Fullan, 2000: 54)

To involve students fully in our question for more complex thinking about education and mentoring, we will need to devise additional strategies which involve students in the analysis of their own situations and also require them to position their research within a wider frame of inquiry – philosophically, socially and humanistically. The current economic analysis, which permeates all analyses of education, needs to be critically considered by professionals who are working within the education system. Medical personnel are aware of the prioritisation of treatment procedures for economic reasons. Teachers apparently still need to inform themselves about how they are working to an agenda primarily based on financial determinants.

Educating the critically reflective mentor requires that experienced mentor teachers need to become mentor researchers through membership of broader public spaces and study circles within sustained networks of educationalists, researchers and policymakers. We assert that mentoring is complex and relational. Educating the critically reflective mentor requires the collective capacity of system-wide reform. Fullan (2010) challenges teacher educators, policymakers, schools and society alike to cultivate the aspiration and co-inspiration necessary to sustain change beyond reacting to crises:

> The role of government is to set the direction … and then crucially to engage in a two-way partnership necessary to resolve problems and to develop individual and collective capacity … (while) other levels of the sector, districts and schools, must become more proactive with respect to the new agenda, engaging vertically and horizontally in purposeful networks. (2010: 100)

We contend that the continuing professional learning and development of all teachers needs continuing education alongside teacher educators. We contend that to offer teachers anything less merely serves to approach teaching as a continuum from a deficit model, reinforcing rigid expert–novice relationships and leaving little or no opportunity for reform of the professional learning of teachers or schools. National policymakers in the Republic of Ireland have yet to acknowledge the complexity and challenge of the mentoring construct or the cultural stance taken by schools to resist change and the development of a critical discourse. This study indicates the extent of cultural resistance to generating a critical discourse of inquiry and the difficulties experienced by motivated mentor teachers attempting to critically interrogate practice at the school site.

We recognise the continuing struggle involved in educating the critically reflective mentor to become a critical thinker and a creative, caring co-professional in the trajectory of teaching within the context of a rapidly changing and challenging society. We leave the last word as a message of hope and inspiration, for the *right conditions* to be created, to Kavanagh in this regard:

> What has become clear to me during my three year study of mentoring is that, given the right conditions, mentoring can have a significant positive impact, not only on mentor teachers and mentees but on all teachers and all schools. The principles employed in mentoring, those of collaboration, reflection and inquiry, can be applied to schools and the education system and transform the way we perceive teaching and learning, and lead eventually to schools being developed as learning organizations. (2009: 131–132)

REFERENCES

Ball, S. J. (2009). *The Education Debate*. Bristol: The Policy Press.

Bernard, M. (2009). The implications for whole school development in mentoring newly qualified teachers in one primary school. Unpublished masters thesis, University of Limerick.

Bernstein, B. (1990). *The Structuring of Pedagogic Discourse (Volume IV) Class, Codes and Control*. London: Routledge.

Bernstein, B. (2000). *Pedagogy, Symbolic Control and Identity: Theory, Research, Critique*. Oxford: Rowman and Littlefield.

Brookfield, S. (1995). *Becoming a Critically Reflective Teacher*. San Francisco: Jossey-Bass.

Cain, T. (2009). Mentoring trainee teachers: how can mentors use research? *Mentoring & Tutoring, Partnership in Learning*, 17(1): 53–66.

Clarke, C. (2009). Exploring the attitudes and perceptions of newly qualified teachers in relation to induction and mentoring. Unpublished masters thesis, University of Limerick.

Darling-Hammond, L., and Bransford, J. (Eds). (2005). *Preparing Teachers for a Changing World What Teachers Should Learn and Be Able to Do*. San Francisco: Jossey-Bass.

Dewey, J. (1933). In Pollard, A. (Ed.), *Readings for Reflective Teaching*, p. 4. London and New York: Continuum.

Drudy, S., and Lynch, K. (1993). *Schools and Society in Ireland*. Dublin: Gill and Macmillan.

Fallon, C. (2009). Mentoring as a professional practice to support whole staff development in one post primary school in the west of Ireland. Unpublished masters thesis, University of Limerick.

Ferris, B. (2009). A comparative study of teacher mentoring: from the perspective of Education Specialists in Ireland and Australia. Unpublished masters thesis, University of Limerick.

Fletcher, S. (1998). Attaining self-actualisation through mentoring. *European Journal of Teacher Education*, 21(1), 109–118.

Fletcher, S. (2000). *Mentoring in Schools – A Handbook of Good Practice*. London: Kogan Page.

Freire, P. (1970/1993). *Pedagogy of the Oppressed*. London: Penguin Books.

Fullan, M. (2010). *All Systems Go The Change Imperative for Whole System Reform*. Thousand Oaks, California: Corwin Press.

Gerwirtz, S., and Cribb, A. (2009). *Understanding Education*. Cambridge: Polity Press.

Giroux, H. (1988). *Teachers as Intellectuals Toward a Critical Pedagogy of Learning*. Westport, Connecticut, London: Bergin and Garvey.

Giroux, H. (2009). *Against the Terror of Neo-Liberalism*. London: Paradigm Press.

Hargreaves, A., and Fullan, M. (2000). Mentoring for the new millennium. *Theory into Practice*, 39(1), 50–56.

Hoban, G. F. (2005). *The Missing Links in Teacher Education Design*. Dordrecht: Springer.

Kavanagh, E. (2009). An examination of the benefits of the mentoring relationship to mentors and the implications for teacher development and professional practice. Unpublished masters thesis, University of Limerick.

Kemmis, S. (2007a). Foreword. In Furu, E.M., Lund, T., and Tiller, T. (Eds) (2007). *Action Research A Nordic Perspective*, pp. 11–17. Norway: HøyskoleForolaget.

Kemmis, S. (2007b). Action research. In Martyn Hammersley (Ed.), *Educational Research and Evidence-based Practice*, pp. 167–180. London: The Open University/Sage Publications.

Killeavy, M., and Murphy, R. (2006). *National Pilot Project on Teacher Induction, Report on Phase 1 and 2, 2002–2004*. Dublin: Department of Education and Science.

Lingard, B., Hayes, D., Mills, M., and Christie, P. (2003). *Leading Learning*. Maidenhead: Open University Press.

Lonergan, J. (2010). *School-Based Professional Development in Two Post-Primary Schools in the South West of Ireland*. Unpublished masters thesis, University of Limerick.

Lynch, K. (1999). *Equality in Education*. Dublin: Gill & Macmillan.

Lynch, K., and Lodge, A. (2002). *Equality and Power in Schools Redistribution, Recognition and Representation.* New York: Routledge Falmer.

Maynard, T., and Furlong, J. (1995). Learning to teach and models of mentoring. In Kerry, T. and Shelton Mayes, A. (Eds), *Issues in Mentoring.* Buckingham: The Open University.

McManus, S. (2009). A small scale study on educational mentoring building strong professional practice. Unpublished masters thesis, University of Limerick.

McNamara, G., and J. O'Hara (2006). Workable compromise or pointless exercise? School-based evaluation in the Irish context. *Educational Administration & Leadership*, 34 (4), pp. 564–582.

Mooney Simmie, G., and Moles, J. (2011). Critical Thinking, Caring and Professional Agency: an emerging framework for productive mentoring. *Mentoring and Tutoring: Partnership in Learning*, 19(4), 465–482.

Mullen, C. (2005). *Mentorship Primer*, Volume 6. New York: Peter Lang Primer.

Noddings, N. (2003a). *Caring, a Feminine Approach to Ethics and Moral Education.* London: University of California Press.

Noddings, N. (2003b). *Happiness and Education.* Cambridge: Cambridge University Press.

Noddings, N. (2007). *When School Reform Goes Wrong.* New York: Teachers College, Columbia University.

O'Brien, M. (2009). The potential of developing a mentoring programme for newly qualified teachers (NQTs) of business subjects within the Business Studies Teachers Association of Ireland (BSTAI) Limerick branch. Unpublished masters thesis, University of Limerick.

O'Connor, B. (2009). Using mentoring to promote a culture of teaching for learning. Unpublished masters thesis, University of Limerick.

Ottesen, E. (2007). Reflection in teacher education. *Reflective Practice*, 8(1), 31–46.

Paul, J. L. (2005). *Introduction to the Philosophies of Research and Criticism in Education and the Social Sciences.* New Jersey: Pearson Education.

Rönnerman, K., Furu, E. M., and Salo, P. (Eds) (2008). *Nurturing Praxis Action Research in Partnerships between School and University in a Nordic Light.* Rotterdam: Sense Publishers.

Scannell, B. (2009). Mentoring as a vehicle for better school-university partnership. Unpublished Masters thesis, University of Limerick.

Schön, D. (1983). *The Reflective Practitioner: How professionals think in action.* New York: Basic Books.

Schön, D. (1987). *Educating the Reflective Practitioner.* San Francisco: Jossey-Bass.

Sexton, M. (2007). Evaluating teaching as a profession – implications of a research study for the work of the teaching council. *Irish Educational Studies*, 26(1), 79–105.

Sundli, L. (2007). Mentoring – A new mantra for education? *Teaching and Teacher Education*, 23, 201–214.

Teaching Council (2007). *Codes of Professional Conduct for Teachers.* Maynooth: Teaching Council.

Teaching Council (2011). *Policy on the Continuum of Teacher Education.* Maynooth: Teaching Council.

Wang, J., and Odell., S. J. (2007). An alternative conception of mentor-novice relationships: learning to teach in reform-minded ways as a context. *Teaching and Teacher Education*, 23, 473–489.

8

Politics and Systems of Coaching and Mentoring

Andrew Hargreaves and Jane Skelton

INTRODUCTION

He arrived late for the meeting at the restaurant. Shaking hands warmly, he explained how he had been delayed by a particularly complicated gastro-intestinal procedure. Brent Walton is one of his country's finest surgeons. He serves on its national medical body. And he is a coach.[1]

Like many medical specialists, Brent is also a hospital teacher. He passes on the knowledge of the profession – a kind of mentoring in itself. It's what Brent teaches that distinguishes him. His class consists of surgeons who have faced or will one day face the moment they all dread – the time when they can no longer practice surgery, when the power of life and death is taken from their hands.

The anesthetist is usually the first one to notice something is amiss: a mis-placed incision, perhaps, or a tremble in the fingers at a critical point. Taking the surgeon on one side, the anesthetist might confide that this is the third time there has been such an error within a few days. So another vital act of coaching is also going on here: providing vital feedback about fading powers.

What does Brent advise people who have given their lives to surgery? What does he say they should do when they can no longer practice it? How does he coach them? Placing his large hands on the table – hands that sever intestines and reconstruct entire gastric systems – he explains that he coaches the surgeon to step aside, remaining in the operating theater perhaps, but now advising others when they are new to the job, have an unfamiliar crisis, or experience a momentary lapse of confidence. The ones who have just been coached are now stepping back to rediscover professional meaning by becoming coaches of their own who help others to step forward. This is the essence of coaching at its best – a cycle of professional exchange and advice; a circle of life that is exercised with both candor and emotional sensitivity in ways that serve the interests of those being coached and those patients or clients that they serve in turn.

On the surface, this is a long way from when the concept of coach first entered the English language. The first coach appeared in the fifteenth century. This coach was a large cart, carriage or *kocsi* built in the Hungarian village of *Kocs* for moving people about; initially between Vienna and Budapest. Known as a *Kutsche* in Austrian German and a *coche* in French, this conveyance then developed into the more familiar coach, carriage, stagecoach and railway coach for transporting people, up to the present day. In essence, then, any coach – human or not – carries things from one place or point to another.

As a verb, coaching has a more disputed origin but with similar implications. From the 1600s, the simplest usage was just 'to convey in a coach'. One interpretation is that during a coach journey, a tutor might guide or coach their student through a course of study. This is an especially intriguing point of origin given that the source of the term *curriculum* derives from the Latin *currere* – to run, as in a chariot race. Here, coaching as a process for carrying people along a physical journey or an educational and curricular one amounts to one and the same thing. A second interpretation, attributed to Oxford University in the 1830s, is where 'coaching' applies to a tutor who 'carries' a student through their examination (Merriam Webster, 2010).

The medical tutor carries information about end-of-career concerns; the anesthetist carries feedback about fading powers; and the elder theater surgeon carries advice to novices about complicated or difficult procedures. All of them are coaches – they carry knowledge and learning back and forth between the people who have it and need it, just as much as physical coaches or carriages carry people.

While it is often assumed that coaches and coaching are athletics terms that have subsequently been applied to educational and business practice (Joyce and Showers, 1981; Minihan, 2006), we have seen that the educational usage actually comes first in the sense of carrying people through their studies or their learning. What sports and athletics add to uses and understandings of coaching is the focus on transferring skill through demonstration, practice and feedback, in order to improve performance and results (Quinn, 2004).

This chapter draws on these origins of coaching as the carrying of learning and ideas and later the transfer of skill and performance, in order to understand the dynamics of coaching in educational institutions today. It raises tensions regarding coaching as learning among fellow travelers and coaching as the passing on of specific skills as developed subsequently in the field of athletics (then transferred to areas like literacy coaching) – and it does so with regard to tensions and power dynamics between coaches and coached about what and who is being coached and transported. We will show that there is a world of difference between the carrying of learning and ideas among fellow travelers committed to a journey together, and the required transfer of skills and behaviors to those who are being forcibly transported, like convicts or slaves, to an unwanted or unchosen destination, in a vehicle that is not of their choosing either.

The chapter reviews some of the literature related to the origins and dynamics of coaching through three perspectives that help inform an understanding of these micropolitical and macropolitical tensions, and explores these tensions through our own research and writing at three levels – interactional, cultural and systemic.

COACHING AND EDUCATIONAL REFORM

Coaching has taken on increased importance in education since the 1990s, especially in relation to literacy coaching. Bean and Wilson (1981) documented the progression of the literacy coach from the reading specialist in the 1930s that supported teachers in improving the implementation of their reading program. After World War II, this role shifted to the reading teacher who focused directly on working with students who were struggling readers. The role of the literacy coach evolved from that of the reading specialist supported by US Title I funding through the Elementary and Secondary Education Act of 1963 (Weber, Raphael, Goldman, Sullivan, and George, 2009).

Following evidence of very limited or no impact from the use of reading specialists and pull-out programs, reform programs from the mid-1990s started to target instructional intervention and hands-on, embedded professional development as the levers for change and the adoption of coaching as one key element of strategies of system-wide change began (Showers and Joyce, 1996).

Joyce and Showers (1996) pointed to significant multiplier effects in implementation of new instruction when hands-on, in-class coaching was used rather than one-shot workshops or other kinds of professional development. Modeling, practice, feedback, support, persistence and observation all increased the likelihood that teachers would adopt and sustain new practices – especially through those phases when they were likely to encounter difficulties, lose confidence or want to return to more familiar ways.

Strongly influenced by the research and experience on coaching, New York District 2 developed a highly lauded (though subsequently more criticized) reform model for improving elementary school literacy by introducing a balanced literacy program, having a clearer focus on results, bringing principals into learning communities to become more familiar with and expert in effective instruction, and introducing a widespread system of hands-on classroom coaches in effective literacy – a number of them highly acclaimed literacy experts from the high performing system of Australia (Elmore and Burney, 1997; Ravitch, 2010).

Modern uses of literacy coaching draw on a number of different coaching traditions such as peer coaching, cognitive coaching, and instructional coaching (Cornett and Knight, 2009; Deussen and Riddle-Buly, 2006; Deussen, Coskie, Robinson, and Autio, 2007; Garmston, 1990; Riddle-Buly, Coskie, Robinson, and Egawa, 2006). They are also increasingly bound up with imposed models, and prescribed programs of educational reform in general and literacy reform in particular. Classroom coaching and large-scale reform have come to be integrally intertwined.

Thus, New York District 2's model of system change that incorporated intensive literacy coaching was exported (albeit with little success and questionable impact) to San Diego with less local knowledge and support, a more prescribed agenda and a shorter timescale (Fullan, 2001;Stein, Hubbard, and Mehan, 2004). The city of Boston adapted a version of New York's model in its collaborative coaching and learning (CCL) intervention – this too being criticized by some of its recipients in the classroom for its excessive and inflexible insistence on 'fidelity' (McDonald and Shirley, 2009). England's high profile but much disputed National Numeracy and Literacy Strategy made extensive use of classroom-based consultants combined with a highly prescriptive literacy program (Barber, 2001). And Ontario, borrowing and refining a version of the English model (Fullan, 2010), grew literacy consultants in one of the province's largest districts, then spread them out in a province-wide reform of literacy practices linked to measurable gains in system-wide standards. Coaching has increasingly become the mandated means to an expected and quantifiable end.

Although evaluations of the impact of coaching on achievement as part of these systemic reform models have been boldly asserted by architects of, advocates for, and advisors regarding the reforms themselves, independent evidence of authentic gains that are rooted in instructional change and not in manipulations of student populations or teaching to the test in a high stakes environment are extremely scarce (Hargreaves and Shirley, 2009; Ravitch, 2010). Instead, research on the nature and effects of coaching concentrates more on quantifiable technical issues like tasks that coaches performed, the number of hours they met with teachers, the increase in students' performance on tests, and the fidelity of curriculum implementation (Knight, 2009); or on more cultural questions like dealing with resistant teachers, insufficient time, lack of communication, and balancing coaches' own roles (Weber et al., 2009).

THREE PERSPECTIVES ON COACHING

Two classic articles on educational innovation and reform by McQuillan and House (1998), argue that all educational changes can be examined through three different lenses or perspectives – technological, cultural and political. This is true of areas like assessment reform (Hargreaves, Earl, and Schmidt, 2002), and also classroom coaching.

Technological perspectives draw attention to issues of time and space, roles and responsibilities, skills and procedures. In coaching, this perspective draws attention to issues of training and skill development, the time allocated to coaches and coaching, whether coaching is done on-site or off-site, and clarity of roles and expectations and associated coaching protocols regarding coaches and those they coach.

House and his colleagues' *cultural perspective* is concerned with questions of communication, understanding, values and beliefs. In coaching, this perspective raises issues of how to develop trust between coaches and those they coach as well as in the wider school community of which they are a part; it addresses the challenges of building common, collaborative understandings about children, instruction and each other; it looks at how to improve communication in the coaching relationship; and it examines the fit or absence of fit between the expectations for collaboration within the coaching relationship, and the strength or weakness of collaborative cultures in the wider school environment.

The third perspective put forward by House and his colleagues – the *political perspective* – raises the most challenging questions about educational change processes and practices. The political perspective is about allocations, distributions and dynamics of power, and about the interplay of different interests within educational change. The political perspective addresses both positive power that engages people in change together; and negative power that imposes change within hierarchical relationships of compliance and control (even though these may be masked by discourses of community and collaboration).

In the general area of school reform, the late Seymour Sarason (1990) argued that the weakness of most reform strategies was that they neglected the power relationships of education. In terms of coaching in particular, Shanklin (2006) calls for more research on the influences of power relationships among teachers, coaches, and administrators and on how teachers' career stage, gender, age, and ethnic identity influence the effectiveness of the coach. Twenty years ago, in an article on 'Coaching as unreflective practice', one of the present authors pointed out that in education and sport, resistance to coaching that was often presented as a problem of poor *skill* or weak confidence among those being coached, was sometimes a difference of *will* or judgment about the desirability or validity of what they were being coached to do (Hargreaves and Dawe, 1990).

The political perspective is most evident in coaching in relation to issues where 'fidelity' to a valid principle turns into compliance with a prescribed program, where evidence-based practices are exaggerated and imposed with coaching 'support', where collaborative teams exploring issues of common concern are transformed into forms of contrived collegiality that implement imposed mandates, where common planning time is colonized by mandated school-based professional development, and where coaches whose roles are legitimized by rhetorics of increased 'support' actually become officers of intrusive surveillance whose primary responsibility is to ensure instructional compliance.

The abiding micropolitical issues of coaching remain much as one of us first characterized them in 1990:

> The socio-political context of teacher development … alerts us to the possibility and the danger that collaborative forms of teacher development may in many instances not be empowering teachers towards greater professional independence at all, but incorporating them and their loyalties within purposes and structures bureaucratically determined elsewhere. They may be fostering training, not education, instructional closure rather than intellectual openness, dispositional adjustment rather than thoughtful critique.
>
> (Hargreaves and Dawe, 1990: 228–229)

Micropolitics is the study of political relationships, of power dynamics, status struggles, and pursuit of competing or common interests and ideologies in relation to personal and professional goals. The micropolitical perspective has been used to show the orchestration and impact of power relationships between teachers and students and, most prominently, between teachers and administrators (Ball, 1987; Blase and Blase, 1998; Iannacone, 1975). Relationships between teachers and coaches in the context of school reform raise many questions about ideological negotiation, teacher resistance, resource allocation and school-based professional development. The presence of a coach in a school often creates ideological dissonance because it represents an external initiative informed by particular beliefs and theories that often change the use of time and the nature of professional conversations among educators who might share different school-based beliefs or ideologies (Achinstein, 2002; Garmston and Wellman, 1995; Hargreaves, 1990).

There is a stark but neglected distinction between teachers' authentic responses to enhanced learning about and reflection on practice that represent some internalization of ideas into their existing knowledge and belief systems, and mere enactment of and enforced compliance with political expectations about particular ways to teach in order to raise performance in tested achievement and highly publicized system-wide measures of improvement.

In the context of mandated reform, coaches are often positioned in the middle of a hierarchical power struggle between teachers and administrators. This hierarchy of power negotiations is evident in how coaches represent themselves as members of the professional community of learning or as representatives of the district and its prescribed reforms in literacy or mathematics. In both these cases, it is important for coaches to understand how and where formal and informal power generates cooperative and conflict-laden actions within this reform process.

These micropolitical and macropolitical tensions and negotiations will now be explored in three instances arising from our own research: the discourse and dynamics of interactions between coaches and teachers; the contrast between collaborative cultures and contrived collegiality within wider professional communities focused on improving achievement; and, different kinds of school-to-school coaching relationships directed at raising overall school performance in the context of systemic reform.

THE POLITICS OF COACHING INTERACTIONS

The micropolitics of education are usually investigated through interview studies of teachers' and others' reflections on their interactions with each other (Ball, 1987; Blase and Blase, 2000; Hargreaves, 2000) on emotional politics. Fewer studies focus on the real-time dynamics and discourse of interactions between teachers and supervisors, coaches or mentors. One way to capture the micropolitical negotiations of interpersonal interaction is through critical discourse analysis, which concentrates on how power issues are evident in oral and written discourse (Fairclough, 1993; Gee, 1999; Rogers, 2004).

Duncan Waite pioneered the use of discourse analysis in professional power relationships when he investigated the discourse of negotiations between supervisors and student teachers about classroom practice and performance. Despite the egalitarian aspirations of supervisors and cooperating teachers, and the use of protocols that encouraged interchange and open-endedness, Waite (1995) found large imbalances between supervisors and those they supervised in areas such as the frequencies of who introduced new topics, who set the agenda, who closed the discussion, who made the most evaluative statements, and who controlled the length of time allocated to different topics. In Waite's work, it becomes clear that in teacher supervision, the discourse devil is often in the details.

The micropolitical elements that are inherent in almost all relations of supervision (since supervision literally means to see or watch over) are magnified when coaches are positioned as the mediators and managers of mandated reforms. Ideally, according to Shanklin (2006), effective coaching at the elementary school level includes being available to all members of the school regardless of their knowledge, age, grade level, or professional experiences; has the depth of knowledge regarding the research that guides the school community toward an effective vision for literacy; maintains focus on the differentiated academic needs of students and how to monitor their progress; and engages teachers in an inquiry approach to learning about their practice and the needs of their students. However, when coaches have to operate in the context of prescribed patterns of curriculum and instruction by their district, it is harder to deliver these essential elements of coaching. The practice of coaching here becomes wracked with and driven by dilemmas about support for teachers versus service or servitude to the district.

This can be seen in a case one of the present authors undertook on how coaches used mandated common planning time so that special education teachers could respond to short vignettes about their work with a prescribed vocabulary curriculum (Skelton, 2010). The 45-minute weekly meetings took place from October to January. The following is an excerpt from the coach's and her teachers' reflections on transcripts of interaction between them.

Coaching in the context of mandated common planning time but of shortage of time more generally, combined with having to steer an agenda related to the district's goals, created difficulties and delicacies for the coach – and also for the teachers.

Coach:	I struggle with having to get the conversation going. Sometimes I feel like I say a lot. I do a lot of 'okay.' Time is always the constraint. It's always the big factor. I've always struggled with what are the questions you have to bring forth in the moment to get things going. You don't want to say too much. You don't want to say too little.
Teacher 7:	It's not a negative thing. You're trying to accomplish something, and you have so much to do, and the time is so limited. You try to rush through. I don't see that as a negative.
Teacher 2:	I do see it as a negative.
Coach:	I do too.
Teacher 2:	There's a point where if you try to do so much you don't get anything done. I understand the time constraints, but I'd rather come out with a little bit of information that I really know and I can really use as opposed to a lot of stuff that is valid information. I'm more into the concrete.
Coach:	I'm not really speaking to accomplishing anything. Getting other folks to talk - that's my struggle. I feel pressures to have other folks speak. So I feel like I say too much up front. [I'm] just trying to get other folks to speak. (*Almost all of the teachers nodded in agreement.*)
Teacher 1:	You're trying to engage [teachers] just as you try to engage your kids.
Teacher 2:	It's really a dance, the kind of back and forth and the planning you're going to do; everybody needs to speak and you need to treat everybody like they have a voice and not disrespect people by cutting them off. You do feel pressured a lot in these meetings. It would be nice to have more time, to relax more; finish a thought.
Teacher 3:	Before the kids start coming down the hallway.
Teacher 7:	We all do it. We all have that problem in the classroom. It's called wait time. We don't wait for them to process their thinking, and we rush to give them the answer. It's something we all needed to learn. It's not [just] for you. It's called wait time.

The coach's dilemmas and teacher's experiences of hurried interactions and closed conversations may initially seem like questions of *skill* – knowing how to manage 'wait time' in coaching just like in the classroom – but it then becomes clear that the difficulties are also a matter of *will*; of having to respond to external pressures for curriculum implementation amid insistent everyday classroom realities and existential anxieties about job security. This profoundly influenced their engagement in the meetings.

Teacher 7:   When we come in here, we have to switch off from that other stuff. We know it's Word Generation, and [we have to] focus on what we're doing.

Teacher 1:   We have so many team meetings. We're at the service of the parents and if the parents come, it's just a matter of us being in two places at once.

Teacher 4:   And that's always been what I would say is the culture of the schools. You have common planning time, you have cluster time, and there's no real sacredness to it. So everything comes before it, and you're flying by the seat of your pants. And, you sit down for a couple of minutes and you want to participate and you find yourself, like everybody else, waiting for the kids to be coming back from gym. So you can never really be relaxed.

Teacher 3:   And then with this year and everyone trying to figure out the job.

Teacher 4:   There it is.

Teacher 3:   Our minds are in different places.

Teacher 4:   Finding work.

Teacher 2:   The [writing prompts] still have to be corrected.

Coach: One final comment: Shifting the gear about coming from one place to the next, [the common planning time] tends to be very coach driven. I think that there are places where I try to invite, but I think that folks feel overloaded with what they are trying to do outside of these meetings. I think that it's a little difficult sometimes. I know that we had talked about questions and a couple of folks had brought them back … you get caught up in things. And so when you think about doing that collaborative piece … I mean they had a parent show up this morning. They had an [individual education plan] meeting this morning. And I feel like – tell me if I'm wrong – I feel lots of times it's like, 'Can you handle this so we can deal with the parent and go to the [individual education plan] meeting? And kind of bring it back together for us week by week so that we can remain focused. (*The teachers were silent.*)

Teacher 2:   I think that it's hard to get a format that would fit every meeting like this … professional development meetings, curriculum-based meeting[s]. Personalities have a huge part of it. No matter what you have in front of you, like this is the manual for it, and we're going to follow this. Forget it. It's not going to happen, because people are different. [They] react to each other differently. They react to the coach differently and vice versa.

Coaching in the context of mandated reform can often fall short of its ideals, therefore, leading to hurried, anxious and one-sided interactions, in required time periods that draw teachers away from compelling classroom concerns in a system where even basic job security can no longer be counted on. Passive resistance results in the form of actions such as withholding full attention or not responding to the coach's requests to complete a survey on what students were learning, because, in the words of one teacher, 'information that I don't know – that's what I take away'. In the technological perspective, it is easy to argue that teachers are just dragging their feet in acquiring new and much needed technical *skills*. But the political perspective highlights how they are actually digging in their heels to assert a contrary *will* that opposes the enforced transportation of unwanted programs and practices into the their classrooms.

COACHING AND SCHOOL CULTURE

Coaching relationships and dynamics cannot be disentangled from the wider cultures of teaching of which they are a part. If a school lacks norms of reciprocity and mutual exchange, or if most teachers do not engage in helping and learning relationships as an integral part of their teaching and professional growth, then the individual assistance offered by coaches, mentors, or supervisors come to be regarded as deviant exceptions to the professional rule – signs of problems that need to be fixed, and deficiencies that have to be remedied (Little, 1990). In many schools, whole networks of professional advice and support are now in place involving literacy coaches, teacher leaders, new teacher mentors, special education resource teachers and many others. The challenges of coaching and mentoring are not only how to connect and integrate these systems of support (Moir, Barlin, Gless, and Miles, 2009), but also how to embed them in a pervasive culture of professional collaboration. Without this embedding, the association of coaching with deficiency will prompt those who are being supported to view their mentors as tormentors, and to detach themselves from coaching relationships as quickly as they can (Hargreaves and Fullan, 2000).

Cultures of professional collaboration, however, also have micropolitical dimensions. In a study of teachers' uses of preparation time, one of us first introduced the concept of *contrived collegiality* to describe forms of professional collaboration that were micropolitically hierarchical and controlling (Hargreaves, 1994).

In collaborative cultures, working relationships between teachers tend to be spontaneous, voluntary, development-oriented, pervasive across time and space, and unpredictable. Contrived collegiality, by comparison, is administratively regulated, compulsory, implementation-oriented, fixed in time and space, and predictable. Collaborative cultures may be administratively supported and facilitated by helpful scheduling arrangements, but ultimately they are sustained by the teaching community's belief in the value of working together for a common cause. Contrived collegiality, however, 'replaces spontaneous, unpredictable, and difficult-to-control forms of teacher-generated collaboration with forms of collaboration that are captured, contained, and contrived by administrators instead' (Hargreaves, 1994: 196).

In time, the idea of and aspiration for collaborative cultures of self-driven improvement (Fullan and Hargreaves, 1991; Lieberman, 1990; Nias, 1989) was supplanted by the concept of *professional learning communities.* This extended the idea of cultures of collaboration into concerted processes of inquiry into professional practice in order to improve the quality and outcomes of professional and classroom learning (Hord, 1997; McLaughlin and Talbert, 2001). Professional learning communities in schools emphasize three key components: collaborative work and discussion among the school's professionals; a strong and consistent focus on teaching and learning within that collaborative work; and gathering assessment and other data to inquire into and evaluate progress and problems over time (Newmann and Wehlage, 1995). At their best, professional learning communities lead to strong and measurable improvements in pupils' learning (Little, 2001; Newmann and Wehlage, 1995) that last over time, because they build the professional skill and capacity to keep the school moving forward (Stoll and Louis, 2007).

Increasingly, though, professional learning communities have been implemented by school districts as technologies to deliver mandated changes in literacy instruction that are closely tied to swift test score gains in student achievement. This has led to a re-emergence of contrived collegiality in yet another guise, which one of us, in a study of professional learning communities, called *performance training sects* (Hargreaves, 2003). Performance training sects are like evangelical religious sects in which there is certainty about the knowledge of effective practice, an unchallengeable monopoly over the truths of effective instruction among the sect's leaders, an insistence on faithfulness or fidelity to the sect's instructional or professional beliefs, demanding standards and training rituals of obeisance and acceptance, and excommunication or banishment of non-believers (often stigmatized as self-centered independent contractors) from the organization and community to another system elsewhere.

In performance training sects, coaches do not build true capacity in terms of helping teachers to help themselves (the original meaning of capacity building within the practice of international development), but under the guise of capacity building, they actually enforce compliance with skill development in externally introduced and non-negotiable practices. This compliance model paradoxically reduce capacity and creativity when those skill areas are confined to instructional basics, or when the skill areas themselves change (for example, in the direction of twenty-first century skills) and teachers have no ingrained capacity to help themselves acquire other needed tools that will enhance their professional work. Instead of the increased capacity brought about in professional learning communities, performance training sects produce short-term gains that actually replace long-term capacity with increased professional dependency. For all their technical complexity and their sophisticated systems of coaching, mentoring and support, performance training sects make support look more like suffocation. They put the sin into synergy!

Most recently, the development of collaboration and helping relationships among teachers has moved from collaborative cultures and professional learning communities to data-driven teams, where teachers systematically analyze more and more complex and sophisticated bodies of data on student learning and performance, to make decisions that guide instructional improvements and interventions.

Amanda Datnow and her colleagues have studied the dynamics of data-driven teams in two school districts (Datnow, 2011). Using the concepts of collaborative cultures and contrived collegiality as a touchstone for their analysis, they found that while the collaboration promoted by both districts was administratively regulated and, designed to meet the districts' purposes through such devices as mandated meeting time and prescribed questions within meeting protocols, many of the negative effects normally associated with contrived collegiality did not take hold. Rather, 'what began as contrived meetings to discuss data evolved into spaces for more genuine collaborative activity wherein teachers challenged each other, raised questions, and shared ideas for teaching' (Datnow, 2011: 156).

With or without structure or prescription, the key factor appears to be found in the quality, integrity, and long-term stability of leadership that, even before the introduction of data-driven improvement, had pursued continuous improvement and been able to 'develop trust among teachers, assuage their concerns about how the data reflected upon them as individual teachers, and promote a positive orientation towards data use' (Datnow, 2011: 156).

The lesson for coaches and mentors is not to underestimate their role in capitalizing on strong professional cultures, or in contributing to the development of such cultures themselves as a context for effective helping relationships. Even where they are constrained by contrived collegiality, or surrounded by performance training sects, coaches can be advocates for their teachers who affirm and reassert their moral purpose of dedication to students within a spirit of genuine inquiry that is open to evidence and not closed about their own or others' solutions that can help all their students succeed. At the same time, systems that operate or introduce systems of coaching support need to understand that where existing leadership is unstable or weak, and cultures of collaboration are underdeveloped, over-reliance on coaching as an isolated intervention will more likely produce negative rather than positive professional and instructional effects.

COACHING AND SYSTEM CHANGE

Since the 1990s, coaching in education has become inseparable from the delivery of large-scale systemic reform. Reviewing different phases of reform patterns over the past 40 years, Hargreaves and Shirley (2009) delineated four ways of change in educational and social policy. Each of them has specific implications and uses for coaching. We focus on the first three ways here.

The First Way of change in the 1960s and 1970s was an expansionist period of government investment and professional autonomy in which innovation was encouraged but inconsistent, and forms of collegial support of any kind were haphazard.

The Second Way of the 1980s and 1990s, replaced the inconsistency and investment of the First Way with market competition between schools on standardized criteria of curriculum and testing. In this Second Way, much of which still persists in the United States, there was high pressure for improvement in tested and examined basics, but diminished or only episodic, short-term support in the form of training and resources.

Coaching is a central element of the Third Way of change. The Third Way, advocated by President Clinton and Prime Minister Blair with intellectual inspiration from Anthony Giddens (1999), argued for something between and beyond the First and Second Ways – mixtures of public and private, pressure and support. In England's National Literacy and Numeracy Strategy, several of the Clinton Administration's Comprehensive School Reforms, and Ontario's educational reforms in the first decade of the twenty-first century, the emphasis switched to more efficient delivery of standardized outcomes and targets that were still imposed from the top. Increasingly, the state commandeered and intruded into the details of pedagogy and instruction, particularly in relation to literacy, and coaching became one of its strategic resources of support to try and ensure that delivery.

While coaching has often been described as a form of *capacity building* – an integral concept of Third Way thinking – in practice, it became more concerned with developing the skills to deliver government and program outcomes rather than helping people to help themselves. In the Third Way, coaching has become part of the politics of delivery rather than the practice of development.

The most advanced forms of Third Way thinking employ what David Hargreaves (2003) called 'lateral capacity building' so teachers can help teachers and schools can coach schools in how to raise achievement. One of the present authors co-led a research team to evaluate one of these lateral capacity building efforts of schools coaching schools (Hargreaves, Shirley, Evans, Johnson, and Riseman, 2006). Raising Achievement/Transforming Learning (RATL), in England was a network of 300 underperforming school partnered with higher performing peers to help raise achievement by employing short-term, medium-term and long-term strategies for change.

The schools' leaders went to national and regional conferences where they attended inspirational presentations, were provided with expert technical assistance on how to interpret achievement data in ways that would help them identify which pupils most needed assistance, and were given access to a range of successful mentor schools and their headteachers (principals) who served pupils similar to their own and who could be contacted and visited for assistance as and when schools required. An annual discretionary budget of £9,000 incentivized schools' involvement, and a web portal gave participating schools access to each other and information about one another's progress, as well as opportunities for communication with mentor schools, before and/or after on-site visits.

At the core of RATL's distinctive change model was an array or menu of short-term, medium-term and long-term strategies for raising achievement that were derived from, and driven by, the experience and judgment (rather than a scientific evidence base) of a group of reputationally successful school leaders.

RATL's improvement strategies and targets were not politically or administratively imposed on schools in given timelines, but made available to, developed by and collaboratively shared among schools working with other schools on improvement and achievement goals together. On the one hand, struggling schools selected their own partners, rather than having mentors thrust upon them. Yet these networks were not ones that merely promoted shared practices. Indeed research on educational networks indicates that sharing practice does not, by itself, increase performance (Chapman, Muijs, Sammons, Armstrong, and Collins 2009). Instead, transparency of participation as well as results in systems where schools support lower performing peers creates peer pressure as well as peer support for measurable improvement. With this contrived but participatory architecture of coaching and support, along with inspired and inclusive leadership, two thirds of the schools improved at double the rate of the national average over 2–3 years.

The major drawback of this more participatory and inclusive yet highly accountable model of laterally driven change of schools coaching schools is that RATL tended to do well in securing short-term gains in high-stakes-tested student achievement, but made little initial progress in bringing about the longer term transformations in teaching and learning that are more compatible with the development of twenty-first century skills, innovation and creativity.

CONCLUSION

In some of its earliest origins, coaching is a learning journey undertaken willingly by travelers together. However, in the context of large-scale systemic reform, coaching has too often turned into enforced transportations from boardrooms into classrooms of unreflective practices based on inflexible ideologies or exaggerated sources of evidence.

A coach is a vehicle. But in education, it is not an inanimate one. Should the coach be a mere deliverer of other people's goods and chattels? Or should the coach carry learners and learning along a self-chosen journey together? Are coaches providers of service learning, or vehicles that deliver people into bureaucratic servitude? Like life coaches, should educational coaches develop people's own capacity to help themselves, or is their role to watch over teachers' fidelity to or compliance with externally prescribed practice. These are the questions that are raised by the politics of coaching.

It takes a big man or woman to step aside from surgery and actively help others take their place at the cutting edge of their profession. And it takes a great coach to stand up for the moral purpose of their work that is or should be at the core of all coaching – developing people, not implementing policies; building capacity rather than enforcing compliance; and giving colleagues a professional service rather than delivering them into ideological servitude.

NOTES

1 This opening vignette is drawn from a study of Performing Beyond Expectations in education, sport, business and health; directed by Andy Hargreaves and Alma Harris and funded by the UK Specialist Schools and Academies Trust and the National College for School Leadership. Brent Walton is a pseudonym.

REFERENCES

Aichenstein, B. (2002). Conflict among community: The micropolitics of teacher collaboration. *Teacher College Record, 104*(3), 421–455.

Ball, S. (1987). *The Micropolitics of the School: Towards a Theory of School Organization.* New York: Routledge.

Barber, M. (2001). High expectations and standards for all, no matter what: Creating a world class education service in England. In M. Fielding (Ed.), *Taking Education Really Seriously: Four Years Hard Labour.* New York: Routledge/Falmer Press.

Bean, R. M., & Wilson, R. M. (1981). *Effecting Change in School Reading Programs: The Resource Role.* Delaware: International Reading Association.

Blase, J., & Blase J. (1998). *Instructional Leadership: How Really Good Principals Promote Teaching and Learning.* Thousand Oaks, CA: Corwin Press.

Blase, J., & Blase, J. (2000). Effective instructional leadership: Teachers' perspectives on how principals promote teaching and learning in schools. *Journal of Educational Administration, 38*(2), 130–141.

Chapman, C., Muijs, D., Sammons, P., Armstrong, P., & Collins, A. (2009). *The Impact of Federations on Student Outcomes.* National College for Leadership of Schools and Children's Services. Nottingham: NCSL.

Cornett, J., & Knight, J. (2009). Research on coaching. In Knight, J. (Ed). *Coaching: Approaches & Perspectives* (pp. 192–216). Thousand Oaks, CA: Corwin Press.

Datnow, A. (2011). Collaboration and contrived collegiality: Revisiting Hargreaves in the age of account-ability. *Journal of Educational Change, 12*(2), 147–158.

Deussen, T., Coskie, T., Robinson, L., & Autio, E. (2007). *'Coach' can mean many things: five categories of literacy coaches in Reading Firs.* Issues & Answers Report, REL 2007–No. 005. Washington, DC: US Department of Education, Institute of Education Sciences, National Center for Education Evaluation and Regional Assistance, Regional Educational Laboratory Northwest. Retrieved from http://ies.ed.gov/ncee/edlabs.

Deussen, T., & Riddle-Buly, M. (2006). Connecting coaching and improved literacy. *Northwest Education, 12*(1), 43–44. Retrieved from http://www.nwrel.org/nwedu/12-01/brief/

Elmore, R. F., & Burney, D. (1997). *Investing in Teacher Learning: Staff Development and Instructional Improvement in Community School District #2 .* New York: National Commission on Teaching and America's Future and the Consortium for Policy Research in Education.

Fairclough, N. (1993). Critical discourse analysis and the commodification of public discourse. *Discourse and Society, 4*(2), 133–168.

Fullan, M. (2001). *Leading in the Culture of Change.* San Francisco: Jossey-Bass

Fullan, M. (2010). *All Systems Go: The Change Imperative for Whole System Reform.* Thousand Oaks, CA: Corwin Press.

Fullan, M. G., & Hargreaves, A. (1991). *What's Worth Fighting For: Working Together For Your School.* Ontario: Ontario Public Schools Teachers' Federation.

Garmston, R. (1990). Is peer coaching changing supervisory relationships: Some reflections. *California Journal of Curriculum and Supervision, 3*(2), 21–27.

Garmston, R. & Wellman, B. (1995). Adaptive schools in a quantum universe. *Educational Leadership, 53*(7), 6–12.

Gee, J. P. (1999). *An Introduction to Discourse Analysis: Theory and Practice.* New York: Routledge.

Giddens, A. (1999). *The Third Way: The Renewal of Social Democracy.* Malden, MA: Blackwell.

Hargreaves, A. (1990). Teachers' work and the politics of time and space. *Qualitative Studies in Education, 3*(4), 303–320.

Hargreaves, A. (1994). *Changing Teachers, Changing Times: Teachers' Work and Culture in the Post-modern Age.* New York: Teacher College Press.

Hargreaves, A. (2000). Mixed emotions: Teachers' perceptions of their interactions with students. *Teaching and Teacher Education, 16*, 811–826.

Hargreaves, A. (2003). *Teaching in the Knowledge Society: Education in the Age of Insecurity.* New York: Teachers College Press.

Hargreaves, A. & Dawe, R. (1990). Paths of professional development: Contrived collegiality, collaborative culture, and the case of peer coaching. *Teaching and Teacher Education, 6*(3), 227–241.

Hargreaves, A., Earl, L., & Schmidt, M. (2002). Perspectives on classroom assessment. *American Educational Research Journal, 39*(1), 69–100.

Hargreaves, A., & Fullan M. (2000). 'Mentoring in the New Millennium,' (with Michael Fullan), *Theory into Practice, 39*(1), Ohio State University, 50–56.

Hargreaves, A., & Shirley, D. (2009). *The Fourth Way.* Thousand Oaks, CA: Corwin Press.

Hargreaves, A., Shirley, D., Evans, M., Johnson, C., & Riseman, D. (2006). *The Long and the Short of Raising Achievement: Final report of the Evaluation of the 'Raising Achievement, Transforming Learning.* Project of the UK Specialist Schools and Academies Trust. Chestnut Hill: Boston College.

Hargreaves, D. (2003). *Education Epidemic.* London: Demos.

Hord, S. M. (1997). *Professional Learning Communities: Communities of Continuous Inquiry and Improvement.* Austin: Southwest Educational Development Laboratory.

Iannaccone, L. (1975). *Educational Policy Systems.* Fort Lauderdale, FL: Nova University Press.

Joyce, B. & Showers, B. (1981). Transfer of training: The contribution of coaching. *Boston University Journal of Education, 16*(2), 163–172.

Knight, J. (Ed.). (2009). *Coaching: Approaches and Perspectives.* Thousand Oaks, CA: Corwin Press.

Lieberman, A. (1990). *Schools as Collaborative Cultures: Creating the Future Now.* London: The Falmer Press.

Little, J. W. (1990). The persistence of privacy: Autonomy and initiative in teachers' professional relations. *Teacher College Record, 91*(4), 509–536.

Little, J. W. (2001). Professional development in pursuit of school reform. In A. Lieberman & L. Miller (Eds), *Teachers Caught in the Action: Professional Development that Matters* (pp. 23–44). New York: Teachers College Press.

McDonald, E., & Shirley, D. (2009). *The Mindful Teacher.* New York: Teachers College Press.

McLaughlin, M., & Taulbert, J. (2001). *Professional Communities and the Work of High School Teachers.* Chicago: University of Chicago Press.

McQuillan, P., & House, E. (1998). Three perspectives of school change. In Hargreaves, A. et al. (Eds), *The International Handbook of Educational Change* (pp. 198–213). Dordrecht: Kluwer.

Merriam-Webster's online dictionary. (2000). Retrieved from http://www.merriam-webster.com/dictionary/coach

Minihan, M. (2006). The foundations of coaching. *OD Practitioner, 38*(3), 4–7.

Moir, E., Barlin, D., Gless, J., & Miles, J. (2009). *New Teacher Mentoring.* Cambridge, MA: Harvard Education Press.

Newmann, F., & Wehlage, G. (1995). *Successful School Restructuring.* Madison, WI: Center on Organization and Restructuring of Schools.

Nias, J. (1989). *Primary Teachers Talking: A Study of Teaching as Work.* London: Routledge.

Quinn, E. (2004). *Qualities of an Effective Athletic Coach.* Retrieved from http://sportsmedicine.about. com/bio/Elizabeth-Quinn-3502.htm

Ravitch, D. (2010). *The Death and Life of the Great American School System: How Testing and Choice are Undermining Education.* New York: Basic Books.

Riddle-Buly, M., Coskie, T., Robinson, L., & Egawa, K. (2006). Literacy coaching: Coming out of the corner. *Voices from the Middle, 13,* 24–28.

Rogers, R., (Ed.). (2004). *An Introduction to Critical Discourse Analysis in Education.* Mahwah, NJ: Lawrence Erlbaum Associates Publishers.

Sarason, S. B. (1990). *The Predictable Failure of Educational Reform: Can We Change Course Before It's Too Late?* San Francisco: Jossey-Bass.

Shanklin, N. L. (2006). *What are the Characteristics of Effective Literacy Coaching?* Literacy Coaching Clearinghouse. Retrieved from http://www.literacycoachingonline.org/briefs/harofLiteracyCoach-ingNLS09-27-07.pdf

Showers, B. & Joyce, B. (1996). The evolution of peer coaching. *Educational Leadership, 53* (6), 12–16.

Skelton, J. (2010). *Micropolitical Negotiations Within School Reform.* Doctoral dissertation, Boston College, Chestnut Hill, MA. ProQuest/UMI for Publishing, No. 10316.

Stein, M., Hubbard, L. & Mehan, H. (2004). Reform ideas that travel far afield: The two cultures of reform in New York City's District #2 and San Diego. *Journal of Educational Change, 5*(2), 161–197.

Stoll, L., and Louis, K. S. (2007). *Professional Learning Communities: Divergence, Depth, and Dilemmas* (pp. 1–14). Berkshire: Open University Press.

Waite, D. (1995). *Rethinking Instructional Supervision: Notes on its Language and Culture.* London: The Falmer Press.

Weber, C., M., Raphael, T., E., Goldman, R. S., Sullivan, M., P., & George, M. (2009). *Literacy Coaches: Multiple Issues, Multiple Roles, Multiple Approaches.* Chicago: University Press at Chicago.

9

Mentoring: Apprenticeship or Co-inquiry?

Tadashi Asada

INTRODUCTION

Is mentoring an apprenticeship or a co-inquiry and what do we mean by 'mentoring' in a Japanese context? This issue is difficult to determine and there are many ways one might approach understanding it. In this chapter, we will explore cultural and epistemological implications for mentoring as 'uchi' and 'soto' concepts that characterize Japanese society. These two notions are deeply embedded in everyday life and permeate aspects of every interaction between individuals and groups in Japanese society. 'Uchi' and 'soto' represent, as relationships, the identity of a social group, a family, a business, a school. 'Uchi' is the inner self, the core, the part that belongs to a whole and 'soto' is an outsider, well respected and treated honorably, but not part of the 'self' of the 'uchi' social group.

Mentoring has also been defined in many ways and can differ from context to context to some extent though retaining core characteristics that can distinguish it from coaching. Coaching tends to be short term, less about induction by a senior or more learned person, where mentoring is a school-based form of ongoing professional development that leads to fundamental changes in values, in skills, as well as knowledge and understanding about teaching in school. Fletcher (2000) signals the value of mentoring as critical engagement with teaching as a professional necessity. Brooks and Sykes (1997) offer insights into the apprenticeship model of mentoring with the mentor described as a skilled craftsperson.

> The novice was inducted into teaching by an experienced practitioner by 'sitting next to Nellie', observing the teacher at work and then attempting to emulate them. (1997: 17)

Suggesting an inquiry-based approach to mentoring the authors propose:

> injecting a degree of rigour and system into what many teachers already do intuitively. Whether they do so consciously or not many teachers do take an inquiry or action-research-based approach to their work. (ibid. 148)

Fletcher (2007) proposed that a useful approach to mentoring is to integrate it with self-study action research using an appreciative inquiry approach as it stimulates a growth of knowledge by the mentor as well as by the mentee. Ideally, mentoring is a process of sustained mutual development of abilities and knowledge for the mentor and the mentee. There is reciprocal benefit and a mentoring relationship changes as the dynamics within it evolve. In this chapter we focus on mentoring rather than coaching but they are closely related activities.

Furlong and Maynard (1995) proposed four stages in mentoring and student teachers' development. In this schema, the mentoring role changes along with the student teacher's development; that is, as a model, a coach, a critical friend, and a co-enquirer. At the same time, this issue also relates closely to the teacher's culture. Elliot and Calderhead (1993) pointed out that support is an essential component for a novice's professional development in any mentoring relationship. This means it is very important for the teachers in a school to provide support for one another, since the culture of the teaching environment needs to be supportive to enable school-based teacher education. In general, however, teaching in the classroom is not collaborative, but revolves around individuals' work. School teachers endeavor to teach pupils as well as they possibly can and improve their teaching to improve learning and professional benefit; for example, by developing teaching materials, creating worksheets as well as journal writing to note down reflection on their teaching. But there is not always a supportive culture among school teachers, especially in Japan, and the culture in which teaching is embedded exerts a strong impact upon mentoring relationships. It is closely related to a teacher's sense of 'self', to social order in a school, and to the teacher's language. By focusing on mentoring observed from a viewpoint of the culture in which teachers practice their professional craft, we can understand its nature.

TEACHER'S CULTURE AND UCHI/SOTO (INSIDE/OUTSIDE)

McCallion (2007) denotes an in-group as a social unit an individual belongs to, interacts with and shares a sense of 'we-ness' with. An out-group, on the other hand is a social unit or group of people nether belongs to nor identifies with.

This description is a useful way for understanding some of the implications of 'uchi' and 'soto' for educating teachers who are seeking to gain acceptance within their profession. Both 'uchi' and 'soto' have further and deeper implications too, relating to the way language is used in Japanese grammar,

As Professor Seiichi Makino explained about 'uchi' and 'soto' in 2007:

> Things that are uchi relate to the home, one's self, the present, reality, the visible, and the internal. Soto refers not only to what is outside, but also to otherness, foreigners, the past and the future, idealizations, the invisible, and abstractions.

Hadden and Lester (1978) explain that the process of emergent identity in an in-group changes over time and as the membership of the in-group define its values and culture.

In Japan, a supportive environment depends on directional movements, which can best be described as 'looking', 'zooming in', and 'reaching'. These processes by which we come to join a social group are part of a broader system of basic orientations through which all of us, in every known language and society, constantly locate ourselves in relation to the world. Through them, we define not only our physical orientations in space but also our social and our psychic orientations as well (Bachnik, 1994). In Japanese society, there exists a concept of social orientation that can be expressed as 'inside' and 'outside' ('uchi' and 'soto'). If you are 'uchi', you are regarded as an associate and all members, as 'uchi', are supportive of you. However, 'uchi' seems to depend on a rigid social order on the basis of seniority. So, typically, the experienced teacher tends to have direct responsibility for teaching or instructing a newly qualified teacher in a school, and thus this kind of mentoring has strong characteristics of apprenticeship. This is even more pronounced where student teachers tend to regard a mentor teacher as their ideal model, and look for direction in everything in their teaching, classroom management and school affairs by following their mentor teacher's lead. This is how a mentoring relationship becomes 'apprenticeship'.

Eliott and Calderhead's concept of mentoring (1995) emphasized support and challenge as the components necessary for professional growth. The level of *support* school teachers have determines how far they are enabled to reflect on their teaching and engage within reflective discourses among themselves. These processes would be far more difficult to maneuver without a supportive school environment and in order to benefit from such mutual support, teachers need to respect one another as members of an in-group ('uchi'). 'Challenge', in Eliott and Calderhead's model, indicates the level of cognitive dissonance between teachers, which stimulates individuals to reflect upon their own beliefs about teaching. Without support, challenge would probably be perceived by a mentee as an uncomfortable experience and he or she would feel there was no growth being enabled by their mentoring relationship.

THE FUNCTION OF MENTORING IN STUDENT TEACHING IN JAPAN

In Japan, for several years now, many educational reforms have been implemented by the Ministry of Education, Culture, Sports, Science and Technology.

In some of these agendas, teacher training is seen as a serious problem. There are two teacher-training programs, the pre-service teacher training program and the in-service teacher training. Asada (2006) has focused on the pre-service element of teacher training. To sustain their continuing professional development, periods of school-based teaching experience are very important for student teachers. However, most Japanese student teachers teach in schools only during the latter stages of their university studies and the length of student teaching practice is only four weeks (see Figure 9.1). Problems are exacerbated because university staff seldom visit their student teachers in school and so it is mainly school teachers who train student teachers. Because of the nature of the Japanese pre-service teacher training, mentoring by teachers plays a crucial role in initial teacher preparation.

Case study I

Asada's case study (2006) explores the function of school-based mentoring in student teaching, introduced to improve Japanese pre-service teacher training programs. The data subjects are three student teachers (one is male, others are female) and three mentors who are working as teachers in a kindergarten. Together, these mentors have more than 15 years' teaching experience. Using the teachers' journal writings and undertaking surveys about professional identity and reflections on the relationship between mentor and student teacher, Asada's study sets out findings relating to investigation into student teachers' professional identities and their mentoring relationships.

First, on the subject of a teacher's *identity*, student teachers tend to expect to personify 'being a teacher ' from the outset. They come to be aware of the responsibility of being a teacher later on. Student teaching seems to lead to an awareness of a reality that is akin to a mixture of teaching and nursing. One student teacher in Asada's study held an expectation of becoming a teacher in spite of perceiving herself as inexperienced as a teacher, while another student teacher seemed to have worries about being inexperienced as a teacher and seemed well

Pre-service teacher training course	Fresher	Sophomore	Junior	Senior	Number of credits
Special subjects	←			→	More than 34 credits
Teaching professional subjects	←		→		High School 25 credits
					Junior High School 31 credits
Practical training			←→ 4 weeks		5 credits (High School is 3 credits)
Special subjects: mathematics, physics, chemistry, and so on					
Teaching professional subjects: teaching method, educational psychology, school counselling and so on					

Figure 9.1   Pre-service teacher training curriculum

aware of the responsibility of teaching. Students cannot establish their identity as a teacher in such a short practicum in Japan, but at least they seem to find out how unskilled they are and learn about the responsibility of teaching.

Second, where student teachers' perceived their occupation as a combination of nursing and teaching in the kindergarten, and of looking after a young child, student teachers did not appear to change their views of either nursing as teaching or of looking after a young child throughout their teaching practice. As far as the teaching-as-nursing perspective is concerned, their views mainly focused on the impact of nursing a small child and learning how to nurse a small child. While the perspective of one student teacher in Asada's study was akin to that of a young child, another's view was that of being a teacher. The student teacher who operated from a viewpoint of 'being a teacher' kept that expectation throughout their teaching practice. In addition, she was aware of expectations and skills required of a school teacher. The student teacher approaching teaching practice from the perspective of a young child, on the other hand, did not actually recognize what a young child was, but tended to adopt a perspective of what teachers learn from a child and how a teacher is influenced in their work by that young child. They are thought not to grasp the reality of being a small child, so that their views do not, in fact, change as they teach.

Third, when it came to the mentoring relationship, student teachers were asked to illustrate the relationship between their mentor and themselves and add a brief explanation about their illustration. Each relationship between the mentor and the student teacher changed during the student's teaching. In particular, the psychological distance between mentor and student teacher became narrowed. Each pairing of mentor and student teacher became closely related, but the student teacher became increasingly dependent upon their mentor. The mentor is like a mother and an idealized teacher to the student teachers. If mentoring is continuing for several years, the relationship is thought to become equal because mentoring should facilitate a shift to a position where mentor and mentee learn many things from one another related to teaching, a way of life, values and so on, and thus the mentoring relationship should involve reciprocal benefits.

The points highlighted above shows there are a few changes in student teachers' perceptions about the identity of being a teacher and their relationship with a mentor.

Nevertheless, this study indicates that mentoring in student teaching does not serve the purpose of pre-service teacher training on account of the short period of student teaching and their image of mentoring as an apprenticeship system.

In this case study, the Japanese pre-service teaching system seems to be based upon apprenticeship. The possible reasons for this include: (1) the length of the newly qualified teacher's (see Figure 9.2) practicum is very short, being only four weeks; (2) most mentors retain a strong belief that mentoring *is* apprenticeship and the role of mentoring is to instruct about many things related to teaching and school affairs; (3) the immediate feedback from mentor is effective for stimulating reflective teaching; and (4) newly qualified teachers have little time

Figure 9.2   Illustrations of a newly qualified teacher

to exchange information about teaching because they need a lot of time to prepare for their teaching.

Although Franke and Dahlgrem (1996) noted that mentoring has three functions for the novice teacher: (1) to facilitate development of their vocational identity as a teacher; (2) to provide support for them to experience reflective teaching; and (3) to establish an equal relationship between mentor and student teacher, this study did not support their model, especially with regard to *equality* within a mentoring relationship. This might suggest, therefore, that it is worthwhile exploring the notion of 'uchi/soto' as an underlying principle of Japanese teachers' culture since it so deeply embedded in everyday life.

TEACHER'S CULTURE AND THE ETHOS OF EQUALITY

While the notion of 'uchi' embodies a hierarchical social order, Japanese school culture is taken to embody an ethos of equality. Thus, if a newly qualified teacher is recognized as an associate, he or she is regarded as being of equal status to other experienced teachers. One wonders how this kind of teaching culture might facilitate co-inquiry between mentors and mentees. In fact, there is little co-inquiry in Japanese schools, largely as a result of teachers' values system and their understandings of equality. Therefore, each school teacher mainly learns about teaching through imitating an experienced teacher's ways. This is a kind of *observational* learning, and in Japan this learning process is called 'Shu, Ha, Ri'. 'Shu' means that a novice emulates an expert through observing his/her behavior. A novice is an imitator or a copier of an expert. After a while, a novice can imitate an expert's behaviors perfectly as he/she begins to incorporate his/her own behavior into the mastered behavioral pattern and this process of divergence from the mould or model is called 'Ha'. 'Ha' means to break through an expert's behavioral pattern. 'Ri' means to establish a unique behavioral pattern. By this stage, the novice will have developed his or her own and original behavioral patterns. It is because of this that almost all Japanese teachers regard equality as meaning 'not teaching'. In effect, all newly qualified teachers must observe and copy an expert's teaching as their own model to emulate. The ethos of equality as Japanese teacher's culture leads to apprenticeship, not thus not co-inquiry, in school-based teacher learning.

This characteristic is stronger in elementary schools than in secondary schools. In Japan, elementary school teachers basically teach all subjects and manage their own tutor group. The Japanese elementary school system is class-based around teacher assignments. This means each class is a closed system, so it has its own educational goals, classroom atmosphere, rules, relationship between classroom teacher and its pupils, and so on. The ethos of equality means elementary school teachers do not interact with or teach with one another. It is difficult for school teachers to share school-based issues, so there is little co-inquiry in Japanese schools, especially at elementary level.

A LACK OF COLLEGIALITY IN JAPANESE TEACHERS' CULTURE

There are two distinct and polarizing aspects of Japanese school teachers' culture, 'inside' and 'outside' and 'the ethos of equality'. The latter is supposed to open up the possibility of enabling co-inquiry among school teachers within a school. However, little co-inquiry in Japan can emerge, owing to a general lack of collegiality within schools. As Asada's case study shows, it is rare for Japanese mentor-teachers to use a problem-solving approach in discussion with their newly qualified teachers. Rather, they adopt rigid teaching steps for their mentee to follow during their first year of their newly qualified teacher training program.

Case study II

In Japan there is no formal mentoring system, but a kind of informal mentoring system exists for all newly qualified teachers who must take an in-service teacher training program during their year in post ('Shonin-ken'). In 2008, Asada compared a sample of mentors' ongoing comments on newly qualified teachers undertaking the second stage of teacher training in Japan, the in-service teacher training program. This program consists of two training courses of which one is training within school and the other is out of school. During the training within school, the mentor takes on the job of working with four newly qualified teachers. In the training that occurs out of school, some supervisors give lectures about the education act, teaching methods, classroom management and related issues at the prefecture educational training institute, and newly qualified teachers engage in social service during the school's summer vacation. The in-school system does not always work well because of the variations in mentoring. Mentors are usually assigned by the Prefecture and the City Board of Education according to how long they have been teaching. This can result in major differences in the quality of the mentoring provided. In considering this situation, the purpose of Asada's study was to explore the kinds of comments mentors give to their mentees while they observed the mentees' teaching. The subjects were two mentors and two newly qualified teachers. Two mentors were male and had more than 20 years of teaching experience between them. One mentee was a male junior high mathematics teacher and the other a female elementary school teacher. Using morphological analysis and content analysis of each mentor's ongoing comments to each mentee's teaching in June, October and February, the study revealed four main findings.

First, the total number of mentors' comments was limited in February, the beginning of the school year in Japan. One reason for this might have been that the mentors knew that they could not continue their mentoring relationship for longer than one year. Because of the spirit of egalitarianism in Japanese teachers' culture, the newly qualified teachers are regarded as fully fledged from the start of their second year of teaching. Because of this, mentors did not really appear to provide substantial comments for their mentees in February. Later on it would appear that one mentor observed shifted his focus from discussing teaching skills to lesson planning, focusing on the process of setting teaching and teaching objectives. Because this mentor recognized it was difficult for a newly qualified teacher to construct a lesson plan logically to achieve teaching objectives, the mentor appeared to concentrate on the importance of the process of teaching through showing relationships between teaching objectives/teaching skills and learning activities. Crucially, the mentor appeared to sustain emotional support for the mentee through the year. In the beginning the mentor pointed out the mentee's aptitude for teaching and as time went on gave positive feedback through showing pupils' achievements as evidence of the mentee's growth.

Second, the elementary school mentor (Mentor A) shifted his focus from teaching skills to lesson planning while he pointed out his mentee's aptitude for and attitude towards teaching in the beginning and he came to recognize her growth by taking account of facts about her pupils. The junior high school mentor (Mentor B) displayed a similar tendency until October, but in February he focused on his mentee's (Teacher C's) teaching skills while he showed clear evidence of his mentee's growth.

Third, in June, while Mentor A gave positive feedback to Teacher A, he also indicated what she should do and offered an alternative based on his observation of her teaching. More than 50 per cent of his comments about alternative teaching strategies included facts about the children. He appeared to model how to reflect upon teaching. In October, he appeared to provide self-confidence in his mentee's teaching by referring to children's development and furthermore he acknowledged her teaching skills. On the other hand, he did not point out the problems with her teaching, although he offered many alternatives strategies for her to consider. Because pointing out her teaching problems had a negative feed-back function, it would appear that he thought his positive emotional support was more important than his negative feedback. In February, while he conceded her growth as a teacher, he provided her with teaching tasks and showed her how to interpret and use teaching materials. He appeared to motivate her to continue her professional development and showed her tasks to tackle during her second year of teaching.

Fourth, in June, Mentor B offered many alternatives based on children's learning. He also pointed out problems related to children's learning. Like Mentor A, Mentor B also appeared to demonstrate his reflective thinking. Though the acknowledgement score for this aspect of mentoring was only 3 per cent, it was very important for their relationship. His comment was, 'Because by now I've insisted it is important that he shows what pupils learn this lesson clearly, today he did very well.' In October, essentially he allocated all his comments in relation to children's learning. He appeared to focus on children's learning as a kind of role modeling in his mentoring and on his mentee's professional growth in observing his mentee's teaching. In February, the limited number of his comments was restricted to expressing his concerns. Mentor B could not understand the teaching content or pupils' thought processes because he had no experience of teaching mathematics. He did not appear to refer to the teaching content and mathematics curriculum in any depth, but focused on how to think about teaching in a reflective way. A further aspect of the study undertaken into in-service education by Asada (2008) was that mentors appeared to offer both career and emotional support to their mentees:

Examples of mentors' comments relating to career support

Mentor A:

October: It is better if she could use a variety of reading methods in her lessons that reflect her teaching objectives because there are a several reading methods for teaching Japanese language, silent reading, reading aloud, intensive reading, the appointed pupil's reading to name a few.

Mentor B:

October: This teacher appoints a few pupils who can read well and show other pupils how to read.

February: I cannot see how the first learning activity where pupils fold papers leads from today's teaching objectives.

Examples of mentors' comments relating to emotional support

Mentor A:

June: I feel she (he mentee) tries to improve her teaching by aspiring to adopt creative strategies.

February: Though pupil A has been a high-maintenance child from the beginning of the school year, he has come to engage in his learning actively through her teaching and caring.

EGALITARIAN ASPECTS OF TEACHER EDUCATION REFLECTING 'UCHI'

In Japan, the newly qualified teacher must be on an equal footing with everyone else within the school. As this case study shows, however, mentoring relationships cannot be equal, even though mentoring is for just one year and it comes under the category of formal mentoring. Rather, the mentoring process seems to follow the apprenticeship model based on the individual mentor's teaching experience. This kind of Japanese formal mentoring (Shonin-ken) appears to display the three following characteristics:

First, a mentor continues to give positive feedback to a mentee for one year. It would appear that it is very significant for newly qualified teachers to receive emotional support and be recognized as a fully fledged teacher by their mentor. In the beginning, the mentor points out a mentee's aptitude or attitude for teaching and later on shows the pupils' development (i.e., pupils' learning in the classroom) as evidence of the mentee's growth. If a mentee has difficulty teaching, the mentor tends to give emotional support rather than demonstrating how to teach, offering alternatives as a form of instrumental and informational support.

Second, a mentor can show a mentee how to think about teaching in a reflective way while another mentor might not reveal his reflective thinking. It appears to depend somewhat on a mentee's teaching ability as to whether a mentor can show his reflective thinking. If the mentor does not show his reflective thinking, the mentoring relationship seems to evolve into an apprenticeship. Namely, a mentor frequently indicates what a mentee should do in teaching.

Third, it would appear that the mentoring process has three stages (i.e., model, coach, critical friend and co-enquirer) where Furlong and Maynard (1995) agued for four stages. In this study, mentors appeared to direct their mentees towards becoming autonomous reflective practitioners and shift their mentoring role from modeling reflective thinking and being an instructor, a sympathizer or motivator towards being a critical friend. As mentioned earlier, although a mentor continues to offer emotional support for one year, in the early stages a mentor gives instruction in how to accomplish basic teaching skills and classroom management, as soon as he or she becomes aware of problems through observing the mentee teaching). In addition, the role of sympathizer and motivator appears to be important in establishing a sound basis for the mentoring relationship in the early stages. At the second stage, the role of motivator seems to be important.

It would appear to be necessary for a mentor to recognize the mentee as a teacher, as a member of the in-group ('uchi') because otherwise he or she feels anxious about his or her professional growth. In parallel, throughout both the first and second stage, the mentor shows the mentee how to think about teaching in a reflective way based on observation of their teaching. This role is thought to act as a model for becoming a reflective thinker. Concurrently, the mentor as an instructor gradually shifts his focus from commenting on teaching skills to the process of teaching. It would appear that a mentor adopts this order as he initially instructs the mentee about teaching skills and classroom management and then, later, shows how to create a lesson plan that will be fairly likely to lead to the achievement of the teaching objectives. At the third stage, a mentor mainly points out problems that arise in teaching, which means that a mentor's opinion originates as a critical viewpoint. At this stage, his role can be thought of as that of a critical friend.

FROM THE VIEW POINT OF EPISTEMOLOGY

Hofner (2008) has explored the role that personal epistemology can play in intellectual development, learning, and education. The enactment of mentoring as apprenticeship, or as co-inquiry, may depend mainly on the epistemology of the mentor and mentee (see Figure 9.3). A mentor who does not accept the mentee's view could be said to adopt a stance of 'objectivism'. In other words, if the mentor regards the mentee as an outsider to the social group ('soto'), the mentee will be put at a disadvantage because of being regarded as an 'outsider' to the profession of teaching. Subsequently, the mentee, who encounters an objectivist position from his or her mentor, is likely to internalize the mentor's view by emulating the mentor's words and deeds. The learning outcome is likely to be a kind of equilibrium as this type of mentoring depends on the characteristics of the mentor and the mentee. It is subject to reproduction, by a mentee, of a mentor's epistemology. This kind of mentoring, which is the 'reproduction model', is characterized by its replication.

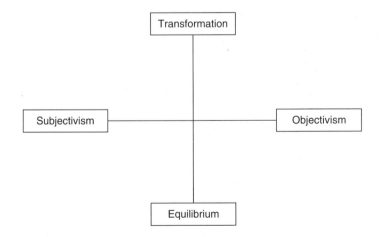

Figure 9.3   A map of mentoring (from Brockbank, A., McGill, I., 2006)

If a mentor focuses on school problems from the stance of objectivism, he/she tries to facilitate changing the school's organization or school structure. However, it does not become possible to change the school structure without considering each school teacher's thinking, which may be flawed, since many school problems stem from what is simply taken for granted in a school. In this scenario, the main aim of mentoring is to raise awareness about the mentee's flawed thinking. This type of mentoring will evolve into the imposition of the mentor's views upon the mentee.

If a mentor adopts a 'subjective' stance, mentoring develops humanistic tendencies for a mentee. Certainly, in this mentoring process a mentor is likely to respect the mentee's views, in contrast to a situation where a mentor intends to maintain the school structure. In that scenario, mentoring directs a mentee to accept the existing school structure even though a mentee might feel autonomous. This mentoring mode can be identified as the 'humanistic reproduction model'.

If a mentor stands for subjectivism and wants to change the school structure or resolve the problems in school alongside his/her mentee, this kind of mentoring will embody co-inquiry. In a co-enquiry mentoring process, the inter-subjective approach is important to generate new practical knowledge. This is a similar process to the participatory action research approach (Kemmis and McTaggart, 2000). It is clear from their model that unless the mentor and mentee respect one another there cannot be the kind of dialogue that leads to a growth of practical knowledge. The mentee is unable as is the mentor to contribute to a growth of learning through sustained and mutual valuing of the other.

DEFINING APPRENTICESHIP WITHIN MENTORING

An apprenticeship approach in initial teacher training has often been recommended in literature relating to developing newly qualified teachers' skills (Hillgate Group 1989; O'Hear, 1988). Maynard and Furlong (1995) critique this standpoint and emphasize that apprenticeship cannot, by itself, be sufficient. They draw attention to Catherine Burn's 'collaborative teaching' model by way of illustration (1995: 19) which apparently has several advantages:

- learning to plan lessons carefully through being involved in joint planning with an experienced teacher, finding out what the teacher takes account of and identifying with the planning and its consequences;
- learning certain skills of classroom teaching through having responsibility for a specified component of the lessons, while identifying with the whole lesson and recognizing the relationships of the past to the whole; and
- gaining access to the teacher's craft knowledge through observation of the teacher's actions, informed by a thorough knowledge of the planning and probably through discussion of the lesson afterwards, with a heightened responsibility for the lesson.

Maynard and Furlong (1995) express concern that if newly qualified teachers learn to teach only with individuals and small groups of students, they will not learn classroom management strategies or experience what taking full responsibility for teaching a lesson might entail. The problem is that newly qualified teachers in Japan spend only four weeks teaching in a school. Collaborative teaching is desirable but time for implementing Burn's model is limited. Becoming part of the teaching profession is possible to some extent via apprenticeship but, ideally, newly qualified teachers need to understand that learning to teach is a process that takes time and a willingness to examine one's own practice and learn.

DEFINING CO-ENQUIRY WITHIN MENTORING

Where a mentor expects a novice simply to imitate his or her own teaching strategies, the novice is unlikely to learn how to approach teaching as enquiry. Realizing that there are no hard and fast rules in classroom teaching (and that every lesson is different) is crucial if a newly qualified teacher is to be a proficient learner. However, if the mentor presents class teaching as too open to change in each lesson, the novice is likely to feel very concerned about the uncertainty of planning and delivering a lesson. The mentor needs to become aware of how far the novice is capable of approaching teaching as enquiry. It takes much skill on the part of a mentor who needs to reveal how he or she uses enquiry, on a limited scale, to improve teaching. Some aspects of teaching are better taught in apprenticeship mode when time is limited such as how to take an attendance register. Working closely with a newly qualified teacher who is making good progress in basic classroom management and is able to make choices about how to approach teaching aspects of the lesson, is a strong starting point for co-enquiry. The mentor can usefully adopt a participatory action research approach to teaching alongside a newly qualified teacher. Together they can address problems as they ask themselves, 'How might we improve our teaching?' This approach, in itself, can be seen as a form of apprenticeship. As the novice sees the mentor reflect on how best to teach some aspects of the lesson by considering a range of different strategies he or she can become part of the 'uchi' by working as a co-enquirer.

THE BENEFITS OF MENTORING AS APPRENTICESHIP

In principle, then, a practical problem-solving approach requires that mentors think dialectically about practice. Significantly, mentoring cannot generate new practical knowledge unless the mentor and mentee are able to respect each other as part of their social group. Whether mentoring is apprenticeship or co-inquiry is likely to depend on the epistemology of both mentor and mentee. Certainly, many studies have pointed out the characteristics of mentoring relationship and the nature of mentor. Jacobi (1991) proposed, for example, that five factors (age difference, duration of mentoring, gender and ethnicity, whether the mentoring style is formal or informal, and mentor's motivation) can all influence a mentoring relationship. Rowley (1999) proposed six qualities for a good mentor:

- to be committed to the role of mentoring;
- to be accepting of the newly qualified teacher;
- to be skilled at providing instructional support;
- to be effective in different interpersonal contexts; and
- to be a model of a continuous learner.

Hobson, Ashby, Malderez and Tomlinson (2009) have pointed out similar characteristics.

> Effective mentors must also be willing and able to 'make their work public' and make explicit the factors underlying their classroom practices and they must be supportive, approachable, non-judgemental and trustworthy, have a positive demeanour, and possess good listening skills and the ability to empathize, as well as the willingness and ability to take an interest in newly qualified teachers' work and lives. Importantly, mentors should also want to do the job and be committed to the work of mentoring. (2009: Section 2.3.2)

Many studies about the mentoring relationship have not necessarily been conducted from the viewpoint of both mentor's and mentee's epistemology. That is the uniqueness of the study in this chapter. Whether the mentee is perceived by the mentor to be on the inside ('uchi') of the social structure in the school or the outside ('soto') will have a lasting and marked effect on the mentoring relationship that evolves and, correspondingly, on the kind of teaching that the mentee develops over time. If both the mentor and the mentee generate new practical knowledge through the mentoring process, their interaction must be dialectic or inter-subjective and is likely to manifest the kind of experiential learning theory that Kolb (1986) described. If mentoring generates new knowledge to improve practice, it is important that its process is dialectic. In our future research on mentoring we will focus on the interaction between mentor and mentee from the viewpoint of the epistemology as well upon the characteristics of the mentor.

CONCLUSION

The purpose of learning to teach is to be able to take responsibility for planning lessons that can enable students to learn. In order to do this, a teacher needs to be a learner too. Newly qualified teachers can only spend a short time learning to teach in schools and so this limits the opportunities for learning to teach other than as an apprenticeship. Ideally, a newly qualified teacher will learn that teaching is a process of learning that benefits from action research approaches with a view to developing knowledge about how to improve student learning. The greater the opportunity for a mentor and a newly qualified teacher to learn together, the more likely they can generate knowledge between them about how to teach effectively. Collaborating closely will build feelings of rapport and the novice is more likely to become accepted as a member of the teaching community ('uchi'). This presents a problem because the time for learning to teach in Japanese schools is short. It is not, however, impossible to approach some aspects of teaching as co-enquiry, even though school practice is so limited. If the newly qualified teacher takes full responsibility for a part of a lesson rather than working with individuals or small groups, he or she can become a co-enquirer with the mentor. This approach would be innovative for most school teachers in Japanese schools where learning to teach is regarded as apprenticeship, not co-enquiry.

EDITOR'S NOTE

It has been my pleasure and privilege to assist Tadashi with completing this chapter. Sarah J. Fletcher (March 2011).

REFERENCES

Asada, T. (2008) 'An analysis of mentor's on-going comments for mentee's teaching', paper presented to the European Educational Research Association annual conference, Goteborg, Sweden.

Asada, T. (2006) 'A study of the mentoring system for beginning teachers', paper presented at the annual conference for the British Educational Research Association, University of Warwick, 7 September 2006.

Bachnik, J. (1994) *Situated Meaning: Inside and Outside in Japanese Self, Society, and Language*, Princeton, NJ: Princeton University Press.

Brooks, V. and Sikes, P. (1997) *The Good Mentor Guide: Initial Teacher Education in Secondary Schools*, Buckingham: Open University Press.

Burn, C. (1992) 'Collaborative teaching', in Wilkin, M. (1992) *Mentoring in Schools* (pp. 133–143). London: Kogan Page.

Elliott, B. and Calderhead, J. (1993) 'Mentoring for Teacher Development: Possibilities and Caveats', in McIntyre, D., Hagger, H. and Wilkin, M. (1993) *Mentoring: Perspectives on School-Based Teacher Education* (pp. 166–189). London: Kogan Page.

Fletcher, S. (2007) 'Educational research mentoring and coaching as co-creative synergy', *International Journal of Evidence-based Coaching and Mentoring*, 5 (2), 1–11.

Fletcher, S. (2000) *Mentoring in Schools; A Handbook of Good Practice*. London: RoutledgeFalmer.

Franke, A. and Dahlgren, L. O. (1996) 'Conceptions of Mentoring: An empirical study of conceptions of mentoring the school-based teacher education' in *Teaching and Teacher Education*, 12(6), 627–641.

Furlong, J. and Maynard, T. (1995) *Mentoring Student Teachers: The Growth of Professional Knowledge*. London: Routedge.

Hadden, S. C. and Lester, M. (1978) 'Talking identity: The production of "self" in interaction' in *Human Studies*, 1 (1), 331–356.

Hillgate Group (1989) *Learning to Teach*. London: Claridge Press.

Hobson, A. J., Ashby, P., Malderez, A. and Tomlinson, P. D. (2009). 'Mentoring beginning teachers: what we know and what we don't. ...' *Teaching and Teacher Education*, 25(1), 207–216.

Hofner, B. K. (2008) *Knowing, Knowledge and Beliefs*. Sydney: Springer Press.

Jacobi, M. (1991) 'Mentoring and Undergraduate Academic Success: A Literature Review', in *Review of Educational Research*, 61 (4), 505–532.

Kemmis, S. and McTaggart, R. (2000) 'Participatory action research', in N. K. Denzin and Y. S. Lincoln (Eds), *Handbook of Qualitative Research* (2nd edn). London: Sage.

Kolb, D. A. (1986) *The Learning Style inventory: Technical manual.* Boston, MA: McBer and Company.

Makino, S. (2007) 'What is Uchi?, What is Soto?: The Cultural Implications of Japanese Grammar' reported in *The Daily Gazette*, accessed on 2 February 2011 at http://daily.swarthmore.edu/2007/2/12/what-is-uchi-what-is-soto-the-cultural-implications-of-japanese-grammar/

Maynard, T. and Furlong, J. (1995) 'Models of mentoring', in Kerry, T. and Mayes, A. S. (Eds), *Issues in Mentoring*. London: Open University/Routledge Press.

McCallion, M. J. (2007) 'In-groups and out-groups', *Blackwell Encyclopedia of Sociology*, accessed at: http://www.sociologyencyclopedia.com/public/tocnode?query=McCallion&widen=1&result_number=2&from=search&id=g9781405124331_yr2010_chunk_g978140512433115_ss1-48&type=std&fuzzy=0&slop=1

O'Hear, A. (1988) *Who Teaches the Teachers?* London: Social Affairs Unit.

Rowley, J. B.(1999) 'The good mentor', *Educational Leadership*, 56(8), 20–22.

10

Effects of Race and Racial Dynamics on Mentoring

Juanita Johnson-Bailey

INTRODUCTION

Even the Greek goddess Athena knew that humans judge others' abilities and worth based on superficial appraisals of physical appearance and status. According to Greek mythology, Athena wisely disguised herself as a mortal man, Mentor, who would become an advisor to Odyessus' son, Telemachus. Why would a goddess create such an elaborate pretext? The answer is quite simple. Doing so helped her to avoid suspicions and allowed her the privilege of having her advice valued and accepted. Would the plan have worked if Athena had appeared as a kindly Moor who was visiting while Odysseus was away fighting in the Trojan War and who only wanted to offer unsolicited help to the family? In all probability the differences in the mentor and the protégées' lived experiences and the possible misconceptions held towards the other's diverse existence would have fundamentally made problematic the counselor and protégé relationship. Mentor had to be older, male, and European. And so it is from this account that we have come to know a *mentor* as someone in a position of power, who is usually male, always senior, part of the majority culture, and an insider who can guide the career of a more junior person. One possible moral of the story is that positionality – who we are and who we are perceived to be in society – are important matters that affect mentoring relationships.

Another possible lesson to take from Mentor's experiences is that possessing a different positionality can limit access or at best affect one's ability to negotiate freely in society. If this was true for Mentor, the person who was charged to give help, then a difference in appearance might also have impacted the inexperienced person needing help and guidance.

WHY DOES RACE MATTER?

To situate the importance of race in this discussion of mentoring, I first need to explore race and racial dynamics in Western society. A glance at the distribution of power and resources in Western society seems to answer the question of whether race matters. The allocation of wealth, education, authority and leadership is not extended uniformly across diverse groups: People of color are reflected disproportionately among the socioeconomically disadvantaged (Chietji and Hamilton, 2006; Hacker, 2008), suggesting that race does indeed matter. Additionally, American society maintains patterns of homogeneity rather than full desegregation in voluntary settings such as social clubs and churches.

Race is but one of the hierarchical systems that gets used in Western society to privilege some and deny others. Many variables drive our transactions in higher education and race counts amongst them as one of the most significant. Undeniably, race can be used in informative and meaningful ways as a critical lens for assessing our higher education experiences (Nettles and Millett, 2006), which includes mentoring relationships and processes.

Studies suggest that racial group membership is a powerful force in the structured lives of minority students and faculty members, affecting what happens in academic classrooms (Hayes and Colin, 1994; Swim, Hyers, Cohen, Fitzgerald, and Bylsma, 2003) and academic careers (Ronstein, Rothblum, and Solomon, 1993; Thomas and Hollenshead, 2001; Thompson and Louque, 2005). So it is reasonable to infer that the unstructured lives of students and faculty are affected by racial group membership and racial dynamics. Hence voluntary subjective interpersonal relationships such as mentoring would be especially affected by race (Alvarez, Blume, Cervantes, and Thomas, 2009; Blake-Beard, Murrell, and Thomas, 2007; Bowman, Kite, Branscombe, and Williams, 1999; Hu, Thomas, and Lance, 2008; Moore and Toliver, 2010; Thomas, 1993a,b). Several studies have found that mutual attraction, a psychological basis of mentorship, is significantly influenced by demographic similarities, especially race (e.g., Byrne, 1971; Ensher and Murphy, 1997; Thomas, 1993a,b). Coincidentally, discomfort in mentoring is also influenced by demographic difference, particularly race (Hu et al., 2008).

Race and racial group membership are defining markers in our world; consequently, these signs of membership and exclusion are powerful forces in the academy. However, race often remains invisible to the privileged White majority in academia, and racism in this setting is characteristically shrouded in rational discourse (Bowman et al., 1999; Frankenberg, 1993; Giroux, 1997). When we talk of race in Western society, we are referring primarily to people of color

(Denzin, Lincoln, and Smith, 2008; Gregory and Sanjek, 1994; Hayes and Colin, 1994; Hytten and Warren, 2003). Depending on the context and geographical location, the racial minority can be Hispanics, Asians, or Native Americans. When we speak of race as educators we are using the same frame of reference and are referring to every group except White Americans.

Our American discourse communicates the fact that race does not include White and that race always means the *other* (Frankenberg, 1993; Giroux, 1997; Gregory and Sanjek, 1994). Since Whites have for so long been the majority population in the United States, it might appear to be a simple matter of convenience to forego naming Whites as the unidentified subject. But this innocuous matter hides a powerful truth: Giving the semblance of normalcy to Whiteness accords it power, allows it to determine and define all other races, and permits it to remain the unseen perfect entity against which all other groups are measured. For instance, when any stereotype is constructed it is Whiteness that is the absent benefactor (Cohen and Steele, 2002; Diekman, and Eagly, 2000; Johnson-Bailey and Cervero, 2000). When we speak of the lazy African American, the hot-blooded Latino, the model Asian, and the alcoholic Native American, who stands in contrast to these images as the good and true norm? The White American.

By ascribing what one group is, the underlying message is that the norm group is not this negative embodiment. It is important not only to note that it is Whiteness that stands to profit from such inaccurate classifications, but that it is also Whiteness that has participated in creating these classifications (Frankenberg, 1993; Giroux, 1997; McIntosh, 1995). And it is not an accident that a ready stereotype does not exist relative to what is a White American. Although race is a social construct, it is an invisible presence that acts in a major role to determine how American society functions. This ordering of the world along set queues is part of a system of categorization and in each classification there are accompanying rights, privileges, and baggage (Frankenberg, 1993; Giroux, 1997; McIntosh, 1995). Therefore, to be of Asian ancestry in the US means one thing and to be White in the US means another. The chance of an Asian American being asked how long she or he has been living in the US is quite probable. In contrast, this would not happen to a White American, for to be White in America means to be the norm. And it is this ability to always blend in, to be the rule and not the exception, and this position of seeming neutrality, that is the currency of access to all things better in our society.

Racism is systemic, with structured inequalities that support a schema, replete with policies and practices, norms and traditions that automatically disadvantage and exploit one social group for the advantage of another group (Sensoy and DiAngelo, 2009). Oppression, the visible operant tool of racism, 'involves institutional control, ideological domination, and the imposition of the dominant group's culture on the target group' (Sensoy and DiAngelo, 2009: 345). White privilege, the unseen partner to oppression, is 'an invisible package of unearned assets that [Whites] can count on cashing in each day, but about which [they are] meant to remain oblivious' (McIntosh, 1995: 291). Academia is not exempt from the effects of systems of White privilege and oppression: Racism, and its corollary, White privilege, are institutionally supported. White privilege constitutes a large part of the hidden infrastructure of American society, directing, driving, and often invisibly and subtly determining outcomes such as employment, housing, education, and even relationships (Chietji and Hamilton, 2006; Giroux, 1997; Hayes and Colin, 1994; Omi and Winnat, 1994; Turban, Dougherty, and Lee, 2002).

RACE AND MENTORING

Students and faculty of color routinely experience higher education as a racially insensitive or hostile environment, which causes psychological distress (Allen, 1985; Fleming, 1984; Thompson and Louque, 2005) that can result in withdrawal, feelings of loneliness, self-doubt, and lowered self-concept (Allen, 1985; Bova, 2000; Fleming, 1984; Thomas and Hollenshead, 2001; Webster, Sedlack, and Miyares, 1979). Such factors significantly affect student satisfaction. A compounding dilemma results because student satisfaction has been shown to influence the performance and completion rate for racial minority students more than for White college students (Taylor, 2000). Additionally, lack of social integration, infrequent participation in campus organizations and activities, and limited interaction with peers and faculty have more of an impact on the grade point averages of these disenfranchised students. Inevitably such issues as isolation, loneliness, self-doubt, and lowered self-concept have had a negative effect on progression rates for students (Allen, 1985; Cokley, 2000) and have impacted career progression for faculty of color (Ronstein, Rothblum, and Solomon, 1993; Winkler, 2000).

Since studies have indicated that mentoring relationships can positively affect development and advancement of students and faculty of color, mentoring takes on even more importance for students and faculty of color (Allen, Eby, Poteet, Lentz, and Lima, 2004; Constantine, Smith, Redington, and Owens, 2008; Crutcher, 2007; Moore and Toliver, 2010). Good mentoring helps the protégé to reach his or her full potential, with benefits of effective mentoring including increased competence, increased feelings of confidence in one's abilities, and higher esteem (Constantine et al., 2008; Crutcher, 2007). Mentors routinely help protégés by providing inside information and access to informal information about one's organization, as well as tips on navigating the process, securing resources, and understanding the institutional climate – unwritten rules for which insiders have insight.

CROSS-RACIAL MENTORING

Most students of color attend predominately White institutions (Bowen and Bok, 1998; Fleming, 1984; Nettles, 1988). The percentage of faculty of color is also increasing at these institutions. The research that examines their presence attests that these students and faculty routinely struggle with isolation and loneliness, discrimination and indifference/insensitivity (Allen, 1985; Cokley, 2000; D'Augelli and Hershberger, 1993; Nettles, 1998). Although the relationship between a mentor and protégé is less conflictual when both share similar experiences, worldviews, cultural backgrounds, and belief systems (Alvarez et al., 2009; Dreher and Cox, 1996; McGoldrick, Giorando, and Pierce, 1996; Tatum, 1997), the reality is that White males make up the critical mass in the academy. People of color are more represented as students and junior faculty than possible mentors for students and faculty. White males, the power brokers and decision makers in academia, are faced with mentoring opportunities and challenges across cultural, ethnic, and gender lines. While mentoring can be a crucial component that positively affects academic advancement, scholars and faculty of color continue to have difficulty finding mentors, especially of the same racial background as themselves (Bierema, 2005; Blake-Beard, et al., 2007; Hansman, 2002, 2005; Thomas, 1990).

As a result of a legacy of segregation in American higher education, students and faculty of color routinely doubt the expressed good intentions of higher education representatives (Cohen and Steele, 2002; Johnson-Bailey, Valentine, Cervero, and Bowles, 2009; Swim, Hyers, Cohen, Fitzgerald, and Bylsma, 2003). And lack of knowledge and limited familiarity, compounded by discomfort can negatively impact cross-cultural and cross-racial mentoring (Bova, 2000; Grier and Cobbs, 1968; Johnson-Bailey and Cervero, 2004, 2008). Kovel (1970) contends that the historical tension between Whites and people of color tends to construct racial barriers. Mentoring across cultural boundaries is an especially delicate dance that juxtaposes group norms and societal pressures and expectations with individual personality traits. To ease the possible apprehension that can occur from attempting to balance multiple concerns embedded in the cross-cultural mentoring process, Blake (1999) believes that cross-cultural mentoring teams need to spend considerable time acknowledging the burden of racism encountered.

Establishing trust in a cross-cultural mentoring relationship is crucial to developing such a relationship, more so than in a same-race mentoring relationship (Blake-Beard et al., 2007; Bowman et al., 1999; Brinson and Kottler, 1993; Thomas, 2001) and it an essential tenet for successful cross-cultural mentoring relationships. Working through trust on the individual level is routinely discussed in the mentoring literature, but one must also recognize that the mentoring relationship is much broader than an association between two persons. On the surface, the concept of trust as it applies to mentoring appears simplistic, but it needs to be present and reciprocal in nature between the mentor and protégé.

However, in cross-cultural mentoring what should be a simple matter of negotiation between two persons becomes arbitration between historical legacies, contemporary racial tensions, and societal protocols (Blake-Beard, et al., 2007; Brayboy, 2003; Johnson-Bailey and Cervero, 2004, 2008). Moreover, a cross-cultural mentoring relationship is an affiliation between a mentor and a mentee who are conducting their relationship on a hostile American stage, with a societal script that could undermine the success of the partnership. It is against this backdrop of American history that trust must be built across the races before cross-cultural mentoring can be successful.

Mentoring occurs on two dimensions: the internal aspect transpires between the mentor and the protégé, and an external aspect takes place between the mentoring pair and their institution (O'Neill, Horton, and Crosby, 2000). The reality that the mentor and the protégé have differing experiences and reactions in their shared work environment is a source of unease and uncommon ground that can weaken the bonds of trust and possibly contribute to feelings of anger and guilt in cross-cultural mentoring. Bowman et al. (1999) draw attention to how White guilt can be a major impediment to the development and success of cross-race mentoring teams.

However, the literature neglects to suggest why White guilt intrudes into a cross-cultural mentoring situation and, at the same time, fails to propose any solution for the dilemma. White guilt on the part of the mentor could be a reaction to the awareness of unearned White privilege, or it might be a natural defensive reaction to Black anger. For an answer, it seems practical to refer to two frequently touted recommendations that stress the importance of honest, ongoing discussions about race and racism and the pairing of mentors and protégés with similar worldviews in cross-cultural mentoring situations (Crutcher, 2007; Johnson-Bailey and Cervero, 2004, 2008; Thomas, 1993b). Indeed, the continuous foregrounding of candid conversation about race and the important stipulation of matching mentors and protégés on the basis of life philosophy are plausible solutions for creating an environment where trust is likely to grow between like-minded individuals.

Two other obstacles faced by minority protégés and White mentors are the paternalistic and political nature inherent in the mentoring process. The hierarchically prescribed mentor–protégé relationship resembles the paternalistic model of the authoritative superior and deferential subordinate that is a painful part of a racist American legacy. Most definitions of mentoring frame the relationship between mentor and protégé as one of *intense caring* where a person with more experience works with a less experienced one to promote both personal and professional development (Hansman, 2002, 2005). However, this framing of the mentoring relationship in purely psychological terms, though partly true, ignores the central dynamic of any mentoring relationship – its hierarchical nature (Bowman et al., 1999). This power relationship is further magnified in cross-cultural mentoring where the people are in differing locations in society. As Ragins explains, 'Diversified mentoring relationships are composed of mentors and protégés who differ in group membership associated with power differences' (1997: 482). The power relations that order our social lives cannot possibly be suspended. Likewise, the learning dimensions of the cross-cultural mentoring relationship are enacted within the political and social circumstances in which we live.

A final point is that studies have shown that mentors in cross-race relationships successfully carry out career development and psychosocial functions when both members share similar strategies for dealing with struggle in the relationship (Bowman et al., 1999). However, when the mentor and protégé engage in 'protective hesitation' (Thomas, 2001) where they refrain from raising touchy racial issues, then the relationship lacks psychosocial support. Bowman and colleagues (1999) have offered that an effective strategy when mentoring people of color is to see/treat the protégé as an individual and not as a category: that is, simultaneously remembering and forgetting. This matter of valuing an individual that is part of a culture but not finitely defined by the culture should be reciprocal, as the White mentor is also an individual and not a category or representative of the larger White society. As Crutcher cautions, 'Mentors need not have the same cultural or social background as their mentees, but they must pay close attention to the implications of the differences' (2007: 21). However, while recognizing that racial differences are a necessary part of daily interactions, the mentor and mentee must also connect as human beings. This is the first and most important step in getting beyond the barriers and boundaries. According to Johnson-Bailey and Cervero (2004), five guidelines should be used to assist White mentors in their cross-racial mentoring efforts: (1) a willingness to extend beyond normal mentoring expectations; (2) an understanding of the psychological and social effects of racism; (3) cultural competence; (4) an understanding of their White privilege, and (5) an acceptance of the risk and possible discomfort implicit in mentoring across racial lines.

INTRA-RACIAL MENTORING

As the numbers of minority faculty increase in higher education and as these individuals move up the career ladder, the prospect of faculty of color becoming mentors also grows. While the literature in higher education is replete with empirical studies that examine the impact of culture, gender, and race (Allen, 1985; Cohen and Steele, 2002; Cokley, 2000; Tinto, 1993) researchers have much more work to do in the area of racial mentoring and the impact of racial mentoring on student experiences. One seminal examination of the affect of mentoring focused on the interpersonal interactions between Black faculty and Black students (Moore and Toliver, 2010), with only a cursory conclusion on mentoring. The researchers concluded that Black faculty can offer more empathy and greater understanding to Black students since they have shared a similar experience that 'empowers them with knowledge of the undertows that many Black students are prone to succumb to in navigating the academy' (Moore and Toliver, 2010: 933).

Interestingly, Moore and Toliver (2010) also found that despite the theory of homogeneity (a preference for mentoring those from the same ethnic group), an uneasy alliance exists between minority students and minority mentors. And the reason for this disjuncture? Some students did not believe that Black faculty possessed the knowledge or power needed to be their most effective mentors. This issue of same-race mentoring dyads is more fully explored in the human resources literature, which examines mentoring in the corporate sector among minority and women mentors and protégés. There were participants in two organizational studies (i.e., Bierema, 2005; Palmer and Johnson-Bailey, 2008) who perceived their same race/same gender mentors as being less powerful and less altruistic than their White counterparts. Additionally, the women and people of color in these same studies felt that their same race/same gender mentors possessed positional power, but held limited referent power.

Another misgiving noted in research on homogeneous mentoring is the suspicion that the successful minority or woman mentor is a 'member of the club' who has conformed. In the study on executive women and mentoring, the junior women believed that senior executive women did not behave 'in ways that improve opportunities for women at lower echelons of the organization" and maintained that the behavior of the senior women sometimes harmed junior women (Bierema, 2005: 16).

Another factor that can impact intra-racial mentoring is the scarcity of mentors of color. While recruiting minority faculty has been accepted as a way to develop the pool of diverse mentors, and positively influence minority recruitment and retention (Grant-Thompson and Atkinson, 1997; Hickson, 2002; Nettles and Millet, 2006; Tinto, 1993), these incoming minority faculty have been inundated with requests to fulfill the diversity initiatives of their universities. Faculty of color are under demand to assume the difficult and complex responsibility of leading the institution's diversity mission, acting as a moral campus compass regarding racial issues, and mentoring students of color (Brayboy, 2003). This burdensome role expectation that is required of minority faculty results in them being overstressed. Many faculty of color find that even if they wanted to mentor students of color, they have to refrain from doing so because the effort goes unrecognized and does not count towards promotion and tenure.

In a case study that explored intra-racial mentoring in a learning community that consisted of a Black woman professor and five Black women students (Johnson-Bailey, 2006), it was noted that the mentoring was culturally bound. The Black woman professor used the concept of othermothering, intense student-centered caring that exceeded the traditional mentoring relationship (Foster, 1993; Guiffrida, 2005). In this case, the teacher assumed a role that not only educated but also socialized and nurtured the students. The professor operated from a position where the cultural background she shared with the students provided a righteous basis for understanding and crossing the usual professional boundaries for the greater good of 'racial uplift'. The Black women students in the study described the *othermothering* style of their professor as 'necessarily authoritative,' 'empathetic tough love,' and 'ancestrally based mothering.'

In this study (Johnson-Bailey, 2006) the Black women students and professor acknowledged and confronted power differences based on age, status, abilities, and class backgrounds. However, they held the central truth that they lived in a world that was racist, sexist, and hierarchically based – one that views Black women as second-class citizens. Nevertheless, the collective were deliberate in expressing themselves as equals who intended to work together to claim their place as one of importance. Using this foundational stance, they attempted to make sense of their mutual struggles in the academy and to analyze, heal, and resist. Drawing from the communal strength of the body, the members of the group individually and jointly honed their teaching and learning practices. Furthermore, the professor and students formulated the basis for scholarship in environmental justice, feminist pedagogy, multicultural education, Black women's leadership, and race and gender in education. For this community of scholars, the professor's mentoring was organically determined by group and individual needs.

This case study set forth the idea that intra-racial mentoring includes a mandatory reciprocity that exists between students and professors. Such give-and-take is apparent and necessary among groups of scholars who exist in an oftentimes hostile academic environment where their numbers are limited. On their common ground as educators, professors, teaching assistants, and students, the study group recognized the frailty of the power negotiated in the teaching/learning setting. Power was interpreted by them as ambiguous and diffusive in nature.

This intra-racial mentoring case study operated with a holistic approach that attended to three areas of existence – the mind, body, and spiritual development. The group studied understood that higher levels of stress induce psychological discord and illness among Black women more so than among White women or men (Boyd, 1993; Gutierrez, 1990; Scott, 1991). The experience of psychological support allowed the group to (1) find the power to reason past personal and cultural pain; (2) act in the face of fear, and (3) forge an intellectual space despite the unreceptive Eurocentric nature of the academy. Moreover, the concept of self-mentoring and participating in a mentoring collective was raised in this study as a promising means for fulfilling the needs of a growing body of minority scholars. This study contributes racial meaning to the issue of psychological support in mentoring relationships and learning processes in the literature (Dingus, 2008; Patton and Harper, 2003).

MENTORING STUDENTS AND FACULTY OF COLOR

Whether students or faculty of color are being mentored across cultural boundaries or within cultural boundaries, there are principles that are deemed effective. First and foremost, a mentor should always place the mentee's needs ahead of their own. A second essential rule is that the mentor should recognize and appreciate the protégé's individuality, remembering that the intent of the mentoring process is not to shape the mentee in the mentor's image and likeness. Getting to know one's mentee as a person involves an investment of time. But the dividends can yield unforeseen benefits such as providing insights into understanding and guiding the mentee. Additionally, devoting time engenders caring and trust, and alleviates tension, providing the basis for a successful mentoring relationship.

Another strategy that helps with the psychosocial aspect of mentoring is finding the common ground shared by the mentor and mentee (Johnson-Bailey and Cervero, 2004). After establishing a good foundation, a mentor who is working with a student or faculty member of color must be aware that effective mentoring extends beyond imparting system knowledge and context-specific strategies on how to maneuver in an academic setting. It is critical for the mentor to understand how race affects the academic environment and then plan how to best manage and advocate for her or his mentee. This process of critiquing a system of which one is a part requires a theoretical awareness of how systems operate and the ability to see the big picture. So it is especially helpful in discussions with the protégé to develop a case-specific agenda for navigating a system, without denigrating the system as intentionally evil. A possible method for achieving this can include conducting a private inventory where the mentor does a personal appraisal and understanding of his or her own cultural history; develops a functional grasp of the sociopolitical forces that affect the mentee's environment; and performs an evaluation relative to whether the mentor is part of the solution or the problem.

On the whole, the task of mentoring is not simple or easy, especially when it involves managing issues of race and racial dynamics. Mentoring students or faculty of color involves being flexible, responsive, and steadfast; for, no matter how far one travels, one never reaches a final destination of establishing a place that is safe and fair. As hooks (1989) reminds us, power continuously co-opts. So being satisfied with one's efforts sanctions a sense of false comfort. Whether you are a person of color or an empathetic majority member there is no complete perfect understanding of what a mentee is experiencing. All mentoring situations are a continuous process of learning and adjusting for both the mentor and the person being mentored. It involves work. But, it is work that is worth the endeavor because mentoring offers an opportunity for making a difference in the academy by helping students and junior faculty navigate a culture that can be hostile and unfamiliar to them.

Ultimately, mentoring students and faculty of color has an important place in the academy as a component of the struggle to promote equity and provide access for this underrepresented group. And working towards equality and providing opportunity are important missions of higher education systems. Less than 50 years ago, higher education looked different. The membership was restricted by race and others factors like gender, class, national origin, and physical ability. Now the once fortified gateway to higher education is more open and the academic landscape is more reflective of American society; however, in the US we have not reached nirvana. Mentoring is sorely needed so that our academic culture can become much more of a welcoming environment that provides equal access and opportunity to all students and faculty who enter the gates.

REFERENCES

Allen, T. D., Eby, L. T., Poteet, M. L., Lentz, E., & Lima, L. (2004). Career benefits associated with mentoring for protégés: A meta-analysis. *Journal of Applied Psychology*, *89*, 127–136.

Allen, W. R. (1985). Black student, White campus: Structural, interpersonal, and psychological correlates of success. *Journal of Negro Education*, *54*, 134–147.

Alvarez, A. N., Blume, A. W., Cervantes, J. M., & Thomas, L. R. (2009). Tapping the wisdom of tradition: Essential elements to mentoring students of color. *Professional Psychology: Research and Practice*, *40*(2), 181–188.

Bierema, L. L. (2005). Women's executives' concerns related to implementing and sustaining a women's network in a corporate context. *Organization Development Journal*, *23*(2), 8–20.

Blake, S. (1999). At the crossroads of race and gender: Lessons from the mentoring experiences of professional black women. In A. J. Murrell, F. J. Crosby, & R. J. Ely (Eds.), *Mentoring Dilemmas: Developmental relationships within multicultural organizations* (pp. 83–104). Mahwah, NJ: Erlbaum.

Blake-Beard, S. D., Murrell, A., & Thomas, D. (2007). Unfinished business: The impact of race on understanding mentoring relationships. In B. Ragins & K. Kram (Eds.), *The Handbook of Mentoring at Work: Theory, research, and practice* (pp. 223–247). Los Angeles: SAGE.

Bova, B. (2000). Mentoring revisited: The Black woman's experience. *Mentoring & Tutoring: Partnership in Learning*, *8*(1), 5–16.

Bowen, W. G., & Bok, D. (1998). *The Shape of the River: Long-term consequences of considering race in college and university admissions*. Princeton, NJ: Princeton University Press.

Bowman, S. R., Kite, M. E., Branscombe, M. E., & Williams, S. (1999). Developmental relationships of Black Americans in the academy. In A. J. Murrell, F. J. Crosby, & R. J. Ely (Eds.), *Mentoring Dilemmas: developmental relationships within multicultural organizations* (pp. 21–46). Mahwah, NJ: Erlbaum.

Boyd, J. A. (1993). *In the Company of my Sisters: Black women and self-esteem*. New York: Penguin.

Brayboy, B. M. J. (2003). The implementation of diversity in predominantly White colleges and universities. *Journal of Black Studies*, *34*(1), 72–86.

Brinson, J., & Kottler, J. (1993) Cross-cultural mentoring in counselor education: A strategy for retaining minority faculty. *Counselor Education and Supervision*, *32*(4), 241–253.

Byrne, D. (1971). *The Attraction Paradigm*. New York: Academic Press.

Chietji, N., & Hamilton, D. (2006). Estimating the effect of race and ethnicity on wealth accumulation and asset-ownership patterns. In J. G. Nembhard & N. Chiteji (Eds.), *Wealth Accumulation and Communities of Color in the United States* (pp. 67–90). Ann Arbor: University of Michigan Press.

Cohen, G. L., & Steele, C. M. (2002). A barrier of mistrust: How negative stereotypes affect cross-race mentoring. In J. Aronson (Ed.), *Improving Academic Achievement: Impact of psychological factors on education* (pp. 303–327). San Diego: Academic Press.

Cokley, K. (2000). An investigation of academic self-concept and its relationship to academic achievement in African American college students. *Journal of Black Psychology*, *26*(2), 148–164.

Constantine, M. G., Smith, L., Redington, R. M., & Owens, D. (2008). Racial microaggressions against Black counseling and counseling psychology faculty: A central challenge in the multicultural counseling movement. *Journal of Counseling and Development*, *86*, 348–355.

Crutcher, B. N. (2007). Mentoring across cultures. *Education Digest*, *73*(4), 21–25.

D'Augelli, A. R., & Hershberger, S. (1993). African American undergraduates on a predominantly White campus: Academic factors, social networks, and campus climate. *Journal of Negro Education*, *62*(1), 67–81.

Denzin, N. K., Lincoln, Y. S., & Smith, L. T. (Eds.). (2008). *Handbook of Critical and Indigenous Methodologies*. Thousand Oaks, CA: SAGE.

Diekman, A. B., & Eagly, A. H. (2000). Stereotypes as dynamic constructs: Women and men of the past, present, and future. *Personality and Social Psychology Bulletin*, *26*, 1171–1188.

Dingus, J. E. (2008). I'm learning the trade: Mentoring networks of Black women teachers. *Urban Education*, *43*(3), 361–377.

Dreher, G. F., & Cox, T. H., Jr. (1996). Race, gender, and opportunity: A study of compensation attainment and the establishment of mentoring relationships. *Journal of Applied Psychology, 81*(3), 297–308.

Ensher, E. A., & Murphy, S. E. (1997). Effects of race, gender, perceived similarity, and contact on mentor relationships. *Journal of Vocational Behavior, 50,* 460–481.

Fleming, J. (1984). *Blacks in College.* San Francisco: Jossey-Bass.

Foster, M. (1993). Othermothers: Exploring the educational philosophy of Black American women teachers. In M. Arnot & K. Weiler (Eds.), *Feminism and Social Justice in Education: International perspectives* (pp. 101–123). Washington, DC: Falmer.

Frankenberg, R. (1993). *The Social Construction of Whiteness: White women, race matters.* Minneapolis, MN: University of Minnesota Press.

Giroux, H. A. (1997). Rewriting the discourse of racial identity: Towards a pedagogy and politics of whiteness. *Harvard Educational Review, 67*(2), 285–320.

Grant-Thompson, S. K., & Atkinson, D. R. (1997). Cross-cultural mentor effectiveness and African American male students. *Journal of Black Psychology, 23*(2), 120–134.

Gregory, S., & Sanjek, R. (Eds.). (1994). *Race.* New Brunswick, NJ: Rutgers University Press.

Grier, W., & Cobbs, P. (1968). *Black Rage.* New York: Bantam.

Guiffrida, D. (2005). Othermothering as a framework for understanding African American students' definitions of student-centered faculty. *Journal of Higher Education, 76*(6), 702–723.

Gutierrez, L. M. (1990). Working with women of color: An empowerment perspective. *Social Work, 35*(2), 97–192.

Hacker, A. (2008). *Two Nations: Black and White, separate, hostile, unequal.* New York: Ballentine Books.

Hansman, C. A. (2002). Diversity and power in mentoring relationships. In C. A. Hansman (Ed.), *Critical Perspectives on Mentoring: Trends and issues* (pp. 39–48). Columbus, OH: *ERIC Clearinghouse on Adult, Career, and Vocational Education.* Retrieved January 31, 2011, from http://calpro-online.org/eric/docs/mott/mentoring1.pdf

Hansman, C. A. (2005). Reluctant mentors & resistant protégées. *Adult Learning, 14*(1), 14–16.

Hayes, E., & Colin, S. A. J., III. (1994). Racism and sexism in the United States: Fundamental issues. In E. Hayes & S. A. J. Colin, III (Eds.), *Confronting Racism and Sexism. New Directions for Adult and Continuing Education* (p. 61). San Francisco: Jossey-Bass.

Hickson, M. G. (2002). What role does the race of professors have on the retention of students attending historically Black colleges and universities? *Education, 123*(1), 186–189.

hooks, b. (2003). *Teaching Community: Pedagogy of hope.* New York: Routledge.

Hu, C., Thomas, K., & Lance, C. (2008). Intentions to initiate mentoring relationships: Understanding the impact of race, proactivity, feelings of deprivation. *Journal of Social Psychology, 148*(2), 727–747.

Hytten, K., & Warren, J. (2003). Engaging Whiteness: How racial power gets reified in education. *Qualitative Studies in Education, 16*(1), 65–89.

Johnson-Bailey, J. (2006). Transformative learning: A community empowerment conduit for African American women. In S. B. Merriam, B. Courtenay, & R. M. Cervero (Eds.), *Global Issues in Adult Education: Perspectives from Latin America, Southern Africa, and the United States* (pp. 307–318). San Francisco: Jossey-Bass.

Johnson-Bailey, J., & Cervero, R. M. (2000). The invisible politics of race in adult education. In A. L. Wilson & E. R. Hayes (Eds.), *Handbook of Adult and Continuing Education* (pp. 147–160). San Francisco: Jossey-Bass.

Johnson-Bailey, J., & Cervero, R. M. (2004). Mentoring in Black and White: The intricacies of cross-cultural mentoring. *Mentoring & Tutoring: Partnership in Learning, 12*(1), 7–21.

Johnson-Bailey, J., & Cervero, R. M. (2008). Different worlds and divergent paths: Academic careers defined by race and gender. *Harvard Educational Review, 78*(2), 311–332.

Johnson-Bailey, J., Valentine, T., Cervero, R. M., & Bowles, T. A. (2009). Rooted in the soil: The social experiences of Black graduate students at a Southern research university. *Journal of Higher Education, 80*(2), 178–203.

Kovel, J. (1970). *White Racism: A psychohistory*. New York: Vintage.

McGoldrick, M., Giorando, J., & Pierce, J. K. (Eds). (1996). *Ethnicity and Family Therapy*. New York: Guilford.

McIntosh, P. (1995). White privilege and male privilege: A personal accounting of coming to see correspondences through work in women's studies. In M. L. Andersen & P. H. Collins (Eds.), *Race, Class, and Gender: An anthology* (2nd ed., pp. 76–87). Belmont, CA: Wadsworth.

Moore, P. J., & Toliver, S. D. (2010). Intraracial dynamics of Black professors' and Black students' communication in traditionally White colleges and universities. *Journal of Black Studies, 40*(5), 932–945.

Nettles, M. T. (Ed.). (1988). *Toward Black Undergraduate Student Equality in American Higher Education*. Westport, CT: Greenwood.

Nettles, M. T., & Millett, C. M. (2006). *Three Magic Letters: Getting to Ph.D.* Baltimore, MD: Johns Hopkins University Press.

Omi, M., & Winant, H. (1994). *Racial Formation in the United States: From the 1960s to the 1990s*. New York: Routledge.

O'Neill, R. N., Horton, S., & Crosby, F. J. (1999). Gender issues in developmental relationships. In A. J. Murrell, F. J. Crosby, & R. J. Ely (Eds.), *Mentoring Dilemmas: Developmental relationships within multicultural organizations* (pp. 63–80). Mahwah, NJ: Erlbaum.

Palmer, G. A., & Johnson-Bailey, J. (2008). The impact of mentoring on the careers of African Americans. *Canadian Journal of Career Development, 7*(1), 45–51.

Patton, L. D., & Harper, S. R. (2003). Mentoring relationship among African American women in graduate and professional schools. *New Directions for Student Services, 104*, 67–78.

Ragins, B. R. (1997). Diversified mentoring relationships in organizations: A power perspective. *Academy of Management Review, 22*, 482–521.

Ronstein, P., Rothblum, E., & Solomon, S. E. (1993). Ivy halls and glass walls: Barriers to academic careers for women and ethnic minorities. *New Directions, 53*, 17–31.

Scott, K. (1991). *The Habit of Surviving: Black women's strategies for life*. New York: Ballantine.

Sensoy, O., & DiAngelo, R. (2009). Developing social justice literacy. *Phi Delta Kappan, 90*(5), 345–352.

Swim, J., Hyers, L., Cohen, L., Fitzgerald, D., & Bylsma, W. (2003). African American college students' experiences with everyday racism. *Journal of Black Psychology, 29*(1), 38–67.

Tatum, B. D. (1997). *Why are all the Black Kids Sitting Together in the Cafeteria? And other conversations about race*. New York: Basic Books.

Taylor, G. S. (2000). Talking to the dream keepers: Culturally responsive teachers on the educational experiences of African American students. *Action in Teacher Education, 21*(4), 101–109.

Thomas, D. A. (1990). The impact of race on managers' experiences of developmental relationships (mentoring and sponsorship): An intra-organizational study. *Journal of Organizational Behavior, 11*, 479–492.

Thomas, D. A. (1993a). Mentoring and irrationality: The role of racial taboos. In L. Hirschhorn & C. K. Barnett (Eds.), *The Psychodynamics of Organizations* (pp. 191–202). Philadelphia: Temple University Press.

Thomas, D. A. (1993b). Racial dynamics in cross-race developmental relationships. *Administrative Science Quarterly, 38*, 169–194.

Thomas, D. A. (2001). The truth about mentoring minorities: race matters. *Harvard Business Review, 79*(4), 98–107.

Thomas, G. D., & Hollenshead, C. (2001). Resisting from the margins: The coping strategies of Black women and other women of color faculty members at a research university. *Journal of Negro Education, 70*(3), 166–175.

Thompson, G. L., & Louque, A. C. (2005). *Exposing the "Culture of Arrogance" in the Academy: A blueprint for increasing Black faculty satisfaction in higher education*. Sterling, VA: Stylus.

Tinto, V. (1993). *Leaving College: Rethinking the causes and cures of student attrition*. Chicago, IL: University of Chicago Press.

Turban, D. B., Dougherty, T. W., & Lee, F. K. (2002). Gender, race, and perceived similarity effects in developmental relationships: The moderating role of relationship duration. *Journal of Vocational Behavior*, *61*, 240–262.

Webster, D.W., Sedlack, W.E., & Miyares, J. (1979). A comparison of problems perceived by minority and White university students. *Journal of College Student Personnel*, *2*, 165–170.

Winkler, J. A. (2000). Faculty reappointment, tenure, and promotion: Barriers for women. *Professional Geographer*, *52*, 737–750.

Mentoring Innovation Through Online Communications in a Digital Culture

Helga Dorner

INTRODUCTION

The mentoring process is being rethought in teacher training and teachers' professional development. A shift from the hierarchical, one-to-one, expert-to-novice transfer into making mentoring a reciprocal and mutual process has emerged. Consequently, the view on mentoring has broadened to include learning communities that enable supportive interpersonal relationships that enhance teachers' professional growth. Various terms refer to such learning communities: teacher research groups (Grimmett, 1995), learning circles (Collay, Dunlap, Enloe, and Gagnon, 1998), teacher networks (Lieberman, 2000), and democratic learning communities (Mullen, 2009). These communities provide for supportive interpersonal relationships where the expert–novice transfer and the hierarchies attached to it are reduced and relationships are more equal and collegial (Lieberman, 2000, Mullen, 2009). Through such communities, teachers are supported to engage in pedagogical practices resulting in changes that seem inevitable for effective teaching and learning processes in the twenty-first century.

With the emergence of new technologies and expectations towards schools and education in general, it has become necessary to transform the Hungarian educational system into a more adaptive learning organisation capable of efficient growth and development. It is well known that teachers' personal and professional knowledge are chief constituents of the educational system. However, the personal and professional growth of teachers is virtually impossible without proper training and professional feedback. A potential way to guide teachers in this development process, especially as concerning the pedagogical use of new technologies, is to invite them to participate in international educational research projects as active collaborating members. This should be considered as a step towards the research-based teacher training and teachers' professional training in Hungary (Csapó, 2007).

The study I describe here includes a brief overview of the design principles and practical applications of the Mentored Innovation Model (MIM). This had been employed as the instructional context for the research-based training of Hungarian preservice and inservice teachers. The MIM was used to collaborate with online teacher communities using the framework of international projects where mentors (facilitators) provide professional mentoring. Peers and mentors endeavour to 'scaffold' participants' knowledge creation in virtual learning environments to support innovative practices.

THEORETICAL SOURCES OF INNOVATION AND COLLABORATION

Theories of social learning such as Vygotsky's (1978) ideas on social mediation and Engeström's (2001) activity theory claim that cognition is a situated activity rooted in social practices. These espouse that the study of individuals' learning is embedded in social, cultural contexts, and interactions. Both approaches served as a source of inspiration when developing the model. A key idea connecting Vygotsky's and Engeström's ideas is mediation on which the MIM strongly relies. Vygotsky's model included three elements: subject, object, and mediating artefact. A stimulus–response relationship transcended by a mediated act described the relationship between the elements of this triad. Opposed to this, Engeström (1987) proposed a more complex model that involves expansive cycles of development in which he refers to learning as an 'activity-producing activity' and a 'mastery of expansion from action to a new activity' (1987: 125).

Based on the tenet of social mediation, teachers' development is assumed to be better achieved if these educators are participating in shared activities. In the MIM, such activities are the innovative educational programme and the professional development exercise. Similar to the ideal–typical cycles of Engeström's (1987) model and opposed to the traditional (dialogical) model for mentoring, the MIM is integrated in school practice and has a spiral structure. This is contrary to the traditional dialogical model, which is linear. In this spiral structure, cycles of exploration, learning, and creation of new knowledge are iterated on higher levels. Accordingly, the model includes these steps (Dorner and Kárpáti, 2008, 2010):

1 Problems are identified and elaborated separately by teams of teachers and researchers.
2 A common research and development agenda is negotiated, with the involvement of local community stakeholders (policy makers, parents, etc.).

3   Supporting structures to solve complex pedagogical problems are provided by researchers and training experts (mentoring).
4   Shared objects of activity are identified and developed (mentored innovation).
5   Cognitive tools are employed to promote scaffolding through structuring inquirers' activities in a way that facilitates complex problem solving.
6   Design-based research in the form of school experiments is performed in several iterations to test problem-solving strategies, refine shared pedagogical objects (teaching programmes and aids, evaluation instruments, social involvement campaign strategies, etc.).
7   Local and national level dissemination of results is organised through a wide variety of channels (ranging from community campaigns to educational conferences).
8   Teachers redefine professional self. Both teachers and participating educational researchers (who collaborate with teachers) act as innovators and mentors for new adaptors of teaching programmes.

In the preservice teacher training, an adjusted form of the MIM is used (Dorner and Major, 2009). Mentoring events are organised to initiate teacher novices to a professional culture and create or share artefacts through interactions with peers and experts. It encompasses most of the previously described features of the MIM; however, joint research agendas are created in small groups of preservice teachers and dissemination occurs within study groups. The adjusted model involves role modelling with respect to the roles of the practicing teacher (teacher trainer), educational researcher, and the education policymaker. Preservice teachers follow the process of making curricular decisions, planning for authentic teaching and learning processes, collecting, creating or adapting digital and traditional teaching aids (Dorner and Major, 2008).

In the MIM, the tenet of collaborative knowledge building (Scardamalia and Bereiter, 1994) is considered as learning theory, pedagogical theory, and even pedagogical strategy. Members of preservice and inservice teacher communities learn from each other because they engage criticality, adaptation, or adoption of resources in online mentoring scenarios, which trigger specific learning mechanisms. When mentoring is successful, individual cognition is encouraged in peer interaction: interaction among participants generates extra activities (explanation, disagreement, mutual regulation), which in turn perpetuate extra cognitive mechanisms (Dillenbourg, 1999, 2002; Dorner and Major, 2009; Kárpáti and Dorner, 2008).

In the current context, the role of the other individual as a mediator of meaning is inevitable. In the MIM, social mediation (Vygotsky, 1978) and scaffolding learning with expert guidance are online mentors' responsibilities. Preservice and inservice teachers in their communities participate in inquiries at the frontiers of knowledge. Their activities with online mentors can be characterised as transformative communication for learning (Kárpáti and Dorner, 2008).

PILOT RESEARCH AND INITIAL PRACTICAL APPLICATIONS

In Hungary, the nationwide educational computerisation and the potential pedagogical innovations attached to it evolved in three phases (Kárpáti, 2004).

Phase 1 was characterised by the immense investment campaigns into information communication technology (ICT) within the infrastructure of schools. In the second phase, however, both policymakers' and researchers' attention turned to the training of inservice teachers, with focus on ICT skills and discipline-based methodology in computer usage. The third phase (including the most recent developments) is substantially defined by digital (educational) content development and the diffusion of methodologies on ICT usage.

Pilot studies about the efficacy of ICT-related investments emerged in the second and third phase of national educational computerisation. In Hungary, the Organisation for Economic Cooperation and Development (OECD) initiated the research project 'ICT and the Quality of Learning.' This was among the first pilot studies that investigated the relation between ICT use and the quality of teaching in school-based qualitative case studies (Venezky and Davis, 2001). Altogether, 91 case studies were documented in 23 countries. In Hungary, two primary schools and four secondary schools, private and public alike, were involved (Kárpáti, 2003). Findings revealed that the presence of ICT infrastructure does not necessarily lead to educational innovation. It turned out that teachers' teaching philosophies and skills impact immensely on the success of the pedagogical implementation of ICT tools within primary and secondary schools. A direct relation was detected between the quality of ICT-based teaching and the pedagogical inventory of the teacher (Kárpáti, 2003). Hence, the potential of inservice teachers during educational innovation was realised. Nevertheless, Hungarian school studies involved only institutions with previous innovatory experiences, that is, ICT pioneers or innovators (Rogers, 1995). Even in their case, teachers and school leaders were sceptical about the possibilities hidden in the frequent pedagogical implementation of the ICT tools and their costly maintenance. Accordingly, as an immediate reaction to the local needs, *ad locum* mentoring scenarios were initiated involving groups of inservice teachers and university staff members, instead of formalised inservice teacher training (Kárpáti, 2003).

A more formalised mentoring, essentially a role modelling method, was utilised in another OECD initiated effort, 'Promoting Equity through ICT in Education'. This was accomplished in Hungary by the active involvement of the research team of the UNESCO Centre for ICT at the Eötvös Loránd University (ELTE). The Romani (Gypsy) Education Through ICT Project (2003–2005) promoted the use of ICT as part of a modern educational culture in schools and communities that had no previous innovatory experience and were situated in the economically most disadvantaged areas of the country. In this project, inservice teachers were grouped in discipline-based ICT study circles facilitated by mentors (research team members), experienced teachers, and specialists in educational technology (Kárpáti, 2004). They monthly participated in organised face-to-face mentoring scenarios focusing on providing resources and discussing useful experience in peer groups. Research mainly focused on the learning efforts of the involved learners, such as their general thinking skills, operational abilities, reading comprehension, and learning abilities (Kárpáti and Molnár, 2004). However, teachers' abilities and competences were not tested for research purposes, and neither was the efficacy of the mentored innovation (role modelling method) nor that of the mentoring dialogues measured. Content prepared by the inservice teachers (e.g., web pages, presentations) and informal feedback from the inservice teachers and their mentors provided a source of information for further developments. Feedback revealed that mentors most often had to be competent as social workers, fundraisers, helpdesk technicians, and moral supporters (Fehér, 2004; Kárpáti, 2004).

The European Pedagogical ICT Licence (EPICT) project (which Hungary joined in 2004) was the first initiative involving research efforts. It focused on the assessment of the MIM, a standardised inservice teacher-training programme based on the online collaboration of practitioners' groups facilitated by online mentors experienced with ICT. Results of the competence development study showed that, through the MIM, teachers' ICT competence and communicative competence were enhanced and their attitude and methodological inventory concerning the pedagogical ICT use changed in a positive way (Kárpáti and Ollé, 2007). As concerns teachers' pedagogical toolkit, results suggested that teachers relied less frequently on static and rigid techniques and instead designed lessons allowing for learner initiatives otherwise unplanned but useful activities in the classroom. The teachers' intention to apply techniques reliant on learner cooperation enhanced, whereas the frequency of teacher–learner cooperation incentives decreased (Kárpáti and Ollé, 2007).

THE MENTORED INNOVATION MODEL IN PRACTICE

The previous studies I reviewed generally suggested that one of the key factors in teachers' professional development and competence enhancement was the quality of mentoring. This recognition resulted in a more concentrated effort in studies of online mentoring dialogues and the mentor's roles in the MIM in the two European Union funded research-and-development projects (Dorner and Kárpáti, 2010; Kárpáti and Dorner, 2008).

The Calibrate and the Knowledge Practices Laboratory (KP-Lab) projects both provided a unique opportunity for reconsidering the content of teacher training and teachers' professional development programmes. In both projects, online mentoring interactions were examined in the context of collaborative practices and activities, with the goal of revealing any changing participant behaviour from individual professional to professional team player.

For the in-depth analysis of online mentoring interactions, data source, and methodological triangulation were used. In the macro-level analysis of interaction patterns, Social Network Analysis (SNA) was used, which relies on quantitative (surface-level) data gained from the *a posteriori* analysis of evolving interactions in online mentoring.

Content analysis (CA) allowed for an *a posteriori* micro-level analysis of online interactions – the texts created by the participants in the online processes. In both projects, CA was an adjusted version of Garrison, Anderson, and Archer's (2000) model (and indicators) of a community of inquiry (CoI). It is a model that maps and defines educational presence (Garrison and Cleveland-Innes, 2005). Educational presence is composed of social, teaching, and cognitive presence, thus the CoI considers these three pillars and integrates them (Garrison and Anderson, 2003). The complete structure of the CoI has been validated (see, e.g., Arbaugh, 2007; Arbaugh and Hwang, 2006; Garrison and Cleveland-Innes, 2005).

The main findings of the CA and the SNA from both projects and their pedagogical implications are next elaborated. With the SNA, quantification and visualisation of the interaction patterns with special attention to the position and parameters of the mentor were provided. In the process of CA, complete messages were coded by using the CoI indicators, and Holsti's coefficient of reliability served as intercoder reliability measure. However, no inferential statistical tests were conducted with respect to the quantitative data; results were used to make comparisons in relative terms. Further, results of the CA and the SNA were not tested against learning outcomes but were interpreted in a comparative research manner.

MENTORING IN INSERVICE TEACHER COMMUNITIES

The aim of the European Calibrate project supported by the Information Society Technologies (IST) programme and coordinated by the European Schoolnet (EUN) was to catalyse the collaborative use of learning resources in pedagogical scenarios. Eight Ministries of Education linked their national digital learning content repositories, investigated new search functions like curriculum mapping of resources, and established a new open-source web community for finding, authoring, and sharing learning resources.

The project had two iterations (Calibrate 1 and Calibrate 2) where Hungarian inservice teachers ($n_1 = 23$ and $n_2 = 20$) worked in collaboration with their colleagues, pupils, facilitators, and educational researchers using the framework of introducing the European Learning Resources Exchange (LRE).

Activities of the first iteration were hosted in the Future Learning Environment (FLE3), which is the third version of a web-based, open source software to support computer-supported collaborative learning (CSCL). In the second iteration, the community platform and social software LeMill, newly developed for the support of the repository, was used for collaboration purposes.

Results of the Calibrate project revealed that mentoring differed in the two iterations. In the first iteration, the online mentor's teaching presence most often focused on the pedagogical or instructor role (Hootstein, 2002). The mentor as a consultant and resource provider offered scaffolding to the participants in their growing understanding through direct instruction and facilitating discourse by initiating questions and provoking responses from them, and focusing discussions on crucial points. Also, actions related to the mentor's managerial role were manifested in the online interactions: designing instructional methods, negotiating timelines for activities and tasks, and providing guidelines and tips concerning the appropriate use of the medium. In the second iteration, the mentor relied on a wider scale of mentoring assets; when providing direct instruction and scaffolding online discussions, s/he made more use of subject matter and pedagogical expertise and less often adopted the role of a manager and organiser of online processes.

The two iterations differed not only in the mentors' approaches (teaching presence) but also in the social presence; that is, the extent to which inservice teachers experienced each other as 'real' in the mentoring process. They most often relied on communication in which social presence had predominantly manifestations of linguistic nature. Messages of this type included salutations, address forms, and reference to the group by using inclusive pronouns. In the second iteration, participants disclosed and exchanged personal information and shared the 'community' experience. Hence, social interactions allowed for the formation of individualised impressions of the group members and the network displayed a more balanced, horizontal interaction pattern.

As the social network analysis revealed, in a network where activities were more intensively connected to the facilitator, as in the first iteration, the mentor's teaching presence focused considerably on the design of instructional methods, negotiation of timelines for activities and tasks, and provision of the appropriate use of the medium. While in a network with less intensive relations, and with participants less dependent on the mentor's involvement as in the second iteration, the mentor's teaching presence was predominantly defined by the instructional role. In this case, facilitation of discussion was usually integrated within direct instruction and *in situ* design of instructional activity.

With the analysis of mentoring interactions, it was revealed that inservice teacher participants relied mostly on elementary levels of cognitive engagement in both iterations. They most often contributed by responding to a message in which they offered feedback or described a problem. One-fourth of the participant messages were informative statements, which contained anecdotal or personal information related to the discussion topic. These informative types of messages demonstrated comprehension of the issues under discussion and often involved in-depth clarification. The highest cognitive engagement manifested in the explanatory and analytical messages. However, despite these types of messages, discussions did not generate synthesising or evaluative statements. Only a minority of statements presented information with limited personal opinions and demonstrated negotiation of meanings or thoughtful analysis.

The lower level of cognitive engagement found in these cases suggests similarities with the findings of previous research (Kanuka and Anderson, 1998; Zhu, 2006). It was revealed that an extensive part of online communication was of sharing and comparing kind. However, lower cognitive engagement in the online discussions does not necessarily mean that participants had not profited from the online mentoring. These moderated interactions captured only part of the mentoring experience, which also incorporated collaboration around shared objects and the development and testing of digital contents in classroom context. In fact, the participant satisfaction survey (which was summative) revealed that among the four investigated aspects – participants' global satisfaction, mentor's role, online communication in the CSCL environments, and perceived social presence – the moderated online interactions and the mentors' role had the greatest impact on inservice teachers' satisfaction with the mentoring experience. Moderated interactions and the mentor's role were identified as the most important (direct) indicators of participant satisfaction in the MIM (Dorner and Kárpáti, 2008, 2010).

Content analyses also revealed that cognitive engagement in the first iteration was higher than in the second. Accordingly, mentoring where the mentor adopts the pedagogical and instructional role that generates a robust network consisting of strong and weak ties respectively – but without the support of a network centred on the involvement of the mentor – does not necessarily result in higher cognitive engagement. In reality, the present scenarios revealed that in a socially less active network with a more directive type of 'guide on the side' facilitation, higher cognitive level was reached.

MENTORING IN PRESERVICE TEACHER COMMUNITIES

In the KP-Lab project, ICT tools are employed to catalyse change from individual to collective knowledge creation practices and agents of the knowledge society (students, teachers, professionals, designers, and researchers) work together on new models for professional skills development based on the concept of trialogical knowledge creation (Paavola, Lipponen, and Hakkarainen, 2002). The Hungarian cases focus on the collaborations among the participants of teacher training courses ($n_1 = 20$; $n_2 = 20$; $n_3 = 18$; $n_4 = 21$; $n_5 = 19$; and $n_6 = 18$) designed in a blended form. In each case, within the large group, micro-communities of five to six preservice teachers worked to create course artefacts and practice pedagogy in an authentic learning environment.

The Moodle platform hosted the online activities (https://elearning.elte.hu). The choice of the online platform lies in the constructivist philosophy of Moodle, which is grounded in the theories of social learning.

Activity analyses showed that in densely knit networks (intensive communication among group members) less intensive teaching presence relied on a wide range of facilitator assets and on the conscious use of pedagogical expertise. In these networks, direct instruction and content provision were maintained by skilful scaffolding of online interactions. Also, increasing cognitive engagement or high levels of cognitive presence and deeper levels of information processing were typical of these networks where discussions were maintained on a group level with all the members involved. The group did not necessarily include the mentor. Instead of her or his active involvement, interactivity (mutually established relations) and a proactive manner of communication prevailed. Interestingly, increasing cognitive engagement prevailed in certain loosely knit networks with participants working in pairs or triads. In their case, however, social presence and the mentor's teaching presence resembled that of the dense communities. Low-level cognitive engagement and surface-level information processing were linked to loose networks where participants worked in pairs or triads, mostly together with the facilitator. In such networks, intensive teaching presence based on an assistive role prevailed.

Social presence, in the previously referenced communities, was characterised by interpersonal interactions with socially appreciative nature where despite group commitment less emotional presence was typical. As opposed to this, social presence in highly interactive networks manifested itself in socially meaningful interactions, and sense of community and emotional presence, which allowed for personalised impressions to form.

Less intensive teaching presence resulted in direct instruction and either content provision maintained by skilful scaffolding or generated mentoring focusing on reinforcement. Both approaches favoured the evolving of socially meaningful interactions. The effect of an intensive teaching presence focusing on reinforcement was reciprocal. This type of teaching presence was associated with social passivity and the lowest level of cognitive engagement.

ONLINE MENTOR ROLES

Based on the results from both projects, two overarching mentoring approaches emerged: guide on the side and resource provider (see Table 11.1). (Hootstein [2002] when he described characteristics of the facilitator's instructional role

Table 11.1   Mentor types in Hungarian preservice and inservice teacher communities

Mentor types	Guide on the side	Resource provider
Approach	Interactive approach	Directive approach
Facilitation style	Proactive facilitation	Reactive facilitation
Network characteristics	Group-level interactions Less intensive facilitator behaviour Densely knit networks A network consisting of strong and weak ties Supportive environment for collaborations	Individual work, pair work, or triads Facilitator as key person Network structure more centred on the facilitator – strong ties with facilitator Loose networks Less supportive environment for collaborations

first introduced the latter category, while the other one is referred to as a commonly used notion in the professional terminology of mentoring.) As the term suggests, the 'guide on the side' mentor was an online instructor who attended to a socially active community and maintained horizontal group architecture. The 'resource provider' mentor, even if s/he applied collaborative instructional design, relied on a stronger instructor presence and a more directive facilitation. This latter approach was characterised by a vertical structure of the workflow and a hierarchical group architecture where the socially less active mentor and eventually a few members obtained the 'top positions'. Under such circumstances, the participants' performance or activity acknowledged by the mentor had a strong impact on participants' satisfaction with the learning experience.

Further in-depth participant activity analyses showed that online facilitation in the mentoring process is more than mere direct instruction. It encompasses providing a comfortable learning experience and the online mentor's social engagement. However, successful professional scaffolding and mentors' pedagogical or instructor role aiming at effective 'instruction' were not necessarily accompanied by socially active mentor behaviour.

Consequently, in line with previous research findings (de Lièvre, Depover, and Dillenbourg, 2006; Young, Bullough, Draper, Smith, and Erickson, 2005), directive mentors who aimed at mainly direct instruction and interactive mentors were differentiated. The former approach was based on reactive mentoring where the instructor reacted exclusively to the participants' requests, whereas the latter type of instructor facilitated in a proactive manner. Proactive mentoring encompassed the mentor's own initiative for entering the participants' learning process by not only supporting on-task professional discussions but also providing a comfortable learning experience by acting as a socially engaged member of the learning community.

MENTORING APPROACH, NETWORK INTERACTION STRUCTURE, AND COLLABORATION

Case studies (of the two empirical research projects) described herein suggested that more mentor messages as well as increased intensive participation in the online interactions did not necessarily guarantee balanced group-level communication patterns and a mutual, intensive, community-level interaction. Neither did reduced mentor activity hamper intensive communication and evolving collaboration in a network. Instead, the incoming and the outbound mentor relations should be in balance. This is the case when the instructor receives and creates the same number of messages or the mentor's activity is characterised by slightly more outgoing linkages than incoming ones. In such networks, more intensive and broad-based participation evolves. This generates mutual interactions and higher level of community, considered prerequisites of group collaborations. Accordingly, interactive mentors, who facilitated in a proactive manner provided better for the preconditions of collaborations. If, however, the mentor's activity shifted to either extreme – mentor outbound communication dominated participant contributions, or s/he was the recipient of most of the incoming linkages – then this most probably hampered the development of balanced interaction patterns and the horizontal flow of information among participants. Hence, the preconditions of collaboration were not met. Analogously, the case when the incoming and outbound mentor communication was in balance but the mentor established strong links exclusively with the same (in most cases a limited number of) participants was not ideal either. This type of interactive pattern was characteristic of reactive mentoring. It must be noted for the sake of completeness and validity that in those groups where participant activity stayed low throughout the mentoring process the mentor's efforts of any kind did not result in an interactive mentoring event. Thus, the importance of group composition (the ratio of active and passive communicators) is assumed a success factor in online mentoring scenarios.

COGNITIVE ENGAGEMENT AND NETWORK TIES

As concerns the relation between cognitive engagement and the strength of connectedness, weak ties were not adequate for transmitting complex knowledge and mediating new information in the pedagogical scenarios. This finding does not necessarily contest the paradigm according to which weak connections make a network robust (Csermely, 2005), but especially in the case of small networks (with five to eight members) defining the minimum strength of weak ties is vital. In the presented scenarios, one-directional linkages and links providing for one-time information exchange were identified as the 'minimum' strength. However, these were inadequate for sharing in-depth expertise or knowledge. Consequently, higher activity level of the participants and more intensive communication could contribute to evolving group-level discussions, and presumably provide the backbone for collaborations and cognitive engagement.

PEDAGOGICAL IMPLICATIONS OF FINDINGS AND MIM DEVELOPMENTS

The MIM has gone a long way since the first application of ad hoc mentoring scenarios as a reaction to inservice teachers' local needs and its transformation into an intentionally designed face-to-face mentoring method and finally to its online adaptation. Naturally, the most current and future challenges are still ahead of the developers of the model. Many rounds of evaluation, revision, and development are needed in order to assess the efficacy of the MIM; the aim is to identify and use mentoring scenarios where mentors are the most efficient. The analysis of online interactions is one possible tool in the evaluation process.

In the scenarios I presented, it proved an effective one in the in-depth analysis of underlying group mechanisms (including the mentors' actions) in online learning communities, leading to the pedagogical implications.

ONLINE MENTORS' TEACHING PRESENCE IN ONLINE MENTORING

Online communication is a crucial element, which may be on-task or off-task, and can take the form of one-to-one, one-to-many, or many-to-many interactions. Agents involved in the design and conduction of online mentoring processes such as those involved in the MIM should devote attention to well-designed, purposeful online communication that aims at facilitating interactions to contribute to participants' growing understanding and joint knowledge construction. Online mentors' teaching presence has an overarching magnitude with regard to educational presence in online mentoring and involves course design and organisation, facilitating discourse (including social aspects of communication and community building) and employing direct instruction at the same time (Anderson, Rourke, Garrison, and Archer, 2001). Accordingly, online mentors should be trained and prepared in the framework of formal education so they can apply the tenet of collaborative learning when involved in online group learning projects. Findings of the two international research projects in which the MIM was used as an instructional context are relevant for the further development of the model itself and for the design and the implementation of such trainings.

Mentors' online activity and mentoring dialogues are indicators of participant satisfaction since purposeful online mentoring interactions optimally contribute to participants' understanding of the content and their knowledge construction.

In the reported cases, despite the mentors being experienced practitioners and experts in the field, they managed to succeed, albeit to a limited extent. Successful in this context means scaffolding higher levels of cognitive engagement and as socially active community members encouraging online collaboration and joint work. Taking this into consideration, requirements concerning mentors' role and their online activity should be clearly formulated; teaching and learning aims and the pedagogical realisation of them must be defined precisely and eventually benchmarked with special focus on online communication among peers and with the mentor. Shared objects of activity should be described in advance in collaboration with the participants of the mentoring process.

Also, mentors and designers of the model have to acquire a common understanding of the most fitting philosophies and effective mentoring approaches so they can use the most appropriate strategies for facilitating ad hoc interactions (even if shared objects of activity are pre-defined jointly). They will also want to strive to provide support to address or solve complex pedagogical problems. Even if this seems trivial, it still has not been repeated enough times that mentors should be sensitive towards group mechanisms and they should adjust their mentoring approach to the given target population. In our studies, experienced, well-prepared mentors made the mistake of relying on their so-far applied mentoring techniques. They thus failed to 'ride the waves of interactions' as they developed and followed the community workflow. Naturally, mentors' communicative competence in facilitating knowledge construction is the most difficult to address, since it largely depends on the mentor's character and identical scenarios with the same wording do not occur. Nevertheless, developers of the model and mentors who collaborate with them should all face this challenge.

MENTORING APPROACH AND MENTORS' ONLINE ACTIVITY

Based on the findings of the two studies, mentors and developers of the mentoring model should jointly plan the online mentoring scenarios in advance with special focus on the learning outcomes of online interactions. Prerequisites of this effort are knowledge and application of the methodology of collaborative instructional design including theoretical background, design principles, and applicable pedagogical tools and strategies. Flexibility and sensitivity towards online group mechanisms are inevitable when designing mentoring scenarios and their potential outcomes. As results showed, group composition, the ratio of active versus passive, or experienced versus less experienced online communicators in a network impacts the strength of interactions and participants' cognitive engagement. In this context, the minimum strength of linkages, which are appropriate for sharing knowledge and in-depth expertise should be pre-defined. Interactive and proactive facilitator behaviour (as opposed to reactive and directive manner) proved more efficient in supporting interactivity, a higher level of participant activity, and group discussions, in addition to collaboration.

Online mentoring is more than direct instruction. It is also about providing a comfortable learning experience. Beyond mentors' teaching presence (including facilitating online mentoring interactions), flexible tool mediation provided by the actual means of communication – in the present study CSCL environments – are to be considered since it is the online communication tool that supports various online activities. Being able to operate the tool itself correlates with participants' skills and competencies involved in computer and Internet usage. Consequently, ICT skills analyses and sufficient (formal or informal) preparation for the online mentoring process are indispensable. The lack of these contributes to participant dissatisfaction and an unsuccessful and inefficient mentoring experience, which causes withdrawals and dropouts. Finally, since ICT skills and competencies are crucial prerequisites of the online mentoring experience, it is also a must for mentors. Beyond their pedagogical or instructional roles and as social directors they must be efficient in their guiding role and technical help (Hootstein, 2002) as well.

ACKNOWLEDGEMENTS

This paper is based on research supported by two EU funded research and development projects, Calibrate (2005–2007, www.calibrate.eun.org) and Knowledge Practice Laboratory Project (2006–2011, KP-Lab, www.kp-lab.org,).

REFERENCES

Anderson, T., Rourke, L., Garrison, D. R., & Archer, W. (2001). Assessing teaching presence in a computer conference context. *Journal of Asynchronous Learning Networks*, *5*(2), 1–17.

Arbaugh, J. B. (2007). An empirical verification of the community of inquiry framework. *Journal of Asynchronous Learning Networks*, *11*, 73–85.

Arbaugh, J. B., & Hwang, A. (2006). Does 'teaching presence' exist in online MBA courses? *The Internet and Higher Education*, *9*(1), 9–21.

Collay, M., Dunlap, D., Enloe, W., & Gagnon, G. (1998). *Learning Circles: Creating Conditions for Professional Development.* Thousand Oaks, CA: Corwin.

Csapó, B. (2007). A tanári tudás szerepe az oktatási rendszer fejlesztésében [translated: Teachers' knowledge in developing the educational system]. *Új Pedagógiai Szemle*, *3–4*, 11–23.

Csermely, P. (2005). *A rejtett hálózatok ereje. Mi segíti a világ stabilitását?* [translated: The strength of hidden networks. What contributes to universal stability?] Budapest: Vince Kiadó.

de Lièvre, B., Depover, C., & Dillenbourg P. (2006). The relationship between tutoring mode and learners' use of help tools in distance education. *Instructional Science*, *34*, 97–129.

Dillenbourg, P. (1999). What do you mean by 'collaborative learning'? In P. Dillenbourg (Ed.), *Collaborative Learning: cognitive and computational approaches* (pp. 1–19). Oxford: Elsevier.

Dillenbourg, P. (2002). Over-scripting CSCL: The risks of blending collaborative learning with instructional design. In P.A. Kirshner (Ed.), *Three Worlds of CSCL: Can we support CSCL?* (pp. 61–91). Heerlen: Open Universiteit Nederland.

Dorner, H., & Kárpáti, A. (2008). Mentorált innováció virtuális tanulási környezetben [translated: Mentored innovation in virtual learning environments]. *Magyar Pedagógia*, *108*(3), 225–246.

Dorner, H. & Kárpáti, A. (2010). Mentoring for innovation: Key factors affecting participant satisfaction in the process of collaborative knowledge construction in teacher training. *Journal of Asynchronous Learning Networks*, *14*(3), 63–77.

Dorner, H., & Major, É. (2008). Developing common collaborative discourse – a model in teacher training. A paper presented at the 3rd European Practice Based and Practitioner Research Conference on Learning and Instruction, November, Bergen, Norway.

Dorner, H., & Major, É. (2009). Evolving collaboration among teacher trainees – analysis of collaborative discourse. *WoPaLP*, *3*, 76–96. Retrieved January 23, 2011, from http://langped.elte.hu/W3Dorner_Major.pdf

Engeström, Y. (1987). *Learning by Expanding.* Helsinki: Orienta-Konsultit.

Engeström, Y. (2001). Expansive learning at work: Toward an activity theoretical reconceptualisation. *Journal of Education and Work*, *14*(1), 133–156.

Fehér, P. (2004). Az OECD Roma Informatikai Projektjének eredményeirol [translated: About the results of the OECD Roma Informatics Project]. *Új Pedagógiai Szemle.* Retrieved January 24, 2011, from http://www.oki.hu/oldal.php?tipus=cikk&kod=2004-06-in-Feher-OECD

Garrison, D. R., & Anderson, T. (2003). *E-learning in the 21st Century: A Framework for Research and Practice.* London: Routledge.

Garrison, D. R., Anderson, T., & Archer, W. (2000). Critical inquiry in a text-based environment: Computer conferencing in higher education. *The Internet and Higher Education*, *2*(2–3), 87–105.

Garrison, D. R., & Cleveland-Innes, M. (2005). Facilitating cognitive presence in online learning: Interaction is not enough. *American Journal of Distance Education*, *19*(3), 133–148.

Grimmett, P. (1995). Developing voice through teacher research: Implications for educational policy. In J. Smyth (Ed.), *Critical Discourses on Teacher Development* (pp. 113–129). London: Cassell.

Hootstein, E. (2002). *Wearing Four Pairs of Shoes: The Roles of E-learning Facilitators.* Retrieved January 24, 2011, from http://www.learningcircuits.org/2002/oct2002/elearn.html

Kanuka, H., & Anderson, T. (1998). Online social interchange, discord, and knowledge construction. *Journal of Distance Education, 13.* Retrieved January 22, 2011, from http://cade.athabascau.ca/vol13.1/kanuka.html

Kárpáti, A. (2003). ICT and the quality of learning at Hungarian school—results of the OECD study. In C. Dowling, & L. Kwok-Wing (Eds.), *Information and Communication Technology and the Teacher of the Future* (pp. 235–246). Boston, Dordrecht, London: Kluwer.

Kárpáti, A. (2004). *Promoting Equity Through ICT in Education.* Paris: OECD.

Kárpáti, A., & Dorner, H. (2008). Mentored innovation model in teacher training using two virtual collaborative learning environments. In J. Zumbach, N. Schwartz, N. Seufert, & L. Kester (Eds.), *Learning and Instruction with Computers, Beyond Knowledge: The legacy of competence meaningful computer-based learning environments* (pp. 29–41). Wien: Springer Verlag.

Kárpáti, A., & Molnár, É. (2004). Képességfejlesztés az oktatási informatika eszközeivel [translated: Competence enhancement by using ICT tools]. *Magyar Pedagógia, 104*(3), 293–317.

Kárpáti, A., & Ollé, J. (2007). Tanárok informatikai képességeinek és pedagógiai stratégiáinak integrált fejlesztése [translated: An integrated development of teachers' ICT competence and pedagogical strategies]. *Iskolakultúra 4*, 14–23.

Lieberman, A. (2000). Networks as learning communities, shaping the future of teacher development. *Journal of Teacher Education, 51*(3), 221–227.

Mullen, C. A. (Ed.). (2009). *The Handbook of Leadership and Professional Learning Communities.* New York: Palgrave Macmillan.

Paavola, S., Lipponen L., & Hakkarainen, K. (2002). Epistemological foundations for CSCL: A comparison of three models of innovative knowledge communities. In G. Stahl (Ed.), *Computer-supported Collaborative Learning: Foundations for a CSCL community. Proceedings of the Computer-supported Collaborative Learning 2002 conference* (pp. 24–32). Hillsdale, NJ: Erlbaum.

Rogers, E. (1995). *Diffusion of Innovations.* New York: Free Press.

Scardamalia, M., & Bereiter, C. (1994). Computer support for knowledge-building communities. *Journal of the Learning Sciences, 3*, 265–283.

Venezky, R., & Davis, C. (2001). *Quo vademus? The Transformation of Schooling in a Networked World.* Draft executive summary of the OECD/CERI project 'ICT and the Quality of Learning.' Retrieved January 22, 2011, from http://www.oecd.org/dataoecd/48/20/2073054.pdf

Vygotsky, L. S. (1978). *Mind in Society: The Development of Higher Psychological Processes.* Cambridge, MA: Harvard University Press.

Young, J. R., Bullough, R. V., Draper, R. J., Smith, L. K., & Erickson, L. B. (2005). Novice teacher growth and personal models of mentoring: Choosing compassion over inquiry. *Mentoring & Tutoring: Partnership in Learning, 13*(2), 169–188.

Zhu, E. (2006). Interaction and cognitive engagement: An analysis of four asynchronous online discussions. *Instructional Science, 34*, 451–480.

12

Perspectives on Culture and Mentoring in the Global Age

Frances Kochan and
Joseph T. Pascarelli

INTRODUCTION

Mentoring has become an international phenomenon (Wedding, McCarney, and Currey, 2009). As such, it is impacted by and impacts the cultural milieu within which it functions. This cultural milieu is in a state of flux and transformation and is evolving in ways not previously imagined (Carroll, 1990). We believe that this new cultural context makes it imperative that those engaged in mentoring endeavors view culture as a central focus in their work. Here we present our case for this premise and provide ideas about future directions that must be taken. We begin with an overview of this evolving culture.

A GLOBAL CONTEXT OF MENTORING

Mead (1970) announced the emergence of a new cultural context four decades ago by anticipating the global communications revolution. This worldwide communication environment is impacting individual and world cultures in ways as yet undiscovered and undefined (Wedding, et al., 2009).

In this interconnected global world, culture has become a central consideration in our ability to work and live together (House, Hanges, Mansour, Dorfman, and Gupta, 2004). Understanding cultural differences and the ways in which leaders and followers think, act, and feel in order to create worldwide solutions to the many problems we face is becoming a critical skill in our world

(Hofstede, Hofstede, and Minkov, 2010). Earley and Mosakowski suggest that cultural intelligence is an essential element in the global society; they define *cultural intelligence* as 'an outsider's seemingly natural ability to interpret someone's unfamiliar and ambiguous gestures the way that person's compatriots would' (2004: 140). Developing such intelligence requires a foundational understanding of the definition and attributes of culture.

Capturing the essence of culture

Culture is a multidimensional concept. It contains many elements and resides within individuals as well as within the contextual situations in which they function and in the society within which they operate (Choi and Lemberger, 2010). There are myriad definitions of culture. We find Nowottny's broad definition useful:

> '[C]ulture may now be said to be the whole complex of distinctive spiritual, material, intellectual and emotional features that characterize a society or social group. It includes … value systems, traditions, and beliefs' (2008: 12).

Culture gives people a sense of order in their daily lives. In similar ways, all organizations and societies have cultures within which many subcultures exist (Earley and Mosakowski, 2004). Although no standard definition of organizational culture exists, Hofstede et al. (2010) propose that organizational culture is: holistic, historically determined, related to anthropological issues, socially constructed, soft, and difficult to change.

Hofstede (1980) initiated germinal research on organizational culture to identify concepts of leadership and management within an organization from a national perspective. This study, conducted in 49 countries, led Hofstede to posit four value dimensions in national cultures: power distance, individualism–collectivism, masculinity–femininity, and uncertainty avoidance.

Hofstede and colleagues (2010) correlated Hofstede's early work with that conducted in the GLOBE study (House et al., 2004), the World Values Survey (2010), and the Chinese Value Survey (Bond, 2004). Based on these correlations, the authors suggest that in addition to the four national values, we must address the degree to which cultures focus on the past, the present, and the future in terms of indulgence or restraint when examining cultural issues.

Although the findings of all of these studies are too extensive to have coverage herein, we believe that the cultural dimensions addressed can be used when researching the mentoring process. We begin this discussion with an overview of mentoring, followed by a review of the literature, which examines the relationships between mentoring and culture.

CHARACTERISTICS OF MENTORING

Mentoring, like culture, is multidimensional. The relationship formed is transactional, reciprocal, interdependent, and developmental (Mullen, 2008).

We conceive of mentoring as dealing not only with knowing and doing, but also with the process of becoming.

Although mentoring, coaching, and tutoring are all relational in nature and have elements of caring and empowering others, we make a distinction among them. We view tutoring as focusing primarily on fostering the development of a skill or ability. It is closely related to teaching and deals with knowing, understanding, and doing. We define coaching as a broader concept, which tends to be directive, as we view the tutor as encouraging the tutee to develop skills and/or replicate actions or behaviors that are considered exemplary. The focus in this case is on modeling, acting and implementing. Mentoring, we believe, is more complex than tutoring and coaching. Admittedly, it might deal with transmitting a skill or behavior, but we view it as more inclusive in nature than the other two concepts.

Mentoring programs and relationships range from those involving two individuals focused on a specific goal to those sponsored or operated by a state or worldwide association or group (Gallimore, Tharp, and John-Steiner, 1990). Mentoring is an important element in developing human capital (Maldonado, Quarles, Lacey, and Thompson, 2002), expanding organizational potential (Mullen and Lick, 1999), and fostering societal improvement (Single and Single, 2005).

In recent years, many mentoring initiatives have had a powerful impact on successfully integrating minorities, women, and other underrepresented groups into professions and into management and leadership positions within them. This has enabled individuals from differing cultures to live and work together; thus promoting diversity in schools, businesses, and the broader community, and assisting societies to move in new directions to improve life for all (Austin, 2005; Patchell, 2005). Such programs tend to consider cultural issues as a part of their development and implementation stages.

RESEARCH, CULTURAL DIVERSITY, AND MENTORING RELATIONSHIPS

Most of the educational research on mentoring dealing with cultural issues examines this topic from the perspective of diversity as the central focus. We briefly review this research to describe how culture has been researched within the mentoring literature and to share some of the most pertinent findings.

Mentoring relationships and diversity

Much of the research on diversity in mentoring is focused on issues of matching and the interactions between mentoring pairs with similar and dissimilar backgrounds. Some researchers suggest that it is important that mentor and mentee share similar ethnic backgrounds as this creates a stronger bond, more satisfaction, or better outcomes (Liang and Grossman, 2007; Orland-Barak, 2003). Other studies have identified problematic effects in cross-cultural mentoring groups (Chan, 2008; Rass, 2010).

A number of researchers have found that it is essential to consider multiple diversity issues when creating mentoring matches (Clutterbuck, 2001; Mullen, 2008; Warren-Sams, 2001). Additionally some researchers discovered that pre-conceived negative notions about one another sometimes create barriers in these pairings (Davis, 2008; Kochan and Pascarelli, 2003).

Wales (2003) found no differences between male and female abilities to mentor potential women leaders in a business setting. Davis (2008) suggests that matching mentoring pairs by race is not important and calls it a myth that should not be accepted. She urges institutions to deal with changing structural barriers to success rather than focusing on whether the mentoring pairs are matched solely by race or ethnicity. Likewise, Crutcher states,

'Mentors need not have the same cultural or social background as their mentees, but they must pay close attention to the implications of the differences' (2007: 2).

Other researchers have reported benefits when pairs are not matched by demo-graphic factors. For some of these pairs, working together has caused them to change previously held negative attitudes toward the 'other' (Kochan and Pascarelli, 2003; Veugelers, 2003). Sperandio found that when working women of a higher class mentored young street girls in Bangladesh, who are often 'treated like dirt' and were used to 'being ordered about,' they reassessed 'their view of the girls' (2002: 218).

Liang and Grossman (2007) suggest that while research indicates that youth–mentor pairs from similar backgrounds have more successful relationships than those from dissimilar backgrounds, there is also evidence that mutual chemistry and cultural values such as collectivism are important elements in successful mentoring relationships (Lee, 1999). Evans (2003) states that while factors such as gender, race, religion, and socioeconomic factors should be considered in matching decisions, other elements such as a mentor's academic history and availability of transport should also be included in this decision. Some research-ers indicate that the quality of mentoring relationships depends on attitudes, more than on having similar cultural dynamics (e.g., Lee, 1999).

In summary, it appears that in some situations having mentors and mentees with similar demographic characteristics is advantageous, while in other instances it is problematic and unsuccessful. Having dissimilar demographic backgrounds can sometimes result in both mentors and mentees gaining new insights and understandings of one another and broaden cultural understandings.

What seems important about matching is that those involved are aware of and sensitive to cultural elements and that they develop strategies to assure that cul-tural factors do not negatively impact their relationships. This finding under-scores the importance of cultural intelligence, previously discussed (Early and Ang, 2003; Earley and Mosakowski, 2004) in mentoring success.

Mentoring and cultural influences in organizations and societies

While research in the area of mentoring and culture, in its broadest sense, is not widely discussed in the educational research literature, it has emerged as a primary issue in the business literature (House et al., 2004). Many studies have examined the degree to which mentoring programs and practices are similar or different within varied types of organizations to determine if there is a particular type of culture related to certain areas (i.e. public/private sector; education/business/health setting) (Kochan, 2002). While some studies have found some unique characteristics in specific environments (Austin, 2005), most research seems to indicate that while practices and policies may differ based on the type of organizational setting, mentoring methods and techniques used are more alike than different (Ely, Rhodes, and Allen, 2007).

The overall culture of the organization impacts the success or failure of any mentoring program which exists within it. For example, Kizilos (1990) notes that a mentoring program in the Internal Review Service was successful because the organizational culture within which it functioned perceived a need for it; accepted it as important; believed in its values; and supported it. Conversely, Mertz and Pfleeger (2002) discovered that when individuals in a corporation were not committed to a mentoring program to assist women to become managers, numerous problems hindered program and individual success. Likewise, Chikunda (2008) found that cultural belief systems held by practicing teachers in Zimbabwe interfered with the espoused beliefs and purposes of a planned mentoring program for new teachers.

Examining cultural issues in e-technology interactions, Fay and Hill (2003) discovered that practitioners experienced difficulties in understanding the cultural aspects of distance learning. The authors suggest that conversations regarding this issue must occur when people are beginning to operate within this new culture for first time. Despite this caution, numerous benefits related to culture may be inherent in an e-mentoring environment. Among them are impartiality, interorganizational connections, overcoming time and space, and operating in an unbiased environment (Single and Single, 2005).

From an international perspective, Parsloe and Wray (2002) found a difference between what they label as 'American style' career-oriented mentoring, which emphasizes the importance of having a mentor in a position of professional influence, and the 'European style' developmental mentoring, in which the primary focus is on the mentee's personal growth and learning, not necessarily on career advancement. Looking at perceptions of power related to mentoring, Bright and Yang (2002) noted that in Asia leadership power comes from factors of seniority and social class, whereas in the United States, leadership usually comes from experience, personal ability, or position and these beliefs impact the mentoring experience.

Investigating cultural differences in African American and Euro-American perspectives related to mentoring, Harris and Smith (1999) suggest that while the African American view perceives the community as central, the Euro-American view sees communalism as dependence, which can impact the way in which mentoring programs are structured and perceived. Manwa and Manwa (2007) found that in Zimbabwe a conception for mentoring based upon the 'homeboy/

girl syndrome' (2007: 31) – a more personal type of involvement – is more appropriate than the mentoring Western model.

Blake-Beard (2009) suggests that Hofstede's cultural value dimensions should be used to enable individuals to become more culturally aware of similarities and differences in order to strengthen mentoring relationships and programs. She points to work done by Apospori, Nikandrou, and Panayotopoulou (cited in Blake-Beard, 2009) as an example of how the dimensions might be used. In their study of mentoring, these authors concluded that it is difficult to develop mentoring programs in Greece because, as one issue, the culture has a high power distance, making it difficult to develop trusting mentoring relationships between individuals at differing management levels.

In our previous work, we analyzed 19 mentoring initiatives occurring on local and national levels. We found powerful cultural effects on mentoring programs and systems including program purposes; funding sources and requirements; levels of control; the intended scope of the change; institutionalization, and issues dealing with sociopolitical tensions between governmental initiatives and local control (Kochan and Pascarelli, 2005).

While the research studies cited in this chapter have uncovered some important insights about the impact of culture upon mentoring programs and relationships, as noted previously, we believe that our field must develop a broader focus on the cultural aspect of mentoring. We propose the use of a framework – a mental model – which captures the essence of interactions between mentoring and culture and provides a comprehensive basis upon which to understand and further study the cultural complexities involved.

Cultural and mentoring conceptual framework

Our Cultural and Mentoring Conceptual Framework is based on an adaptation of Mead's (1970) classic work on culture in which she identifies three basic types of cultures: postfigurative, cofigurative, and prefigurative. Carroll (1990) describes them as traditional, transitional, and learning cultures. While we do not presume to present a thorough construct of the concept of culture from an anthropological or sociological perspective, we have adapted Mead's cultural types as interpreted by Carroll, renaming them Traditional, Transitional, and Transformative. For each type of culture, we describe several mentoring initiatives to illustrate how this framework can be used.

Mentoring in traditional cultures

In traditional cultures, people acquire knowledge primarily from their elders, who are, viewed as keepers of the culture. It is their responsibility to transmit the culture to others, who are to maintain it for future generations. These cultures hold values, beliefs, policies, and ways of operating as timeless. Swoboda and Millar (1986) refer to this type of mentoring as 'grooming' in which the mentee is expected to learn his or her lessons well and follow the model emulated.

Many cultures use traditional forms of mentoring to transmit their culture to the next generation. Some Native American cultures, such as the Pueblo and the Cherokee, view mentoring as a means of cultural transmission integrated with the notion of learning and teaching (Gallimore et al., 1990; Patchell, 2005). Generally speaking, Buddhist Asian cultures, which revere their elders, mentor their children and families in this way. In such cultures, there is a filial obligation on the part of the elder and the entire family to assure that traditions are transmitted across generations even after death.

Although these ceremonies differ in Japan and Thailand, there are three primary means used to transmit culture to youth, while simultaneously mentoring the elders into elderhood. First, the elders are expected to share their knowledge of the cultural ethics of growth and respect and reverence of the elders to their children and families. Second, the journey into elderhood is marked by ceremonies such as celebrations at which adult children honor their parents and learn how they will want to be treated as elders. Third, after the death of the elders, memorials are held to reinforce connections between the living and the dead and cultural traditions themselves (Nakasone, 2008).

Often, countries engage in activities and foster mentoring programs that seek to foster the assimilation of the culture by new immigrants entering the country. For example, during the nineteenth and twentieth centuries in the American culture, new immigrants were encouraged and mentored by those in schools, by other immigrants, and by the society to relinquish their home cultures and assume the values, mores, and beliefs of their adopted home.

One of the dangers of this type of mentoring is the degree to which the mentee may be expected to adopt another person's values and lose his/her own identify (Enomoto, Gardiner, and Grogan, 2000; Haring and Freeman, 1999). While these problems can often be overcome, they sometimes can cause difficulties in the mentoring process.

Another difficulty in a traditional mentoring setting is that the mentee may rebel against this model (or the traditional ways) and may resent or even resist having someone 'tell' them what to do (Patchell, 2005). In other situations, there may be a stigma attached to having a mentor that may be perceived by the mentee or others as being needed to fulfill a deficit the mentee may have (Haring, 1999).

Metaphorically, in this type of arrangement, the mentor is viewed as the teacher or sage and the mentee is viewed as the learner or student. Traditional mentoring is firmly grounded in passing on values, beliefs, and norms in uninterrupted continuity from generation to generation, yet conflict and clashes can arise that challenge the role of the mentor, the mentee, and the mentoring process. The result of such conflict is examined in the next cultural frame.

Mentoring and transitional culture change

As described, traditional cultures, for the most part, remain static based on their focus on sustaining the norms and values of the past. They are tested, however, when recognition or heightened awareness and increased sensitivity of certain sociocultural conditions or dilemmas emerge. These may relate to issues such as social justice and marginalized groups, the condition of youth in society, economic conditions, and workforce changes. When these conditions exist, the stage is set for transitional cultural change.

This stage can be characterized by a questioning of the status quo, emergence of innovation and creativity to solve newly identified problems, and the reshuffling of priorities and directions. Ambiguity, mixed messages, and clashes of perspectives take center stage. Generally, tension emerges – a dilemma concerning which values, beliefs, norms, and practices need to be preserved from the traditional culture and to what extent changes must be made to ensure that mentoring remains relevant, useful, and aligned with the needs of a new 'present.'

This uncertainty understandably places a strain on the mentor, the mentee, and the mentoring relationship, since the role of the mentor is to bridge cultural gaps, and/or to translate the culture for the mentee without expecting or encouraging the mentee to abandon his/her own culture. Questions emerge: Which values and beliefs does a mentor stand for? What changes in the role of mentor need to occur? To what extent do mentees value the advice and indeed the role of the mentor?

On the social stage of the US, the Civil Rights movement was played out in the 1960s – perhaps the most significant US transitional cultural shift of the twentieth century marked by a dramatic change in societal beliefs, including equity and pluralism, and a new chapter of American history was written. This shift in the US and even in other parts of the world, saw the entry of women and minorities into previously inaccessible social arenas such as business and law.

These cultural changes led to an increase in the focus of mentoring and the need for mentors who could translate the messages of these movements (a dramatic cultural revolution) and, at the same time, ensure that those traditional values and beliefs that were important to preserve remained intact. This marked the beginning of a new kind of cultural awareness – the acceptance of new ways of thinking, doing, acting, and accepting, and the need to unravel centuries of injustices, bringing changes that increased the need for new kinds of mentoring programs in a wide variety of settings.

A recent successful initiative, exemplifying such a program, the statewide Puente project in California, illustrates the tension of the roles of the mentor, the mentee, and the mentoring relationship itself when functioning in a mentoring program within a transitional culture frame (Laden, 2000). The program focuses on increasing underserved operates in over 60 high schools and community colleges in California. A critical component of this initiative matches students with mentors from the business community and community college campuses.

The roles of mentors are similar to traditional roles of mentors in terms of guiding, support, and coaching. However, their focus is twofold: to help develop the emerging academic identities of the mentees, while ensuring that they continue to value their cultural identities as Latinos. As learners, mentees engage in sense-making in terms of how to integrate these two roles – maintaining respect and pride about their cultural identity while, at the same time, moving into an unfamiliar academic role with values and norms considerably different from those in their backgrounds.

A cultural shift in South Africa led to similar dilemmas for university faculty members faced with social justice issues relating to disenfranchisement (Geber, 2003). A mentoring program was established to assist with the early academic career development of Black academics in a university in which the faculty body is predominantly White. Findings suggest that while the traditional role of the mentor in this context was effective, there emerged unexpected role expectations for mentors they were not prepared to address. For example, mentees expected mentors to support and to 'use their positions of power and authority to overcome overt displays of prejudice and discrimination' (Gerber, 2003: 124). Another expectation had to do with the acceptance of these new academics into departments and to ensure that they were not being exploited because of their new minority status.

A primary learning from this initiative is that the traditional role of mentor is sometimes insufficient in cross-cultural settings. Special knowledge and skill sets are necessary for mentors in such contexts so that they are prepared to guide and advise mentees with regard to pressing matters involving acculturation, the university context, and pathways to success. Selection of mentors, professional development, and careful guidance of mentors in these contexts need to be addressed to maximize their effectiveness with mentees.

Perhaps the most dramatic challenges, dilemmas, and tensions we have encountered in a mentoring program within a transitional cultural frame is on a national level. It relates to a professional mentoring program that impacts the entire Israeli school system consisting of the Jewish, Arab, and Druze school sectors.

In response to the educational reform movement and specifically student achievement, the Israeli Ministry of Education has mandated this program and supported it with resource allocation. All levels of the system are impacted: the national policy level, teacher preservice and inservice programs, regional and local educational units, and local schools. In addition to these levels, cross-cultural issues permeate across all levels of the system relating to Jewish, Arab, and Druze communities (Orland-Barak, 2003).

Approximately 5,000 teachers have assumed the role of 'national counselors' or 'inservice mentors' whose responsibilities are to provide ongoing technical assistance to classroom teachers. The orientation to mentoring takes two forms: an 'instrumental narrative' and 'a developmental narrative.' The former is closely associated with the traditional role of mentor with a focus on student achievement and the teacher's role. The latter, the developmental role, focuses on the personal and professional growth of the teacher as change agent. These are perceived as competing narratives and pose a dilemma for the mentor. Mentors are to provide technical assistance for teachers and, at the same time, evaluate and report teacher performance to administrators and policymakers. This is perceived as dual accountability – one to the teacher and the other to system (project inspectors). Mentors in this context experience role conflict.

A metaphor for transitional mentoring is partnership. It involves co-mentoring in which those involved gain and learn from one another. Mentoring that encompasses transitional cultural change is, to borrow Orland-Barak's (2003) phrase, 'between worlds' – a dynamic tension that brings forward past values, beliefs, and integrating them with ones emerging to meet current conditions. It is fraught with uneasiness, dilemmas, and continued questioning.

Mentoring and transformational culture change

The transformational cultural frame looks beyond what is to what might be – a more intensified questioning of beliefs, patterns, and habits occurs than in the transitional frame. An increased recognition is that past structures and processes simply will not work, along with a willingness to become 'unstuck' in one's present. Scharmer (2007) views this 'being stuck,' as our tendency to engage continually in 'downloading' – that is, stubbornly persisting to act on past patterns of habit. Instead he suggests we must 'let go' of the past in order to 'let in' (Scharmer, 2007) a new present of possibility. The roles of mentor and mentee become more fluid in this process.

This 'letting in' requires a commitment to having a fresh mindset, to engage in new, creative, and continual learning, and to begin taking collective action (Daszko and Scheinberg, 2005). For this reason, transformation is viewed as a matter of discovery grounded in a continual process of evolution with the only constant being evolution. The lexicon of this stage includes such descriptors as adaptable, flexible, emerging, connected, moving forward and the ability to sense and respond (Daszko and Scheinberg, 2005). These very same descriptors become applicable to mentoring programs and indeed the roles of the mentor and mentee.

We present two very different types of mentoring programs that reflect transformational cultural change: one is global and systemic and concerns a global crisis, and the other is more anchored in personal growth. Each program captures the essence of transformational change – a sense of urgency and an open mindset required for the establishment of a new learning culture.

Global crises, a commitment to creating a new global learning model, and a recognized sense of responsibility to promote individual leadership were the catalysts that inspired the development of the Global Action Network (Klein, 2003) – the world's largest membership alliance dedicated to saving lives by improving health throughout the world. Those involved in creating it recognized the limited access to reproductive and sexual health services and education worldwide. For differing reasons, the old way of communicating, educating, and supporting youth health professionals was not working. The world was continuing to struggle with issues relating to HIV/AIDS, high maternal mortality, sexually transmitted diseases, and adolescent health concerns. What the group 'let in'

(Scharmer, 2007) was a willingness and an open mind for creating a new system that responded to world health and developing of leaders in reproductive health and human rights.

Using the Internet, the Network installed a worldwide mentoring program linking young health professionals (aged 16–35) with senior health professionals. With a website platform and a loosely designed curriculum, Network facilitators carefully matched mentors with mentees to foster sustained dialogue via email. This online global community presently includes participants from 20 different countries – 57 per cent from global south, 43 per cent from global north. Feedback loops have indicated that the program is very effective in connecting and sharing a much-needed knowledge base with young professionals and in providing these mentees with guidance and empowerment as young leaders in the health professions. The Network, now part of the Global Health Council, is internationally recognized for its work. One of the most significant challenges in this initiative is sustaining the e-dialogue between mentor–mentee pairs. Beyond the normal prompting that such communication networks frequently require, there are embedded cross-cultural issues to which those involved have to be sensitive. Without this sensitivity, feelings, attitudes, and the mentoring relationship itself can be injured. Some of these elements were cited by Klein in her work. They also directly related to the cultural dimensions Hofstede (1980) identified.

The Network is sensitive to such factors as uncertainty – characteristic of mentoring programs set in transformational cultures – and the impact it can have on mentoring relationships. For example, when national or regional conflict exists in the countries or regions represented by the mentor and mentee, it is challenging to maintain the trust, openness, and mutual respect that must underscore a mentoring program. In such situations, the relationships become strained. Similarly, the program recognizes that cultural expectations and differences must be considered when forging a mentoring partnership (Klein, 2003).

A second mentoring model operating within a transformational cultural frame is the New Scholars Network (NSN) (Angelique, Kyle, and Taylor, 2002). This program involves a group of entry-level professionals who are committed to a feminist ideology and determined to obtain support to become empowered change agents in their college through collective action. Community-building and collective action are critical outcomes of their work.

Prior to the establishment of NSN, a traditional mentoring model was established with the intent of having senior faculty mentor new tenure-track mentees. While some mentoring arrangements were successful, problems emerged for several reasons. This traditional model was characterized by peer mentoring and focused on information-sharing, career planning, and providing feedback. While there were several advantages to this peer mentoring, these were overpowered by several important drawbacks. Peer mentoring was limited in terms of the matched dyads. Although mentors and mentees were peers, there were perceived differences in the status of certain individuals with respect to their involvement in grants and favoritism in certain departments or campuses. Finally, the 'sameness' in terms of tenure-track roles and expectations was perceived by the mentees as fostering competition for recognition.

A group of these new professionals recognized the limitations of this traditional mentoring program as it related to both traditional and transitional culture change. They envisioned a group that transcended formal mentoring. Holding fast to their intent of creating a proactive group based on building relationships and sharing power as potential change agents, they designed a new structure allowing for peer growth to occur based on collaboration, openness, and vulnerability and named it the New Scholars Network (Angelique et al., 2002: 205). Presently, this Network perceives itself as being engaged in 'musing' rather than mentoring and members view themselves as being in a better position to influence their acculturation into the professional world of higher education. Their dialogues include sharing and assisting each other with research projects, supporting one another to navigate through the tenure track, sharing information about grant and teaching strategies, as well as community and socialization issues.

The group has evolved into a more natural professional community whose culture is mutually respectful, rewarding, and empowering. They have deliberately 'let go' of the past and 'let in' new thinking to create a model that is self-organizing based on changing needs. This model is fluid in structure, flexible with respect to boundaries, adaptable to changing conditions with respect to their professional journeys, and has a strong sense of group commitment and cohesion. This dynamic, organic model has even displaced the traditional word 'mentoring' with 'musing'.

Metaphorically, mentoring in both of these programs can be viewed as social networking. In such programs, mentoring is evolving and transforming, with roles changing continuously. There is no finite endpoint for the work. All involved and the initiative itself are constantly 'becoming'.

REFLECTIONS AND FUTURE DIRECTIONS

We have presented a perspective on fostering a broader conversation and a more comprehensive research agenda around the cultural aspects of mentoring. Past research has provided some guidance in understanding the processes and interactions involved and in developing a research base. We have attempted to expand our ability to understand and research the relationships between mentoring and culture through the creation of a framework for future discussion and study.

Although the cultural categories in the framework appear as discrete, neat, and simply-defined units of classification, this is the antithesis of actuality. Cultural change is based on fluidity, complexity, and emergence. For this reason, there is considerable overlapping, connectivity, and synchronicity when we consider the three categories – traditional, transitional, and transformative. In fact, these cultural realities may exist simultaneously and alongside one another, each with distinct rhythms of continuity and discontinuity.

We encourage others to examine their programs using the insights from the Cultural and Mentoring Conceptual framework to engage in dialogue about the cultural purposes of their programs, the role of mentors and mentees, cultural barriers to success, and cultural factors that facilitate success. Further, we hope this framework will facilitate more extensive and intensive research on the symbiotic relationship of culture and mentoring and perhaps more importantly, the sustainability of the human condition.

REFERENCES

Angelique, H., Kyle, K., & Taylor, E. (2002). Mentors and muses: New strategies for academic success. *Innovative Higher Education, 26*(3), 195–209.

Austin, Z. (2005). Mentorship and mitigation of culture shock: Foreign-trained pharmacists in Canada. *Mentoring & Tutoring: Partnership in Learning, 13*(1), 133–149.

Blake-Beard, S. (2009). Mentoring as a bridge to understanding cultural difference. *Adult Learning, 1–2,* 14–18.

Bond, M. H. (2004). Culture-level dimensions of social axioms and their correlates across 41 cultures. *Journal of Cross-Cultural Psychology, 35,* 548–570.

Bright, L. K., & Yang, F. J. (2002, April). *Crouching Tiger in a Corn Field: Doctoral Mentoring for East-West Cultural Understanding.* Paper presented at the Annual Meeting of the American Educational Research Association, San Diego, CA. [ERIC Document Reproduction No. ED429 523].

Carroll, T. G. (1990). Who owns culture? *Education and Urban Society, 22*(4), 346–355.

Chan, A. W. (2008). Mentoring ethnic minority, pre-doctoral students: An analysis of key mentor practices. *Mentoring & Tutoring: Partnership in Learning, 16*(3), 263–278.

Chikunda, C. (2008). Inconsistencies within attachment teaching practice in Zimbabwe: Call for a participatory model. *Mentoring & Tutoring: Partnership in Learning, 16*(2), 141–146.

Choi, S., & Lemberger, M. E. (2010). Influence of a supervised mentoring program on the achievement of low-income South Korean students. *Mentoring & Tutoring: Partnership in Learning, 18*(3), 233–248.

Clutterbuck, D. (2001). Building and sustaining the diversity–mentoring relationship. In D. Clutterbuck & B. Ragins (Eds.), *Mentoring and Diversity: An International Perspective* (pp. 87–113). London: Butterworth-Heinemann.

Crutcher, B. N. (2007). Mentoring across cultures. *Educational Digest, 73*(4), 21–25.

Davis, D. J. (2008). Mentorship and socialization of underrepresented minorities into the professoriate: Examining varied influences. *Mentoring & Tutoring: Partnership in Learning, 16*(3), 278–293.

Daszko, M., Macur, K., & Sheinberg, S. (2005). *Transformation: A definition, a theory, and the challenge of transforming.* Santa Clara, CT: Marcia Daszko and Associates.

Earley, P. C., & Ang, S. (2003). *Cultural Intelligence: Individual Interactions across Cultures.* Stanford, CA: Stanford Business Books.

Earley, P. C., & Mosakowski, E. (2004). Cultural intelligence. *Harvard Business Review, 8*(2), 139–146.

Ely, L. T., Rhodes, J. E., & Allen, T. D. (2007). Definition and evolution of mentoring. In T. D. Allen & L. T. Eby (Eds.), *The Blackwell Handbook of Mentoring: A Multiple Perspectives Approach* (pp. 7–20). Malden, MA: Blackwell.

Enomoto, E., Gardiner, M. E., & Grogan, M. (2002). Mentoring women in educational leadership. In F. K. Kochan (Ed.), *The Organizational and Human Dimensions of Successful Mentoring Programs and Relationships* (pp. 207–220). Greenwich, CT: Information Age.

Evans, A. (2003). Creating connections across new learning systems in the UK's National Mentoring Pilot Project. In. F. K. Kochan & J. T. Pascarelli (Eds.), *Global Perspectives on Mentoring: Transforming Contexts, Communities, and Cultures* (pp. 5–21). Greenwich, CT: Information Age.

Fay, R., & Hill, M. (2003). Educating language teachers through distance learning: The need for culturally-appropriate DL methodology. *Open Learning, 18*(1), 9–27.

Gallimore, R., Tharp, R. G., & John-Steiner, V. (1990). *The Developmental and Sociocultural Foundations of Mentoring.* New York: Institute for Urban and Minority Education.

Geber, H. (2003). Fostering career development for black academics in the New South Africa. In F. K. Kochan & J. T. Pascarelli (Eds.), *Global Perspectives on Mentoring: Transforming Contexts, Communities, and Cultures* (pp. 107–128). Greenwich, CT: Information Age. Haring, M. J. (1999). The case of a conceptual base for minority mentoring programs. *Peabody Journal of Education, 74*(2), 5–14.

Haring, M. J., & Freeman, K. (1999). Editors' Introduction. *Peabody Journal of Education, 74* (2), 1–4.

Harris, F., & Smith, J. C. (1999). Centricity and the mentoring experience in academia: An Afrocentric mentoring paradigm. *Western Journal of Black Studies, 23*(4), 229–238.

Hofstede, G. (1980). *Culture's Consequences.* Thousand Oaks, CA: SAGE.

Hofstede, G., Hofstede, G., & Minkov, M. (2010). *Cultures and Organizations: Software of the Mind.* New York: McGraw Hill.

House, R. J., Hanges, P. J., Mansour, J., Dorfman, P. W., & Gupta, V. (Eds.). (2004). *Culture, Leadership, and Organization: The GLOBE Study of 62 Societies.* Thousand Oaks, CA: SAGE.

Kizilos, P. (1990). Take my mentor, please. *Training, 4*(27), 49–55.

Klein, J. (2003). *International E-Mentoring for a Healthy Future: The Global Action Network Experience.* In F. K. Kochan & J. T. Pascarelli (Eds.), *Global perspectives on mentoring: Transforming contexts, communities, and cultures* (pp. 295–310). Greenwich, CT: Information Age.

Kochan, F. K. (2002). Examining the organizational and human dimensions of mentoring: A textual data analysis. In F. K. Kochan (Ed.), *The Organizational and Human Dimensions of Successful Mentoring Programs and Relationships* (pp. 269–286). Greenwich, CT: Information Age.

Kochan, F. K., & Pascarelli, J. T. (2003). Culture, context, and issues of change related to mentoring programs and relationships. In F. K. Kochan & J. T. Pascarelli (Eds.), *Global Perspectives on Mentoring: Transforming Contexts, Communities, and Cultures* (pp. 417–428). Greenwich, CT: Information Age.

Kochan, F. K., & Pascarelli, J. T. (2005). *Creating Successful Telementoring Programs.* Greenwich, CT: Information Age.

Laden, B. V. (2000). The Puente project: Socializing and mentoring Latino community college students. *Academic Exchange Quarterly, 4*(2), 90–99.

Lee, W. (1999). Striving toward effective retention: The effect of race on mentoring African American students. *Peabody Journal of Education, 74*(2), 27–43.

Liang, B., & Grossman, J. M. (2007). Diversity and youth mentoring relationships. In T. D. Allen & L. T. Eby (Eds.), *The Blackwell Handbook of Mentoring: A Multiple Perspectives Approach* (pp. 239–258). Oxford: Blackwell.

Maldonado, N. L., Quarles, A., Lacey, C. H., & Thompson, S. T. (2002). Mentoring at-risk adolescent girls: Listening to 'little sisters.' *Mentoring & Tutoring: Partnership in Learning, 16*(2), 223–234.

Manwa, H., & Manwa, F. (2007). Applicability of the western concept of mentoring to African organizations. *Journal of African Business, 1*(8), 31–43.

Mead, M. (1970). *Culture and Commitment.* Garden City, NY: Natural History Press/Doubleday.

Mertz, N., & Pfleeger, S. L. (2002). Using mentoring to advance females and minorities in a corporate environment. In F. K. Kochan (Eds.), *The Organizational and Human Dimensions of Successful Mentoring Programs and Relationships* (pp. 221–242). Greenwich, CT: Information Age.

Mullen, C. A. (Ed.). (2008). *The Handbook of Formal Mentoring in Higher Education: A Case Study Approach.* Norwood, MA: Christopher-Gordon.

Mullen, C. A., & Lick, D. W. (Eds.). (1999). *New Directions in Mentoring: Creating a Culture of Synergy.* London: Falmer.

Nakasone, R. (2008). Journeying into elderhood: Reflections on growing old in Asian cultures. *Generations, 32*(2), 25–29.

Nowottny, M. (2008). *Putting Culture First.* London: Commonwealth Foundation.

Orland-Barack, L. (2003). In between worlds: The tensions of in-service mentoring in Israel. In F. K. Kochan & J. T. Pascarelli (Eds.), *Global Perspectives on Mentoring: Transforming Contexts, Communities, and Cultures* (pp. 191–210). Greenwich, CT: Information Age.

Parsloe, E., & Wray, M. (2002). *Training Mentors is not Enough: Everything Else Schools and Districts Need To Do*. Thousand Oaks, CA: Corwin.

Patchell, B. (2005). Mentoring in multiple dimensions. *Journal of Cultural Diversity, 2*(12), 56–58.

Rass, R. A. (2010). The new teacher induction programme in Bedouin schools in the Negev, Israel. *Journal of Education for Teaching, 1*(36), 35–55.

Scharmer, O. (2007). *Theory U: Leading from the Future as it Emerges*. Cambridge, MA: The Society for Organizational Learning.

Single, P. B., & Single, R. M. (2005). Mentoring and the technology revolution: How face-to-face mentoring sets the stage for e-mentoring. In F. K. Kochan & J. T. Pascarelli (Eds.), *Creating Successful Telementoring Programs* (pp. 7–28). Greenwich, CT: Information Age.

Sperandio, J. (2002). Alternative mentoring of street girls in Bangladesh: New identities and non-traditional opportunities. *Mentoring & Tutoring: Partnership in Learning, 16*(2), 207–221.

Swoboda, M. J., & Millar, S. B. (1986). Networking-mentoring: Career strategy of women in academic administration. *Journal of NAWDAC, 49*, 8–13.

Veugelers, W. (2003). Possible futures envisioned by student mentees in Amsterdam. In F. K. Kochan & J. T. Pascarelli (Eds.), *Global Perspectives on Mentoring: Transforming Contexts, Communities, and Cultures* (pp. 39–52). Greenwich, CT: Information Age.

Wales, S. (2003). *Breaking Barriers in Business: Coaching Women for Career Advancement in the United Kingdom*. In F. K. Kochan & J. T. Pascarelli (Eds.), *Global perspectives on mentoring: Transforming contexts, communities, and cultures* (pp.165–186). Greenwich, CT: Information Age.

Warren-Sams, B. (2001). *Mentors Confirm and Enhance Girls' lives*. Newton, MA: WEEA Equity Resource Center.

Wedding, D., McCartney, J. L., & Currey, D. E. (2009). Lessons relevant to psychologists who serve as mentors for international students. *Professional Psychology: Research and Practice, 40*(2), 189–193.

World Values Survey. (2010). Retrieved December 30, 2010, from www.worldvaluessurvey.com.

School Contexts

13

Mentoring and Coaching for School Teachers' Initial Teacher Education and Induction

Pete Sorensen

INTRODUCTION

This chapter examines developments in mentoring and coaching in Initial Teacher Education (ITE) and the induction period. It draws on models and approaches from US and UK contexts to illustrate a range of practices developed internationally and examines innovative practices which have had positive impacts on teacher development in specific contexts. We draw out themes and identify possibilities and challenges for mentoring practice, in relation to teacher knowledge and the context in which it emerges. This discussion is necessarily framed by the broader context of debates about policy and practice in teacher education.

Though frameworks defining 'mentoring' and 'coaching' have been adopted at state or national levels in some countries, including the UK (CUREE, 2005), the terms are often used interchangeably. Some use the term 'coaching' to refer to approaches that are more directive, involving a more skilled practitioner advising others or showing them how to do things, and 'mentoring' as a less directive process, involving guidance and support for individuals in questioning and reflecting on their learning. For others, the use of these terms is reversed. In the main body of this chapter, we will use the term 'mentoring' as an overarching term, referring to both more and less directive approaches. We return to this issue in the final section.

Across countries, different terms are used to describe students on courses leading to teacher accreditation, including 'pre-service', 'teacher candidates', 'interns' and 'trainees'. For purposes of consistency we will refer to them throughout as 'student teachers'. Equally, periods of support and expectations for confirmation of status for teachers starting their careers after gaining initial certification vary from country to country. We will refer to this early career period, normally between ten months and two years, as the 'induction' period and teachers at this stage of their career as 'beginning teachers'.

POLICY, CERTIFICATION AND CONTEXTS

In examining mentoring and coaching practices for ITE and induction it is important to consider developments in the light of policy considerations, certification processes and contexts of provision. Language can give an important insight into policy. For example, in some jurisdictions there is a discourse of *delivery* and *teacher training*. Such discourse tends to suggest more directive approaches to mentoring. However, others lay stress on *reflective processes* and *teacher education*, suggesting less directive approaches. Variations in certification requirements reflect views about the knowledge, attitudes and skills deemed essential for a teacher entering the profession and will also clearly affect the role of the mentor. Teacher education programmes across the world vary from those largely or wholly-based in school, with or without support from external agencies, to those largely designed and managed by higher education institutions (HEIs), with practicum placements in schools. Such varied contexts, with their attendant assessment approaches, have also led to different expectations of mentors.

State involvement in ITE in England can be traced back to apprenticeship models in the nineteenth century (see, e.g., Aldrich, 1990). This model disappeared in the early years of the twentieth century, with the education profession gradually taking more control and responsibility for teacher education moving from schools to HEIs. By the 1970s the most prevalent entry routes to the profession were either a four-year Bachelor of Education degree or a three-year undergraduate degree followed by a one-year Post Graduate Certificate of Education (PGCE). During this period the ITE curriculum had developed, with a more academic base and a clear divide between the HEI and school. Faculty in HEIs had considerable autonomy and the state exercised only very indirect control. Similar developments in teacher education over this time period were seen in other countries (see, e.g., Sorensen, Young and Mandzuk, 2005, for a comparison of Canada and England).

The move to an increasingly HEI-dominated model was accompanied by extensive debate and controversy concerning the nature of theory and its relationship to practice (Darling-Hammond, 1999; Shulman, 1987). The model most commonly involved a theoretical course taught by the HEI followed by a teaching practicum. This led to some characterising it as privileging theoretical over professional knowledge and assuming that an understanding of theory precedes effective practice (Pring, 1996, discusses challenges faced by HEIs in responding to this critique).

In 1976, James Callaghan, the then British Prime Minister, made a speech at Ruskin College that was seen as challenging the teaching profession, including the dominant models of teacher education (Furlong, 2001). In the years following, the HEI-led models came under further attack and the balance of power started to shift back towards the state. In 1984, the government set out requirements for all ITE courses and set up the Council for the Accreditation of Teacher Education (CATE) to ensure compliance (DES, 1984). One stated aim was to develop partnership between schools and higher education. Though nationally effects were initially small, one or two more significant changes did occur. An important example of this was seen in the Oxford University Department of Educational Studies Internship Scheme, introduced in 1987. Here teachers in schools took on a mentoring role, following training, and a much higher degree of collaboration developed between schools and the university (Benton, 1990). A strong motive was to try to bridge the theory–practice divide (McIntyre, 1997). Whilst other ITE partnerships were also developing at the time, this was the first scheme in England to put stress on a mentoring role.

Further impetus to promoting use of school-based mentors came through development of alternative routes into teaching in England during the late 1980s, against a backdrop of commitment to modernisation and marketisation at national policy level (Furlong, 2005). Government intervention in the ITE curriculum also grew, with sets of competences defined (DfE, 1992, 1993), later to be replaced by regularly revised sets of standards, with the latest version (TDA, 2007) currently under review. In 1994, the Teacher Training Agency (TTA), later to become the Training and Development Agency (TDA), was set up to manage ITE and given responsibility for developing alternative routes as part of its remit. ITT providers, as they were now termed, were to be regularly inspected by the newly formed Office for Standards in Education (OFSTED), to determine 'compliance' and assure quality.

Two important early manifestations of alternative routes were the Articled and Licensed Teacher schemes, introduced in 1989. In the former, 80 per cent of the two-year training was based in school, with an HEI organising and coordinating the scheme. In the latter trainees were appointed directly to schools for on the job training organised by an LEA or governing body of a school, with no requirement for HEI involvement, though in practice most Licensed Teacher schemes still chose to use HEI support (Furlong, Barton, Miles, Whiting and Whitty, 2000). These were the first national programmes to specify significant mentoring roles, now built into current dominant alternative routes: the Graduate Teacher Programme (GTP), almost entirely school-based in its conception; and the School-Centred Initial Teacher Training (SCITT), where consortia of schools take responsibility.

In terms of induction, though England had a probationary year for beginning teachers prior to its abolition in 1992, for many there had been little formal support in schools. However, in 1999, a new 'induction year' was introduced, supported by funding and clear entitlements of support, including a mentoring role for a school-based teacher colleague (Bleach, 1999).

It is important to note these changes to teacher education in England took place during a period of increasing government intervention and control over the education system, with the implementation of a national curriculum in 1990. Similar patterns of influence on the knowledge base, jurisdiction, structure and control of teacher education can be seen in many countries. However, models of teacher education that have *any* HEI involvement have been challenged. In the US, some faculty members have described a sustained assault on HEI-based teacher education courses, feeling they are 'under siege' (Sleeter, 2008: 1947). In particular, courses that support inquiry-based approaches within a critical pedagogy of teacher education have been criticised from a neoliberal perspective, with various responses suggested (e.g., Groenke and Hatch, 2009; Zeichner, 2009). The position taken in relation to such arguments has considerable implications for mentoring structures and practices.

MENTORING AND THE DEVELOPMENT OF PARTNERSHIP

Mentoring that emphasises support for questioning and reflecting on learning, as an alternative to the more directive approaches seen in some of the early apprenticeship models, started to be seen in teacher education from the early 1980s. In the US, part of the impetus for this was a response to concerns about a high drop-out rate in the early years of teachers' careers. Better support during the induction period was viewed as critical and mentors in school were regarded as an important facet of such an approach (Little, 1990). As a result, many states mandated the use of mentoring in the 1990s.

At the same time as looking to provide mentor support for beginning teachers, US policy makers were turning their attention to ITE and calls were made for closer relationships between what were termed 'teacher candidates' and experienced teachers through the introduction of professional development schools (PDS) designed to serve as contexts for internships (Holmes Group, 1990). However, clarity concerning the roles of mentors was often lacking and control of partnership remained very largely with the HEI (Arthur, Davison and Moss, 1997).

The growth in mentoring in the US and UK was mirrored in other parts of the world. Some models, such as one from the Netherlands (Korthagen, 2001), again stressed the importance of bringing theory and practice closer together. In Australia there was particular emphasis on seeking to deepen partnerships (Grundy, Robinson and Tomazos, 2001). Menter, Hulme, Dely and Lewin (2010), in their extensive Literature Review of Teacher Education in the twenty-first century, noted that some models in Australia stress large-scale collaborations drawing on the notion of 'scholarly teachers' working in schools (2010: 28). However, their overview of practice across countries indicated that the locus of control of many partnerships remained largely with the HEI, often because statutory responsibility and accountability ultimately lay with the HEI. Hagger and McIntyre's (2006) review of partnership approaches suggests that this structural factor needs to be rebalanced if the full potential of school-based teacher education is to be realised and argue that putting 'teachers at the centre of the task of renewing their profession' (2006: 181), is an important factor in this regard.

There have been several extensive literature reviews examining partnership models. Brisard, Menter and Smith (2005) note the emphasis placed on the development of collaborative partnerships between HEIs, schools and other stakeholders. Smith, Brisard and Menter (2006: 147) highlight arguments that stress 'the desirability of developing models which are truly collaborative in nature between higher education institutions (HEIs) and other stakeholders'. This presents serious challenges for policy makers as such reviews also show that funding remains limited and investment in support for mentors is often poor. Zwozdiak-Meyers, Cameron, Mustard, Leask and Green (2010) conclude that partnership arrangements should aim to incorporate: a 'strong mentoring programme'; a critical mass of trainees, including the use of 'paired/multiple placements' (2010: 47); 'joint reflection and evaluation between mentor and trainee' (ibid. 48); 'formalised mentor training' (ibid. 103); 'mentoring at all levels' (ibid. 104). However, they also state that the issue of providing 'adequate levels of funding' (ibid. 108), is vital for these notions of extended partnerships to be achieved. Smith et al. (2006: 161) note that currently teachers do not desire such an extended role and to shift such attitudes will require much greater government commitment.

In England, the government has supported several reviews of ITE and induction to try and develop an evidence base for decision making. Four studies are particularly relevant here. First, Moyles and Stuart (2003) attempted to identify which elements of the school-based ITE practicum supported professional development and found there was some evidence to support the value of regular constructive dialogue between student teachers and mentors and the value two student teachers working together in a classroom. However, their main conclusion was that more research into specific practices was needed. Second, in reviewing the impact of organisational structures and conceptual frameworks on the quality of ITE, Bills, Briggs, Browne, Gillespie, Gordon, Husbands et al. (2007) found a paucity of research but concluded that 'increased time in schools appears to be beneficial' (2007: 1). Third, the same team (Bills, Briggs, Browne, Gillespie, Gordon, Husbands et al., 2008), in looking at international perspectives on quality found 'agreement that effective partnership between the provider and schools is central to the quality of initial teacher education' (2008: 1). However, they noted significant differences in the nature of these partnerships and the processes taking place in different countries, as well as views on measures of quality. Fourth, a review by Totterdell, Woodroffe, Bubbs and Hanrahan (2004) focussed on induction programmes. This review found many positive impacts, including benefits for those in the mentoring roles as well as the newly qualified teachers, but also cited studies emphasising the need for mentors to be given time to fulfil the role and to feel valued as part of professional communities.

The potential contributions of involvement with ITE and induction to broader professional development have often not been recognised or valued within school development plans and structures (Child and Merrill, 2003). One of the reasons for this has been the way in which other systemic pressures, including accountability measures under high stakes testing and inspection regimes, can tend to sideline work with beginning teachers, leading to a lack of recognition of the work of mentors and coaches. However, Darling-Hammond, Chung Wei, Andree, Richardson and Orphanos (2009), in their status report on teacher development, suggest that collaborative approaches to professional learning bring important gains, including improved pupil attainment. They further argue for investment in the role of the 'teacher mentor' through training and release time (2009: 12) and point to examples across the world where investment in professional development is greater in some higher achieving education systems, including Sweden, the Netherlands and Singapore, with mentoring and coaching systems more firmly embedded as part of induction programmes and continuing professional development (ibid. 19).

MODELS OF MENTORING

There is now a wealth of literature to support mentors in developing and understanding their practice (e.g., Fletcher, 2000; Hawkey, 1997; Mullen, 2005; Tomlinson, 1995) and this chapter identifies some of the models that have emerged. Hagger, Burn and McIntyre (1993) used the findings from initial work on the Oxford Internship Scheme to define essential skills and strategies for working with student teachers. Alongside a stress on planning, observation and supervision, there was emphasis on collaborative teaching, critical discussion of student teachers' ideas and support for student teachers' self-evaluation, features that were not common in many partnerships at that time and which have continued to remain elusive (Hagger and McIntyre, 2006; Menter et al., 2010).

Maynard and Furlong (1993) identified three models of mentoring from the literature: the apprenticeship, competency and reflective practitioner models. They argued that each model was 'partial and inadequate' but 'taken together … may contribute to a view of mentoring that responds to the changing needs of trainees' (1993: 78). Some supporting the apprenticeship model as the *only* necessary one, were generally concerned with removing much of the content of current teacher education courses and the role of the universities within them (e.g., Hillgate Group, 1989). Much of the attack on teacher education in the US today comes from a similar perspective. However, Maynard and Furlong (1993) argued that the work of a mentor involves apprenticeship, noting that modelling within collaborative teaching arrangements was a good way to access teachers' professional knowledge and skills.

The second model, the competency model, with defined sets of skills to be achieved, was the attempt to use research into effective teaching as a basis for training. Though some questioned the use of competences, with critiques raising issues of centralisation and control, this model became a strong feature of mentoring in the UK. It has been strongly critiqued by those arguing for the third reflective practitioner model, which puts critical evaluation at the heart of learning. Furlong et al. (2000) noted that concentration on standards and competences meant that mentoring appeared to have had limited impact on encouraging reflective practice with critical evaluation, learning and the development of professional knowledge at its heart. Maynard and Furlong note that this reflective model presents challenges and a shift in the role of the mentor, away from that of 'a model and instructor to being a co-enquirer' (1993: 82).

In the US, strong critique of competency-based models of mentoring has also emerged. In developing her arguments for the preparation of teachers to develop democratic participation and recognise diversity, Sleeter (2008) highlights the need to develop inquiry-based approaches embedded in multiple classrooms in diverse communities, working with teachers who model stances of advocacy and social justice. This is needed to counter unnecessary replication of conventional practice in some mentoring practices (Feiman-Nemser, 2001). Along with many other commentators on the US system (e.g., Darling-Hammond, 2006), she argues for equity and diversity to be strongly woven throughout programmes. This suggests that the dispositions of mentors selected for working in ITE are going to be critical. Yet evidence suggests that the role is given relatively low status or importance in many schools (Child and Merrill, 2003) and the selection of mentors may lack attention to desirable skills.

Zeichner (2006) argues strongly for four key actions to strengthen ITE: redefining the debate about the relative merits of alternative and traditional certification programmes; broadening the goals of teacher education; strengthening the role for schools and communities in teacher education; and taking teacher education seriously as an institutional responsibility (2006: 326). Drawing on Darling-Hammond (2000), he states that the practicum needs to be 'as carefully planned as any other college or university course' and 'closely integrated with the rest of the teacher education programme' (ibid. 334). He notes the growing body of evidence for the value of community-based learning in supporting student teachers' learning and argues that 'the realization of a more decent and humane society for everyone's children should be the core principle underlying all forms of teacher education whether they are sponsored by colleges and universities or not' (ibid. 337). He thus argues for mentoring models that are more transformative in nature, echoing Cochran-Smith's (1991) call for mentors to be reformers. Menter et al.'s (2010) review suggests that there are four influential paradigms of teacher education: 'the *effective* teacher, the *reflective* teacher, the *enquiring* teacher and the *transformative* teacher' (ibid. 21); many challenges remain if the aspiration to move to more transformative approaches is to be met.

Many researchers have written about the attributes of effective mentors. Hobson et al. (2009a) argue that attention to the affective needs of teachers is critical and this is more likely to happen in schools with more a holistic commitment to ITE, induction and further professional development. However, Hobson, Ashby, Malderez and Tomlinson (2009b) also note that significant problems can arise through hierarchical, judgemental approaches to mentoring that relegate a student or beginning teacher to the 'bottom of the heap'. The same research team (Ashby, Hobson, Tracey, Malderez, Tomlinson, Roper et al., 2008) cite studies from a variety of cultural contexts suggesting the need for inclusive, supportive environments for teacher retention. They argue that ITE providers and schools should support student teachers and newly qualified teachers in: 'assessing their own skills and characteristics', 'recognising their own individual teacher identity', 'discussing their professional concerns and needs', and 'taking a proactive approach to in-school relationships' (ibid. 76). Some experts in the field have developed resources that reflect these arguments. Boreen et al.'s guide to mentoring is underpinned by 'a philosophy that advocates listening, questioning, and collaborating' (2009: xi). Poseen and Denmark's (2007) resource tool highlights the skills associated with particular mentoring and coaching approaches, with emphasis on the personal attributes required of a mentor as well as the mentoring models adopted.

Reviews from Australia (Long, 2009) and the US (Berry, Smylie and Fuller, 2008; Parker, Ndoye and Imig, 2009) show that collaborative mentoring approaches during induction foster commitment and retention. In Australia several innovative collaborative projects took place in the 1990s, including those where university teacher educators and practising teachers researched aspects of practice together. In reporting on this, Grundy et al. (2003) highlighted the potential for the development of a much deeper professional learning community. However, Peters (2002), examining projects aimed at fostering collaborative partnerships, identified significant barriers to effective mentoring that resonate with findings in many other contexts. These included institutional and structural factors, incorporating differing cultures and valuations of particular aspects of teacher knowledge, as well as from the demands of time, energy and effort. Barrera, Braley and Slate (2010) note in particular the tensions that exist for mentors working in high stakes testing environments which limit the time available for critical reflective practices.

Some studies suggest that the quality of mentoring is among the most crucial factors in teacher preparation. In the PDS schools model in the US, Utley, Rhodes and Basile (2003) describe how a 'master teacher' can take a lead role in teacher education, and help foster the development of mentoring cultures. Research also indicates that the quality of mentoring is a crucial aspect of the success of alternative routes to accreditation. The National Academy of Education (2009) concluded that variations in the effectiveness within pathways are as great as those across them. Drawing on a substantial body of research into a range of alternate and more traditional route programmes, Feistritzer (2008) concludes that the most important factor in the efficacy of any programme is that they enable student teachers to work in classrooms with mentor teachers. Evidence from the National Academy paper (2009) suggests that those programmes which include the involvement of an expert mentor teacher during a sustained school practicum and a university offering accreditation at masters level are producing positive results in terms of retention. This approach is also seen elsewhere and accords with attempts to strengthen partnerships through collaboration and the concept of 'extended professionalism' (Menter et al., 2010).

MENTORING AS COLLABORATIVE PRACTICE

In conventional HEI-led ITE programmes it has been common practice to place a single student with a single teacher for the practicum, implicitly reflecting an apprenticeship model. Bullough, Young, Erickson, Birrell, Clark, Egan et al. (2002), reviewing research across Europe and North America, noted how little had changed over the preceding 50 years. However, with initiatives such as PDS schools in the US and expectations that student teachers spend at least two-thirds of their course in schools in England, the role of the school-based teacher had evolved in some settings to a mentoring role involving greater collaboration between faculty tutors and student teachers.

Research into mentoring and collaborative practices led to publication of a considerable volume of literature in the last decade of the twentieth century (e.g., Arthur et al., 1997; Furlong and Maynard, 1995; Hagger et al., 1993). It also became clear that mentoring programmes had grown across the world and comparative studies began to appear that identified issues for programme development and economic implications (e.g., Wang, 2001). Pierce and Millar's (1994) review of the implementation of mentoring in the US identified funding pressures as a major factor in implementation and it was clear from studies in a number of contexts that issues of time and recognition were preventing some of the collaborative practices advocated from developing (e.g., Wynn and Kromrey, 1999).

Hargreaves and Fullan (2000: 54–55) identify three important strategic approaches to mentoring programs: first, to 'conceptualize and design mentoring programs so that they are explicitly seen as instruments of school reculturing'; second, 'mentoring must be explicitly connected to other reform components … [it] must address the needs of *all* teachers new to the district or school, not just beginning teachers'; third, to recognise the potential of mentoring to 'recreate the profession'. Thus the role of the mentor would move away from that of 'hierarchical dispensations of wisdom to shared inquiries into practice'. Such changes in approach would clearly emphasise the importance of developing a shared discourse in the promotion of learning.

A number of theoretical frameworks may be drawn on to support the arguments for changes to the nature of mentoring made by Hargreaves and Fullan (2000). At the core of many ITE and induction programmes is the notion of the development of the reflective practitioner (Schön, 1987), someone who is able to develop their own sense of identity, through reflecting on their practice with the support of others (Loughran, 2002). Key to school improvement has been an emphasis on teachers learning from each other and the establishment of professional learning communities (Fullan, 1999) that promote a shared sense of inquiry into practice. This is supported by Lave and Wenger's (1991) concept of 'legitimate peripheral participation', which involves situating learning in ways that involve social co-participation in the development of practice.

Sorensen and Sears (2005) have drawn on the arguments for collaboration and collegiality in developing and reporting on the use of peer mentoring as part of paired and multiple placements in the school practicum. This adds to research (e.g., Bullough et al., 2002; Cornu, 1995) showing that the use of peer learning and mentoring can have positive benefits in the school practicum. Nokes and colleagues' (Nokes, Bullough, Egan, Birrell and Hansen, 2008) report on the use of paired placements puts particular stress on the way the relationship could lead to deepening dialogue and reflection on practice and support for experimentation through collaboration. They point out that 'one of the surprising results of [their] study was that even with very little guidance almost all of the student teachers and mentors had positive learning experiences', but suggest that 'with guidance the benefits of pair-placed student teaching can be magnified, especially for pupils, and the negative outcomes reduced' (2008: 2175).

Notions of deepening dialogue and exercising agency are also at the heart of co-teaching models, involving teaching with someone else in the classroom and discussing such teaching episodes in praxis (Tobin and Roth, 2006). The model has been applied to mentors working with student and newly qualified teachers as co-inquirers. Such approaches draw on Schon's (1987) ideas on the importance of reflection-in-action and resonate with Whitehead and Fitzgerald's (2006) call for reconceptualising the role of the mentor, with more emphasis on reflective dialogue and the involvement of all partners in 'the formation and reformation of the knowledge base of the profession' (2006: 40). In adopting this approach they found that new relationships were formed between mentors and trainees and staff became more collaborative, forming a 'community of practice' (Wenger, 1998).

The establishment of collaborative practices through the use of new technologies is now becoming a more common feature of teacher education programmes. Zwozdiak-Myers et al.'s (2010) review points to considerable variation in the education sector in relation to 'communities of practice and ways of working with web 2.0 technologies and collaborative tools through virtual online environments' (2010: 77). While there is clearly a need to explore and research this area further, the potential for such technologies to provide support for the development of new approaches to mentoring is clearly highlighted by such reviews.

CONCLUSION

At the start of the chapter we indicated that 'mentoring' would be used as an overarching term. This reflected the fact that mentoring has featured more strongly than coaching in the language of teacher education and that there is no agreed distinction between the two terms in much of the literature. The CUREE (2005) framework adopted in England is one national model aimed at providing clarification. In this framework 'mentoring' is characterised as a structured and sustained process of support through significant career transitions, 'specialist coaching' as structured support for the development of specific skills or practices and 'collaborative (co-) coaching' as a process where professionals support each other in embedding new knowledge and skills in their practice. A variety of support materials for teacher educators followed (see DfE, 2011), the impact of which cannot yet be judged. However, a shared conceptual framework has the potential to provide a language for both research and practice.

It is clear from the research discussed in this chapter that many mentors and coaches have limited opportunities to consider and develop their roles. Yet, these roles need to be valued highly at individual, institutional and state levels if they are to have a major impact. Time and energy need to be invested to prepare teachers for mentoring and coaching roles, which need to be seen as an integral part of professional and school development. A wider understanding of the opportunities offered by the presence in schools of student and beginning teachers is also needed. Where this is recognised and collaborative processes are more integrated there is evidence that this enhances both the professional learning of all participants and the development of schools.

REFERENCES

Aldrich, R. (1990) The evolution of teacher education. In Graves, N. (ed.) *Initial Teacher Education: Policy and Progress.* London: Kogan Page.

Arthur, J., Davison, J. and Moss, J. (1997) *Subject Mentoring in the Secondary School.* London: Routledge.

Ashby, P., Hobson, A. J., Tracey, L., Malderez, A., Tomlinson, P. D., Roper, T., Chambers, G. N. and Healy, J. (2008) *Beginner Teachers' Experiences of Initial Teacher Preparation, Induction and Early Professional Development: A Review of Literature.* DCFS Research Report No DCSF-RW076. Available at: http://gtce.org.uk/documents/publicationpdfs/bat_litreview1108.pdf [accessed 10.10.10]

Barrera, A., Braley, R. T. and Slate, J. R. (2010) Beginning teacher success: an investigation into the feedback from mentors of formal mentoring programmes *Mentoring and Tutoring* 18(1): 61–74.

Benton, P. (Ed.) (1990) *The Oxford Internship Scheme: Integration and Partnership in Initial Teacher Education.* London: Calouste Gulbenkian Foundation.

Berry, B., Smylie, M. and Fuller, E. (2008) *Understanding Teacher Working Conditions: A Review and Look to the Future Centre for Teacher Quality* Available at: http://www.teachingquality.org/pdfs/TWC2_Nov08.pdf [accessed 12.10.10]

Bills, L., Briggs, M., Browne, A., Gillespie, H., Gordon, J., Husbands, C., Shreeve, A., Still, C. and Swatton, P. (2007) *Structures, Management and Process in Initial Teacher Education: A Systematic Review.* In Research Evidence in Education Library. London: EPPI-Centre, Social Science Research Unit, Institute of Education, University of London.

Bills, L., Briggs, M., Browne, A., Gillespie, H., Gordon, J., Husbands, C., Shreeve, A., Still, C. and Swatton, P. (2008) *International Perspectives on Quality in Initial Teacher Education: An Exploratory Review of Selected International Documentation on Statutory Requirements and Quality Assurance.* In Research Evidence in Education Library. London: EPPI-Centre, Social Science Research Unit, Institute of Education, University of London.

Bleach, K. (1999) *The Induction and Mentoring of Newly Qualified Teachers.* London: David Fulton Publishers.

Boreen, J., Johnson, M. K., Niday, D. and Potts, J. (2009) *Mentoring Beginning Teachers: Guiding, Reflecting, Coaching.* Stenhouse Publishers.

Brisard, E., Menter, I. and Smith, I. (2005) *Models of Partnership in Initial Teacher Education.* Edinburgh: General Teaching Council for Scotland.

Bullough, R. V., Young, J., Erickson, L., Birrell, J. R., Clark, D. C., Egan, M. W., Berrie, C. F., Hales, V. and Smith, G. (2002) Rethinking field experiences: Partnership teaching vs single-placement teaching. *Journal of Teacher Education* 53(1): 68–80.

Child, A. J. and Merrill, S. J. (2003) Professional mentors' perceptions of the contribution of school/HEI partnerships to professional development and school improvement. *Journal of In-Service Education* 29(2): 315–324.

Cochran-Smith, M. (1991) Learning to teach against the grain. *Harvard Educational Review* 61(3): 279–310.

Cornu, R. L. (2005) Peer mentoring: engaging pre-service teachers in mentoring one another. *Mentoring and Tutoring* 13(3): 355–366.

CUREE (2005) *National Framework for Mentoring and Coaching.* Available at: http://www.curee-paccts. com/resources/publications/national-framework-mentoring-and-coaching [accessed 10.10.10]

Darling-Hammond, L. (1999) The case for university-based teacher education. In Roth, R. (ed.) *The Role of the University in the Preparation of Teachers.* Philadelphia: Falmer. 13–30.

Darling-Hammond, L. (2000) *Studies of Excellence in Teacher Education* Washington, DC: American Association of Colleges for Teacher Education.

Darling-Hammond, L. (2006) *Powerful Teacher Education.* San Francisco: Jossey-Bass.

Darling-Hammond, L., Chung Wei, R., Andree, A., Richardson, N. and Orphanos, S. (2009*) Professional Learning in the Learning Profession: A Status Report on Teacher Development in the United States and Abroad.* NSDC, Stanford University. Available at: http://www.nsdc.org/news/NSDCstudy2009. pdf [accessed 14.10.10]

Department of Education and Science (1984) *Initial Teacher Training: Approval of Courses.* (Circular 3/84). London: DES.

DfE (1992) *Initial Teacher Education (Secondary phase)* (Circular 9/92). London: Department for Education.

DfE (1993) *The Initial Training of Primary School Teachers: New Criteria for Course Approval.* (Circular 14/93) London: Department for Education.

DfE (2011) *Mentoring and Coaching in Initial Teacher Education: Review and Development.* Available at: http://nationalstrategies.standards.dcsf.gov.uk/node/83265 [Accessed 30.3.11]

Feiman-Nemser, S. (2001) From preparation to practice: Designing a continuum to strengthen and sustain teaching. *Teachers College Record* 198(6): 1013–1055.

Feistritzer, E. (2008) *Building a Quality Teaching Force: Lessons Learned from Alternate Routes.* Upper Saddle River, NJ: Pearson Merrill Prentice Hall.

Fletcher, S. (2000) *Mentoring in Schools: A Handbook of Good Practice.* Abingdon: Routledge.

Fullan, M. (1999) *Change Forces: The Sequel.* London: Falmer Press.

Furlong, J. (2001) Reforming teacher education, re-forming teachers. In Phillips, R. and Furlong, J. (eds.) *Education, Reform and the State: Twenty-five Years of Politics, Policy and Practice.* New York: RoutledgeFalmer.

Furlong, J. (2005) New Labour and teacher education: the end of an era. *Oxford Review of Education* 31(1): 119–134.

Furlong, J., Barton, L., Miles, S., Whiting, C. and Whitty, G. (2000) *Teacher Education in Transition: Re-forming Professionalism?* Buckingham: OUP.

Furlong, J. and Maynard, T. (1995) *Mentoring Student Teachers.* London: Routledge.

Groenke, S. L. and Hatch, J. A. (Eds) (2009) *Explorations of Educational purpose 6: Critical Pedagogy and Teacher Education in the Neoliberal Era.* New York: Springer.

Grundy, S., Robinson, J. and Tomazos, D. (2001) Interrupting the Way Things Are: exploring new directions in school/university partnerships. *Asia-Pacific Journal of Teacher Education* 29(3): 203–217.

Hagger, H., Burn, K. and McIntyre, D. (1993) *The School Mentor Handbook.* London: Kogan Page.

Hagger, H. and McIntyre, D. (2006) *Learning Teaching from Teachers: Realizing the Potential of School-based Teacher Education.* Maidenhead: Open University Press.

Hargreaves, A. and Fullan, M. (2000) Mentoring in the new millennium. *Theory Into Practice* 39(1): 50–56.

Hawkey, K. (1997) Roles, responsibilities and relationships in mentoring: a literature review and agenda for research. *Journal of Teacher Education* 48(5): 325–335.

Hillgate Group (1989) *Learning to Teach*. London: Claridge Press

Hobson, A. J., Malderez, A., Tracey, L., Homer, M. S., Ashby, P., Mitchell, N., McIntyre, J., Cooper, D., Roper, T., Chambers, G. N. and Tomlinson, P. D. (2009a) Becoming a Teacher. *Teachers' Experiences of Initial Teacher Preparation, Induction and Early Professional Development: Final Report*. DCFS Research Report No DCSF-RR115. Available at: http://www.education.gov.uk/research/data/upload-files/DCSF-RR115.pdf [accessed 10.10.10]

Hobson, A. J., Ashby, P., Malderez, A. and Tomlinson, P. D. (2009b) Mentoring beginning teachers: What we know and what we don't. *Teaching and Teacher Education* 25(1): 207–216.

Holmes Group (1990) *Tomorrow's Schools: Principles for the Design of Professional Development Schools*. East Lansing, MI, USA.

Korthagen, F. (Ed.) (2001) *Linking Practice and Theory: The Pedagogy of Realistic Teacher Education*. New Jersey: Lawrence Erlbaum.

Lave, J. and Wenger, E. (1991) *Situated Learning: Legitimate Peripheral Participation*. Cambridge: Cambridge University Press.

Little, J. W. (1990) The mentor phenomenon and the social organization of teaching. In Cazden, C. (Ed.), *Review of Research in Education* 16: 297–351. Washington DC: American Educational Research Association.

Long, J. (1997) Mentoring for school based teacher education in Australia. *Mentoring and Tutoring* 4(3): 11–18.

Loughran, J. J. (2002) Effective reflective practice: in search of meaning in learning about teaching. *Journal of Teacher Education* 53(1): 33–43.

Maynard, T. and Furlong, J. (1993) Learning to teach and models of mentoring. In McIntyre, D., Hagger, H. and Wilkin, M (Eds), *Mentoring: Perspectives on School-based Teacher Education*. London: Kogan: 69–85.

McIntyre, D. (1997) *Teacher Education Research in a New Context: The Oxford Internship Scheme*. London: Paul Chapman Publishing.

Menter, I., Hulme, M., Dely, E. and Lewin, J. (2010) *Literature Review on Teacher Education in the 21st Century*. Edinburgh: Education Analytical Services.

Moyles J. and Stuart, D. (2003) *Which School-based Elements of Partnership in Initial Teacher Training in the UK Support Trainee Teachers' Professional Development?* In Research Evidence in Education Library. London: EPPI-Centre, Social Science Research Unit, Institute of Education, University of London.

Mullen, C. A. (2005) *Mentorship Primer*. New York: Peter Lang Publishing.

National Academy of Education (2009) *Teacher Quality: Education Policy White Paper*. Available at: http://www.naeducation.org/Teacher_Quality_White_Paper.pdf [accessed 10.10.10]

Nokes, J. D., Bullough, R. V., Egan, W. M., Birrell, J. R. and Hansen, J. M. (2008) The paired-placement of student teachers: An alternative to traditional placements in secondary school. *Teaching and Teacher Education* 24(8): 2168–2177.

Parker, M. A., Ndoye, A. and Imig, S. R. (2009) Keeping our teachers! Investigating mentoring practices to support and retain novice educators. *Mentoring and Tutoring* 17(4): 329–341.

Peters, J. (2002) University-school collaboration: Identifying faulty assumptions. *Asia-Pacific Journal of Teacher Education* 30(3): 229–242.

Pierce, T. and Miller, S. P. (1994) Using peer coaching in preservice practica. *Teacher Education and Special Education* 17(4): 215–223.

Poseen, I. J. and Denmark, V. (2007) *Coaching and Mentoring First Year and Student Teachers*. Larchmont: Eye on Education.

Pring, R. (1996) Just desert. In Furlong, J. and Smith, R. (Eds) *The Role of Higher Education in Initial Teacher Training*. London: Kogan Paul. 8–22.

Schön, D. (1987) *Educating the Reflective Practitioner*. San Fransisco: Jossey-Bass.

Shulman, L. (1987) Knowledge and teaching: Foundations of the new reform. *Harvard Education Review* 57: 1–22.

Sleeter, C. (2008) Equity, democracy, and neoliberal assaults on teacher education. *Teaching and Teacher Education* 24(8): 1947–1957.

Smith, I., Brisard, E. and Menter, I. (2006) Models of partnership developments in initial teacher education in the four components of the United Kingdom: recent trends and current challenges. *Journal of Education for Teaching* 32(2): 147–164.

Sorensen, P. and Sears, J. (2005) Collaborative practice in initial teacher education: the use of paired subject placements in the school practicum. *International Journal of Learning* 14: 619–631.

Sorensen, P., Young, J. and Mandzuk, D. (2005) Alternative routes into the teaching profession. *Interchange* 36(4): 371–403.

TDA (2007) *Professional Standards for Teachers: Why Sit Still in Your Career?* London: TDA.

Tobin, K. and Roth, W.-M. (2006) *Teaching to Learn: A View from the Field.* Rotterdam: Sense Publishers.

Tomlinson, P. (1995) *Understanding Mentoring: Reflective Strategies for School-based Teacher Preparation.* Buckingham: Open University Press.

Totterdell, M., Woodroffe, L. Bubbs, S. and Hanrahan, K. (2004) *The Impact of NQT Induction Programmes on the Enhancement of Teacher Expertise, Professional Development, Job Satisfaction or Retention Rates: A Systematic Review of Research on Induction.* In Research Evidence in Education Library. London: EPPI-Centre, Social Science Research Unit, Institute of Education.

Utley, B. L., Rhodes, L. K. and Basile, C. G. (2003) Walking in two worlds: master teachers serving as site coordinators in partner schools. *Teaching and Teacher Education* 19(5): 515–528.

Wang, J. (2001) Contexts of mentoring and opportunities for learning to teach: A comparative study of mentoring practice. *Teaching and Teacher Education* 17(1): 51–73.

Wenger, E. (1998) *Communities of Practice: Learning, Meaning and Identity.* Cambridge: Cambridge University Press.

Whitehead, J. and Fitzgerald, B. (2006) Professional learning through a generative approach to mentoring: lessons from a Training School partnership and their wider implications. *Journal of Education for Teaching* 32(1): 37–52.

Wynn, M. J. and Kromrey, J. (1999) Paired peer placement with peer coaching in early field experiences: Results of a four year study. *Teacher Education Quarterly* 26(1): 21–38.

Zeichner (2006) Reflections of a university-based teacher educator on the future of college- and university-based teacher education. *Journal of Teacher Education* 57(3): 326–340.

Zeichner (2009) *Teacher Education and the Struggle for Social Justice.* London: Routledge.

Zwozdiak-Myers, P., Cameron, K., Mustard, C., Leask, M. and Green, A. (2010) *Literature Review: Analysis of Current Research, Theory and Practice in Partnership Working to Identify Constituent Components of Effective ITT Partnerships.* TDA, Brunel University, West London. Available at: http://www.scribd.com/doc/29847198/T35416-Literature-Review-Final-February-2010 [accessed 10.10.10]

14

Mentoring and Coaching for Teachers' Continuing Professional Development

Philippa Cordingley and Natalia Buckler

INTRODUCTION

Here we consider links between mentoring and coaching and broader evidence about continuing professional development (CPD) that has an impact on pupil outcomes. We explore these concepts by attempting to embed relevant evidence in policy and practice in England. More specifically for this purpose, we use theoretical foundations, key concepts, and principles of the English National Framework for Coaching and Mentoring.

The National Framework for Coaching and Mentoring – commissioned by the then Department for Education and Skills (DfES) (see Centre for the Use of Research & Evidence in Education [CUREE], 2005) – was a way of translating evidence into policy and practice from three systematic research reviews. Each review focused on the impact of CPD on teaching and learning with regard to empirical studies about outcomes for both pupils and teachers. However, the reviews also built upon theory. For example, the review's core definition of CPD was from Day's (1999) work on teacher development as part of lifelong learning. The review also drew on Joyce and Showers (2002) in exploring connections between CPD and pupil outcomes, and Adey's (2002) practice of long-term exploration of the effects of coaching within programs for accelerating learning in science. The goal of the commission from the Department was to create a national policy framework that could be endorsed by the government and that national agencies and practitioners at regional, local, and school levels could adopt. The process of translating review findings into such a framework involved these elements:

- fieldwork to establish the ways in which CPD practice current in 2002 related to the review findings;
- analysis of policies current at that time to ensure that the resulting framework complemented other statutory frameworks;
- consultation with leading research experts in the field including Bruce Joyce (see Joyce and Showers, 2002) who has since updated his original 1988 study;
- analysis of lessons from the evaluations of national programs, such as the Department for Education and Skills (DfES) (2004) and Earl and colleagues' (Earl, Watson, Levin, Leithwood, Fullan, and Torrance, 2003) evaluation of national literacy and numeracy strategies;
- wide-ranging consultation with school leaders and CPD local and regional leaders from local authorities and higher education institutions.

Lessons from the experiences and development work of national agencies in England, including the General Teaching Council for England (GTCE), Becta, National College for School Leadership (NCSL), Training and Development Agency for Schools (TDA), Specialist Schools and Academies Trust (SSAT), and the DfES were also investigated collaboratively with key representatives. All of these agencies subsequently adopted the principles outlined in the Framework.

The Framework was grounded in research findings indicating the importance of peer support, specialist expertise, and the professional learner's role in mentoring and coaching and broader CPD. The Framework aimed to offer to the English education system a consistent and evidence-based combination of principles, skills, and core concepts. These were drafted in a summary of the what, who, how, why, and when of mentoring and coaching to bring key aspects of research evidence to the attention of practitioners and policy makers. An aspect of the evidence particularly emphasized by the Framework was the value of combining specialist coaching with the co-coaching of professional learners, both of whom take risks and so are reciprocally vulnerable. This was something that had not been featured strongly in practice, as the fieldwork highlighted, and might otherwise have been overlooked.

COLLABORATION AND SPECIALIST EXPERTISE IN CPD

Three systematic reviews of the research about CPD and its impact on pupils as well as their teachers (e.g., Cordingley, Bell, Rundell, and Evans 2003) found that evidence about benefits to pupils in studies of teacher development was strongly linked to a combination of specialist and peer support. Indeed, a review comparing individual and collaborative CPD showed that only in two studies of individually oriented CPD were there positive benefits for both pupils and teachers. In both cases, the specialists had intensely worked alongside teachers for the equivalent of a day a week, and so were becoming in effect peer collaborators.

In other cases of individually oriented CPD, evidence of impact tended to be restricted to fewer benefits for both teachers and pupils. Some researchers referred to the collaborative element as *peer support*, others as *peer coaching*, and still others as *collaborative inquiry* or *conferencing*. Similarly, the specialist contributions were variously labeled *coaching*, *tutoring*, *mentoring*, and *conferencing*. What was common in each case was a sustained professional development relationship between pairs or small groups of colleagues working to specific development goals through both peer and specialist support. This professional relationship took the form of extended dialogue between professionals that explored evidence from experiments with new practices in classrooms. Emphasized was the development of increasing control over the learning process by the teachers involved. In effect, even though it was not labeled as such, both specialist and collaborative coaching were identified as the golden thread running through the wide range of CPD programs with evidence about positive outcomes.

The fourth systematic review of research on CPD linked to positive student outcomes (Cordingley, Bell, Isham, Evans, and Firth, 2007) focused explicitly on the nature of the expert or specialist contribution to teacher learning. The review identified three main areas of specialist support to initiate and embed change so that pupils as well as teachers are beneficiaries:

- specialist knowledge of a particular subject area and/or effective pedagogical approaches;
- specialist knowledge and skills in framing, initiating, and sustaining the CPD process; and
- understanding of the dynamics, challenges, and facilitators of professional learning in practical ways, within the fast-paced dynamics of daily school life.

The studies from which the evidence was drawn were all set within the context of CPD processes. These might well be described as a mix of (mostly) in-school specialist coaching supplemented by in-school peer or collaborative coaching (i.e., co-coaching).

ROLE OF SPECIALIST EXPERTISE

A key finding in relation to the role of specialists was that they introduced new knowledge and/or skills *and* they employed a repertoire of support mechanisms to help embed learning and bring about changes in teachers' practice. In particular, the specialists helped teachers connect the wider evidence base, underpinning theory for new practices, and knowledge about the ways in which pupils learn and develop in response to such approaches. In doing so, they helped teachers identify and review existing practices and beliefs in the context of new evidence. Coaching techniques and strategies for supporting teachers' learning were present during various stages and in different contexts throughout this process. They included the use of modeling, workshops, observation, and feedback, plus strategies for introducing and supporting peer working, usually in the teachers' own schools and classrooms. These key strategies helped motivate teachers to persist with new approaches in the face of difficulties, and ensured that adaptations for context were informed by direct evidence about how students were responding to the changes teachers were making.

Timperley, Wilson, Barrar, and Fung's (2007) best evidence synthesis reinforced all of these findings. It also identified in more detail elements that were important for promoting professional learning in ways that impacted positively and substantively on a range of student outcomes. When engaging with external expertise, she found that 'experts' needed more than knowledge of the content of changes in teaching practice that might make a difference to students. They also needed to know how to make the content meaningful to teachers and manageable within the context of daily teaching practice:

> 'Expecting teachers to act as technicians and to implement a set of "behaviours" belies the complexity of teaching, the embeddedness of individual acts of teaching, and the need to be responsive to the learning needs of students'
>
> (Timperley et al., 2007: xxix).

Effective CPD for teachers involved sustained support in processing new understandings and their implications for the participants' professional practice: 'Challenging problematic beliefs and testing the efficacy of competing ideas' (Timperley et al., 2007: xxx) was highlighted as another aspect of such CPD.

LEADERSHIP OF CPD

Leadership was also a strong feature of Timperley et al.'s findings. Their review found that school-based interventions in the core research studies had leaders who facilitated one or more of these conditions:

- an actively organized supportive environment that promoted professional learning opportunities and the implementation of new classroom practices;
- a focus on developing a learning culture within the school that applied to both teachers and students;
- provisions of alternative visions and targets for student outcomes and monitoring of whether these were met; and
- explicit development of conditions for distributing leadership by developing others' leadership.

Teacher learning and leadership are connected concepts that need more exploration. Timperley et al. (2007) quoted Stein and Nelson who argued that 'teachers must believe that serious engagement in their own learning is part and parcel of what it means to be a professional' (2007: 192). They emphasized that, along with providing opportunities for staff professional development, school leaders needed to 'hold teachers accountable for integrating what they have learned in professional development into their ongoing practice' (cited in Timperley et al., 2007: 192). Research published by GTC on the strategic leadership of CPD (CUREE, 2007) in schools also highlighted, *inter alia*, the importance of locating the leadership of CPD at senior management level and using a mix of specialist expertise and collaborative coaching. Bolam and Weindling (2006) identified the key role of heads and senior staff in promoting and supporting CPD. Robinson's (2009) extensive systematic review of what school leaders do that has the most impact on student outcomes found that their engagement with CPD was the single most important factor. School leaders' involvement in both leading and participating in professional development, thus modeling professional learning, had twice as much statistically significant impact (effect size = 0.84) as the next nearest leadership contribution (effect size = 0.42).

PROFESSIONAL LEARNING

The contribution of teachers participating in CPD has been curiously overlooked in mainstream CPD research and practice. Years ago, Zeichner and Liston (1996) argued that unless teachers take control over their development and become committed to their learning, their CPD will be 'miseducative'. Evidence from the CPD research reviews about the importance of peer support led to the inclusion of specifically identified professional learning skills alongside the coaching skills within the National Framework for Mentoring and Coaching. Such skills include responding proactively to specialist expertise, understanding one's own learning needs, and observing, analyzing, and reflecting on one's own and the coach's practice.

Slowly, recognition of teachers' increasing responsibility and ability to control learning is growing in both policy and practice in England. For example, the General Teaching Council for England (GTCe) has developed the Teacher Learning Academy (TLA) as a way of recognizing teachers' contributions to professional learning. The pilot introduction of a funded masters degree in teaching and learning (MTL) for new teachers in 2010 by the outgoing Labour Government had at its heart the recognition of the important role that developing a 'learning mindset' had to play in increasing the status and success of the profession.

Timperley et al.'s (2007) best evidence synthesis defined professional learning by contrasting it with professional development. She quotes the definition of professional development put forward by Guskey, which refers to 'those processes and activities designed to enhance the professional knowledge, skills, and attitudes of educators so that they might, in turn, improve the learning of students' (cited in Timperley et al., 2007: 3). Professional learning, on the other hand, is interpreted as an internal process of creating professional knowledge and expertise, 'an umbrella term under which professional development of the "delivery" kind is just one part' (ibid.). In this context, school-based coaching relationships span both professional development and professional learning.

PROFESSIONAL LEARNING AND EXPERIMENTATION

Much of both teachers' professional learning and development is increasingly seen as work-based learning. Lave and Wenger's (1991) study gave impetus to a number of models and theories of workplace learning. Their work challenged the prevailing orthodoxy, which linked adult learning to participation in formal education or training. Based on the ethnographic studies of how people learn at work, Lave and Wenger proposed the interrelated concepts of *legitimate peripheral participation* and *communities of practice*, which explored how novices progress to full participant status. Their vision of learning as a process involving collaboration of newcomers with more experienced peers became a foundation for theories of apprenticeship and learning in non-specialist educational settings.

When describing the nature of work-based learning, Eraut (2000) highlighted that it was driven by demands, challenges, and interactions at the workplace and often happened though experimentation. Teacher professional learning, a form of adult learning (Wald and Castleberry, 2000), occurs over time, is reflective and experimental by nature, is fuelled by various sources of information, and is driven by the professional learner around relevant issues. Young (2004), on the other hand, argues that not all knowledge can be viewed as situated or context-specific. Some kinds of knowledge or models of understanding offer support that is more generic to practitioners. Fuller (2006) proposed to provide professional learners with knowledge of theories and strategies that are not limited to their daily practice, integrating workplace learning with learning from other sources. Evidence about teacher CPD places particular emphasis on the role of specialist coaches in creating and recognizing such learning opportunities.

Exploring teacher learning in new contexts, Hagger, Burn, Mutton, and Brindley (2008) found that student teachers' orientations towards risk and the aspirations of this group played an important role in sustaining learning. Student teachers whose aspirations for their pupils were limited and who assumed that their practice and skills would automatically flow from increased experience, tended to 'plateau'. Based on their research, Hagger et al. (2008) suggested that encouraging new teachers to experiment during their own teaching could counteract this problem and help secure their commitment to sustained professional development at the same time as becoming competent classroom practitioners. Leat (1993) identified a link between experimenting, taking risks, and making decisions in the classroom and teachers' emotions. He argued for the necessity of taking seriously the feelings of teachers along with their knowledge and behavior when discussing issues of teacher competence and development. This perspective advances the importance of teacher feelings and emotions during professional learning and development as an important context for coaching relationships.

HOW TRANSFERABLE IS PROFESSIONAL LEARNING?

Wallace (1996) who warned about the 'myth' of 'automatic transfer,' which can be thought of as another type of boundary crossing between learning that occurs inside and outside the workplace. This researcher argued that 'simulating' new skills during external training courses will not necessarily result in the ability or readiness to perform them in the workplace context. Joyce and Showers (2002) found that theoretical input should be accompanied by demonstration, opportunities to try out new knowledge/theory in practice, elicitation of feedback, and support via coaching to make the biggest impact on improving teachers' performance. Cordingley et al. (2007) also found that effective teacher learning and development comprised not only the introduction of new knowledge and skills by specialists but also a range of measures for supporting and embedding their use via coaching-based collaboration with peers and specialists, modeling, and experimentation.

For the purposes of this discussion, perhaps the most important messages from the wider evidence base about effective CPD (i.e., CPD that has a demonstrably positive impact on both teacher and learner outcomes) are that CPD is most effective when it is collaborative, sustained, embedded in real-life learning contexts, and supported by specialists. And, when used properly, mentoring and coaching provide tailor-made in-school strategies for making the most of all four of these approaches.

COACHING AND MENTORING BENEFITS FOR TEACHERS AND PUPILS

Mentors, specialists, co-coaches, and professional learners all have to take into account a wide range of factors, including staying abreast of research and best practice and ensuring that their work occurs in complementary ways. This leads to the question, what benefits might motivate teachers and schools to tackle such complexity on a serious, sustained basis? Consistent messages across the systematic reviews of CPD related to positive links between collaborative, sustained CPD and teachers' self confidence in taking risks, as well as their ability to make a difference; willingness to continue professional learning; ability to make changes to practice; deeper knowledge and understanding of subject and pedagogy; and use of a wider repertoire of strategies and ability to match to pupil needs.

The reviews also found that teachers' involvement in collaborative and sustained CPD, including through mentoring and coaching, was linked with pupils' enhanced motivation to learn, better performance, improved organization of work, better questioning skills and responses, improved participation in group work, and increased ability to select and use a variety of learning strategies.

USING COACHING IN SCHOOLS

The development of research- and policy-based frameworks for coaching in England was firmly in place by 2010. The use of the evidence from systematic reviews and of the National Mentoring and Coaching Framework by all of the national agencies and by many local authorities and schools has increased the consciousness of schools, teachers, and CPD leaders about the importance of coaching. The system is now 'talking the talk' and this represents progress, as can be seen from two successive thematic reviews by the English schools inspectorate, Ofsted. The first Ofsted report (2006), for example, highlighted that whilst many are talking the talk with regard to coaching there was some concern that the potential of coaching and mentoring was yet to be fully realized:

> The schools had developed their own interpretations of coaching and mentoring, and consequently the usefulness of this valuable form of CPD was limited. Often staff used the terms only to refer to a system of peer support in an area of common interest. (2006: 14)

Some of the common issues identified by the report included lack of peer observations and lack of input from expert specialist coaches. Another area of concern was school managers being 'unaware of what was going on' (ibid.) and thus ill-equipped to evaluate the effectiveness and value of mentoring and coaching processes.

In the follow up report, Ofsted (2010) highlighted 'the need for confidentiality between coach and colleague' (2010: 22) as one of the key features of successful mentoring and coaching. It was also found that collaboration 'carried out in an atmosphere of trust' enabled staff to 'talk openly about their concerns and problems. In order to preserve this openness, some of the schools visited had deliberately separated their coaching work from their formal procedures for performance management' (ibid.).

The report (Ofsted, 2010) noted that while successful schools were making increasing use of coaching and mentoring, a common understanding about the terms used was lacking. This knowledge deficit concerning 'different forms of mentoring and coaching' often meant that schools were not able to 'use them to best effect' (2010: 20).

EMBEDDING COACHING IN SCHOOLS

So, although there is evidence that the profession is more supportive of coaching and mentoring, many school professionals are not yet 'walking the walk'. One context in which CPD in general and coaching more specifically are likely to be in demand and supported by schools is the introduction in England of new curriculum frameworks – particularly as this is happening at the same time as the removal of much of the national infrastructure of support for schools. For the first time since 1988, curriculum design is becoming a key responsibility of all teachers.

Recent research in schools – which had been identified as highly effective in curriculum development (CUREE and University of Wolverhampton, 2008, 2010) – helps us understand what coaching and mentoring can achieve when they are used 'to best effect'. Heads and curriculum leaders in these schools had developed strategies for teachers to experience one-to-one specialist or co-coaching, or both, as part of a cycle of continuous school improvement. In one school, for example, eight teachers worked together to develop an integrated year 7 humanities curriculum. The teachers also worked in pairs as co-coaches (e.g., a history and geography teacher) to support each other in teaching areas of the curriculum outside their specialism.

Whilst the practical details of the approaches to coaching (number of sessions, elapsed time between sessions, pairing arrangements, etc.) differed, the learning processes at the heart of the coaching were consistent. All models relied on joint planning that involved observation and debriefing. Teachers were expected to experiment with new lesson plans and resources on behalf of the group and to reflect on the outcomes for learners and for their practice. School and curriculum leaders were also actively involved in coaching. They used curriculum-oriented observation to help shape the focus for coaching sessions and spot areas where old practices, which had been earmarked for replacement, were persisting because of other pressures. The schools used both internal and external specialist expertise. The latter included creative arts practitioners and local authority advisers. However, it was the identification and deployment of internal specialist curriculum expertise that particularly characterized these schools.

Cordingley and Bell (2007) have reviewed evidence from the international research base. This work suggests that actual transfer of learning – that is, walking the walk, as well as talking the talk, resulting in embedded and sustainable change – depends on a combination of measures to encourage engagement and thus facilitate the development of ownership and control of new practices. One of the most important of these measures was coaching. Coaching in this context was defined as a sustained and collaborative process, and allows 'demonstration and modeling, simulation, experimentation, observation, reflecting on evidence, building on individual starting points and structured dialogue that explores beliefs, internalized practice, and the rationale for approaches' (2007: 11).

MAKING COACHING AND MENTORING HAPPEN

As the Ofsted reports underline, it is one thing to make a strong case for coaching but quite another to achieve this in the school context. School leaders may understand the link established between teachers' learning and development, and school improvement, as a recent guidance report on coaching published by the National College (Lofthouse, Leat, and Towler, 2010) indicates. The study sees coaching as a means of realizing the core principles of teacher professional learning. The principles that apply to successful CPD provision were put forward by Timperley (2009) and included creating conditions that allow:

> teachers to experience and develop understanding of an integration of knowledge and skills; teachers to gain multiple opportunities to learn and apply information; teachers' beliefs to

be challenged by evidence which is not consistent with their assumptions, teachers to have opportunities to process new learning with others. (2009: 9)

However, alongside the appreciation of the imperative for coaching is an equally strong awareness of the complex and challenging nature of teaching, and the difficulties inherent in potentially bringing about a major cultural change to the school ethos. The National College report identified that coaching was often offered to a minority of staff 'who fall into pre-determined categories', or was offered to any member of staff who wanted to 'fit it into their pre-existing workload' (Lofthouse et al., 2010: 11).

In the midst of this complexity, it is worth returning to the National Framework (CUREE, 2005) and the attempt to embed within coaching practice a series of principles. These principles provide some guidance to CPD leaders in such areas as considering the establishment of coaching and mentoring within schools, expressed as activities that underpin effective coaching and mentoring. Such principles address issues such as the importance of: learning conversations and a learning agreement, combined support from colleagues and specialists, development of self direction, challenging and personal goal setting, understanding why different approaches work, acknowledging benefits to mentors and coaches, experimenting and observing, and using resources effectively.

The National Framework also establishes the core concepts of mentoring, specialist coaching, and collaborative coaching (or co-coaching). It enables coaching and mentoring to become operational through answering such practical questions as: Why would your colleagues use coaching and mentoring? Who would be involved? What activities would they do? When would the coaching and mentoring take place? Where would the activity take place?

The Framework's list of skills needed by coaches and mentors encompasses building relationships, modeling, tailoring learning to goals, observing, analyzing and reflecting, providing information (or sharing interpretation for co-coaches), recognizing and reinforcing learners' increasing control over their learning – easy to say but hard to do. What is made clear is that mentors, coaches, and professional learners 'learn to do' many of these skills on a continuing basis. Here, the importance of linking support for learning to specialist knowledge and expertise, to the wider public evidence base, and to the underpinning rationale are emphasized in practical ways. As already noted, a distinctive feature of the Framework is the defining and highlighting of the skills of a professional learner, as well as those of the coach or mentor who helps colleagues feel more empowered to seek out the help of specialists. It replaces passive models of professional development with a proactive approach to enhancing their own confidence, clarity, and self-evaluation, and so makes a critical contribution to the process of building a professional learning community. Moreover, it relieves some of the pressure from coaches and mentors to be ultra-skilled, and reinforces the learning opportunities offered to them and the modeling of professional learning that is crucial to fostering these key skills.

CONCLUSION

What we have sought to argue is that a strong empirical and theoretical evidence base exists for the value of coaching. And, in England at least, there is an increasing interest in and awareness of its potential, but there are challenges too. In particular, the removal of a wide-ranging infrastructure of support and proposed reforms of initial teacher education suggest a possible fragmentation of specialist support. Identifying and working with specialist coaches is likely to bemore challenging in the future. And, whilst models of coaching like GROW (Goal–Current—Reality–Options–Will, http://www.what-is-coaching.com/grow-coaching-model.html) emphasize the need for specialist knowledge of coaching rather than specialist content knowledge, the evidence we have pointed to suggests a need for both. This is especially true when coaches are supportingcolleagues who are not self aware and who lack a specific diagnostic assessment of their own developmental needs.

An emphasis on the development of collaborative or peer coaching alongside specialist coaching would do much to alleviate this problem, since it would start subject specialists down the road of developing coaching skills and, effectively executed, would inevitably whet their appetite for further learning. Alongside subject specialists developing their coaching skills, a parallel emphasis is required for professional learners themselves as well as school leaders. Teachers need to develop their skills as professional learners in order to make good use of coaching opportunities. School leaders wishing to embed coaching and ensure effectiveness of CPD in their settings need to be prepared to model coaching and professional learning. This commitment to professional development from the major players on the CPD scene in schools could help the educational system in England and other countries reach the kind of critical mass of coaching skills that could create a virtuous learning cycle.

REFERENCES

Adey, P., Robertson, A., & Venville, G. (2002). Effects of a cognitive stimulation programme on Year 1 pupils. *British Journal of Educational Psychology*, 72, 1–25.

Bolam, R., & Weindling, D. (2006). Synthesis of research and evaluation projects concerned with capacity-building through teachers' professional development: GTC report. Retrieved January 31, 2011, from http://www.gtce.org.uk/133031/133036/133039/133112/full_report

Cordingley, P., & Bell, M. (2007). Transferring learning and taking innovation to scale (1–27). (The Innovation Unit). Coventry: CUREE/Crown. Retrieved January 31, 2011, from http://www.innovationunit.org/images/stories/files/pdf/transferring_learning.pdf

Cordingley, P., Bell, M., Rundell, B., & Evans, D. (2003). The impact of collaborative CPD on classroom teaching and learning. In: *Research Evidence in Education Library*. London: EPPI-Centre, Social Science Research Unit, Institute of Education, University of London. Accessible at: http://www.eppi.ioe.ac.uk/cms/Default.aspx?tabid=132

Cordingley, P., Bell, M., Thomason, S., & Firth, A. (2005). The impact of collaborative continuing professional development (CPD) on classroom teaching and learning. In: *Research Evidence in*

Education Library. London: EPPI-Centre, Social Science Research Unit, Institute of Education, University of London.

Cordingley, P., Bell, M., Isham, C., Evans, D., & Firth, A. (2007). What do specialists do in CPD programmes for which there is evidence of positive outco*mes for pupils and teachers? In: Research Evidence in Education Library.* London: EPPI-Centre, Social Science Research Unit, Institute of Education, University of London.

CUREE. (2005). National framework for mentoring and coaching. Retrieved January 30, 2011, from http://www.teachernet.gov.uk/_doc/8864/4.4.10.pdf

CUREE. (2007). Qualitative study of school-level strategies for teachers' CPD (GTC report). Retrieved January 30, 2011, from http://www.gtce.org.uk/133031/133036/133039/curee_cpd_strategies

CUREE and University of Wolverhampton. (2008). What are the characteristics of effective continuing professional development (CPD) for teachers undertaking curriculum development? What are teachers involved in? Who supports them, how and with what results? Coventry: CUREE.

CUREE and University of Wolverhampton. (2010). In schools that are successfully developing the curriculum, how are the changes required by curriculum innovation being managed by school leaders? Coventry: CUREE.

Day, C. (1999). *Developing Teachers: The Challenges of Lifelong Learning.* London: Falmer.

DfES. (2004). Primary national strategy: Intensifying support programme. Retrieved January 30, 2011, from http://www.education.gov.uk/publications/eOrderingDownload/DfES-0037-2004.pdf

Earl, L., Watson, N., Levin, B., Leithwood, K., Fullan, M., & Torrance, N. (2003). Final report of the external evaluation of England's national literacy and numeracy strategies. Retrieved January 30, 2011, from http://eric.ed.gov/PDFS/ED472214.pdf

Eraut, M. (2000). Teacher education designed or framed. *International Journal of Educational Research*, 33(5), 557–574.

Fuller, A. (2006). Participative learning through the work-based route: From apprenticeship to part-time higher education. *European Journal of Vocational Education*, 37, 68–81.

Hagger, H., Burn, K., Mutton, T., & Brindley, S. (2008). Practice makes perfect? Learning to learn as a teacher. *Oxford Review of Education*, 34(2), 159–178.

Joyce, B. R., & Showers, B. (2002). *Student achievement through staff development* (3rd ed.). Alexandria, VA: Association for Supervision and Curriculum Development (ASCD).

Lave, J., & Wenger, E. (1991). *Situated learning: Legitimate peripheral participation.* Cambridge: Cambridge University Press.

Leat, D. (1993). A conceptual model of competence. *Journal of In-Service Education*, 19(2), 35–40.

Lofthouse, R., Leat, D., & Towler, C. (2010) Coaching for teaching and learning: A practical guide for schools. Nottingham: National College. Retrieved January 31, 2011, from http://www.nationalcollege.org.uk/docinfo?id=133111&filename=coaching-for-teaching-and-learning.pdf

Ofsted. (2006). The logical chain: CPD in effective schools. London: Ofsted. Retrieved January 31, 2011, from http://www.ofsted.gov.uk/Ofsted-home/Publications-and-research/Browse-all-by/Education/Leadership/Management/The-logical-chain-continuing-professional-development-in-effective-schools

Ofsted. (2010). Good professional development in schools: How does leadership contribute? London: Ofsted. Retrieved January 30, 2011, from http://www.ofsted.gov.uk/Ofsted-home/Publications-and-research/Browse-all-by/Documents-by-type/Thematic-reports/Good-professional-development-in-schools

Robinson, V., Hohepa, M., & Lloyd, C. (2009). School leadership and student outcomes: Identifying what works and why (BES). Wellington: Ministry of Education. Retrieved January 30, 2011, from http://www.educationcounts.govt.nz/

Timperley, H. (2009). Teacher professional learning and development. Educational Practices Series. Retrieved January 30, 2011, from http://www.ibe.unesco.org/fileadmin/user_upload/Publications/Educational_Practices/EdPractices_18.pdf

Timperley, H., Wilson, A., Barrar, H., & Fung, I. (2007). Teacher professional learning and development: Best Evidence Synthesis Iteration (BES). Wellington: Ministry of Education. Retrieved

January 31, 2011, from http://www.educationcounts.govt.nz/__data/assets/pdf_file/0017/16901/TPLandDBESentire.pdf

Wald, P. J., & Castleberry, M. S. (2000). *Educators as learners: Creating a professional learning community in your school*. Alexandria, VA: Association for Supervision and Curriculum Development (ASCD).

Wallace, M. (1996). When is experiential learning not experiential learning? In G. Claxton, Atkinson, T., Osborn, M., & Wallace, M. (Eds.), *Liberating the learner: Lessons for professional development in education* (pp. 16–31). London: Routledge.

Young, M. (2004). Conceptualizing vocational knowledge: Some theoretical considerations. In H. Rainbird, A. Fuller, & A. Munro (Eds.), *Workplace learning in context* (pp. 185–200). London: Routledge.

Zeichner, K. M., & Liston, D. P. (1996). *Reflective teaching: An introduction*. London: Routledge.

15

A Critical–Constructivist Perspective on Mentoring and Coaching for Leadership

Gary M. Crow

INTRODUCTION

During the last several years, attention on school leadership has increased significantly. Research evidence has emphasized the importance of school leadership for student learning, teacher workplace conditions, and school climate and renewal (Day, Sammons, Hopkins, Harris, Leithwood, Gu et al. 2009; Wahlstrom, Louis, Leithwood, and Anderson, 2010). Although the preponderance of evidence suggests an indirect relationship between principal leadership and student achievement, the significance of the leader's role is nonetheless critical. Due to this growing recognition of the importance of school leadership, more emphasis has been placed on how school leaders themselves are prepared and then supported during induction in schools (Young, Crow, Murphy, and Ogawa, 2009). Research, policy, and practice have focused on how leaders are prepared to engage in school reform and transformation. Among the more popular forms for the preparation and professional development of school leaders are mentoring and coaching. Although the research on these two leadership development strategies has not kept pace with their use in practice, the regard for mentoring and coaching has taken on almost panacea-like power in the leadership development of school leaders (Barnett and O'Mahony, 2008).

Herein, I focus on mentoring and coaching for leadership – definitions, perspectives, and practical applications. My intention is not to provide an exhaustive literature review on mentoring and coaching for leadership but rather to present a particular conceptual perspective and to apply this to policy, leadership development, and research. Relevant conceptual and empirical literature will, however, be used to reinforce this discussion.

DEFINING MENTORING AND COACHING FOR LEADERSHIP

Beginning with definitions of mentoring and coaching seems an obvious place to start. However, defining these two leadership development strategies has proven to be one of the more difficult conceptual tasks undertaken in the literature.

Mentoring

Defining mentoring is problematic in at least four ways. First, historically definitions of mentoring have identified attributes rather than the meaning of the concept (Bozeman and Feeney, 2007). For example, Kram's (1985) classic work on mentoring defined the concept as an intense relationship where a senior expert colleague supports a junior colleague in at least two ways: career advancement and psychosocial development. However, this definition takes the meaning of intense relationship for granted and focuses instead on the functions of mentoring. A more recent definition of mentoring, based on Kram's concept, is equally ambiguous. Stated by Eby (1997):

> Mentoring is an intense developmental relationship whereby advice, counseling, and developmental opportunities are provided to a protégé by a mentor, which, in turn, shapes the protégé's career experiences … This occurs through two types of support to protégés (1) instrumental or career support and (2) psychological support. (1997: 126)

An example from education seems equally ambiguous. A mentor is someone 'with the experience, expertise, wisdom and/or power who teaches, councils and helps less experienced or less knowledgeable persons to develop professionally and personally' (Danielson and McGreal, 2000: 251). This lack of clarity regarding the meaning of mentoring leads to other definitional difficulties.

A second problem with defining mentoring is the expanding types of mentoring practices; for example, co-mentoring, peer mentoring, multiple mentoring, team mentoring, and e- mentoring (Mullen and Lick, 1999; Scandura and Pellegrini, 2007) have developed in various organizational sectors. This expansion of types of mentoring has effectively tried to move the field away from overly narrow definitions characterized by mentor–protégé dyads, formal-only programs, single rather than multiple mentors, and static as opposed to dynamic features of mentoring relationships.

Third, the difficulty in defining mentoring is also intensified by the lack of boundaries of the concept. Mertz (2004) identified the confusion of mentoring in the literature with other supportive roles, including teacher, coach, role model, peer pal, sponsor, patron, counselor, advisor, and guide. This lack of definitional boundaries leads to the question of what differentiates mentoring from any other supportive role: 'Are all of the relationships referred to in the literature as mentoring talking about the same kind of relationship, or are there fundamental differences in their relationships, differences that can be distinguished?' (Mertz, 2004: 544).

A fourth problem in defining mentoring, also identified by Mertz (2004), involves unexamined assumptions about mentoring in the literature. Assumptions about the goals of the mentoring relationship, the agreement about these goals between the mentor and protégé, the benefits to each party, the degree to which mentor and protégé value these benefits, and the willingness of each party to exert effort to acquire these benefits are all preconceptions rarely investigated in the mentoring literature. In addition, one of the most widespread beliefs about mentoring is its effectiveness not only for the protégé but also for the organization.

Far from being an academic exercise, these problems of definition are important for several reasons. First, because the explanatory power of the concept is missing, definitional ambiguity limits the ability to develop theories of mentoring. Second, definitional problems make it difficult to build a research base due to the methods assuming certain definitions of mentoring. Merriam emphasized this problem, having said that 'how mentoring is defined determines the extent of mentoring found' (1983: 165). Third, the difficulties in defining mentoring affect our ability to talk with one another about mentoring (Mertz, 2004) and to develop practical ways of implementing mentoring programs.

One attempt by educational leadership researchers to define mentoring comes from Mertz's (2004) definition, which integrated the concepts of intent and involvement. This researcher argued that various supportive roles, including mentoring, can be identified based on *intent*, which is the perceived purpose of the activity and whether that intent is sought or valued; and *involvement*, which is the time and effort required to achieve this purpose. About the purpose of the activity, Mertz's model is built on three functions of mentoring. Two of these, career development and psychosocial development, come from Kram (1983). Later, role modeling was added as a third function (Burke, 1984; Scandura, 1992). Crow and Matthews (1998) identified three functions of mentoring for leaders as career development, psychosocial development, and professional development. This model allows Mertz to distinguish mentoring from other roles such as patron, sponsor, advisor, coach, or role model. Mentoring entails the highest level of involvement on the part of individuals participating in the process and emphasizes career advancement as the primary intent of the mentoring relationship. Although mentoring may also include professional or psychosocial development purposes, the major intent is career advancement in which the mentor sponsors or becomes an advocate for the protégé.

Coaching

The definition of coaching has provided less difficulty in the literature on leadership development; however, there are problems. Barnett and O'Mahony (2008) used Robertson's definition that 'coaching involves two people setting and achieving professional goals, being open to new learning, and engaging in dialogue for the purpose of improving leadership practice' (cited in Barnett and O'Mahony, 2008: 245). Several authors (Hobson, 2003; Male, 2006) referred to mentoring as a more encompassing and generic term than coaching, in fact seeing coaching as a form of mentoring.

> A coach … provides continuing support that is safe and confidential and has as its goal the nurturing of significant personal, professional, and institutional growth through a process that unfolds over time. A coach brings outside perspective and has no stake in the status quo in an organization.
>
> (Bloom, Castagna, Moir, & Warren, 2005: 10)

Other than characterizing coaching as less comprehensive than mentoring, these definitions actually do little to define the concept. Mertz's (2004) model (described previously) characterized coaching as including much less involvement than mentoring and as focusing primarily on professional development rather than career advancement. In the case of leadership, coaching usually focuses on some skill-set, such as teacher conferencing.

A THEORETICAL PERSPECTIVE ON MENTORING AND COACHING

The literature on mentoring and coaching for school leaders tends to be based on an atheoretical perspective, focusing primarily on the functions, roles, and practices of mentoring. However implicit in this treatment of mentoring and coaching is a functionalist perspective, which makes certain assumptions about the nature and processes of mentoring/coaching school leaders. In this section, I describe this traditional, functionalist perspective in terms of its elements and how it influences a particular way of viewing and practicing mentoring and coaching. I then propose a critical–constructivist perspective on mentoring and coaching, and discuss the nature, relationships, goals/outcomes, and functions of mentoring and coaching. This perspective provides a guide for the final section in which I discuss practical applications of this viewpoint of mentoring and coaching for policy, leadership development, and research.

Traditional perspective

The traditional perspective from which mentoring and coaching have historically been understood is functionalist. Brockbank and McGill (2006) described this perspective as focusing on organizational efficiency and equilibrium. The fundamental nature of mentoring and coaching involves transmitting knowledge to enable a newcomer to support the efficient and stable continuation of the organization. The embedded goal of mentoring and coaching is to maintain organizational status quo. The functionalist perspective assumes a power relationship in mentoring and coaching in which the mentor or coach possesses expert power and the protégé is the recipient of this knowledge. In the origin of the term 'mentor', Odysseus leaves the care of his son Telemachus in the hands of Mentor. Mentor is regarded as possessing power and knowledge that enables him to protect and guide the growth and development of Telemachus.

A recent conceptual analysis of mentoring, which attempts to deal with some of the difficulties I identified in my discussion of the definition of mentoring, slightly modifies this functionalist perspective but retains the same power relationship: 'Mentoring: a process for the informal transmission of knowledge, social capital, and psychosocial support perceived by the recipient as relevant to work, career, or professional development' (Bozeman and Feeney, 2007: 731). These authors specified mentoring as a form of knowledge transmission and acknowledged that the knowledge and support must be pertinent to the protégé. However, they assumed that the mentor alone possesses the relevant expert knowledge, social capital, and support that are transmitted to the protégé.

In the typical case of mentoring and coaching school leaders, formal mentoring programs assume this functionalist perspective. The definition I quoted from Danielson and McGreal (2000) reflects this when the authors state that a mentor is someone 'with experience, expertise, wisdom and/or power who teaches, counsels and helps less experienced or less knowledgeable persons to develop professionally and personally' (2000: 251). Moreover, the purpose or outcome of these mentoring programs for school leaders tends to emphasize maintaining the status quo. In one study of a district mentoring program for aspiring school leaders, the researchers found that the successful candidates were those who were 'able to recognize and reproduce district norms in terms of leadership style and values. The aspirants who recognized and understood this dynamic were able to move into leadership positions with relative ease and speed' (Tooms, 2010: 169).

This functionalist perspective of mentoring has several weaknesses, especially in relation to the mentoring and coaching of school leaders. First, it ignores the likelihood that individuals have multiple mentors and/or coaches rather than an individual mentor or coach. The prevalence of peer mentoring and the likelihood of multiple mentors serving various functions argue for viewing mentoring and coaching as more dynamic, fluid, and complex than the functionalist perspective suggests. Mentoring scholars have been referring to mentoring relationships as a constellation of relationships (Higgins and Kram, 2001). Thus, rather than having one mentor, an individual school leader is likely to have several mentors who perform different functions including career advancement, professional development, and psychosocial support.

Second, the functionalist perspective ignores the reciprocal nature of mentoring and coaching. Various writers both inside and outside of education have pointed to the benefits of mentoring for both mentors and protégés (Barnett and O'Mahony, 2008; Daresh, 2004; Megginson and Clutterbuck, 1995). Thus, it is likely that the protégé is contributing to the relationship as well as the mentor. I return to this reciprocal notion in the next section.

Third, and perhaps most damning, a functionalist framework perpetuates a conservative view of mentoring and coaching. As mentioned, this framework emphasizes the goal of maintaining the status quo; that is, ensuring that newcomers accept and further the goals of the organization and contribute to an emphasis on equilibrium over innovation. In educational leadership settings in particular, such a conservatizing force contradicts current trends to reform and, more importantly, transform schools. Mentoring school leaders to enable them to turn around schools, ensure the learning of all students, and provide ethical and transformative leadership must go beyond the efficiency and equilibrium goals of the functionalist perspective (Crow and Matthews, 1998).

Critical–constructivist perspective for mentoring and coaching

In order to overcome these weaknesses of the functionalist framework, I propose a critical-constructivist perspective for mentoring and coaching school leaders. Put simply, a critical-constructivist perspective blends the understanding of learning as a co-constructed endeavor between mentor and protégé in which both are active participants with a critical activism in which this understanding is used to influence changes in the practice of leadership. Next, I describe that perspective relative to the nature of mentoring, the relationships involved, goals/outcomes, and elements/functions.

Nature of mentoring and coaching

From a critical–constructivist perspective, the essential nature of mentoring and coaching is learning. Mentoring and coaching, after all, are learning activities, but this learning does not simply involve a transmission of knowledge. The learning that takes place with these strategies involves the social construction of knowledge, in which knowledge is co-constructed through the social negotiation process of relationships. Thus, rather than identifying and transmitting a set of facts, skills, and practices, mentoring and coaching involve a creative process in which mentors and protégés together construct the knowledge of school leadership and make sense of the protégé's practice.

Certainly, mentoring and coaching involve the development of skills and practices for leadership. But, in a critical constructivist perspective the fundamental quality of mentoring and coaching is learning in which inquiry, sense making, and reflection are foundational. Barnett (1995) stated that the 'image of a successful mentor is that of someone who … encourages a protégé to become a more reflective, inquiring professional' (1995: 54). This reflection and inquiry focus on several types of knowledge. Barnett and O'Mahony (2008) used Lieberman and Miller's (1991) three types of knowledge to understand the focus of mentoring. According to these authors, there is knowledge *for* practice, *in* practice, and *of* practice. The last two, relevant to mentoring, involve reflection on exemplary practices (in practice) and reflection on one's own practices (of practice). Cognitive coaching (Costa and Garmston, 1994) illustrates a similar focus on reflection and inquiry and thereby on learning in coaching practices. One of the goals of cognitive coaching is to create an autonomous learner who consistently uses inquiry and reflection on her or his own practices.

Mentoring and coaching relationships

A critical–constructivist perspective for mentoring and coaching school leaders also includes a way to think about the mentoring and coaching relationship. In contrast to a narrow power relationship or even a vague 'intense relationship' (Kram, 1985) in which only one side possesses the power or expertise, namely the mentor, in this framework the relationship is a social and political negotiation between mentor and protégé in which knowledge and learning are reciprocal, shared, and created. The mentoring and coaching relationship remains a power relationship but not in a unidirectional way where the mentor has all the power. Rather the power relationship is used to negotiate and create knowledge. This shared power relationship reflects the kind of learning organization and organizational socialization in which power and learning are multidirectional (Crow and Matthews, 1998). When knowledge is co-constructed, a relationship must be multidimensional and the learning must be reciprocal. As previously mentioned, mentoring in particular has recently been described as a relationship constellation. These webs and networks increase the potential not only for an enriched set of skills and practices but also for expanded opportunities for reflection, inquiry, and creation. This type of perspective of mentoring and coaching also reflects a more distributed form of leadership (Spillane, Camburn, and Pareja, 2007).

Goals and outcomes of mentoring and coaching

What makes this perspective of mentoring and coaching a critical one relates to the goals and outcomes of mentoring and coaching. Rather than aiming to maintain the organizational status quo, mentoring and coaching from a critical–constructivist perspective focus on transformation. In what they call evolutionary mentoring, Brockbank and McGill (2006) described the kind and consequences of collective and reflective learning for transformation that occurs in this kind of mentoring and coaching. Both mentors and protégés engaged in this type of transformative learning 'have been able to see beyond, above, below and beside the taken-for-granted assumptions; the outcomes may be threatening to the status quo, and sometimes the consequence is that the individuals choose to leave or are excluded' (Brockbank and McGill, 2006: 17).

Merriam (see Merriam, Caffarella, and Baumgartner, 2007) contrasted transformational learning with informational learning. *Transformational learning* is focused on 'fundamental change in the way we see ourselves and the world in which we live' (2007: 130). In contrast, informational learning extends currently existing cognitive capacities. This transformational goal of mentoring is reflected in Gehrke's (1988) notion of mentoring as gift giving, where the mentor shares wisdom and awakening: 'There is a stirring, a recognition of the import of the gift, of the strength or talent, of the possibilities of one's life – a point where someone sees potential for genius in you' (1988: 191). In this view, the mentor provides a new vision of life and encourages the protégé to realize this vision. Although Gehrke's notion of mentoring as gift giving is probably more unidirectional than I have argued with regard to a critical–constructivist perspective, the notion of the goal of mentoring as transformational clearly fits the perspective.

The practice of this transformational learning focuses on the mentoring dialogue. In their reflective dialogue, mentors and protégés make sense of leadership practices and engage in the kind of learning that awakens them both to new kinds of possibilities for schools and the individuals who inhabit them. This dialogue can take many forms. According to Daloz's (1999) notion of transformational learning, stories become a critical part of the learning process: 'The first business of the guide is to listen to the dreams of the pilgrim. How are our students moving? What do they want for themselves? How do they tell their own stories?' (1999: 21). It is not surprising that the stories that administrators tell become so important in making sense of their practices and in the mentoring interaction (Denning, 2007).

Mentoring and coaching functions

As mentioned, three primary functions of mentoring are professional development, psychosocial development, and career development. In the case of coaching, professional development is the primary function. In the case of school leaders, the professional development function focuses on the development of knowledge, skills, and values necessary to perform the job. Psychosocial development emphasizes the personal and emotional wellbeing of the individual in relation to role expectations, clarification, and conflict. Career development focuses on career satisfaction, career awareness, and career advancement (Crow and Matthews, 1998).

Much of the literature on mentoring and coaching has centered on the acquisition of knowledge and the development of skills necessary to perform successfully the functions of the job, to adjust to the work environment, and to internalize the values of the profession (Feldman, 1976). Although coaching certainly gives weight to the development and acquisition of skills necessary to perform these job functions, a critical–constructivist perspective suggests a broader set of functions for mentoring. Recent trends in leadership development, both generally and specifically to school leadership, have tended to emphasize a technocratic orientation to the role focused on skills and competencies (Leicht and Fennell, 2001; Lumby and English, 2009; Scribner and Crow, 2010). Such an emphasis has tended to overshadow a professional orientation to the role in which values, beliefs, motivations, energy, and identities are emphasized and which go beyond the professional's personal satisfaction and motivate the individual to accept and invest in a particular professional role (Burke and Stets, 2009). Lumby and English (2009) argued that such a technocratic orientation with its emphasis on skills and competencies 'evades and miniaturizes the performance of leadership' (2009: 95). Although they did not propose that we should ignore the development of skills for school leaders, they encourage decentering technical skills and focusing instead on 'the meaning of the leader's role, script, and performance and how these relate to the identity construction of self, students, and the wider school community' (ibid. 112). In a critical–constructivist perspective, this identity construction is seen as a major function of mentoring.

The identity literature focuses on role identity, social identity (membership in a group) or person identity (unique meanings that define an individual apart from roles and groups) (Burke and Stets, 2009). Although mentoring for school leaders could certainly deal with all three of these kinds of identity, for purposes of this critical–constructivist perspective I focus on role identity. According to Burke and Stets, role identity is 'the internalized meanings of a role that individuals apply to themselves' (2009: 114). This type of identity involves how the individual makes sense of the role and provides the motivations for taking on and enacting the role: 'The energy, motivation, drive that makes roles actually work require that individuals identify with, internalize, and become the role' (ibid. 38). But, far from being an individual process the development of role identity involves the social negotiation with others. An individual does not simply designate oneself as being of a certain identity, but rather in the social and political give-and-take of work relationships identities are developed.

The literature on identity theory suggests that identity is dynamic, multiple, contextual, embedded with degrees of ambiguity and/or certainty, and socially negotiated. First, rather than being a static, unchanging notion of self, identity is fluid. This does not mean that identity is in constant flux but rather that events, experiences, and people contribute to the modification of various identities. Second, individuals have multiple identities related to the various constituencies with whom they work. Lumby and English (2009) acknowledged these multiple identities of school leaders but also argue that these leaders struggle with the need to maintain and construct a sense of self. Third, these multiple identities tend to be contextual. School leaders respond to multiple constituencies – teachers, students, parents, district superiors, community members – who make demands and communicate expectations that sometimes conflict with each other. Fourth, an individual's identities do not come to the mentoring relationship totally developed. Frequently, individuals experience confusion, ambiguity, as well as certainty regarding their role identities. Finally, these role identities are socially negotiated with the various constituencies that confirm or disconfirm the identities. This need for negotiation also results in individuals' own expectations of their identities in relation to the identities of others.

In a critical–constructivist frame, mentoring is part of this co-constructed, socially negotiated identity development. In their dialogue with protégés, mentors both negotiate identities with protégés and assist them in understanding those identities and the process of their development. As they reflect, coach, share stories, and engage in other mentoring activities, mentors and protégés engage in an identity development process. Wenger's (1998) description of the dynamic nature of identity and five dimensions of professional identity reinforce the mentoring process of identity construction.

> (1) identity as *negotiated experiences* where we define who we are by the ways we experience our selves through participation as well as the way we and others reify our selves; (2) identity as *community membership* where we define who we are by the familiar and the unfamiliar; (3) identity as *learning trajectory* where we define who we are by where we have been and where we are going; (4) identity as *nexus of multi membership* where we define who we are by the ways we reconcile our various forms of identity into one identity; and (5) identity as a *relation between the local and the global* where we define who we are by negotiating local ways of belonging to broader constellations and manifesting broader styles and discourses.
>
> (Cited in Sachs, 2001: 154)

Following Wenger's five dimensions, a critical–constructivist process of mentoring includes these five mentoring functions:

1 Mentors engage with protégés in understanding and navigating negotiated experiences.
2 Mentors reflect with protégés on the various communities of membership in which school leaders reside.
3 Mentors support and prod the protégés' active and transformative learning development.
4 Mentors stimulate the protégés internal integration of multiple identities.
5 Mentors awaken the protégé to a broader sphere of influence, responsibility, and practice.

These functions reflect a co-constructivist notion of learning that go beyond the traditional conceptions of mentoring and present the opportunities for a more transformative process for both mentors and protégés.

Understanding mentoring in a critical–constructivist perspective has the potential to move the development of school leaders from reproducing technocrats who maintain the status quo focused primarily on school equilibrium to enabling educational change agents engaged in a collective, transformative process.

APPLICATIONS OF A CRITICAL–CONSTRUCTIVIST PERSPECTIVE

Here I apply the critical–constructivist perspective of mentoring and coaching to policy, leadership development, and research. Obviously, such applications could be quite extensive, but I have focused them on areas that seem most pertinent to current education reform contexts.

Policy applications

A critical–constructivist perspective on mentoring and coaching raises policy issues at federal, state, and local levels. First, the federal approach to turning around schools and the 'Race to the Top' funding available to some states underscore an approach to leadership development that is almost exclusively skill-oriented. As noted, the mentoring of school leaders needs to address professional development in terms of the skills necessary for changing the direction of failing schools. However, such a technocratic orientation to mentoring specifically and leadership development in general runs counter to a more transformational perspective. The policy rhetoric, while stressing transformation, usually consists of the preference for corporate models of reform, which are not new or transformative to educational leadership practice (Callahan, 1962). A critical–constructivist perspective emphasizes the need to see mentoring as a leadership development strategy to awaken new models, paradigms, and approaches to schooling.

In most states, school leadership preparation programs continue to be licensed by individual states. Although there are certainly attacks on the value of licensure, a more deliberate and valuable approach is to raise the expectations of and standards for preparation programs. Current attempts to raise these standards have, similar to the federal approach, stressed the identification and measurement of skills and competencies (Crow, 2009). Such a technocratic orientation forces university and alternative preparation programs to ignore or de-emphasize values, beliefs, dispositions, and identities that guide and motivate aspiring leaders to lead the work involved in an authentic transformation of schools and schooling. I maintain that state regulations and support for both preparation and professional development need to focus attention on mentoring and coaching programs that establish and reinforce the kinds of identities that school leaders need in order to challenge as well as guide school transformation.

At the local level, districts frequently create formal mentoring or coaching programs for the induction of school leaders. Although it is often necessary to create formal programs, a more effective strategy for the kind of mentoring and coaching I have described involves support to create a learning community in the district and the school in which peer-mentoring, e-mentoring, team mentoring, coaching, and other forms evolve from a community context in which transformational learning is expected and supported. By providing time, training, and other resources that encourage the development of a learning community, districts can send strong signals to leaders of the kind of mentoring and coaching that are likely to be more effective than typical formal programs that frequently perpetuate inauthentic and unsustainable leadership development.

Leadership development applications

A critical–constructivist perspective of mentoring and coaching has several implications for leadership development – both preparation and induction. First, mentoring and coaching is a potentially potent form of leadership development, but it is not a panacea to correct all ills. Where these strategies are appropriate as tools to create significant change, not just to survive, the focus needs to be on transformational learning. As I have said, leadership development certainly can and should include skill development. However, that type of development is unlikely to be as creative and transformative as identity development. Mentoring for identity development should include opportunities for both mentors and protégés to engage in creative inquiry and reflection.

Second, this creative inquiry and reflection requires effective mentors. The selection and preparation of mentors and coaches is clearly an important part of the mentoring/coaching process. Selecting mentors who are not only effective school leaders but have the types of skills, and more importantly, dispositions and values, to encourage creative thinking and critical reflection is necessary. Preparing all mentors to ask insightful questions, guide reflective conferencing, use storytelling effectively, build rewarding relationships, actively listen, and so forth, must not be taken for granted (Matthews and Crow, 2010).

Third, I have raised the point about the value of storytelling as a tool of mentoring and coaching. Storytelling has a bad reputation coming out of leadership development programs of some time ago when the focus was on telling war stories about the mentor's experiences in order to provide recipes for aspiring leaders. However, perhaps it is time to re-energize and re-value the storytelling tradition in educational leadership. If stories that mentors and protégés tell can be used as instruments for critical reflection and inquiry, they can be channeled as powerful tools that awaken, prod, expose, and create new ways of thinking about the roles and impact of leaders (Denning, 2007).

Research applications

Research on mentoring and coaching has tended to be atheoretical, cross-sectional, and process focused, without much attention on outcomes (Barnett and O'Mahony, 2008; Grogan and Crow, 2004). Policymaking and leadership development could benefit from rigorous, insightful research on the nature, relationships, outcomes, and functions of mentoring and coaching in schools. A critical–constructivist perspective has implications for research on mentoring and coaching.

First, researchers in mentoring need to be clear about their definitions, in keeping with Merriam's (1983) point about the definition of mentoring determining the extent of mentoring. I have argued that attempts to define mentoring beyond simplified notions of intense relationship, offer the opportunity to investigate more extensively the nature of mentoring and this relationship. Mertz's (2004) identification of intent and involvement as critical elements of mentoring deserves rigorous empirical investigations in order to help us understand the extent to which mentoring of school leaders occurs in schools as well as the quality of that mentoring.

Second, although coaching is less problematic concerning the issue of definition, the research is no less troublesome. Coaching, like mentoring, has been assumed to be a panacea especially for the remediation of ineffective principals. However, there is little empirically rigorous evidence on the effects of coaching (West and Milan, 2001).

Third, longitudinal research, especially on the effects of mentoring and coaching, would be extremely valuable for testing the intended and unintended consequences of mentoring and determining the contextual factors that facilitate or impede the effectiveness of these strategies. West and Milan (2001) identified three suggestions to improve research on mentoring and coaching: increase the respondents sampled within and across programs; obtain information from stakeholders other than mentors, coaches, and their protégés; and incorporate control groups of school administrators who have not been mentored or coached. Research using these suggestions would provide the opportunity to investigate the nature, relationships, outcomes, and functions of mentoring and coaching.

Finally, mentoring and coaching can be significant developmental strategies to prepare, guide, and support leaders to be change agents committed to bringing about school transformation or they can transmit skills and competencies geared to maintaining the status quo of schools. In this writing, I have offered a critical–constructivist perspective to encourage scholars and practitioners to rethink the nature of mentoring and coaching in order to ignite their transformative learning potential.

REFERENCES

Barnett, B. G. (1995). Developing Reflection and Expertise: Can Memtors Make the Difference? *Journal of Educational Administration, 33*(5), 45–59.

Barnett, B. G., & O'Mahony, G. R. (2008). Mentoring and Coaching Programs for the Professional Development of School Leaders. In J. Lumby, G. Crow, & P. Pashiardis (Eds.), *International handbook on the preparation and development of school leaders* (pp. 232–262). New York: Routledge.

Bloom, G., Castagna, C., Moir, E., & Warren, B. (2005). *Blended Coaching: Skills and Strategies to Support Principal Development.* Thousand Oaks, CA: Corwin.

Bozeman, B., & Feeney, M. K. (2007). Toward a Useful Theory of Mentoring: A Conceptual Analysis and Critique. *Administration and Society, 39*(6), 719–739.

Brockbank, A., & McGill, I. (2006). *Facilitating Reflective Learning Through Mentoring and Coaching.* London: Kogan Page.

Burke, P. J. (1984). Mentors in Organizations. *Group and Organizations Study, 9,* 353–372.

Burke, P. J., & Stets, J. (2009). *Identity Theory.* New York: Oxford University Press.

Callahan, R. (1962). *Education and The Cult of Efficiency: A Study of the Social Forces That Have Shaped the Administration of Public Schools.* Chicago: University of Chicago Press.

Costa, A. L., & Garmston, R. F. (1994). *Cognitive Coaching: A Foundation for Renaissance Schools.* Norwood, MA: Christopher-Gordon.

Crow, G. M. (2009). The Development of School Leaders' Professional Identities: Challenges and Implications for Interprofessional Practice. In Forbes, J. & Watson, C. (Eds.). *Research into Professional Identities: Theorizing Social and Institutional Identities.* Aberdeen, Scotland: School of Education, University of Aberdeen.

Crow, G., & Matthews, L. J. (1998). *Finding One's Way: How Mentoring Can Lead to Dynamic Leadership.* Thousand Oaks, CA: Corwin.

Daloz, L. (1999). *Mentor: Guiding the Journey of Adult Learners.* San Francisco: Jossey-Bass.

Danielson, C., & McGreal, T. L. (2000). *Teacher Evaluation to Enhance Professional Practice.* Princeton, NJ: Educational Testing Service.

Daresh, J. (2004). Mentoring School Leaders: Professional Promise or Predictable Problems? *Educational Administration Quarterly, 40*(4), 495–517.

Day, C., Sammons, P., Hopkins, D., Harris, A., Leithwood, K., Gu, Q. et al. (2009). *The Impact of School Leadership on Pupil Outcomes.* Nottingham: University of Nottingham.

Denning, S. (2007). *The Secret Language of Leadership*. San Francisco, CA: Jossey-Bass.

Eby, L. T. (1997). Alternative Forms of Mentoring in Changing Organizational Environments: A Conceptual Extension of the Mentoring Literature. *Journal of Vocational Behavior, 51*, 125–144.

Feldman, D. (1976). A Contingency Theory of Socialization. *Administrative Science Quarterly, 21*, 433–452.

Gehrke, N. (1988). Toward a Definition of Mentoring. *Theory into Practice, 27*(3), 190–194.

Grogan, M., & Crow, G. M. (2004). Mentoring in the Context of Educational Leadership Preparation and Development – old wines in new bottles? *Educational Administration Quarterly, 40*(4), 463–467.

Higgins, M. C., & Kram, K. E. (2001). Reconceptualizing Mentoring at Work: A Developmental Network Perspective. *Academy of Management Review, 26*, 264–288.

Hobson, A. (2003). *Mentoring and Coaching for New Leaders*. Nottingham: National College for School Leadership.

Kram, K. E. (1983). Phases of the Mentor Relationship. *Academy of Management Journal, 26*, 608–625.

Kram, K. E. (1985). *Mentoring at Work: Developmental Relationships in Organizational Life*. Glenview, IL: Scott, Foresman and Company.

Leicht, K., & Fennell, M. (2001). *Professional Work: A Sociological Approach*. Oxford: Blackwell.

Lieberman, A., & Miller, L. (Eds). (1991). *Staff Development: New Demands, New Realities, New Perspectives* (2nd ed.). New York: Teachers College Press.

Lumby, J., & English, F. (2009). From Simplicism to Complexity in Leadership Identity and Preparation: Exploring the Lineage and Dark Secrets. *International Journal of Leadership in Education, 12*(2), 95–114.

Male, T. (2006). *Being an Effective Headteacher*. London: Paul Chapman Publishing.

Matthews, L .J., & Crow, G. M. (2010). *The Principalship: New Roles in a Professional Learning Community*. Boston: Allyn & Bacon.

Megginson, D., & Clutterbuck, D. (1995). *Mentoring in Action*. London: Kogan Page.

Merriam, S. (1983). Mentors and Protégés: A Critical Review of the Literature. *Adult Education Quarterly, 33*, 161–173.

Merriam, S., Caffarella, R., & Baumgartner, L. (2007). *Learning in Adulthood: A Comprehensive Guide* (3rd ed.). San Francisco: John Wiley & Sons.

Mertz, N. T. (2004). What's a Mentor, Anyway? *Educational Administration Quarterly, 40*(4), 541–560.

Mullen, C. A., & Lick, D. W. (Eds.). (1999). *New Directions in Mentoring: Creating a Culture of Synergy*. London: Falmer.

Sachs, J. (2001). Teacher Professional Identity: Competing Discourses, Competing Outcomes. *Journal of Education Policy, 16*(2), 149–161.

Scandura, T. A. (1992). Mentorship and Career Mobility: An Empirical Investigation. *Journal of Organizational Behavior, 13*, 169–174.

Scandura, T. A., & Pellegrini, E. K. (2007). Workplace Mentoring: Theoretical Approaches and Methdological Issues. In T. D. Allen & L. T. Eby (Eds.), *The Blackwell Handbook of Mentoring. A Multiple Perspectives Approach* (pp. 71–92). Malden, MA: Blackwell.

Scribner, S., & Crow, G. (2010). Employing Professional Identities: Case Study of a High School Principal in a Reform Setting. Paper Presented at the University Council for Educational Administration, New Orleans, LA.

Spillane, J., Camburn, E., & Pareja, A. (2007). Taking a Distributed Perspective to the School Principal's Workday. *Leadership and Policy in Schools, 6*(1), 103–125.

Tooms, A. (2010). Socializing Aspiring School Leaders: The Politics of a Grown Your Own Administrator Program. In W. K. Hoy & M. DiPaola (Eds.), *Analyzing school contexts: Influences of principals and teachers in the service of students* (pp. 169–190). Charlotte, NC: Information Age.

Wahlstrom, K., Louis, K., Leithwood, K., & Anderson, S. (2010). *Investigating the Links to Improved Student Learning*. Minneapolis, MN: University of Minnesota.

Wenger, R. (1998). *Communities of Practice: Learning, Meaning, and Identity*. Cambridge: Cambridge University Press.

West, L., & Milan, M. (2001). *The Reflecting Glass: Professional Coaching for Leadership Development*. Basingstoke, England: Palgrave.

Young, M. D., Crow, G. M., Murphy, J., & Ogawa, R. T. (Eds.). (2009). *Handbook of Research on the Education of School Leaders*. New York: Routledge.

16

Mentoring and Coaching for Leadership Development in Schools

Christopher Rhodes

INTRODUCTION

There is a well-established international focus on school performance and school improvement framed by social, economic and political considerations. National conceptions of desirable performance and improvement therefore vary between countries and regions according to the prevailing modifiers of culture, central policy and socio-economic background coupled with local parameters pertaining to the immediate context of individual schools themselves. A large international literature has placed the professional development of school staff as an important factor in enabling achievement to be raised against measures set by national norms and expectations. Amongst reports showing the potential benefits of staff development, the development and engagement of high-quality school leaders has been repeatedly linked with the growth of improving and effective schools (DfES, 2005; Hallinger and Snidvongs, 2005; Teddlie and Reynolds, 2000). The appointment of senior leaders, particularly a new head, will be influential in consolidating a continuing, or perhaps changed, direction for the improvement journey of a particular school (Hargreaves and Fink, 2006). The importance of good leadership and good change leadership as a precursor to school improvement is now recognised in school systems around the world. Prompted by the linkage of good leadership and school improvement, a burgeoning international interest in leadership development as an important facet of school improvement has now arisen (Brundrett and Crawford, 2008; Bush, 2008). For example, in the United States (US), Crow (2006) has emphasised the importance of school leader preparation in contributing to the quality of subsequent leadership practices. In the United Kingdom (UK), Rhodes and Brundrett (2008) have identified the importance of establishing schools as good training grounds for leadership development. The ongoing establishment of new networks and collaborations between schools in the UK, such as federations (Chapman, Lindsay, Muijs, Harris, Arweck and Goodall, 2010; Jones, 2009; Moore and Kelly, 2009) increasingly provides additional potential for staff and school leaders to share resources and ideas and therefore effect better staff learning and leadership development. Interest in leadership development has been further stimulated by a crisis in the recruitment and retention of school leaders in many parts of the world. For example, MacBeath (2006) reports leadership shortages in the Netherlands, Sweden, France and parts of Germany and shortages of middle and senior leaders have been reported in the UK, the US, Australia and New Zealand (see Cranston, 2007; Rhodes and Brundrett, 2006, 2009). In these terms, learning to lead has never been as important as it is now.

A wide variety of leadership development mechanisms have been reported in the literature and include: leadership internships in the US (Crow, 2005) and in the UK (Earley, 2009), National training courses (Brundrett and Crawford, 2008; Bush, 2008; Rhodes, Brundrett and Nevill, 2009), networking (Bush and Glover, 2004), in-school training (Earley and Jones, 2009) and coaching and mentoring (Bush, Glover and Harris, 2007; Simkins 2009; Simkins, Coldwell, Calliau, Finlayson and Morgan, 2006). Leadership development which engages the use of coaches or mentors has been established in many countries. For example, in a study of leadership preparation in Hong Kong, Walker and Dimmock (2006) have emphasised the efficacy of learning linked to school contexts coupled with the involvement of experienced principals as mentors. Formal and informal workplace learning has increasingly become an important inclusion in the development of school leaders. Along with this contextualised learning, the use of incumbent heads as role models, mentors and coaches for deputies and other staff aspiring to or preparing for headship has been seen as a powerful element in the journey to headship. In a US study, contact with serving principals has been judged to positively influence role-conceptualisation, initial socialisation and role-identity transformation for aspirant principals (Browne-Ferrigno, 2003). In the UK, staff positioning with respect to incumbent heads raises the confidence and determination of those aspiring to leadership roles (Rhodes and Brundrett, 2006) and contact with serving heads has been judged to provide realistic perspectives of the job for those in leadership training programmes such as the National Professional Qualification for Headship in England (Rhodes et al., 2009).

In this chapter, I shall commence by exploring the rise of coaching and mentoring in education. An international perspective will be taken as the nature of coaching and mentoring is examined and a focus on the use of these mechanisms in leadership development is established. The chapter will seek to identify persistent issues in coaching and mentoring that may serve to block the desired benefits associated with these learning mechanisms. With specific focus on the use of coaching and mentoring in leadership development, the chapter will consider leadership preparation, early headship and later headship incumbency as distinct phases where these mechanisms have an important but differing role to play. An exploration of the 'problematic and unresolved' side of coaching and mentoring will be included. Finally, the chapter calls for a renewed view of this field and a new and expanded research agenda is suggested which may provide better understanding and deployment of these mechanisms for the benefit of leaders their staff and ultimately to the better advantage of those pupils in their care.

THE RISE OF COACHING AND MENTORING IN PROFESSIONAL DEVELOPMENT IN EDUCATION

Whether in business or in education, coaching and mentoring are based upon a wish to improve performance, raise the skills, knowledge and attributes of staff appropriately, consolidate staff commitment and assist in change and the sustainability of change (Rhodes, Stokes and Hampton, 2004). Coaching and mentoring are based upon trusting collaboration between individuals so that they may work and learn together. Such professional learning can occur at a variety of career stages. For example, teachers in the UK begin their professional learning with initial teacher training and this continues into the newly qualified teacher induction year spent teaching in a school. The use of school-based mentors in both these phases is thought essential in order to induct, socialise and support these new recruits as they first enter the profession. The transition of newly qualified teachers into their early years within the profession has been viewed as a crucial time in which new teachers can be supported to adapt to school working practices, make a firm commitment to the profession and develop a mindset which enables them to see benefits in their ongoing professional learning and development.

However, it is not only at the beginning of a teaching career that induction mentoring is deployed. For many experienced staff, starting a new post as a teacher, middle leader, senior leader or head, the use of internal and external mentors is commonplace within the UK education system. The challenging nature of headship and particularly early headship is well documented (Briggs, Bush and Middlewood, 2006; Hobson, Brown, Ashby, Keys, Sharp and Benefield, 2003; Holligan, Menter, Hutchings and Walker, 2006) and heads need to consider their own continued learning as well as helping teachers and others to learn and improve their practice. The conceptualisation and establishment of 'the learning centred school' has emerged and denotes that a school places both pupil and staff learning at the core of its work. The leadership of such a venture may be termed 'leadership for learning' (see Rhodes and Brundrett, 2010). The implication here is that leaders are charged with the task of helping to create a school culture that will foster learning. The place of coaching and mentoring in professional learning has been very much a part of this debate and many have shown the potential benefits of these learning approaches. For example, Rhodes and Beneicke (2002) and Rhodes et al. (2004) review the benefits of coaching and mentoring and a rich international literature pertaining to coaching and mentoring has developed.

THE NATURE OF COACHING AND MENTORING IN EDUCATION

Coaching is a learning relationship between individuals that has long been associated with raising individual performance (see Downey, 2001; Parsloe and Wray, 2000; Whitmore, 1995). Mentoring is a learning relationship which includes coaching but also includes broader support in the form of counselling, career development and access to wider learning opportunities (see Clutterbuck, 1991; Dignard, 2002; Landsberg, 1996). Coaching and mentoring are based upon trusting relationships between individuals and in themselves may help to foster additional collaboration between staff in schools. For collaboration to occur there must be a willingness to collaborate and in some schools it is likely that staff have had previous good experiences of collaborating with their colleagues. Conversely, in other schools trust and collaboration may be impeded by presumed threats to personal self-conception and identifying the need to learn may be more difficult or met with hostility as issues of power and territoriality may occur. Blockages to coaching and mentoring may also be exacerbated by worries about the true locus of control in these learning relationships and by the time and effort needed to plan, agree learning needs, undertake the agreed learning and evaluate whether or not useful learning has taken place. Good practices in coaching and mentoring schemes would tend to ensure that learners are aware of their need to learn and enable consideration of a plan for personal development in conjunction with the learner. Careful choice of coaches and mentors, their training and their matching with learners is thought essential so that the conditions for learning are fostered. Importantly, the recognition of time constraints upon the learning relationship needs to be recognised and overcome.

In 2005, the Department for Employment and Skills in England, supported by the Centre for the Use of Research and Evidence in Education (CUREE), produced a National Framework for Mentoring and Coaching with the intention of informing mentoring and coaching schemes in schools. This National Framework is located on the Teacher Development Agency website (TDA, 2005). The framework offers ten principles of effective mentoring and coaching. In summary, the principles encompass the centrality of learner reflection, mutual trust and accommodation of power differences between individuals and access to resources. The principles also include the importance of fostering learner self-direction, enabling appropriate goal-setting, flexibility depending on the individual and the context, realisation that the coaches and mentors may also benefit from the relationship, ensuring space for learners to experiment and the effective use of learning time. The framework describes mentors as experienced colleagues with knowledge of the requirements of a particular role who are able to support learners through significant career transitions. Coaching is described as a process for enabling the development of a specific aspect of a learner's professional practice and specialist coaches are described as those with knowledge and expertise relevant to the goals of the learner. The framework also introduces the notion of collaborative coaching where two or more learners work together to embed new knowledge and skills into their practice. Although coaching and mentoring have become an integral part of professional development and leadership learning in education and offer great promise, they do not offer a certain solution to all the problems of career transition and poor performance. The appropriateness of mentoring and coaching to professional development situations should be closely thought through as each context is different and the establishment of successful learning relationships may, in some cases, be problematical.

PERSISTENT ISSUES IN COACHING AND MENTORING IN EDUCATION

Being a mentor entails the sharing of professional knowledge between individuals, promoting reflection as well as offering support at times of career transition and development. It is a complex relationship and may make many difficult demands upon the mentor as well as the mentee. In a US school-based study, Kilburg (2007) explored the operation of mentoring teams and elucidated a range of problems that occurred during formal mentoring between more experienced staff mentors and new teachers. Kilburg states that a variety of institutional barriers were found to impact negatively on the success of these learning relationships. For example, potential problems were found to reside in cost, mentor selection and training, time availability, poor interpersonal skills, understanding learner needs and the need for support from the principal. The study suggested that a clear focus on emotional support for newly-qualified teachers should be established and that, in turn, mentors' should have the ability and skills to provide that support. Bullough and Draper (2004) have explored mentoring relationships from the point of view of the emotional cost to mentors who feel insufficiently trained. It is clear that the extent of emotional cost that can be expended by both mentors and their learners needs to be better understood if sufficient emotional support for all those involved in these adult learning relationships is to be provided. The complexity of potential emotional cost is further highlighted by consideration that these learning relationships might, for example, involve people of different ages, genders, values, seniority and those who may be prone to become too emotionally dependent upon their mentor. Stead (2006) has reported the possibility for feelings of vulnerability on the part of mentees and issues of power and power differences are raised along with constraints upon openness and trust. In coaching, which typically involves training, reflection and skill gains so that performance is increased, it is reasonable to assume that similar difficulties in the relationship between coach and learner may arise. A question arises about the correct balance and the correct changing balance between coach instruction and the space for learner reflection and voice. Getting this right demands a high level of skill on the part of the coach who must resist the transition of necessary authority into the misuse of power. The place of coaching and mentoring in leadership development will now be explored. The available literature deals mostly with the development of leaders as individuals, but the importance of team development must not be lost and must maintain a high place on the agenda of team leaders.

COACHING AND MENTORING FOR LEADERSHIP DEVELOPMENT

In leadership development, incumbent school leaders may act as coaches or mentors for staff either within or outside their own school and help identify and assist talented aspirant leaders to make the journey towards headship or another leadership role. For example, this may involve an incumbent head assisting a deputy or other senior colleague so that they may become better socialised with respect to headship and its demands (see Browne-Ferrigno and Muth, 2004; Stead, 2006). Incumbent school heads may also become involved in forms of peer-coaching or peer-mentoring to assist fellow heads acclimate to their roles or increase the effectiveness of their performance. For example, support may be offered to a colleague who is in the early stages of a new headship or a more experienced colleague who needs to overcome a particular problem within their school. Sometimes referred to as 'executive coaching', heads may engage with learning supported by experts from outside their school who have experience of leadership and leadership development in schools. Coaching and mentoring may be formal or informal and as mentoring may include elements of coaching it is not surprising that there is some blurring of these terms within the literature on leadership development. In the US, Villani (2006) describes mentoring as extended support from a more experienced colleague to enable a new head to develop personally and professionally. Also in the US, Bloom, Castagna, Moir and Warren (2005) describe coaching as the provision of support to help an individual clarify and achieve goals. West and Milan (2001) distinguish between skills coaching (short term), performance coaching (job performance) and development coaching (longer-term development). Notwithstanding this complexity, this chapter now addresses the use of coaching and mentoring as pertinent to leadership development in three distinct phases, the journey to headship, early incumbency and later incumbency.

The preparation of those making the journey to headship

Browne-Ferrigno and Muth (2006) place leadership mentoring and situated learning as important components in the effective preparation of candidates for school principalship in the US. Leadership mentoring and situated learning are thought to best enable aspirant principals to build confidence and socialise into the community of educational administrators they wish to join. Leadership mentoring is described as:

> the formal and informal social construction of professional performance expectations developed through purposeful interactions between aspiring and practicing principals in the context of authentic practice. (2006: 276)

The importance of learning from experienced heads during the journey to headship appears widely in the literature. For example, in the US, Browne-Ferrigno (2003) firmly links contact with serving principals as a key element in an aspirant principal's conception of the role and in the ongoing transformation of their identity to that of principal. In England, Rhodes et al. (2009) have identified that participants' undertaking the National Professional Qualification for Headship as a precursor to their transition to headship highly rated meetings with experienced heads as part of this experience. Also in the UK, John (2008) refers to leadership mentoring as a central component of the National Professional Qualification in Integrated Centre Leadership (NPQICL) intended to develop children's centre leaders. Children's centres offer support for disadvantaged families and provide a variety of services to these children and their families. Here the emphasis is on new leaders being able to talk to someone experienced about the difficulties they encounter in their work. Mentoring in this case is seen as essential to help to sustain leaders who often work in very difficult circumstances. Lim (2003) reports on the training of aspiring school principals in Singapore which includes learning via shadowing a mentor who is an incumbent and experienced principal. This formal mentoring takes place within the mentor's own school. Despite apparent success, Lim points to the need for additional study to ensure that learning gains are transferred to the aspirant heads' own practice. The question of the success transfer of leadership learning between individuals and contexts, when those contexts might be quite different, is again raised.

Simkins et al. (2006) point out that for some time mentoring has been the predominant term used within education in England, especially within the contexts of initial teacher training and the induction of new heads. However, the term of coaching has now entered usage especially in the context of the continuing professional development of teachers. These authors report on a national middle leader development programme called 'Leading from the Middle' offered by the National College for School Leadership in England from 2003. This was the first large-scale national leadership development programme to include a high profile inclusion of in-school coaching. Coaching was mostly undertaken by senior staff within a participant's own school and had the intention of raising general job performance. Simkins et al. (2006) report on the wide variety of approaches and the variable quality of coaching experienced by participants. The study concludes that the skill of the coach, the receptiveness of the participant, the constraints of immediate context, time limitations, the background culture of the school, the expectations placed upon coaching and the power relationships between coach and participant were influential in participant learning and the chances of subsequent school improvement. This further indicates that the persistent institutional barriers already highlighted in this chapter can permeate the development of leaders in many schools. More recently, the National College for School Leadership, now renamed the National College for Leadership of Schools and Children's Services, has put forward six propositions about the importance of coaching and the role of incumbent school leaders (NCLSCS, 2010). These propositions encompass the notion that incumbent leaders have a moral responsibility to support the learning of the next generation of school leaders and that coaching should be promoted as valuable in supporting professional development and school improvement. Finally, it is suggested that learning conversations are important in engaging staff in debate and dialogue within a culture of high-quality in-school coaching. A recent publication from the College authored by Hanbury (2009) concludes that coaching has the potential to be highly influential and an effective strategy for the development of school leaders and has much importance in supporting succession planning and enabling new heads to develop in the role. The availability of trained coaches in schools with the time and resources to effect a less variable and high-quality learning experience for leadership learners in their schools is an item calling for attention internationally as leadership talent pools diminish and the recruitment of excellent leaders becomes increasingly challenging in some countries.

Early headship incumbency

Mentoring leaders is difficult given the complexity of the leadership role (Clutterbuck, 2004). However, it is important that new heads are supported, especially during the potentially difficult early years of headship. Mentors of new heads would, for example, be able to convey the day-to-day realities of the job, answers questions drawing on their own experience and enable the confidence of the new head to be raised. Hobson and Sharp (2005) undertake a review of literature pertaining to the mentoring of new head teachers. These authors report that all formal mentoring programmes for new heads included in their review indicate perceptions of both merit and effectiveness in the mentor support provided. Hobson and Sharp (2005) also refer to Malderez and Bodoczky (1999) and suggest that mentors of new heads may enable new heads to better assimilate an existing professional culture, gain additional access to resources and people who can help, give emotional support, reduce feelings of isolation and increase confidence and assist new heads in their professional learning and in their change of professional identity. Daresh (2004) conveys that many US states have adopted mentoring schemes to help develop and support new principals. In a study located in the US, Silver, Lochmiller, Copland and Tripps (2009) have identified the intensive support needed by new principals in the early years of their incumbency as they make a journey to become effective school leaders. Reporting on a university-based coaching programme for new principals, these authors also identify the importance of personalising coaching to meet the individual needs of new principals in the different contexts in which they work and the different challenges they face. Silver et al. (2009) also suggest that whilst studies of principal mentoring schemes are abundant in the US, few studies can be found with respect to leadership coaching programmes for principals and attribute this to the relative newness of principal coaching endeavours. A question emerges as to whether mentoring or coaching support for all new heads is feasible and attainable and whether this should be a mandatory requirement given this investment may result in more effective heads more quickly. In addition to the issues of time and cost, a willingness of new heads to understand that their learning could be helped by collaboration with mentors and coaches in this way would be helpful. Given that the support offered was high quality, constructive and sufficiently contextualised to the immediate daily practice of headship, any reticence for new heads to participate may be reduced.

Later headship incumbency

Learning during headship is an essential component of an ongoing professionalism and an essential component in sustaining the need to address the leading professional role within the context in which the senior leadership is being enacted. Over years of endeavour, heads may become tired and their creativity diminished due to the relentless pressures of responsibility and accountability required in contemporary educational settings. Intervention and support emerging from coaching and mentoring may enable longer serving heads to remain enchanted, motivated and passionate about their work and the profession. As in the case of support for new heads, support for heads in later incumbency may help to reduce feelings of isolation and enable work difficulties to be shared, discussed and reflected upon in a constructive and forward looking way.

Mentors and coaches of senior leaders' inevitably need to show that they are good practitioners, trained to a high level and sufficiently skilled to allow space for experienced heads to reflect, learn and accommodate the complexity associated with change and continued improvement. Stead (2006) found that mentoring for senior leaders was helpful in their development and stands as an important learning mechanism amongst others in fast-changing educational environments. Robertson (2008) has firmly linked the coaching of leaders in education contexts with improvements in their leadership practice. The coach is identified as a means to enable new thinking to better inform the achievement of improvement goals for the school. In a US study, Wise and Jacobo (2010) use socio-cultural and organisational learning theory to suggest a framework of leadership coaching in which the school principal acts as a change agent in school improvement assisted by an external coach who can help the principal in developing new thinking to inform change and increase chances of improvement success. The field continues to portray both mentoring and coaching as established and still-developing mechanisms in the continued learning of senior leaders. A question emerges as to how to best employ these mechanisms for experienced leaders, and in what contexts, so that they are not threatened by the presence of another senior mentor or coach figure involved in the work of headship, but rather that they are reinvigorated and remain passionate about the important role that they have play.

COACHING AND MENTORING AND NEW AGENDAS IN LEADERSHIP DEVELOPMENT

As highlighted in this chapter, there is an established role for coaching and mentoring in schools as a means of induction, teacher learning and leadership development. However, it is also clear that potential problems in the organisation, process and impact of these learning mechanisms may detract from the benefits they appear to offer. According to Sundli (2007), the concept of mentoring remains confused and issues of power, control and dependency in these relationships are seldom put forward as potential drawbacks. This author cites Colley who contends that 'the meteoric rise of mentoring has not been matched by similar progress in its conceptualisation' (2002: 258).

In a Norwegian context, Sundli (2007) reports that student teachers who are mentored find it difficult to engage in reflection as part of their learning. It is suggested that student teachers may just blindly follow the model set by the mentor without suitable reflection and adaptation into their own developing practice. In these terms, Sundli (ibid.) suggests that mentoring may actually represent a barrier to student teacher reflection. As reflection constitutes an important part of coaching and mentoring relationships, questions about the promotion of reflection in leadership development are also raised. Are coaches and mentors sufficiently skilled to enable the linkage of theory to practice? Not all coaching and mentoring relationships are necessarily successful and the possibility of failure needs to be considered. Is there a possibility for competing agendas between the coach or mentor and the learner? For example, a learner may wish to promote their own success and progress in a different way to that which is desired by the host school. Whilst learner needs are very much part of the learning relationship, consideration of school needs is also present and these needs are perhaps strongly framed within a desired improvement journey. In addition to difficulties which may arise from competing agendas between coaches, mentors and their learners, Daloz (1998) has identified potential problems which may damage intended learning stemming from differing ethics, possible misuse of power or excessive control, or from exaggerated emotional dependence by either party. A recent review of ineffective coaching behaviours by managers in a variety of work contexts has been undertaken by Ellinger, Hamlin and Beattie (2008). This study found that along with poor communication, predominant ineffective behaviours included the adoption of a style that was autocratic, directive, controlling or dictatorial.

There is the potential for high emotional interaction within mentoring and coaching relationships. Stead (2006) has identified the emotional intensity, power, trust and commitment involved. In leadership development, these relationships may be experienced as open and trusting or alternatively as overbearing and potentially oppressive. Leadership has often been framed as a social interaction in which individuals with authority and 'people skills' can engage with others and secure their followership. Developing the professional identity of a leader suggests interaction with other people and context as new and experienced leaders adapt and readapt their identity to the necessities of immediate school circumstances. Rhodes and Greenway (2010) have begun to identify and characterise some of the professional identities that heads adopt in the enactment of their day-to-day leadership. This leadership 'as' performance is likely to entail repeated submergence and contradiction of true 'self' as heads seek to lead and influence others successfully. The possibility of significant emotional cost to the 'actor' head is self-evident. How can heads be helped to 'perform' better and in a variety of different contexts with a variety of individuals and groups? Such considerations have implications for our thinking about leadership learning, the journey and transition to headship and the enactment of leadership. Mentoring and coaching potentially have an important role to play in this learning and enactment, but it presently remains a difficult and underexplored aspect of leadership development.

Coaching and mentoring have become established as models of professional development in education (Kennedy, 2005). However, in the research literature it is possible to detect a tendency towards instrumental approaches often with focus on prescriptive descriptions of actions at the expense of a more critical approach to these learning relationships. In order to explore coaching and mentoring relationships more deeply, the establishment of a broader conceptual map of the field may assist in building a new research agenda which is better able to identify priorities and better able to inform the field in general and leadership development in particular. This is an ambitious task. Facing similar challenge in the field of leadership studies, the excellent work of Gunter and Ribbins (2002) established an approach to mapping the field of leadership studies based upon a typology of knowledge domains. These authors identified five knowledge domains which include the above-mentioned instrumental domain. The four other identified domains consist of: the conceptual domain, which encompasses research engaging with issues of values and rights; the critical domain, which encompasses social injustice, power and oppression; the humanistic domain, which includes research that explores biographies and lived-lives; and finally the evaluative domain, which includes research pertinent to measurement of effectiveness. Transposed to the field of coaching, mentoring and leadership development, a conceptual approach might lead us, for example, to further consider participant dissent in leadership coaching and mentoring relationships, a humanistic approach could lead to an exploration of important differences in the experience of coaching and mentoring in different leadership contexts and a critical approach may lead us to ask whose interests does leadership coaching and mentoring really serve? In summary, the creation of a wider field of research engagement could offer new opportunities for us to understand, develop and deploy these mechanisms in smarter informed ways to the benefit of all those engaged in leadership development and ultimately to the better advantage of those learners in their care.

REFERENCES

Bloom, G., Castagna, C., Moir, E. and Warren, B. (2005) *Blended Coaching: Skills and Strategies to Support Principal Development.* Thousand Oaks, CA: Corwin Press.

Briggs, A. R. J., Bush, T. and Middlewood, D. (2006) From Immersion to Establishment: The Challenges Facing New School Heads and the Role of 'New Visions' in Resolving Them. *Cambridge Journal of Education*, 36(2), 257–276.

Browne-Ferrigno, T. (2003) Becoming a Principal: Role Conception, Initial Socialization, Role-identity Transformation, Purposeful Engagement. *Educational Administration Quarterly*, 39(4), 468–503.

Browne-Ferrigno, T. and Muth, R. (2004) Leadership Mentoring in Clinical Practice: Role Socialisation, Professional Development and Capacity Building. *Educational Administration Quarterly*, 40(4), 468–494.

Browne-Ferrigno, T. and Muth, R. (2006) Leadership mentoring and situated learning: catalysts for principalship readiness and lifelong mentoring. *Mentoring and Tutoring*, 14(3), 275–295.

Brundrett, M. and Crawford, M. (2008) (Eds) *Developing School Leaders: An International Perspective.* London: Routledge.

Bullough, R. V. and Draper, R. J. (2004) Mentoring and the emotions. *Journal of Education for Teaching*, 30(3), 16–24.

Bush, T. (2008) *Leadership and Management Development in Education.* London: Sage.

Bush, T. and Glover, D. (2004) *Leadership Development: Concepts and beliefs.* Nottingham: National College for School Leadership.

Bush, T., Glover, D. and Harris, A. (2007) *Review of School Leadership Development.* Nottingham: National College for School Leadership.

Chapman, C., Lindsay, G., Muijs, D., Harris, A., Arweck, E. and Goodall, J. (2010) Governance, leadership, and management in federations of schools. *School Effectiveness and School Improvement*, 21(1), 53–74.

Clutterbuck, D. (1991) *Everyone Needs a Mentor.* London: Institute of Personnel and Development.

Clutterbuck, D. (2004) *Everyone Needs a Mentor: Fostering Talent in your Organisation*, 4th edition. London: CIPD.

Colley, H. (2002) A 'rough guide' to the history of mentoring from a Marxist Feminist perspective. *Journal of Education for Teaching*, 28(3), 257–273.

Cranston, N. C. (2007) Through the eyes of potential aspirants: another view of the principalship. *School Leadership and Management*, 27(2), 109–128.

Crow, G. (2005) Developing leaders for schools facing challenging circumstances, in M. Coles and G. Southworth (Eds) *Developing Leadership: Creating the schools of tomorrow.* Maidenhead: Open University Press, 65–79.

Crow, G. (2006) Complexity and the beginning principal in the United States: Perspectives on socialization. *Journal of Educational Administration*, 44(4), 310–325.

Daloz, L. (1998) Mentorship, in M. W. Galbraith (Ed.) *Adult Learning Methods: A Guide to Effective Instruction.* Florida: Krieger, 353–372.

Daresh, J. C. (2004) Mentoring school leaders: Professional promise or predictable problems? *Educational Administration Quarterly*, 40(4), 495–517.

DfES (2005) *Higher Standards, Better Schools For All: More choice for parents and pupils.* London: Stationery Office.

Dignard, K. (2002) *Mentoring Handbook – Department of Family Medicine.* Ottawa: University of Ottawa.

Downey, M. (2001) *Effective Coaching*. London: Texere.

Earley, P. (2009) Work, learning and professional practice: the role of leadership apprenticeships. *School Leadership and Management*, 29(3), 307–320.

Earley, P. and Jones, J. (2009) Leadership development, in B. Davies (Ed.) *The Essentials of School Leadership*, 2nd edition. London: Sage Publications. 179–201.

Ellinger, A. D., Hamlin, R. G. and Beattie, R. S. (2008) Behaviour indicators of ineffective managerial coaching: a cross-national study. *Journal of European Industrial Training*, 32(4), 240–255.

Gunter, H. and Ribbins, P. (2002) Leadership studies in education: Towards a map of the field. *Educational Management Administration and Leadership*, 30(4), 387–416.

Hallinger, P. and Snidvongs, K. (2005) *Adding Value to School Leadership and Management: A review of trends in the development of managers in the education and business sectors*. Available online at: http://www.ncsl.org.uk/publications (accessed 10 December 2009).

Hanbury, M. (2009) *Leadership Coaching: An evaluation of the effectiveness of leadership coaching as a strategy to support succession planning*. Available online at: http://www.ncsl.org.uk/publications (accessed 1 September 2010).

Hargreaves, A. and Fink, D. (2006) *Sustainable Leadership*. San Francisco: Jossey-Bass.

Hobson, A., Brown, E., Ashby, P., Keys, W., Sharp, C. and Benefield, P. (2003) *Issues for Early Headship – Problems and Support Strategies*. Nottingham: National College for School Leadership.

Hobson, A. and Sharp, C. (2005) Head to head: a systematic review of the research evidence on mentoring new head teachers. *School Leadership and Management*, 25(1), 25–42.

Holligan, C., Menter, I., Hutchings, M. and Walker, M. (2006) Becoming a head teacher: the perspectives of new head teachers in twenty-first-century England. *Journal of In-Service Education*, 32(1), 103–122.

John, K. (2008) Sustaining the leaders of children's centres: the role of leadership mentoring. *European Early Childhood Education Research Journal*, 16(1), 53–66.

Jones, J. (2009) The development of leadership capacity through collaboration in small schools. *School Leadership and Management*, 29(2), 129–156.

Kennedy, A. (2005) Models of continuing professional development: a framework for analysis. *Journal of In-Service Education*, 31(2), 235–250.

Kilburg, G. M. (2007) Three mentoring team relationships and obstacles encountered: a school-based study. *Mentoring and Tutoring*, 15(3), 293–308.

Landsberg, M. (1996) *The Tao of Coaching*. London: Harper Collins.

Lim, L. H. (2003) Educational practice in leadership mentoring: The Singapore experience. *Educational Research for Policy and Practice*, 2, 215–221.

MacBeath, J. (2006) The talent enigma. *International Journal of Leadership in Education*, 9(3), 183–204.

Malderez, A. and Bodoczky, C. (1999) *Mentor Courses: a resource book for trainer trainers*. Cambridge: Cambridge University Press.

Moore, T. A. and Kelly, M. P. (2009) Networks as power bases for school improvement. *School Leadership and Management*, 29(4), 391–404.

NCLSCS (2010) *About Coaching*. Available online at: http://www.nationalcollege.org.uk (accessed 1 September 2010).

Parsloe, E. and Wray, M. (2000) *Coaching and Mentoring*. London: Kogan Page.

Rhodes, C. P. and Beneicke, S. (2002) Coaching, mentoring and peer-networking: challenges for the management of professional development in schools. *Journal of In-Service Education*, 28(2), 297–309.

Rhodes, C. P. and Brundrett, M. (2006) The identification, development, succession and retention of leadership talent in contextually different primary schools: A case study located within the English West Midlands. *School Leadership and Management*, 26(3), 269–287.

Rhodes, C. P. and Brundrett, M. (2008) What makes my school a good training ground for leadership development? *Management in Education*, 22(1), 21–27.

Rhodes, C. P. and Brundrett, M. (2009) Growing the leadership talent pool: perceptions of heads, middle leaders and classroom teachers about professional development and leadership succession planning within their own schools. *Professional Development in Education*, 35(3), 381–398.

Rhodes, C. P. and Brundrett, M. (2010) Leadership for learning, in T. Bush, L. Bell and D. Middlewood (Eds), *The Principles of Educational Leadership and Management*. London: Sage Publications. 153–175.

Rhodes, C. P., Brundrett, M. and Nevill, A. (2009) Just the ticket? The National Professional Qualification and the transition to headship in the East Midlands of England. *Educational Review*, 61(4), 449–468.

Rhodes, C. P. and Greenway, C. (2010) Dramatis personae: enactment and performance in primary school headship. *Management in Education*, 24(4), 149–153.

Rhodes, C. P., Stokes, M. and Hampton, G. (2004) *A Practical Guide to Mentoring, Coaching and Peer-networking: Teacher professional development in schools and colleges*. London: Routledge.

Robertson, J. (2008) *Coaching Educational Leadership: Building leadership capacity through partnership*. London: Sage.

Silver, M., Lochmiller, C. R., Copland, M. A. And Tripps, A. (2009) Supporting new school leaders: findings from a university-based leadership coaching programme for new administrators. *Mentoring and Tutoring: Partnership in Learning*, 17(3), 215–232.

Simkins, T., Coldwell, M., Calliau, I., Finlayson, H. and Morgan, A. (2006) Coaching as a strategy: Experiences from Leading from the Middle. *Journal of In-Service Education*, 32(3), 321–340.

Simkins, T. (2009) Integrating work-based learning into large-scale national leadership development programmes in the UK. *Educational Review*, 61(4), 391–405.

Stead, V. (2006) Mentoring: A model for leadership development? *International Journal of Training and Development*, 9(3), 170–182.

Sundli, L. (2007) Mentoring – A new mantra for education? *Teaching and Teacher Education*, 23, 201–214.

TDA (2005) *National Framework for Mentoring and Coaching*. Available online at: http://www.tda.gov.uk (accessed 20 August 2010).

Teddlie, C. and Reynolds, D., (Eds) (2000) *The International Handbook of School Effectiveness Research*. London: Falmer Press.

Villani, S. (2006) *Mentoring and Induction Programs that Support New Principals*. Thousand Oaks, CA: Corwin Press.

Walker, A. and Dimmock, C. (2006) Preparing leaders, preparing learners: The Hong Kong experience. *School Leadership and Management*, 26(2), 125–147.

West, L. and Milan, M. (2001) *The Reflective Glass: Professional coaching for leadership development*. London: Palgrave.

Whitmore, J. (1995) *Coaching for Performance: A practical guide to growing your own skills*. London: Nicholas Brealey.

Wise, D. and Jacobo, A. (2010) Towards a framework for leadership coaching. *School Leadership and Management*, 30(2), 159–169.

Dialogical Mentoring and Coaching in Early Years Leadership

Paul Watling and Mike Gasper

INTRODUCTION

In this chapter we describe the context of Early Years and multi-agency working, the background and nature of dialogical mentoring and illustrate key aspects of how it can work in practice. The examples used in the chapter are purely fictitious. While they are based in our experience, any resemblance to real examples, groups, individuals or organisations is entirely coincidental and unintended. The examples are intended to illustrate issues concerned with mentoring in a context of Early Years practice rather than focus on the fictional individuals or settings.

Background to the development of Early Years

Since the early 1980s, the small voice of Early Years has grown and matured. Early Years pioneers like Tina Bruce, Chris Pascal, Margy Whalley, Margaret Edgington, Gillian Pugh, and Tony Bertram, have contributed to preschool and Early Years workers being recognised as professionals in their own right with a key role in laying the foundations for lifelong learning. Through the 1990s, reports and commentaries supported the pioneering voices building a strong case for a more coherent approach to Early Childhood Care and Education (ECEC). Two reports in particular stand out: Rumbold's (1990) *Starting With Quality*, which emphasised the importance of the context and process of learning, not simply content, and Ball's (1994) *'Start Right*, which drew on the knowledge of and research by respected professionals. While identifying the failure to provide Margaret Thatcher's promised 'Nursery Education for all', *Start Right* went on to state: 'Investment in high-quality and effective early education provides a worthwhile social and economic return to society' (Ball 1994: 6).

The importance of quality was stressed identifying the following requirements (ibid.):

- the integration of education and care;
- unified responsibility for provision;
- targets for growth by a specified year;
- effective and continuing training for early-year teachers and carers;
- an appropriate curriculum encouraging active 'purposeful play';
- partnership between parents and educators; and
- adequate resources.

The next 16 years saw increased investment and resourcing for the new Early Years. The 1997 New Labour Government raft of initiatives to improve ECEC included:

- Early Years Development and Care Partnerships (EYDCPs), where each Local Authority provided a partnership group comprising all interested parties within ECEC services, including private and independent providers and service users;
- Early Excellence Centres (EECs), which were developmental partnerships, including all preschool and Early Years, Health, Social Care and Education providers, local community service providers including police, job centres, adult education and parents;
- Sure Start Local Programmes, which were set up in clearly defined reach areas of high social deprivation and need, to identify local needs and design services to meet them in partnership with service users and other agencies; and
- Neighbourhood Nurseries, to provide affordable child care and education for those parents who could not afford private provision.

The last three initiatives merged into Sure Start Children's Centres.

There is now in the Early Years Professional Status (EYPS), a nationally recognised qualification for practitioners. Improved training has produced greater awareness of the value of practice grounded in research and theory. Increasing complexity in Early Years partnerships has brought recognition of the need for high-quality, trained leadership. Now leaders of ECEC centres and services have to be confident in practicing the skills of multi-agency partnership working and specific training programmes have been developed by the government and universities, in particular the National Professional Qualification in Integrated Centre Leadership (NPQICL), which has parity with the National Professional Qualification for Headteachers (NPQH).

NPQICL was developed by Pen Green Research Centre in partnership with the then National College for School Leadership, now the National College. Whalley, Whitaker, Thorpe, and John (2004) developed a unique, experiential, rather than didactic, programme grounded in andragogical approaches (Knowles, 1970; Whalley, 2004[1]) and including mentor support for participants. Participants, facilitators and mentors join in a sensitive partnership to explore leadership of multi-agency settings (Figure 17.1).

The acceptance of mentoring as a valid and valuable practice in leadership support and development has only relatively recently become accepted. Over the past six years, in the context of Early Years, it has been shown to be essential, particularly to those leading services and centres. Mentoring actively helps them understand more clearly the complexity of the context in which they work. This includes their own identity and as leaders, the interpersonal forces at work within their organisations and the strategies and skills required to develop a shared vision, sense of purpose and direction.

Definitions

Mentoring has been around for a long time. In Greek mythology Mentor is Odysseus's trusted counsellor to his son, Telemachus, whilst he was away on his long journey.

Freedman (1993) highlights that in the 1820s the Brothers Grimm wrote a story called Iron John, which is about a 'wild man' who becomes a mentor to a prince against the odds. This reworks the Odysseus story from another angle, exploring the idea that somebody who was not seen as a trusted and respected person could also offer the mentor role. This again highlights a classic teacher/ student and parent/child role and the conflict between process-centred and task-centred approaches. The latter is not the mentoring process that I and others on the National Professional Qualification in Integrated Centre Leadership experienced. In the 1970s, the idea of coaching staff and an achievement-based mentoring approach developed in the corporate world. The task-centred approach of latter twentieth-century business was an anathema to me.

Bell (2002) uses the term building blocks like surrendering, accepting, gifting, and extending to identify his philosophy of mentoring. However, like the Brothers Grimm, he sees mentoring as a way of a senior partner passing on

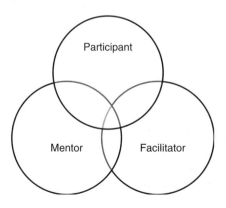

Figure 17.1

wisdom to a junior partner. The senior and junior may not just be to do with chronology; it could be to do with length of service in an organisation or purely that you are a hub in the organisation. He tells the story of a security guard in a firm that he was working at, who at his retirement party received accolades as a mentor from everybody from the chief executive to the cleaners and that a very famous surprise visitor, a well-known business guru, even came back to say thank you. Bell also links these building blocks with effective leadership. He suggests that great leaders are confident enough to show humility, are courageous and foster curiosity within those they lead. He also suggests that great leaders are generous with advice and feedback, stories and support.

Whilst leading a community development project for a national children's charity in the 1990s in inner city Birmingham, I came across my first formal mentoring project, the Ashanti Project. This project worked specifically with young black men in the education system, offering a behaviourist mentoring approach. The main ideas were to model good behaviours and explore with the young people the reasons why they behaved in an unacceptable way. I found this to be what I now know as a deficit model and at times I felt uneasy with this process, because it seemed to reinforce what Merton (1968: 477) calls a self-fulfilling prophecy. On the surface we were supporting the young people, but this could also strengthen negative behaviour; they were special and getting the attention of the mentor because of their unhelpful behaviour.

An alternative and more positive approach is encouraged by Karen John, drawing on Adlerian psychology, who, in her 2006 lecture to the Adlerian Society, referred to 'the courage to be imperfect'. This allows us to identify the 'I' as a generative and positive force and, therefore, encourages the mentee participant in the dialogical mentoring process to focus on their positive attributes and to see themselves as 'the intervening variable' (op cit). This is the basis of the model of mentoring used in NPQICL with which we have been involved with for the last six years. Its stated aim is to help leaders achieve greater self-awareness and professional integration, with the intended outcomes for participants that include (NPQICL, 2008):

- a clarification of their passions and goals;
- an exploration of their work practices and needs;
- a reflection on their work based relationships;
- an understanding of their wider work-based context;
- increasing their self awareness;
- allowing them to feel more confident and authentic as a leader;
- reflecting on and finding ways to address challenges;
- prioritise their workload and tasks; and
- explore problem solving.

These outcomes are shared with other methods of mentoring and indeed coaching, but the difference lies in the way that the relationship between the mentor and the mentee is developed. We have identified this approach as 'dialogical mentoring' where the mentor, whilst having an understanding and experience of the professional challenges that the mentee is facing, is not set up as an 'older and wiser' mentor or even the coach to 'help you get it right'. The relationship between the dialogical mentor and the mentee should predominantly be a relationship of equals, jointly exploring experiences and issues.

The NPQICL mentoring approach has adopted the values of the British Association of Counselling and Psychotherapy (BACP) which are given in Box 17.1.

The importance of these values to dialogical mentoring is fundamental. The mentor needs to become a trusted and important part of the leadership learning journey of the mentee. They have to be seen not as an expert but as a confidante acting as a mirror of the mentee's practice to offer positive, critical reflection.

SO WHY USE DIALOGICAL MENTORING RATHER THAN THE MORE TRADITIONAL MENTORING AND COACHING APPROACHES?

Clutterbuck (2004) identifies that mentoring draws from other learning styles. This includes the prerequisite that mentors have sufficient sensitivity to the needs of the mentee and can adjust and respond with the appropriate behaviour. Robertson's (2008) view of coaching is linked to these ideals. She draws a clear distinction between leadership mentoring and life/executive/personal coaching. We believe the clear difference between the coaching and dialogical mentoring is the reciprocity and mutuality of the dialogical mentoring approach. The mentors are also the receivers of new knowledge and learning if the relationship is truly reciprocal.

This is evidenced in the work of Bokeno and Gannt (2000: 237) who state that 'dialogical mentoring has advantages over both conventional mentoring

---

Box 17.1   NPQICL leadership mentoring support values (adapted from BACP, 2002)

The values adopted from the BACP ethical framework on NPQICL are:
- respecting human rights and dignity;
- ensuring the integrity of the mentor–participant relationship;
- enhancing the quality of professional knowledge and its application;
- alleviating personal distress and suffering;
- fostering a sense of self that is meaningful to the leader;
- increasing personal effectiveness;
- enhancing the quality of relationships between people;
- appreciating the variety of human experience and culture; and
- striving for the fair and adequate provision of mentoring support.

Source: NPQICL (2008: Section 2, p. 4)

relationships and extant practices for generative learning in organizations [sic]'. This supports our argument that, unlike more traditional coaching and mentoring approaches, the symbiotic nature of dialogical mentoring gives additional value to both organisations and participants.

Saarnivaara and Sarja (2007: 5) describe dialogic mentoring as 'a fruitful pedagogical tool in preventing and reducing work based stress'. They have identified that the dialogic method supports individuals making the transition into a new environment by both supporting and encouraging positive qualities and dispositions. This again reinforces our view that dialogical mentoring offers something different from more traditional approaches. Hargreaves and Fink (2006: 248) exhort sustainable leaders to 'take mentoring seriously', urging a move away from the more traditional, automatic, construct of the older wiser expert and towards a shared and equal exploration of 'values in common' and 'differences'. This is further supported by Stopp (2008) who advocates a move from traditional analysis and feedback of observed teaching sessions to *dialogic review*, thus encouraging a shared reflection on wider issues than a simple focus on numerical scores.

The task-centred nature of coaching lends itself to skills development and the attainment of a certain level of performance. Dialogical mentoring does not start with the premise that the input of the mentor will achieve a certain level of performance, therefore as Clutterbuck (2004: 23) asserts there is far less of the 'tell, show, suggest' style and much more of the 'stimulate' style. The traditional view of a coach is of one who says, 'When you are doing this think about these things', whilst the dialogical approach would encourage one to say, 'What are the things that would change this situation do you think?' so the answers are intrinsic to the mentee. The dialogical approach is used to support their leaders: we would suggest the traditional coaches' 'tell, show and suggest' approaches are not only inappropriate, but impossible due to the ever-changing external service environment.

SO WHY NOT THE OLDER–WISER MENTOR MODEL?

The role model approach as described by Murray (2001) needs the mentor to be performing the same activities and therefore be held in high regard and seen in a favourable light. Role models often exhibit:

- success in the field;
- commendable behaviour in attainment and flair;
- aptitude for getting things done;
- knowledge of the organisations policy and philosophy; and
- apparent enjoyment of position and accomplishment.

This is different from dialogical mentoring because in this the mentor is a peer rather than a more successful, older and wiser person. Murray uses the word 'protégé' which we believe gives a value to the relationship which implies a power that we believe can be unhelpful when trying to describe a more dialogical approach.

This leads us to the basic principle of our view of dialogical mentoring, that of a 'non-deficit' model. By this we mean that for the mentoring process to be most successful the mentee must feel that the mentor is not judging them. In the true Rogerian tradition (Rogers, 1980) the mentee should be central to the relationship rather than the organisation, the task or the mentor.

We believe that the use of a non-deficit approach to dialogical leadership mentoring is essential. This means that we start from where the mentee is rather than where we think they should be and allows the mentor to respectfully challenge poor practice, behaviour or style, if required. This is not an easy situation, especially when poor practice is evidenced by the mentor. The need for good support/supervision, training and CPD for mentors is essential for both the efficacy and the safety of both mentors and mentees.

If we have Clutterbuck's (2004) starting point suggesting that everyone needs a mentor then we should look at the advantages of this type of dialogical mentoring for organisations. Through our research over the last four years we have identified the benefits of dialogical mentoring for both mentees and mentors. We believe that more research needs to be carried out to identify the organisational benefits.

Clutterbuck (2004) identifies organisational issues that can block the mentoring process, which includes poor planning and preparation, poor clarity of role, failure to set and measure clear outcomes, too little or too much formality, failure to quality control the mentor pool and being too elitist. We would add to this list the importance of the quality of initial induction and ongoing training for the mentor pool. If this is not included it is more likely that individual mentors will drift from the purpose and vision of the particular mentor programme.

We see the process of group supervision/support for experienced mentors as a cost effective and useful process for organisations, where a lead mentor brings together a group of mentors to use the same dialogical approach used with mentees to support each other and discuss broad areas of concern regarding the mentor programme. The mentors have an opportunity to share concerns, good practice tips and also highlight common issues identified by their mentees whilst the lead mentor is then able to feedback to the organisation and identifies any common areas for development.

In the ever-changing world of integrated children's services in England we believe that it is essential that the newly forming children's services departments are supporting their leaders by using the new knowledge that is developing within them. One of the main reasons for this assertion is that these new organisations are developing their own cultures. This is, as Tuckman (1965) relates, a 'storming' time where decisions don't come easy and people position themselves in opposition to leaders. We believe that it is essential for the future development of effective children's services that the lessons learnt from these reflective organisation are noted by leaders of integrated children's services at all levels.

HOW DOES IT WORK?

Case study 1: Failing leader – hopeful setting

The hypothetical leader describes the children centre:

> We are a school based phase 2 Children's Centre with me as co-ordinator and one part-time family support worker and one part-time Early Years worker. The deputy head at the school is the Children's Centre teacher and I am nominally line managed by the head teacher, although I have been getting support from the Children's Service officer who has a district wide approach. The services are just starting but I find it difficult to access our funds which are managed by the school bursar. We have a small new build which the school have been using as a library, now the team are in place we need the space and resources but I am finding it hard to negotiate with the head and other school staff.

In this case the mentor could start with questions like, 'How do you think the Children's Centre, you and your team are seen by the head and senior management team (SMT)?', 'Why do you think they are seen that way?', 'Where are the aims of the school and the Children's Centre similar and where are they different?'

This would enable the mentee to begin to get a clearer view of the perceptions and feelings of each of the parties involved as well as how they themselves were feeling about their current situation. The mentor here would need to be aware of the useful acronym that Clutterbuck (2004: 53) incorporates:

Manages the relationship
Encourages
Nurtures
Teaches
Offers mutual respect
Responds to the mentees needs

In terms of managing the relationship the mentor needs to allow the mentee to identify where the issues are for themselves. It would be easy to give answers and to identify the power relationship issues for the leader, but this would not be managing the relationship. We need to be clear that the leader feels comfortable to share where they feel they are with the issue they have bought up. If we take the non-deficit approach (see previously), focusing on successes and on what the leader has achieved, where things are working well, there is the possibility of building on success, however small, and of their gaining confidence in the mentor as an appreciative listener.

By active listening and by employing supplementary questions the mentor encourages the mentee; for example, a question like, 'How does the school SMT see the core offer for children's centres?' would allow the leader, who has a clear view of the core offer and how to implement it but is stifled by the school's lack of knowledge around the agenda, to understand more clearly why there is a lack of appreciation of the Children's Centre and to begin to spend time reflecting on their role and the power they have to change things. Another approach might be introduced with a question like, 'What kind of support do you think is important for the co-ordinator at your centre?' This encourages mentee reflection on their own, legitimate, support needs, which are often pushed to the back of the business queue in the minds of leaders. This could lead to a supportive discussion about how to get their own needs met, especially when feeling like a minor partner within the organisation. It is not unusual for the discussion to begin to show up what are and what are not, realistic aims, what areas lie within and what areas beyond, the mentee's sphere of influence. This in itself often releases the mentee from their inner feelings of frustration and even guilt and produces a sense of relief, as their understanding becomes clearer.

Nurturing the mentee is a subtle process: picking up on ideas that they express, sometimes not as coherent theories, but as 'by the way' points; drawing attention to things that they can reflect on, that will draw out their own experiences and understanding, help to pass the initiative to the mentee and increase their empowerment to take charge of their own direction. Using pointers like, 'I heard you say' or 'I'd like you to expand on something you said' is a mode of questioning that helps the mentee to get a clearer picture of their own situation. As experienced mentors we can say that the 'aha moments' that some mentees have during this part of the process can be the most revelatory for the mentee and therefore the most useful when planning their future actions. In this case the need to explore the power relationship between the Children's Centre and the school is evident, finding the right key phrases that will nurture the mentee to move from victim to active partner would be important.

Teaching is an interesting role for the mentor. Freire (1972) states that dialogue is teaching and it should not involve one person acting *on* another, but rather people working with each other. Freire argues that formal education relies too much on the educator 'banking' by depositing knowledge in those being educated. We see the mentor role in dialogical mentoring to be encouraging shared dialogue that enlightens both the mentor and mentee alike, rather than imparting knowledge, or 'getting the mentee to see the pathway the mentor has set out for them'. Our research has enabled us to see this in action. Mentors on the NPQICL programme have themselves expressed that the 'aha' moments for them have come when in dialogue with their mentees. Drawing out the learning from the mentee leads to what Freire (1972) describes as *praxis*, action that is informed and linked to certain values, and is a key issue for this part of the dialogical mentoring process. For this to happen, trust and mutual respect must be at the centre of the mentor–mentee relationship. In this example the shared experience of what it is like working in a situation where there is a dominant culture and where there is little or no understanding of the 'new' culture needed to move things forward, can be shared through dialogue but without falling into the trap of sharing too much from the mentor's own past experiences, no matter how relevant they may seem.

Ensuring that we are working in response to the mentees' identified needs is essential. Throughout the process the principle of non-deficit mentoring must prevail for it to be effective. This can be encouraged by using techniques of summing up and reflecting with the mentee, clarifying together what has been discussed and what has become clearer for them as a result, suggesting further points for reflection that the mentee can consider in between mentoring sessions and bringing these reflections back next time. Reviewing where the discussion started, how it progressed and how the mentee *feels* at the end is a powerful and satisfying conclusion for both mentor and mentee.

Case Study 2: Failing setting – hopeful leader

The leader describes their Children's Centre:

> It was a social services-run Family Centre and some of the day care and family support staff have been there since it opened. The previous leader had been on long term sickness leave and two temporary appointments had been made until I was appointed. The nursery was originally private using spare classrooms and was added to the centre leadership portfolio three years ago. The nursery manager was appointed a year ago from the children's centre staff and budget but the nursery is staffed and run for the centre by the private provider. Two years ago the building work to refurbish and extend the old school buildings was begun and was completed 18 months later, when I took up post. There are now specially equipped rooms for midwives to use, two large and two small training rooms and smaller consultation rooms, a community area and a large office space which is shared by all the teams and admin. I have an office of my own across the hallway from the main office. The reception office and desk are where the old school entrance used to be. The building is on one floor and there is space outside but this was not included in the refurbishment.

Before starting it is useful to reflect on the following. What kind of picture this creates? What has not been mentioned? What additional information would be helpful? What impression do you gain of the speaker by the way they tell their story? Questions like these while the mentee is speaking can help decide how you would begin.

The picture described is of separate staff teams, of hierarchies and isolated individuals and of partner agencies who use rooms on the site but without connection to the setting as a whole. The worst effects are magnified by the lack of leadership of the centre over at least a three-year period. Despite this, the head is optimistic in their outlook and although frustrated, demonstrates a positive attitude, retaining their sense of humour.

The mentor's role is primarily to listen and, by questioning, to help the mentee to clarify each of the interwoven threads and clear the 'fog'. At the same time considering how they might gauge the head's feelings and how these might affect particular aspects. Relationships are often key aspects: clues about the overall situation and any particular parts may involve, returning to one aspect, tone changes when talking about an aspect or individual, avoiding eye contact when describing certain roles or relationships, not mentioning a role or person that you might expect to be.

As in each of these examples the first step is to build the confidence in the mentee to trust the mentor and the process of mentoring. Listening actively enables appropriate questioning and a degree of respectful challenge by the mentor.

This is aimed at honest appraisal of the context and its elements which will allow the mentee to stand back and to acknowledge what might previously have been only vague feelings or impressions and to crystallise these into clearer perceptions. Once this is achieved the mentor can encourage the mentee to reflect on the clarified issues and relationships, the emotions involved and how these have affected the mentee, balancing and prioritising as they do so.

Parsle and Leedham's four questions encourage more focused exploration of critical questions progressing from the 'what and why' of what has occurred and extending to include the resulting feelings and thoughts, specific learning or sense that can be made and how this experience will inform future actions.

In the example given, reflection on the whole and its parts can help focus the enthusiasm of the new leader in an unpromising setting, to help them understand what they can and cannot influence and to identify how they might begin to move the organisation forward by steps. Friedman (2005) describes how important it is for tasks to be shared and understood, and for people and teams to recognise where they are starting from. Once this is clear they can begin to understand what is achievable, in gradual steps of change, with successes celebrated along the way, in the movement of a curve to turn rather than a straight line with a fixed point which alone signifies 'success' if achieved or 'failure' if not reached, irrespective of the gains and improvements on the way.

One aspect of reflection is to help the mentee to have the confidence to understand different perceptions and to see the potential in positive elements of their team. Hargreaves and Fink urge their readers to 'Take mentoring seriously' (2006). They go on to identify that 'A central task of leadership is to organize mentoring, provide mentoring, and find mentoring for oneself' (ibid. 248).

In doing so they recognise the importance of shared values and a degree of difference in developing shared understanding and the value of past knowledge and experience to the process of building the future. In this example one important aspect for the mentee to begin to reflect on is whether they want change, and if so, what kind of change they want and how might they begin. Change cannot happen instantly but understanding this fact can.

Case Study 3: Autocratic to reflective learning

The centre head is a teacher who has now to lead the multi-disciplinary team in a phase 1 Children's Centre:

> I expect staff to get on with their roles if they are qualified; there is too much shilly shallying and beating about the bush. We have targets and have to meet them. I get frustrated by the lack of action. In our centre people want too much supervision, I blame the previous manager who was a social worker, I want to run the centre in a way that good school runs, with little management intervention!

The role of the mentor in this case is interesting. A strong, confident leader with a successful track record in her chosen profession, who really did not see the purpose of leadership mentoring and saw it initially as an interference to her usual routine.

The initial contact with this mentee would be important in building a credible relationship with them, respecting their professional heritage and identifying their achievements, finding out how you can work together and laying out the mentor contract verbally and in clear, unambiguous terms. Starting with a brief history of the centre and the structure of the team and asking questions about what the leader thinks is good and not so good about the current situation is useful. Empathy, in this case, is the most important emotion, understanding the situation from the perspective of the mentee and trying to unpick the intricacies of the emotions and disequilibrium that the mentee is feeling with the new situation that they find themselves in.

Clutterbuck (2004) highlights the following, amongst others, as keys to successful graduate mentoring schemes. In this case we can see how important they would be to ensure positive movement for the mentee.

- *Managing the 'power distance'.* Ensuring the mentee is comfortable with the role and experience of the mentor. The trick here is to ensure that the mentor has enough experience to get the mentees respect and not so far apart as to damage the rapport.
- *Timing the start of the relationship.* In this case the mentoring relationship is linked to a CPD experience. It is important that the mentoring process is in line with the development of the mentee: too early in their work life experience could lead to them being unable to articulate some of the issues they are struggling with.
- *Linking with competencies.* In this case it would be linking to the National Standards for Integrated Centre Leadership (DCSF, 2007) especially the standard around building and developing multi-disciplinary teams.
- *Focus on the practical.* Mentoring sometimes fails because the process moves away from the practicable-solution-based approach; in this case looking at the intricacies of multi-disciplinary leadership and identifying the small step approaches that the leader may use.
- *Focus on opportunities not problems.* Again looking at a solution-based approach with this mentee. Identifying the win: win opportunities with the mentee is essential.

The role of the mentor here then would be to make the links to their own experience and develop the trusting relationship with the mentee to allow them to gently move the mentee to the next step in dealing with some of their issues.

It is often difficult for an individual leader with an espoused theory and established theory in action to allow themselves to contemplate any other possible way of *doing*. Dialogical mentoring seeks to encourage mentees to consider the possibility of other ways of *being* while still respecting the mentee's starting point. Respectful challenge can help the mentee to begin to see new possibilities but can often take time to achieve. It is also important to avoid being judgemental: the mentor can help the mentee to see new possibilities but if they choose not to adopt them the mentor must respect their choice and try to offer the best quality approaches within the mentee's willingness to engage. The mentor must recognise the 'art of the possible' as well as encouraging the mentee to do the same.

Case Study 4: Depleted potential to conscious capability

I am head of a Children's Centre. I have been in post for a year and feel I have a good view of each of the parts that make up the centre. My background is in education and my previous post was as deputy of a nursery school. In my last post all the staff were very committed and supportive and we had gradually built up our outreach and work with parents. We had good relationships with partner agencies especially in social care and health. Gradually all the staff had come to see the value of working together and really worked well to support families. My new situation is very different. The nursery and day care manager is very authoritarian in her approach. The staff are scared to take any initiative and have become demoralised and there have been increasing cases of sickness absence. One assistant who had been on long-term sick leave has left. The work being carried out is at best routine and lacks any imagination. There is little or no contact with the Children's Centre although we are in the same building. The Family Support Team have given up trying to approach the nursery. I introduced supervision for the nursery and day care staff shortly after taking up post, which was already set up in the Children's Centre but this was a mistake as it has made things worse. I am not sure what to do. I can feel the atmosphere getting worse and feel I am losing my way.

The concept of depleted potential is relatively simple to understand. Most people have experienced occasions when either the context of their life or relationships constrict their activity and constrain their practice and their emotional engagement with tasks and people. Leaders in Early Years settings are not immune and depleted potential can exert a negative influence on them and their setting at all levels.

In this case the mentor's role is essentially to listen and to encourage the mentee to explore the identified issues, reflecting on the relationships, interactions and feelings. A useful tool used in NPQICL is emotional mapping. The mentee is encouraged to create a pictorial representation of their setting using images to symbolise how they feel about particular parts. In this case there does potentially appear to be a good deal to celebrate. Helping the mentee towards a better balance in their perceptions of how things are can help them to begin to identify what makes the 'good' parts good and the 'uncomfortable' parts bad. Exploring how they feel and why they feel as they do can help to identify the debilitating and disempowering aspects and to understand them.

If the mentor–mentee relationship is established well, the mentor can respectfully challenge and ask the more difficult questions: 'Have you noticed that each time we have started talking about different areas, you have brought it back to [name]? Why is that?', or, 'You say you aren't really concerned about [name] but their name keeps turning up – why do you think that is?'. In some circumstances it may help for the mentee to write down their own answers but not share them. Showing this degree of sensitivity encourages the developing trust with their mentor and can help the mentee to come to terms with hard and difficult areas which they may be unwilling to acknowledge even to themselves.

Once the 'elephant in the room' has been acknowledged the mentee can be encouraged to consider what strategies and approaches may be available and what the consequences and requirements of each may be. Again this is not the mentor telling them what to do; rather, it is helping them to improve and answer their own questions to explore possibilities. A great deal of the power of mentoring lies in its ability to boost and restore the mentee's sense of self-belief, self-confidence and a more balanced view of reasonable expectations of themselves and others.

Once there is recognition of the real issue, the mentee may be in a better place to consider why, in this case, an individual is acting in the way they are. Exploring this avenue can be productive in opening possibilities which the mentee may not have considered while being too close and 'closed'. Restoring a better balance can enable the mentee to draw on their past experience and knowledge to see more than one perspective and a more positive way forward. Where this involves difficult tasks, especially where it is necessary to adopt positions or procedures which emotionally aware leaders are reluctant to resort to, the role of the mentor is to support the exploration. Respectful questioning: 'Is doing nothing an option?', 'What do you feel you should do?', 'What are the alternatives as you see them?', 'Do you feel able to take this forward yourself or do you need additional advice or support?', 'How do you think (name) will react?', 'What can you put in place to help them?', 'How do you feel the rest of the team will feel?' can help. Once action appears it may be useful to use the 'five whys', starting with 'Why do I want to do this?' (see Box 17.2).

This possible set of responses based on the current example brings the mentee to a new understanding of the individual at the heart of the issue. It doesn't solve the problem but it does open new lines of thought and possible approach. Questions seek to encourage the mentee to think things through, to appreciate other perspectives but also to recognise their choices and to move towards a decision on future action. The aim of this is to help them move towards 'conscious capability', to take charge of their leadership role even though they may not like the choice or the situation.

Box 17.2

1   Why do I want to challenge this individual? Because their style is having a negative effect.
2   Why is it having a negative effect? The staff aren't able to contribute or use their imagination.
3   Why can't staff contribute or use their imagination? Because they lack confidence and are being dominated.
4   Why do they lack confidence? Because they are being suppressed.
5   Why are they being suppressed? Because the manager is afraid.

Source: Megginson and Clutterbuck (2009)

In these difficult dilemmas it may be tempting for the mentor to sympathise and to begin to see parallels with their own experience but this may not be helpful to either party. As Parsloe and Needham point out:

> It is wise to follow the advice of Adler (2002) when he says: 'Assume difference until similarity is proven.' Often there are different ways of achieving the same common understanding. The coach-mentor should try to sensitively help the learner find alternative approaches that will work sympathetically within the specific culture or diversity while retaining the learner's own identity.
>
> (Parsloe and Leedham, 2009: 96)

CONCLUSION

This chapter has examined the nature of dialogical mentoring and its importance for supporting leaders of integrated ECEC settings. We have made a distinction between coaching, which is based in approaches focused on outcomes, and mentoring, which is focused on helping mentees to explore issues and identify emotional responses, see other perspectives and move towards finding their own solutions, by understanding more about the processes and interactions involved. The view of the mentor as the all-knowing, wiser professional which creates a deficit model is rejected in favour of an approach which places the mentor alongside the mentee as a fellow traveller on their journey.

NOTE

1 Knowles describes andragogy as the art of facilitating adult learning. For more information on Knowles's principles of andragogy see Knowles (1970).

REFERENCES

Adler, N. J. (2002) Global Companies, Global Society: There is a Better Way. *Journal of Management Enquiry*, 11 (3), 255–260. Selected as 'Editors choice' in Parsloe, E. and Leedham, M. (2009) *Coaching and Mentoring: Practical conversations to improve learning* London: Kogan Page, p. 96.

Ball, C. (1994) *Start Right*. London: Royal Society for the Encouragement of Arts, Manufactures and Commerce (RSA).

Bell, C. (2002) *Managers as Mentors*. San Francisco: Berret Koehler.

Bokeno, R. M. and Gantt, V. W. (2000) Dialogic Mentoring: Core Relationships for Organizational Learning. *Management Communication Quarterly*, 14 (2): 237–270.

Clutterbuck, D. (2004) *Everybody Needs a Mentor*. London: CIPD.

DCSF (2007) *National Standards for Leaders of Sure Start Children's Centres*. London: DCSF

Freedman, M. (1993) *The Kindness of Strangers*. San Francisco: Jossey-Bass.

Friedman, M. (2005) *Trying Hard Is Not Good Enough: How to Produce Measureable Improvements for Customers and Communities*. Victoria BC: Trafford.

Freire, P. (1972) *Pedagogy of the Oppressed*. London: Penguin.

Hargreaves, A. and Fink D. (2006) *Sustainable Leadership*, San Fransisco, Jossey-Bass.

Honey, P. and Mumford, M. (1986) *Using Your Learning Styles*. Maidenhead: Peter Honey Publications.

John, K. (2006) *Encouraging the Disencouraged to Encourage the Disencouraged.* Adlerian Society, Herta Orgler Lecture, Oxford Adlerian Society and Institute of Psychology, Oxford.

Knowles, M. (1970) *The Modern Practice of Adult Education: From Pedagogy to Andragogy* Cambridge Book Company, Cambgridge.

Merton, R. K. (1968) *Social Theory and Social Structure.* New York: Macmillan.

Megginson, D. and Clutterbuck, D. (2009) *Further Techniques for Coaching and Mentoring.* Oxford: Butterworth-Heinemann, p. 174.

Murray, M. (2001) *Beyond The Myths and Magic of Mentoring.* San Francisco: Jossey-Bass.

NPQICL (2008) *NPQICL Tutor Manual.* Nottingham: NCSCSL.

Parsloe, E. and Leedham, M. (2009) *Coaching and Mentoring: Practical Conversations to Improve Learning.* London: Kogan Page.

Rumbold, A. (1990) *Starting With Quality.* London: DfES.

Robertson, J. (2008) *Coaching Educational Leadership.* London: Sage.

Rogers, C. (1980) *A Way of Being.* Boston: Houghton Mifflin.

Saarnivaara, M. and Sarja, A. (2007) From University to Working Life: Mentoring as a Pedagogical Challenge. *Journal of Workplace Learning,* 19(1): 5–16.

Stopp, P. (2008) *From Feedback to Dialogic Review: Using Reflective Dialogue in Post-Lesson Observation Sessions on an ITT Placement.* MA dissertation, Bishop Grosseteste University College, University of Leicester.

Thorpe, S. and Gasper, M. (2003) *Who Cares for the Carers? An Exploration of Support Provided for Leaders of Integrated Early Years Centres.* DfES Leadership & Management Bursary Report. London: DfES.

Tuckman, B. W. (1965) Developmental Sequence in Small Groups. *Psychological Bulletin,* 63, 384–399. Reprinted in *Group Facilitation: A Research and Applications Journal* 3, (2001).

Whalley, M., Whitaker, P., Thorpe, S. and John, K. (2004) *NPQICL Training Programme Materials.* Nottingham: National College.

Whittaker, P. (2007) *Developing Academic Capability.* Nottingham: NCSL.

18

Coaching in the K-12 Context

Joellen Killion

INTRODUCTION

Coaching, a form of professional development, supports the transfer of new learning into practice and promotes continuous improvement. Professional development engages teachers in developing knowledge and skills; however, the acquisition of new knowledge and skills does not automatically guarantee that they will be integrated into teachers' practice. As one form of continuous teacher development, coaching provides personalized, school and classroom-based support for teachers as they continue to expand their professional capacity throughout their career.

Putnam and Borko (2002) in their examination of the nature of teachers' knowledge and skills, support needed for teacher learning, and the dimensions of teacher learning distinguish between cognitive theorists who believe learning is devoid of context and situative theorists who conclude that learning occurs in context. Putnam and Borko suggest that the social and physical contexts in which learning occurs are an integral part of the learning process. Coaching is both a situative and interactive process for adult learning that moves learning from 'knowing about' to implementation within the classroom environment.

What occurs within a coaching interaction affects the results of coaching. Killion (2009, 2010) distinguishes between light coaching, which is more focused on providing encouragement and support; and heavy coaching, which is focused on improving practice and producing results. Coaches working from the premise of cognitive theorists who believe that learning is the process of acquisition of knowledge and skills fail, according to Putnam and Borko, to recognize that learning is more than the acquisition of knowledge and skills. Learning is the integration of new knowledge and skills into practice within the classroom context. Coaches who only provide opportunity, stimulation, and encouragement for the individual construction of knowledge rather than interact with teachers in their classroom environment about how to implement what they are learning, restrict both what is learned and how learning takes place.

Because coaching, according to Hargreaves and Dawe (1989), is a process of active learning, and engages more than a single perspective, the situative theory of learning serves as a strong foundation for professional learning associated with coaching: 'What is to be coached in teaching cannot be reduced solely to matters of technical skills and competence, but involves choices of personal, moral, and socio-political nature' (1989: 20). Understanding how learning for teachers occurs is core to understanding the role of coaching in professional learning. One of the greatest challenges in professional learning that occurs outside the school is bringing that learning back into the school and integrating it into the classroom practice. Coaching bridges the gap between learning that occurs outside the school or classroom and classroom practice. In her early research, Showers (1982, 1984) found across several studies that teachers who received coaching were more likely to implement newly learned teaching practices with greater fidelity than teachers who did not receive coaching support. To ensure that professional development for practicing teachers transforms their practice and supports student learning, learning must move into the school and classroom.

Coaching as a form of professional development is unlike more conventional forms that occur in courses, workshops, conferences, or professional development days. Coaching focuses on goals generated from the needs of teachers and their students, occurs within the context in which teachers will apply their learning, and provides personalized support. Some of educators' common complaints about more conventional forms of professional development are that it is unrelated to daily work, that it is facilitated by experts from outside the school or school system who have only limited understanding of the context in which the learning will be applied, and that there is limited, if any, follow-up support (Russo, 2004). Researchers and practitioners alike recommend that professional development, to have its greatest impact on educator practice and student achievement, must be 'deeply embedded into teachers' classroom work with children, specific to grade-level or academic content, and focused on research-based approaches' (2004: 2). It must also promote strong collaboration among educators within a school (Saunders, Goldenberg, and Gallimore, 2009).

WHAT IS COACHING

Coaching is a professional development practice that bridges the gap between training and application of new learning in classrooms.

Coaching models recognize that if professional development is to take root in teachers' practice, ongoing and specific follow-up is necessary to help teachers incorporate new knowledge and skills into classroom practice both in the short and long-term ... [S]chool-based coaching generally involves experts in a particular subject area or set of teaching strategies working closely with small groups of teachers to improve classroom practice and, ultimately, student achievement. In some cases coaches work full-time at an individual school or district; in others they work with a variety of schools throughout the year. Most are former classroom teachers, and some keep part-time classroom duties while they coach.

(Darling-Hammond, Wei, Andree, Richardson, and Orphanos, 2009: 14)

Definitions of coaching range from specific and narrow to imprecise and broad. Broadly, coaching is the practice of providing deliberate support to another individual to help him/her to clarify and to achieve goals' (Bloom, Castagna, Moir, and Warren, 2005: 5). 'The Department for Education and Skills (DfES/CUREE, 2005) defines coaching as a structured process for enabling the development of a specific aspect of a professional learner's practice' (Galanouli, 2009: 12). Simkins, Coldwell, Caillau, Finlayson, and Morgan (2006) describe coaching more specifically as a form of professional development that is narrower in scope than mentoring. Coaching, as they conceive of it, focuses on skill development and job-specific tasks rather than career development. 'Similar in many aspects to teacher mentoring in which newly qualified teachers pair with a more experienced teacher or a team of teachers, coaching involves a collaborative relationship between a teacher and an expert, who has developed specific knowledge and skills related to instructional practice' (Neuman and Cunningham, 2009: 538).

The National (England) Framework for Mentoring and Coaching, grounded in evidence from research, identifies ten principles for successful coaching and mentoring:

- participating in a learning conversations;
- setting challenging and personal goals;
- developing a thoughtful relationship;
- understanding why different approaches work;
- having a learning agreement;
- acknowledging the benefits two mentors and coaches;
- combining support from fellow professional learners and specialist;
- experimenting and observing; growing self-direction; and
- using resources effectively.

(Creasy and Patterson, 2005: 13)

These principles serve as the fundamental assumptions that drive effective coaching and mentoring.

In informal coaching teachers volunteer to support one another in a collegial way. Informal coaching engages peers as equals in providing feedback to one another to promote shared learning. Formal coaching, often with a person designated as a coach who is a specialist or knowledgeable other and who has had some formal preparation to serve in that capacity, focuses on developing a specific body of knowledge or pedagogy. Both informal and formal coaching may focus on developing expertise in a specific discipline area, as occurs often in literacy and numeracy, with specific pedagogical practices such as strategies for differentiating instruction, or may focus on more general instruction or management of classroom environment. Table 18.1 explains the distinction between informal and formal coaching.

Joyce and Showers (1981) offer two versions of definitions of coaching. Coaching 'usually involves a collegial approach to the analysis of teaching for the purpose of integrating mastered skills and strategies into: a) curriculum: b) a set of instructional goals; c) a time span; d) a personal teaching style' (1981: 170). They later refine their definition by adding that coaching functions to provide companionship, give technical feedback, analyze application, and adapt to the students (1983). Sometimes coaching is short-term, occurring only once or twice, especially when the coaching is provided by an external specialist who makes occasional visits to schools (Cordingley, Bell, Isham, Evans, and Firth, 2007; Rhodes, 2004). Other times coaching is intensive and continuous, especially when a coach works within a school and is assigned to the specific role of coach (Killion and Harrison, 2006). Coaches who are teacher leaders spend a significant portion of their work day in direct contact with teachers in their schools and classrooms assisting teachers in learning and applying new knowledge and skills to improve the academic performance of all students (Killion and Harrison, 2006).

Broader definitions of coach and coaching exist. The International Coaching Federation defines coaching as 'partnering with clients in a thought-provoking and creative process that inspires them to maximize their personal and professional potential … Coaching honors the client as the expert in his/her life and work, and believes that every client is creative, resourceful, and whole.' In their review of research on coaching, Cornett and Knight (2009) state that the International Reading Association adopted Dole's definition of literacy coach, 'anyone who supports teachers in their daily work (2004: 462)'. They note that this definition fails to define specific 'common core duties, a theory, or the manner in which coaches perform their jobs' (ibid. 203).

Vaguer and less specific definitions of coaching may lead to an ambiguous understanding of what coaching is and result in coaches having a weak sense of

Table 18.1   Informal versus formal coaching

	Formal	*Informal*
Defined knowledge and skills about teaching and learning	Provided by a skillful coach focused on specific content or pedagogical skills, often as a part of a curriculum implementation process or follow-up to a training program	Provided by a peer partner focused on specific content or pedagogical skills, often as a part of a curriculum implementation process or follow-up to a training program
Undefined knowledge and skills about teaching and learning	Provided by a skillful coach focused on general pedagogy	Provided by a peer partner focused on general pedagogy

purpose, lack of focus for their work, or inadequate accountability for results. Killion (2009) describes this problem by delineating two forms of coaching: light and heavy. Coaching light is focusing on relationship issues and affirmation without promoting deep learning. Coaching heavy means that coaches take significant responsibility for the academic success of the students of teachers being coached and focus their work on transformative learning that deeply reforms practice and results in student learning.

BENEFITS OF COACHING

A common theme among the definitions of coaching is educators engaging in collaborative work for the purpose of improving their practice. Koh and Neuman (2006) summarize the benefits of coaching as a form of professional development:

- To receive support and encouragement through the opportunity to review experiences, discuss feelings, describe frustrations, and check perceptions with a partner;
- To fine-tune skills or strategies through technical feedback and technical assistance from a coaching partner;
- To analyze practices and decision making at a conscious level;
- To adapt or generalize skills or strategies by considering what is needed to facilitate particular outcomes, how to modify the skill or practice to better fit interactions with specific families or practitioners, or what results may occur from using the skill or practice in different ways; and
- To reflect on what they perceive or how they make decisions, which helps improve their knowledge and understanding of professional practices and activities.

(Koh and Neuman, 2006: 1)

Creasy and Paterson (2005) identify the key benefits of coaching as 'improving a whole school or department, personalizing professional learning for staff, promoting self-directed professional learning, creating a learning-centered mode of professional dialogue, and building capacity for leadership' (2005: 20).

WHO ARE COACHES?

Classroom teachers, former classroom teachers, school administrators, curriculum and/or instructional specialists, university faculty, or others engaged in teacher professional development and who receive at least basic preparation to serve as coaches may serve as coaches. Coaches may be internal or external to the school. Some are members of a school staff who have a full- or part-time position as a coach or resource person within the school. Other coaches work outside the schools and visit teachers in multiple schools.

TYPES OF COACHING

Coaching occurs in a variety of formats and for an array of purposes. The most common form of coaching is face-to-face, one-to-one coaching. This type of coaching transpires in schools, coffee shops, classrooms, district offices, and other places in which the coach and the person being coached can hold a private conversation or small teams can meet without interruption. Group or team coaching, an emerging practice, recognizes that one-to-one coaching can be both costly and inefficient in promoting transformation in instructional practice. Team coaching occurs in small groups of colleagues who share common interests. Several premises lie behind team coaching. Coaching several people in a small group setting exponentially increases the benefits of coaching. Team coaching, according to Cockerham, maximizes 'the combined energy, experience, and wisdom of individuals' (Cockerham, as cited in Britton, 2010: 6) and models and encourages the skills of self- or peer-coaching among the members of the team.

Peers and experts provide coaching in one-to-one, team, or virtual settings. Coaching practices includes one-to-one meetings observations with feedback, discussions sometimes held via telephone or other electronically mediated means. Some coaching sessions follow training or occur between training sessions. Other coaching occurs naturally as a part of educator's workday as routine professional practice, during mentoring programs, as a component of a research lesson process, or in co-teaching situations.

Virtual coaching is another form of coaching. Sometimes conducted via telephone or the Internet, virtual coaching can be either one-to-one or group coaching. Sometimes referred to as e-coaching, this form of coaching might occur live between a coach and the client or a group of clients, or it can be a resource through which employees tap into an online coach who is ready to provide guidance, support, answers, and encouragement. Bud-in-the-ear technology is a form of synchronous coaching or cybermentoring (Johnson, Maring, Doty, and Fickle, 2006) in which a remote coach is able to observe a teacher live via webcast and is able to speak directly to the client via an ear bud. This form of 'real time' coaching allows the coach to provide just-in-time input or feedback to a client during the lesson. The client has the capacity to make 'on-the-spot' changes to his or her instruction (Goodman, Brady, Duffy, Scott, and Pollard, 2008; Johnson et al., 2006; Rock, Gregg, Thead, Acker, Gable, and Zigmond 2009). In other forms of virtual coaching 'an electronic coach can serve as a lower-cost tool that replicates the benefits of a live session while allowing content to be accessed privately and conveniently – at any time' (Ahrend, Diamond, and Webber, 2010: 44). Ahrend et al. make it clear that e-coaching will not replace face-to-face coaching or personal coaching. However, e-coaching will continue to grow as a mean of filling the void between day-to-day work and achieving performance improvement goals. Seventy-five percent of respondents to a survey of e-coaching users in the US and Europe, according to these authors, indicated that e-coaching is clear and easy to use, taught them something, and helped them handle a work-related situation.

In their book, Killion and Harrison (2006) describe nine varieties of coaching.

Challenge coaching focuses on persistent problems teachers experience (Garmston, 1987).

Cognitive Coaching[SM] engages teachers in conversations about planning, reflecting on practice, and problem solving (Costa and Garmston, 2002).

Collegial coaching promotes collaboration about instruction to promote shared responsibility and professional dialogue about teaching and learning (Garmston, 1987).

Content-focused coaching focuses on the tasks of planning, assessing, teaching, and reflection on the curriculum standards, instruction, and lesson design related to a particular discipline (West and Straub, 2003).

Instructional coaching more generally focuses on implementing research-based instructional practices, making appropriate decision about instructional methodologies, and reflecting on the effectiveness of instructional decisions.

Mentoring is a form of coaching that occurs when an experienced teacher works closely with the novice teacher to improve teaching and classroom management and facilitates acculturation of the novice into the school culture.

Peer consultation is a naturally occurring form of teacher support that includes informal interactions among teachers as they seek to improve their practice and understand their work. Neither teacher in peer consultation assumes to take a leadership role and the relationship is guided by the principle of reciprocity (Blasé and Blasé, 2006).

Peer coaching is the process in which teams of teachers regularly observe one another and provide support, companionship, feedback, and assistance (Valencia and Killion, 1988).

Technical coaching generally follows training in specific teaching methods to support accurate implementation of new strategies or techniques (Garmston, 1987).

Common among the various types of coaching is the goal to improve teaching practices and increase student learning. While there are many forms and practices of coaching, the consensus among applications appears to be that coaching is a form of professional development that involves ongoing classroom modeling, supportive critiques of practice, and specific observations (Shanklin, 2006).

COACHING IN US SCHOOLS

In the US, coaches come from a wide variety of roles within and outside the education system. For example, some states hire external coaches, often retired educators, as school coaches for chronically underperforming schools. State departments of education or their designees select, prepare, and place coaches in schools that have been identified as 'in need of improvement'. These coaches work either part-time or full-time within the schools providing guidance to school administrators, leadership teams, or individual or teams of teachers. In the state of Michigan, through specialized federal and state funding, coaches support low-performing schools in mathematics and literacy instruction and using data to improve instruction. To promote increases in student achievement in literacy, the state of Florida provided funding to hire, prepare, and place a reading coach in every elementary and middle school. To serve in the capacity of a reading coach, teachers completed a series of courses offered collaboratively by universities throughout the state to receive a special certificate that they were prepared to be literacy coaches. In the small school district of Springfield, Vermont, the district partners with a local college to provide professional development for its teachers. The college faculty teach courses on topics identified as important to the district's instructional framework such as problem-based learning. As a component of the agreement between the school district and the college, the college faculty provide school and classroom coaching to participants in their courses.

In some school systems, such as Allen Independent School District in Allen, Texas, district curriculum coaches, who are curriculum specialists in literacy, mathematics, science, and social studies, provide coaching to teachers in multiple schools. They use a visitation schedule that places coaches in residence within a school for several days contiguously to allow them to meet with numerous teachers and provide a variety of services such as model lessons, classroom observations with feedback, team planning, and instructional guidance. In other school systems, either through specialized funding or through staff allocations, full- or part-time coaches work with teachers in that single school. Sometimes these school-based coaches have a specific focus such as literacy or mathematics; others serve more generally as instructional facilitators.

Some districts, such as in Fargo Public Schools, in Fargo, North Dakota, are beginning to prepare non-instructional staff such as school librarians to serve as coaches. Their ability to provide resources to teachers and their frequent interactions with teachers about instruction make them excellent candidates to add a coaching dimension to their support of teachers. In some school districts too, teachers who previously worked directly with special needs students are learning to serve as learning coaches and work in a consultative manner with teachers in their classrooms as special needs students are more widely included in regular education classrooms.

Retired school administrators or teachers serve as coaches in some school systems. For example, novice principals in DeKalb County School District in Georgia, as in many districts across the country, have a leadership coach who supports them through their first few years as principals. Novice teachers receive coaching provided by retired teachers who serve as mentors or as instructional coaches. When novice teachers need additional support beyond what a mentor might typically provide, they may see the support of an instructional or curriculum specialist. Many school systems have programs through which principals can request additional support for teachers.

Central office curriculum specialists are incorporating more school-specific support into their work. Rather than just developing the curriculum, they now work more closely with teachers and teacher leaders to implement it. Central office staff members may serve as coordinators of coaching programs and provide both preparation and ongoing development and support to coaches working in schools. In schools, department chairs and team- or grade-level division leaders are shifting their work to include more classroom-focused support for teachers. Rather than serving as managers of budgets and books, they are now coaching individual teachers and teams as a part of their work as teacher leaders.

Coaches are evident in both large, urban school districts and in small, rural ones. Larger districts, because of flexibility in their funding to reallocate resources, use specialized funding to support coaching positions. Larger districts are also more likely to have public or private foundation grants and other types of programs that support coaching. Schools and school districts, motivated by stringent accountability generated by No Child Left Behind, are hiring coaches to improve instruction and student achievement. Federally funded grants in special areas such as STEM (science, technology, engineering, and mathematics) make resources available to support coaching. At Clemson University, in Clemson, South Carolina, with a federally funded grant, university faculty created a math and science coaching program that has resulted in impressive increases in student achievement over the last several years (iCoach Student Achievement Analysis, 2008).

In the last few years, however, limited public funding for education as a result of the national and state-level economic challenges has caused school systems to re-evaluate how they allocate their resources. Many are eliminating coaches and coaching programs. Two reasons cited most often for this action are the high cost of coaching and the limited evidence that coaching improves teaching and student results. School systems that are committed to rigorous evaluation of their coaching program and to continuous improvement of their coaching program and coaches' competencies, such as Fairfax County Public School District in Virginia, continue to fund coaching positions in its lowest performing schools.

IN THE LITERATURE

The emerging research base about coaching provides some clarity about how coaching, combined with training and other forms of professional development, increase both teachers' use of specific pedagogical strategies and student learning. The research on coaching and its effects is limited. This review of research focuses on the effects of coaching on systems, teachers, teaching practices, and student achievement. Yet it is also evident from the research on coaching that not all coaching is equally effective.

Common problems in examining the research on coaching are evident in the meta-analysis of professional development studies conducted by Timperley, Wilson, Barrar, and Fung (2007). Researchers studied the impact of professional learning and development on student-achievement outcomes in mathematics and science. Their findings support the general consensus that professional development, when sustained longer than one year, has higher effect sizes especially in those studies that focused on teachers' content knowledge and pedagogical knowledge than in those studies that focused on content knowledge alone (Yoon, Duncan, Lee, Scarloss, and Shapley, 2007). The research team also notes that nearly all interventions studied included workshops with coaching. The research team observes, however, that the term *coaching* is not used consistently in the literature and often refers to various forms of teacher and expert interaction, making it difficult to determine what is learned in a coaching episode (Timperley et al., 2007). How coaching is defined and how it is enacted in the studies reviewed are either insufficiently described or widely varied, making the analysis of the effects of coaching across studies especially challenging.

Effects on systems

Effects for organizations identified by Lord, Atkinson, and Mitchell (2008), in their synthesis of research on mentoring and coaching in school systems and other social care organizations, include changes in the organization's culture that resulted in increased research and learning, reflection, collaboration, professionalism and recognition, high aspirations, and vitality. Other effects noted include improved leadership, professional and career development, greater external links, enhanced knowledge and skills shared within the organization, recruitment and retention, and improved organization policy practices and systems and processes. Finally, the study identified impacts for young people that included increases in learning benefits for students and school improvement outcomes.

Effects on teachers

Early and clear evidence of the impact of coaching resulted from studies of the implementation of new teaching skills. Cornett and Knight (2009) report on a longitudinal study conducted by Bush in 1984 involving 80 schools that examines whether peer coaching increased teachers' use of new instructional skills. Only ten percent of the teachers who received a description of new instructional skills used those skills in their classroom. When other components were added, such as modeling, practice, and feedback, teacher use of the skills increased by 2–3 percent for each added component. Bush (1984: 197) states, 'Description, modeling, practice, and feedback resulted in a 16–19 percent transfer of skill to classroom use. However, when coaching was added to the staff development, approximately 95 percent of the teachers implemented the new skills in their classrooms.' Truesdale (2003) finds that the transfer of professional development to classroom practice increases when coaching was added. Teachers receiving coaching increased transfer of training over the 15 weeks of the study while teachers who did not receive coaching stopped using the new practices.

In a study of peer coaching to support literacy teaching, teachers engaged in watching videotapes of their own teaching while working with a coach to receive feedback on lessons taught and receiving guidance on literacy instruction. Coaches provided three kinds of support: procedural, affective, and reflective. As a result of peer coaching teachers changed their technical expertise, their sense of efficacy and confidence, as well as their skillfulness in reflecting upon teaching and learning. In addition to the impact of coaching on teachers being coached, coaches also report becoming more experienced and challenged in their thinking (Swafford, Maltsberger, Button, and Furguson, 1997).

In the study by Lord et al. (2008), mentioned previously, two categories of benefits for mentees are identified. These include:

- increased reflectivity and clarity of thinking;
- improved psychological well-being and confidence;
- better problem solving skills;
- increased practitioner knowledge and skills;
- improved sharing of practice;
- better communication and relationships;
- more positive attitudes towards professional and career development; and
- self-management and learning skills.

Effects identified in the same study for mentors and coaches include:

- improved knowledge and skill;
- improved psychological well being and confidence;
- increased reflectivity;
- added professional and career development;
- better problem solving skills; and
- improved sharing a practice.

In a study in Dutch secondary schools, researchers explored the relationship between five characteristics of reciprocal peer coaching and teacher learning.

> A main outcome of the current study is that within a context of reciprocal peer coaching, teachers learn when they are intrinsically motivated to take part in professional development programs; when they feel a certain pressure toward experimenting with new instructional methods; and when they are able to discuss their experiences within a safe, constructive, and trustworthy environment. Those teachers who reported trying out new teaching strategies while being observed in their classrooms (a *trajectory characteristic*) displayed greater changes in their behavior according to the students, and they also reported more learning themselves.
>
> (Zwart, Wubbels, Bergen, and Bolhuis, 2009: 253)

Effects on teachers and student learning

Research conducted by Showers (1982) identified benefits for both teachers and students when coaching followed training. She found that training followed by peer coaching increased teachers' use of a new instructional practice. In another study, Showers (1984) examined the impact on the performance of students whose teachers demonstrated high implementation rates of the specific teaching practices they were learning. Showers randomly assigned teachers to two groups. The treatment group worked with a peer coach while the control group received no coaching. Showers concluded that teachers who received coaching were more likely to incorporate new teaching practices into their classrooms than non-coached teachers. In addition, student achievement scores in the coached classrooms yielded significantly higher gains than students in the non-coached classrooms.

In his study of teacher technology integration to enhance student learning, Jacobsen (2001) explored expert support provided to teachers at three primary schools. He concluded that when experts provide onsite mentorship and support, teachers engage in professional dialogue, observe how other teachers integrate technology, and share student work. These practices encouraged and helped teachers to understand the advantage of integrating technology within their classrooms. The General Teaching Council for England (2005) acknowledged that teachers risk uncertainty, plan to change their roles, and demonstrate willingness to develop both their technology and teaching skills when they have the support of experts to guide them.

Suggett (2006) studied how senior leaders used coaching in the six schools and concluded that:

1 Coaching impacts staff and pupils and enhances the social and emotional atmosphere of the school;
2 Coaching is a generic process that can be used opportunistically with staff, pupils and parents – self coaching, one-to-one coaching and team coaching;
3 A coaching approach could be anything from an intuitive leadership style to a structured, whole-school process;
4 Coaching strategies should be tailored to suit the organizational readiness of each school, reflecting its unique context in particular circumstances;
5 Coaching is an investment programs in time and money programs that produces gains for staff and pupils and builds individual and organizational capacity; and
6 Coaching is most effective when coaches have had a planned development program and peer support structures are in place. (2006: 15)

Studies of content-focused coaching demonstrated that student achievement as well as teacher practice increased when coaching focused specifically on content knowledge and content-specific pedagogy. A study by The Learning Network (2006) reported a steady growth in student achievement over a five-year period in fourth-grade student reading scores when teacher leaders worked in schools in the capacity of literacy coaches. The gains in student achievement were substantial, from 29 percent in 1999 to 86 percent in 2004, yet the research design makes it difficult to determine if the presence of teacher leaders was responsible for any variation in student performance. In another study of the implementation of math and science coaching in schools in South Carolina, substantial increases in student achievement on state assessments (iCoach Student Achievement Analysis, 2008) were noted. In a study of the value added by literacy coaching, preliminary conclusions show a 16–29 percent increase in student literacy learning in years one and two of implementation of a literacy coaching model (Biancarosa, Bryk, and Dexter, 2008).

Since the research literature on the effects of coaching is not yet fully developed, many claim that the investment in coaching is an 'act of faith, based on the belief that it will build personal and organizational capacity' (Suggett, 2006: 12). Emerging research on the benefits of coaching, however, conducted in the last decade, show substantive promise that implementing coaching for professional learning and school improvement leads to improvement in teacher practice and student learning. The key to success with coaching is in how coaching is defined, initiated, implemented, monitored, and evaluated.

IN PRACTICE

Successful coaching depends on careful planning and preparation. There is, however, no simple formula for developing the conditions for effective coaching. The amount and specificity of planning and preparation depend to a large degree on the type of coaching and the formality of the coaching program. For example, a peer-coaching program in which teachers volunteer to support one another without a particular focus on a specific set of instructional methodologies or specific content will require far less preparation than a formal coaching program. A coaching program designed to support the implementation of specific instructional methodologies or content-specific curriculum in which coaches serve as specialists and coach full- or part-time and hold a formal responsibility for the success of their colleagues will require a more formal preparation to ensure success. The sequence listed below describes a general process for initiating, implementing, and evaluating coaching programs:

1   define coaching;
2   create a supportive culture;
3   establish goals and parameters;
4   clarify coach roles;
5   engage school and district leader support;
6   select coaches;
7   prepare coaches;
8   place coaches;
9   support coaches;
10 evaluate coaching and coaches; and
11 overcome barriers to coaching.

Define coaching

The first step of this process is to define coaching and determine the type of coaching to be implemented. While the specific form of coaching may be a hybrid, clarity about the kind of coaching is essential to plan for successful implementation. A school may determine, for example, that it wishes to implement a peer-coaching program as a follow-up to system-wide training on a particular set of instructional strategies. This form of coaching combines peer coaching with aspects of technical coaching and instructional coaching. A more formal type of coaching may be provided to support the implementation of a new curriculum. This form of coaching is technical coaching provided by specialists or experts who have had specialized training in the curriculum. With a clear understanding of the type of coaching, there will be strong alignment among those responsible for coordinating the coaching program, those providing coaching, and those being coached (Killion and Harrison, 2006; Knight, 2009; Moran, 2007; Sweeney, 2010).

Create a culture for coaching

A second important consideration is creating a culture within the school which supports coaching. Characteristics of this culture are norms of collegiality and experimentation (Little, 1982) in which a high degree of trust and collaboration exist. Crafting this culture will take considerable time and is best done while implementing coaching. However in some school settings, it is considered an indication of ineffectiveness to ask for and receive support. When schools are places in which everyone learns, both teachers and students, coaching will be welcomed as a routine form of professional development. Such a culture requires trust among the adults, deprivatization of practice, a willingness to take risks without fear, and routine opportunities for conversation and reflection about practice. School leaders including principals, team and division leaders, and chairs contribute to shaping an open, productive, learning-focused, and risk-free culture by establishing school-wide agreements about the confidentiality of coaching conversations, the reporting structure between coaches and school principals, and the non-evaluative nature of coaching. They foster a sense of collective responsibility, one which holds each teacher responsible for the success of each student within a school. They can initiate and sustain the development of such a culture by facilitating conversations designed to promote inquiry, problem solving, and reflection, facilitating opportunities for learning, modeling examining one's own practice, and engaging in continuous improvement (Killion and Harrison, 2006; Knight, 2009: Moran, 2007; Sweeney, 2010).

Establish goals and parameters

Understanding the goals and parameters of the coaching program are another important early preparation step. Some coaching programs focus specifically on strengthening teaching practices and increasing student academic success. Other coaching programs might focus more on building a collaborative culture within the school. Some coaching programs attempt to accomplish both of these goals simultaneously. Parameters include who receives coaching, how often, who decides the focus of coaching conversations, how much time is devoted to coaching, and how confidential coaching interactions are. In some coaching programs teachers may volunteer to receive coaching. Other coaching programs are designed so that all teachers participate. When the goals and parameters of a coaching program are explicit, both coaches and teachers will understand expected results of coaching and how they will contribute to achieving those results (Killion and Harrison, 2006).

Clarify roles

Clarifying the roles coaches fill helps focus coaches' work. This is especially true in a formal coaching program where coaches are given partial or full-time release to serve in the role of a coach. An evaluation study of a coaching program in a school district in Florida concludes that how coaches spend their time impacts the school's overall performance in its efforts to improve. The more time a coach spends on core coaching responsibilities, the greater the increase in a school's overall improvement (Schultz Center for Teaching and Leadership, 2008).

Killion and Harrison (2006) described ten roles for coaches. These roles include resource provider, data coach, curriculum specialist, instructional specialist, classroom supporter, mentor, learning facilitator, school leader, catalyst for change, and learner. Most coaches serve in several of the ten roles simultaneously. Which role they take depends on the definition of coaching and the goals and parameters of the coaching program. Some roles work naturally together, such as the roles of curriculum specialist and instructional specialist. The curriculum specialists assist teachers in determining what to teach, what is developmentally appropriate for the students' age and academic readiness, and what is required by the adopted curriculum. Following the decision about what to teach is the decision about how to teach. The instructional specialist assists teachers with decisions about the appropriate pedagogical approach, how to differentiate for the needs of students within the classroom, and how to assess students' learning. Data coaches help teachers use data about student performance from a variety of formal and informal assessments to make informed decisions about classroom instruction in lesson planning. Learning facilitators act as facilitators for the study of research lessons, learning communities, action research, or other forms of professional learning. School leaders serve on a school's leadership team or other school-wide committees. Mentors work closely with experienced teachers who are new to the school and novice teachers with little or no teaching experience to ensure that they have adequate support and continue to build their instructional expertise. Resource providers help teachers access information and resources in both print and non-print forms to support their instruction. Catalysts for change frequently challenge the status quo to assess whether current actions lead to desired results. Often acting as the irritant within the system in a humane and productive way, the catalyst for change is the impetus for positive change within the school. All coaches, regardless of the kind of coaching, the goals of the coaching program, or the other roles they have are learners. By engaging in career-long learning, they serve as models of continuous improvement.

Engage leaders

Formal coaching programs require established roles for school and district leaders. Those roles include coaching the coaches by giving feedback to the coaches on their practice, maintaining the agreements established for coaching, and addressing any violations of those agreements. Formal leaders within schools and school systems demonstrate visible support for coaching by participating in their own coaching, by minimizing disruptions that pull coaches away from their primary responsibility, and by making time to meet with coaches to provide them feedback. Informal coaching programs also require leadership support which comes in the form of encouragement, providing time and resources, and seeking and receiving feedback from teachers about how their experiences and how they are benefiting (Killion and Harrison, 2006; Sweeney, 2010).

Selecting coaches

Some coaching programs create a designated position for a coach. These programs require a more formal selection and screening process. Schools and district leaders, often with the support of teachers, use the definition of coaching and its goals and parameters as a starting point for determining the criteria for selecting coaches. Criteria might include, as Killion and Harrison (2006) describe, dispositions suitable to being in a helping role, teaching expertise, relationship skills, content expertise, and leadership skills. Key to the selection of coaches is their status as a recognized and respected colleague who engages in continuous improvement, works well with others in a collaborative way, and has potential for developing the knowledge and skills needed to be an effective coach. Once the criteria are established, school and district leaders, again with the support of teachers, create a process for selection. The process incorporates application, portfolios, demonstrations, and/or interviews. When finalized, the criteria and the selection process are widely distributed and thoughtfully followed (Killion and Harrison, 2006).

Coach preparation

Once coaches are selected, they participate in professional development to develop the knowledge and skills that align with the type of coaching and the goals of the coaching program. Typical content of a coach-preparation program includes building trusting relationships; communication skills, especially listening and questions; adult development and human change; gathering, analyzing, and using data; and giving and receiving feedback. Some coaches take on a broader role that includes presenting and facilitation, so skills in both those areas may be added to the preparation program. The scope of coaches' initial preparation is balanced with their ongoing professional development. Some coaches engage in extensive preparation before they step into the role of a coach. Others have basic preparation and simply follow up with an ongoing plan for continuous development. Beyond developing competencies in coaching, content-focused coaches or those supporting the implementation of a particular program of instruction usually receive in-depth training and development in competencies specific to the content area or program (Killion and Harrison, 2006).

Place coaches

Following preparation is the coach placement, the assignment of coaches to specific schools, regions, grades, departments, or divisions. How coaches are placed in schools or assigned coaching responsibilities is another decision that requires careful thought. One consideration is whether to place coaches in the schools in which they were teachers. There are advantages and disadvantages to each. Regardless of the decision, it will be important to provide adequate opportunity for newly placed coaches to develop productive relationships with the teachers and school leaders with whom they will work.

Another aspect of placing coaches is the decision about who supervises and supports coaches. If coaches are placed in a single school, the school's headmaster typically supervises them. If a coach serves in multiple schools, a central office staff member usually supervises their work (Killion and Harrison, 2006).

Support coaches

Ongoing development continues throughout a coach's career. Regardless of the extensiveness of coaches' preparation, they benefit from ongoing support and continuous professional development. A designated coach champion provides support as coaches encounter new experiences, challenges, or obstacles in their practice. This support comes from both within the school from school leaders, who take time to provide feedback and guidance to coaches, as well as from school system or other external specialists who assist them to be successful in their new positions. The work of a coach is unpredictable, therefore the continuous refinement of their expertise is essential for their continued success (Killion and Harrison, 2006).

Evaluating coaching and coaches

Sophisticated coaching programs, regardless of their formality or informality, invest in evaluation of coaching and coaches. The evaluation of coaching measures the operations of the coaching program such as support for coaches and resources available to them, as well as the achievement of the goals of the coaching program. By examining critically the coaching program on a regular basis, coaching program supervisors have the data needed to recommend.

Evaluation of coaches occurs outside the evaluation of the coaching program. Providing coaches with feedback about their effectiveness and identifying their strengths and areas for continuous development assists coaches to set goals for

their continuous improvement to refine their knowledge and skills. Coaches'
evaluation is based on a pre-determined set of specific performance expectations
against which coaches are evaluated and for which they develop plans for their
ongoing professional development (Killion and Harrison, 2006).

Overcome barriers

Barriers fall into two categories, operational and interpersonal. Typical
operational barriers include role uncertainty, lack of leadership support, time
allocation, inadequate resources, and coaching load. Many of these barriers
stem from a lack of clarity or inadequate communication about the purpose
and goals of a coaching program. Some result from inadequate planning or
resources. Common interpersonal barriers include the lack of trust, resistance, or
professional jealousy. These barriers too can result from lack of clarity and
inadequate planning and preparation. They also are products of the school culture. Working to reduce those barriers from the earliest stages will minimize the
negative impact on the success of coaching. District staff and school principals
are primarily responsible for addressing operational barriers while the coach has
primary responsibility to address the interpersonal barriers.

THE FUTURE OF COACHING

Coaching that supports the implementation of effective teaching practices
will continue to be an extended and essential component of professional
development and school improvement. Coaching provides continuous teacher
professional development by differentiating and personalizing opportunities to
learn and by supporting the transfer of new learning into practice. As coaching
increasingly becomes routine practice in schools, it will be important for all
teachers, not just some, to have equal opportunity to develop the professional
competencies of a coach. A novice interacting with and providing feedback to a
more experienced teacher gains the opportunity to more deeply understand pedagogy. When that same novice teacher only receives feedback and rarely has
opportunities to be the provider of the feedback, she misses learning the skills
of coaching, core skills of the profession, and skills useful in interaction with
students. School systems and schools should provide opportunities for teachers,
regardless of their career stage, to receive coaching and provide coaching.
Membership in a profession carries with it the commitment to engage in continuous development.

Coaching is one means through which school systems support continuous
development while simultaneously building a collaborative community of professionals committed to student success. When teachers work together in a collaborative, open, and supportive community of practice, all teachers and their students benefit. Coaching creates constructive, trusting professional relationships

that result in continuous learning, improving teaching practice, and increasing student achievement.

It is likely too that, with continued improvement and access to technology such as 'bud-in-the-ear' and 360-degree digital cameras, more virtual, cyber-, or e-coaching will occur. To maintain the integrity of coaching as a form of professional development, virtual coaching should adhere to the same stringent expectations for integrity that face-to-face coaching meets including clear goals, parameters, preparation of coaches, and continuous evaluation. Virtual coaching is best as a supplement to, rather than a replacement of, face-to-face coaching because coaching is deeply personal and human.

CONCLUSION

Coaching will not solve every challenge facing schools. It has the potential, though, to develop and refine expertise among educators and empower and encourage them to resolve the knotty issues within schools to making teaching more satisfying and professionally rewarding. Research about coaching, now in the early stages, provides insights into the effects of coaching on teachers, student learning, and school organizations. However, not all coaching is of the same high quality or produces results for teachers or their students. To ensure that any investment in coaching pays exponential dividends for students, teachers, and school systems, coaching programs must be thoughtfully planned, carefully implemented, and regularly evaluated. Coaches too must be carefully selected, thoroughly developed, continually supported, and regularly evaluated. When the coaching program and coaches have integrity in practice, results for teachers and students will follow.

REFERENCES

Ahrend, G., Diamond, F., & Webber, G. (2010). Virtual Coaching: Using Technology to Boost Performance. *Chief Learning Officer, 9*(7), 4447.

Biancarosa, G., Bryk, A., & Dexter, E. (2008). *Assessing the Value-Added Effects of Literacy Collaborative Professional Development on Student Learning.* A Paper Presented at the Annual Meeting of the American Educational Research Association, New York.

Blasé, J., & Blasé, J. (2006). *Teachers Bring Out the Best in Teachers: A Guide to Peer Consultation for Administrators and Teachers.* Thousand Oaks, CA: Corwin Press.

Bloom, G., Castagna, C., Moir. E., & Warren, B. (2005). *Blended Coaching: Skills and Strategies to Support Principal Development.* Thousand Oaks, CA: Corwin Press.

Britton, J. J. (2010). *Effective Group Coaching: Tried and Tested Tools and Resources for Optimum Group Coaching Sessions.* Mississauga, ON: John Wiley and Sons Canada.

Bush, R. N. (1984). Effective Staff Development. In *Making Our Schools More Effective. Proceedings of Three State Conferences* (pp. 223–238). San Francisco: Far West Laboratories.

Costa, A., & Garmston, R. (2002). *Cognitive Coaching: A Foundation for Renaissance School.* Norwood, MA: Christopher-Gordon.

Cordingley, P., Bell, M., Isham, C., Evans, D., & Firth, A. (2007). *Continuing Professional Development (CPD): What do specialists do in CPD programmes for which there is evidence of positive outcomes for pupils and teachers? Report no. 1504T.* London: EPPI-Centre, Social Science Research Unit, Institute of Education, University of London.

Cornett, J., & Knight, J. (2009). Research on Coaching. In J. Knight (Ed.), *Coaching Approaches & Perspective* (pp. 192–216). Thousand Oaks, CA: Corwin Press.

Creasy, J., & Patterson, F. (2005). *Leading Coaching in Schools. Leading Practices Seminar Series.* Nottingham: National College for School Leadership.

Darling-Hammond, L. Wei, R., Andree, A., Richardson, N., & Orphanos, S. (2009). *Professional Learning in the Learning Profession: A Status Report on Teacher Development in the United States and Abroad.* Oxford, OH: National Staff Development Council.

Duessen, T., Cookie, T., Robinson, T. L., & Autio, E. (2007). *'Coach' can mean many things: Five categories of literacy coaches in Reading First.* Issues & Answers Report, REL, 2007-No. 005. Washington, DC: US Department of Education, Institute of Educational Sciences, National Center for Educational Evaluation and Regional Assistance, Regional Education Laboratory Northwest.

Galanouli, D. (2009). *School-based Professional Development: A Report for the General Teaching Council for Northern Ireland.* Belfast: General Teaching Council for Northern Ireland.

Garmston, R. (1987). How Administrators Support Peer Coaching. *Educational Leadership, 44*(5), 18–26.

General Teaching Council for England. (2005). Research for Teachers: Teachers Professional Learning. London: Author. Retrieved from: http://www.gtce.org.uk/teachers/rft/prof_learn1205/

Goodman, J., Brady, M., Duffy, M., Scott, J., & Pollard, N. (2008). The Effects of 'Bug-in-Ear' Supervision on Special Education Teachers' Delivery of Learn Units. *Focus on Autism and Other Developmental Disabilities, 23*(4): 207.

iCoach Student Achievement Analysis (2008). Clemson, SC: Clemson University Math and Science Unit.

International Coaching Federation. (n.d.). *What is coaching?* Retrieved from: http://www.coachfederation.com/find-a-coach/what-is-coaching/, accessed August 10, 2010.

Jacobsen, D. (2001). *Building Different Bridges: Technology Integration, Student Engagement, and New Approaches to Professional Development.* Paper Presented at the Annual Meeting of the American Educational Research Association. Seattle, Washington. 10–14 April 2001.

Johnson, T., Maring, G., Doty, J., & Fickle, M. (2006). Cybermentoring: Evolving High-end Video Conferencing Practices to Support Preservice Teacher Training. *Journal of Interactive Online Learning, 5*(1), 59–74.

Joyce, B., & Showers, B. (1981). Transfer of Training: The Contribution of 'Coaching.' *Boston University Journal of Education, 162*(2), 163–172.

Joyce, B., & Showers, B. (1983). *Power in Staff Development Through Research in Training.* Alexandria, VA: Association for Supervision and Curriculum Development.

Killion, J. (2009). Coaches' Roles, Responsibilities, and Reach. In J. Knight (Ed.), *Coaching Approaches & Perspectives* (pp. 7–28) Thousand Oaks, CA: Corwin Press.

Killion, J. (2010). Reprising Coaching Heavy and Coaching Light. *Teachers Teaching Teachers,* 6(4), 9–10.

Killion, J., & Harrison, C. (2006). *Taking the Lead: New Roles for Teachers and School-based Coaches.* Oxford, OH: National Staff Development Council.

Knight, J. (2009). *Coaching Approaches & Perspective.* Thousand Oaks, CA: Corwin Press.

Koh, S., & Neuman, S.B. (2006). Exemplary Elements of Coaching: Ann Arbor MI: University of Michigan Research Program on Ready to Read. Retrieved from: http://www.umich.edu/~rdytolrn/projectgreatstart/docs/ElementsofCoaching.pdf

Little, J. (1982). Norms of Collegiality and Experimentation: Workplace Conditions of School Success. *American Educational Research Journal, 19*(3), 325–340.

Lord, P., Atkinson, M., & Mitchell, H. (2008). *Mentoring and Coaching for Professionals: A Study of the Research Evidence.* London: Training and Development Agency for Schools.

Moran, M. C. (2007). *Differentiated Literacy Coaching: Scaffolding for Student and Teacher Success.* Alexandria, VA: ASCD.

Neuman, S. B., & Cunningham, L. (2009). The Impact of Professional Development and Coaching on Early Language and Literacy Instructional Practices. *American Educational Research Journal, 46*(2), 532–566.

Putnam, R. T., & Borko, H. (2000). What do new views of knowledge and thinking have to say about research on teacher learning? *Educational Researcher, 29*(1), 4–15.

Rhodes, C., Stokes, M., & Hampton, G. (2004). *A Practical Guide to Mentoring, Coaching and Peer-Networking.* London: Routledge.

Rock, M., Gregg, M., Thead, B., Acker, S., Gable, R., & Zigmond, N. (2009). Can you hear me now? Evaluation of an online wireless technology to provide real-time feedback to special education teachers-in-training. *Teacher Education and Special Education, 32*(1), 64.

Russo, A. (2004). School-based Coaching: A Revolution in Professional Development or just the latest fad? *Harvard Education Letter, 20*(4), 1–3.

Saunders, W., Goldenberg, C., Gallimore, R. (2009). Increasing Achievement by Focusing Grade-level Teams on Improving Classroom Learning: A Prospective, Quasi-experimental Study of Title I schools. *American Educational Research Journal, 46*(4), 1006–1033.

Schultz Center for Teaching and Leadership. (2008). *School Instructional Coaches and the Coaches Academy 2007–08.* Jacksonville, FL: Schultz Center for Teaching and Leadership. Retrieved from: http://www.schultzcenter.org/pdf/coaching_academy_brief.pdf

Shanklin, N. (2006). *What are the characteristics of effective literacy coaching?* Denver, CO: Literacy Coaching Clearinghouse.

Showers, B. (1982). *Transfer of Training. The Contribution of Coaching.* Eugene, OR: Centre or Educational Policy and Management.

Showers, B. (1984). *Peer Coaching: A Strategy for Facilitating Transfer of Training.* Eugene, OR: Centre for Educational Policy and Management.

Simkins, T., Coldwell, M., Caillau, I., Finlayson, H., & Morgan, A. (2006). Coaching as an in-school leadership development strategy: Experiences from Leading from the Middle. *Professional Development in Education, 32*(3), 321–340.

Suggett, N. (2006). *Time for Coaching.* Research Associate Report. National College for School Leadership.

Swafford, J., Maltsberger, A., Button, K., Furguson, P. (1997). Peer coaching for facilitating effective literacy instruction. In Kinzer, C. K., Hinchman, K. A., & Leu, D. J. (Eds), *Inquiries in literacy theory and practice* (pp. 416–426). Chicago: National Reading Conference.

Sweeney, D. (2010). *Student-centered coaching: A Guide for K-8 Coaches and Principals.* Thousand Oaks, CA: Corwin Press.

The Learning Network. (2006). *Data Sheet: The Learning Network in Battle Creek, Michigan.* Katonah, NY: Richard C. Owen Publishers.

Timperley, H., Wilson, A., Barrar, H., & Fung, I. (2007). *Teacher Professional Learning and Development.* Wellington, New Zealand: New Zealand Ministry of Education, Iterative Best Evidence Synthesis Program.

Truesdale, W. T. (2003). The Implementation of Coaching on the Transferability of Staff Development to Classroom Practices in Two Selected Chicago Public Elementary Schools. *Dissertation Abstracts International, 64*(11), 3923. University Microfims No. 3112185.

Valencia, S. & Killion, J. (1988). Overcoming obstacles to teacher change: Directions from school- based efforts. *Journal of Staff Development, 9*(2), 168–174.

West, L., & Staub, F. (2003). *Content-focused Coaching: Transforming Mathematics Lessons.* Portsmouth, NH: Heinemann.

Yoon, K., Duncan, T., Lee, S., Scarloss, & Shapley, K. (2007). *Reviewing the evidence on how teacher professional development affects student achievement.* Issues & Answers Report, REL 2007–No. 033. Washington, DC: US Department of Education, Institute of Education Sciences, National Center for Education Evaluation and Regional Assistance, Regional Educational Laboratory Southwest. Retrieved from: http://ies.ed.gov/ncee/edlabs

Zwart, R. C., Wubbels, T., Bergen, T., & Bolhuis, S. (2009). Which characteristics of a reciprocal peer coaching context affect teacher learning as perceived by teachers and their students? *Journal of Teacher Education, 60*(3), 243–257.

19

Using Mentoring and Coaching for Professional Learning in UK Secondary Schools

Cathy Pomphrey and Suzanne Burley

THE NEED FOR A BROAD PERSPECTIVE ON MENTORING AND COACHING IN SECONDARY SCHOOLS

Mentoring and coaching processes are now commonly used in secondary schools in the UK to develop and support professional learning. These processes have evolved over a number of years and have drawn on uses of mentoring and coaching from a wide range of professional areas and contexts.

This chapter is informed by theoretical perspectives from texts which consider the dimensions of mentoring and coaching related to a range of professional areas; for example Brockbank and McGill (2006), Clutterbuck (2003), Garvey, Stokes and Megginson (2009), as well as a variety of texts which outline the development of processes of mentoring and coaching in secondary schools; for example, Hagger (1993), Stephens (1996), Arthur, Davison and Moss (1997), Furlong and Maynard (1995), Fletcher (2000), Hampton, Rhodes and Stokes (2004). This enables the application of a diversity of perspectives on mentoring and coaching to be considered in relation to the secondary school context.

THE INFLUENCE OF BEHAVIOURISM AND SOCIAL CONSTRUCTIVISM

The ways in which mentoring and coaching processes have evolved in school contexts are heavily influenced by the professional cultures and philosophies within education. These cultures and philosophies are not always explicit but their impact shapes the approaches to mentoring and coaching adopted by schools. Two contrasting approaches which influence mentoring and coaching and their relationship to professional learning in education are those of behaviourism and social constructivism.

A behaviourist approach relies on fixed definitions and purposes in order to improve professional performance. This improvement could be aimed at either an individual or institutional level. Brockbank and McGill (2006) use the term 'functionalist' to describe approaches to mentoring and coaching where the key purpose is to improve individual or institutional performance to serve the 'perceived "needs" of the organisation or society' (2006: 12). This approach is not concerned with the questioning of established values and norms. Brockbank and McGill also employ the term engagement mentoring or coaching to describe a more 'humanistic version of functionalist mentoring or coaching' (ibid. 13).

Engagement mentoring or coaching fits well with the humanistic concerns of the education profession and tempers the more mechanistic processes and outcomes that could result from competence-based, assessment-led, more functionalist approaches. Thus in engagement mentoring or coaching, the quality of the collaboration between participants in the mentoring or coaching relationship is essential to the achievement of predetermined outcomes. Elements of a behaviourist approach are often attractive to schools as such an approach can produce clear structures and quick responses where professional learning is determined by the requirements of statutory policy.

The alternative approach of social constructivism, originally conceived by Vygotsky (1978), underpins the dominant discourse in education about learning, including professional learning. From this perspective, mentoring and coaching is concerned with the social construction of new professional knowledge leading to individual and institutional transformation. Brockbank and McGill's (2006) 'evolutionary' approach to mentoring and coaching can be related to social constructivism as it is an approach where underlying values and power structures can be challenged and questioned in order to bring about transformation in professional learning. Such an approach can produce longer-term structural and systemic change which is also subject to continual review and development. Social constructivism relies heavily on the use of critical dialogue. The use of critical dialogue within mentoring and coaching is key to the quality of the professional learning that takes place. A social constructivist approach also identifies collaboration as a central focus for professional learning. Thus the collaborative nature and quality of mentoring and coaching relationships is of central importance in order to effect transformation through professional learning. Garvey et al. (2009)

highlight how the relationships within mentoring and coaching are dynamic and change over time.

Within secondary schools there are a plethora of mentoring and coaching practices which are influenced by these two different philosophies. Despite this secondary schools tend to identify similar key purposes for mentoring and coaching which are:

- developing a process of professional learning; and
- achieving a level of individual or institutional change.

However, the mentoring and coaching processes used in schools to achieve these two purposes and the outcomes from them can differ substantially. These differences often depend on the degree to which criticality and transformation are applied within the mentoring and coaching relationship.

A FRAMEWORK FOR ASSESSING MENTORING AND COACHING POLICY AND PRACTICES: CONTEXT, PROCESS AND OUTCOME

In order to examine the differences in mentoring and coaching, Clutterbuck (2003) suggests a framework for assessing mentoring and coaching policy and practices which identifies three key variables as context, process and outcome. A consideration of mentoring and coaching context will include a number of factors such as school location, diversity issues, power relationships and institutional organisation and ethos. Clutterbuck (2003) recognises that variables of process can have a major impact on the outcomes of mentoring and coaching. Process variables will include the nature and quality of dialogue and collaboration within the mentoring and coaching relationships and models and strategies used for professional learning. These different contexts and processes result in a range of different outcomes. Consideration of outcome includes examining the nature of the learning resulting from the mentoring and coaching, the development of collaborative professional learning relationships and the transfer of professional learning to other situations.

THE USE OF MENTORING AND COACHING IN UK SCHOOLS

In the last few years there has been considerable interest in developing teachers' professional learning, together with the growth of and investment in processes of mentoring and coaching as a tool for achieving professional learning. Also in the last two decades there has been an increasing formalisation within national policy of mentoring and coaching processes and relationships. This has led to changes in the training and development of secondary school teachers from initial teacher training through to senior leadership development.

The early 1990s was a key time for changes to initial teacher training policy and practice. In 1992 the government required that initial teacher training establish the use of experienced school-based teachers to act as mentors who provide training and support for trainee teachers (Department for Education,1992). Arthur et al. (1997) show how processes for the mentoring of trainee teachers arose from this requirement and also led to the creation of different partnership structures between schools and higher education institutions. Arthur et al. (1997) compare two models of school and higher education partnership. The first is a collaborative partnership, (the 'internship scheme') developed at Oxford University in 1987, and the second a competence-based model of partnership as developed by a number of teacher training providers. Their comparison shows how collaborative partnerships produce a reflective practitioner model of discursive mentoring whilst competence-based models tend to produce what Arthur et al. refer to as 'pragmatic mentoring' (1997: 95). These contrasting approaches to mentoring can be related to differences in the underlying philosophies of social constructivism and behaviourism discussed earlier.

FURTHER APPLICATIONS OF MENTORING AND COACHING IN SECONDARY SCHOOLS

In secondary schools today there exist a range of mentoring and coaching relationships for teachers, which can broadly be categorised as follows, according to who is determining the processes and outcomes for the relationship:

1   those governed and determined by external national policy requirements;
2   those associated with accreditation; and
3   those which give greater autonomy and determination to the teachers involved.

The first category includes mentoring relationships such as those between an experienced teacher and a trainee teacher or newly qualified teacher. These are bound by government statutory requirements, professional competencies and nationally set assessment procedures which influence the nature, process and quality of the mentoring relationship. Within initial teacher training there is a statutory requirement for a substantial part of the training to take place in schools to enable trainee teachers to demonstrate that they have met the standards for Qualified Teacher Status (Training and Development Agency for Schools (TDA) 2008: R2.8). There is also a requirement for schools to work with training providers (such as universities) in order 'to ensure that partners work together to contribute to the selection, training and assessment of trainee teachers against the QTS standards' (R3.2). Currently, schools meet this requirement by the use of an experienced teacher acting as a mentor to work alongside a trainee teacher during school-based experience. These experienced teachers or mentors are given training and guidance for their role by the training provider. A similarly formal structured process is also applied to the process of mentoring newly qualified teachers (NQT) based on the Department for Children, Schools and Families (DCSF) (2008) guidance on NQT induction. This requires a school-based induction tutor to 'provide, or co-ordinate, guidance and effective support including coaching and mentoring for the NQT's professional development'. The process also requires the formal assessment of the NQT against a nationally determined set of professional standards.

The second category is concerned with the use of coaching for the formal accreditation of teachers' professional learning. Depending on the accreditation pathway the coaching can be provided from either within or external to the school. Although these coaching relationships are working with accrediting bodies' requirements, which fit broad national frameworks for professional learning, they tend to offer more scope for the processes and outcomes of the relationship to be negotiated by the participants. For example, a recently implemented Masters in Teaching and Learning (MTL) programme (TDA, 2009b), which was first introduced as a pilot in 2009 and rolled out nationally in 2010, requires coaches to be trained and identified within school settings according to a set of national criteria. The role of the MTL coach is firmly based on the 'National Framework for Mentoring and Coaching' (DSCF, 2005; see further discussion later in this chapter). Like the induction tutor for newly qualified teachers, the school-based coach is expected to provide 'support and professional challenge', but also to 'motivate and inspire, encourage on-going enquiry and reflection … identifying needs relevant to the participants' school contexts, apply evidence and educational theory to real-life situations' (TDA, 2009a). This implies a relationship which can be more personalised and open to establishing negotiated processes and outcomes as well as supporting masters-level academic study.

Coaching has also become a key tool for professional learning in national school leadership programmes such as those offered by the National College for Leadership of Schools and Children's Services (www.nationalcollege.org.uk). These include the 'National Professional Qualification for Headship', 'Leading from the Middle', and 'Leadership Pathways', all of which make use of external coaches who are trained to support the development of teachers in relation to the specific goals of the programme. These programmes identify some common aims for the coaching relationship such as facilitating in-school learning and establishing a trusting and purposeful relationship with participants. As with MTL these programmes also carry some form of professional accreditation.

The third category is concerned with the use of co-coaching and specialist coaching relationships for the continuing professional learning of all teachers. The determination of the degree of formality and structure within these relationships will depend on the institutional context and the desired process and outcomes for the coaching relationship. Unlike the previous two categories these relationships are generally developed by the participants rather than determined by institutional or statutory requirements. So, for example, a teacher or group of teachers may use specialist coaching and/or co-coaching to enhance their subject and professional knowledge in a specific area. (For specific examples of the use of specialist and co-coaching in secondary schools see the inquiries discussed in Burley and Pomphrey, 2011.) A further example is the use of executive coaching, where an external coach is selected by an individual teacher. This relationship usually occurs at senior leadership level and the processes and outcomes for the coaching are determined and negotiated according to the needs of the individual and/or broader institutional aims. Coaching at this level often makes use of processes used by a range of professions such as the GROW model (Whitmore, 1996) or the Skilled Helper Model (Egan, 1990) to structure a process which includes both personal and professional goal-setting and considers options to support individual learning.

INTRODUCTION OF A NATIONAL FRAMEWORK FOR MENTORING AND COACHING

As the use of different mentoring and coaching relationships developed in secondary schools, a 'National Framework for Mentoring and Coaching' was established in 2005. This arose from a study by CUREE (Centre for the Use of Research Evidence in Education) in 2004–2005, which gives an overview of research into professional development for teachers and the contribution of mentoring and coaching to successful professional learning. The national framework has been endorsed by a number of influential organisations, including the Department for Education (formerly the Department for Children, Schools and Families (DCSF)), the General Teaching Council (GTC), the National College for Leadership of Schools and Children's Services (NCLSCS) and the Training and Development Agency for Schools (TDA).

The aim of this framework is to use mentoring and coaching as a vehicle for developing teachers' professional learning in order to improve student learning in schools. The framework draws on a number of studies related to teacher professional learning including Joyce and Showers (2002), Cordingley et al. (2003) and Adey et al. (2004).

It is divided into three parts, identifying ten principles for mentoring and coaching, core concepts for mentoring and coaching and skills for mentoring and coaching. It also offers a comparison of the overlapping roles between mentoring and coaching.

Principles

The ten principles identified in the framework are as follows:

- a learning conversation;
- a thoughtful relationship;
- a learning agreement;
- combining support from fellow professional learners and specialists;

- growing self direction;
- setting challenging and personal goals;
- understanding why different approaches work;
- acknowledging the benefits to the mentors and coaches;
- experimenting and observing; and
- using resources effectively.

These 'principles' provide useful guidelines for establishing the processes used in mentoring and coaching relationships. They refer to the nature of the relationship, the aims and structure of the relationship and the importance of the learning within mentoring and coaching. They also suggest that the relationship offers both parties the opportunity to experiment and extend professional understanding and practice. However, the ten 'principles' represent a mixture of functions, processes and outcomes rather than making explicit the overarching principles (such as commitment to professional learning and development of autonomy) which underpin the mentoring and coaching processes that they advocate.

Concepts

The framework also specifies as three core concepts the roles of mentoring, specialist coaching and collaborative co-coaching. Mentoring is defined as 'a structured, sustained process for supporting professional learners through significant career transitions' National Framework for Mentoring and Coaching, (DCSF, 2005). Specialist coaching is defined as 'a structured, sustained process for enabling the development of a specific aspect of a professional learner's practice' whilst collaborative (co-) coaching is 'a structured, sustained process between two or more professional learners to enable them to embed new knowledge and skills from specialist sources in day-to-day practice'. These roles clearly carry a great deal of overlap but still provide some useful guidelines for the ways in which the mentoring and coaching relationships can be used to support different learning purposes. However by using the term 'concept' to describe a mentoring or coaching role, this part of the framework is limited to a set of behaviours and actions. In this way it fails to identify the key concepts which underpin the mentoring and coaching process, such as collaboration and the nature of professional knowledge and learning.

Skills

The skills which are identified in the framework are also separated into the three roles of mentoring, specialist coaching and co-coaching. Once again there is a great deal of overlap, but they offer useful insights and guidance into the processes of mentoring and coaching for both mentor/coach and professional learner. The list of skills includes the need for listening and sensitivity by both participants, together with the use of reflection and evidence in order to improve professional practice and promote ownership of the learning. However, the framework provides a limited account of how professional learning can be maximised through the skillful use of collaboration and critical dialogue.

The National Framework for Mentoring and Coaching (DCSF, 2005) acknowledges the overlap in principles, concepts and skills related to mentoring and coaching. This demonstrates the difficulties which exist in distinguishing between mentoring and coaching as practices. Garvey et al. highlight 'the confusing array of definitions found in modern discourses' (2009: 27). Brockbank and McGill have a similar view, stating that the 'terminology of mentoring and coaching in the literature has been confused and confusing' (2006: 1). It would seem that attempts to make clear distinctions between mentoring and coaching as professional practices have failed to produce agreed understandings and definitions of the terms. Garvey et al. offer an explanation for this by suggesting that 'the meaning of coaching and mentoring is fundamentally determined by the social context' (2009: 25). They argue that because the relationships within mentoring and coaching are dynamic and change over time it is difficult to set boundaries around mentoring and coaching as separate activities. As a result of this confusion the European Mentoring and Coaching Council avoid the use of the terms mentoring and coaching and have adopted the idea of a 'one-to-one developmental dialogue' (Garvey et al., 2009: 224) to describe all mentoring and coaching relationships (see Garvey et al., 2009).

THE IMPORTANCE OF PROFESSIONAL LEARNING TO MENTORING AND COACHING

Brockbank and McGill (2006) identify three clear aims for professional learning. These are:

- learning for improvement of professional performance;
- meta-learning, learning about the process of professional learning; and
- transformative learning.

The National Framework for Mentoring and Coaching (DCSF, 2005) is essentially concerned with the first of these aims, namely the improvement of both individual and institutional professional performance. Learning for improvement tends to focus on the importance of experiential learning within the workplace (Marsick and Watkins, 1990). Marsick and Watkins draw on Kolb's (1984) four-stage learning cycle of experiential learning. This cycle moves from actual experience to reflection on experience which generates new learning and ends with a stage of acting on the outcomes of this process. Ponte (2010) describes experiential learning as situated learning, or 'learning from experience of what is immediately to hand'. She points out the limitations of this type of learning suggesting that 'learning from experience only produces direct, context-based practical knowledge, for direct application; knowledge geared to competent practice and not to describing and understanding reality from a distance' (2010: 72).

She advocates an alternative type of professional learning which she calls 'mediated learning' (ibid. 72).

Mediated learning combines understanding of theory with reflection on experience in order to go beyond the immediate context and synthesise knowledge derived from a range of sources such as theoretical reading, understandings of policy and reflections on professional practice. Thus mediated learning aims to construct new knowledge and learning that can be applied to other contexts. Mentoring and coaching have the potential to support the development of mediated learning, although there is limited emphasis on encouraging it in the national framework.

The second aim of professional learning identified by Brockbank and McGill (2006) is learning about learning (meta-learning). Watkins, Carnell, Lodge, Wagner and Whalley (1998) add to Kolb's (1984) four-stage learning cycle a cycle of meta-learning which they define as 'the process of making sense of your experience of learning'. A concern for learning about learning can help teachers develop greater understanding of their own professional learning in order to transfer successful learning processes to future situations. As with mediated learning, mentoring and coaching have the potential to provide an ideal vehicle for developing meta-learning.

Brockbank and McGill's third aim of transformative learning is a more radical concept which refers to the development of processes of criticality in order to question and challenge existing values and practices and create new understandings of professional practice and learning. Transformative learning encompasses meta-learning and learning for improvement of professional performance. However it also goes beyond these in allowing for the possibility of a critique of underlying ideologies and values, questioning national standards and policies as well as institutional and individual practices.

In their work on effective teacher professional learning, Carnell and Lodge (2002) include all three aims for learning identified by Brockbank and McGill in 2006. They recognise the importance of the day to day professional context (experiential learning) as well as of opportunities for reflection on learning (meta-learning) and the potential for teacher dialogue and collaboration to develop actions for change (transformative learning).

The mentoring or coaching relationship is the perfect vehicle for developing all three types of professional learning identified by Brockbank and McGill (2006). The mentoring and coaching relationship allows for effective dialogue and collaboration between teachers which supports the co-construction of new professional knowledge and learning.

EFFECTIVE PROFESSIONAL LEARNING THROUGH MENTORING AND COACHING

Burley and Pomphrey (2011) identify three components of effective professional learning which contribute to the co-construction of professional knowledge and learning within mentoring and coaching: reflection, dialogue and criticality.

Reflection

Reflection within mentoring and coaching can be compared to Boud's (2010) notion of group or team-based reflection within professional settings as opposed to individually centred reflection. Boud (2010) extends previous definitions of reflection derived from Schoen (1983) by viewing professional learning and practice as essentially collaborative and 'co-produced' (2010: 25).

Dialogue

Dialogue is an essential process for the co-construction of meaning through the collaborative interaction of mentoring and coaching and Brockbank and McGill (2006) recognise its importance for transformative professional learning. Boud describes the challenge of 'creating common ground' (2010: 34) through dialogue which 'involves the questioning of the taken-for-granted assumptions … being able to step aside from one situation and view it from the perspective of another' (ibid.). It is this collaborative engagement with different ideas and perspectives which means that mentoring and coaching is well placed to challenge thinking and provide opportunities for the co-construction of new professional knowledge.

Criticality

Fook (2010) sees criticality as strongly related to transformative learning and emphasises the importance of professional learning leading to a change in perspective. Criticality enables this change of perspective through 'a willingness to wonder, to ask questions, and to seek to understand by collaborating with others in the attempt to make answers to them' (Wells, 1999: 121). Nelson (2005) uses the term 'knowledge negotiation' (Slavit and Nelson, 2009: 8) to describe this process of examining 'alternative perspectives and questioning one's own knowledge and beliefs' (ibid.).

MENTORING AND COACHING AS A METAPHORICAL SPACE FOR REFLECTION, DIALOGUE AND CRITICALITY

Mentoring and coaching can be conceptualised as providing a metaphorical space in which the three key processes of reflection, dialogue and criticality can take place in order to generate and construct transformative professional learning. The metaphor of a platform has been used to describe a space for professional learning by Smith (2000) in relation to initial teacher education and by Ponte (2007) in relation to postgraduate continuing teacher education. Ponte (2010) reinforces Smith's (2000) notion of the platform as 'a meeting place, where … others can learn from each other and engage in debate. The central idea is that the participants consult each other to decide what they will learn and how.' (2010: 71). Ponte identifies criticality as an essential process and outcome for professional learning with a number of 'mediated learning' interactions taking place on the platform (ibid. 74).

Smith's (2000) and Ponte's (2007) notions of the platform can also be applied to mentoring and coaching where participants meet to determine goals and processes for transformative professional learning. This metaphorical space enables the mentoring and coaching relationship to operate alongside immediate day-to-day practice. However, this process can be problematic. For example, there may be a tension for teachers between intrinsically (self) motivated learning and extrinsically directed, externally regulated learning or a difference in the status, power and range of experience of the teachers involved. In such cases, the platform of mentoring and coaching provides a space where such tensions may be explored through collaboration and dialogue.

CHARACTERISTICS OF EFFECTIVE PROFESSIONAL LEARNING IN MENTORING AND COACHING

Mentoring and coaching as a space for collaboratively co-constructed professional learning can be characterised by the following:

- mediated professional learning drawing on all types of knowledge and experience;
- the co-construction of new professional knowledge;
- the use of dialogue and collaborative reflection;
- the use of criticality to develop transformative professional learning; and
- an understanding of mentoring and coaching as a place of shared goals and processes that are continuously reviewed and contested.

This chapter has examined the terminology, roles and relationships and processes that comprise mentoring and coaching in UK secondary schools. It has considered the influence of different theoretical and national policy frameworks on the development of mentoring and coaching in UK secondary schools. It examines the usefulness as well as the limitations of the National Framework for Mentoring and Coaching (DCSF, 2005). This framework identifies a range of detailed roles, skills and processes but omits to recognise the full potential of mentoring and coaching to promote collaborative professional learning which is critical and transformative. The chapter has argued for an understanding of professional learning to underpin policies, practices and definitions of mentoring and coaching. It goes on to identify the components of effective professional learning and cites mentoring and coaching as a metaphorical space which allows for these components to be realised. Finally, the chapter offers a summary of characteristics of mentoring and coaching collaborations which would support transformative professional learning at both individual and institutional levels. This provides a way forward for the development of effective mentoring and coaching in UK secondary schools.

REFERENCES

Adey, P. Hewitt, G., Hewitt, J. & Landau, N. (2004) *The Professional Development of Teachers: Practice and Theory.* Dordrecht: Kluwer Academy.

Arthur, J., Davison, J. & Moss, J. (1997) *Subject Mentoring in the Secondary School.* London: Routledge.

Boud, D. (2010) 'Relocating reflection in the context of practice' in Kilminster, S. Zukas, M. Bradbury, H. & Frost, N. (eds), *Beyond Reflective Practice: New approaches to professional lifelong learning,* pp. 25–36. Abingdon: Routledge.

Brockbank, A. & McGill, I. (2006) *Facilitating Reflective Learning Through Mentoring and Coaching.* London: Kogan Page.

Burley, S. & Pomphrey, C. (2011) *Mentoring and Coaching: Professional Learning through Collaborative Inquiry.* Abingdon: Routledge.

Carnell, E. & Lodge, C. (2002) *Supporting Effective Learning.* London: Sage.

Clutterbuck, D. (2003) *The Problem With Research in Mentoring.* The Coaching and Mentoring Network, Clutterbuck Associates. Retrieved from: http://www.coachingnetwork.org.uk/resourcecentre/articles/ViewArticle.asp?artId+82

Cordingley, P., Bell,M., Rundell, B. and Evans, D. (2003) 'The impact of collaborative CPD on classroom teaching and learning' in *Research Evidence in Education Library.* London: EPPI-Centre, Social Science Research Unit, Institute of Education, University of London.

CUREE (Centre for the Use of Research Evidence in Education) (2004/2005) *Mentoring and Coaching for Learning: Summary Report of the Mentoring and Coaching CPD Capacity Building Project.* Coventry: CUREE.

Department for Children, Schools and Families (2005) *National Framework for Mentoring and Coaching.* London: DCSF.

Department for Children, Schools and Families (2008) *Statutory Guidance on the Induction Period for Newly Qualified Teachers (NQTs) in England.* London: DCSF.

Department for Education (1992) *Initial Teacher Training (Secondary Phase) Circular 9/92.* London: DfE.

Egan, G. (1990) *The Skilled Helper: a systematic approach to effective helping,* 4th edn. Pacific Grove: Brooks/Cole.

Fletcher, S. (2000). *Mentoring in Schools: A Handbook of Good Practice.* London: Kogan Page.

Fook, J. (2010) 'Beyond reflective Practice: Reworking the "critical" in critical reflection' in H. Bradbury, N. Frost, S. Kilminster, S. & M. Zukas (eds) *Beyond Reflective Practice: New Approaches to Professional Lifelong Learning,* pp. 37–51. Abingdon: Routledge.

Furlong, J. & Maynard, T. (1995) *Mentoring Student Teachers: The Growth of Professional Knowledge.* London: Routledge.

Garvey, R., Stokes , P. & Megginson, D. (2009) *Coaching and Mentoring: Theory and Practice.* London: Sage.

Hagger, H. B. (1993) *School Mentor Handbook.* London: Kogan Page.

Hampton, G. Rhodes, C. & Stokes, M. (2004) *A Practical Guide to Mentoring, Coaching and Peer-networking: Teacher Professional Development in Schools and Colleges.* London: Routledge.

Joyce, B. & Showers, B. (2002) *Student Achievement Through Staff Development,* 3rd edn. London: Longman.

Kolb, D. (1984) *Experiential Learning: Experience as the Source of Learning and Development.* New Jersey: Prentice Hall.

Marsick, V. J. & Watkins, K. E. (1990) *Informal and Incidental Learning in the Workplace.* London: Routledge.

Nelson, T. H. (2005) Knowledge interactions in teacher-scientist partnerships: negotiation, consultation and rejection. *Journal of Teacher Education* 56(4): 382–395.

Ponte, P. (2007) 'Postgraduate education as platform: a conceptualisation' in J. Van Swet, P. Ponte & B. Smit (eds) *Postgraduate Programs as Platform: a Research-led Approach,* pp. 19–39. Rotterdam: Sense Publishers.

Ponte, P. (2010) 'Postgraduate programmes as platforms: Coming together and doing research for a common moral purpose' in A. Campbell & S. Groundwater-Smith (eds) *Connecting Inquiry and Professional Learning in Education: International Perspectives and Practical Solutions,* pp. 68–82. Abingdon: Routledge.

Schoen, D. (1983) *The Reflective Practitoner: How Professionals Think in Action.* New York: Basic Books.

Slavit, D. & Nelson, T. H. (2009) 'Supported collaborative teacher inquiry' in D. Slavit T. H. Nelson, & A. Kennedy (eds) *Perspectives on Supported Collaborative Teacher Inquiry.* Abingdon: Routledge. 1–15.

Smith, R. (2000) The future of teacher education: principles and prospects Asia Pacific. *Journal of Teacher Education* 28(1): 7–28.

Stephens, P. (1996) *Essential Mentoring Skills: A Practical Handbook for School-based Educators.* Cheltenham: Stanley Thornes.

Training and Development Agency for Schools (2008) *Professional Standards for Qualified Teacher Status and Requirements for Initial Teacher Training (Revised 2008).* London: TDA.

Training and Development Agency for Schools (2009a) *Guidance to accompany the Professional Standards for Qualified Teacher Status and Requirements for Initial Teacher Training (Revised 2008).* London: TDA.

Training and Development Agency for Schools (2009b) Masters in Teaching and Learning Coaching Strategy V1.0, 18 November 2009. London: TDA.

Vygotsky, L. (1978) *Mind in Society: the Development of Higher Psychological Processes.* Cambridge MA: Harvard University Press.

Watkins, C., Carnell, E., Lodge, C., Wagner, P. & Whalley, C. (1998) *Learning about Learning.* Coventry: NAPCE.

Wells, G. (1999) *Dialogic Inquiry: Towards a Sociocultural Practice and Theory of Education.* Cambridge: Cambridge University Press.

Whitmore, J. (1996) *Coaching for Performance.* London: Nicholas Brealey.

20

Multidimensional Understandings of School-based Mentoring

Po-yuk Ko, Mun-ling Lo and
John Chi-kin Lee

INTRODUCTION

Novice teachers in the K-12 school context frequently have problems adjusting to the teaching environment. Many find difficulty in bridging the gap between theory and practice, especially in the areas of lesson planning, motivating students to learn, and evaluating students' work (Grossman and Thompson, 2004; Howe, 2006). Recognition of the vulnerability of novice teachers and their need for emotional support has led to the instigation of mentoring in schools (Hargreaves and Fullan, 2000; Huling-Austin, 1992). Acknowledgement of the benefits of mentoring in supporting novice teachers in schools has grown to the extent that mentoring is now seen as a fundamental part of the teacher induction system in some countries (Britton, 2006).

Benefits of mentoring have been much promoted (e.g., Hobson, Ashby, Maldarez, and Tomlinson, 2009), and various studies have shown that it is valuable for both mentors and mentees. Mentoring provides emotional support for novice teachers (Driscoll, Peterson, and Kauchak, 1985), helps them satisfy requirements related to induction and certification and to meet standards, supports them in adjusting to the culture of the school system (Roehrig, Bohn, Turner and Pressley, 2008), and contributes to the reduction of teacher attrition (Smith and Ingersoll, 2004). However, not all structured mentoring relationships necessarily support reform-minded teaching practice. It is equally possible for mentoring to foster conventional norms and practices. In such cases, new teachers may be induced to follow traditional approaches and practices that are considered less effective than those newly promoted ones in bringing about student learning (Cochran-Smith and Paris, 1995; Feiman-Nemser, 1996; Martinez, 2004).

The meaning of, as well as approaches to, mentoring have changed over time and across educational systems. No consensus on a common definition for mentoring has been reached. Roberts (2000) identifies the essential attributes of mentoring from the perspectives of relationship, process, and development. These include a process form, an active relationship, a helping process, a teaching–learning process, reflective practice, career and personal development, a formalized process, and a role constructed by or for the mentor. Nonetheless, mentoring is not just about processes and practices *per se.*

The purpose, approach, and focus of mentoring for novice teachers are shaped by how novice teachers are perceived within schools (e.g., as well-trained, partially trained, or life learners), how mentors' roles are regarded (e.g., whether they are seen as buddies, advisors, critical friends, or coaches to mentees), and the view of how teachers' professional development is best achieved. The only feature common to the different forms of mentoring is the main purpose of mentoring – to support novice teachers in accordance with their perceived needs – although the understanding of such needs may vary across systems (e.g., emotional support, meeting standards, professional growth). However, to aim mentoring only at supporting novice teachers is a relatively narrow view of what mentoring can achieve. As it is important for the teaching profession to continue to develop knowledge and grow, we frame mentoring support from a learning perspective. We see mentoring as providing a platform for the construction of a professional learning community (PLC) in which everyone involved learns and grows together, and all benefit from the process.

To begin to understand mentoring for novice teachers in all its complexity, we propose a multidimensional analytical framework. The dimensions of the framework should be regarded as variations, not as dichotomies. Adhering to any extreme position or pole is likely to lead to problems. The five dimensions of mentoring are as follows.

1 *Policy/context:* from mandatory, top-down to bottom-up approaches.
2 *Focus:* from enculturation and socialization to having a teaching and learning focus.
3 *Format and involvement:* from a one-to-one mentor-mentee approach to group mentoring or a learning community approach.
4 *Structure:* from formal to informal mentoring structure.
5 *Key players:* shift from mentor as teacher and mentee as learner to both as learners.

We next discuss each dimension in turn. However, because it is not possible to discuss each dimension in isolation, we also discuss the interactions of them with each other where appropriate. The system has to be understood as a complex, dynamic system with multiple dimensions, each subject to multiple levels of consideration, with each dimension and level affecting the other. The most desirable system for any school is to find the optimum or favorable position among the dimensions best suited to the context and people involved.

DIMENSIONS OF MENTORING

Policy/context: the need for bottom-up approaches

Teachers do not work in a vacuum. The interplay between the policy environment and classrooms cannot be ignored (Grossman and Thompson, 2004). Trends in mentoring practice are often shaped by contextual factors and national, state, or local policies in the broader educational landscape. For example, with ongoing educational reforms that call for accountability and a steady supply of qualified new teachers for all students, the focus of mentoring has turned from enculturation, counseling, and guidance to improving teaching and learning and helping teachers to meet state-mandated standards (Martinez, 2004). Britton's (2006) study of teacher induction in China, Switzerland, France, New Zealand, and Japan suggests that different mentoring practices are embedded in different school and curriculum contexts. The practice of mentoring also varies across cultural settings, ranging from a top-down, centralized, and mandatory approach to a school-based, bottom-up approach, with distinct degrees of teacher autonomy and great variation in the degree of centralization.

As induction programs for novice teachers have gradually become institutionalized (Darling-Hammond and Sclan, 1996), some countries have adopted a more centralized approach to mentoring. In some places, teacher induction programs have become mandatory and serve a gatekeeping function in securing a quality teaching force to ensure better learning outcomes (Britton, Pain, Pimm, and Raizen, 2003). For example, in many states in the United States mentoring practice is being extended, even mandated (Feiman-Nemser, 1996; Mullen, 2010; Portner, 2002). Many US states provide new teachers with various kinds of support, of which formal mentoring programs are a key component (Smith and Ingersoll, 2004). State educational policies frame the socialization and conception of new teachers, especially when they prescribe instructional practices and assessment outcomes (Achinstein, Ogawa, and Speiglman, 2004). Local school and district contexts likewise exert a profound influence on the socialization of novice teachers and, implicitly, on their teaching and learning practices.

There is some debate in the literature on whether a formal or mandatory system of mentoring, as opposed to an informal or school-based system, is a more favorable model (Mullen, 2008). Those who favor an informal or school-based system criticize formal systems for reinforcing the imbalance of power in the mentoring process, and for forcing teachers who are not committed to teaching to become mentors, which results in a technical approach to mentoring. It has been suggested that in both the US and the UK mentoring as a reform strategy often becomes a technical, evaluative activity as opposed to a symbiotic process of cultivating a professional culture of learning and collaboration (Mullen, 2008, 2010; Wynn, Carboni, and Patall, 2007).

Some countries have adopted mentoring policies that are school-based and bottom-up. For example, novice science teachers in New Zealand find help in every direction (Britton, Raizen, and Huntley, 2003; Britton, 2006), both from within schools and from outside. Studies have revealed that school-based induction can be a success if there is a commitment throughout the educational system to novice teacher support (e.g., Carter and Francis, 2001). However, actors at all levels of the system need to assume that new teachers have particular needs, and the system must then pay explicit attention to addressing these (Britton, 2006). Problems associated with an informal approach to mentoring include a lack of structure for the mentoring process, a lack of training for mentors, and a lack of resources (e.g., workload reduction for mentors). Further, novice teachers who most need mentoring may not opt to join the process (Ehrich, Hansford, and Tennent, 2004).

As Fullan (1994) pointed out, wholly neither top-down nor bottom-up strategies for educational reform are effective. Mentoring policies should instead be top-down or bottom-up to different degrees depending on teacher autonomy. What is required is perhaps a blend of the two, with top-down mandates coordinated with bottom-up initiatives that local players shape.

Toward a teaching–learning focus

The focus of mentoring has changed over time. As mentoring entered the vocabulary of educational reform in the 1980s, particularly in the US, it was described by concepts such as psychological and technical support and guidance (Wang and Paine, 2001). Mentoring approaches mainly focused on emotional support, adjusting to school cultures, short-term assistance, and acculturation to the teaching profession (Feiman-Nemser, Schwille, Carver, and Yusko, 1999; Wang, Odell, and Schwille, 2008). Research on teacher effectiveness and teacher development strongly suggests that the socialization process needs to incorporate more collaborative and intentional experiences during which neophyte and experienced professionals can share and grow together. Although socialization plays a vital part in novice teacher development and adaptation to the school culture, emotional and technical support alone do not do enough to help novices learn to teach (Feiman-Nemser et al., 1999). Moreover, the erroneous socialization of entrenched and predefined behavior, attitudes, and values may hinder teaching effectiveness and disadvantage certain sectors of the student population that are already underachieving (Martinez, 2004). Unfortunately, the celebration of mentoring and emphasis on socialization in the literature and the prominence accorded contextual and cultural matters in mentor–mentee interactions over actual questions about teaching tend to direct mentoring away from teaching and learning (Da Ros and Swick, 1995; Gratch, 2001).

Nevertheless, some researchers argue that mentoring should aim to help novice teachers acquire further skills and knowledge. An early study by Driscoll, Peterson, and Kauchak (1985) showed that novice teachers rated instructional and curricular support as more important than emotional support. Many researchers similarly stress that effective mentoring should in fact focus on teaching and learning. A mentoring relationship that focuses on the central tasks of teaching (such as enacting teachers' repertoire in purposeful ways and creating a classroom community conducive to student learning) is highly regarded by novice teachers and expected by them (Feinman-Nemser, 2001). Wang and Paine (2001) argue that mentor support for novice teachers that helps them learn to teach appears to be more effective than merely accepting the preconceived role of facilitating teachers' entry into the teaching profession. Supporting teachers to achieve independence in teaching and learning should be a fundamental objective of mentoring. Hargreaves and Fullan (2000) see mentoring as preparing teachers to become effective agents of change who will transform the teaching profession into an improvement-oriented profession. Wang and Odell also advocate 'reform-minded mentoring' (2002: 534). In the US, this concept had little impact in practice until recently when the success of schools became more standards-driven due to the implementation of accountability measures, which changed the focus of teachers' work. In line with this, the focus of mentoring shifted from socialization and enculturation to teaching and learning. As the current climate in many countries (including the US) emphasizes teachers' responsibility for student achievement, novice teachers are expected to become 'effective' quickly in boosting student performance (Roehrig et al., 2008).

In China, the focus of mentoring has always been on helping novices to develop a deep understanding of the subject matter, curriculum, and professional ethics, as suggested by the state's centralized curriculum and subject-based teaching. However, mentoring in China also connotes a hierarchical relationship and draws on an apprenticeship model in which the mentor transmits knowledge and skills to the mentee (Lee and Feng, 2007; Wang and Paine, 2001). Britton (2006) argues for a much broader model and a 'developmental' view that both cultivates and motivates novice teachers to learn more about teaching and learning, assessment, instructional practices, and subject matter, and to develop an awareness of educational issues and the importance of working with stakeholders such as parents.

Toward group mentoring and learning community

There are many different forms of mentoring, including one-to-one, co-mentoring, and group mentoring. In many schools, one-to-one mentoring is the dominant or sole strategy for supporting new teachers (Wong, 2004). For example, a tradition in China is one of experienced teachers helping novice teachers. Lee and Feng's (2007) study in Guangzhou, China, reveals that teacher mentors provide at least four forms of support: provision of information, mutual lesson observation, collaborative lesson preparation, and formal discussions in the school office.

Recently, increasing numbers of studies have adopted the view that group mentoring strengthens and supports the one-to-one mentor–mentee model, as the mentor may not have all the skills needed to support the mentee. A form that is less hierarchical and individualistic is preferred, as 'all teachers are more effective when they can learn from and be supported by a strong community of colleagues' (Hargreaves and Fullan, 2000: 52). In a similar vein, Britton (2006) suggests that novices can also learn from each other through peer support groups facilitated by someone with experience. Johnson and Birkeland (2003) advocate the development of school-wide structures that promote the frequent exchange of information and ideas among novice and veteran teachers. Group mentoring emphasizes collegiality and collaboration (Bullough, Young, and Drapera, 2004). In the same vein, Williams, Prestage, and Bedward (2001) suggest that 'even where effective collaborative work is limited largely to the interaction between mentors and newly qualified teachers, the newly qualified teacher is able to have a positive and successful induction experience' (2001: 264). Britton et al. (2003) and Wong (2004) concur that collaboration and support among peers is the strength of the successful, cross-cultural induction programs that they studied.

The findings of a plethora of studies indicate that a PLC effectively facilitates professional teacher development. Howe (2006) argues that a successful teacher induction program should include opportunities for experts and neophytes to learn together in a supportive environment that allows time for collaboration, reflection, and gradual acculturation into the teaching profession. To shift the mentor–protégé relationships from 'structured support' to 'emerging colleagueship' as proposed by Spindler and Biott (2000), Glazer and Hannafin (2006) developed a model of teacher induction that initiates collaboration and collegial support within a PLC. The collective PLC model starts with an induction phase that functions to engender a sense of group identity and treat new teachers as colleagues and cohorts. Collaborative group work is understood, fostered, illuminated, and accepted as a part of the wider teaching culture. The existence of shared experiences, shared practices, shared tools, and a shared language among novice teachers facilitates and contributes to a meaningful, comprehensive induction (Britton et al., 2003).

From formal to informal mentoring structure

Mentoring programs may be formal or informal. A formal induction program usually follows a team approach (group mentoring) involving different people, including mentors, administrators, and representatives from higher education. This is different from the informal program, which usually incorporates a buddy system (one-to-one mentor–mentee model) (Klug and Salzman, 1990).

Formal mentoring programs differ greatly in nature, focus, and outcomes (Ehrich and Hansford, 1999; Ehrich et al., 2004; Smith and Ingersoll, 2004).

In the US, it has been demonstrated that different conceptions of learning and teaching may arise depending on district resources, professional culture, and degree of curriculum centralization. Some district administrators emphasize the use of structured instructional programs to attain state-mandated standards for academic performance, whereas others encourage creativity and autonomy among teachers. Achinstein et al. (2004) found that, more often than not, fewer professional development opportunities are available to novice teachers in schools in lower-income districts that have a vested interest in strictly adhering to legislative mandates. In such schools, novice teachers are expected simply to 'learn and follow the procedures of the school' (2004: 590). In schools in high-income districts, in contrast, teachers are not required to adhere to centralized curricula. These teachers are exposed to an extensive array of professional development opportunities that encourage the inquiry and co-construction of knowledge alongside peer collaboration. This situation benefits novice mentees, as mentors have greater autonomy to pursue, push for, and direct innovative teaching and mentoring methods, which in turn enhances individual student learning.

Stevenson and Baker (1991) found that under a centrally controlled curriculum, teachers' decisions are more likely to be associated with rigid curriculum standards and requirements, whereas under a non-centrally controlled curriculum, their decisions more closely relate to individual teachers' preferences and students' characteristics. Their findings suggest that even if mentor teachers are teaching using reform-standard and consistent methods, the potential effects of such mentoring behavior is limited by how the novice teachers respond to them and by the instructional contexts in which the mentoring relationship is situated (Strong and Baron, 2004; Wang, 2001; Wang et al., 2008). Special attention should be paid to the influences that instructional contexts may have on mentoring, and consequently teaching, and on the kinds of learning opportunities that mentoring creates for novice teachers in different contexts.

Interestingly, in addition to formal mentoring programs and officially assigned mentors, novice teachers also solicit support from informal mentors (Coburn and Russell, 2008). Hochberg, Hawkinson, Cannata, Desimone, and Porter (2009) found that novice middle school mathematics teachers in the US tend to spend more time with informal mentors than with their formally assigned mentors. The mentees regard the interactions with informal mentors as being more helpful than those with formal mentors in some areas, such as classroom management, expectations, and emotional support. Another study has shown that novice teachers in New Zealand receive support through informal means such as conversations at 'intervals' and lunchtimes with teachers of subjects other than their own (Britton, 2006). This raises the question of whether the mentor's location, personality, and background affect the content and helpfulness of mentoring interactions. Another study of novice teacher mentorship from Saskatchewan, Canada reveals that the compatibility of the mentor and mentee is an important issue. The researchers propose that 'rather than creating and implementing a province-wide, government-mandated mentorship or induction program, the mentorship of teachers could be developed through an adaptation of the PLC model focused on student learning' (Hellsten, Prytula, Ebanks, and Lai, 2009: 725). In other words, engaging the novices in an informal mentoring structure that focuses on improving student learning, rather than a formal one, may better help them to adapt to and improve on their practices in the school.

Formal mentoring programs are usually more well planned and structured. It ensures that mentorship is extended to individuals (Ehrich and Hansford, 1999). However, some literature outlines its drawbacks. Feiman-Nemser (2001) criticizes the conventional practices of formal teacher induction of having too narrow a vision. Therefore, even when formal programs exist, sometimes it only reinforces traditional norms and practices rather than promoting more powerful teaching. Long (1997) points out that mentoring relationship can be detrimental to the mentor, mentee or both parties under some conditions; for example, a lack of time, poor planning of mentoring process, mismatch between mentors and mentees, as well as a lack of understanding about the mentoring process. He proposes that such negative outcomes may be minimized by a more sustained sequence of institutional activity and follow up support in teacher induction. Feiman-Nemser (2001) argues that practices of mentoring should include appropriate assignments, programs with multiyear timeframes and a 'developmental' stance, the integration of assistance and assessment, careful selection, preparation and support of the mentors themselves, and the building of partnerships and collaborations.

Toward mentor and mentee as learner

The conventional model regards the mentor as someone who is senior in rank and more experienced, knowledgeable, and skillful in teaching. This suggests that there is no need for training for mentors, which results in the danger of novices being inducted into the norms and expectations of the profession and school culture, but not necessarily taught good practices. It is self-evident that quality mentors need to have both expertise in teaching and competence in mentoring (Evertson and Smithey, 2000; Wang and Odell, 2002).

Feiman-Nemser (1996) and Zachary (2000), among other researchers, point out that a dramatic improvement in mentoring practice results if the mentoring relationship is defined in terms of learning, with both parties regarded as learners. Mentoring has the potential to facilitate professional growth by making practices explicit, allowing what has been taken for granted to move to the fore and improvements to be made in teaching. New teachers should be taken seriously as learners, but mentors must also be adequately equipped, and should be relieved of some of their responsibilities so that they have time to reflect (Ballantyne, Hansford, and Packer, 1995). The provision of ongoing support for mentors is vital (Feiman-Nemser, 1994), and the preparation of competent teacher mentors is crucial if mentoring support is to be recognized as a key component in the infrastructure of teacher internship or induction (Cochran-Smith and Paris, 1995).

However, the reality is that many mentors are unwilling or unable to move beyond their role of simple 'local guide' (Feiman-Nemser and Parker, 1992) or safety net, especially where fiscal motivation or other reward for mentoring is lacking. Tang and Choi (2005) contend that the organization of curriculum components, such as coursework (e.g., lesson analysis and conferencing skills) and structured practical work in mentoring, facilitates the connection of theory and practice.

How mentors and mentees perceive their roles also affects their actions. One function of mentoring support is to help novice teachers to recognize their institutional role and the tensions that may exist in the modern teaching profession. Teachers are expected 'to take personal and collective responsibility for improving their skills and subject knowledge' (Dymoke and Harrison, 2006: 72). Mentees need to be open to critiques and suggestions, and they should have sufficient self-reflective, metacognitive skills to enable their appropriate use of information. Roehrig et al. (2008) found that novice teachers' skills in openness and metacognition interact with the skills of mentors, underscoring the importance of mentor–mentee communication. Clearly, both mentors and mentees need relevant knowledge and skills in order to benefit from the mentoring process. Preparation for mentors should ensure that they are able to model effective practice for novice teachers to observe and to provide suggestions on a broad repertoire of effective teaching strategies. Preparation for mentees should focus on the development of reflective, metacognitive skills to process, contemplate, and use information.

MENTORING FOCUSED ON STUDENT LEARNING

The ideas derived from the foregoing literature review and analysis, while meaningful, do not explicitly enlist one of the key stakeholders in education: the student. In part, the provision of quality mentoring support for teachers is driven by the hope that through mentoring support novice teachers will become more effective or better teachers, which will enhance student learning and achievement. Thus, in addition to decisions about the kind of mentoring approach or system to be adopted from the perspective of the professional growth and personal development of teachers (both mentors and mentees), the choice of mentoring approach should also be considered from the perspective of student learning outcomes. This perspective warrants more attention, as research suggests that 'evidence for the direct impact of mentoring on newly qualified teachers' development, especially their teaching skill, is somewhat limited' (Hobson et al., 2009: 209). There is also a lack of evidence on 'the impact of mentoring in the short or longer term on the learning of pupils taught by mentors and mentees' (ibid. 213). Effort has yet to be made to researching the direct impact of mentoring, if any, on both the learning of newly qualified teachers and students taught by mentors and mentees.

Tang and Choi (2005) describe the introduction in 2001 of a mentoring model by the Hong Kong Institute of Education (HKIEd) that focused on student learning. In addition to the one-to-one approach to mentoring, the model also sought to establish an infrastructure in schools to facilitate collaborative enquiry among teachers into teaching and learning by engaging in lesson study. In this kind of study, teachers plan lessons and evaluate classroom practices carefully and collaboratively specifically for improving student learning, and in the process learn to improve their own teaching (e.g., Lewis, 2002). According to Lewis (2005), lesson study improves teachers' thinking and practice by (1) increasing their knowledge of the subject matter, (2) expanding their knowledge of instruction, (3) improving their ability to observe students, (4) establishing stronger collegial networks, (5) forging a stronger connection between daily practice and long-term goals, (6) generating stronger motivation and a sense of efficacy in their own teaching, and (7) improving the quality of available lesson plans (2005: 115). Puchner and Taylor (2006) similarly find that the implementation of the lesson study model stimulates the dynamics and promise of teacher change and teacher efficacy. The resulting learning community that is formed changes the culture of the school, and makes the environment more conducive to ongoing professional learning (Cheng and Chan, 2009).

With the lesson study approach, mentoring is not confined to learning by the mentee, but also provides an opportunity to build a community of learners in school, the aim of which is ultimately to improve student learning. During the process, all those participating in the lesson study gain and grow professionally. This conception of mentoring situates learning at the center of the mentoring process. An obvious advantage to this approach is that one does not have to be a mentor or mentee to make professional gains. Every teacher can gain professionally by viewing the practice of others and using the critical points that arise as benchmarks for the evaluation of their own practice. This is an important point, as a lesson conference in which all participate and each is considered a learner, regardless of how experienced a teacher he or she may be, supports the notion of the school as a learning community. In this way, this model has the advantages of having the features of both the one-to-one mentor–mentee model and the learning community model.

The Hong Kong Institute of Education (HKIEd) offered intensive mentoring courses to partnership schools from 2000 to 2010. At the same time, the government of Hong Kong recognized the need for mentoring support for novice teachers and launched a series of mentoring courses to prepare teachers for this role. HKIEd was commissioned by the Education and Manpower Bureau to run the Mentoring Support Development Programme, which was open to all schools in Hong Kong. In this way, a bottom-up approach was coupled with a top-down approach, as schools saw the model as being endorsed by the government.

HKIEd offered mentoring courses to schools at three levels. The first comprised a 30-hour course for frontline teachers aiming to become mentors. The course covered lesson analysis and conferencing skills, structured practical work in mentoring, and the theory and practice of lesson study. The second level comprised a 60-hour course for senior teachers and department heads, which equipped these teachers who may have greater influence on other teachers to become mentors. With this approach, in addition to preparing participants to become competent mentors, it also helped them to develop a mentoring structure and to prepare other teachers in their school to be mentors. The final level consisted of a 15-hour course for principals to provide them with the knowledge to support the mentoring system and lesson studies as a platform for developing a learning community in their schools. Through the program, teachers received both formal and informal training in mentoring. The positive impact of the learning community using lesson studies as a platform on the professional learning of teachers, and the learning of students, is supported by both statistical and qualitative evidence (Lo, 2009).

CONCLUSION

We have proposed that mentoring be regarded as a complex and dynamic system with multiple dimensions. In addition to nurturing and supporting novice teachers, a good mentoring system should also facilitate the professional growth of mentors and other teachers in the school. Schools can establish their own mentoring system in accordance with their own circumstances and needs.

We understand there is no perfect mentoring and induction system. The most desirable system for any school is to find the optimum position within the different dimensions of the multidimensional analytical framework described, and to adopt the most suitable combination of approaches for the context and people involved. In choosing the most suitable mentoring system, schools should question what the mentoring system aims to achieve, the ways in which different approaches to mentoring can coexist in the school, and the best combination of approaches and extent to which the school should adopt them. Another vital question is the kinds of support that should be incorporated for the school to benefit from the mentoring system once the optimum position has been identified.

These questions have no easy answers. They serve as a framework for future inquiry and the development of high-quality mentoring practices for novice teachers. Regardless of which approach a school adopts in offering mentoring support to novices, it is important to recognize that all stakeholders must make an effort to support the chosen mentoring system. This includes policymakers and school principals who provide supportive policies and resources; district leaders and university academic leaders, who build and nurture platforms for teachers' professional development; and fellow teachers and students, who provide feedback and generate positive interactions with novice teachers and their mentors. It is also vital to provide concrete support to mentors and mentees and to equip them with essential knowledge and skills, so both parties know how to take advantage of the mentoring process and benefit from it. When both mentors and mentees learn from each other and grow professionally, students ultimately benefit.

REFERENCES

Achinstein, B., Ogawa, R. T., & Speiglman, A. (2004). Are we creating separate and unequal tracks of teachers? The effects of state policy, local conditions, and teacher characteristics on new teacher socialization. *American Educational Research Journal, 41*(3), 557–603.

Ballantyne, R., Hansford, B., & Packer, J. (1995). Mentoring beginning teachers: A qualitative analysis of process and outcomes. *Educational Review, 47*(3), 297–307.

Britton, E. D. (2006). Mentoring in the induction system of five countries: A sum greater than its parts. In C. Cullingford (Ed.), *Mentoring in education* (pp. 107–120). Aldershot: Ashgate.

Britton, E. D., Paine, L., Pimm H. D., & Raizen, S. (2003). *Comprehensive Teacher Induction: Systems for Early Career Learning.* Dordrecht: Kluwer.

Britton, E. D., Raizen S., & Huntley, M. A. (2003). Help in every direction: Supporting beginning science teachers in New Zealand. In E. Britton (Ed.), *Comprehensive Teacher Induction* (pp. 141–193). Dordrecht: Kluwer.

Bullough, R. V. Jr., Young, J., & Drapera, R. J. (2004). One-year teaching internships and the dimensions of beginning teacher development. *Teachers and Teaching, 10*(4), 365–394.

Carter, M., & Francis, R. (2001). Mentoring and Beginning Teachers' Workplace Learning. *Asia-Pacific Journal of Teacher Education, 29*(3), 249–262.

Cheng, C. K., & Chan, W. Y. (2009). *Managing Learning Study Communities for Leveraging Pedagogical Content Knowledge.* Paper presented at the World Association for Lesson Studies in International Conference, Hong Kong.

Coburn, C. E., & Russell, J. L. (2008). District policy and teachers' social networks. *Educational Evaluation and Policy Analysis, 30*(3), 203–235.

Cochran-Smith, M., & Paris, C. (1995). Mentor and Mentoring: Did Homer have it right? In J. Smyth (Ed.), *Critical discourses on teacher development* (pp. 181–202). London: Cassell.

Da Ros, D., & Swick, S. W. (1995). The socialization of beginning teachers. *Journal of Early Childhood Teacher Education, 16*(1), 13–17.

Darling-Hammond, K., & Sclan, E. M. (1996). Who Teaches and Why: Dilemmas of building a profession for 21st century schools. In J. Sikula, T. J. Buttery, & E. Guyton (Eds.), *Handbook of research on teacher education* (pp. 67–101). New York: Macmillan.

Driscoll, A., Peterson, K., & Kauchak, D. (1985). Designing a mentoring system for beginning teachers. *Journal of Staff Development, 6*(2), 108–117.

Dymoke, S., & Harrison, J. K. (2006). Professional Development and the Beginning Teacher: Issues of teacher autonomy and institutional conformity in the performance review process. *Journal of Education for Teaching, 32*(1), 71–92.

Ehrich, L. C., & Hansford, B. C. (1999). Mentoring: Pros and cons for HRM. *Asia Pacific Journal of Human Resources, 37*(3), 92–107.

Ehrich, L. C., Hansford, B. C., & Tennent, L. (2004). Formal Mentoring Programs in Education and other Professors: A review of the literature. *Educational Administration Quarterly, 40*(4), 518–540.

Evertson, C. M., & Smithey, M. W. (2000). Mentoring Effects on Protégés Classroom Practice: An experimental field study. *Journal of Educational Research, 93*, 294–304.

Feiman-Nemser, S. (1994). *Mentoring in Service of Reform.* Paper presented at the annual meeting of the American Educational Research Association, San Francisco.

Feiman-Nemser, S. (1996). *Teacher Mentoring: A Critical Review.* Retrieved from http://www.eric.ed. gov/PDFS/ED397060.pdf, accessed December 15, 2010.

Feiman-Nemser, S. (2001). From Preparation to Practice: Designing a continuum to strengthen and sustain teaching. *Teachers College Record, 103*(6), 1013–1055.

Feiman-Nemser, S., & Parker, M. B. (1992). *Mentoring in Context: A comparison of two U.S. programs for beginning teachers* (NCRTL Special Report). East Lansing: Michigan State University, National Center for Research on Teacher Learning.

Feiman-Nemser, S., Schwille, S., Carver, C., & Yusko, B. (1999). *A conceptual review of literature on new teacher induction.* Washington, DC: National Partnership for Excellence and Accountability in Teaching.

Fullan, M. (1994). Coordinating top-down and bottom-up strategies for educational reform. In R. F. Elmore & S. H. Fuhrman (Eds.), *The governance of curriculum* (pp. 186–202). Alexandria, VA: Association for Supervision and Curriculum Development.

Glazer, E. M., & Hannafin, M. J. (2006). The Collaborative Apprenticeship Model: Situated professional development model within school settings. *Teacher and Teacher Education, 22*(2), 179–193.

Gratch, A. (2001). The culture of teacher and beginning teacher development. *Teacher Education Quarterly, 28*(4), 121–136.

Grossman, P., & Thompson, C. (2004). District Policy and Beginning Teachers: A lens on teacher learning. *Educational Evaluation and Policy Analysis, 26*(4), 281–301.

Hargreaves, A., & Fullan, M. (2000). Mentoring in the new millennium. *Theory Into Practice, 39*(1), 50–56.

Hellsten, L.-a. M., Prytula, M. P., Ebanks, A., & Lai, H. (2009). Teacher Induction: Exploring beginning teacher mentorship. *Canadian Journal of Education, 32*(4), 703–733.

Hobson, A. J., Ashby, P., Malderez, A., & Tomlinson, P. D. (2009). Mentoring Beginning Teachers: What we know and what we don't. *Teaching and Teacher Education, 25,* 207–216.

Hochberg, E. D., Hawkinson, L. E., Cannata, M. A., Desimone, L. M., & Porter, A. C. (2009). Formal and informal mentoring in the first year of teaching. Paper presented at the annual meeting of the American Educational Research Association, San Diego. Retrieved from http://www.cpre.org/images/stories/cpre_pdfs/aera2009_hochberg_et_al.pdf, accessed December 15, 2010,

Howe, E. (2006). Exemplary teacher induction: An international review. *Educational Philosophy and Theory, 38*(3), 287–297.

Howey, K. (1988). Mentor-teachers as inquiring professionals. *The Education Digest, 54,* 19–22.

Huling-Austin, L. (1992). Research on learning to teach: Implications for teacher induction and mentoring programs. *Journal of Teacher Education, 43*(3), 173–180.

Kagan, D. M. (1992). Professional growth among preservice and beginning teachers. *Review of Educational Research, 62*(2), 129–169.

Kardos, S. M., & Johnson, S. M. (2007). On their own and presumed expert: New teachers' experience with their colleagues. *Teachers College Record, 109*(9), 2083–2106.

Klug, B. J., & Salzman, S. A. (1990). *Formal induction vs. informal mentoring: Comparative effects and outcomes.* Paper presented at the annual meeting of the American Educational Research Association, Boston, MA.

Lee, J. C. K., & Feng, S. (2007). Mentoring Support and the Professional Development of Beginning Teachers: A Chinese perspective. *Mentoring & Tutoring: Partnership in Learning, 15*(3), 243–262.

Lewis, C. (2002). *Lesson Study: A handbook of teacher-led instructional change.* Philadelphia, PA: Research for Better Schools.

Lewis, C. (2005). How do teachers learn during lesson study? In P. Wang-Iverson & M. Yoshida (Eds.), *Building our understanding of lesson study.* Philadelphia, PA: Research for Better Schools.

Lo, M. L. (2009). The Learning Study – a framework for enhancing school–university collaboration that focuses upon individual Lessons. In D. Boorer, J. S. H. Quintus Perera, K. Wood, S. P. Loo, &

S. Sithamparam (Eds.), *Evolving pedagogies: Meeting the global challenges of diversity and interdependence* (pp. 162–181). Bandar Seri Begawan: Universiti Brunei Darussalam.

Long, J. (1997). The dark side of mentoring. *Australian Educational Research, 24*, 115–123.

Martinez, K. (2004). Mentoring new teachers: promise and problems in times of teacher shortage. *Australian Journal of Education, 48*(1), 95–108.

Mullen, C. A. (Ed.). (2008). *The handbook of formal mentoring in higher education: A case study approach.* Norwood, MA: Christopher-Gordon.

Mullen, C. A. (2011). New teacher mentoring: A mandated direction of states. *Kappa Delta Pi Record, 47*(2), 63–67.

Portner, H. (2002). *Mentoring new teachers.* Thousand Oaks, CA: Corwin.

Puchner, L. D. & Taylor, A. R. (2006). Lesson study, collaboration and teacher efficacy: Stories from two school-based math lesson study groups. *Teaching and Teacher Education, 22*, 922–934.

Roberts, A. (2000). Mentoring revisited: A phenomenological reading of the literature. *Mentoring & Tutoring: Partnership in Learning, 8*(2), 145–170.

Roehrig, A. D., Bohn, C. M., Turner, J. E., & Pressley, M. (2008). Mentoring beginning primary teachers for exemplary teaching practices. *Teaching and Teacher Education, 24*, 684–702.

Smith, T. M., & Ingersoll, R. M. (2004). What are the effects of induction and mentoring on beginning teacher turnover? *American Educational Research Journal, 41*(3), 681–714.

Spindler, J., & Biott, C. (2000). Target setting in the induction of newly qualified teachers: Emerging colleagueship in a context of performance management. *Education Research, 42*(3), 275–285.

Stevenson, D. L., & Baker, D. P. (1991). State control of the curriculum and classroom instruction. *Sociology of Education, 64*(1), 1–10.

Strong, M., & Baron, W. (2004). An analysis of mentoring conversations with beginning teachers: Suggestions and responses. *Teaching and Teacher Education, 20*(1), 47–57.

Tang, S. Y. F., & Choi, P. L. (2005). Connecting theory and practice in mentor preparation: mentoring for the improvement of teaching and learning. *Mentoring & Tutoring: Partnership in Learning, 13*(3), 383–401.

Veenman, S. (1984). Perceived problems of beginning teachers. *Review of Educational Research, 54*(2), 143–178.

Wang, J. (2001). Contexts of mentoring and opportunities for learning to teach: A comparative study of mentoring practice. *Teaching and Teacher Education, 17*(1), 51–73.

Wang, J., & Odell, S. J. (2002). Mentored learning to teach according to standards-based reform: A critical review. *Review of Educational Research, 72*(3), 481–546.

Wang, J., Odell, S. J., & Schwille, S. A. (2008). Effects of teacher induction on beginning teachers' teaching: A critical review of the literature. *Journal of Teacher Education, 59*(2), 132–152.

Wang, J., & Paine, L. W. (2001). Mentoring as assisted performance: A pair of Chinese teachers working together. *Elementary School Journal, 102*(2), 157–181.

Wideen, M., Mayer-Smith, J., & Moon, B. (1998). A critical analysis of the research on leaning to teach: Making the case for an ecological perspective on inquiry. *Review of Educational Research, 68*(2), 130–178.

Williams, A., Prestage, S., & Bedward, J. (2001). Individualism to collaboration: The significance of teacher culture to the induction of newly qualified teachers. *Journal of Education for Teaching, 27*(3), 253–267.

Wong, H. K. (2004). Induction programs that keep new teachers teaching and improving. *NASSP Bulletin, 88*(638), 41–58.

Wynn, S. R., Carboni, L. W., & Patall, E. A. (2007). Beginning teachers' perceptions of mentoring, climate, and leadership: Promoting retention through a learning communities perspective. *Leadership and Policy in Schools, 6*(3), 209–229.

Zachary, L. J. (2000). *The mentor's guide: Facilitating effective learning relationships.* San Francisco, CA: Jossey-Bass.

21

Mentoring Student Teachers in Professional Development Schools in Israel

Maureen Rajuan

INTRODUCTION

The metaphorical space in which teacher educators perform their work can be seen as a calm island in the midst of a storm, a still place in the eye of a tornado. Teacher educators are often surrounded by the proliferation of demands of outside forces compounded by inside forces shaped by the specific contexts in which they work. Many are confused by the complexity of theories of professionalism that call for teaching according to a constructivist perspective that is learner-centered while being faced with the hard, cold reality that what seems to really matter are pupils' scores from standardized assessment tests. Teacher educators are often surprised by the rapid worldwide changes in globalization that require them to prepare preservice teachers to cope with the new challenges of technology and multiculturalism while policymakers in local contexts demand greater involvement in work with parents and the community, and practice that aligns with policy. These factors and others contribute to the feeling that teacher educators today must fulfill an impossible role in the changing world of teaching others to teach (Ben-Peretz, 2001).

This grave situation is replicated in the teacher mentor literature which is characterized by a plethora of theories and perspectives concerning the role of the mentor that are in need of economical integration for the generation of effective, multifunctional practitioners. Here, I present a framework for mentoring that seeks to integrate some of the major theories that reflect the current state of research and philosophy. I propose a framework for student teacher development and suggest ways that cooperating teachers can contribute to this learning process shaped by different orientations to teaching and teacher education. I refer to Calderhead and Shorrock (1997) who include orientations that range from the academic, the technical and the practical to the personal and culminate in the critical.

Teacher education programs are increasingly in need of a more negotiated teaching–learning contract between the institution and participants (Montecinos, Cnudde, Ow, Solis, Suzuki, and Riveros 2002). The goal is to arrive at a model that is all-inclusive of the ideology and vision of the institution, while providing the basic knowledge and skills needed for learning to teach. Fuller (1969) advocates a better fit between the curriculum of teacher education and the concerns of newly qualified teachers. Since teacher preparation programs include practical teaching experiences throughout the coursework, the curriculum must contribute to the effectiveness of student teachers' work in the classroom. Conversely, student teaching experiences must be explicitly linked to the practical implementation of educational goals and theories. Korthagen (2010) claims that teacher education is in need of providing student teachers with practical situations of 'situated learning'. This means that they need to be supported through sufficient, suitable, and realistic experiences that promote reflection within a professional community, leading to the development of an intrinsic need by student teachers to create meaning by using theory to promote understanding.

Whereas many researchers and educators have argued for the need to reconceptualize and rebuild the basic beliefs, theories, and structures underpinning preservice teacher education, past orientations to teaching and teacher education can be utilized as a basis upon which to attain higher educational goals. Hargreaves and Fullan (2000: 50) refer to this pyramid model as 'an evolutionary model of professionalism', as I next describe.

RATIONALE FOR A CYCLICAL HIERARCHY OF EDUCATIONAL GOALS

Stages of professional development in teaching and mentoring parallel Maslow's (1943) Hierarchy of Needs model; in it, the lowest stage is described as 'survival'. In this initial stage, technical and practical tools of the trade, as well as subject matter, are acquired, which allow teachers to fulfill basic teaching functions. Management techniques enable the feeling of control and safety in the classroom. In the middle stage, the feeling of belongingness in the classroom and the school's culture present a challenge in which teachers are motivated to gain personal self-esteem and respect through experience and confidence-building. At the top of the pyramid – the highest level – is self-actualization, the stage in which teachers are able to act spontaneously with creativity and morality.

Not only is the development within the higher stages dependent upon those that support them from below, but sustaining achievements in each stage demands an ongoing effort to repeatedly bring about renewed learning of knowledge, skills, and attitudes. Progress through the different stages can be seen as an ongoing spiral that is continuously repeated within each level, leading to subsequently higher levels of development. Thus, basic level skills are reinforced through repetition and initial skills become automatic with time and practice (Fairbanks, Freedman, and Kahn, 2000), while higher order skills are introduced as a continuing challenge. This dynamic process is in accordance with learner diversity, providing an ongoing opportunity for student teachers and experienced teachers alike to progress at their own pace throughout their formal education and professional development. The goal is to foster the student teacher's capacity to learn for future experiences (Zeichner, 1993) and, ultimately, to produce teachers who see themselves as lifelong learners.

Calderhead and Shorrock (1997) claim that while different orientations have competed for dominance in educational innovation in different times and places around the world, the various orientations can be seen as complementary and thus as completing one another. Zeichner (1993) agrees that teacher education programs cannot be classified according to a single orientation, but rather as a synthesis of multiple commitments to various orientations. However, he claims that these commitments do not occupy equal positions in programs because institutions choose to emphasize priorities that reflect select educational and social philosophies. Whereas Maslow's model has been criticized for its choice of needs based on American values of individualism with autonomy and self-actualization at the top of the pyramid (Hofstede, 1984), I wish to emphasize universal democratic and ethical goals of teachers as agents of social change (Calderhead and Shorrock, 1997) as the highest level of conceptualization. I am making this claim with reference to my own cultural background and the national and local milieu in which I work.

Orientations to teaching and teacher education can be seen as a hierarchical framework inclusive of many overlapping, and seemingly conflicting, education theories. In the proposed framework, the academic, technical, and practical orientations comprise the basic level of academic knowledge, technical skills, and practical experiences. In the middle level, the personal orientation deals with practitioners' reflection upon the transition from student teacher to teacher and from experienced teacher to mentor that are connected to the need for feelings of belonging to a community and self-worth. The critical orientation emphasizes aspirations for social and moral change as the highest level on the hierarchy of educational goals.

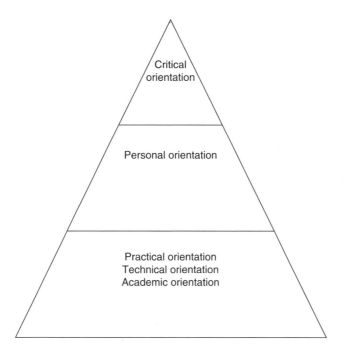

Figure 21.1   Hierarchy of educational goals based on the orientations to teaching and teacher education of Calderhead and Shorrock (1997)

CONTEXT OF THE TEACHING PRACTICUM

Although mentoring of student teachers in schools preceded mentoring of novice teachers by many years, more attention and resources are being allocated to the latter. National and regional mentoring programs for new teachers are gaining in size, funding, and recognition by policymakers in an attempt to counteract the high attrition rate of new teachers, as well as to encourage educational reform through professional development opportunities for experienced teachers. Full-length courses for mentor teachers are increasing in numbers (often with academic accreditation), while guidance for cooperating teachers varies between meetings with the college supervisor in the schools to orientations held at the training institutions.

In the Israeli context, personnel from the training institutions often approach principals or teachers in the schools on an individual basis. Agreement to participate in practicum programs is often voluntary, not mandatory, as it is for all schools that employ first-year teachers. While mentor teachers receive increments and incentives that may translate into an additional rung on the career ladder, cooperating teachers usually do not receive the same kinds of benefits, including recognition.

School principals and staff perceive the immediate benefits of investing in retaining novice teachers in their schools, so many are motivated to assign the best teachers for the job as mentors. This kind of arrangement potentially provides the novice teacher with maximum support. In contrast, school staff members rarely appreciate the long-term effects of mentoring student teachers who are 'visitors' (Martin, 1996) and whose commitments to helping teachers in the building are limited. This disparity largely occurs because student teachers usually do not continue as teachers in the same schools in which their practicum placement is assigned.

For the dual purpose of guidance and assessment, the mentor teacher is required to observe the novice while s/he teaches in classes that are part of her work employment. In contrast, the cooperating teacher must open up her own classroom to student teachers who observe her as she teaches. She must relinquish control over her class and pupils to student teachers who assume the full responsibility of teaching for a scheduled number of hours weekly. The mentor teacher is therefore able to maintain privacy behind closed doors, whereas the cooperating teacher is more vulnerable.

Formal assessment of the work of the novice is part of the requirements of school personnel to the Israeli Ministry of Education, rendering the role of mentor both formally significant and organizationally part of the school system. Mentor teachers are allocated meeting time in which to guide novice teachers through feedback and coaching, and are required to document observations and assessments in written reports submitted to the Ministry. Cooperating teachers, on the other hand, while exempt from this time-consuming obligation, enter into a role whose organization is often vague and undefined with little or no recognized time allocation in which to perform the job. However, the lack of formal assessment by cooperating teachers in many practicum programs allows for a more open and trusting relationship to develop between student teachers and themselves.

Varying conditions of the student teaching practicum and the first-year internship create different and overlapping contexts, each with its own unique set of strengths and challenges. This affects the nature of the mentoring relationships that are formed within diverse organizational structures. Because of such challenges, practicum programs in the Israeli teacher education context are increasingly based on Professional Development School (PDS) models for creating future communities of teacher educators. Next, I suggest ways that theory can be implemented in mentoring programs with student teachers in order to attain goals as well as cope with some challenges experienced within specific practicum contexts.

ORIENTATIONS TO TEACHING AND TEACHER EDUCATION

The traditional orientation: academic, technical and practical

Traditionally, in the preprofessional era, as Hargreaves and Fullan (2000) describe, three of the orientations (i.e., academic, technical, and practical) served in a combinational form as the necessary basis of teaching knowledge and skills.

The academic orientation to teacher education emphasizes the teacher's role as a subject matter specialist and the teacher's own academic expertise as a professional. Recently, a pendulum swing has occurred in which the academic orientationhas been brought back into vogue in many teacher education programs and placed at the top of the pyramid. This is a reaction to low scholastic achievement of pupils in general, as well as the widening gap between pupils of high and low socioeconomic background. Together with a greater emphasis on academic preparation, many teacher education programs now emphasize higher-order thinking skills, metacognition, and self- and peer-assessment of knowledge from a constructivist orientation with the purpose of developing learner autonomy. These approaches have renewed the emphasis on teacher quality with respect to teachers' academic education. Consequently, this emphasis has often neglected other important orientations that are perceived as overly practical or value-laden.

Their college-level course load burdens student teachers as they attempt to fulfill their student teaching responsibilities. Student teachers and cooperating teachers perceive the learning of academic subject matter to be the realm of the training institution, not the school (Williams and Soares, 2000). However, student teaching provides opportunities for narrowing the gap between academic knowledge learned in the training institution and pedagogical content knowledge necessary for the classroom (Ball, 2000). Supervision of cooperating teachers should emphasize the role of the cooperating teacher in acquiring and implementing academic subject matter knowledge in the classroom, thereby connecting college curriculum with practical implementation. This also enhances the feeling of professionalism among mentors in the stage of confidence building (Casey and Claunch, 2005).

The technical orientation emphasizes the behavioral skills, rules, and regulations that create structure and control for class management. Traditionally, mentoring consisted of modeling, practical tips, and techniques such as microteaching, simulations, and models for skills training from a behaviorist approach that sought to determine systematically the competencies needed for teaching.

The mentor course for cooperating teachers in the Israeli context for which I have familiarity begins with the perceptions of the participants in the first stage of mentoring. Participating teachers are encouraged to reveal their uncertainties and doubts concerning the new mentoring role that they have undertaken, in what Casey and Claunch (2005) call the stage of 'disequilibrium'. Through metaphor, one cooperating teacher revealed her lack of confidence as 'the blind leading the blind'. She continued to explain her self-doubts concerning basic technical and practical aspects of her work: 'My classroom management, for example, leaves much to be desired in my eyes, although it has improved. I don't feel that I am organized with checking assignments, etc. and I am desperately trying to get this accomplished this year.' In my educational context, I work with others to encourage our cooperating teachers to recognize their own need for support (Hargreaves and Fullan, 2000) and to share their difficulties with their student teachers.

The practical orientation views the teacher as an artist or craftsperson and attaches importance to classroom experience and apprenticeship models of learning to teach. Traditionally, based on coursework in the college, student teachers acquired the building blocks of practice through an apprenticeship model, as they observed their cooperating teachers and learned by trial and error. The practical orientation in Shulman's (1987) approach is elevated to pedagogical knowledge through which educators seek to integrate subject matter and teaching skills with learners' needs.

Whereas the apprenticeship approach to mentoring may seem outdated today, basic knowledge and skills among new teacher candidates cannot be taken for granted and should be taught in an explicit manner. The constructivist view of learning is based on the assumption that learning is an individual endeavor and that each learner comes to a program with a unique lens and set of experiences, as has been shown by research on student teachers' personal theories (e.g., Knowles and Holt-Reynolds, 1991). The curriculum today must accommodate the diversity of student teachers of different sociocultural backgrounds and life histories that give rise to diverse beliefs and theories concerning education. Teacher candidates must be encouraged to move beyond the knowledge and beliefs of their past by encountering a wide array of different kinds of knowledge and skills in their training program. This demands the creation of a supportive, nonjudgmental climate in which personal theories of individuals are a foundation for further development through learning and practice.

Casey and Claunch (2005) describe the initial stage of mentoring as the 'disposition' phase in which experienced teachers seek professional growth and desire to assist and nurture others. In mentoring relationships in this stage of development, concerns for practical and technical knowledge and skills necessary for survival are often common to both student teachers and cooperating teachers. These form a mutual goal for all participants involved in the mentoring relationship. Whereas student teachers are concerned with immediate survival strategies for classroom management (Fuller, 1969), it has been found that cooperating teachers perceive their mentor role as transferring a body of technical skills to novice teachers (Eraut, 1985; Hargreaves and Fullan, 2000). Recognition of basic needs as a foundation for the mentor relationship aids participants in seeing each other as partners in the classroom for the benefit of their pupils. Building current practices based on respect for the professional expertise of the experienced teacher that has deep roots in the past places the cooperating teacher in the position of role model and facilitator of basic subject matter knowledge and practical wisdom (Hargreaves and Fullan, 2000). The opportunity for cooperating teachers to work with student teachers provides exposure to innovation and renewal as student teachers bring updated teaching ideas and methods fresh from their training programs. Synergy integrates the new energy of student teachers with the perspectives, knowledge, and wisdom of cooperating teachers, all of whom actively teach and learn from one another (Mullen, 2000).

The modern orientation: personal

The personal orientation emphasizes the teacher's interpersonal relations in the classroom and views learning to teach as a process of 'becoming' or personal development. The personal orientation emphasizes the process of internalization and automatic implementation of basic skills, making them one's own and personalizing them to fit one's self and teaching style, resulting in the empowering of student teachers to develop their own teacher identities (Beijaard, Verloop, and Vermunt, 2000). This stage is concerned with personal relationships and the ability to collaborate with pupils, teachers, parents, and administrators in order to build confidence and the feeling of belonging to the school culture (Ben-Peretz and Schonmann, 2000). Similarly, Casey and Claunch (2005) see this stage of mentor development as the 'transition' stage in which mentors develop trusting relationships with colleagues. The personal orientation is the 'cement' that holds the relationship together and allows all forms of collaboration and learning to take place. Research findings point to student teachers' feelings of neglect and lack of caring attributed to their cooperating teachers (Rajuan, 2008). Empathy, communication, and listening skills can be taught to both student teachers and cooperating teachers for the enhancement of interrelationships. Underlying variables that allow for the creation of the student teacher–cooperating teacher relationship that create an optimal match (such as cognitive styles, personality traits, background characteristics, and educational orientations) are in need of more research (Rajuan, 2008).

In practice, during this stage, student teachers are given the opportunity to create their own teaching style and personal professional identity, thus making the transition from passive recipient to active participant in the process of learning to teach (Beijaard et al., 2000). Similarly, Casey and Claunch (2005) depict mentor development in the 'transition' stage as the ability to replace personal agendas with the mentee's agenda. Therefore, teacher education programs must give adequate time for, and emphasis to, reflection as a personal process through which student teachers are permitted some degree of freedom for experimenting in the classroom.

Caring for pupils (Noddings, 2002; Oplatka, 2007) is often taken for granted as part of the teacher' role. However, attention should be given to questions of boundaries and personal involvement, which are often unclear to student teachers who may still identify more with the pupils in their classroom than with the teacher role (Martin, 1996). Similarly, cooperating teachers may view the student teachers as pupils who are mere competitors for their time and resources in their need for attention. The personal orientation deals with the transition from student to teacher role, as well as the transition from teacher to mentor role.

A Western individualistic perspective dominates the current view of the professional self (Hofstede, 1984). There is a need to broaden the personal orientation by encouraging teachers to develop a wider perspective concerning diverse communal and ethnic styles of interaction and learning in relation to the growing multicultural pupil population of school contexts (Doye, 1999), and the greater need to involve parents and other stakeholders (Bekerman and Tatar, 2009) in school life. The personal orientation should be expanded to include the principles of a learning community in which constructivist concepts promote connected learning (Belenky, Clinchy, Goldberger, and Tarule, 1997), which legitimizes learners' knowledge and personal theories. Teacher trainers and education researchers must also take part in the attempt to assume a more balanced position 'with colleagues who are equal but different' (Mullen, 2000: 4) by engaging in learning with cooperating teachers and student teachers. Much research has been carried out for the purpose of uncovering the beliefs (Pajares, 1992), perspectives (Rajuan, 2008), and theories (Knowles and Holt-Reynolds, 1991) of both student teachers and cooperating teachers so these can be integrated into educational theory and practice.

In relation to community, I have worked with others in the Israeli practicum context to create Professional Development School (PDS) models in which principals and their staff engage with university supervisors and student teachers to promote the best possible learning environment. I have experimented with untried ways in our attempts to meet different challenges presented by specific school contexts in order to create viable partnerships in which we perceived the needs of the school as challenges, not impediments, to our own ways of thinking and planning. We designed a school–university partnership model in which student teachers were responsible for after-school hours, both as teachers of new material for gifted children and as providers of reinforcement for remedial help. In another program, we traveled to low-income schools in order to support and strengthen the teaching staff; in these schools, our student teachers became exposed to ways of coping with children of broken homes, who were often hungry and unable to buy school supplies.

Peer mentoring in pairs, or as Korthagen (2010) calls it 'peer supported learning', has always been part of our student teaching framework, as well as experimentation with alternative forms of student teachers working in small groups. Many of these programs have taken creative and innovative forms due to the needs of the schools in which student teachers were seen as an important commodity in lieu of qualified teachers or as additional 'manpower' in overcrowded classrooms. In order to accommodate larger numbers of student teachers in classrooms, cooperating teachers were encouraged to take an active part in co-planning alternative techniques for group work and were, thereby, externally motivated to work in new ways due to the practical benefits of gaining extra helping hands in their demanding classrooms.

Ongoing professional development can be seen in our growing community of teacher educators as more of our graduates accept the cooperating teacher role, complete mentor courses, and participate jointly in educating student teachers. We have been inviting experienced cooperating teachers to study days at the college and to mentor courses to share their experiences with novice mentors. These activities are designed to create a continuum to empower our teaching staff on all levels and to strengthen and sustain our community of educators (Feinam-Nemser, 2001). We hope that some of our experienced cooperating teachers and mentor teachers will one day join our college staff of student teaching supervisors.

The postmodern orientation: critical

The critical orientation emphasizes the role of the teacher in promoting democratic values and reducing social inequities. Theoretically, the last and highest dimension of teacher education should culminate in the awareness of sociopolitical and moral issues within an ecological learning community. In such a community, all participants serve as learners and co-mentors for mutual emotional support and as sources of cognitive knowledge and insight (Le Cornu and Ewing, 2008; Mullen, 2000). In the final stage, students should become aware of the larger context of the school in society, what has been called moral education (van Veen, Sleegers, Bergen, and Klaassen, 2001) or induction into the socialization process in teacher education (Kelchtermans and Ballet, 2001). In addition, there is a need to expose student teachers to universal issues of a pluri-cultural world, peace education, and equal opportunity for the attainment of self-actualization among all world citizens through education (Doye, 1999).

The final stage of mentor development, according to Casey and Claunch (2005), describes the confidence and efficacy of the mentor as the attainment of a personal mentoring style and the recognition of personal strengths with a move from intuitive to intentional practices (see Chapter 6).

In practice, many programs today seek to promote multicultural education in explicit and intentional ways. Israeli endeavors include student teaching programs in which students of different ethnic and national groups (Jewish and Palestinian, religious and nonreligious, veterans and immigrants) teach in each other's schools. Whereas student teachers initially say that teaching in a school very different from the kind of school in which they anticipate teaching in the future is not personally beneficial, they come to understand the value of placement in a school in which past assumptions and habits are no longer valid. Openness to the development of attitudes to other cultures and contexts of diversity serve them well in their teaching careers since the pupil population is becoming more diversified in classrooms worldwide. In addition, pairing student teachers of different ethnic and sociocultural backgrounds has provided rewarding opportunities for student teachers to learn from their peers. In the classroom, these student teaching pairs serve as role models of coexistence to pupils through which subject matter connected to topics of the heritage culture is taught, thus promoting intercultural awareness, communication, and comprehension (Doye, 1999). Based on Allport's (1954) principles, it has been found that sustained interaction between members of different cultural groups decreases fear of the other and builds confidence for interacting more openly with those who are different, with the effect of promoting intergroup coexistence in a natural setting. Mixed student teaching pairs have designed and engaged in projects as leaders in educational change, such as a school play in a religious school in which parents were involved for the first time. Jewish–Bedouin pen pal letter-writing and meetings between Jewish and Bedouin schoolchildren also occurred. These projects were only possible with the vision and support of cooperating teachers, who became enthused and motivated to engage actively with student teachers as agents of change.

Action research has assumed a place of greater significance in teacher education programs as part of student teachers' documentation of their learning and teaching. Action research can be seen as a framework for progression through the stages of learning to teach: Student teachers begin with the practical planning and implementation of lesson plans, progress to reflections on their teaching that produce insights about learning outcomes for pupils and, finally, arrive at ideas about instruction that have social and moral implications.

In our program, action research is carried out within a community of peers of fellow student teachers, supported by the practices of cooperating teachers in the schools and informed by theoretical knowledge that college lecturers facilitate. Projects such as these provide support for student teachers in the multifaceted aspects of learning to teach and present them with an integrated model of theory and practice that connect to their everyday work in the practicum. In my work with other educators, we have encouraged student teachers to incorporate observations and feedback from their cooperating teachers in their pedagogical journal as data in an effort to expand cooperating teachers' involvement in action research. Mullen (2000) presents one ideal model for the co-mentoring of teachers as equal in the design, implementation, and reporting of action research. As in her work, relational inquiry through such forms as joint publications released on an international scale have resulted from some of these collaborative efforts between schools of education and teaching laboratories in schools (Mullen and Lick, 1999).

According to research findings, student teachers need to retain at least some degree of their initial idealism so that their commitment to teaching can be sustained (e.g., Day, Elliot, and Kington, 2005; Shkedi and Laron, 2004). Although student teachers may not always perceive the social relevance of these issues (Martin, 1996), they express many conflicts concerning values and goals of education that have implications that surpass the confines of the classroom. Student teachers should be encouraged to confront their underlying perceptions and beliefs about education even when they are in conflict with those held by cooperating teachers and with what they encounter in the school system. For this purpose, a safe and nonjudgmental environment is facilitated using the framework of supervision for dialogue between student teachers and cooperating teachers: Self-efficacious mentors make the healthy emotional shift to detachment and minimal response in order to nurture mentee's autonomy and independence in the final stage of 'efficacy' (Casey and Claunch, 2005; see also Chapter 6).

In the last stage of our mentor course, we focus on the sociopolitics of the school as reflected in discussion about the teachers' lounge (Ben-Peretz, 2000). This practical focus leads to critical reflection on the school system and its underlying agendas (Kelchtermans and Ballet, 2001). One cooperating teacher cited an educational dilemma that has social implications: 'Our school prepares students for high achievements to enter the high school and those that have the ability will continue and those that don't will leave. We can't meet everyone's needs.' The heated discussion that ensued exposed the cooperating teachers to dilemmas embedded in their work as part of the sociopolitical inequalities of a democratic society and the contested role of teacher as agent of change.

Table 21.1   Overview of educational theories representing developmental stages of the mentoring relationship

Theory	Researchers	Description
	TRADITIONAL	
Basic physiological needs of survival	Maslow (1943)	Breathing, food, shelter, safety
Academic, technical, and practical orientations	Calderhead and Shorrock (1997)	Basic knowledge and skills Classroom management
Age of the pre-professional	Hargreaves and Fullan (2000)	Practical apprenticeship
'Survival' stage	Fuller (1969)	Basic teaching concerns
	MODERN	
Love, belonging, esteem	Maslow (1943)	Friendship, family, self-esteem, confidence, achievement, respect of and by others
Personal orientation	Calderhead and Shorrock (1997)	Transition from student role to teaching role
Age of the autonomous professional Age of the collegial professional	Hargreaves and Fullan (2000)	Individualism and autonomy School cultures of collaboration
Teaching self	Beijaard, Verloop, and Vermunt (2000)	Personal and professional identity
Caring	Noddings (2002) Oplatka (2007)	Emotional relationships
	POSTMODERN	
Self actualization	Maslow (1943)	Morality, creativity, spontaneity, problem solving, lack of prejudice
Critical orientation	Calderhead and Shorrock (1997)	Promoting teachers as change agent
Age of postmodern professionalism	Hargreaves and Fullan (2000)	Diverse clientele and moral uncertainty
Connected learning	Belenky et al. (1999)	Giving 'voice' to minorities and gender equality
Intercultural dimension	Doye (1999)	Retention of pupils' ethnic background; promote understanding of other cultures
Value education	Shkedi and Laron (2004)	Retention of idealism
Micropolitics of teacher education	Kelchtermans and Ballet (2001)	Socialization as micropolitical literacy

CONCLUSION

While the suggestions I have presented are based on one theory of orientations to teaching and teacher education, other equally valid theories may be substituted. The formulation by Calderhead and Shorrock (1997) describes a model of the multiple roles my colleagues and I wish to promote for cooperating teachers, as well as a multifactored framework of knowledge and skills necessary for learning to teach for student teachers. We recommend implementing teaching orientations as a professional language (Hawkey, 1997) through which the goals of the program are conveyed to student teachers, cooperating teachers, and academic staff. Academic preservice training courses can implement orientations to teaching and teacher education to build a framework for including a wide array of education theories to which student teachers are exposed. Complex theories like the orientation framework can be complementary or conflicting. The approach I described promotes the creative development of a personal theory of education among student teachers, rather than their passive socialization or confusion concerning diverse beliefs and perspectives (Zeichner and Gore, 1990). In addition, as Korthagen (2010) claims, teacher education experiences are not as fragmented as the curriculum of some programs may suggest.

In practice, boundaries between the different orientations are blurred and overlap. In our specific context, we endeavor to guide student teachers and their mentors in the acquisition of academic, technical, and practical knowledge and skills through a constructivist approach of personal relationships of care within a community of sharing that reflects social and ethical values. However, because cultures orient differently (Hofstede, 1984), I recommend that educators and researchers assess their own teacher education programs according to different orientations in order to explicitly recognize dominant orientations as products of national and local contexts and to identify implicit orientations that may need additional emphasis.

Teacher education programs undergo changes in perspective and ideology according to a myriad of social, political, and economic factors (Ben-Peretz, 2001). The inclusive formulation of Calderhead and Shorrock (1997) of different orientations to teaching and teacher education can be used to make sense of the wave of change that is compounding feelings of uncertainty and fear in educational workplaces worldwide (Hargreaves and Fullan, 2000). Teacher education programs that are based on a curriculum of diversity will more easily promote flexibility among future teachers to survive 'storms of change' and adapt to novel situations in the ongoing development of their teaching selves (Beijaard et al., 2000). As teacher educators and mentors of mentors, we must assume an inquiry stance in the present in order to withstand the unforeseen 'winds' of the future.

REFERENCES

Allport, G. W. (1954). *The Nature of Prejudice.* Cambridge, MA: Addison-Wesley.

Ball, D. L. (2000). Bridging Practices: intertwining content and pedagogy in teaching and learning to teach. *Journal of Teacher Education, 51*(3), 241–247.

Bekerman, Z. & Tatar, M. (2009). Parental choice of schools and parents' perceptions of multicultural and co-existence education: The case of the Israeli Palestinian–Jewish bilingual primary schools. European Early Childhood Education Research Journal, 17(2), 171–185.

Beijaard, D., Verloop, N., & Vermunt, J. D. (2000). Teachers' Perceptions of Professional Identity: An exploratory study from a personal knowledge perspective. *Teaching and Teacher Education, 16,* 8–23.

Belenky, M. F., Clinchy, B. M., Goldberger, N. R. & Tarule, J. M. (1997). *Women's ways of knowing.* New York: Basic Books.

Ben-Peretz, M. (2001). The impossible role of teacher educators in a changing world. *Journal of Teacher Education, 52*(1), 48–56.

Ben-Peretz, M., & Schonmann, S. (2000). Behind Closed Doors: *Teachers and the role of the teachers' lounge.* Albany, NY: SUNY.

Calderhead, J., & Shorrock, S. (1997). *Understanding teacher education.* London: Falmer.

Casey, J., & Claunch, A. (2005). The Stages of Mentor Development. In H. Portner (Ed.), *Teacher mentoring and induction: The state of the art and beyond* (pp. 95–108). Thousand Oaks, CA: SAGE.

Day, C., Elliot, B., & Kington, A. (2005). Reform, Standards and Teacher Identity: Challenges of sustaining commitment. *Teaching and Teacher Education, 21,* 563–577.

Doye, P. (1999). *The intercultural dimension: foreign language education in the primary school.* Berlin: Cornelsen Verlag.

Eraut, M. (1985). Knowledge creation and knowledge use in professional contexts. *Studies in Higher Education, 10,* 111–133.

Fairbanks, C. M., Freedman, D., & Kahn, C. (2000). The role of effective mentors in learning to teach. *Journal of Teacher Education, 51*(2), 102–112.

Feinam-Nemser, S. (2001). From preparation to practice: Designing a continuum to strengthen and sustain teaching. *Teachers College Record, 103*(5), 1013–1055.

Fuller, F. (1969). Concerns of teachers. A Developmental Conceptualization. *American Educational Research Journal, 6,* 207–226.

Hargreaves, A., & Fullan, M. (2000). Mentoring in the new millennium. *Theory Into Practice, 39*(1), 50–56.

Hofstede, G. (1984). The cultural relativity of the quality of life concept. *Academy of Management Review, 9*(3), 389–398.

Hawkey, K. (1997). Roles, Responsibilities and Relationships in Mentoring: A literature review and agenda for research. *Journal of Teacher Education, 48*(5), 325–336.

Kelchtermans, G., & Ballet, K. (2001). The Micropolitics of Teacher Induction. A narrative–biographical study on teacher socialization. *Teaching and Teacher Education, 18,* 105–120.

Knowles, G. J., & Holt-Reynolds, D. (1991). Shaping pedagogies through personal histories in preservice teacher education. *Teachers College Record, 93,* 87–111.

Korthagen, F. (2010). Situated learning theory and the pedagogy of teacher education: Towards an integrative view of teacher behavior and teacher learning. *Teaching and Teacher Education, 26,* 98–106.

Le Cornu, R., & Ewing, R. (2008). Reconceptualising professional experiences in pre-service teacher education: Reconstructing the past to embrace the future. *Teaching and Teacher Education, 24,* 1799–1812.

Martin, S. (1996). Support and Challenge: conflicting or complementary aspects of mentoring novice teachers? *Teachers and Teaching: Theory and practice, 2,* 41–56.

Maslow, A. H. (1943). A theory of human motivation. *Psychological Review, 50*(4), 370–396.

Montecinos, C., Cnudde, V., Ow, M., Solis, M. C., Suzuki, E., & Riveros, M. (2002). Relearning the meaning and practice of student teaching supervision through collaborative self-study. *Teaching and Teacher Education, 18,* 781–793.

Mullen, C. A. (2000). Constructing co-mentoring Partnerships: Walkways we must travel. *Theory Into Practice, 39*(1), 4–12.

Mullen, C. A., & Lick, D. W. (Eds.). (1999). *New Directions in Mentoring: Creating a culture of synergy.* London: Falmer.

Noddings, N. (2002). *Educating Moral People: A caring alternative to character education.* New York: Teachers College Press.

Oplatka, I. (2007). Managing Emotions in Teaching: toward an understanding of emotion displays and caring as nonprescribed role elements. *Teachers College Record, 109*(6), 1374–1400.

Pajares, M. F. (1992). Teachers' Beliefs and Educational Research: Cleaning up a messy construct. *Review of Educational Research, 62,* 307–332.

Rajuan, M. (2008). *Student teachers' perceptions of learning to teach as a basis for supervision of the mentoring relationship.* Eindhoven: Technical University Eindhoven Press.

Shkedi, A. & Laron, D. (2004). Between Idealism and Pragmatism: a case study of student teachers' pedagogical development. *Teaching and Teacher Education, 20,* 693–711.

Shulman, L. S. (1987). Knowledge and Teaching: Foundations of the new reform. *Harvard Educational Review, 57,* 1–21.

van Veen, K., Sleegers, P., Bergen, T., & Klaassen, C. (2001). Professional orientations of secondary school teachers towards their work. *Teacher and Teacher Education, 17,* 175–194.

Williams, A., & Soares, A. (2000). The role of higher education in the initial training of secondary school teachers: the views of the key participants. *Journal of Education for Teaching, 26,* 225–244.

Zeichner, K. M. (1993). Traditions of practice in U.S. preservice teacher education programs. *Teaching and Teacher Education, 9*(1), 1–13.

Zeichner, K. M., & Gore, J. M. (1990). Teacher socialization. In W. R. Houston (Ed.), *Handbook of research on teacher education* (pp. 329–348). New York: Macmillan.

Adult and Higher Education Contexts

22

Mentoring Doctoral Students in Educational Leadership Programs

Ken Young and Sandra Harris

INTRODUCTION

The attrition rate for students in doctoral programs in the United States and Canada is approximately 50–60 percent (Mullen, Fish, and Hutinger, 2010; Smallwood, 2004). Within the United Kingdom, completion ranges from 57 to 71 percent for full-time students and 19 to 34 percent for part-time doctoral students (Higher Education Funding Council for England, 2005). The attrition rate may be even higher for women and minorities as well as for US students when compared with international students (Council of Graduate Schools (CGS), 2008; Mullen et al., 2010). Smallwood (2006) noted that doctoral students in education are approximately 42.5 years old, compared to 33 in other disciplines. Additionally, education doctoral students take an average of 13 years to complete their program compared to 8.2 years for students in other disciplines.

Researchers suggest that across all demographics and areas of study, the high attrition of doctoral students occurs at the point of transition from coursework to the dissertation (CGS, 2008; Mullen et al., 2010). However, Creighton, Parks, and Creighton (2009) argued that doctoral completion rates actually reveal little about experiences of graduate research students while in their programs. Most studies focus on entry into doctoral programs based on the Graduate Record Examination (GRE) scores and degree completion rates. Little information regarding the student's relationship with faculty is known. Further, there have been limited investigations of doctoral mentoring programs. Evidence suggests that mentoring enhances doctoral student success in terms of retention, persistence, and graduation and that it helps close gaps across demographic groups and academic disciplines (CGS, 2008; Mullen et al., 2010; Nettles and Millett, 2006; Nyquist and Woodford, 2000). For example, Creighton (2007) investigated the relationship between doctoral graduation rates in educational administration at US public universities affiliated with the University Council for Educational Administration (UCEA) and the percentage of students from underrepresented populations, finding that graduation rates ranged from 20 to 30 percent to as high as 94–98 percent. When looking at only those universities with graduation rates of 70 percent or higher, in the same study Creighton found that mentoring of some type was part of every program. Even though some doctoral research students report excellent mentoring experiences (Diamond, 2010; Heinrich, 1991), and others report very poor mentoring experiences (Nyquist and Woodford, 2000), Gonzalez suggested that graduate students need access to 'existing knowledge and values that personal interactions with the faculty bring' (2001: 1625). More recently, Mullen (2005, 2009) urged that proactive mentoring is essential to the success of university students, both academically and professionally, and that it can be seen as an investment for reducing program attrition and increasing satisfaction.

Agreement on a definition of mentoring still proves difficult (Creighton, 2007; Mertz, 2004; Mullen, 2005, 2009; Santos and Reigadas, 2005). Most scholars emphasize the career advancement or professional development of a protégé by someone in a position of authority (Kram, 1985; Mertz, 2004). Within academic environments, mentoring is often viewed primarily as a means for passing along academic norms and values (Goodwin, Stevens, and Bellamy, 1998). Mullen (2005) suggests that mentoring in academic settings extends beyond formal job-related issues and required coursework and that it is a lifelong commitment. In essence, Mullen (2009) has argued that mentoring is integral to the development of human and organizational systems. Further, both formal and informal mentoring networks are valuable to the success of students within academia; specifically graduate students (Mullen, 2006). With this in mind, we borrow Nettles and Millett's (2006) definition, stating, '[A] mentor is a faculty person who establishes a working relationship with a student and shepherds her or him through the doctoral process to completion' (2006: 98). We also recognize that mentoring networks, both formal and informal, exist within academic settings to serve what Mullen (2006) has referred to as ranging from a traditional mentoring to an alterative co-mentoring role.

Because adult learners come to the learning experience with a specific set of characteristics, Grady and Hoffman (2007) suggested that adult learning characteristics have relevance for advising and mentoring education doctoral students. Building on adult learning theory, Brown argued that 'transformative learning is a process of experiential learning, critical self-reflection, and rational discourse that can be stimulated by people, events, or changes in contexts that challenge the learner's basic assumptions of the world' (2006: 706). Transformative learning leads to viewing one's experiences through a new lens, fostering new interpretations. The purpose of the transformative learning experience is not to change values but to examine the experience for possible continued acceptance, revision, or rejection of currently held interpretations of one's worldview (Cranton, 1992). What follows is a brief summary of adult learning theory, specifically the works of Knowles (1980) and Mezirow (1991, 2000), as a lens for providing mentoring opportunities for graduate students. We then describe strategies, formal and informal alike, for mentoring adult graduate students to become practitioner–researchers.

ADULT LEARNING THEORIES

Andragogy and mentoring

The best mentoring practices are thought to be consistent with the principles of andragogy (English, 1999; Zachary, 2000). Knowles' (1980) theory of andragogy suggested that adults learn best when involved in decisionmaking about learning (planning, implementing, and evaluating learning), have a supportive facilitator, and are self-directed. Although adult learning theory has developed into a broad and diverse field since Knowles' seminal work (Merriam, Caffarella, and Baumgartner, 2007), his tenets remain foundational to adult learning. According to English (1999), the way mentoring should take place is through an embodiment of adult learning principles. As such, andragogy provides an important framework for mentoring adult graduate students.

Transformative learning theory and mentoring

Mezirow (1991), Freire (1970), and Brown (2003) argued that transformative andragogy moves beyond the knowledge acquisition model, focusing on connecting theory to practice. This transformation is consistent with Middlebrooks' (2004) challenge that 'the leadership curriculum in higher education must instill a sense of responsibility in potential leaders for being role models and for bringing about positive changes in the school, workplace, and the community' (2004: 443). Senge (1990) noted learning that results in bringing about changed understandings and practice rarely occurs when education programs fail to recognize a shared vision. Indeed, learning in isolation of changing behavior and practices is of little value – thus, learning that transforms practice is 'driven by the heart and soul of the learner's personal/professional goals' (Harris, 2005: 160). Transformative theory provides a framework for facilitating such learning experiences.

Much attention in the adult learning literature has been given to Mezirow's (2000) transformative learning theory, which emphasizes rational thought and reflection in a ten-step recursive learning process, as follows:

1 experiencing a disorienting dilemma;
2 experiencing fear, anger, guilt, or shame;

3 critically assessing assumptions about the world;
4 realizing others have gone through what they are feeling;
5 revising one's old belief system and exploring new ones;
6 planning a course of action;
7 gaining the knowledge and skills for implementing new plans;
8 trying on the new role;
9 becoming competent and confident with the new change; and
10 reintegrating into one's life based on a new perspective.

(Mezirow 2000: 22).

Mezirow (1991) viewed rational discourse as requisite for fostering transformation in learners. Brown (2003) added to this idea, noting that participating in critical self-reflection requires self-awareness, planning, skill, support, and discourse. Although there has been some criticism regarding Mezirow's emphasis on rationality in the meaning-making process (Merriam et al., 2007), the role of experience and critical reflection in learning strengthens the argument for this being a viable and important framework for the mentoring of graduate students. Transformative learning not only facilitates graduate students becoming more knowledgeable practitioners in their field, but also potentially influences their worldview as developing practitioner–researchers.

Many adults who pursue formal education do so to help deal with external changes, such as career advancement or occupational transition, but rarely realize the many internal changes their endeavor will engender (Taylor, Marienau, and Fiddler, 2000). In two studies, Harris (2005, 2007) reviewed 29 reflective essays written about doctoral student experiences, noting that each of the students wrote of personal and professional life changes. These included increasing personal capacity through changed understandings, nurturing service to others through dialogue and building relationships, recognizing the need for authentic leadership that is responsive to all learners, and becoming self aware through critical reflection. Doctoral students acknowledged that mentoring by faculty and other leaders, and the cohort members consistently laid the foundation for this growth to occur. Mezirow's (1991) transformational learning theory provides a mentoring framework for allowing adult learners to reflect critically upon those changes. As Daloz (1999) indicated, adult learning is a transformational journey during which mentors serve as guides. Within the context of doctoral studies in educational leadership, faculty and cohort members have served as mentors who facilitate critical reflection on current practices and paradigms, as well as models for embodying leadership within educational settings. For a relevant case study, see Mullen et al. (2010).

Mentoring strategies

Effective mentoring of adult doctoral students requires the development and implementation of what Mullen (2006, 2009) refers to as 'intentional mentoring' through promising practices and refined strategies. According to Mullen (2006), 'The most successful programs offer a wide variety of interconnected, ongoing activities that students are informed of and participate in and, where appropriate, assume leadership in their developing roles as organizers, presenters, authors, and researchers' (2006: 17). Those programs that are intentional in their mentoring structures or scaffolds provide both formal and informal networks in which graduate students engage in learning. When mentoring networks are formed with the adult learner in mind, they provide mentoring opportunities that support educationally oriented processes of the graduate student and their goals (Mullen, 2006).

Often, the mentoring process is conceptualized narrowly by being limited to technical supervising and advising. As such, the mentoring focuses primarily on 'how to' questions rather than more creative approaches that investigate 'why' or 'what if' questions generated from reflective, open dialogue (Mullen, 2009). Creighton, Parks, and Creighton (2007) conceptualized a cyclical model of planning, practicing, and evaluating to better understand effective mentoring beyond the scope of supervision, and suggested that '[mentoring] is a well-designed *plan* that shapes our specific *practice* and further helps to create an effective *evaluation* of the process' (2007: 166). They recommended two components for effective mentoring and the planning of it: frequency of contact and monitoring of academic progress. Practicing effective mentoring includes providing early and continuous opportunities for doctoral students to become productive in research activities. The evaluation component of the cycle includes a mentoring survey to be used for designing, assessing, and altering mentoring systems.

Alternative ways to mentor are also to be considered as individual faculty members mentor beyond the context of teaching and supervising students (Mullen, 2005). For example, alternative mentoring occurs when mentors take risks by experimenting with educational ideas and seek opportunities for guiding others; when they embrace ideals of equitable opportunity for the traditionally underserved; and when they advocate for their students in concrete ways (Mullen, 2009). Mezirow (1991) argued that adults can change their points of view and that a goal of transformation theory is to encourage reflective processes that enable the evaluation of values, beliefs, and experiences to occur. Thus, alternative ways of mentoring that encourage personal self-evaluation and critical reflection while addressing social justice, democratic ideals, and marginalized populations are framed within an extension of adult learning theory to transformation theory.

Zachary (2000) suggested that there are four phases of an effective mentoring relationship, which are enveloped and operationalized in Chapter 6 by Mullen and Schunk:

- *Preparing.* Mentors take time to critically reflect on the process and skills, as well as mutual interests, learning needs, and assumptions brought into the relationship by both parties.
- *Negotiating.* Mentors and their protégés reach agreement on learning goals, processes for maintaining the relationship, and for defining its content.
- *Enabling.* This is the longest phase of the process in which the protégé is nurtured through open conversations, affirming learning cultures, being asked the right questions at the right time, and by the mentor providing thoughtful and timely constructive feedback. (Zachary, 2000)

- *Coming to closure*: A short phase in which the mentor and protégé establish a strategy for closure of the learning relationship. It encompasses the evaluation of learning that occurred, acknowledging progress, and celebrating achievement.

Whether a mentoring program or group dynamic is individualized, mentoring is built on a trusting relationship that exhibits full acceptance, active participation, and transparency of the protégé as well as the mentor (Levinson, Darrow, Klein, Levinson, and McKee, 1978; Mullen, 2009). Successful mentoring relationships facilitate numerous benefits for all involved (Ehrich, Hansford, and Tennent, 2004).

We next provide practical examples of mentoring in one graduate program, the Center for Doctoral Studies in Educational Leadership (CDSEL). The CDSEL, over a five-year period, had a graduation rate of 96 percent for doctoral students in educational leadership, generally completing their programs within a three-year period. In addition to examples of formal mentoring, such as supervision, instruction, professional development, and training, we also discuss several informal mentoring strategies. These mentoring strategies not only develop collaborative, democratic relationships and extend the notion of mentoring as an ethical act fostering lifelong learning, but they are also grounded in adult learning and transformative theory principles.

Formal mentoring strategies

Although formal mentoring programs and relationships vary in structure and how they are evaluated, they tend to be planned, structured, and coordinated within the context of the institutions (Ehrich et al., 2004). For example, there is considerable variation among undergraduate programs and how or if mentors are formally trained by the institution for service as a mentor, how protégés are assigned to mentors (or *vice versa*), and how or if processes for evaluating the mentoring program exist (Jacobi, 1991). Formal mentoring relationships in academia may also take various forms in that they can occur one-on-one, as in the traditional mentor–protégé relationship (Daloz, 1999; Ehrich et al., 2004), or they may occur in alternative forms such as co-mentoring or in groups (Mullen, 2009). In essence, the primary characteristic of formal mentoring is that the various components of the formalized mentor–protégé relationship (e.g., relational boundaries, objectives, and expectations) are established from the beginning of the program (Mullen, 2009).

When adult learning theory informs formal mentoring strategies, these facilitate transformative learning for the adult learner (Taylor, 2005). Mentoring relationships, regardless of the form (dyads or groups), are created in such as way that the parties intentionally engage in practices that enable adult students to examine their self-conceptions and their existing worldview and to formulate a new or more developed perspective (Daloz, 1999; Merriam et al., 2007). Therefore, the pre-entry interviews, cohort structure itself, aspects of the curriculum (e.g., coursework) and the dissertation proposal all are components of formal mentoring strategies.

Pre-entry interviews

The selection of applicants is critical to the success of doctoral programs (Young, 2005). In the US, many university faculty members use standardized measures such as the Graduate Record Exam (GRE) and Miller Analogies Test (MAT), as well as grade point averages (GPA), as part of the admissions criteria for their graduate programs. While Young found that GRE or MAT scores, as well as graduate and undergraduate GPA, have some utility for determining program entry, they vary considerably in importance. The CDSEL uses this objective information, in addition to years of leadership experience and current professional position, to determine whom to invite for an interview. It is at the pre-entry interview that the formal mentoring of a potential doctoral student in educational leadership begins. During the interview, two faculty members engage the doctoral applicant in a discussion regarding his or her background, motivations, understanding of cultural issues, and personal/professional goals. Throughout the interview process, the interviewers assess adult learner skills in such critical areas as problem analysis, range of interest, ability to plan, self-direction, communication skills, vision, and goals. At the conclusion of the interview, the interviewers communicate to the applicant information about the program, expectations for research quality and other matters, and the dissertation process.

Cohort models

Sometimes within formal mentoring situations, the mentor has the opportunity to mentor groups. Intentional mentoring promotes a satisfying learning environment through cohort learning (Mullen, 2009). The formalized cohort model in graduate programs consists of a group of individuals organized to follow a common course of study at the same time. Mullen et al. (2010) and Nimer (2009) suggest that a cohort model increases the graduation rate of individuals who complete their degrees within a specified timeframe. Nimer (2009) also points out that a cohort model provides a higher rate of continued interaction among members over the lifetime of their professional careers. Within the cohort model, direct communication and socialization among faculty, students, and sometimes other cohorts take place, resulting in an increased chance for individual success. The use of a co-mentoring relationship strategy – a process of reciprocal learning between cohort members and faculty members – contributes to peer mentoring, collaboration, co-leading, and synergistic learning (Diamond, 2010; Mullen, 2009).

Emphasizing facilitation of co-mentoring occurs in the CDSEL program when cohort members are identified. The cohort size averages 20 to 25 members. Faculty members intentionally seek cohort members with diversity in age, gender, ethnicity, experiences, and long-range goals. Although there is research to suggest the importance of mentor pairings or groupings that are similar with respect to gender, ethnicity, age, and discipline, this is less valuable when cohorts are intentionally configured to reflect diversity (Mullen, 2009).

Indeed, in the CDSEL program we have found that diversity among cohort members increases the opportunity for cognitive connections to be made and rational discourse to occur, as students and faculty build on one another's experiences and meanings. Although the process might be enhanced with formal contracts, which could be used to establish cohort ground rules and psychological safety (Mullen, 2006), the time cohort members spend together and the direction faculty mentors provide tend to facilitate these processes. In every evaluation, students comment on what they have referred to as the 'power of the cohort' to support one another through the doctoral process. Not only do students exhibit adult learning and transformative characteristics such as being critically reflective and self-directed, but they also acknowledge and accept their responsibility to support others and participate in discourse that challenges their basic assumptions of the world. One student recently pointed out that the cohort provides him a 'safe place to try on new ideas'. Another student commented that because of the ongoing dialogue with fellow cohort members, she felt that she had '20 mentors who were always ready to offer their support'. Kram (1988) noted that mentoring incorporated project-related support and interpersonal support. Thus, the cohort, created with the intention to provide support in both of these areas, has the inherent potential to serve as a formal mentoring strategy.

Curriculum structuring

Another strategy for enhancing formal mentoring is the intentional structuring of curriculum, including coursework. The primary mission of a research university is not to carry out research, according to Gonzalez (2001), but rather to model how to conduct research and to inspire in students the 'passion for discovery' (2001: 1624). Gonzalez reported that doctoral students express a deep interest in teaching and mentoring and 'want to acquire good teachers and mentors while becoming good teachers and mentors themselves' (ibid. 1625). Consequently, professors are challenged to provide students with learning experiences necessary for accomplishing their needs through exploring ideas for their dissertation, reading relevant literature and reviews, and understanding research methodologies (Mullen, 2010). In every core and elective course, the CDSEL professors focus on connecting theory with practice, which is an important component for adult learners because it addresses the ever-present 'why?' of adult learning (Knowles, 1984). Mentoring procedures are developed intentionally as courses are designed to facilitate mentoring strategies.

The importance of learning to write scholarly for research is a crucial element in the process of earning the graduate degree (Mullen, 2009). Acknowledging this need for students to be successful in a program that culminates in a traditional dissertation, scholarly research writing is emphasized in every course. From the onset of the program, students are mentored through identifying a worthy problem to explore for their dissertation study. Thus, the first semester of the CDSEL program requires a three-hour scholarly writing course, the purpose of which is to prepare students to become research writers. As students write, they receive immediate and detailed feedback from their professors.

Framed within adult learning principles, constructivist-teaching strategies are also emphasized. For example, in a qualitative research course in this program, students are grouped to collaborate on a simulated qualitative research project. They identify a research problem, collect and analyze data, and draw conclusions. This project is presented to the larger cohort and deconstructed for optimal learning. Another course focuses on writing for publication and how to publish in the current scholarly community. The course's professor functions as a mentor and editor, as s/he works with each student to identify an appropriate place of publication for their work and then assists the students with formatting their work according to publication guidelines and the required submission process.

In two core classes (Cultural Influences in American Education and Quantitative Research), professors collaborate to help students individually and in small groups complete a research paper on a cultural issues topic. Identifying a topic related to a problem in their work setting aids in connecting theory to practice, an important component for transformative learning. Thorough, frequent feedback is given to students in the formulation and writing of their problem statement, data collection and analysis, as well as in the presentation of findings. Professors shepherd the student through the process of submitting the paper that is produced to a regional branch of the American Educational Research Association (AERA) association for possible presentation at a conference. These are just a few of the intentional mentoring strategies that are built into the coursework in this 60-hour doctoral program. All of the mentoring opportunities are grounded in adult learning and transformative theory and each one is designed for the optimum success of students in this program.

Pre-dissertation process
The most formal mentoring opportunity at the CDSEL occurs during the dissertation research process. In fact, Grogan, Donaldson, and Simmons (2007) advocate that an 'essential competency of a quality educational leadership practitioner is the capacity to engage in research that fosters organizational learning and transformation' (2007: 83). However, a critical issue in doctoral advising and mentoring is the number of students who have completed all required coursework and examinations, but have not completed their dissertation. In doctoral programs within the US, the students who have achieved this status are often referred to as ABD ('All But Dissertation').

Grady and Hoffman challenge doctoral advisers to commit to 'encouraging the student to completion' (2007: 105). Along with encouraging students to decide on a topic early in their program, the CDSEL initiates the formal dissertation process with a pre-prospectus meeting that is held prior to the proposal defense. Dissertation chairs and committee members acting as supportive facilitators acknowledge the student's self-direction and internal motivation for learning and they provide timely, critical feedback. At the pre-prospectus meeting, held in the fourth semester of the typically eight-semester program, the student presents a ten-page paper that contains the tentative research question(s) to be investigated, background of the problem, possible methodology to be used, and an outline of some relevant literature. The meeting is collaborative and geared towards promoting dialogue, constructive feedback, and power sharing as student and committee work to define and refine the process of dissertation investigation.

The typical result of the pre-prospectus meeting is that students have a sense of direction and confidence as they begin work on the actual proposal, which is usually presented five months later. This additional requirement in the dissertation process strengthens personal and professional relationships among the student, doctoral chair, and committee members. The proposal defense and the dissertation defense that follow continue to provide opportunities for effective mentoring strategies as the committee guides the student to completion of the dissertation and degree.

Informal mentoring strategies

Informal mentoring relationships have traditionally been conceived as those in which a mentor and his or her protégé serendipitously meet (Kram, 1988) and for which the mentor plays a significant role in teaching and developing the novice professional (Ehrich et al., 2004). As Mullen (2005, 2010) points out, the informal mentoring relationship may, like formal mentoring, extend beyond the traditional mentor–protégé relationship to groups and cultures as lifelong mentoring opportunities are sought out. Mullen (2005) also advocates addressing sociocultural learning conditions and the particular cultural mores of one's program setting and discipline when fostering mentoring (Mullen et al., 2010). While the mentoring group model can be formal or informal, it is particularly evident as peers collaborate on shared interests and build developmental networks around them to support their expanding academic and career opportunities (Mullen, 2009).

Although informal mentoring relationships, as characterized in the mentoring literature, take on a less structured form, this does not mean that graduate programs cannot be intentional in providing opportunities for them to occur. One might argue that the existence of graduate programs provides a ripe context for informal mentoring relationships to exist and flourish. What follows are specific strategies within the CEDSEL that incorporate adult learning theory practices and have facilitated the opportunity for informal mentoring opportunities.

Orientation

Prior to the first fall semester when students begin the doctoral program, students attend an orientation. They receive information about the program and meet their new cohort colleagues and professors. Informal mentoring begins at this point because students begin to identify students with similar experiences and interests. They also meet with the cohort that started a year earlier and they have opportunities to learn from the members and begin networking early in the program.

Cohorts

Informal mentoring opportunities occur as conversations that take place within diverse settings, including cohorts. Mezirow (1991) explained that transformation theory is the process of being 'critically aware of one's own tacit assumptions and expectations and those of others and assessing their relevance for making an interpretation' (1991: 4), a process crucial for change. Once again, the intentional diversity of the cohort model leads to this type of learning opportunity. For example, in the CDSEL program some students have experience in K-12 education, while others have professional backgrounds in post-secondary education. The conversations that arise through coursework invariably emphasize the different perspectives students bring to this learning. Students consider this a rich opportunity to hear about education from perspectives other than their own.

Another example of informal mentoring occurred recently in a CDSEL course called Communication in a Global Society, which emphasizes the importance of building relationships through communication with people from differing cultural contexts. After a particularly active cohort discussion regarding minority issues, one student wrote in a critical reflection statement: 'I didn't realize some of the negative stereotypes I had about others, until this class. Now I can begin to overcome these feelings. I can see myself already changing … for the good.' Intentionally creating a cohort membership that is diverse in membership and perspective enhances opportunities for critical reflection.

Research presentations

Nimer (2009) recommended that students have opportunities to expand beyond their comfort zones. One way the CDSEL facilitates this is the seeking out of presentation opportunities for students. A state leadership group sponsors a Graduate Research Exchange, an informal sharing of research projects with other doctoral students and university faculty. We support CDSEL students in voluntarily presenting at this group. A regional group of AERA meets every year; students in the CDSEL are required to attend it in their first year of the program in order to experience how educational research is presented. In their second year, they are required to submit a paper they wrote in a required course. In the spring of every year, the CDSEL hosts a dissertation forum in which cohort students are required to attend and graduating students present their completed research. Through intentional activities like these, informal mentoring occurs as students are given the chance to practice their new learning and to network and build relationships with other doctoral students throughout the region.

E-mentoring

Electronic mentoring or e-mentoring within graduate programs and specifically online doctoral programs is an emerging field that needs further investigation

(Columbaro, 2009). Existing research suggests that many administrators in higher education responsible for hiring new faculty are especially concerned with the mentoring experience of potential faculty hires, while candidates who earned their terminal degree through an online program were more concerned with the convenience of completing their degree from a distance (Adams and DeFleur, 2005; Flowers and Baltzer, 2006). Columbaro (2009) has suggested that e-mentoring relationships in online doctoral degree programs should focus on successful research, teaching, and overall preparation for academic careers in both land-based and online institutions. Further, she encouraged institutions that offer online doctoral programs and e-mentoring study the efficacy of their mentoring program offerings. In doing so, they potentially improve the quality of their programs and address negative feelings that include the quality of mentoring associated with online doctoral degrees.

Mentoring beyond degree completion

Smallwood (2004) reported the attrition rate in doctoral programs could be as high as 50 percent. Mentoring is a critical component for improving the graduation rate of students seeking advanced degrees. As mentors and facilitators of mentoring at the CSDEL, we have intentionally interwoven formal and informal mentoring strategies for adult learners to direct their learning process, critically reflect on their changing worldviews, and translate their learning into action. The results support that mentoring has a positive influence on degree completion. The CDSEL for the past five years has a doctoral student graduation rate of 96 percent; most CDSEL students completed their doctoral degree requirements within a three-year period.

Daloz (1999) challenged educators to not only be concerned with how much students know, but also with how they make meaning with that knowledge and how it affects their continued participation in the learning process. Mentoring accomplishes far more than just completion and attainment of a graduate degree. It also fosters and supports lifelong personal and professional growth. When mentoring is framed with the principles of adult learning and transformative theory, ongoing support is provided for adult students to complete the degree in a manner that honors and challenges them as adult learners.

Recently, a second-year doctoral student in the CDSEL submitted a proposal for presentation at a conference. He shared this reflection illustrating the learning that can occur when a program emphasizes quality of learning, regardless of whether that mentoring is formal or informal: 'I appreciate the expectations that challenge us to grow both personally and professionally. Without these targets, we most likely would never pursue or even attempt these lofty goals that we now comfortably call our own.' This student also shared that the program was helping him 'reevaluate what I currently believe and understand while also testing the validity of my body of knowledge as I gain new ideas'.

Finally, we believe that the effective mentoring of doctoral students can provide the support needed to transition them from coursework to completion of the dissertation to ongoing growth as lifelong learners.

REFERENCES

Adams, J., & DeFleur, M. (2005). The acceptability of a doctoral degree earned online as a credential for obtaining a faculty position. *American Journal of Distance Education, 19*(2), 71–85

Brown, K. (2003). Leadership for Social Justice and Equity: Weaving a transformative framework and pedagogy. *Educational Administration Quarterly, 42*(5), 700–745.

Brown, K. (2006). Leadership for Social Justice and Equity: Evaluating a transformative framework and andragogy. *Educational Administration Quarterly, 42*(5), 700–745.

Columbaro, N. L. (2009). E-mentoring Possibilities for Online Doctoral Students: A literature review. *Adult Learning, 20*(3/4), 9–15.

Council of Graduate Schools (CGS) (2008). *PhD Completion and Attrition: Analysis of baseline demographic data from the PhD completion project.* Retrieved February 4, 2011, from http://www.phd-completion.org/information/book2.asp.

Cranton, P. (1992). *Working with adult learners.* Toronto: Wall & Emerson.

Creighton, L. (2007). Factors affecting graduation rates of university students from under-represented populations. *International Electronic Journal for Leadership and Learning, 11*(7), 1–15.

Creighton, T., Parks, D., & Creighton, L. (2007). Mentoring Doctoral Students: The need for a pedagogy. In C. A. Mullen, T. B. Creighton, F. L. Dembowski, & S. L. Harris (Eds.), *The handbook of doctoral programs in educational leadership: Issues and challenges* (pp. 160–172). Houston, TX: The NCPEA Press.

Creighton, L., Creighton, T., & Parks, D. (2009). Mentoring to Degree Completion: Expanding the horizons of doctoral protégés. *Mentoring & Tutoring: Partnership in Learning, 18*(1), 39–52.

Daloz, L. A. (1999). *Mentor: Guiding the journey of adult learners.* San Francisco: Jossey-Bass.

Diamond, C. T. P. (2010). A Memoir of Co-mentoring: The 'we' that is 'me'. *Mentoring & Tutoring: Partnership in Learning, 18*(2), 199–209.

Ehrich, L. C., Hansford, B., & Tennent, L. (2004). Formal mentoring programs in education and other professions: A review of the literature. *Educational Administration Quarterly, 40*(4), 518–540.

English, L. M. (1999). An adult learning approach to preparing mentors and mentees. *Mentoring & Tutoring: Partnership in Learning, 7*(3), 195–202.

Flowers, J., & Baltzer, H. (2006). Hiring Technical Education Faculty: Vacancies, criteria, and attitudes of online doctoral programs. *Teacher Education, 43*(3), 29–44.

Freire, P. (1970). *Pedagogy of the oppressed.* New York: Seabury Press.

Gonzalez, C. (2001). Undergraduate research, graduate mentoring, and the university's mission. *Science, 293*, 1624–1616.

Goodwin, L. D., Stevens, E. A., & Bellamy, G. T. (1998). Mentoring among faculty in schools, colleges, and departments of education. *Journal of Teacher Education, 49*, 334–343.

Grogan, M., Donaldson, J. F., & Simmons, J. (2007). Disrupting the Status Quo: The action research dissertation as a transformative strategy. In C. A. Mullen, T. B. Creighton, F. L. Dembowski, & S. L. Harris (Eds.), *The handbook of doctoral programs in educational leadership: Issues and challenges* (pp. 76–89). Houston, TX: The NCPEA Press.

Grady, M. L., & Hoffman, S. C. (2007). Guiding the Dissertation Proposal: A student advocacy approach. In C. A. Mullen, T. B. Creighton, F. L. Dembowski, & S. L. Harris (Eds.), *The handbook of doctoral programs in educational leadership: Issues and challenges* (pp. 104–115). Houston, TX: The NCPEA Press.

Harris, S. (2005). *Changing mindsets of educational leaders to improve schools: Voices of doctoral students.* Lanham, MD: Rowman & Littlefield Education.

Harris, S. (2007). Critical reflections on doctoral learning. *Mentoring & Tutoring: Partnership in Learning, 15*(4), 331–332.

Heinrich, K. T. (1991). Loving Partnerships: Dealing with sexual attraction and power in doctoral advisement relationships. *Journal of Higher Education, 62*(5), 515–538.

Higher Education Funding Council for England. (2005). *PhD research degrees: Entry and completion.* Retrieved February 5, 2011, from http://www.hefce.ac.uk/pubs/hefce/2005/05_02/.

Jacobi, M. (1991). Mentoring and undergraduate academic success: A literature review. *Review of Educational Research, 61,* 505–532.

Knowles, M. S. (1980). *The Modern Practice of Adult Education: From pedagogy to andragogy* (2nd ed.). New York: Cambridge Books.

Knowles, M. S. (1984). *The Adult Learner: A neglected species* (3rd ed.). Houston, TX: Gulf.

Kram, K. E. (1988). *Mentoring at Work: Developmental relationships in organizational life.* Lanham, MD: University Press of America.

Levinson, D. J., Darrow, C. M., Klein, E. G., Levinson, M. H., & McKee, B. (1978). *Season's of a man's life.* New York: Ballantine.

Merriam, S. B., Caffarella, R. S., & Baumgartner, L. M. (2007). *Learning in adulthood: A comprehensive guide* (3rd ed.). San Francisco: John Wiley & Sons.

Mertz, N. T. (2004). What's a mentor, anyway? *Educational Administration Quarterly, 40,* 541–560.

Mezirow, J. (1991). *Transformative dimensions of adult learning.* San Francisco: Jossey-Bass.

Mezirow, J. (2000). Learning to Think Like an Adult: Transformation Theory: Core concepts. In J. Mezirow & Associates (Eds.), *Learning as transformation: Critical perspectives on a theory in progress* (pp. 3–33). San Francisco: Jossey-Bass.

Middlebrooks, G. H. (2004). Professionalism and Teacher Leadership Preparation. *Teacher Education and Practice, 17*(4), 432–450.

Mullen, C. A. (2005). *Mentorship Primer.* New York: Lang.

Mullen, C. A. (2006). *A graduate student guide: Making the most of mentoring.* Lanham, MD: Rowman & Littlefield Education.

Mullen, C. A. (2009). Re-imagining the Human Dimension of Mentoring: A framework for research administration and the academy. *Journal of Research Administration, 40*(1), 10–22.

Mullen, C. A., Fish, V. L., & Hutinger, J. L. (2010). Mentoring doctoral students through scholastic engagement: Adult learning principles in action. *Journal of Further and Higher Education, 34*(2), 179–197.

Nettles, M., & Millett, M. (2006). *Three magic letters: Getting to Ph.D.* Baltimore, MD: John Hopkins University Press.

Nimer, M. (2009). The Doctoral Cohort Model: Increasing opportunities for success. *College Student Journal, 43*(4), 1373–1379.

Nyquist, J. D., & Woodford, B. J. (2000). *Re-envisioning the Ph.D.: What concerns do we have?* Seattle, WA: Center for Instructional Development and Research/ University of Washington.

Santos, S., & Reigadas, E. (2005). Understanding the student–faculty mentoring process: Its effects on at-risk university students. *Journal of College Student Retention, 6*(3), 337–357.

Senge, P. (1990). *The fifth discipline.* New York: Doubleday Business.

Smallwood, S. (2004). Doctor dropout. *The Chronicle of Higher Education, 50*(19), A10.

Smallwood, S. (2006). Driven by foreign students, doctoral degrees are up 2.9% in 2005. *The Chronicle of Higher Education, 53*(15), A12.

Taylor, E. W. (2005). Making meaning of the varied and contested perspectives of transformative learning theory. In D. Vlosak, G. Kielbaso, & J. Radford (Eds.), *Proceedings of the 6th international conference on transformative learning* (pp. 459–464). East Lansing, MI: Michigan State University.

Taylor, K., Marienau, C., & Fiddler, M. (2000). *Developing adult learners: Strategies for teachers and trainers.* San Francisco: Jossey-Bass.

Young, I. P. (2005). Predictive validity of applicants' reference information for admission to a doctoral program in educational leadership. *Educational Research Quarterly, 29*(1), 16–25.

Zachary, L. (2000). *The mentor's guide: Facilitating effective learning relationships.* San Francisco: Jossey-Bass.

23

Mentoring and Coaching in Further Education

Janet Oti

INTRODUCTION

The intention of this chapter is to outline mentoring and coaching as seen in further education (FE) in England and Wales. A brief overview of FE and its importance to policy makers will initially set the scene. An exploration of the meaning of mentoring and coaching and its role in FE then follows. The change in initial teacher training through a more formalised and focused emphasis on mentoring is discussed and the possible implications highlighted. Relevant research is investigated and a research agenda identified. Later sectors of the chapter draw upon the author's own personal experiences of mentoring within FE and why mentoring is so important for students as well as staff within the sector. The rise of mentoring as an important concept and process is observed; for example, with the introduction of a new BTEC qualification for peer mentoring (Edexcel, 2010). Barriers to effective mentoring are identified and the potential for future research and development is discussed.

CONTEXT AND BACKGROUND

Until the 1960s, when the grammar, technical and secondary modern schools began to be replaced by comprehensive schools, those who did not go to grammar school were unable to study A-levels. Adults who wanted a second chance to improve their academic qualifications were able to attend technical college. The numbers of young people who preferred to study within an adult environment of a college increased (Hall, 1990). The Russell Committee Report (1973) perceived adult education as meeting the needs of three kinds of people: those who wished to continue with formal education, those who wished to pursue creative studies and those who wished to expand their role in society. Hence, adult education was variously provided by FE colleges, adult colleges and centres, and by voluntary bodies. The link was made in the 1960s between education and economic prosperity. The economic crisis of 1973 and the resulting world recession then followed. High unemployment levels and the 'Great Debate' over education, started by James Callaghan in 1976, further promoted the link with education and particularly FE to that of training (Chitty, 1991; Chitty and Simon, 1993; Green, 1991). This link between education and the economy has not diminished and appears particularly relevant for FE today.

FE has always been dynamic in its educational approach and proactive rather than reactive regarding change (Pring, 1995). FE has always been linked to social and economic needs. Indeed Fowler, Moris and Ozgat (1973: 183) stated: 'The Virtue of FE is that it is as flexible as a rubber hose and highly sensitive to social demand.' Many government policies have influenced FE and the post-compulsory sector. Once referred to as the post-16 sector, the expansion of compulsory education with the 14–19 Learning Pathways (which encourages greater partnerships and creative provision between schools and colleges), has resulted in uncertainty. Blending of the boundaries between the ages of 14 and 19 and what defines post-compulsory education leaves some individuals, including teachers, feeling confused. Confusion is augmented by the titles given to this sector including community colleges, technology colleges, adult education, tertiary and FE colleges. All come under the umbrella of post-compulsory education and training, often referred to as the Life Long Learning and Skills sector. While it is often defined as all the provision available after the age of 16 years (excluding universities), it has increasingly been seen to include some 14-plus age group provision.

FE is seen as a main driver for skills development throughout the UK, but for FE to be successful support is required. Today FE colleges are at the heart of the drive to meet the skills and productivity challenge of the economy. This can be seen in report such as the Leitch report (2006) and to some degree the Webb report (2007) which centred on the role of FE in Wales. However, with the economic climate being in recession, change is again on the agenda as outlined by the Innovation, University, Science and Skills Committee in 2009.

Lord Leitch published his review of skills two years ago, in December 2006. It set out ambitious targets for 'up-skilling' the UK population which government adopted enthusiastically. But since then the economic climate has worsened, and our evidence was taken at a time when the thrust of skills policy was already under review ... Re-skilling, rather than up-skilling, is increasingly becoming the norm and it is our view that targets and the government allocation of resources must change to reflect that.

Innovation, University, Science and Skills Committee, 2009: 3

Debbie Andolo (2007) in the *Guardian* newspaper provides an article heading that spells it out: 'When you need someone to lean on: Young people at risk of dropping out of further education benefit from mentoring support system'. With the recent shift in government power, from New Labour to the present coalition government of Liberal and Conservative parties (2010), educational change is once again on the agenda. The concept and importance of mentoring was raised by Michael Gove, Secretary of State for Education, in his speech made to the National College Annual Conference in Birmingham on the 16 June 2010:

> Mentoring others is often the best form of professional development … As well as giving teachers more control over their classrooms I want to give them control over their careers.

Indeed Michael Gove was promoting the benefits of mentoring back in 2008 in a speech entitled 'Why Conservative social policy delivers progressive ends':

> [W]e want state help to be as personal, intimate, human and responsive as possible, reinforcing relationships and working with the grain of human nature. There when you need it, not when it suits the Government. Freely available mentoring.

One wonders exactly what Gove means by 'mentoring'. The hope is that it is not perceived as a cheap alternative to staff development in order that budgets and finance can be effectively reduced even further by government. Oti (2008: 184) discussed policies and their implementation and observed the need to take 'note of past problems'. In other words, if policies are to be successful in the future then we must learn from the past.

MENTORING AND COACHING

As we begin to explore the notion of mentoring in FE, we would do well to focus on its counterpart, coaching. A symbiotic relationship between these concepts is reinforced by Wallace and Gravells (2005: 73), where they explain: 'As a mentor in FE we sometimes need to coach our mentees in order to help them improve their performance in specific areas'.

But is mentoring and coaching the same or are they conceptually different; to be kept segregated at all costs? Are there areas of overlap, subtle changes according to the context they are used in? For some there is little difference between the terms (Carpenter, 2009; Oti, 2009). Others do see subtle differences between the role of mentor and coach as outlined in the National Framework of Mentoring and Coaching by the Centre for the Use of Research and Evidence in Education (CUREE), but they still agree there is much overlap (CUREE, 2010).

Mentoring can involve a closer and more meaningful relationship with an individual, be formal or informal in nature and cover a substantial period of time. Coaching on the other hand may be viewed as being more impartial with greater critical assessment. It may be more short term, be task specific and involve either one individual or a group of people. Mentoring and coaching relate closely to tutoring and counselling and can be seen as two sides of the same coin within FE. They overlap with teaching: '[M]entoring is not simply a leadership or supervisory role, but … qualities and skills implicit in what we think of as good teaching' (Wallace and Gravells, 2005: 104).

Coaching is viewed as a more practical activity, more inclined towards sports and physical education. Mentoring is more concerned with guidance and counselling in the academic arenas relating to study, career and life choices. However, Wallace and Gravells, (2005: 2), remind us that

> mentoring takes several different guises within FE colleges … some relationships or arrangements … currently referred to loosely as 'mentoring' would not be recognised as such by the world of industry and commerce.

The Brefi Group website highlights the difference between mentoring and coaching as well as counselling and coaching in relation to commercial industries and how the Chartered Institute of Personnel and Development (CIPD) list characteristics which many organisations agree with. They explain:

> The CIPD differentiates between coaching, mentoring and counselling. It is helpful to understand these differences as, although many of the process are similar, they are generally delivered by individuals with different qualifications and different relationships with their client'.
>
> Brefi Group, 2010

Mentoring also involves reflection; something that is replaced in coaching by repetition if it is purely skill based. Reflection is seen as a pivotal activity in the role of mentoring, in order that progression can be effective. Roffey-Barentsen and Malthouse (2009: 99) explained it as follows:

> [A]ll reflection requires a level of self awareness. This may not always be a comfortable process: looking at your own values, behaviours, questioning them and acknowledging where they came from, may be a bit unsettling. It requires honesty and commitment.

For Boud and Walker, (1998), mentoring can stimulate students to reflect in an educational setting, or otherwise. Indeed it could be argued that it is the context which dictates whether mentoring or coaching occurs. 'The DfES recognises that the ways mentoring and coaching are used depend on the context' (CUREE, 2010). This context factor was also uncovered in the findings from a small research project completed in FE (Oti, 2009). As Tedder and Lawy (2009: 423) also observed from their research in UK, 'there is no simple or consistent understanding of what "mentoring" means'.

Because little difference is perceived between these terms in FE, the terms 'mentoring' and 'coaching' will be used interchangeably through this chapter and we therefore subsume 'coaching' within 'mentoring'. Mentoring between teachers and students aims to promote learning and personal development, and also is used between members of staff to aid one another's professional development. Thus, mentoring can be seen as a tool to improve organisational effectiveness through increased motivation, supporting change, improving staff retention, increasing recruitment and promoting learning and training. Research by Allen and Eby (2004) suggests that individuals who hold roles as mentors advance more rapidly in an organisation, earn higher salaries, have a favourable work attitude and are more retainable. Even where a very informal approach is taken to mentoring, the key aspect will be development of the mentee's personal (and professional) development. Crucially, it is the mentee who exerts control in this process and has ownership, not the mentor.

In FE mentoring relationships are usually voluntary and trust-based and may be subject to formal or informal arrangements. Mentoring can be seen in relationships between staff and students, (some being developed through tutorial systems), between experienced and new staff members of the organisation, via management shadowing and of course relationships with trainee teachers. Carpenter (2009: 63), cites Miller (2002) explaining the difference between informal and formal mentoring as 'natural or planned'. In FE, as elsewhere, successful mentoring schemes require matching the right mentor to the mentee. However, as O'Connor and Laidlaw (2006) explain: 'The matching of mentor to mentee is one of the most important parts of a mentoring programme but can also be one of the most problematic' (2006: 46).

With the introduction of mentoring as a main facet of teacher training in recent years, more formalised, structured mentoring is being established. This was in response to an Office for Standards in Education (Ofsted) report on FE teacher training in 2003, which highlighted the lack of 'systematic mentoring and support in the workplace' (Ofsted, 2006: 1). Few opportunities for trainee teachers were identified regarding subject specialism mentoring, a weakness of the practical elements of the teacher training programmes provided. Those teachers in FE on part-time contracts pursing teaching qualifications often had no mentor support at all.

> In many colleges, senior management still give insufficient attention to the quality of ITT provided for their staff, despite the obvious link between the quality of teacher training and the standards of teaching and learning in the colleges they manage.
>
> Ofsted, 2006: 2

Tedder and Lawy (2009) suggest that although there remains a clack of clarity about the meaning of mentoring, it is being used by government and the Office for Standards in Education (Ofsted) as an assessment tool, forming a judgemental model, with informal or natural mentoring, which still takes place with new colleagues (peer mentoring), being described as a developmental model.

> [T]he role of mentors and teacher trainers has shifted to one where they are required to ensure that trainees write action plans to set targets that can become evidence of achievement of the LLUK standards. There is a move away from the developmental model underpinning *Mentoring for excellence* and towards a model that is more judgemental but is favoured by agencies like Ofsted.
>
> Tedder and Lawy, 2009: 417

Thus, the increase in formal mentoring roles in FE is set to rise. But, as Ofsted (2006: 2) identify, 'these schemes are at a very early stage of development and the quality of specialist support given to trainees is uneven'. Indeed the results from Tedder and Lawy's (2009) research project confirmed that the quality of the mentor and mentee relationship was more important and 'more significant to successful mentoring' (2009: 424) than subject specialism mentoring. This is also borne out by Glasson (2008), whose findings confirm that the relationship between mentor and mentee is vital for good mentoring experience. 'In some cases the mentees have actively sought out someone who they respected and liked even if they had been officially allocated another person' (Glasson, 2008: 13).

RESEARCH, REFLECTIONS AND DISCUSSIONS

Research literature relating to mentoring and coaching in the UK tends to focus upon initial teacher training (ITT) programmes in Higher Education (HE) and trainee teachers in the workplace. Data is also available regarding mentoring used within business as an organisational tool. As Carpenter (2009: 64), observed

> much research on the utilisation of mentoring for initial teacher training (is available) … but the majority of information … was orientated at mentoring practice within the business/ industry settings.

In the past the mentoring role appears to have had a much higher and professional profile in schools than in post-compulsory education. In FE mentoring trainee teachers in a formal capacity was seen as an additional burden for overstretched staff (Oti, 2009). Perhaps this is because some FE establishments failed to see the financial gain for the department, school or faculty involved in the process. To compound the issue, staff ratios involved in mentoring trainee teachers in FE tend to fluctuate year on year; quite often with new members of staff taking on this role, some being fairly new to the teaching profession (ibid.).

Naturally, each establishment is different and some colleges may take the role of mentoring trainee teachers quite seriously; therefore a blanket negative impression of all FE institutions would be wrong. Indeed mentoring has taken on a much more significant role as mentioned above, especially since the introduction of compulsory training for all post-compulsory teachers. This can be seen with the introduction of the Further Education National Training Organisation (FENTO) standards in 2001 and guidelines from the Office for Standards in Education (Ofsted) in 2001 and 2003. Other interested bodies have also become involved such as the Department for Education and Science (DfES, 2004) and the Lifelong Learning and Skills UK department. Mentoring, and its importance in teacher training, is highlighted by Catapano (2006: 95):

> Through reflection and discussion with a mentor, pre-service teachers learn to peel away the layers of an issue to unearth the underlying problem and then brainstorm possible solutions.

Although we are able to gain an insight into initial teacher training, as yet scant attention has been focused on mentoring as a teaching aid in FE, and the perceptions of students and staff to the mentoring role. Carpenter (2009) and Miller (2002) refer to informal mentoring being natural and formal being planned but this may be a somewhat simplistic view of mentoring. Mentoring can occur through friendships made and therefore be classed as natural but informal mentoring can also be planned.

Little research seems evident on the difference between mentoring and coaching in FE. Silver, Lochmiller, Copland and Tripps (2009) report on supporting new school leaders through a university based leadership coaching programme. They suggest 'there are few research studies concerning the effectiveness of coaching programs … [but there are] a number of empirical studies related to principal mentoring programmes' (2009: 218).

Some Australian authors have argued that mentoring in the western world is now being driven by assessment and judgement.

> Today, mentoring of academic staff is undergoing a process of transformation. Staff activity is monitored and mentoring is increasingly assuming an audit function.
> Buchanan, Gordon and Schuck, 2008: 241

Indeed, this same conclusion is argued by Tedder and Lawy (2009) from the UK. Hence, care is needed with formalised staff (peer) mentoring. However, peer mentoring for students is seen through a different lens, and is viewed as important in the fight against bullying. Indeed Edexcel (2010) has introduced a new BTEC qualification available at level 2, entitled Peer Mentoring.

Research also suggests some gender differences in the mentoring role in that male mentors reported providing more career mentoring whereas female mentors more psychosocial mentoring (Allen and Eby, 2004). Woodd (2001) argues that different individuals would perceive and interpret the role of mentoring differently from one another. Also, the level of skills would differ in each individual (e.g., communications), depending upon their subject background. Perhaps it is here that we can see more clearly the link to coaching being more male dominated in that it relates to the more hardened subjects of physical prowess. The female gender aligned more to the caring and communicative aspects of mentoring. However, this is an aspect which deserves more research so will not be fully discussed here.

Oti (2009), in a small research study, found that FE staff were unanimous in their perceptions that mentoring was an important part of teaching. Findings suggested that the terms coaching and mentoring were used interchangeably in the work place, according to teaching subject disciplines. For some staff there was a little confusion regarding the most appropriate term to use. Those who taught more active subjects were more familiar with the use of coaching as a term, but perceived its role as the same or similar to that of mentoring. Results from this small study indicated that staff felt that their mentoring role (which included tutoring and pastoral care) was squeezed out by other demands made by external influences including data gathering exercises and bureaucracy. Informal and formal mentoring schemes were in evidence although formal mentoring was on the decline due to workload pressures. Formal staff mentoring (peer mentoring) was not seen generally, although management in some FE establishments was slowly introducing mentoring as an organisational tool for new managers (management shadowing). To date there has been little evidence of sustained research into FE mentors' perceptions of their role but in the next section we redress this by exploring the author's own experiences.

A MENTOR IN THE FE SECTOR: A NARRATIVE AUTOBIOGRAPHY

With over 18 years of teaching in FE, my experience has covered formal and informal mentoring roles involving both staff/colleagues as well as students. Within my teaching role, I had responsibility for a group of students and held formal tutorial sessions. In the early days (late 1980s), pastoral care was important and was included in these sessions. Some sessions were arranged for one-to-one appointments and others for whole group tutorial sessions. The individuals within the group were guided, advised and mentored, even after leaving college in many cases.

Over the years, the context of the tutorial sessions changed to ensuring documentation was completed and records updated. Attainment of key skills became important and other issues more relevant than the role of effective mentor. However, good teachers still wanted to mentor individuals they saw had potential and so mentoring carried on but in a more informal, ad hoc and casual manner for students generally. When students had problems one could now refer them to the college counsellor. This was someone who was a 'professional' and had the time to sort out some of the personal problems that faced students which tutors had dealt with or advised in earlier times. Concerns such as potential pregnancy, homelessness due to fights with parents and court/police procedures for petty crimes are examples of some of the student problems I encountered.

Hence, mentoring, and indeed counselling for some students, was clearly evident in those early days in my career. Throughout my career, and even today, colleagues I work closely with have been informally mentored (either by me or another). Those who entered the profession as a trainee or newly appointed teacher in FE were encouraged and supported until they felt confident in their abilities and in dealing with the processes and systems in place. In the main these mentoring relationships tended to be informal, although newly appointed staff and trainee teachers may need some formal elements included in the mentoring role. These formal elements could be progress reports, for example, or monitoring and signing off direct teaching hours that trainee teachers have been required to complete as part of their 'on the job' work experience.

Within my role in FE, I also managed a group of teachers who were seconded to a curriculum initiative that I project managed within the college. This covered a period of approximately six years and again a mentoring role to staff and colleagues was evident. This curriculum initiative project involved a variety of different staff with different backgrounds; including teachers, support staff and other project managers. Thus, the mentoring relationships were different and somewhat multi-layered. Each mentoring relationship needed to be tweaked according to individual needs and requirements. Indeed some mentees are still in contact with me from those days and a mentoring relationship still exists.

On reflection, most of my experience in FE rests upon informal mentoring, whether this is for students or colleagues. I would argue that most informal mentoring is voluntary, and must be so to be successful. However today in FE most informal mentoring is not recognised or rewarded. For many FE lecturers and teachers with a heavy workload and demotivated students, mentoring is just an additional burden they can ill afford to do. My role today in education involves supervising PhD and MA students with their research. This also involves a mentoring role. Mentoring seems synonymous with teaching in many ways. Perhaps this is because for teaching to be successful, barriers to learning must be removed. Teachers need to be aware of personal barriers that may inhibit learning and provide support and guidance as appropriate. When viewed under this lens it is easy to see why counselling, coaching and mentoring are often confused and used interchangeably. This is due to the fact that all have some similar elements and make-up. The dividing line between them is therefore easily blurred.

THE IMPORTANCE OF MENTORING IN FE: A PERSONAL PERSPECTIVE

FE is a dynamic, varied sector of education. It deals not only with mature students but young adults and adolescents. Some of these students could be classified as vulnerable, their backgrounds and social welfare potentially being more disadvantaged than others. Not doing well in school has forced some adults to return to FE to address their educational needs. Others return to develop or broaden their skills. Some may attend purely for social reasons and to make new friends or acquaintances. Younger students attending FE do so because their school may not provide the course or programme of study they want to pursue. For some it may be because their friends are attending college. Whatever their purpose in attending college students need mentoring. In recent years even younger students are seen in the corridors and classrooms of many colleges (14-year-olds) due to the partnership programmes existing between colleges and their local schools. More adolescents turned to college in order to obtain the Educational Maintenance Allowance (EMA), finding this preferable than being on the dole or staying on at school (although the EMA is soon to disappear in England). All this has had an influence on the culture and environment of colleges, and particularly for staff who have to deal with many of the issues these students bring. Thus, what we see is a pressing need for more student mentoring overall and certainly not less.

However, formalised mentoring in FE between student and tutor has been on the decline over the past two decades. I use the word formalised in this context to emphasise identified and recognised mentoring roles. With other pressing documentation needing completion during tutorial time, there is little if no time left to mentor students effectively. Pastoral care, as mentoring was described in my early years of teaching, needs to return to education. From the earlier discussions, we see illustrated the need for mentoring in FE. To ensure a society that feels nurtured, guided and supported, mentoring is a vital tool. Rather than individuals who are unknown to students providing help, such as the college counsellor and careers officer, let mentoring with the support from these specialists along with the tutor return to FE and be recognised. Informal mentoring will still go on but perhaps it is time for some of this to change to a more highly recognised and valued activity and role. I am not saying 'turn the clocks back', but instead incorporate the positive and fruitful elements of the past and incorporate mentoring and pastoral care for students to reduce barriers to learning.

EXTENDING THE INCIDENCE OF MENTORING IN FE: POTENTIAL IMPLICATIONS

Time is required for effective mentoring. This has a cost implication and impacts on funding. Time to mentor, and therefore funding, is perceived as being the main implication if FE is to have effective mentoring for both students and staff. Indeed effective mentoring can help staff to cope and manage the constant change FE has experienced and is likely to continue to experience.

Unfortunately, with increasing financial pressures, it seems unlikely that greater funding will be made available anytime soon. Mentoring students regarding their career and future prospects, social, medical and personal problems undoubtedly brings great rewards, enabling progression and academic and/or vocational achievement. Staff mentoring can be a useful organisational tool, reducing the costs of staff development yet being more effective in the long term. Indeed continuous professional development (CPD) is now a 'hot' topic in the world of FE and is seen by some managers as a cheaper alternative to staff development. As Roffey-Barentsen and Malthouse (2009: 3) observed:

> [T]hose teaching in the lifelong learning sector now have to partake in and reflect on their professional development. If you are a full-time teacher you are expected to show evidence of at least 30 hours of continuing professional development (CPD) each year.

According to Klasen and Clutterbuck (2002), short courses used for staff development purposes are not effective and are forgotten by more than three-quarters of staff within a month of the time of the training. Soft skills and emotional intelligence are becoming more important, particularly in a leadership role, and has added to the interest in mentoring as a concept and development strategy. Greater emphasis on mentoring throughout an establishment may be pursued by FE management, especially if seen as a cost-saving exercise, but again, implementation may prove to be more difficult.

> There is a lot of anecdotal evidence that formal training of mentors and mentees has been an important component of a number of successful mentoring programmes.
>
> O'Connor and Laidlaw, 2006: 46

Little remission in many cases is given for mentoring in FE and some staff may decline the mentoring role due to work pressures. Others may take the role on and areas of responsibility as part of their workload under protest, or complete this role purely as a gesture of goodwill only. Teaching staff may be persuaded to take on the mentoring role, as Cunningham (2007: 287) points out from a 'no one else available syndrome' to the current position. Admittedly, he adds, this remains rare.

Today, formal mentoring for trainee teachers is an important aspect and is being highlighted as such in teacher training programmes in the UK. On some part-time programmes, for example, mentoring is so important that in order to gain admission a potential student must identify a mentor who will support them. With more formalised mentoring roles encouraged in teacher training programmes, workloads for staff in FE are likely to increase. In a meeting in June 2010 with franchised centres (who deliver higher education (HE) in an FE environment), the following was recommended. Professional training and development should be offered to all FE mentors; remission or some form of recognition for the mentoring role must be evident making it more appealing to staff, and a database of subject mentors should be established to aid continuity. Clarification was identified as being needed regarding the role of mentors and investigations into whether coaching, as a distinct but related activity, would be useful.

Examining the role of (FE) mentoring for initial teacher training, Tedder and Lawy (2009: 425), make a valid point, applicable to all mentoring roles in FE, when they explain that:

> [d]ifferent colleges make use of ... staff in different ways and this has an impact on the provision of mentoring ... Mentoring raises issues for college managers in sorting out roles and responsibilities, how roles like advanced teachers and subject learning coaches should relate to mentoring functions.

However, an interesting observation is made by Cunningham (2007: 293), when discussing teacher training: '[W]e may find colleges placing successful mentoring far more prominently in their criteria for the award of "advanced skills" status.'

CONCLUSION

In FE, the use of the terms 'mentoring' and 'coaching' are used interchangeably as it is the context that differentiates their practice. More active subjects such as physical education and sports use the term coaching whilst those courses with subjects viewed as more academic use the term mentoring. However, great similarities between the two are indeed apparent. This is an area where further research should be pursued, aiding transparency between these concepts. Like Saunders and Welsh Assembly Government (2008), who investigates the role of the learning coach, I strongly uphold greater clarity between the roles of mentor and coach.

Student motivation and achievement have a high profile today, especially as they are linked to FE funding. In view of the present restrictive economic climate, this is likely to increase in importance as taxpayers' money and the way it is spent is scrutinised more closely. Hence, student mentoring is becoming more important and not less so.

Some authors have argued that formalised mentoring in FE is not as effective as informal mentoring and that care will be needed to ensure mentoring is not turned into a formalised judgemental tool, used by management and government as an assessment implement (Tedder and Lawy, 2009). But whichever method is adopted, whether it is formalised of informal mentoring, one thing is certain and that is 'time' is required. This is important to enable the relationship between mentor and the mentee to flourish by organising regular meetings. Such regularity is necessary whether the mentoring relationship is between staff and colleagues or involves trainee teachers or students. But time has a cost element and with cutbacks in education budgets this may not be regarded as feasible by management. Clearly, care is needed as effective mentoring brings additional responsibilities to the workloads of existing FE staff (Oti, 2009).

In order to make the role of mentoring more attractive, incentives need to be in place. There is a pressing need for experienced and qualified staff who are capable and willing to take on the role and the responsibilities attached to being a mentor. As Cunningham (2007: 283) has identified:

> The college sector has not presently been able to claim that a large pool of suitably qualified and motivated mentors has been coming forward to take up the challenges presented by Government and Ofsted.

FE plays a vital role in educating, skilling and upskilling the working population by providing a strong foundation for economic success. However, little research into mentoring in FE has been undertaken in comparison to mentoring (and coaching) in schools and universities. As Gravatt and Silver (2000: 115) have observed:

> Schools are compulsory. Universities are selective. Colleges are the adaptive layer in the education system. Shock waves from the world of work, politics or the family often rebound off school walls or ivory towers, but frequently permeate further education.

It is hoped that policy makers and management will investigate the benefits of funding effective mentoring schemes. This is particularly important in the teaching context between tutor and student, reducing barriers to learning and aiding progression. Although the mentoring of trainee teachers in the workplace has a high profile, other mentoring roles are just as significant. More research into mentoring in FE is undoubtedly (and urgently) needed.

REFERENCES

Allen, T. D. and Eby, L. T. (2004) Factors relating to mentor reports of mentoring functions provided: gender and relational characteristics. *Sex Roles Journal, 50*(1/2), 129–139.

Andolo, D. (2007) When You Need Someone to Lean On: Young people at risk of dropping out of further education benefit from mentoring support system, *The Guardian*, 19 December 2007. Retrieved from: http://www.guardian.co.uk/society/2007/dec/19/youngpeople/, accessed April 2008).

Boud, D. and Walker, D. (1998) Promoting Reflection in Professional Courses: The challenge of context, *Studies in Higher Education Journal, 23*(2), 191–206.

Brefi Group (2010) *Coaching and Mentoring – What's the Difference?* Retrieved from: http://www.breifigroup.co.uk/coaching/coaching_and_mentoring.html, accessed October 2010.

Buchanan, J., Gordon, S. and Schuck, S. (2008) From mentoring to monitoring: the impact of changing work environments on academics in Australian universities, *Journal of Further and Higher Education, 32*(3), 241–250.

Carpenter, A. (Ed.) (2009) Experiences in HE:FE Mentoring, *The Research and Development Bulletin*, pp. 61–78.

Catapano, S. (2006) Teaching in Urban Schools: Mentoring pre-service teachers to apply advocacy strategies, *Mentoring and Tutoring, 14*(1), 81–96.

Chitty, C. (1991) *Post-16 Education: Studies in Access and Achievement.* London: Kogan Page.

Chitty, C. and Simon, B. (1993) *Education Answers Back: Critical Responses to Government Policy.* London: Lawrence and Wishart.

Cunningham, B. (2007) So where do I go from here? College mentors' continuing professional development, *Journal of Further and Higher Education, 31*(3), 283–295.

CUREE (2010) *National Framework of Mentoring and Coaching.* Retrieved from: http://www.curee-paccts.com/files/publication/1219925968/National-framework-for-mentoring-and-coaching.pdf, accessed 2 November 2010.

DfES (2004) *Equipping our Teachers for the Future: Reforming Initial Teacher Training for the Learning and Skills Sector.* Nottingham: DfES.

Edexcel (2010) *BTEC Specialist Qualifications/Peer Mentoring (L2).* Retrieved from: http://www.edexcel.com/quals/specialist/peer-mentoring-lvl2/Pages/default.aspx, accessed 2 November 2011.

FENTO (2001) *Mentoring towards Excellence.* London: Further Education National Training Organisation.

Fowler, G., Morris, V. and Ozgat, J. (1973) *Decision Making in British Education.* London: Heinemann/Milton Keynes: Open University Press.

Glasson, M. (2008) Case Studies in Mentoring in FE/ITE, *Peninsula CETT Bulletin.*

Gove, M. (2008) Why Conservative social policy delivers progressive ends. Speech made at the Institute for Public Policy Research in London on 4 August 2008. Retrieved from: http://www.conservatives.com/News/Speeches/2008/08/Michael_Gove_Why_Conservative_social_policy_delivers_progressive_ends.aspx

Gove, M. (2010) Heads and teachers are the best people to run schools – not politicians or bureaucrat. Speech made by the Secretary of State for Education to the National College Annual Conference 16 June 2010. Retrieved from: http://www.michaelgove.com/content/national_college_annual_conference, accessed 22 July 2010.

Gravatt, J. and Silver, R. (2000) Partnerships with the community, in Smithers, A. and Robinson, P. (Eds) *Further Education Re-formed.* London: Falmer Press.

Green, A. G. (1991) Comprehensive Education and Training: Possibilities and Prospects, in Chitty, C. (Ed.) *Post-16 Education: Studies in Access and Achievement.* London: Kogan Page.

Hall, V. (1990) *Maintained Further Education in the United Kingdom.* Bristol: The Further Education Staff College.

Innovation, Universities, Science and Skills Committee (2009) *Re-skilling for Recovery: After Leitch, Implementing Skills and Training Policies – Volume 1 (First Report of Session 2008–09).* London: The Stationery Office.

Klasen, N. and Clutterbuck, D. (2002) *Implementing Mentoring Schemes – A Practical Guide to Successful Programs.* Oxford: Butterworth-Heinemann.

Leitch, S. (2006) *Skills Review Final Report: Prosperity for all in the Global Economy – World Class Skills.* London: HMSO. Retrieved from: www.hm-treasury.gov.uk/leitch.

Miller, A. (2002) *Mentoring Students and Young People: A Handbook of Effective Practice.* London: Kogan Page.

O'Connor, S. and Laidlaw, K. (2006) *Mentoring for Business in Wales: Learning from Good Practice: Final Report for Welsh Assembly Government-DELLS.* Cardiff: LEED.

Ofsted. (2001) *The Common Inspection Framework.* London: Ofsted.

Ofsted. (2003) *The Initial Training of Further Education Teachers: A Survey.* London: Ofsted.

Ofsted. (2006) *The Initial Training of Further Education Teachers; findings from 2004/5 inspections leading to national awarding body qualifications,* (HMI 2485). London: Ofsted.

Oti, J. (2008) Conflict in the policy process: Examples of power struggles in a Welsh initiative, *Contemporary Wales, 21,* 174–186.

Oti, J. (2009) Mentoring in FE: Staff Perceptions. Draft working paper presented at the BERA conference, Manchester University, September 2009.

Pring, R. A. (1995) *Closing the Gap: Liberal Education and Vocational Preparation.* London: Hodder and Stoughton.

Roffey-Barentsen, J. and Malthouse, R. (2009) *Reflective Practice in the Lifelong Learning Sector.* Exeter: Learning Matters.

Russell Committee Report (1973) *Russell Committee Report.* London: HMSO.

Saunders, D. and Welsh Assembly Government (2008) *Learning Coaches of Wales – Executive Summary Document.* Retrieved from: http://wales.gov.uk/dcells/publications/publications/guidanceandinformation/learningcoaches/learningcoachesofwalese.pdf;jsessionid=srcQMvFGTyCXTmGQvgJkfbtK22RvT90dRkXBqgxJQ2zqVJ5LhG1L!-2135057422?lang=en, accessed October 2010.

Silver, M., Lochmiller, C. R., Copland, M. A. and Tripps, A. M. (2009) Supporting new school leaders: findings from a university-based leadership coaching programme for new administrators *Mentoring and Tutoring: Partnership in Learning Journal, 17*(3): 215–232.

Tedder, M. and Lawy, R. (2009) The pursuit of 'excellence'; mentoring in further education initial teacher training in England, *Journal of Vocational Education and Training, 61*(4), 431–429.

Wallace, S. and Gravells, J. (2005) *Mentoring in Further Education.* Exeter: Learning Matters.

Webb, A. (2007) *Promise and Performance: A Review of FE Colleges in Wales.* Cardiff: Welsh Assembly Government.

Woodd, M. (2001) Learning to leap from a peer: a research study on mentoring in a further and higher education institution. *Research in Post- Compulsory Education, 6*(1), 97–104.

24

Empowerment in the Faculty–Student Mentoring Relationship

Catherine A. Hansman

INTRODUCTION

During a search committee meeting for a tenure-earning assistant professor position, my departmental colleagues and I were examining the 34 applications when something caught my attention. Several committee members were commenting on the lack of 'professionalism' some applicants had displayed. We learned from each other that many of the early-career applicants, most who were just completing their doctorates, did not send the required certified transcripts; other applicants had not bothered to include letters of recommendation or even the names of references. One applicant had submitted a poorly written letter with misspellings. The chair of the search committee shared that one of these applicants had called her several times, requesting to meet so he could get to know her and the university where he hoped to teach. She explained to him that, at least in our university, committee members cannot have contact with the applicants until the screening process was complete. We collectively shook our heads in bewilderment as we discussed these 'gaffes' in applying for a highly competitive professional position. We wondered where their mentors were, and why it seemed that they had not guided these neophytes in the norms of academic culture.

That same evening, while teaching, my qualitative research students discussed an article about the importance of graduate students learning the culture of academe. Doctoral students asked me about the academic cultural norms of putting together a dissertation committee, along with other matters they view as mysterious customs and norms in academe. As I discussed these issues with my class, it became clear that the knowledge of 'how things work', in which faculty members and administrators participate and perpetuate as academic insiders, is not at all transparent to students, who for the most part are academic outsiders. Further, faculty members who fail to help their students understand academic culture may be operating from a stance of power; withholding information is as powerful an action as sharing information. Sharing hidden norms and expectations can empower students, particularly those hoping for a career in academe.

Students who wish to form helpful mentoring relationships with faculty members may encounter difficulties. In my own experience as a female doctoral student, there were no women faculty members in my department to act as mentors. The all-male faculty members were helpful to female students, but for the most part, they saved their publication and presentation invitations and job announcements for promising male doctoral students, seeming to assume female students were not interested in these opportunities or mentoring relationships. However, despite this gender unfriendly context, I was fortunate to find an empowering male faculty mentor. John was my tour guide to academia, helping me understand some of the hidden processes and norms. John accomplished this in several ways. First, as a fairly new faculty member at our university, he discussed feeling ambivalent about his role as a junior professor in the university, sharing some of his achievements as well as challenges and concerns, which deepened my comprehension of academic enigmas. Second, he patiently read multiple drafts of my conference proposals and papers, sharing helpful information about how to submit articles to journals for publication review. He also discussed those professional associations and conferences that could be useful for my future career as a faculty member. Consistent with what Johnson-Bailey and Cervero (2004, 2008) discuss relative to their own cross-cultural mentoring relationship, John challenged me to submit papers whenever I procrastinated. But, perhaps his most empowering action was his expressed belief that I could do the work of an academician; that I had the definite potential to become a productive, contributing faculty member.

John is only one of many empowering mentors with whom I have been fortunate to study. In my personal and professional life, these mentors have played various roles, from inspiring me to complete class assignments as a doctoral student to encouraging me to apply for promotion as a faculty member. Through their examples, support and actions, my mentors guided me. In my work as a university professor engaged in mentoring students, I try follow their examples of mentoring, with the goal of being helpful and empowering as a mentor to my students and colleagues.

This discussion raises the question, what does empowerment in faculty student mentoring relationships mean? *Empowerment* is defined as promoting self-actualization, influencing and enabling another person. 'Enable' means 'to make possible, practical or easy' (Merriam–Webster Dictionary, 2011). None of the positive mentors I have had in my life has made things easy. Instead, they have challenged me to set goals and strive toward attaining them while promoting my self-actualization and self-direction with respect to teaching, writing, and learning. My mentors have allowed me to envision, imagine, and realize a future possible self (Fletcher, 2007) within these contexts.

Many, but not all, faculty members may choose to empower students through supportive mentoring relationships. Fresko and Wertheim (2006: 149) contend that 'mentoring is an educational tool of empowerment'. In this writing, I explore the concept of power and empowerment in faculty–student mentoring relationships. I examine models that reflect these ideals and include reflective discussion aimed at improving mentoring practice to encompass principles of empowerment.

DEFINING MENTORING RELATIONSHIPS

Varied discussions of power and empowerment within mentoring relationships are available in the mentoring literature. Some authors bestow upon mentors mystical powers, assigning a spiritual component to mentoring relationships. For instance, Daloz (1999: 18) contends that 'mentors give us the magic that allows us to enter the darkness; a talisman to protect us from evil spells a gem of wise advice, a map, and sometimes simply courage'. Others describe mentoring in less enchanted terms, focusing more on learning and structured relationships between mentors and protégés. Among them, Zachary (2005: 3) describes *mentoring* as 'reciprocal and collaborative learning between two or more individuals who share mutual responsibility and accountability for helping a mentee work toward achievement of clear and mutually defined learning goals'. Additional definitions of mentoring imply that mentors are superiors who have little personal interest in their protégés, instead focusing on how mentors guide and support career development (Blake-Beard, Murrell, and Thomas, 2007; Dreher and Cox, 1996; O'Neil and Marsick, 2009; Ragins and Kram, 1997).

Classifications of mentoring relationships include informal, formal, career-related, psychosocial, and peer mentoring (Kram, 1983). All of these types of relationships may characterize faculty–student mentoring. Informal mentoring relationships are usually psychosocial in nature, formed to enhance the protégé's self-esteem through the interpersonal dynamics between mentors and protégés who may commit to a mentoring relationship through their mutual interests. Typically, faculty members and students enter into informal mentoring dyad arrangements for thesis or dissertation advisement, although as these projects progress and committees are formed, mentoring relationships may become more formal. Informal mentoring relationships may also encompass personal goals and, thus, may take place not only in organizations but also in more personal or social spaces, such as churches, clubs, or coffee houses. Other types of informal mentoring may include peer or cohort groups that provide mentoring to their peers and psychosocial as well as career help to each member.

In contrast to informal mentoring, formal mentoring programs can be promoted by organizations to provide opportunities for mentoring in a more structured and possibly democratic fashion, matching mentors with protégés (Hansman, 1999, 2002). Organizational leaders may develop formal mentoring programs to promote mentoring relationships for diverse groups and address racial, class, gender, and other inequalities in the workplace. In higher education institutions, formal mentoring programs may be designed, for example, to help assimilate first-generation students or assist a cohort of graduate students with their research projects or theses/dissertations. However helpful the intent of formal mentoring programs is, some studies (i.e., Brinson and Kottler, 1993; Hansman, 2003; Koberg, Boss, and Goodman, 1998; Thomas, 2001) have shown that discrimination may prevent protégés from engaging in helpful mentoring relationships. In short, perceptions based on race, gender, class, sexual preferences, and ability can impact the formation of successful mentoring relationships. When discussing their mentoring relationships, mentors and protégés do not always address issues of power (Hansman, 2002, 2003, 2005), yet awareness of power dynamics can affect the quality and helpfulness of mentoring relationships, as well as how empowering the relationship can be to both mentors and protégés.

POWER ISSUES AND MENTORING RELATIONSHIPS

Ragins (1997: 485) defines *power* as the 'influence of one person over others, stemming from an individual characteristic, an interpersonal relationship, a position in an organization, or from membership in a societal group'. All teaching/learning relationships are comprised of acknowledged and unacknowledged power structures. Likewise, mentoring relationships, socially constructed relationships formed to enhance learning and development for both mentors and protégés, inherently include unequal power relationships – with mentors typically holding more power than protégés.

Power comes from several sources. First, by virtue of having more experience and knowledge, mentors have advantages in the relationship, and they can use the power they have to hurt or help their protégés, such as withholding important information (hurting), or by passing onto their protégés new career information or opportunities (helping). Second, because mentors have more experience than their protégés, they may adopt hierarchical paternalistic lenses of their protégés, assume they know what is best, and further, may not ask for input from their protégés or engage in joint discussions and shared decisions concerning learning goals or desired outcomes for the mentoring relationship. Because of this paradigm of power, mentors may simply pass on information or dominant organizational values rather than assist their protégés to develop self-directed learning objectives or support them to critically examine their own goals and the values they represent. Third, mentors may exercise power by not aiding protégés to understand and navigate the organizational politics or contexts that may assist or impede their careers. Finally, perhaps the biggest oxymoron surrounding mentoring relationships is that although mentors should seek to empower their protégés, mentoring relationships themselves are entrenched in power dynamics that are often unacknowledged and unaddressed by mentors or protégés (Hansman, 2002, 2003, 2005).

Two kinds of power may be inherent in mentoring relationships: internal relationship power; that is, the power existing between the mentor and the protégé; and external power, which influences the relationship and which may reflect the power and political dynamics in the organization (Ragins, 1997). In academe, within faculty–student mentoring relationships, internal relationship power may manifest as the hierarchical power the faculty member holds as part of the dominant university culture (Driscoll, Parkes, Tilley-Lubbs, Brill and Pitts Bannister 2009) that s/he may use to support or hurt the protégé.

An example of internal and external power is Hansman's (2003) study of student teacher protégés and their faculty mentors in an accelerated masters degree. In this teacher licensing program, faculty mentors delayed and potentially damaged their protégés' progress through intentionally or unintentionally withholding vital information concerning meetings, assignments, and faculty mentors' expectations. Some of the faculty mentors interviewed revealed their assumptions that student-teacher protégés 'should have known' faculty mentors' expectations and other information related to their student teaching experiences, so they did not make announcements and otherwise share information with their protégés. The resulting miscommunications led to misunderstandings that perpetuated throughout the program. Faculty mentors also did not return teaching observation evaluations of their protégés in time for the student teachers to review them before their next observation by a mentor, thus inhibiting the improvement of their teaching demonstrations.

As Searby (2009) asserts, faculty mentors who are part of the dominant university culture may make assumptions about their protégés and the culture from which they come, which can impede the advice and help they give. In Hansman's (2003) study, it seems that faculty mentors assumed that student-teacher protégés understood academic expectations. Even when it was clear there was a breakdown in communication, the mentors did not move quickly to correct these miscommunications, which would have helped produce productive and successful student teaching experiences. The faculty mentors, for the most part, did not play an empowering role with their student teacher protégés.

MAKING A DIFFERENCE THROUGH EMPOWERED MENTORING

Many times when empowerment in faculty–student mentoring relationships is discussed, it is inferred that the mentor is 'bestowing gifts on the protégé in a highly altruistic way' (Johnson-Bailey and Cervero, 2004: 17). Formal dyadic mentoring, when a senior mentor is assigned to a single protégé based on their mutual interests or when an individual protégé selects a mentor (Mullen and Hutinger, 2008), may be successful if the individuals in the dyads are compatible.

But dyadic relationships have the potential to reinforce hierarchical organizational or societal power structures. Highly paternalistic views of mentoring do not take into account the two-way street that mentoring can be, and that mentors, as well as protégés, can gain and become empowered from the relationships.

Mentors empower their protégés through sharing knowledge, advice, and insights, and evaluations of their protégés' work, while allowing for discourse and reflection. However, protégés may also contribute to the relationship, sharing their own insights and reflections with their mentors. Faculty mentors might also benefit from engaging in research studies with students in areas that may contribute to their knowledge. As Fletcher (1998: 110) argues, 'Good mentors are critical friends, personal guides, counselors, and fully engaged in a relationship that has the potential to become as fundamental to the personal development of the mentor as to the development of the mentee'. Thus, empowered faculty–student mentoring relationships involve give-and-take, with mentors potentially benefiting from the relationship as well.

Galbraith and Maslin-Ostrowski (2000) contend that mentors make the difference between an individual's success and failure through his or her life journey. Many graduate students desire mentoring relationships with their faculty members to prepare them for their future roles in higher education or other professions. Rishel (2006: 218) argues that

> [m]entoring should be flexible and interactive, not ... a self-absorbed activity where only the mentor possesses knowledge that he or she can choose to share with protégés, or mentors act as entrenched professionals who are unwilling to change or think in a new way about teaching and students.

Mentors can empower their protégés through building a climate of trust and respect in the mentoring relationship. Positive mentors support protégés through learning experiences that will build their self-confidence. They challenge students to reflect upon their assumptions and develop new levels of knowledge and understanding, providing opportunities for students to achieve their goals and empathetically helping them to be self-reflective of their successes and failures. Empowered mentors also engage in their own self-reflection in order to grow as teachers and as mentors. In discussing engaged pedagogy, which may resemble empowered mentoring, hooks (1994: 15) says that teachers 'must be actively involved and committed to a process of self-actualization that promotes their own well-being if they are to teach in a manner that empowers students' (ibid.). Not all faculty members may wish to engage students in mentoring relationships, but those who do should strive to empower their protégés.

MENTORING MODELS AS EMPOWERMENT IN ACTION

Mentoring models, as well as research that furthers understanding of empowerment in student–faculty mentoring relationships, can help advance knowledge of enriched mentoring relationships. Empowered mentoring relationships can take many forms, such as individual mentoring dyads with one-on-one mentoring relationships, formally organized cohort mentoring programs, informal mentoring relationships between faculty members and students, and peer mentoring among graduate students. Next I discuss several models of mentoring that encompass these ideas.

Complete Mentor Framework

Many traditional models of mentoring presume that a mentoring dyad consists of an experienced mentor and less experienced protégé, and at times assume that the protégé is a passive recipient of knowledge (Galbraith and James, 2004; Hansman, 2002). However, mentoring dyads can be empowering to mentors and protégés. In their Complete Mentor Framework, Galbraith and James (2004) discuss six interrelated behavioral functions of mentorship that can be significant to relationships between mentors and protégés:

- *Relationship emphasis:* Creates a psychological climate of trust between mentor and protégé so that free exchange of information is possible.
- *Information emphasis:* The mentor requests information from the protégé in order to provide the best advice for achieving personal, educational, or career goals.
- *Facilitative focus:* The mentor poses hypothetical questions to expose underlying assumptions while presenting diverse viewpoints that foster more in-depth understandings of current and future decisions and actions.
- *Confrontive focus:* The mentor challenges the protégé's procrastination and avoidance behaviors in completing relevant educational or developmental tasks. While confronting their protégés, the mentor's objective is to promote the protégé's self-assessment of incongruences in their beliefs and behavior in order to find strategies for growth and development.
- *Mentor model:* Mentors share with protégés their own personal and professional experiences to motivate their protégés to make decisions and overcome difficulties.
- *Mentor vision:* Mentors encourage their protégés to take on the roles of independent adult learners through managing and negotiating transitions throughout their lives.

Galbraith and James contend that all six functions are required to constitute a 'complete mentor'. Although their model seems more appropriate for mentoring dyads consisting of one mentor and one protégé, it may point to ways in which mentors can empower their protégés to move forward in their careers and personal lives. It may also be adapted into cohort or peer group mentoring relationships; peer protégés could serve as mentors to each other, moving through Galbraith and James' functions and playing the role of mentor in a reciprocal fashion.

Mentoring Best Practices

Other models of mentoring also emphasize partnership in mentoring relationships, such as Fischler and Zachary's (2009) model, in which mentor and protégé 'work to achieve goals that they mutually define to develop skills, abilities, knowledge and/or thinking' (2009: 6). Their model of mentoring consists of seven elements that can empower both mentor and protégé: *reciprocity, learning, relationship, partnership, collaboration, mutually defined goals*, and *development*. *Reciprocity* refers to the understanding between mentor and protégé that their relationship is an equal partnership, from which both can learn and profit. *Learning* refers to active learning where protégés gain insider knowledge and perspectives of organizational culture and/or professions, and, through this deeper understanding, critically reflect on how to apply this new knowledge to 'transform and apply learning in new ways' (ibid. 7). Fischler and Zachary describe *relationship* as something that both mentors and protégés need to develop from both inside and outside, getting to know each other and to value the contributions each makes to the relationship. They argue that '*partnership* is the essence of the learner-centered approach to mentoring' (ibid. 7), and that through viewing mentoring relationships from this lens, protégés play a more active role in the relationship, shifting away from a paternalistic model of mentoring where the mentor 'fills' the protégé with knowledge that is passively received. Through *partnership*, mentors become less authoritarian and more engaged in the learning relationship. *Collaboration* describes the shared learning process in which mentors and protégés engage through an exchange of knowledge in active dialogue. Within this discourse, mentor and protégé may formulate *mutually defined goals* and steps for achieving them. Finally, in *development*, the relationship becomes future-directed, and mentors assist their protégés with developing their knowledge and abilities for achieving their goals.

Galbraith and James's Complete Mentoring Framework and Fischler and Zachary's Mentoring Best Practices each address elements that may help empower both mentor and protégés in mentoring dyads. However, other models of mentoring extend the concept of mentoring dyads to include peer and cohort mentoring, offering expanded and alternative ways of designing mentoring relationships.

Action Learning Conversations

O'Neil and Marsick (2009) propose Action Learning Conversations (ALCs), a structured protocol for facilitating peer coaching and mentoring, as critically reflective practice in groups of no more than seven to address challenges. In ALCs, insightful questions combine with 'reflection and critical reflection to produce a process of group mentoring' (2009: 19). These researchers identify critical reflection as a process to 'identify underlying values, beliefs, and assumptions … it enables people to see how they can change a situation by changing the way they frame it and act on it' (ibid. 19).

The ALCs model consists of three phases: framing and engaging (phase 1); advancing (phase 2), and disengaging (phase 3). In phase 1, a member of the group, the problem holder, brings a problem or issue to the group. Group members then write about it, turning the problem into written questions that each member shares so that dialogue can occur with each other and questions are asked that clarify contexts and situations. This phase ends with the person who brought the problem 'framing' the support s/he needs to further consider the problem. Phase 2 is the 'heart of the process' (Marsick and Maltbia, 2009: 163), consisting of four kinds of questions designed to expand thinking about the problem: objective, reflective, interpretative, and decisional. Peer members explore assumptions about the problem identified. Also, peer members write down the assumptions they feel the problem holder may have or ones they may have if they were in a similar situation. In phase 3, the member who has been leading the peer mentoring session reviews the questions for alignment with commitments made to address the problem or issue. This allows for feedback and acknowledgement of gained insight and knowledge, upon which group members may then choose to act. Through group discourse, the ALCs mentoring model can help develop and empower those involved as well as provide support for transformational learning (Mezirow, Taylor, and Associates, 2009).

Mentoring cohorts

Mullen (2003) asserts that many current faculty members do not experience steadfast traditional or innovative mentoring in their journey to the professorate and/or have not had the opportunity to study mentoring as a learning process, so they are lack familiarity with mentoring in its varied forms. She suggests that steadfast mentoring interventions are needed, such as cohort mentoring or informal doctoral mentoring. Through her research concerning informal mentoring of doctoral students, Mullen (2003) offers the concept of *mentoring cohorts* as another perspective of faculty student mentoring relationships. In her study, she defines a *mentoring cohort* 'as a collaborative faculty–student support group that brings together doctoral students and their academic mentors' (2003: 412) so that they may practice the thinking and skills necessary to take their future place in academe as scholars and teachers. The many benefits to cohort mentoring that Mullen described includes students benefiting from professional development while completing university degree requirements, opportunities to practice scholarly writing skills, and enhanced focus for completing tasks and coursework and for meeting goals.

In Mullen's 2003 study, she formed an informal mentoring cohort consisting all of the doctoral students for whom she was a dissertation supervisor. The students were at various stages in their degree program, from taking courses to writing their dissertations. The cohort set their goals as a 'commitment to building relationships dedicated to dissertation research and creating a safe place for critiquing work' (2003: 416). Students in the cohort critiqued each other's writing through regular meetings, thus a 'thriving mentoring network was built and sustained' (ibid.). In Mullen's analysis of the data based on the participants' perceptions, she found that the following patterns seemed evident in the group's learning process.

- 'A sense of identity and belonging' (ibid. 418) through the socialization within the doctoral mentoring cohort that built capacity beyond one-to-one faculty–student mentoring dyads.
- 'Support for learning and attaining dreams' (ibid. 419) that allowed the members to achieve their goals, making them realistic and realizable.
- 'Experiencing a faculty–student support model' (ibid. 420) that enhanced the cohort's learning through power sharing, mutual respect, and identity formation as scholarly writers.

Importantly, in addition, cohort members discussed how the dynamics of power and empowerment encouraged through their mutual critique of their scholarly writing encouraged 'reflective learning about scholarly development' (ibid. 421).

The advantages of informal mentoring cohort with students at various stages of completion of their doctoral degree seem clear. More experienced students in the cohort can perform important mentoring functions through partnering with less experienced peers, empowering everyone in the cohort to work towards their goals and scholarly achievements. In the Urban Education doctoral program in which I teach at my university, our students are enrolled in cohorts formed each year by program administrators. Although communication among members of different cohorts is encouraged by faculty and administrators, most students primarily interact with the members of their own cohort, who are all at the same stage of the doctoral program. This may limit helpful peer mentoring and the types of assistance they give each other. In contrast, the informal cohort Mullen describes in her 2003 study is not a cohort group of students and faculty members formed for convenience by administrators; instead, this dynamic group facilitated powerful developmental and transformative support for its members across programmatic stages and as an outgrowth of their non-institutionalized drive to work together. In the mentoring cohort model, faculty and peer mentors gained reciprocal benefits from their participation in the cohort.

Mentoring mosaics

Another model for formal or informal peer group mentoring is *mentoring mosaics*, which Mullen, Fish, and Hutinger (2010: 181) claim functions as 'a network, a community or simply a resource'. Mentoring mosaics exemplifies the ideals of empowering its members through nonhierarchical and reciprocal mentoring interactions that can, for example, address scholarly writing, presentation skills, and graduate student life. The mosaics can be primary or secondary mentoring relationships for graduate students, providing opportunities for students to be engaged in mutual processes of learning and development that increases their abilities to nurture, advise, and instruct each other. Members of the mosaic act as critical friends to other members while challenging their long-held beliefs, while at the same time encouraging critical self-reflection among each of them.

Mosaic members engage in co-mentorship, where 'mentors and mentees (or students) proactively teach each other in ways that are completely respectful while being critically supportive' (Mullen et al., 2010: 182). In short, mosaic members, acting as mentors, are adult educators, promoting self-direction among their protégés, as well as fostering transformational learning among the group. Additionally, the group mentoring may diffuse the power dynamic that can be present in mentoring dyads, where a mentor may typically have more experience and power. Learning strategies may include 'power sharing, turn taking, co-leading, dialogue and constructive feedback, as well as transparency and authenticity' (ibid. 182).

In their research on the mentoring mosaics model, Mullen et al. (2010) collected data from five triangulated sources to gain understanding of the success of this mentoring model. Participants in their research study reported many benefits from their involvement, including their growth as learners, leader, scholars, and writers in academe. Through the interactions within the mosaic, members engaged in empowering mentoring relationships that fostered their individual development and learning. Mentoring mosaics have the potential to promote nonhierarchical peer mentoring, where each individual functions as mentor and protégé, emphasizing mutual interdependence among the members (Mullen, 2005).

IDEAS FOR FUTURE RESEARCH

Mentoring relationships can encompass many different formats and models beyond traditional one-on-one dyads. Embracing models of mentoring beyond traditional formal mentoring models can further understandings of how adult learners can 'take responsibility for their professional development and create a scaffold rather than a straitjacket within which they can continue to develop' (Fletcher, 2007: 84). These 'scaffolds', similar to Wenger's (1998) concept of communities of practice, can permit mentors and protégés to dialogue about the knowledge they have developed, empowering them through collaboration, conversation, and reflections on learning (Hansman, 2007). Continued research on mentoring models and understandings of mentoring relationships, such as those I have discussed, are needed.

Mentoring relationships can be educational tools of empowerment, allowing protégés to reflect upon their learning and development while being guided on this path by caring yet critical mentors. However, mentors, as well as their protégés, can gain much from mentoring relationships. Positive outcomes for mentors can include the development of greater self-confidence, awareness of their own strengths, improved managerial skills, and enhanced abilities to work with groups (Clinard and Ariav, 1998). Correspondingly, more research is needed to further explore how faculty members' past mentoring experiences as student protégés may affect their teaching and mentoring practices, particularly pedagogical practices that promote empowerment and transformation in learning relationships. Additionally, further research should address cohort and peer mentoring groups and how protégés, acting as mentors to their peers in these groups, become empowered in their own learning and development. Other future research may address empowerment in faculty–student mentoring relationships and how mentoring experiences affects mentors' and protégés' development in their personal as well as professional lives.

As can be inferred from the mentoring models and research previously discussed in this chapter, trust is an essential ingredient of empowered mentoring. Trust can be present in traditional mentoring dyads as well as formal or informal cohort or peer mentoring groups. Galbraith and James (2004) discuss how mentors can establish trust with their protégés through allowing and facilitating free exchanges of information between mentor and protégé, while at the same time challenging protégés' avoidance behaviors (e.g., procrastination) in completing tasks. Successful mentoring necessitates the mentor's commitment to building trust with their protégés through responsive listening and providing feedback about concerns involving protégés' learning. Johnson-Bailey and Cervero (2004: 11) concur, asserting that 'certainly, the foundation of any successful mentoring relationship is trust'.

Hansman (2009) expanded the idea of trust between mentors and protégés through her mentoring maxims: first, mentors should strive to never unintentionally or intentionally take action that may impair the learning of their protégés, or 'do no harm' (2009: 61); second, mentors need to communicate honestly with their protégés, defining the 'roles, goals, and outcomes' (ibid.) of the relationship. Third, mentors should always carefully consider how the power they hold as a faculty member can potentially help or harm their protégés and channel their power wisely to support the work of the mentoring relationship and the development of their protégés.

Finally, the work of mentors and protégés, whether they are faculty, students, or peers, should be infused with empowerment ideals through undertakings such as those I have covered. Mullen's (2003) model of mentoring cohorts that are comprised of reciprocal peer mentoring to improve written communications and presentations can endow graduate students with the skills needed for their future professional or academic careers. Similarly, the mentoring mosaic described by Mullen et al. (2010) provides primary or secondary mentoring to students so that they can hone their abilities to advise and instruct each other. Such a learning process can assist protégés to learn the skills they need to become empowering mentors themselves in the present and future.

FULL CIRCLE

One of the stories I began with introduced John, an empowering faculty mentor I was fortunate to encounter during my doctoral journey. In reflecting on John's actions as a mentor, I realize that his mentorship exemplifies some of the ideas presented in the models I have discussed, especially those in Galbraith and James' (2004) Complete Mentor Framework. John established trust in our mentoring relationship through nonjudgmental listening to my questions and concerns about academic culture and by responding sincerely in ways that furthered my understanding about academic culture and careers. He helped me realize that I had a place in academe through diplomatically providing descriptive and helpful feedback to me on written assignments and presentations. But, all the while, he challenged me to continually strive to 'do better' while at the same time unfailingly expressing the belief that I possessed the ability to become a faculty member. He was the 'critical friend' embodied in Fletcher's (1998) definition of a mentor. His confidence in me enhanced my own self-assurance concerning my future career in academe. Furthermore, our mentoring relationship did not end when I earned my doctoral degree; instead, over the years our mentoring relationship has morphed into a friendship and professional association that I believe has benefited us both.

As a professor, although I try to emulate John's actions as a mentor, I have experienced both successes and failures as a mentor to my protégés. I continually reflect upon these relationships and try to learn from each of them in order to improve my mentoring abilities. Nevertheless, I know that I was fortunate to have had a powerful mentor who believed in me and my abilities, and, through his mentoring actions, enabled me to succeed. Faculty members who have not experienced empowering mentoring relationships in their own doctoral careers may not have developed the skills to mentor their own students, which may be why some are reluctant to engage in mentoring relationships. Through expanding the vision of enriched and empowering mentoring beyond dyads to include peer and cohort mentoring and other models, the opportunity exists to not only successfully mentor students but to develop them so they will themselves become empowered mentors to their students and colleagues one day.

REFERENCES

Blake-Beard, S. D., Murrell, A. J., & Thomas, D. A. (2007). Unfinished business: The impact of race on understanding mentoring relationships. In B. R. Ragins & K. F. Kram (Eds.), *The Handbook of Mentoring* (pp. 223–247). Thousand Oaks, CA: SAGE.

Brinson, J., & Kottler, J. (1993). Cross-cultural mentoring in counselor education: A strategy for retaining minority faculty. *Counselor Education and Supervision, 32*(4), 241–253.

Clinard, L. M., & Ariav, T. (1998). What mentoring does for mentors: A cross-cultural perspective. *European Journal of Teacher Education, 21*(1), 91–108.

Daloz, L. A. (1999). *Mentor: Guiding the journey of adult learners.* San Francisco: Jossey-Bass.

Dreher, G. F., & Cox, T. H. (1996). Race, gender, and opportunity. A study of compensation attainment and establishment of mentoring relationships. *Journal of Applied Psychology, 81*(3), 297–308.

Driscoll, L. G., Parkes, K. A., Tilley-Lubbs, G. A., Brill, J. M., & Pitts Bannister, V. R. (2009). Navigating the lonely sea: Peer mentoring and collaboration among aspiring women scholars. *Mentoring & Tutoring: Partnership in Learning, 17*(1), 5–21.

Fischler, L. A., & Zachary, L .J. (2009). Shifting gears: The mentee in the driver's seat. *Adult Learning, 20*(1–2), 5–9.

Fletcher, S. (1998). Attaining self-actualisation through mentoring. *European Journal of Teacher Education, 21*(1), 109–118.

Fletcher, S. (2007). Mentoring Adult Learners: Realizing possible selves. In M. Rossiter (Ed.), *New Directions for Adult & Continuing Education, 114* (pp. 75–86). San Francisco: Jossey-Bass.

Fresko, B., & Wetheim, C. (2006). Learning by Mentoring: Prospective teachers as mentors to children at-risk. *Mentoring & Tutoring: Partnership in Learning, 14*(2), 149–161.

Galbraith, M. W., & James, W. B. (2004). Mentoring by the community college professor: One role among many. *Community College Journal of Research and Practice, 28*, 689–701.

Galbraith, M. W., & Maslin-Ostrowski, P. (2000). The Mentor: Facilitating out-of-class cognitive and affective growth. In J. L. Bess & Associates (Eds.), *Teaching alone teaching together* (pp. 133–150). San Francisco: Jossey-Bass.

Hansman, C. A. (1999) Mentoring and women's career development. In L. L. Bierema (Ed.), *Women's career development: Implications for adult education* (pp. 63–72). San Francisco: Jossey-Bass.

Hansman, C. A. (2002). Diversity and power in mentoring relationships. In C. A. Hansman (Ed.), *Critical Perspectives on Mentoring: Trends & Issues* (pp. 39–48). Information series no. 388. ERIC Clearinghouse on Adult, Career, and Vocational Education (ED99CO0013). Columbus, Ohio.

Hansman, C. A. (2003). Power and learning in mentoring relationships. In R. Cervero, B. Courtenay, & M. Hixson (Eds.), *Global perspectives, 3* (pp. 101–121). Athens, GA: University of Georgia.

Hansman, C. A. (2005). Reluctant mentors & resistant protégées. *Adult Learning, 14*(1), 14–16.

Hansman, C. A. (2007). Adult learning in communities of practice: Situating theory in practice. In C. Kimble, P. Hildreth, & I. Bourdon (Eds.), *Communities of practice: Creating learning environments for educators, 1* (pp. 279–292). Charlotte, NC: Information Age.

Hansman, C. A. (2009). Ethical issues in mentoring adult learners in higher education. In L. Burge (Ed.), *Ethical Issues in adult education. New directions for adult and continuing education, #123* (pp. 53–64). San Francisco: Jossey-Bass.

hooks, b. (1994). *Teaching to Transgress: Education as the practice of freedom.* New York: Routledge.

Johnson-Bailey, J., & Cervero, R. M. (2004). Mentoring in black and white: The intricacies of cross-cultural mentoring. *Mentoring & Tutoring: Partnership in learning, 12*(1), 7–21.

Johnson-Bailey, J., & Cervero, R. M. (2008). Different worlds and divergent paths: Academic careers defined by race and gender. *Harvard Educational Review, 78*(2), 311–332.

Koberg, C. S., Boss, R. W., & Goodman, E. (1998). Factors and outcomes associated with mentoring among health-care professionals. *Journal of Vocational Behavior, 53*(1), 58–72.

Kram, K. E. (1983). Phases of the Mentoring Relationship. *Academy of Management Journal, 26*, 608–625.

Marsick, V. J., & Maltbia, T. E. (2009). The Transformative Potential of Action Learning Conversations: Developing critically reflective practice skills. In J. Mezirow, E. W. Taylor, & Associates (Eds.), *Transformative learning in practice: Insights from community, workplace and higher education* (pp. 160–181). San Francisco: Jossey-Bass.

Merriam–Webster Dictionary (2011). Retrieved January 30, 2011, from http://www.merriam-webster.com/

Mezirow, J., Taylor, E., & Associates (2009). *Transformative learning in practice: Insights from community, workplace and higher education.* San Francisco: Jossey-Bass.

Mullen, C. A. (2003). The WIT Cohort: A case study of informal doctoral mentoring. *Journal of Further and Higher Education, 27*(4), 411–425.

Mullen, C. A. (2005). *The mentorship primer.* New York: Peter Lang.

Mullen, C. A., & Hutinger, J. L. (2008). At the tipping point? Role of formal faculty mentoring in changing university cultures. *Journal of In-Service Education, 34*(2), 181–204.

Mullen, C. A., Fish, V. L., & Hutinger, J. L. (2010). Mentoring doctoral students through scholastic engagement: Adult learning principles in action. *Journal of Further and Higher Education, 34*(2), 179–197.

O'Neil, J., & Marsick, V. (2009). Peer mentoring and action learning. *Adult Learning, 20*(1–2), 19–24.

Ragins, B. R. (1997). Diversified mentoring relationships in organizations: A power perspective. *Academy of Management Review, 22*(2), 482–521.

Ragins, B. R., & Kram, K. E. (1997). The roots and meaning of mentoring. In B. R. Ragins & K. E. Kram (Eds.), *The handbook of mentoring at work: Theory, research and practice* (pp. 3–15). Thousand Oaks: SAGE.

Rishel, T. J. (2006). Rethinking the roles of mentor and mentee in the context of student suicide. *Mentoring & Tutoring: Partnership in Learning, 14*(2), 207–226.

Searby, L. (2009). 'But I thought....' An examination of assumptions in the mentoring relationship. *Adult Learning, 20*(1–2), 10–13.

Thomas, D. A. (2001). The truth about mentoring minorities: Race matters. *Harvard Business Review, 79*(4), 99–107.

Wenger, E. (1998). *Communities of Practice: Learning, meaning, and identity.* Cambridge: Cambridge University Press.

Zachary, L. J. (2005). *Creating a Mentoring Culture: The organization's guide.* San Francisco: Jossey-Bass.

25

Student Peer Mentors as a Navigational Resource in Higher Education

Jenepher Lennox Terrion

INTRODUCTION

Many undergraduate students travel through their university or college programs with relative ease, graduating after the requisite three or four years with countless papers, exams, and assignments completed. For these students, higher education can be likened to a manageable stroll. For many others, however, the journey is fraught with difficulties and obstacles, much like a challenging hike through dark woods. Some of these obstacles can be insurmountable, and this leads to failure or withdrawal: outcomes that are costly to both the student and the institution. Thus, college administrators have long sought to identify the support mechanisms necessary to improve the academic success, performance, and retention of their students by providing them with the compass necessary for navigating 'the woods' of higher education. Here I look at the role of student peer mentor as metaphorical compass guiding undergraduates through their educational journey.

Peer mentoring is defined as a formal relationship in which a qualified student provides guidance and support to another student to enable that individual to better navigate his or her education (Kram, 1983). Peer mentoring is based on the traditional mentoring model in which an older, more experienced person provides either task/career-related support (such as helping a protégé to use new equipment or to take on a new role in an organization) or psychosocial support (such as providing guidance during difficult emotional times) (Kram, 1983). The traditional form of mentoring consists of a hierarchical relationship in which the mentor is considerably older and more experienced than the mentee. In contrast, peer mentors tend not to possess a vast differential in experience and age compared to their protégés (Philion, 2005). According to Kram and Isabella (1985), the peer-mentoring model can be a valuable alternative to the traditional concept and practice of mentorship.

IMPACT OF PEER MENTORING ON STUDENT MENTEES

Peer mentoring and the task/career function

In terms of fulfilling the task/career-related function, a similarity of age and experience of peer mentors to their protégés may limit their ability to provide career-enhancing support where work experience is lacking. Given their own background as college or university students, peer mentors can, however, fulfill the immediate task functions related to the requirements of post-secondary education (e.g., study skills, course selection, exam preparation, navigating the higher education culture). This guidance is important to students at all stages of their educational programs, whether their concerns are related to surviving within an unfamiliar academic terrain or whether they are course-related, including such challenges as essay writing and test taking. Thus, task-motivated needs tend to drive the mentoring requirements of many students. Peer mentoring helps meet these needs.

Peer mentoring and psychosocial function

In addition to fulfilling the task function, studies have shown that the psychosocial function of mentoring is largely met through peer-mentoring programs (e.g., Loots, 2009; Rose, 2005). Furthermore, research shows that fulfilling psychosocial needs is essential to the experience of student mentees and that it may be more important than the task/career-related function for first-year students in particular (Allen, Russell, and Maetzke, 1997). This finding can be explained by the observation that younger students are more likely than their older counterparts to experience greater 'uncertainty about expectations and requirements' of the university or college environment (ibid. 500) and, as a result, may experience emotional difficulties that the mentoring relationship can help alleviate.

Further, similarities between peer mentor and mentee may create the conditions for a highly effective mentoring relationship. As Loots (2009) found, because senior students have already 'been through the mill' (2009: 231) and probably understand something valuable about their academic field or discipline and the important role that support plays, their connection with new students makes them especially well suited for serving as peer mentors. That is, in addition to providing information about resources and services of potential value to the mentee, peer mentors may be able to 'offer confirmation, emotional support, personal feedback, and friendship' to a greater degree than would traditional mentors (Angelique, Kyle, and Taylor, 2002: 199). In fact, peer mentors may have more success than professionals at connecting with struggling students, given that peer mentors can draw 'upon their own immediate experiences [and] ... offer empathetic emotional support rather than just sympathetic support' (ibid.). Indeed, it may be the proximity and similarity between partners in a peer-mentoring relationship that builds trust through establishing common ground, thus fulfilling the psychosocial function.

Psychosocial support may be particularly important, given research that shows that poor academic performance is rarely the reason for student withdrawal and that a perceived poor fit between student and institution explains withdrawal in many cases (Finnie and Qiu, 2009). Most withdrawals are associated with factors beyond failing marks, such as lack of fit and loneliness and financial issues, and some of these may be mitigated by enhanced psychosocial support. In fact, according to Mills, Heyworth, Rosenwax, Carr, and Rosenberg (2009), one benefit of peer-mentoring programs is their capacity for positively influencing what is referred to as 'student fit' by introducing students to the culture and practices of their institution, encouraging participation in campus activities, and, in general, supporting their transition to higher education.

Likewise, supportive relationships in university are one of the most important sources of stress reduction (Tinto, 1993). Therefore, the mentor who provides psychosocial support can help reduce the stress that a younger and less experienced student experiences. If the college or university's objective in implementing a peer-mentoring program is to decrease student attrition, then partially reducing student stress by providing support via peer-mentoring relationships may help achieve this outcome.

Peer mentoring impact on social and academic integration

In addition to providing task and psychosocial support, peer mentoring may enhance the social and academic integration of students. In his research on academic success, Tinto (e.g., 1998) has asserted that the integration of students into the learning community is critical to their success. Further, the more academically and socially involved individuals are – that is, the more they interact with students and faculty – the more likely they are to persist. Tinto argues that two forms of integration exist. The first, *social integration*, is defined as 'the development of a strong affiliation with the college social environment both in the classroom and outside of class [and] includes interactions with faculty, academic staff, and peers but of a social nature (e.g., peer group interactions, informal contact with faculty, involvement in organizations)' (Nora, 1993: 237). The second, *academic integration* reflects these same linkages with students and staff but emphasizes those that are academic in nature (e.g., peer tutoring, study groups).

Clearly, then, forming connections with others is a primary task for students to undertake. According to Pascarella and Terenzini (1983), the effect of integration on academic success is most powerful when both forms of integration – academic and social – occur, but the two forms are also reciprocal in that they act as a vehicle for integrating the other form. Further, Tinto (1998) suggests that while the two forms of integration play different roles for students in various contexts – that is, for some students it is social integration that matters most while, for others, academic integration is most critical to persistence – when it comes to retention, academic integration is more important.

Peer mentoring has been shown to stimulate the cultivation of both social and academic integration. Tinto (1998) suggests that the shared experience of participants in learning communities, such as those created through peer-mentoring relationships, helps students develop a support network that not only connects them to their peers but also more fully engages them in academic life. This connection, he argues, explains to a significant degree why some students persist in their studies while others, less integrated, withdraw.

Research on peer mentoring in higher education has shown that student satisfaction and engagement, as well as persistence, can be enhanced through peer-mentoring relationships because of the integration that such programs facilitate. For example, Terrion and Daoust (2011–2012) evaluated a group peer-mentoring program, which included a supplemental instruction component (a review of course material) called the Residence Study Group Program (RSGP) for residence students registered in freshman courses associated with high failure or attrition. The study compared final grades and re-enrolment rates (i.e., whether the student registered at the university for the semester following the research study) of students in these courses after controlling for personal motivation. The researchers found that while those who participated in the RSGP did not receive higher final grades than non-participants, they were more likely to persist in their studies. While this peer-mentoring intervention did not have a significant effect on grades, it contributed in many important ways to the academic and social integration of first-year students, enabling connections to be made that are critical to persistence beyond the entry year.

Regarding the issue of linkages forged with peer mentors, Sanchez, Bauer, and Saronto (2006) studied the effects of a university freshman peer-mentoring initiative. They found that students who were peer mentored reported greater satisfaction with their university during the semester of the mentoring intervention and at the end of the following semester. In terms of commitment and actual graduation rates, however, there was no significant difference between the mentored and non-mentored students. Sanchez et al. concluded that the mentoring intervention seemed to have a positive impact on satisfaction and integration but not on academic performance indicators such as GPA or graduation.

Peer mentoring thus fosters vital connections with other students that contribute to social integration. In terms of academic integration, peer mentoring provides mentees with extra help through reviewing material covered in class (particularly problematic areas), answering questions, and providing feedback on homework and assignments. In addition, peer mentors can offer course-related information (e.g., what content to study for an exam). These activities have been shown in numerous studies to enhance self-confidence, particularly if they are offered in an individualized format (see Arendale, 1997, for a review).

Impact of peer mentoring on social capital

In addition to enhancing the social and academic integration of undergraduates, peer mentoring seems to build social capital for students. In their study of engineering students' perceptions of factors that influenced their academic success, Amenkhienan and Kogan (2004) found that participation in peer-mentoring relationships through formal study groups allowed students to work collaboratively with others on difficult material and to learn by teaching peers. These connections, which are a form of social capital, offer a tangible value that may help explain the positive impact of peer mentoring on the academic success and retention of mentees.

Recently, there has been much discussion about the social capital concept since Coleman (1988) introduced it as an extension of prior research on financial and human capital. While financial capital describes a family's wealth or income and human capital is measured by parents' education, Coleman defines social capital by referring to its function, viewing it as a valuable resource that can be drawn upon for support, information, access to opportunities, positive role modeling, and so on. Putnam (2000) refined social capital to include the norms of reciprocity and trustworthiness that exist in social networks.

Researchers have examined the impact of social capital on a range of health and wellbeing indicators across the life span including healthy child development (Resnick, Harris, and Blum, 1993), adolescent health (Hendry and Reid, 2000), family functioning (Terrion, 2006), high school retention (Teachman, Paasch, and Carver, 1996), healthy aging (Keating, Swindle, and Foster, 2005), and even neighborhood mortality rates (Lochner, Kawachi, Brennan, and Buka, 2003). The consensus among these studies is that positive human relationships function as an invaluable resource to those who benefit from such connections.

In addition to contributing to these positive outcomes, Putnam (2000: 312) argues that the value of social networks lies in part in the 'enforcement of positive standards' or the modeling of desirable values and effective practices. Putnam refers to research (conducted by such researchers as Pascarella and Terenzini as well as Astin), suggesting that 'involvement in peer social networks are powerful predictors of college dropout rates and college success, even holding constant pre-collegiate factors, including aspirations' (ibid.). Further, as Packard (2004–2005) suggests, mentoring as social capital for postsecondary students in the sciences influences the decision to remain in one's program of study by connecting students with more senior students, tutors, faculty members and professionals and thus to the science community, reinforcing their commitment to be part of the broader community. Likewise, Roberts, Clifton, and Etcheverry (2001) found that undergraduate students' perceptions of social capital, particularly in the form of support from other students, had a positive impact on the quality of academic experience and even grades.

IMPACT OF PEER MENTORING ON MENTORS

While peer-mentoring programs benefit mentees in important ways, the literature shows that mentors also reap positive outcomes from the mentoring experience. In the workplace, mentors can enjoy greater salary, greater promotion rates, and stronger subjective career success than individuals without any previous mentoring experience (Allen, Lentz, and Day, 2006). In addition, mentors may experience career revitalization, social recognition, and personal satisfaction (e.g., Jacobi, 1991).

In the university context, researchers have found that peer mentors gain confidence in facilitating small group learning, a deeper understanding of subject matter, and enhanced problem-solving skills (Topping, 1996). Terrion, Philion, and Leonard (2007) concluded that the mentoring experience enabled peer mentors to establish and maintain networks – fundamental to building social capital – with people throughout the university, including other students, professors, and university administrative staff. Research on student engagement (Chickering and Gamson, 1987) and integration (Tinto, 1998) suggests that these connections contribute significantly to a positive student experience.

Similarly, in his study of the university peer-mentoring experience, Harmon (2006) found that mentors learned through observation and self-reflection. These processes led to changes in their own practice as university students and in their beliefs about influencing other students and personal responsibility in the learning process. In peer-mentoring relationships for highly technical courses such as accounting, mathematics, and chemistry, peer mentors also have the opportunity to relearn and reinforce their knowledge by virtue of explaining what they know and, through this exercise, reviewing or thinking about assimilated learning in greater depth (Jackling and McDowell, 2008; Potter, 1997).

Policy and policymaking in peer-mentoring programs

Given that peer mentoring has such potential for positive impact on students and peer mentors themselves, formal programs would be recommended as a standard practice in colleges and universities. As Jacobi (1991) reported in her review of peer-mentoring programs, a broad range of models can be drawn on for designing and implementing such a service. In more formal programs, mentors are hired, trained, and supervised, with mentees assigned to a specific mentor and the relationship and outcomes of the mentoring program evaluated by program administrators. Some programs may match mentees to a single mentor, while others offer group-based mentoring to students. More casual or informal approaches may assign mentors to mentees through volunteer networks and may have limited evaluation mechanisms in place. Ultimately, different approaches require special considerations and specific conditions. Next, I briefly examine some of the variations in mentoring programs and, with recourse to the literature explore the effectiveness of different approaches.

Comparing informal and formal peer-mentoring models

The development of an informal peer-mentoring relationship can be enjoyed more readily by students who possess certain characteristics. First, they must have access to a supportive listener who possesses knowledge of the higher education context. Second, they must have the ability to seek help and guidance from this peer. Finally, they will benefit if they can weigh a peer mentor's feedback and judge how best to implement it. Finally, the student must have the self-efficacy to put into practice the advice received. Clearly, however, this ideal scenario does not exist for many students, in particular those who represent vulnerable populations, including first-generation postsecondary students, students with learning or other disabilities, students who enter postsecondary programs with a low high school GPA, international students, students coping with mental illness or addiction, and students from a lower socioeconomic status. Such student populations tend to be more at risk for academic failure or early withdrawal from university (Finnie and Qiu, 2009; Pizzolato, 2003; Yeh, 2002). They may not possess the social capital or the rich network from which to draw psychosocial or task support that would enable informal peer mentoring. In other words, many students may not be able to somehow find or be found by a mentor. As Ehrich, Hansford and Tennent (2004) suggest, either seeking help or being found by a peer is the means by which most informal mentoring relationships are formed.

For those students who do not find their own peer mentor, formal programs administered by college and university support services are necessary. Programs such as these provide formal peer mentoring whereby a structured relationship is established between mentees and trained peer mentors who offer support and guidance. The formal nature of these programs may serve to legitimize and publicize the service, thus attracting students who might need the support but do not know to whom to turn for help. Such programs can also enable collaboration with professors, administrators, and other students who advise students in need of support in order to be able to make effective use of mentoring programs.

Comparing individual and group-based peer mentoring

Peer mentoring can be offered in many forms, including the more traditional one-on-one model or in a group format. A benefit of the one-on-one model is that mentoring can be tailored to the individual needs and concerns of the mentee and thus can be efficient in offering appropriate and effective support. In addition, the confidentiality of the one-on-one meeting encourages student mentees to be honest and seek support for problems that may be too embarrassing or personal to share in a group setting.

Group-based mentoring, such as the 'study group', is an approach where the peer mentor leads mentees in reviewing and understanding course material. The study group, also known as supplemental instruction (SI) (Arendale, 1997), may be offered as one of a myriad of student support services in university residences to student athletes, specific groups, such as international students, or a student body. Unlike programs that focus on at-risk students, SI targets difficult courses, is open to all students within the target population, and uses peer-assisted study sessions to supplement professors' lectures. Study groups are most often offered to supplement introductory science, engineering, and math courses, given the difficulty that many students experience in these subjects. Through their interaction with the other study group members, participants establish trust, form relationships, share information and resources, and experience belonging. *Sense of belonging* is defined as a 'subjective sense of affiliation and identification with the university community' (Hoffman, Richmond, Morrow, and Salomone, 2002–2003: 228). This forms as students are integrated into the academic and social spheres of the university, which has ramifications for retention and withdrawal, particularly after the first year (Tinto, 1993, 1998).

Training in peer-mentoring programs

Given the responsibility and professional skills necessary for peer mentors to effectively fulfill both the psychosocial and task function of peer mentoring, formal training of mentors is considered critical to the success of these relationships (Garvey and Alred, 2000; Mee Lee and Bush, 2003; Tierney and Branch, 1992; Tindall, 1995). In fact, in their review of the literature on formal mentoring programs, Ehrich et al. (2004) report lack of mentor training as a key issue that can cause problems in the mentoring relationship. Likewise, Garvey and Alred (2000) state that the skills and knowledge required of a peer mentor should be not assumed and that the organization instituting a peer-mentoring program must commit resources to training. Ongoing training, whereby mentors meet regularly to discuss issues and challenges related to their role and receive instruction to enable them to continue in their skill development, is considered much more effective than 'one-shot' training at the beginning of the mentoring experience (Philion, 2007).

Before establishing a training program, competencies required of the peer mentors need to be identified, as necessary. According to Terrion et al. (2007), peer mentors in training need a solid grasp of the content or information that mentees will seek and that training might be required in these areas. Other examples of the areas requiring training might be topics such as services that mentees can make use of, where specific resources can be found on campus, and how to manage certain university or college-specific tasks such as taking notes in a large lecture hall. In addition, mentors need to learn the dynamics of establishing and maintaining a helping relationship. Finally, in the role of support service providers, peer mentors need the skills and the confidence to work with other professionals in order to effectively share information, understandings, and expertise, in effect enhancing the overall competency of a university's support services.

To enable peer mentors to take on their role and hone these competencies, a training program needs to be developed. One such service, a Peer-Mentoring Training Program (PMTP) designed and implemented at the University of Ottawa in Ottawa, Canada, enabled student peer mentors to develop skills and knowledge. While the immediate goal of the training program was to facilitate peer mentors' capacity to support mentees, the PMTP also furthered the mentors' own personal and professional development. As a researcher at the University of Ottawa, I evaluated the PMTP (Terrion et al., 2007).

The PMTP began with a three-day intensive training workshop during the week before the fall semester began and then continued throughout the school year with ongoing training during the mentors' regular weekly staff meetings. All modules featured an experiential, hands-on format designed to engage participants in a self-reflective learning experience (Schön, 1987). According to Philion (2005), this reflective practice allowed mentors to describe their mentoring practice in terms of its perceived effectiveness while enabling them to adapt as a result of the learning process they had experienced in training.

To facilitate the self-reflexive practice of the peer mentors, an ongoing electronic dialogue, taking the form of a journal, was maintained between mentors and their supervisor. In Terrion and Philion (2008), we, the researchers, argued that the journal, particularly in its electronic form, provided the conduit for a supervisor or trainer to guide peer mentors in developing metacognitive (self-reflexive) skills. The development of these skills was facilitated because the journal required mentors to be conscious of their thought processes and ability to regulate these processes and articulate them in writing for the purpose of supervisory feedback, and, as a result, for further reflection.

Regarding the impact of this training program, Terrion et al. (2007) reported that participants demonstrated statistically significant learning in the competencies that the training was designed to achieve. The least change was reported with respect to establishing a helping relationship. On the one hand, we suggested that this was not surprising, given that mentors were hired with the expectation that they already possessed the interpersonal communication skills, based on previous experience and personality type, required to establish and maintain a helping relationship. On the other hand, we found it noteworthy, given that numerous studies have found that the establishment of the helping relationship is one of the most important components in the training of peer mentors (Baudrit, 2000; Mee Lee and Bush, 2003; Philion, 2005). We recommended, therefore, that attention be paid to ensuring that this aspect of training be well conceived and presented.

Comparing paid and unpaid peer mentors

Whether peer mentors are paid is an issue worth exploring. Researchers (e.g., Terrion and Leonard, 2010) have found that student mentors who are paid a stipend most effectively fulfill the psychosocial and task function in comparison to volunteer peer mentors. In their qualitative study of the motivations of paid and unpaid peer mentors, Terrion and Leonard found that both types of mentors reported being motivated by self-oriented reasons, such as learning about themselves and fulfillment, but that paid mentors were primarily motivated by other-oriented reasons, including a desire to help young people, with many citing their own challenges in first-year university as a reason for wanting to help younger or newer students. Volunteer peer helpers, in contrast, reported being highly motivated to fulfill social needs, such as making friends and becoming integrated into the university. Thus, while both paid and unpaid peer mentors showed a commitment to helping students in need, the social motivation of unpaid mentors could indicate that, if this need were met elsewhere, such as by making new friends outside of the volunteer position, the volunteer could prematurely withdraw from this role.

Evaluation in peer-mentoring programs

The basic premise of program evaluation is to determine a program's viability and how it can be improved (Rossi, Lipsey, and Freeman, 2004). Formal, systematic evaluation should be an integral part of any program design. Interestingly, however, in relation to the evaluation of mentoring programs, Ehrich et al. (2004) suggest, based on their review of over 300 research-based articles about formal mentoring programs, that few programs undergo any kind of rigorous evaluation beyond what Merriam (1983: 172–173) had described as 'testimonials and opinions'. Regardless of the methodology, whether quantitative, qualitative or a combination of the two, Ehrich et al. conclude that '[g]ood practice suggests that there should be ongoing evaluative tasks during the life of a mentoring program and a follow-up assessment some time after the completion of the program' (2004: 536). While program administrators may perceive that they are too busy or lacking skills necessary to conduct program evaluation, it has been found that measuring short-term outcomes and long-term impacts can identify success markers, lessons learned, achievements, ways for improving operations, and steps needed to move forward (Mullen, 2008).

PEER MENTOR AS COMPASS

The peer mentor plays a role similar to a compass by leading the novice student through the difficult-to-navigate terrain of a university or college. Like a compass, the peer mentor provides the support and direction necessary for the student to arrive intact at his or her destination. However, the student has to do the required work to get there. In other words, the peer mentor does not do the tasks or make the decisions for the peer mentee but supports him or her in building the capacity necessary to succeed in higher education. Proper training is necessary for both parties, as is the provision of resources to support the relationship and ongoing feedback for both mentor and mentee. Perhaps a peer mentor is not necessary for every student; however, those students needing a mentor can thrive under the gentle but confident leadership of their guide who assists with the crucial navigation among the intimidating and at times frightening path through higher education. Like novice explorers who must learn to use tools if they are to successfully make their way toward their endpoint, so too must the budding student learn to use such compasses as peer mentoring and other support services to achieve desired goals.

REFERENCES

Allen, T. D., Lentz, E., & Day, R. (2006). Career success outcomes associated with mentoring others: A comparison of mentors and nonmentors. *Journal of Career Development, 32*, 272–285.

Allen, T. D., Russell, J. A., & Maetzke, S. (1997). Formal peer mentoring: factors related to protégés' satisfaction and willingness to mentor others. *Group and Organization Management, 22*, 488–507.

Amenkhienan, C. A., & Kogan, L. (2004). Engineering students' perceptions of academic activities and support services: Factors that influence their academic performance. *College Student Journal, 38*(4), 523–540.

Angelique, H., Kyle, K., & Taylor, E. (2002). Mentors and Muses: New strategies for academic success. *Innovative Higher Education, 26*(3), 195–209.

Arendale, D. (1997). Supplemental Instruction: Review of research concerning the effectiveness of SI from The University of Missouri–Kansas City and other institutions across the United States. *Proceedings of the 17th and 18th Annual Institutes for Learning Assistance Professionals: 1996 and 1997* (pp. 1–25). Tucson, AZ: University Learning Center, University of Arizona. Retrieved January 21, 2011 from http://eric.ed.gov/PDFS/ED457797.pdf.

Baudrit, A. (2000). *Le tutorat dans les Universités Anglo-saxonnes: Des idées pour les Universités Francophones* (translated: Tutoring in anglo-saxon universities: Lessons for French universities). Paris: L'Harmattan.

Chickering, A. W. & Gamson Z. F. (1987). Seven principles for good practice in undergraduate education. *American Association of Higher Education Bulletin*, March, 3–7.

Coleman, J. (1988). Social capital in the creation of human capital. *American Journal of Sociology, 94* (Suppl. 95), S94–S120. Retrieved January 21, 2011 from http://links.jstor.org/sici?sici=0002-9602%281988%2994%3CS95%3ASCITCO%3E2.0.CO%3B2-P

Ehrich, L. S., Hansford, B., & Tennent, L. (2004). Formal mentoring programmes in education and other professions: A review of the literature. *Educational Administration Quarterly, 40*, 518–540.

Finnie, R., & Qiu, H. T. (2009). Is the glass (or classroom) half-empty or nearly full? New evidence on persistence in post-secondary education in Canada. In R. Finnie, R. E. Mueller, A. Sweetman, & A. Usher (Eds.), *Who goes? Who stays? What matters? Accessing and persisting in post-secondary education in Canada* (pp. 179–208). Montreal & Kingston: McGill–Queen's University Press.

Garvey, B., & Alred, G. (2000). Educating mentors. *Mentoring & Tutoring: Partnership in Learning, 8*(2), 113–126.

Harmon, B. V. (2006). A qualitative study of the learning processes and outcomes associated with students who serve as peer mentors. *Journal of the First-Year Experience & Students in Transition, 18*(2), 53–82.

Hendry, L. B., & Reid, M. (2000). Social relationships and health: The meaning of social 'connectedness' and how it relates to health concerns for rural Scottish adolescents. *Journal of Adolescence, 23*, 705–719.

Hoffman, M., Richmond, J., Morrow, J., & Salomone, K. (2002–2003). Investigating 'sense of belonging' in first-year college students. *Journal of College Student Retention, 4*(3), 227–256.

Jacobi, M. (1991). Mentoring and undergraduate academic success: A literature review. *Review of Educational Research, 61*(4), 505–532.

Jackling, B., & McDowell, T. (2008). Peer mentoring in an accounting setting: A case study of mentor skill development. *Accounting Education: An International Journal, 17*(4), 447–462.

Keating N., Swindle J., & Foster, D. (2005). The role of social capital in aging well. In Government of Canada (Ed.), *Social capital in action: Thematic policy studies* (pp. 24–48). Ottawa: Policy Research Initiative. Retrieved January 23, 2011, from http://www.policyresearch.gc.ca/doclib/SC_Thematic_E.pdf

Kram, K. (1983). Phases of the mentor relationship. *Academy of Management Journal, 26*, 608–625.

Kram, K., & Isabella, L. (1985). Mentoring Alternatives: The role of peer relationships in career development. *Academy of Management Journal, 28*, 110–132.

Lochner, K. A., Kawachi, I., Brennan, R. T., & Buka, S. L. (2003). Social capital and neighborhood mortality rates in Chicago. *Social Science & Medicine, 56*, 1797–1805.

Loots, A. G. (2009). Student Involvement and Retention in Higher Education: The case for academic peer mentoring programmes for first-years. *Education as Change, 13*(1), 211–235.

Mee Lee, L., & Bush, T. (2003). Student Mentoring in Higher Education: Hong Kong Baptist University. *Mentoring & Tutoring: Partnership in Learning, 11*(3), 263–271.

Merriam, S. (1983). Mentors and Protégés: A critical review of literature. *Adult Education Quarterly, 33*, 161–173.

Mills, C., Heyworth, J., Rosenwax, L., Carr, & Rosenberg, M. (2009). Factors associated with the academic success of first year Health Science students. *Advances in Health Science Education, 14*, 205–217.

Mullen, C. A. (Ed.) (2008). *The Handbook of Formal Mentoring in Higher Education: A case study approach.* Norwood, MA: Christopher-Gordon.

Nora, A. (1993). Two-year colleges and minority students' educational aspirations: Help or hindrance? *Higher Education: Handbook of Theory and Research, 9*, 212–247.

Packard, B. W-L. (2004–2005). Mentoring and retention in college science: Reflections on the sophomore year. *Journal of College Student Retention, 6*(3), 289–300.

Pascarella, E. T., & Terenzini, P. (1983). Predicting voluntary freshman year persistence/ withdrawal behavior in a residential university: A path analytic validation of the Tinto model. *Journal of Educational Psychology, 52*(2), 60–75.

Philion, R. (2005). *Prise en compte des représentations des étudiants mentors au regard de leur rôle, de leur pratique et de leurs besoins en matière de formation* (translated: Consideration of student peer mentors' perceptions of their role, practices and training needs). Unpublished doctoral dissertation, University of Ottawa, Ottawa, ON.

Philion, R. (2007). L'analyse de construits au service de la co-construction de sens chez les étudiants mentors (translated: The role of construct analysis in the construction of meaning by student peer mentors). *Revue Éducation et Francophonie, 35*(2), 192–216.

Pizzolato, J. E. (2003). Developing self-authorship: Exploring the experiences of high-risk college students. *Journal of College Student Development, 44*(6), 797–812.

Potter, J. (1997). New directions in student tutoring, *Education and Training, 39*(1), 24–30.

Putnam, R. D. (2000). *Bowling alone: The collapse and revival of American community.* New York: Simon & Schuster.

Resnick, M. D., Harris, L. J., & Blum, R. W. (1993). The impact of caring and connectedness on adolescent health and well-being. *Journal of Paediatrics & Child Health, 29* (Sup 1), S3–S9.

Roberts, L. W., Clifton, R. A., & Etcheverry, E. (2001). Social capital and educational attainment: A study of undergraduates in a faculty of education. *Alberta Journal of Educational Research, 47*, 24–39.

Rose, G. L. (2005). Group differences in graduate students' concepts of the ideal mentor. *Research in Higher Education, 46*, 53–80.

Rossi, P., Lipsey, M., & Freeman, H. (2004). *Evaluation: A systematic approach* (7th ed.). Thousand Oaks, CA: SAGE.

Sanchez, R. J., Bauer, T. N., & Saronto, M. E. (2006). Peer-mentoring Freshmen: Implications for satisfaction, commitment, and retention to graduation. *Academy of Management Learning & Education*, *5*(1), 25–37.

Schön, D. (1987). *Educating the reflective practitioner: Toward a new design for teaching and learning in the professions.* San Francisco: Jossey-Bass.

Teachman, J. D., Paasch, K., & Carver, K. (1996). Social capital and dropping out of school early. *Journal of Marriage and the Family*, *58*(3), 773–783.

Terrion, J. L. (2006). Building social capital in vulnerable families: Success markers of a school-based intervention program. *Youth and Society*, *38*(2), 155–176.

Terrion, J. L., & Daoust J-L. (2011–2012). Assessing the impact of supplemental instruction on the retention of undergraduate students after controlling for motivation. *Journal of College Student Retention*, *13*(3), 311–328.

Terrion, J. L., & Leonard, D. (2010). Motivation of paid peer mentors and unpaid peer helpers in higher education. *International Journal of Evidence Based Coaching and Mentoring*, *8*(1), 85–103.

Terrion, J. L., & Philion, R. (2008). The electronic mentor journal as reflection-on-action: A qualitative analysis of communication and learning in a peer-mentoring program. *Studies in Higher Education*, *33*(5), 583–597.

Terrion, J. L., Philion, R., & Leonard, D. (2007). An evaluation of a university peer-mentoring training program. *International Journal of Evidence Based Coaching and Mentoring*, *5*(1), 42–57.

Tierney, J. P., & Branch, A. Y. (1992). *College students as mentors for at-risk youth: A study of six campus partners in learning programmes.* Philadelphia, PA: Public/Private Ventures.

Tindall, J. A. (1995). *Peer programmes: An in-depth look at peer helping, planning, implementation, and administration.* Bristol, PA: Accelerated Development.

Tinto, V. (1993). *Leaving College: Rethinking the causes and cures of student attrition. Second edition.* Chicago: University of Chicago Press.

Tinto, V. (1998). Colleges as Communities: Taking research on student persistence seriously. *Review of Higher Education*, *21*(2), 167–177.

Topping, K. J. (1996). The effectiveness of peer tutoring in further and higher education: A typology and review of the literature. *Higher Education*, *32*, 321–345.

Yeh, T. L. (2002). Asian American college students who are educationally at risk. *New Directions for Student Services*, *97*, 61–71.

Inclusion

26

Using Best Practices for Teaching the Process of Coaching

Hal Portner and Mary H. Portner

INTRODUCTION

The Wisconsin Deafblind Technical Assistance Project (WDBTAP), a unit of the Wisconsin Department of Public Instruction, has a staff of approximately 30 specialists who assist public school teachers in the state of Wisconsin, USA. The teachers they support are those with students with hearing and/or visual impairment mainstreamed into their otherwise regular classes.

These WDBTAP specialists are knowledgeable and experienced in addressing the needs of deaf/blind youngsters. Their task is to provide classroom teachers with materials and advice about how to accommodate hearing and visually impaired students so that those students will function and progress within the general education curriculum. Although the specialists are generally well received and appreciated by the teachers, little change has been evident in the way mainstreamed deaf/blind students are being taught and how well those students learn. The specialists supply relevant information and materials, but their efforts are inconsistent in respect to creating meaningful change in the teachers' day-to-day instructional practices. Simply put, the specialists are not having the desired impact on teacher effectiveness.

INFORMATION AND MATERIALS WERE NOT ENOUGH

It became clear to WDBTAP supervisors that more was needed by teachers from the specialists beyond information and knowledge about teaching students with limited hearing and/or vision. Additionally, teachers had to develop and rely on specialized skills in order to effectively employ the materials and implement relevant practices in their classrooms. A teacher who had these skills would be one who is willing and able to (a) generate and choose purposefully from among viable alternatives; (b) act upon those choices in ways that improve student learning; (c) monitor and reflect upon the consequences of applying those choices; and (d) modify and adjust practices in order to enhance student learning.

In addition, teachers with these pedagogical skills needed to acquire the confidence to use them purposefully and effectively. Bandura (1994) suggested that individuals' confidence and their perceptions of their abilities can affect their efforts and consequently influence outcomes for students. According to Bandura, more than half of the non-special education teachers this educational psychologist surveyed had low confidence when it came to effectively engaging students having disabilities, demonstrating 'helplessness', or exhibiting aggression. General classroom teachers also lacked confidence when using instructional strategies explicit to the needs of students with other disabilities. Bandura also found no significant differences in degrees of confidence across groups by years of teaching experience for general education teachers. This suggests that time alone does not necessarily contribute to increased confidence in classroom teachers to support students with disabilities.

Certainly, knowledge about disability characteristics is important, but so is practical application of this knowledge in the classroom. Part B of US Public Law 108–446, December 3, 2004, the revised Individualized Accommodation Plan process, or IEP, emphasizes that the classroom teacher's *application* of this information is key to ensuring that appropriate goals and objectives are both established and achieved.

Repackage the delivery system, not the product

In fall 2009, after further assessment and discussion, WDBTAP supervisors decided that although the content of the specialists' assistance was appropriate, they needed to present that content to teachers in a new way, one that would result in their advice and materials being effectively applied. The supervisors then reviewed various strategies and determined that the specialists would increase effectiveness by employing coaching strategies into their work. In February 2010, we, the authors, were contracted to present a two-day workshop designed to teach the specialists to coach.[1]

We began by reviewing materials and interviewing WBDTAP staff about the project's mission and procedures, and clarifying mutual goals and expectations. Our next step was to determine what effective training strategies and processes or 'best practices' to use or adapt in order to address these goals and expectations, that is, to teach these specialists to be effective coaches.

A word about best practices

A best practice is a technique or methodology that, through experience and research, has proven to lead reliably to a desired result. A commitment to using a best practice is a commitment to using all the knowledge and technology at one's disposal to ensure success.

Carr (2009) points out that the notion of best practices came out of a national initiative that identified those practices that were soundly based in research and development. The National Center for Education Research (2002) disseminates these practices in order for others to learn about and consider 'adopting' or 'adapting' them. Sweeny (2003) postulated that what is best for one program may not be best for others. This education consultant suggested that the goal is what determines what might be best for a particular program.

Based on our experience, research, and WDBTAP's needs, we designed the workshop and follow up sessions to include elements of the following best practices: cognitive coaching, mastery teaching, constructivism, and peer coaching. We explore these practices in more detail as their application is described.

The two practices or support services that the WDBTAP specialists have already been using to address the project's goals can be categorized as *consulting* and *collaborating*. *Consulting* implies a hierarchical relationship. As described by Lipton and Wellman (2001: 20), consultants inform regarding processes and protocols, advise based on well-developed expertise, or advocate for particular choices and actions. *Collaborating* involves people working together as equals to achieve agreed upon goals. The collaborators act as partners who bring information and resources to their interactions.

WDBTAP's decision to add *coaching* as a third practice to the specialists' repertoire of strategies was consistent with the state's emphasis on coaching as a model for providing technical assistance to educators. It also was reinforced by WDBTAP supervisors' agreement with our four principles that underpin coaching (see Portner, 2008).

1   Coaching places responsibility for decision making with the one being coached.
2   Coaching, like teaching, involves constant decision-making driven by the feedback loop of action, result, and adjustment.
3   A major coaching skill is to ask the questions that will guide those being coached to to uncover their expectations, beliefs, and perceptions thereby empowering them to make their own informed decisions.
4   Change resulting from reflection is not remediation.

From among several concepts of coaching, we selected the cognitive coaching model as the potentially most productive for this particular program. We did this because the elements of cognitive coaching provide not only a process for the coach to guide the teacher to critically analyze and reflect on their teaching of hearing and visually impaired students, but also have the potential to engender in teachers an increase in confidence in their ability to make effective instructional decisions. The focus of the two-day workshop was to teach the elements of cognitive coaching to the participants.

THE COGNITIVE COACHING MODEL

Cognitive coaching is based on Costa and Garmston's (2002) work. The model involves the coach using dialogue and questioning strategies to guide the teacher through a process of reflection, thinking, and decision making. By guiding discussion and asking the right questions the right way, coaches lead teachers through the type of planning and activity that develops competency and confidence. Costa and Garmston (2002: 4) documented research that demonstrates that

> teachers with high conceptual levels are more adaptive and flexible in their teaching style. They produce higher achieving students who are more cooperative and involved in their work. Cognitive coaching increases the capacities for sound decision making and self-directedness.

Cognitive coaching was synthesized by Costa and Garmston from the work of researchers such as Glickman, Gordon, and Ross-Gordon (2001) (developmental supervision); Goldhammer (1969) and Cogan (1973) (clinical supervision); Sergiovanni and Starratt (1998) (supervision theory); Thies-Sprinthal (1986) (teacher as adult learner), Koestler (1972) (holonomy), and Kegan (1982) (adult development).

KEY COMPONENTS OF COGNITIVE COACHING

The process of cognitive coaching, often referred to as the *coaching cycle*, involves observing the teacher teaching, and the reflection, problem-solving, and decision-making that takes place before and after that observation. The three steps in this process – pre-observation conference, classroom observation, and post-observation conference – are next described.

Pre-observation conference

The coach and teacher meet privately to discuss the upcoming class. The coach's objectives are to have the teacher be able to express and clarify learning objectives, fine-tune teaching strategies, anticipate student behaviors, firm-up plans for monitoring student learning, and consider ways to adjust instruction.

During this pre-observation conversation, the coach asks the teacher probing questions about his or her plans and expectations for the lesson.

These conversations are conducted in ways that will encourage the teacher to come up with ideas to enrich the lesson. They will also provide the teacher with the opportunity to gain confidence as a reflective, self-reliant practitioner who thinks through the consequences of plans and actions and makes modifications based on thoughtful consideration of outcomes. Techniques the coach uses during this phase can include probing for detail, pressing for specifics, being patient, acknowledging and validating answers, summarizing, avoiding judgment, and resisting giving advice.

Classroom observation

The coach's objective while observing the class is to gather data. What is primarily observed is the extent to which quality learning takes place. Therefore, what the coach looks for is evidence of student learning and what is contributing to the process or obstructing it. Techniques a coach may use during this phase include sitting where she can best observe, concentrating on agreed upon area(s) to observe, looking for evidence of student learning, considering what helps or hinders learning, taking notes to help guide later review of the observation, and refraining from participating or making comments.

Post-observation conference

The coach's goal here is to encourage the teacher to assess the effectiveness of the lesson, to identify factors that contributed to and interfered with student learning, and to consider why he or she may have used alternative instructional strategies at times. The coach helps scaffold and promote teacher reflection by asking questions that will lead to self-reflection and analysis of the lesson, and learning based on the data collected. It also helps the teacher to consider how the application of the new insights can be applied to future lessons. This is the critical transformation stage that is necessary to ensure that a teacher's instructional decisions consistently impact student learning. Techniques the coach may use during this phase include sticking to objective facts, keeping opinions to him/herself, asking open-ended questions, acknowledging and validating comments, avoiding implied negative questions, considering when to give advice, summarizing, and agreeing on follow-up activities.

A word about giving advice

Practitioners of Cognitive Coaching generally agree that decisions are more likely to be internalized and acted upon when, through guidance and reflection, the receiver of coaching constructs his or her own decisions and actions. However, there is a powerful human urge to give advice and the strong motivation to seek advice from a mentor or coach. Carr (2010) suggests how advice could occur without being a roadblock to effective coaching.

A first step for deciding whether to give advice, Carr proposes, is to determine the degree of risk involved. For example, the less interested in taking advice, the higher the risk that the advice will be meaningless, not heard, or completely rejected. Even worse, the advice receiver may act on the advice and when it does not work, blame the advice giver. When the advice-giver determines that the seeker is in an appropriate low-risk state to receive advice, he or she can then ask whether sharing might be helpful. Carr suggests that the advice-giver draw upon his or her own life experience and frame the advice within that experience ('Here's what I did,' and not, 'You should do this.'). The coach then should ask whether the advice fits the seeker's situation. Throughout this process, the advice giver listens deeply to the reaction of the seeker and through asking powerful questions helps the seeker modify, revise, or otherwise adapt the advice. In addition to selecting cognitive coaching as the *content* of the workshop, we chose mastery teaching as the best-practice model for the session's *process*.

THE MASTERY TEACHING MODEL

For over a decade, Hunter (1982) and her colleagues at the University of California, Los Angeles, studied teaching decisions and their implementation. They concluded that '*regardless of who or what is being taught*, all teaching decisions fall into three categories: (1) what contents to teach next, (2) what the student will do to learn and to demonstrate learning has occurred, and (3) what the teacher will do to facilitate the acquisition of that learning' (1982: 3; emphasis added). Hunter also found that learning would increase if those decisions reflect the teacher's sensitivity to the student and to the situation.

In order for teachers to identify consciously and deliberately the decisions needed to be made in each category, Hunter formulated a research-validated lesson design that she calls 'mastery teaching'. The elements of mastery teaching can be categorized as purpose and objective, anticipatory set, effective content, modeling, and checking for understanding. Although these elements of mastery teaching apply to teaching children, Portner (2005) adapted them to form a framework for teaching adults. A description of these elements and how we applied them to the WDBTAP workshop follows. We consider each of the elements to be a 'best practice' in its own right.

Purpose and objective

Hunter (1982: 29) emphasizes the need for an objective or purpose when she cautions the teacher to 'be sure that when you don't tell students what they will learn, that is what you intended, rather than having the omission result from your [not being clear about it yourself]'. We wanted participants in our WDBTAP sessions to know up front what they could expect to get out of the experience and why it would be worth their time to participate. We know that adults are *goal-oriented*. They appreciate a program that is organized with clearly defined elements. Adults are also *relevancy-oriented*. They need to feel that a workshop will be applicable to their work. In the case of such a workshop, they also need to feel that they will be better coaches and that the teachers with whom they work will become better learners because of their participation.

In designing the workshop, we wanted to be clear about *what* participants will learn and *why* they will need to learn it. Thus, the material we supplied to WDBTAP supervisors and participants prior to the training included the purpose and objective of the sessions.

Anticipatory set

First impressions are important in that they set the tone for what is to follow. A week prior to the event, we sent each participant a personally addressed note introducing ourselves, sharing expectations, and assigning an activity that would be used in the workshop and give a taste of what they could expect. Here is an approximation of that email message.

Dear _____:

We are looking forward to meeting and working with you Thursday and Friday, June 17 and 18. During our time together, you can expect to acquire and fine-tune a set of skills you will use to be a more effective coach.

A major part of our work together will be the opportunity for you to practice coaching and receive feedback. During these practice sessions, you will take turns coaching and being coached. To prepare for this, prior to the sessions, we ask that you develop a brief (about 10 minute) lesson to teach to the small group who will be sharing your table. The lesson can be academic, but preferably not.

Be creative. For example, it can be something like how to do a card trick, hold a golf club, or tie a bowline knot (more fun than teaching the periodic table, perhaps, but just as effective for practicing the coaching process). Bring along any props or materials needed to teach the lesson. Also, make a copy or two of your brief (one page or less) lesson plan.

Yes, you can expect to work hard. You can also expect to learn and have fun while doing so.

Effective content

Hunter (1982: 33) contends that 'teachers must determine which information is basic or essential to understanding the content or process of the lesson'. Once that is done, she writes, teachers can 'separate that information from information which may be desirable but is supplementary and can be acquired later' (ibid.).

Good professional development practice suggests having participants actively engaged as soon as possible, and as much as possible. So, after the usual opening business, we immediately introduced the coaching cycle and had participants practicing, discussing, and reflecting on the cycle's components throughout the workshop's two days.

Theoretical underpinnings and other important aspects of coaching such as trust building, establishing ground rules, and assessing needs and learning styles came into play on a need-to-know basis by relating such issues to the activity of the moment. For this reason, we provided handouts and elaborated upon their content as relevant questions or situations arose. We did, however, briefly touch upon those important underpinnings that were not substantively addressed with the intention of presenting them in detail during possible later sessions.

Modeling

A model is an example such as an activity or object that a student can perceive directly rather than having to rely on memory of some previous learning or experience. During the workshop, we modeled the coaching cycle and its application through demonstration. In order to engage participants and provide an authentic model, the demonstration was conducted as follows.

One participant agreed prior to the workshop to play the role of a teacher. She was given a basic lesson plan. During the actual demonstration, one of the authors role-played the coach and the entire group of participants played the students. The role-playing teacher and coach conducted a mock pre-observation conference followed by a group discussion of the conference's objectives and techniques. The teacher then taught the lesson to the students while the coach observed. A discussion of the objectives and methodology of observing followed. A post-observation conference and a discussion of its objectives and techniques completed the demonstration.

Modeling through demonstration enhanced understanding. However, the difference between observing how something should be done and being able to do it is the quantum leap in learning. The springboard for that leap is developed by guided practice accompanied by feedback that gives the learner information about what is correct, what needs to be improved, and how to improve performance.

We devoted the major part of the workshop to practicing the coaching cycle. In order to provide everyone the opportunity to coach and receive constructive feedback, participants were seated in groups of five. Individuals in each group alternated the roles of teacher, coach, and student. In order to reduce anxiety and inject some levity into the process, the participants' role-playing teachers taught the brief creative lessons they developed prior to the workshop. Each configuration of participants performed the complete coaching cycle.

With each repetition of the cycle, participants became more fluent with what to do and what to look for in coaching. Participants comments such as: 'Having the opportunity to role play all roles – student, teacher, coach – provided a wonderful opportunity for reflecting on how this process will be integrated into my practice,' and, 'Practicing being the coach was amazing. I needed the application to tie together the theory,' confirmed our observations of increasing levels of interest, more creative participant engagement, and overall evidence of authentic learning. As in the demonstration, we processed each phase of the cycle and checked for understanding before moving onto the next phase.

Checking for understanding

Most educators understand that just because they have taught, it does not necessarily mean the students have learned. There are several ways to take occasional 'snapshots' in order to check for understanding along the way. One method used during the workshop was to ask participants how they might apply what had just been discussed. From their responses, we were able to decide whether to move on or revisit a point, perhaps using a different approach.

At the end of each day's session, we checked for understanding by responding to our list of expectations, questions, and concerns that we had elicited from participants at the start of and during the session. We posted the lists on newsprint. We added written clarifications and new understandings to the newsprint alongside the original expectations, questions, and concerns. As anticipated, one of the concerns expressed was the need for specific strategies related to the kinds of situations participants might encounter while actually coaching teachers of mainstreamed deaf/blind students.

Throughout the workshop, our focus was on participants experiencing the *process* of the coaching cycle. However, although we are skilled in teaching the generic coaching cycle process, we had little knowledge of and even less experience in the content to which participants will be applying the cycle. The participants, however, were cognizant of the needs of the visual and hearing impaired and generally experienced in teaching those students.

Thus, we suggested that WDBTAP institute a second round of practice in the near future during which participants would construct their own strategies for applying the coaching cycle to the kinds of situations they could expect to encounter in the field. As they go through the process of devising such 'real-world' strategies, the participants would be experiencing the best practice tenets of constructivism.

CONSTRUCTIVISM AS A RESPONSE TO THE CHALLENGE OF CONTEXT

Constructivism posits that learning is an active, constructive process. The learner is an information constructor who actively constructs or creates their own new knowledge and meaning from interactions between their experiences and their ideas.

Lev Vygotsky, the Russian psychologist, was predominant among several originators and important contributors to the model. According to Crawford (1996), Vygotsky (1978) focused on the connections between people and the sociocultural context in which they act and interact in shared experiences. Vygotsky's theory promotes learning contexts in which students play an active role in learning. Roles of the teacher and student are therefore shifted whereby the teacher collaborates with his or her students in order to help facilitate the construction of meaning.

Our recommendation was to use typical classroom situations for the proposed follow up practice. The goal for participants would be for them, in collaboration with facilitators, to develop strategies and language specific to coaching educators toward becoming self-reliant teachers of hearing and visual impaired students. Prior to gathering for such a practice session, participants would select an authentic situation from among their actual caseloads. They would prepare a summary of the issues encountered along with any pertinent information about the teacher, students, and administration. This 'assignment' would serve as an anticipatory set activity. During practice, participants, under the guidance of a facilitator, would process each phase of the cycle (i.e., pre-observation conference, classroom observation, post-observation conference) with the goal of codifying strategies and techniques for addressing those real-life issues.

IMPLEMENTING NEWLY ACQUIRED KNOWLEDGE

Even if the workshops went well and participants left excited and inspired, we know that demonstration and practice alone do not guarantee implementation of newly acquired knowledge. When Showers, Joyce, and Bennett (1987) released ground-breaking research regarding implementation of training, they reported that although 25 percent of learners will transfer a new skill into their practice as a result of theory, demonstration, practice, and corrective feedback during their training, 90 percent of learners will transfer a new skill into their practice when demonstration, practice, and corrective feedback are followed up with job-embedded coaching. Subsequent research by Joyce and Showers (1995) reinforced these findings.

Based on the Showers et al. (1987) study, which has been reinforced by personal experience over the years, we recommended to WDBTAP that they follow the workshops with peer coaching. This best-practice model extends the use of the coaching cycle from coaching teachers to coaching coaches.

PEER COACHING

Peer coaching evolved out of Edmonds's (1979) research on effective schools and positive school climate. The adaptation of peer coaching as a follow up to the situation described in this case calls for two WDBTAP specialists who have gone through the same workshops to partner and, together, use the coaching cycle to coach each other. Ideally, one of the coaches would invite his or her partner to observe him or her conducting actual pre-conference, observation, and post-conference activities with a teacher. The peer-coach would sandwich that observation between pre- and post- conferences with the partner. The goal would be to determine what does (and does not) work and to develop and try out new strategies. Peer coaching also provides the opportunity to share successful practices, act as a problem-solving vehicle, and reduce isolation among coaches. Additionally, peer coaching helps internalize and more effectively apply what was learned during training.

Sustainability of best-practice outcomes

As a result of the workshop, and assuming our recommended follow up activities would be implemented, the selection, adaptation, and application of best practices should be comprehensive and coherent. However, the use of newly acquired coaching skills needs to be sustained so as not to diminish its effectiveness and, indeed, in order to continuously enhance it. Consequently, we suggested to WDBTAP that it implement the following activities in order to sustain coaching as a strategy in the specialists' repertoire.

- Provide facilitated individual and group sessions where specialists can reflect on successes and challenges experienced while coaching in the field.
- Sponsor workshops in such areas as alternative classroom data-collection methods and the relationship of learning styles to coaching.
- Introduce the process of designing and implementing individual growth plans.
- Distribute pertinent material about coaching.
- Conduct periodic online sessions for purposes of fine-tuning and networking.
- Develop and implement a plan for evaluating the frequency and quality of the application of coaching and its effectiveness on teaching and learning in mainstreamed classrooms.

SUMMARY AND CONCLUSION

The goal of the Wisconsin Deafblind Technical Assistance Project (WDBTAP) was to enhance the ability of specialists to present content and instructional strategies to teachers in mainstreamed classrooms in a way that would allow their advice and materials to be effectively applied. Coaching was the process WDBTAP specified to meet this goal. We were engaged in teaching the specialists to coach, and, to that end, we adapted aspects of these models of educational best practice: cognitive coaching, mastery teaching, constructivism, and peer coaching.

We selected cognitive coaching as the 'best practice' by which to teach the WDBTAP specialists because the model has proven to help teachers critically analyze and reflect on their teaching. The tenets of cognitive coaching also has added value in this particular situation in that it has the potential to increase teachers' confidence for making effective instructional decisions regarding hearing and visually impaired students in mainstreamed classes.

To identify consciously the decisions teachers need to make throughout a lesson, Hunter (1982) formulated a lesson design, Mastery Teaching, based on research-validated knowledge. Although the 'best practice' elements of Hunter's lesson design apply to teaching children, we adapted them to form the framework for use with adult learners.

A desired outcome of professional development is the transfer of learning a new skill into practice. According to research by Showers et al. (1987), workshop strategies that help transfer of learning to occur include practice and corrective feedback. Describing the function of constructive feedback during a workshop, Reeves (2010: para. 3) suggested visiting a practice session led by a great athletic coach or outstanding music teacher: 'After a great practice session, every musician and athlete in the class knows that they are better than when they started.'

Teaching the WDBTAP specialists to coach their particular group of teachers presented a special challenge because we were unfamiliar with the unique situations faced by teachers with deaf/blind-impaired students in their inclusive classes. The best practice we recommended to address this challenge during follow up sessions was an adaptation of constructivism whereby participants develop their own strategies for applying the coaching cycle to the kinds of situations they expect to encounter.

The best practice we recommended for ensuring ongoing improvement and sustainability was peer coaching. We also recommended networking sessions to facilitate individual and group reflection and ongoing training in such areas as classroom data-collection and the adaptation of learning styles to coaching. We additionally saw value in these sessions for developing individual growth plans, occasionally disseminating ideas and pertinent resource material, and using periodic online sessions for the purposes of fine-tuning and networking, as well as for evaluating workshop effectiveness.

We believe that the same best practices we used and recommended for this project can, when properly adapted, effectively address the goals of most training-of-coaches workshops. Finally, we contend that no matter the area in which the workshop participants will later coach, the focus should be on the *process* of coaching.

NOTE

1 Although we use the term *coach*, we consider coach to be synonymous with *mentor*. When done well, each involves aspects of the other; for example, developing a trusting relationship, assessing learning styles and needs, applying observation and feedback, and challenging those being coached/mentored to improve.

REFERENCES

Bandura, A. (1994). Self-efficacy. In V. S. Ramachaudran (Ed.), *Encyclopedia of human behavior, 4,* 71–81. New York: Academic Press.

Carr, R. (2009). Best Practices: Barrier or boost for mentoring? *Peer Bulletin*, 178. Retrieved September 24, 2010, from http://www.peer.ca/Projects/Bulletin178-080.html#Anchor-MENTOR-11481

Carr, R. (2010). *Advice-giving: The forbidden fruit of mentoring and coaching.* Retrieved October 9, 2010, from http://www.mentors.ca/thementornews.html

Cogan, M. L. (1973). *Clinical Supervision.* Boston: Houghton-Mifflin.

Costa, A., & Garmston, R. (2002). *Cognitive Coaching* (2nd ed.). Norwood, MA: Christopher-Gordon.

Crawford, K. (1996). Vygotskian approaches to human development in the information era. *Educational Studies in Mathematics, 31,* 43–62.

Edmonds, R. (1979). Effective schools for the urban poor. *Educational Leadership, 37*(1), 15–24.

Glickman, C. D., Gordon, S. P., & Ross-Gordon, J. M. (2001). *SuperVision and instructional leadership: A developmental approach* (6th ed.). Needham Heights, MA: Allyn & Bacon.

Goldhammer, R. (1969). *Clinical Supervision.* New York: Holt, Rinehart and Winston.

Hunter, M. (1982). *Mastery teaching.* El Segundo, CA: TIP Publications.

Joyce, B., & Showers, B. (1995) *Student achievement through staff development: Fundamentals of school renewal* (2nd ed.). White Plains, NY: Longman.

Kegan, R. (1982). *The evolving self: problem and process in human development.* Cambridge, MA: Harvard University Press.

Koestler, A. (1972). *The Roots of Coincidence.* New York: Vantage Books.

Lipton, L., & Wellman, B. (2001) *Mentoring Matters: a practical guide to learning-focused relationships.* Sherman, CT: Miravia, LLC.

National Center for Education Research. (2002). *U.S. Department of Education Institute of Education Sciences, H.R. 3801-15 Education Sciences Reform Act of 2002, PART B.* Retrieved November 20, 2010, from http://ies.ed.gov/pdf/PL107-279.pdf

Portner, H. (2005). *Workshops that really work: The ABCs of designing and delivering sensational presentations.* Thousand Oaks, CA: Corwin.

Portner, H. (2008). *Mentoring New Teachers* (3rd ed.). Thousand Oaks, CA: Corwin.

Reeves, D. (2010). *Practices, not programs: high-leverage interventions that work. ASCD Express, 6*(1). Retrieved November 18, 2010, from http://www.ascd.org/ascd-express/vol6/601 reeves.aspx?utm_source=ascdexpress&utm_medium=email&utm_campaign=express601 accessed 10/14/2010

Sergiovanni, T. J., & Starratt, R. J. (1998). *Supervision: A redefinition* (6th ed.). New York: McGraw-Hill.

Showers, B., Joyce, B., & Bennett, B. (1987). Synthesis of Research on Staff Development: A framework for future study and a state-of-the-art analysis. *Educational Leadership, 45*(3), 77–87.

Sweeny, B. (2003). *What is common and unique in mentoring across different settings?* Retrieved October 30, 2010, from http://www.mentoring-association.org/MembersOnly/Consult/CommonUniqueList.htm

Thies-Sprinthal, L. (1986). A Collaborative Approach for Mentor Training: A working model. *Journal of Teacher Education, 37*(6), 13–20.

Vygotsky, L.S. (1978). *Mind and Society: The development of higher mental processes.* Cambridge, MA: Harvard University Press.

27

Mentoring Graduate Students of Color

Richard J. Reddick
and Michelle D. Young

INTRODUCTION

The United States is becoming an increasingly diverse, complex and competitive environment. By the year 2020, demographers predict that students of color will constitute 46 percent of the US school-age population (Miller, 1995) and by 2050 the population of non-Hispanic, Whites will grow by 7 percent (US Census Bureau, 2004), a percentage that stands in stark contrast to projected increases for the Hispanic population (projected to increase by 188 percent), the Asian population (projected to increase by 213 percent), and the Black population (projected to increase by 71 percent). Yet, as the nation's population grows increasingly diverse, both K-12 and higher education faculty and administrators are disproportionately White (Turner and Myers, 2000; Young and Brooks, 2008). For example, Gay (1997) estimated that the number of public school teachers of color has declined from 12 percent in the 1970s to 6 percent in the 1990s. The 2003–2004 School and Staffing Survey indicates that statistics for school administrators of color are similarly discouraging, estimating that the total distribution of 'minority' principals in public schools at 17.6 percent, although the minority student population was estimated at 39.7 percent (Strizek, Pittsonberger, Riordan, Lyter, and Orlofsky, 2006).

In higher education, 37 percent of undergraduate students in 2008 were people of color compared to 22 percent in 1988 and 30 percent in 1998 (Brainard, 2010).

Similarly, 17.4 percent of full-time faculty members were Asian, Black, Hispanic, or American Indian in 2007, the most recent year for which data are available. According to Brainard's (2010) analysis, these numbers represent a 58 percent increase in faculty of color since 1997. However, the percentage of faculty of color in higher education is disappointingly low. Many see the comparatively low percentage of faculty of color as a pipeline issue: Compared to their White counterparts, smaller percentages of students of color attend four-year colleges and this is also the case for college graduates of color whose doctorate is sought later on.

The continuing lack of diversity of the professoriate is a problem (Turner and Myers, 2000). McCarthy and Kuh's (1997) longitudinal study of educational administration faculty provides a comprehensive examination of faculty perspectives and attitudes on this issue. The authors administered surveys to educational administration program faculty from across the United States in 1972, 1986, and again in 1994. Analyses of these data suggest a trend toward heightened sensitivity regarding issues of race. For example, in their 1972 survey, 37 percent of professors of educational administration reported that the small portion of professors of color was either rather serious or very serious, but by 1994 that number had swelled to 57 percent. McCarthy and Hackmann's (2011) more recent research indicates very little growth in these percentages. These statistics make a compelling case for the necessity of addressing the diversity of the faculty and leadership pipeline in K-12 and higher education.

Not surprisingly, scholars have called for proactive measures and policies designed to attract people of color into K-12 public education and as higher education faculty and leaders (e.g., Allen, Jacobson, and Lomotey, 1995; Grogan and Andrews, 2002; Jackson, 1988; Leonard, 1988; Marshall, 1989; Marshall and Oliva, 2005; Turner and Myers, 2000; Young, Petersen, and Short, 2002). One oft-heard suggestion for addressing this issue is the development of both formal and informal mentoring programs. Turner and Myers (2000: 160) have stated that 'designing and implementing mentoring programs would help new minority faculty become acclimatized to academia and the campus culture as a whole'.

While the idea of providing mentors to burgeoning scholars in higher education seems straightforward enough, mentoring is complex, dynamic, and riddled with contradictions (Reddick, 2009). Some mentoring is informal and ad hoc, while some is more formalized. Mentoring programs and relationships that last a short time contrast with those that are sustained for years. Some programs are modeled on corporate designs, while others are rejections of corporate/business models. In fact, the very definition of mentoring is contested (Young and Brooks, 2008).

One thing is certain, diversifying the pipeline of faculty and leaders in K-12 and higher education will not happen by chance. It will require a comprehensive effort. While our focus here is the mentoring of graduate students of color, it is important to recognize that mentoring is only one part of a larger agenda for developing and supporting scholars of color. According to Young and Brooks (2008: 397),

> support for graduate students of color can be conceptualized as occurring in five distinct yet interrelated phases of a student's program: (a) recruitment, (b) orientation and induction, (c) faculty and peer mentoring, (d) in-program experiences, and (e) opportunities for career socialization and advancement.

Indeed, mentoring practices would mean little without concerted efforts in each of these five areas.

We next review existing research on mentoring in hopes of serving as a foundation for planning and implementing effective mentoring programs and practices. As such, we address several key issues, including why mentoring is important for graduate students of color, how effective mentoring is currently understood, how that understanding differs when the focal population is graduate students of color, and how the development and implementation of mentoring programs and practices may be shaped by opportunities as well as obstacles.

MENTORING IN PURPOSEFUL GROWTH INITIATIVES

As we discuss the importance and relevance of mentoring interventions for underrepresented minority students in higher education, it is essential to spend some time analyzing the culture of institutions of higher education in the US, particularly predominantly White institutions (PWIs). These institutions are those that typically encounter challenges recruiting and retaining students of color, in large part because of a history of segregation and overt, as well as covert, practices of exclusion (Tuitt and Carter, 2008). While all students may benefit from mentoring experiences, students of color in PWIs in particular may be in need of support from senior scholars as they progress in their educational journey.

Culture at predominantly White institutions

A body of research suggests that Black students at PWIs report more negative experiences, suffer lower academic achievement, and experience higher levels of attrition when compared to White students at the same institutions (Allen, 1992; Freeman, 1999). Similar findings can be found in the literature concerning Asian American, Latino, and Native American students, citing the explicit absence of cultural representation in academic curriculum and campus culture (Ancis, Sedlacek, and Mohr, 2000; Smedley, Myers, and Harrell, 1993; Swail, Redd, and Perna, 2003). Therefore, one of the most significant initial efforts mentors can perform is making clear what students of color can realistically expect at their institutions, should they choose to enroll. For instance, it is imperative to ask whether there is a critical mass of students and scholars of color. If a recruiting event draws significant numbers of persons of color, is that representation parallel to what can be found year round? Have racial incidents occurred at the campus, and, if so, what was the response, both from the student community and the administration? An honest assessment and discussion of these matters serves at least two significant functions: one, it provides potential students with accurate and timely information regarding how they might experience life on campus; and two, it helps to establish trust between mentors and mentees, an essential component of the mentor role.

Indeed, the level of honesty required may place mentors at cross-purposes with institutional goals. Knowledge of a department's emphasis on a 'cutoff' standardized test score, or preferred research foci, will help prospective students find the appropriate fit between their own goals and the department and institution in question. Even if such a discussion leads an applicant to consider another institution, the alternative of a student applying, enrolling, and ultimately being dissatisfied, or even leaving has greater negative repercussions not only for the individual student but also for successive generations of students who might envision that experience as their own. Additionally, opportunities to collaborative and future academic experiences may lead students to an institution at another time, for successive degrees, postdoctoral opportunities, and/or employment.

Unpacking the hidden curriculum and rules for success

Margolis and Romero (1998) have discussed the significance of unearthing norms and structures in academia that advantage majority, middle-class students. They term these invisible norms the *hidden curriculum*, a system of privilege and exclusion embedded in academic contexts. Unsurprisingly, first generation collegians and students of color are often unaware of the hidden curriculum, so effective mentoring of these populations requires exposing the system whenever possible.

The hidden curriculum often inhibits access to opportunities and knowledge; thus, mentors need to make plain the masked rules of academia for their mentees. For instance, when teaching assistant and research assistant positions are posted, they are often awarded to students who have previously indicated interest in such positions. One explicit lesson here for students is to express interest in such positions early and often. Perhaps more importantly, however, is to make mentees aware that many factors, some seemingly related, will serve as linchpins for one's eligibility for opportunities. These factors include but are not limited to demonstrating responsibility, capability, and timeliness; diligently approaching studies and classroom performance; and, as noted, expressing interest in opportunities for growth and learning beyond the classroom. Indeed, these factors may be especially important for mentees of color, as students of color often experience the contrasting experience of being both invisible (i.e., not seeing representative numbers of people of color on campus) and hypervisible (i.e., being asked to respond on issues of racism and inequity in class by professors and classmates) (Brayboy, 2004; Tuitt and Carter, 2008).

Strong mentoring relationships bring these realities to the attention of mentees, empowering students to respond to these concerns. At many predominantly White campuses, advanced students of color hold meetings, alternately termed 'fireside chats', 'charm school', and 'boot camps', providing experiential knowledge of how students of color tend to be noticed when arriving late and leaving early, and even in settings off campus (Griffin and Reddick, 2011). Individual mentors may not feel comfortable holding such meetings; however, being able to refer students to seasoned student colleagues and fostering conditions so that students can share these experiences can advance the progress of underrepresented students in crucial ways.

Networks and sources of support

Another often-veiled aspect of academic culture is knowing how to garner resources and support. The combined experience of being invisible and hypervisible may lead students to internalize concerns rather than sharing them. This, of course, is compounded if students do not feel they have trusted allies in whom to confide. Additionally, traditional academic cultural standards of separating academic performance from the rest of one's life means students weather factors like family stress and financial woes in silence, lest they be perceived as 'whiners'. Students, however, as Harvard University Chaplain Peter Gomes opined, are more than 'brains on a stick' (as quoted in Lewis, 2006: 100).

By definition, a mentor is expressly invested in the totality of the mentee's experience, attending to both psychosocial and instrumental aspects, especially when the two domains merge (Kram, 1988; Kram and Isabella, 1985). Financial concerns often factor heavily into student stress, especially as students approach the end of their studies (Willie, Grady, and Hope, 1991). For such reasons as these, mentors should endeavor to provide information and resources about financial aid policies, and give sound advice concerning how students can best navigate the financial terrain. While specific direction regarding the intricacies of financial aid is beyond the expertise of mentors outside of the field of student services, serving as a sounding board and directing mentees to relevant sources is an equally important function.

Expectations and assumptions about underrepresented populations

Mentors can be essential in helping students of color and first-generation students become aware of the expectations and assumptions associated with their respective populations (Brown, Davis, and McClendon, 1999; McNairy, 1996). Students of color may encounter overt or covert assumptions from the campus community that their presence is due solely to affirmative action, regardless of their actual academic credentials (Solórzano, Ceja, and Yosso, 2000). They may also experience seemingly minor, but draining exchanges with faculty, staff, students, and campus members inferring that they are less deserving of respect – behaviors termed microaggressions (Pierce, 1995; Solórzano et al., 2000; Swim, Hyers, Cohen, Fitzgerald, and Bylsma, 2003). It is also imperative that mentors assist mentees in understanding that faculty of color often share struggles similar to those experienced by students. Cultural taxation occurs for faculty and students of color, meaning that these scholars are often called upon as racial representatives to serve on committees, to function as the manifestation of diversity at PWIs (Brayboy, 2003; Padilla, 1994; Reddick, 2006), and to respond to competing demands on their time from faculty colleagues, community members, and students (Banks, 1984). These conversations in particular may be challenging, and at times uncomfortable for mentors to broach. However, it is our feeling that effective mentoring requires courage and trust, and perhaps those qualities are no better exemplified than in open discussions of these matters.

Certainly, there is no 'one size fits all' approach to mentoring. Individuals will find some strategies more effective than others. Similarly, there is no one approach to mentoring for underrepresented populations. Many of these approaches will prove effective for all student mentees, regardless of background and orientation. However, the issues we have raised may be of particular importance to first-generation students and students of color at PWIs. Mentors should consider personality type, the depth of the relationship, and their own comfort level when engaging mentees about these topics.

EFFECTIVE MENTORING PRACTICES

When exploring what counts as *effective mentoring*, we have to acknowledge that there are multiple definitions of the term. According to Reddick and Griffin (2010), the phenomenon known as mentoring was made popular by Levinson's (1978) work which described mentoring as guiding, counseling, and supporting. However, the term *mentoring* has taken on many more features than Levinson's preliminary set. In fact, Jacobi (1991) and Crosby (1999) identified respectively 15 and 18 distinct definitions of mentoring. Drawing on the growing body of literature in this area, Mertz (2004) developed a conceptual model hoping to clarify what mentoring means, particularly with regard to intent and involvement, and summarized mentoring as 'supportive relationships' (2004: 543). Similarly, Healy described mentoring as a 'dynamic, reciprocal relationship in a work environment between an advanced career incumbent (mentor) and a beginner (protégé) aimed at promoting the career and development of both' (cited in Haring, 1999: 8).

Further building on the mentoring literature, Kram (1988) argued that the act of mentoring can be divided into two spheres: career (or instrumental) functions and psychosocial functions. With regard to the former, mentors typically serve as sponsors. They provide their mentees with exposure and visibility within their professional circles. They may also serve as coaches and, if necessary, provide their mentees with protection. Finally, career mentors give their mentees challenging assignments. According to Kram, psychosocial mentoring looks somewhat different and it may involve role modeling and supervising performance, followed by feedback, acceptance or confirmation. Psychosocial mentoring may also involve counseling and, at times, evolve into friendships. Reddick (2009) explored both approaches to mentoring in his research on the mentoring behavior of White faculty at Harvard College. Although one might assume that instrumental functions would develop first in a mentoring relationship, Reddick (2009) argues that the more 'Maslovian' psychosocial approaches to mentoring should come first in higher education, given the complexities of the environments and the work itself. He further noted that for graduate students of color psychosocial mentoring 'may be more appropriate than sponsorship when the junior person encounters challenges such as perceived racism, or racial microaggressions' (2009: 71).

Ideas about mentoring shared thus far have influenced, though not determined, what counts as mentoring in various professions. With regard to graduate students of color, Guiffrida (2005), Griffin and Reddick (2011), Stanley and Lincoln (2005), and Young and Brooks (2008), among other researchers, assert that robust mentoring programs in which faculty members assume personal and professional roles beyond those of the traditional academic advisor are needed, particularly for students attending PWIs. As Young and Brooks (2008: 399) have stated, 'an effective mentor–protégé relationship is empathetic rather than sympathetic – a proactive partnership wherein each participant commits to an equal share of responsibility and commitment to the others' success'. They further note that these attributes hold true for both faculty–student and student–student mentoring relationships.

Mentoring myths

When putting into practice a mentoring program, there are many issues to consider. Widely held myths exist regarding mentoring students of color (Brown et al., 1999; Young and Brooks, 2008). These include the myth that any senior person can mentor any junior person, that engaging with students during class, seminars, and scheduled offices hours constitutes sufficient mentoring commitment, that mentoring is simply extra advising, that students of color can only be mentored by faculty of color, and that a mentor and protégé's research interests, philosophical, positionality, and 'polisocioecoracial' experiences must be a perfect match (Brown et al., 1999: 114). Each of these myths is next addressed.

- *Myth 1*: Any senior person can mentor any junior person. Faculty–graduate student mentoring relationships should be carefully chosen and entered into freely by each partner. As mentoring is a dynamic reciprocal relationship between two engaged partners, it requires a degree of care and commitment rather than a casual or 'strictly business' approach (Brown et al., 1999; Young and Brooks, 2008).
- *Myth 2:* Engaging with students during class, seminars, and scheduled office hours constitutes a sufficient commitment. Instead, mentoring entails an additional set of commitments, which

includes social and academic advocacy, career counseling, and a commitment to providing opportunities that can contribute to the success of mentee *and* mentor (Brown et al., 1999; Young and Brooks, 2008).

- *Myth 3:* Mentoring is the same as extra advising. Again, advising is not mentoring. The former is a formal academic arrangement focused on program completion and degree attainment that may or may not be entered into freely; the latter requires a substantive personal and professional commitment. It is certainly possible, for example, that someone could be an excellent advisor and a poor mentor (Brown et al., 1999; Young and Brooks, 2008).
- *Myth 4:* Students of color can only be mentored by faculty of color. This assumption is problematic for at least two reasons. First, as scholars of color are not well represented in many educational administration faculty units, faculty of color may carry an inordinately large advising/ mentoring load in relation to other faculty members. Second, leaving faculty of color to serve as mentors for graduate students of color is an absolution of responsibility and an implicit form of racism. Supporting graduate students of color is the responsibility of all faculty members, regardless of race (Brown et al., 1999; Reddick, 2009; Young and Brooks, 2008).
- *Myth 5:* A mentor and protégé's research interests, philosophical positionality, and 'polisocioecoracial' experiences must be a perfect match. An empathetic approach to the relationship and a commitment to an ethic of care, ethic of critique, ethic of community, an ethic of profession (Brooks and Normore, 2004; Furman, 2004; Starrat, 1997), and a reciprocal approach to success is at least as important as having similar research interests, philosophies, and 'polisocioecoracial' experiences (Brown et al., 1999; Young and Brooks, 2008).

Mentoring is a potentially powerful tool for supporting the careers of graduate students of color. While we do not want to create any of our own myths about mentoring relationships, the selection of a mentor can either make or break the relationship. At times the behavior of the mentor is the issue. Within the leadership literature, it is noted that mentors can, at times, have selfish or ulterior motives for taking on a mentee (Crow and Matthews, 1998). Thus, it is suggested that when identifying mentors, efforts be made to understand why a person wishes to be a mentor. Similarly, mentors can be overly controlling (Lashway, 2005). On the other hand, Daresh and Playko (1993) note that mentors can be too protective, undermining mentees' learning and growth. Mentors may also have too strong of an attachment to a certain style of 'being' a professor, which can encourage 'cloning' or constrict innovation (Southworth, 1995).

QUALITY MENTORING PRACTICES FOR STUDENTS OF COLOR

When considering the existing literature on mentoring vis-à-vis the competencies argued to be necessary to serve as an effective mentor for students of color, we have compiled a typology of eight quality mentoring practices: being a race-conscious mentor; having concern for student mentees beyond the instrumental aspects of the relationship; unpacking the hidden curriculum and making transparent the implicit rules of the department and/or institution; developing and sustaining both formal and informal support structures; opening doors and helping to foster networks; having knowledge and respect for newer conceptualizations of mentoring (incorporating technology and new media); and staying current with critical epistemologies and research methodologies that may be of interest to students of color. These practices can aid mentors in their efforts to assist mentees of color in achieving their educational and life goals.

Race-conscious mentoring

Perhaps the most important aspect of working with students of color is having respect and understanding for the influence that issues of race and ethnicity have on their lives. This requires a personal commitment to a race-conscious, antiracist worldview (Brown et al., 1999; Scheurich and Laible, 1995; Young and Brooks, 2008). Similarly, Thomas's (1993, 2001) research on cross-race mentors found that when mentors and mentees shared a similar worldview in regard to the influence race had on their lives and careers, those relationships tended to be beneficial and satisfying to both junior and senior partners. Mentors can engage in antiracist actions in many ways, including acknowledging their own racial identity, communicating high standards to student of color, further educating colleagues and students, integrating multicultural themes in scholarship, challenging discriminatory behaviors among colleagues and the institution, and contributing efforts toward programs for students of color (Lawrence and Tatum, 1997). Further research suggests that proximal experiences – those in which mentors can relate incidents of isolation and/or discrimination – can heighten mentors' awareness of potential concerns, and a willingness to listen to student concerns, can be an effective component of cross-race mentoring practice (Reddick, 2009).

Engaging in race-conscious practice also requires courage on the part of mentors. Confronting discrimination can challenge collegial relationships; however, the returns for addressing maladaptive institutional and interpersonal behaviors are significant, not only for students of color but also for all students and members of the campus community. Mentors are advantaged by holding positions of status and forms of capital such as access to and membership in academic networks, which can be used to challenge inequitable situations, and furthermore can lessen the burden experienced by students.

Demonstrating concern for students

Mentoring, by its definition, incorporates both instrumental (work- or project-related) support with psychosocial (interpersonal and social) support (Kram, 1988); however, some senior partners emphasize the former over the latter. Both aspects of support are equally important to effective mentoring partnerships; in fact, for underrepresented students at PWIs there may be multiple sources for instrumental support, but a limited number of individuals that students feel they can trust and confide in (Museus and Quaye, 2009). Indeed, the qualities that mentors must master parallel those that are found in the best college teachers. Bain (2004: 139), Vice Provost for Instruction and Director of Montclair State

University's Teaching and Learning Resource Center, noted the importance of professors 'displaying not power but an investment in students', caring about students as *people* as well as learners, a bond that is established through trust. Investment and concern for students is a building block for more significant support efforts, as Young and Brooks (2008: 404) noted: 'An overarching ethic of care in the faculty–student relationship and attention to individual needs undergirds specific and personalized support efforts.' Trust, the cornerstone of effective mentoring, provides a starting point for bonding and improving student experiences – even those that are difficult to endure.

Mentors can use personal incidents of struggle to help mentees understand that they, too, experienced setbacks and challenges to their progress as students (Reddick, 2011). Such exchanges serve two purposes: demonstrating that the mentor, though established, did not travel a primrose path to professional success, and missteps and challenges are part of the learning process. Invariably, a significant gap in age, educational attainment, and life experience may inhibit mentees identifying with mentors. Hence, it is essential that effective mentors work to reduce this distance through showing concern and connection to their mentees.

Hidden curriculum and transparency

Our discussion of the hidden curriculum necessitates the importance of unveiling practices and norms that exist in academic environments. Oftentimes, underrepresented students are unaware that they are subject to an invisible system of assessment and ranking, typically from the day their application arrives at the institution. Effective mentors can assist their mentees in interpreting messages, and help position their mentees for optimal opportunities. Students of color and first-generation college students, populations that often overlap, may hesitate to participate in class discussion, utilize office hours, attend academic social events, or voice perspectives and opinions which they feel contradict or challenge those held by faculty (Gay, 2004). Mentors can serve a vital 'intercessory function' by assisting students in maximizing their interactions with fellow faculty and administrators (Willie, 1987). At the same time, mentors can serve as truth-tellers about the importance of opportunities for involvement and the signals sent via how mentees use their time in the academic program. In being privy to 'faculty talk', mentors can give invaluable advice about attending class, engaging in co-curricular activities, and approaching colleagues with questions or concerns.

Opening doors and fostering networks

Effective mentors of students of color leverage their social capital for the benefit of their mentees (Reddick, 2009, 2011; Young and Brooks, 2008). Simply referring a student to a faculty colleague may not be as impactful as calling or e-mailing on behalf of the student. At the same time, an effective mentor ensures that mentees understand that they need to 'put their best foot forward' when interacting with professors and administrators (i.e., being on time for meetings, being prepared, being respectful of time). Similarly, mentors help position their mentees to be noticed by other faculty members, students, and administrators. One of us had a mentor who insisted on working on projects in a highly trafficked part of the library frequented by faculty. When colleagues stopped by to say hello, the mentor made mention of the mentee's efforts on the project – providing visibility (Kram, 1988; Ragins and Kram, 2007) and access to a new cadre of faculty.

Addressing networking for mentees of color is crucial not only for the current student being mentored but also for successive generations of student mentees. Just as students earn reputations based on their efforts, mentors also earn a reputation for the efforts they put forth on behalf of their mentees. Networks rarely exist in a vacuum; they are multi-purpose and operate for social, academic, and professional support (Young and Brooks, 2008). It is likely that prior generations of mentees can assist mentors with successive mentees, demonstrating that the mentor is trustworthy and invests time in long-term relationships with students.

Newer conceptualizations of mentoring

The literature on mentoring reveals many new conceptualizations of the dyad described between Mentor and Telemachus in the *Iliad*. Among these are e-mentoring (utilizing email, social media, and other technologies to interact across distance) (Ensher and Murphy, 2007; Johnson, 2007); frientoring (developmental relationships at the nexus of friendship and mentoring) (Brown et al., 1999); constellation mentoring (utilizing multiple senior partners to assist a junior person) (Johnson, 2007); and team mentoring (bringing together multiple mentees so that mentors can impact more students in one setting). Many of these approaches reflect a departure from the traditional one-on-one dyad and may not be the most comfortable arrangements for some mentors. However, having an open mind about innovations in mentoring, and even allowing mentees to introduce technology to the relationship, addresses the reciprocal nature of mentoring and may enhance and expedite mentoring functions.

Critical epistemologies and research methodologies

Another critical issue for mentors of students of color is their familiarity, engagement, and respect for new, nontraditional research techniques and epistemologies that speak to the experiences and interests to many emerging scholars of color. This is perhaps most commonly observed in the age-old debate regarding the rigor and propriety of qualitative research, which has been articulated many times in the past 40 years (Bryman, 1984; Eisner and Peshkin, 1990). While most researchers have moved beyond this impasse, emergent theoretical innovations, such as those that locate inequities of race, gender, physical ability, sexual orientation, and socioeconomic status at their core, are at times rejected by otherwise supportive faculty. In addition, new research methodologies, such as those incorporating audiovisual and electronic data, and those that reduce the distance between the researcher and those researched are also viewed in some quarters with suspicion. While no faculty member can have equal expertise in all epistemologies and methodologies, effective mentors should work to remain current on innovations in the generation of knowledge. With this knowledge, mentors can educate colleagues concerning the use, validity, and effectiveness of these theories and methodologies, serving in the critical 'intercessory function' of advocate.

MENTORING GRADUATE STUDENTS OF COLOR

In their interdisciplinary review of mentoring research, Hansford, Ehrich, and Tennent (2004: 536) noted that when planning and implementing a formal mentoring program, program leaders face a variety of opportunities and obstacles. They assert that program leaders

> be aware of the growing body of research literature on mentoring, the need for program support at various levels, the importance of mentor training, the careful selection of participants, and the need for ongoing evaluations. If resources (both human and financial) are to be invested in mentoring programs, those responsible for planning and implementing programs must be willing to commit time, resources, and energy to such programs. Indeed, all parties have a responsibility to make mentoring work so that it can be a positive force for individuals and their organizations.

We address a number of these and several other challenges and opportunities below.

Mentor selection

One of the challenges facing those in charge of mentor selection is that many people think that they possess the qualities of a good mentor (e.g., being caring and committed) (Gross, 2009). Within the leadership and management realm, a number of instruments are available to screen potential mentors (see, e.g., Geismar, Morris and Leiberman's (2000) discussion of the Mentor Identification Instrument). Within higher education, we are not aware of the availability of such instruments. However, the literature on mentoring does provide some insight, such as a commitment to a student's success (Reddick, 2009; Young and Brooks, 2008). However, what makes a good mentor may be more of an issue of what they do, rather than who they are.

Mentor preparation

Finding the right mentor is essential but it is only the first step in ensuring that a mentoring relationship works. Other elements include ensuring that the mentor is properly oriented to his or her role (Gross, 2009). Mentors need to know what they are expected to do, such as the instrumental and psychosocial functions we discussed previously (Kram, 1988), as well as the importance of developing trust (Playko, 1991; Reddick, 2009; Young and Brooks, 2008). They need to understand the full spectrum and richness of mentoring, the importance of the mentoring relationship, and the benefits of mentoring for the student and mentor. They also need to know that they may face challenges in developing a relationship with their mentee (Crocker and Harris, 2002).

Mentor training programs could serve a variety of important goals, including orientation, preparation, and ongoing development. According to Crocker and Harris (2002: 190), 'specific guidelines should be available to the mentor outlining roles for the mentee that include meaningful activities and delineate ways to involve mentees'. However, as is the case with selection, there are very few widely used mentor training programs in higher education, particularly programs focused on mentoring graduate students of color. The University Council for Educational Administration (UCEA) does provide such training during its annual meetings for the mentors of the Barbara Jackson Scholars and offers a mentoring guidebook on its organizational website (Crow, 2005). Important factors to consider when developing mentor-training programs include goals of the mentoring relationships, best ways to provide the training, and clarification of how mentoring performance will be assessed (Gross, 2009).

Time and tenure

In their research on Black faculty mentors, Griffin and Reddick (2011) found that finding time to be an effective mentor was a challenge, particularly for junior faculty members who have not yet attained tenure. Barnett (1995) and Crocker and Harris (2002) have emphasized the need for time and constancy for effective mentoring relationships to develop. Given that most mentoring work occurs through dialogues, the issue of time and the scarcity of it is crucial (Barnett, 1991). This is especially true for untenured junior faculty. The tenure review process at many research-oriented PWIs does not reward faculty for engaging in the process of nurturing and developing a new generation of scholars to the same degree that it rewards the advancement of the field via publications and research.

Cultural taxation

Closely related to the issue of time is a phenomenon known as 'cultural taxation' experienced by a large number of faculty of color at PWIs who are given countless additional responsibilities because of their racial or ethnic background (Padilla, 1994). According to Reddick (2011: 319), 'the additional committee work and academic housekeeping around diversity that falls to Black professors, challenges them to balance their efforts on service responsibilities that carry insufficient weight in the tenure process.' This 'cultural taxation' obligates Black faculty and faculty of color to serve on various committees and support cultural groups, thus allowing senior administrators and faculty to create the illusion of diversity at institutions. Faculty of color must navigate these challenges, recognizing that a choice to 'give' may reduce the time available to qualify for tenure (Washington and Harvey, 1989), while a choice to 'withhold' may give them the reputation of 'race traitors'. Such expectations place the burden of representation on their shoulders, typically far more than on White faculty.

Role and gender differences

Another challenge to effective mentoring relationships is related to the authoritative distance between the faculty and graduate student role. Although some students bridge the distance fairly easily, others – particularly students of color, women and first generation students – do not. In his research on Black faculty mentors, Reddick (2011) found that Black students felt they needed to mask their insecurities and worries when interacting with Black faculty.

Role distance is strongly related to a similar challenge concerning gender difference and level of intimacy. In general, faculty report greater feelings of comfort interacting with students of like sex (Griffin and Reddick, 2011; Turner and Myers, 2000). Reddick (2011) found that junior male faculty members tended to have a concern about intimacy in mentoring relationships, particularly with female students, thus preferring to maintain a distance.

MOVING PURPOSEFULLY AND KNOWLEDGABLY FORWARD

As university faculty recruit scholars of color into their programs traditionally and predominantly populated by White faculty and students, organized by White faculty, and informed by a concomitant knowledge base, faculty must be proactive if their efforts are to move from empty (though well-intended) rhetoric toward substantive and equitable change (Young and Brooks, 2008). As we have argued, fostering future generations of scholars of color will require a comprehensive effort. Mentoring is only one piece, albeit a very important one, of a larger agenda for developing and supporting graduate students of color. At a minimum, the agenda must involve concerted efforts in the six areas noted earlier vis-à-vis Young and Brooks (2008).

Further, real change will only come when the institutions in which students will learn and eventually work change. We have identified some of the important obstacles that must be addressed for effective mentoring. Faculty members must also address issues of organizational culture and institutional racism, sexism, and other forms of prejudice. Awareness and concern must be increased among organizational members regarding such matters that include how best to support future scholars of color and their success.

REFERENCES

Allen, W. R. (1992). The Color of Success: African-American college student outcomes at predominantly White and historically Black public colleges and universities. *Harvard Educational Review, 62*(1), 26–44.

Allen, K., Jacobson, S., & Lomotey, K. (1995). African American women in educational administration: The importance of mentors and sponsors. *Journal of Negro Education, 64*(4), 409–422.

Ancis, J. R., Sedlacek, W. E., & Mohr, J. J. (2000). Student perceptions of campus cultural climate by race. *Journal of Counseling and Development, 78*(2), 180–185.

Bain, K. (2004). *What the best college teachers do.* Cambridge, MA: Harvard University Press.

Banks, W. M. (1984). Afro-American scholars in the university. *American Behavioral Scientist, 27*(3), 325–338.

Barnett, B. G. (1991). School–university collaboration: A fad or the future of administration preparation? *Planning and Changing, 21*(3), 146–157.

Barnett, B. G. (1995). Developing Reflection and Expertise: Can mentors make the difference? *Journal of Educational Administration, 33*(5), 45–59.

Brainard, J. (2010). Undergraduate Diversity: More minorities, more women. *The Chronicle of Higher Education,* B45, September 24.

Brayboy, B. M. J. (2003). The implementation of diversity in predominantly White colleges and universities. *Journal of Black Studies, 34*(1), 72–86.

Brayboy, B. M. J. (2004). Hiding in the ivy: American Indian students and visibility in elite educational settings. *Harvard Educational Review, 74*(2), 125–152.

Brooks, J. S., & Normore, A. H. (2005). An Aristotelian framework for the development of ethical leadership. *Journal of Values and Ethics in Educational Administration, 2*(3), 1–8.

Brown II, M. C., Davis, G. L., & McClendon, S. A. (1999). Mentoring graduate students of color: Myths, models, and modes. *Peabody Journal of Education, 74*(2), 105–118.

Bryman, A. (1984). The debate about quantitative and qualitative research: A question of method or epistemology? *British Journal of Sociology, 35*(1), 75–92.

Crocker, C., & Harris, S. (2002). Facilitating growth of administrative practitioners as mentors. *Journal of Research for Educational Leaders, 1*(2), 5–20. Retrieved January 31, 2011, from www.uiowa.edu/~jrel/spring02/Harris_0107.htm

Crosby, F. J. (1999). The developing literature on developmental relationships. In A. J. Murrell, F. J. Crosby, & R. J. Ely (Eds.), *Mentoring Dilemmas: Developmental relationships within multicultural organizations* (pp. 3–20). Mahwah, NJ: Erlbaum.

Crow, G. M. (2005). Developing leadership for schools facing challenging circumstances. In M. J. Coles & G. Southworth (Eds.), *Developing Leadership: Creating the schools of tomorrow* (pp. 65–79). Maidenhead, UK: Open University Press.

Crow, G. M., & Matthews, L. J. (1998). *Finding one's way: How mentoring can lead to dynamic leadership.* Thousand Oaks, CA: Corwin.

Daresh, J. C., & Playko, M. A. (1993). *Leaders Helping Leaders: A practical guide to administrative mentoring.* New York: Scholastic.

Eisner, E. W., & Peshkin, A. (1990). *Qualitative inquiry in education: The continuing debate.* New York: Teachers College Press.

Ensher, E. A., & Murphy, S. E. (2007). E-mentoring: Next-generation research strategies and suggestions. In B. R. Ragins & K. E. Kram (Eds.), *The handbook of mentoring at work* (pp. 299–322). Thousand Oaks, CA: SAGE.

Freeman, K. (1999). No services needed? The case for mentoring high-achieving African American students. *Peabody Journal of Education, 74*(2), 15–26.

Furman, G. C. (2004). The ethic of community. *Journal of Educational Administration, 42*(2), 215–235.

Gay, G. (1997). Multicultural infusion in teacher education: Foundations and applications. *Peabody Journal of Education, 72*(1), 150–177.

Gay, G. (2004). Navigating marginality en route to the professoriate: Graduate students of color learning and living in academia. *International Journal of Qualitative Studies in Education, 17*(2), 265–288.

Geismar, T., Morris, J., & Lieberman, M. (2000). Selecting mentors for principalship interns. *Journal of School Leadership, 10*, 233–247.

Griffin, K. A., & Reddick, R. J. (2011). Surveillance and sacrifice: Gender differences in the mentoring patterns of Black professors at predominantly White research universities. *American Educational Research Journal.* Advance online publication. doi: 10.3102/0002831211405025

Grogan, M., & Andrews, R. (2002). Defining preparation and professional development for the future. *Educational Administration Quarterly, 38*(2), 233–256.

Gross, S. J. (2009). Establishing meaningful leadership mentoring in school settings: Transcending simplistic, rhetoric, self-congratulation, and claims of panacea. In M. D. Young, G. Crow, J. Murphy, & R. Ogawa (Eds.), *Handbook of research on the education of school leaders* (pp. 515–534). New York: Routledge.

Guiffrida, D. (2005). Othermothering as a framework for understanding African American students' definitions of student-centered faculty. *Journal of Higher Education, 76*(6), 701.

Hansford, B., Ehrich, L. C., & Tennent, L. (2004). Formal mentoring programs in education and other professions: A review of the literature. *Educational Administration Quarterly, 40*(4), 518–540.

Haring, M. J. (1999). The case for a conceptual base for minority mentoring programs. *Peabody Journal of Education, 74*, 5–14.

Jackson, B. L. (1988). Education from a Black Perspective: Implications for leadership preparation. In D. E. Griffiths, R. T. Stout, & R. B. Forsyth (Eds.), *Leaders for America's Schools: The report and papers of the National Commission on Excellence in Educational Administration* (pp. 305–316). Berkeley, CA: McCutchan.

Jacobi, M. (1991). Mentoring and Undergraduate Academic Success: A literature review. *Review of Educational Research, 61*(4), 505–532.

Johnson, W. B. (2007). *On Being a Mentor: A guide for higher education faculty.* Mahwah, NJ: Erlbaum.

Kram, K. E. (1988). *Mentoring at Work: Developmental relationships in organizational life.* Lanham, MD: University Press of America.

Kram, K. E., & Isabella, L. (1985). Mentoring Alternatives: The role of peer relationships in career development. *Academy of Management, 28*, 110–132.

Lashway, L. (2005). *Developing instructional leaders.* (ERIC Digest, ED 466023.) Washington, DC: U.S. Department of Education, Office of Educational Research & Improvement.

Lawrence, S. M., & Tatum, B. D. (1997). Teachers in transition: The impact of antiracist professional development on classroom practice. *Teachers College Record, 99*(1), 162–178.

Leonard, P. Y. (1988). Teaching in the year 2000: Minority recruiting push to span the gap. *School Administrator, 45*, 33–40.

Levinson, D. J., Darrow, C. N., Klein, E. B., & Levinson, M. (1978). *Seasons of a man's life.* New York: Random House.

Lewis, H. R. (2006). *Excellence without a soul: How a great university forgot education.* New York: PublicAffairs.

Margolis, E., & Romero, M. (1998). 'The department is very male, very White, very old and very conservative': The functions of the hidden curriculum in graduate sociology departments. *Harvard Educational Review, 68*(1), 1–23.

Marshall, C. (1989). *More than black face and skirts: New leadership to confront the major dilemmas in education.* Charlottesville, VA: National Policy Board for Educational Administration. (ERIC Document Reproduction Service No. ED 318 089).

Marshall, C., & Oliva, M. (2005). *Leadership for Social Justice: Making Revolutions in Education.* Boston: Pearson.

McCarthy, M., & Hackmann, D. (2011). *The Educational Leadership Professoriate.* Charlotte, NC: Information Age.

McCarthy, M. M., & Kuh, G. D. (1997). *Continuity and Change: The educational leadership professoriate*. Columbia, MO: University Council for Educational Administration.

McNairy, F. G. (1996). The Challenge for Higher Education: Retaining students of color. *New Directions for Student Services, 74*, 3–14.

Mertz, N. (2004). What's a mentor, anyway? *Educational Administration Quarterly, 40*(4), 541–560.

Miller, S. (1995). *An American imperative: Accelerating minority educational advancement*. New Haven, CT: Yale University Press.

Museus, S. D., & Quaye, S. J. (2009). Toward an intercultural perspective of racial and ethnic minority college student persistence. *Review of Higher Education, 33*(1), 67–94.

Padilla, A. M. (1994). Ethnic minority scholars, research, and mentoring: Current and future issues. *Educational Researcher, 23*(4), 24–27.

Pierce, C. (1995). Stress Analogs of Racism and Sexism: Terrorism, Torture, and Disaster. In C. V. Willie, P. Rieker, B. Kramer, & B. Brown (Eds.), *Mental health, racism, and sexism* (pp. 277–293). Pittsburgh, PA: University of Pittsburgh Press.

Playko, M. A. (1991). Mentors for administrators: Support for the instructional leader. *Theory Into Practice, 30*(2), 124–127.

Ragins, B. R., & Kram, K. E. (2007). The roots and meaning of mentoring. In B. R. Ragins & K. E. Kram (Eds.), *The handbook of mentoring at work* (pp. 3–14). Thousand Oaks, CA: SAGE.

Reddick, R. J. (2006). The gift that keeps giving: Historically Black college and university-educated scholars and their mentoring at predominantly White institutions. *Educational Foundations, 20*(1/2), 61–84.

Reddick, R. J. (2009). Fostering Cross-racial Mentoring: White faculty and African American students at Harvard College. In S. Sánchez-Casal & A. A. Macdonald (Eds.), *Identity in education* (pp. 65–102). New York: Palgrave Macmillan.

Reddick, R. J. (2011). Intersecting Identities: Mentoring contributions and challenges for Black faculty mentoring Black undergraduates. *Mentoring & Tutoring, 19*(3), 319–346.

Reddick, R. J., & Griffin, K. A. (2010). Black faculty narratives on developmental relationships across stages of life experience: Challenging and expanding traditional conceptions of mentoring theory and practice. Unpublished paper presented at the 2nd Annual University of New Mexico Mentoring Conference, Albuquerque, NM.

Scheurich, J. J., & Laible, J. (1995). The buck stops here – in our preparation programs: Educational leadership for all children (no exceptions allowed). *Educational Administration Quarterly, 31*(2), 313–322.

Smedley, B. D., Myers, H. F., & Harrell, S. P. (1993). Minority-status stresses and the college adjustment of ethnic minority freshmen. *Journal of Higher Education, 64*(4), 434–452.

Solórzano, D., Ceja, M., & Yosso, T. (2000). Critical Race Theory, racial microaggressions, and campus racial climate: The experiences of African American college students. *Journal of Negro Education, 69*(1/2), 60–73.

Southworth, G. (1995). Reflections on mentoring for new school leaders. *Journal of Educational Administration, 33*(5), 17–28.

Stanley, C. A., & Lincoln, Y. S. (2005). Cross-race faculty mentoring. *Change, 37*(2), 44–50.

Starrat, R. J. (1997). Administering ethical schools. In L. Beck & J. Murphy (Eds.), *Ethics in educational leadership programs: Emerging models* (pp. 95–108). Columbia, MO: University Council of Educational Administration.

Strizek, G. A., Pittsonberger, J. L., Riordan, K. E., Lyter, D. M., & Orlofsky, G. F. (2006). *Characteristics of schools, districts, teachers, principals, and school libraries in the United States: 2003–04 schools and staffing survey* (NCES 2006-313). Washington, DC: National Center for Education Statistics. Retrieved February 2, 2011, from http://nces.ed.gov/pubs2006/2006313_1.pdf

Swail, W. S., Redd, K. E., & Perna, L. W. (2003). Retaining Minority Students in Higher Education: A framework for success. *ASHE Higher Education Report, 30*(2), 1–88. San Francisco: Jossey-Bass.

Swim, J. K., Hyers, L. L., Cohen, L. L., Fitzgerald, D. C., & Bylsma, W. H. (2003). African American college students' experiences with everyday racism: Characteristics of and responses to these incidents. *Journal of Black Psychology, 29*(1), 38–67.

Thomas, D. A. (1993). Racial dynamics in cross-race developmental relationships. *Administrative Science Quarterly, 38*(2), 169–194.

Thomas, D. A. (2001). The truth about mentoring minorities: Race Matters. *Harvard Business Review, 79*(4), 98–107.

Tuitt, F. A., & Carter, D. J. (2008). Negotiating atmospheric threats and racial assaults in predominantly White educational institutions. *Journal of Public Management & Social Policy, 14*(2), 51–68.

Turner, C. S. V., & Myers, S. (2000). *Faculty of color in academe: Bittersweet success.* Boston: Allyn & Bacon.

U.S. Census Bureau. (2004). *Census Bureau projects tripling of Hispanic and Asian populations in 50 years; non-Hispanic Whites may drop to half of total population.* Retrieved February 2, 2011, from http://www.census.gov/PressRelease/www/releases/archives/ population/001720.html

Washington, V., & Harvey, W. (1989). Affirmative Rhetoric, Negative Action: African-American and Hispanic faculty at predominantly White institutions. *ASHE-ERIC Higher Education Report 2, 1989.* Washington, DC: Office of Educational Research and Improvement.

Willie, C. V. (1987). *Effective education.* Westport, CT: Greenwood.

Willie, C. V., Grady, M. K., & Hope, R. O. (1991). *African-Americans and the doctoral experience: Implications for policy.* New York: Teachers College Press.

Young, M. D., & Brooks, J. S. (2008). Supporting graduate students of color in educational administration preparation programs: Faculty perspectives on best practices, possibilities, and problems. *Educational Administration Quarterly, 44*(3), 391–423.

Young, M. D., Petersen, G. J., & Short, P. M. (2002). The Complexity of Substantive Reform: A call for interdependence among key stakeholders. *Educational Administration Quarterly, 38*(2), 136–175.

28

The Role of Mentoring in Adult Literacy and Numeracy in Northern Ireland

Shelley Tracey

INTRODUCTION

Most of the mentors who participated in interviews for this chapter spoke of 'going the extra mile' in their reflections on mentoring in the field of adult literacy and numeracy, referred to in Northern Ireland as Essential Skills. Mentors emphasized the need for Essential Skills tutors and mentors to address the complexities of learning and learners in their practice. Essential Skills mentors' voices are included in the body of this chapter. We hear their comments from a survey on mentoring, a training programme, and interviews conducted with past participants. This chapter is a reflective space for the author, who designed and co-delivered the mentor training, for describing the background to and reviewing mentoring in adult literacy and numeracy. This is a valued space, as the mentoring training programme is no longer running and because many mentors have less time to mentor colleagues than previously as result of changes to their workplace contracts. The impact on mentoring and learning in Essential Skills policies is discussed, as is the background to mentoring in Essential Skills.

BACKGROUND

In 2002, the Department for Employment and Learning (DEL, 2002) in Northern Ireland launched a policy for addressing the literacy and numeracy needs of sixteen-year-olds and above. The Essential Skills for Living Strategy was a response to the International Adult Literacy Surveys in the late 1990s, which identified that approximately 24 per cent of the population of Northern Ireland had functional difficulties with literacy and numeracy. The Strategy established standards and qualifications for adult literacy and numeracy, a core curriculum, and a framework for tutor qualifications. Learners work at five levels: Entry Level One learners in literacy struggle with reading and writing, whereas numeracy learners at the same level have difficulties with concepts of number and basic arithmetical operations. Level Two learners would work at the equivalent of GCSE level.

Essential Skills classes take place in further education colleges, training, community and voluntary organisations, in alternative education settings and in prisons. The initial target audience for the adult literacy and numeracy classes was adults who had not been successful at school, and who would respond positively to this opportunity to improve their skills and employability. In subsequent years, policy changes and the government's employability and skills agendas have meant that the majority of learners in Essential Skills classes are aged 16–25, on vocational programmes, and many are not voluntary participants. Learners' reluctance to participate has impacted on the nature of teaching in Essential Skills and on the mentors supporting these teachers. Evelyn, a mentor interviewed for this paper, identified the challenges involved in delivering Essential Skills to reluctant learners:

> Essential Skills learners have changed because of the funding mechanisms. Mentors need to be aware of the wider issues as well as funding, and you're dealing with a group of younger people who don't want to be there – it's motivating young men, dealing with inappropriate behaviour at times, this 16–19 year old disenfranchised group of young people. It's bringing these people around; it can be done, it can be done. You need quite a lot of strength of character and motivation … it's hard work – it's harder work than when I was doing adult literacy. Having said that, the government has put so much money into this, … they want results. When I was a tutor learners didn't have to do exams, now it's output-related funding. It has made it more professional, it has attracted people who might not have thought about Essential Skills.

Bridget pointed out the importance of addressing the challenges of engaging Essential Skills learners:

> We get a second chance with people who feel that they have failed and it's very important they now recognise that they are starting to turn things round, that they can record success, that they can taste success, they can taste it and see how good it feels.

This chapter explores the role of mentors in making the most of this second chance.

MENTORING FOR ESSENTIAL SKILLS COURSE

Queen's University Belfast, tasked with designing and delivering new qualifications for Essential Skills tutors, established a two-year part-time teacher education programme. The majority of new tutors do not come from a formal teaching background, therefore to support them in learning and to strengthen the tutor qualifications framework, an accredited training programme for mentors for Essential Skills practitioners was set up at the outset of the programme. The mentoring course, a 30-hour module on the Open Learning programme in the School of Education at Queen's, ran once a year from the 2002/2003 academic year for six consecutive years. The course team won a Queen's Teaching Award for the mentoring course in 2005. The course was designed as a space for mentors to identify and reflect on their expertise, share ideas about how Essential Skills standards might be addressed, and develop appropriate strategies for supporting new tutors. The programme synthesises two of the models of staff development identified by Crandal (1993): the craft or mentor model, in which experienced practitioners impart their knowledge to those who are less experienced, and the model of reflective practice. The mentor model was based on classical models from business such as that of Clutterbuck (1991). In the classical models of reflective practice on which many teacher education programmes are based (Schön, 1991), reflection takes place through discussion and critical reflection, and is assessed through writing, in the form of reflective learning journals. In the Essential Skills tutor qualifications programme reflection is conceived of as a multimodal system for articulating, reviewing and creating learning, building on Brookfield's lenses for reflection (1995), Valli's typology (1997) of reflection, Tracey's model of guided reflection (2006), and Leitch and Day's call for more complex forms of reflection in teacher education programmes (2000).

The Mentoring for Essential Skills course was conceived as a series of reflective spaces for mentors to consider and develop their practice. A key reflective space is triad work, in which mentor and mentee first role-play a scenario from practice, then receive feedback from an observer. One mentor noted that the triad work was an effective way of developing mentoring skills, and subsequently incorporated this into the programme she managed in a further education college.

Symbols and metaphors generated ideas about mentoring within the reflective space; for example, mentoring might be associated with being a superhero, lighthouse, a helping hand and a ladder. Discussions supported mentors in identifying and challenging their assumptions about their roles. The use of arts-based methods as a further reflective space is illustrated in Figure 28.1.

Each quadrant represents a small-group reflection on the roles and responsibilities of mentors in Essential Skills, using arts-based methods such as props and art materials. Although each piece was created on a different course, similarities suggest that mentors used materials to articulate complex roles and multiple identities they assume as mentors, conveyed by hats and masks. The words 'persuasion', 'calming', 'change' and 'banish/vanquish problems' and images of the chain and sword evoke the challenges involved in engaging reluctant Essential Skills learners. To support reflection on the multiple dimensions of mentoring in

Figure 28.1   Arts-based reflections on mentoring

Essential Skills, an Awareness Model was developed and presented at the start of the course (Figure 28.2).

The first mentoring course took place in the 2002/2003 and the final one in 2007/2008. The first three courses took place from October to January, but participants would have preferred the course to span the whole academic year so they could support their mentees throughout their learning at Queen's and in completing their teaching practice. There were opportunities for exploring personal, professional and contextual aspects of mentoring during the six sessions:

Session One: the nature of mentoring, an introduction to the Awareness Model for mentoring, reflective practice, mentoring models, and to standards for Essential Skills teaching and learning, with documentation for initiating and maintaining a mentoring relationship. Information on course assignments: a reflective learning journal, a portfolio of evidence on the mentoring relationship, and an essay on a mentoring topic pertinent to participants' practice.

Session Two: exploration of mentoring relationships, comparing and contrasting mentoring models; reflection on Cohen's (1995) model of relationships; triads established and contracts drawn up; helping behaviours (advising, informing, supporting and guiding) discussed and potential issues identified with mentors role playing supportive roles with mentees which might otherwise be demeaning or inappropriate.

Session Three: skills practice.

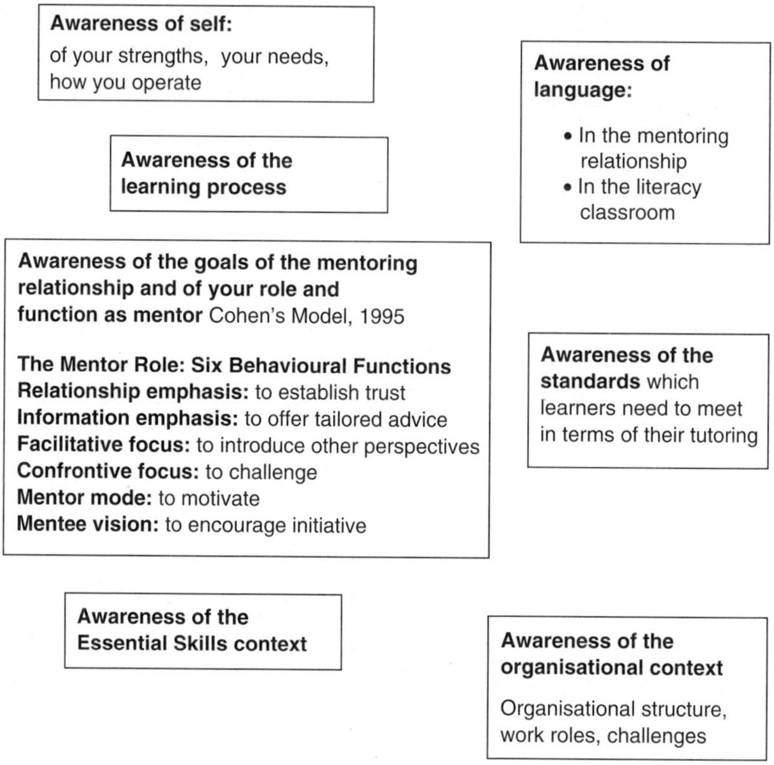

Awareness of self:
of your strengths, your needs, how you operate

Awareness of language:
- In the mentoring relationship
- In the literacy classroom

Awareness of the learning process

Awareness of the goals of the mentoring relationship and of your role and function as mentor Cohen's Model, 1995

The Mentor Role: Six Behavioural Functions
Relationship emphasis: to establish trust
Information emphasis: to offer tailored advice
Facilitative focus: to introduce other perspectives
Confrontive focus: to challenge
Mentor mode: to motivate
Mentee vision: to encourage initiative

Awareness of the standards which learners need to meet in terms of their tutoring

Awareness of the Essential Skills context

Awareness of the organisational context
Organisational structure, work roles, challenges

Figure 28.2   Awareness Model for mentoring

Session Four: exploring mentoring through the use of arts-based methods; sharing issues from practice. Exploring the assessment of mentees.
Session Five: mentoring in organizations and exploring issues relating to power and responsibility.
Session Six: triad work, opportunities to raise questions about assignments; space for mentors to set up peer support networks and plan for developing those already set up. Course evaluations.

Seventy-six mentors participated in the course over the six years, with 55 completing the assignments successfully and gaining the qualification. Those who failed cited lack of time as the reason, although they reported they were practising skills acquired on the course. The majority of the participants were literacy practitioners (44, or 58 per cent), with 17 numeracy experts (22 per cent) and 15 (20 per cent) with qualifications and experience in both areas. The discrepancy between the numbers of qualified literacy and numeracy practitioners reflected the relative lack of numeracy experts in the field. The discrepancy between female and male participants (68 per cent female and 32 per cent male) is a fair representation of the gender balance in Essential Skills, which is female-dominated. Participants were working across the full range of contexts for

Essential Skills, including training organisations, further education colleges, community and voluntary sectors, alternative education projects and prisons. When the participants started the courses, there were no formal mentoring systems in their organisations for Essential Skills practitioners. After completing the course, participants with managerial responsibilities set up mentoring programmes in their organisations. Two such programmes are described in the interviews.

The course evaluation questionnaire offered further reflective space for participants, requiring them to rate and comment on course delivery, contents and handbook. Ratings and comments were positive, the only exception being the role-play. Approximately half of the respondents said they disliked role-play, although they realised its importance for developing mentoring skills. Other illustrative comments identified the personal benefits which participants gained, support networks developed during the course, and the reflective nature of the course:

> I learned a lot from these sessions, plus it helped build my confidence personally and professionally.

> Excellent, support network has evolved during the course.

> Strong support and guidance throughout. Clear and precise directives given. Delivery of each session was lively, reflective and of a very high standard.

SURVEY OF MENTORING EXPERIENCES

In 2006, a survey was sent to the 47 participants who had completed the first three mentoring courses to ascertain their subsequent mentoring experiences. Given the small response rate (23 per cent), it is not possible to establish trends and draw conclusions, but some results are included here because they confirmed ideas about mentoring that were embedded in the course; the results also identified areas for development in subsequent courses. Respondents reported they had mentored between two and six student tutors since completing the course. Participants were asked how much time in total they had spent on the mentoring relationship, including observing lessons. Options ranged from three to over eighteen hours, based on a teaching practice period of twenty to forty weeks. Participants were also asked how they allocated time for mentoring. There was great variation of formal and informal contact, from a regular weekly meeting, to email contact and meetings as required. The nature of support offered varied from observing teaching to sharing ideas and resources, advice and guidance on practice, and help with course assignments for mentees who were enrolled on the Essential Skills tutor qualifications programme at Queen's.

In response to the question as to whether they had been given time in their practice for mentoring, remuneration and/or recognition, all noted that their organisations had allocated time and those who had supported students undertaking Essential Skills qualifications had received a fee from Queen's. One respondent wrote after the word *recognition*: 'GRATITUDE! Acknowledgement: Personal satisfaction, professional recognition'.

Asked to identify the most valuable aspect of their mentoring experiences, respondents referred to the opportunity for reflection in comments such as 'having to think more clearly about what you were teaching and the guidance and support you were giving'. They also referred to the contribution they were making to developing good practice in Essential Skills, and the reciprocal learning process in 'giving advice for those less experienced that they valued and were able to implement in the work. Also, the learning that took place from observing the mentees.' One respondent reflected on the importance of continued mentoring after initial teacher training: 'I think mentoring is particularly valuable for more inexperienced tutors. However, a more informal type of mentoring is useful for all tutors (myself included) for advice and support.'

An additional comment on one respondent's evaluation form referred to the experience of the Queen's mentoring course: Does this require quotation marks?

> This was an excellent course, which helped me raise the standard of my work as a mentor. It gave me a broader understanding of the role and the importance of mentoring in adult learning.

MENTORING FORUM

Evaluations from the first cohort of students on the mentoring course identified a need for a network for mentors to share ideas and offer reciprocal support on an ongoing basis. A network meeting held in October 2004 was attended by 15 mentors who decided to establish a mentoring forum, hosted at Queen's and supported by LSDANI (Learning Skills Development Agency Northern Ireland). The first meeting took place in January 2005. The proposed purpose of the forum was to share information on current and further practice and act as a pressure group to ensure implementation of a structured approach to mentoring in Northern Ireland. Two subsequent meetings were held in December 2005 and February 2006. A lack of infrastructure and opportunities to take time away from the workplace for meetings meant the forum failed to continue after the February meeting; however, a group of six mentors working in the community sector set up a network and continued to meet and share materials for a few years after this.

INTERVIEWS WITH MENTORS

To enable my reflection on the mentoring course in particular and mentoring in Essential Skills in Northern Ireland in general, I decided to interview mentors who had completed the mentoring courses. Participants were selected because they represented a range of contexts, each had attended the course on a different occasion, and they had varied work roles as tutors, managers and Essential Skills coordinators, with from three to more than ten years of experience in Essential Skills and in mentoring preceding the Essential Skills Strategy. Five mentors who participated in the interviews were female and one male; ideally, there should have been another male to reflect the gender balance of course participants. Mentors' names have been changed and work settings anonymised to support confidentiality.

Three participants work in further education colleges in different parts of Northern Ireland in different capacities: Evelyn, who retired recently, is a qualified teacher and comes from adult education where she was the mentoring coordinator for the college where she worked. Mentors whom she managed supported colleagues who were new to teaching. Over 50 tutors have been mentored since the programme began in 2003. Evelyn notes that although tutors from a variety of subject areas were interviewed as potential mentors for the programme, all those appointed were Essential Skills practitioners:

> I'm beginning to think that Essential Skills tutors have that little bit extra, I don't know what it is – maybe it's because they have a more caring attitude, they are more empathetic than people who are teaching, say, A Level physics … maybe it is the personality of the Essential Skills tutor who makes a better mentor, I don't know.

Heather, the principal lecturer and Essential Skills Coordinator for six campuses of a further education college, has eleven years' experience in adult basic education. She mentors a large team of Essential Skills tutors and also uses her mentoring skills in her role as a literacy tutor. She refers to the caring nature of Essential Skills tutors and mentors throughout her interview and notes

> the idiosyncratic nature of Essential Skills – as an Essential Skills teacher you are not only a teacher you are a mother, you are a friend, you are a supporter, you are a counsellor, and you only pick up those skills when you have been effectively mentored. Yes, so you are an all-singing all-dancing type of individual because the type of Essential Skills learners we get can vary from a group of very reluctant adults to a group of very difficult trainees on apprenticeships, who have more disruptive behaviour and problems because they are used to covering up the fact that they are not sure how to spell or to how use an apostrophe or how to communicate. There is such a wide gamut of individuals and roles for an Essential Skills literacy or numeracy course, and the five levels and all of those individuals come with so much baggage and so much experience and awareness of some previous educational experience that perhaps wasn't as attractive as it could be … you are looking and listening … you really have to be an observant person in that classroom.

Heather's words reflect the complex array of personal qualities and skills Essential Skills tutors and mentors need.

Barbara is a full-time literacy lecturer in a further education college, with many years of experience and a special interest in research on the teaching of reading. She believes that low literacy levels are due to inadequate teaching of reading in schools. She notes that when she acted as a placement tutor for students on the Queen's Essential Skills qualifications programme in the years before she attended the mentoring course, she was actually 'mentoring unofficially ... students would ask me about what wasn't working or I would notice that someone was getting tangled up and just help them.' Barbara commented although her mentoring practices did not change substantially as a result of the course, 'doing the course affirmed me that I was doing the job properly ... um ... getting all the assignments done, feeling myself properly qualified, was very important, feeling that I hadn't left anything out, that I was doing this properly'.

Susan was an Essential Skills tutor in the community for many years, mentored five Essential Skills students on the Queen's programme in that time, and has recently become an Essential Skills tutor for adults with acquired brain injury. Her first career was in the business world. She came to Essential Skills as a qualified 'reflective listener'. Susan was unable to attend the interview and sent her reflections via email in response to the questions.

Frank taught on the last mentoring course in 2007/2008. He is the training manager in a training organisation. The learners in his organisation are young people on a vocational programme, Training for Success (TFS), and older learners who are unemployed. Frank started out as a retail tutor 14 years ago in the same organisation and has been working in Essential Skills for about 11 years. He acts as an external verifier for Essential Skills for an awarding body, and is currently delivering a qualification for mentoring learners on work placements. Frank explains that his experience as a student on the Queen's mentoring course initiated the setting up of a mentoring programme for learners in his organisation:

> It was actually when we were doing the mentoring programme here, myself and a colleague, for mentoring Essential Skills tutors and at that time we had a problem with retaining learners and we do the IQ:RS as you know every year [self-evaluation for inspection purposes], and we had a problem with Level 1 learners ... We found that they weren't staying, they were leaving the programme which meant that it was a negative outcome for us and at that time we were mentoring a lot of tutors and we thought, well, everybody was being mentored, but the people who needed it most in the organisation, which was the learners ... umm ... and that's when we came up with the idea of mentoring them to try and retain them, engage them and then trying to move them on so that they would stay.

> ... It's been very worthwhile; it has been one of the successes that we've had. It starts off ... as part of the disciplinary process where we would take them in and discuss the issues with them that have come up and try and keep them on board and try and meet them on a regular basis so that they feel that there is a place for them here. When they reach the disciplinary stage then it [participation in the mentoring programme] isn't voluntary, but we also take on people who want to make use of the mentoring programme here, they could come on board voluntarily.

> ... We have informal mentoring as well, it wouldn't be specific – just a general chat, if you see someone in the corridor, saying how are you doing or if one of the tutors mentioned something I would say I hear you're doing well – so it's kind of supporting, also guidance and advising, but also motivating, it wouldn't take very much, saying well done, you're doing very well. It may not be guidance and advising but its supporting, telling them I hear you've done very well; they get a buzz out of hearing that.

Bridget is a qualified teacher and Essential Skills coordinator in a men's prison:

> I was asked to pilot the Essential Skills qualifications back in the early days, both in literacy and in numeracy, and then went on to pilot it in the prison. We fed back to ETI [Education and Training Inspectorate] who then wrote a report to DEL on Essential Skills and that particular accreditation, our thoughts on the strengths and weaknesses of it. … Obviously as there were new teachers brought on board, some of the teachers didn't have a background in teaching adults, never mind in teaching Essential Skills, so I started mentoring the teachers who had no idea about the – about what Essential Skills was, what literacy and numeracy was, what it meant to teach adults, very simple things, like for example, teachers who came from a school background didn't have a notion that adults were coming with prior learning that they would know things already … so the mentoring developed along those lines and was rolled out to mentoring students now who are … who were Essential Skills students who are now being trained as Essential Skills teachers themselves through Queen's and also student teachers from Queen's and from UU [University of Ulster] who are now working in with us, and who I support and … um … advise really on their teaching and their students' work and learning.

Bridget refers to prisoners participating in a pilot project with Queen's to train them as Essential Skills tutors before they complete their sentences. Her interview revealed engagement in many kinds of mentoring: with prisoners, their tutors, Queen's students on placement in the prison, colleagues, and with learners in Essential Skills classes.

INTERVIEWS: REFLECTIONS

The interviews were designed as reflective spaces for thinking about mentoring and Essential Skills. Participants were asked to reflect on their experiences of the mentoring course, their own mentoring experiences, and the skills and qualities of effective mentors. They reflected on the Awareness Model for mentoring and on mentoring in the context of Essential Skills in NI, referring to current issues in the field. The final part of the interview invited mentors to reflect on a key theme of the course: the relationship between mentoring and power. To support reflections, participants received questions beforehand, as well as a copy of the Awareness Model. All brought along notes which they had prepared in response to the questions to the interviews.

REFLECTIONS ON THE MENTORING COURSE

Every participant commented that they had welcomed the opportunity to work with colleagues from different organisations on the course. As Evelyn notes, 'It was a great experience to meet and learn and share experiences with other tutors'. Heather corroborates this, adding that

> [t]he big thing for me was the networking and the fact that we could share experiences was very important to me and we had a lot of colleges and training organisations represented and there as a nice sort of cohesiveness – the networking and the opportunity to reflect – a

lot of the penny was dropping for me, that I was doing a lot of these skills already but I didn't see it as being mentor, I just saw it as being Heather – I didn't realise that already in my role I had a quite diverse group of people that I was mentoring, and I was thinking, hey I can put a hat on this, I can put a title on what I am doing in the college.

Four participants said they had enjoyed opportunities the course had offered for reflection. Heather notes: 'You were able to give us a talking shop in sharing practice, sharing experiences, to offload, and to reflect. … We were encouraged to reflect and I suppose that up till then there wasn't the opportunity to do that on any academic course that I had done … and there isn't much opportunity to do that in the different curriculum areas.'

REFLECTIONS ON THE QUALITIES AND SKILLS OF GOOD MENTORS

In their reflections, some participants foregrounded the mentoring of learners rather than tutors, while others focused on the student teachers whom they were mentoring. Frank differentiates between mentoring learners and tutors: '[T]utors obviously have to deal with what's in front of them and it can be can be tough, so we're trying to motivate them, trying to keep their confidence up because it's a knock to their confidence when they've got into a situation when they feel that they can't deal with it, there is someone there that they can talk to and throw out the issues and try to come up with some kind of resolution. It can be a bit of pressure off them.'

According to Barbara, effective mentoring is:

professionalism, seeing continuing professional development, professional development is a career-long process. I see teaching as a vocation, you need the willingness to go an extra mile, be nonjudgmental, constructive, have a sense of humour about the pitfalls, you need to be a good communicator … also, where Queen's courses are continually changing I may not be up to speed so I need to resource myself … and of course I need to be reflective.

Barbara's equation of mentoring with effective teaching was echoed by Bridget, who said:

I think … a good mentor has to have patience, I think … um … you have to realise, to take yourself back to when you were starting out as a teacher and not presuppose things that now are second nature to you because you've worked in that role for so long. I think especially in Essential Skills, you have to be inspirational to an extent, I think it's evident to the teacher and to the students you care about – about how things are done about using resources or topics that are of interest to the student in order to gain their interest in order to motivate them, progress them – I think that it's important – to inspire others and to see that what they do is important and how they do it, recognise that.

For Frank, it is important to have

patience, empathy and the ability to get down and dirty with learners, talking at their level if you know what I mean, and empathizing with them and realizing that the issues they have are real issues to them you know when they come to us. A lot of them wouldn't have a secure family background, a lot of them would have social work involvement … when they close the door in the mornings and come to us, we don't know what they've left behind though it's important that we can realize, look, it's not all perfect out there and they have a lot of pressures, trying to get down to the bottom of the root causes of the problems that they're having and that requires you being able to communicate at their level without patronising them.

For Heather, tutors and mentors in Essential Skills require a complex range of personal skills and qualities:

Essential Skills practitioners have to be mentors too to do their job properly, it's a caring and teaching and a compassion, it's all those skills that teachers should have, people say nuns and priests have, a vocation; teachers should have a vocation too ... there is a dual role and you can't really divorce the two, the two go hand in hand really to make it work well; you have all the roles of the administrator, the academic, the practitioner, the teacher; you also have to have the care.

REFLECTIONS ON THE AWARENESS MODEL FOR MENTORING

Evelyn reflected on the overall structure of the model, suggesting that it combined personal and professional skills. Like other participants, she stressed the importance of Awareness of Self.

With regard to Awareness of the Organisational Context, Barbara now realises

how important mentoring is as a cohesive bonding kind of thing within an organisation. I remember thinking, yes, this is very important, because I had actually seen it as this tiny thing between the mentor and the mentee but I began to think – I began to look a bit broader.

Bridget focused on Awareness of the Mentoring Relationship from the perspective of working in a prison environment, reflecting on all of the stages of Cohen's model:

You can teach adults – for example, you can teach adults French or whatever in an FE [further education college], but teaching somebody Essential Skills is more difficult because you know you are getting down to more basic principles with people, you are discussing the curricula, you are helping them with all sorts of skills, skills that are essential for everyday life so it's very important that the relationship you have with that student is a good relationship, is a trusting relationship. You recognize, when you talk about the facilitative focus, you recognize what that adult can bring to the class ... umm ... where they can share with you where they can share with the rest of the group and you are always reflecting on what you do, you confront yourself, you almost confront your ability to do something better.

REFLECTIONS ON POWER IN THE MENTORING RELATIONSHIP

Susan comments on issues of power in the mentoring relationship:

Where the power lies in the student/tutor relationship is a big issue because the teacher is the role model/guide to whom the learner will look for help and support, but the power level has to be equal if the student is to feel comfortable and at ease to learn. If the student is fearful or the balance of power moves towards the tutor then it becomes a barrier to learning as the student does not have full opportunity to thrive as much as when they are given the tools to grow – maybe even beyond their tutor!

Bridget reflected on the issue of power in terms of her mentoring relationship with her ex-learners, now studying to become Essential Skills tutors.

> You can see how the roles have changed now. They now are on an equal footing. You can see not just their development, but also what their strengths are in this role, huge strengths because as prisoners themselves they will have a peer relationship with the students which you never will have.

Evelyn felt that to avoid disempowering the mentee, the mentoring relationship should be horizontal rather than vertical; the deputy director of a college, for instance, should not mentor a colleague much further down in the hierarchy. Evelyn raised the question about the power imbalances that can arise when mentors assess their mentees as well as supporting them, challenging the notion embedded in the Queen's mentoring training that mentors should combine both roles. Evelyn also suggested that mentors and mentees should observe and reflect on each others' classes to equalize the relationship and support learning.

Heather addressed the dependence on mentors that may arise when mentees rely too much on them, commenting that '[y]ou are their little guardian angel; you won't always be there as their guardian angel. It's probably best to help them find their own wings and then to reverse out of that situation.'

There is an organizational dimension to the relationship between mentoring and power. Evelyn and Frank described in their interviews how effectively mentoring worked when it was recognised by the organisation and there were formal structures to support it. (There is no formal recognition of Bridget's role as a mentor in the prison):

> It's not recognised and certainly not valued, although I have to say that it's intrinsic to my work as a coordinator and I recognize that it's perceived as such by the inspectorate when they come in ... they will see systems that I've put in place as a quality assurer, but they will see that I have dealt with things if I feel that somebody needs support. That teachers need support and they see the advice and guidance that I have given them and what I have done to progress things and how I have worked with students and they have remarked as a strength the relationship that there is between the between myself and the students who uh, who are ... because they come from an Essential Skills background, it's very important to have that relationship with them.

Bridget's comment points to the amount of unrecognized mentoring that occurs when practitioners take responsibility for the professional aspects of their practice and their learners' well-being and confidence. Heather expressed this when she declared: 'I am in the business of confidence building.'

DISCUSSION AND REFLECTIONS

The mentoring course provided a reflective space for Essential Skills mentors to learn together and share their experiences. Responses to the course, survey and interviews revealed the commitment of mentors to their practice and their learners, as well as their recognition of the challenges involved in Essential Skills learning and teaching and the multiple skills and personal qualities required. Frank suggested with regard to Essential Skills classes of 16- and 17-year-olds, 'tutoring requires a lot of skills that may not necessarily be involved in other environments'.

Heather declared: 'I see mentoring as the key cornerstone of effective Essential Skills delivery.' While this is a broad claim, acknowledgement of the mentoring programmes by the inspectorate in Evelyn's, Frank's and Bridget's workplaces does suggest that it has made a contribution to good practice in Essential Skills.

CONCLUSION

We have focused on the design, processes and outcomes of a mentoring training programme for adult literacy and numeracy practitioners in Northern Ireland. Responses to the programme suggest that despite its specific agenda, it has relevance for the design of mentoring training programmes and engagement of mentors in reflection in other contexts. Mentors' comments about the Awareness Model suggest the importance of providing a framework in mentoring training to support participants' engagement with personal, professional, organisational and relational aspects of mentoring. Interviews revealed mentors' awareness of their multiple responsibilities in the field of Essential Skills: for inexperienced tutors and Essential Skills learners as well as for development of good practice. The course offered reflective spaces for mentors to explore their responsibilities and practice; similar opportunities might be included in other mentoring programmes, taking cognizance of holistic models of reflection which offer collaborative as well as individual, arts-based and verbal methods for engagement with practice.

The outcomes of course evaluations and interviews concur with Garvey and Alred's notion (2001) that mentoring can play a role in helping employees tolerate complexity in their working environments and in developing learning. This requires skilled and resourceful mentors, aware of multiple dimensions in their practice, from policy requirements to supporting new teachers to engaging learners. Two mentors interviewed designed their own mentoring programmes in their organisations after they had completed the course, indicating the extent of their learning from the mentoring programme.

Responses to the interviews suggest that training programmes mentors attended provided spaces for them to synthesise their knowledge of Essential Skills and to share their experiences. A key finding was the importance of for mentors of interacting with their peers, developing awareness of contexts in which others were working, and sharing materials. The Mentoring Forum was welcomed as it reduced the isolation of individual practitioners and contributed to developing good practice; although it could not be sustained, it has potential applications for other settings.

This participant communicates many of the dimensions of mentoring addressed in this chapter:

Mentorship is a vital two-way support process. It encourages reflective practice, it allows for issues to be instantly reflective practice, it allows for issues to be instantly addressed as they arise, which is vital. The process is of vital importance for the mentee and can provide great insight and thought provocation for mentors. The burning issue is how it can be funded and supported. This will involve an exploration of how one can change the mindsets of senior management to see it not as merely an expense but in the long-term as an investment which will pay dividends.

REFERENCES

Brookfield, S. (1995) *Becoming a critically reflective teacher.* San Francisco: Jossey-Bass.

Clutterbuck, D. (1991) *Everybody Needs a Mentor: Fostering talent at work* (2nd ed). London: Institute of Personnel Management.

Cohen, N. H. (1995) *Mentoring Adult Learners: A guide for educators and trainers.* Florida: Krieger Publishing Company.

Crandal, J. (1993) Professionalism and Professionalization of Adult ESL Literacy. *TESOL Quarterly*, 27(3), 497–515.

Department for Employment and Learning (2002) *Essential skills for living: A framework and consultation paper on adult literacy. Equipped for the future: Building for tomorrow.* Belfast: Department for Employment and Learning.

Garvey, B. and Alred, G. (2001) Mentoring and the Tolerance of Complexity, *Futures*, *33*(6), 519–530.

Leitch, R. & Day, C. (2000) Action research and reflective practice: Towards a holistic view. *Educational Action Research*, *8*(1), 179–193.

Schön, D. (1991) *The Reflective Turn: Case studies in and on educational practice.* New York: Teachers Press, Columbia University.

Tracey, S. (2006) Embedding Reflection in a Teacher Education Programme for Adult Literacy Tutors, What a Difference a Pedagogy Makes: Researching Lifelong Learning and Teaching. Presented at the 3rd International Conference, University of Stirling, 24–26 June. Retrieved from: http://www.leeds.ac.uk/educol/documents/159992.htm, accessed 9 January 2011.

Valli, L. (1997) Listening to other voices: A description of teacher reflection in the United States. *Peabody Journal of Education*, *72*,(1), 67–88.

29

Peer Mentoring and Inclusion in Writing Groups

Dannielle Joy Davis, Kara Provost
and Sonya Clark

INTRODUCTION

Commonalities emerge within the literature regarding the formation of faculty writing groups and the benefits to faculty development. Lee and Boud (2003) advocate the use of research writing groups as developmental initiatives to support productive work environments. Supportive writing groups establish shared goals and values, while maintaining individual members' interests. The established goals of the group contribute to its success and productivity where processes are as important as products (Fassinger and Gilliland, 1992). Writing groups not only provide communities of social support with like-minded individuals, but may also be a means of acculturation into academe for junior faculty members. Such groups have evolved from increasing pressures on faculty to publish, as well as teaching and learning outcomes requiring extensive documentation (Gillespie, Nivas, Kochis, Krabill, Lerum, Peterson et al., 2006).

Literature (e.g., Fassinger and Gilliland, 1992; Mullen, 2005; O'Malley, Bates, Latham, Lucey, Meyer, Spycher et al., 2006) on writing groups advocates cross-disciplinary membership for forging collegial relationships bonded by the commonalities of writing and the writing process. The group writing process also provides a nonhierarchical space for members to grow professionally and offers a forum where each person feels empowered and affirmed (Fassinger and Gilliland, 1992). Individual contributions in a group, regardless of differences in specialization, can increase the knowledge base and empathy of group members (O'Malley et al., 2006). Lee and Boud (2003: 193) assert that members' 'commonalities of interests' in regards to writing and publication, despite field prompts collegiality within a group. Intellectual discourse stimulates writing, which necessitates social interactions (Pastemak, Longwell-Grice, Shea and Hanson, 2009). Lee and Boud (2003: 194) advocate supplementing the older 'laissez-faire notions of collegiality' with attention to mutuality and peer-reciprocation.

PEER MENTORING DEFINITION

Peer mentoring entails the informal sharing of information or expertise from people of the same or similar rank as well as colleagues across rank. Through peer mentoring, writing groups transform the oft solitary act of writing into a collegial experience. This occurs through interactions related to the writing process and addressing barriers to productivity whether professional (i.e., lack of support services for faculty) or personal (i.e., writing phobias; depression).

Marginalized populations, such as racial minorities and women, may not receive quality mentoring during doctoral study (Wilson, 1997), which may negatively influence future professional productivity. Peer mentoring fills this gap, assisting in leveling the academic playing field. The writing groups featured herein offer examples of how peer mentoring includes and embraces traditionally marginalized members of the professoriate. Inclusion in this work refers to respect of minority colleagues' scholarly inquiry and value of their unique contributions within the group and to the academic field at large.

FEATURED MENTORING FRAMEWORK

Research suggests that mentoring influences the individual, interpersonal, collective, and non-program related or extra-programmatic areas of novices' experiences. The individual influence of mentorship impacts protégées' values, aspirations, skill acquisition, self assessment, and personal development. The interpersonal influence of mentorship refers to fostering professional relationships through face-to-face interaction in professional or social contexts. In these contexts, 'regular interaction facilitates positive interpersonal influence and models academic culture' (Davis, 2008: 284). Mentorship's collective influence points to interactions within a group that prompt accountability and communal responsibility. Influence occurring outside of a group or program environment, such as influence upon participants' family members or non-participating coworkers, illustrates the extra-programmatic nature of mentoring. The various influences of mentorship listed serve as the framework for discussing peer mentorship and inclusion.

PRACTICAL APPLICATION: WRITING GROUP LEADERS' EXPERIENCES

The writing component of faculty work can be isolating. The programs described next demonstrate the influence of mentoring within writing groups with respect to inclusion of marginalized groups as shared by two writing group leaders. Their stories and suggestions for practice were informed by participant feedback, observation, program documents, and journaling.

A faculty leader's experiences with academic writing groups

The first author formed her first writing group as a postdoctoral fellow at a research-oriented, predominantly White university via inviting collaborators on a grant project in 2005. Her reason for starting the group centered upon recreating the productivity experienced during her doctoral study, which was fostered by accountability and fellowship with scholars holding similar interests. Members of this first writing group comprised five African-American female academics representing various fields. The majority of participants were new faculty with one tenured member at the associate level. Following completion of the grant, members of the group continued to collaborate or pursued individual projects. Peer mentoring led to strong professional relationships with members attending writing retreats together and meeting to write as recently as fall 2010. Group members also celebrated accomplishments through periodic lunch or dinners on weekends. They mentored each other on writing and publication strategies, teaching, promoting work–life balance, and personal issues negatively affecting writing output. This writing group was highly productive, with all participants completing two to four papers per semester (a four-month period), which were published as refereed journal articles, book chapters, or funded grants.

Following this postdoctoral experience, she continued the development of writing groups as a new tenure-track faculty member at a similar postsecondary institution. During 2006, she invited all new faculty and members of her department to join. This broad invitation yielded a diverse group of five women (one Asian, two Black, and two White) from across the university, including the fields of education, sociology, English, and biology. The group met monthly to review each other's work, which included grant applications, journal articles, and book chapters. Members agreed upon expectations for the group. Group members were encouraged to write daily and to track their writing time. WEBCT (Web course tool for online learning) was used as the medium to share and comment on work. As her writing productivity increased through leadership of this group, so did the faculty leader's interest in accountability and its role in scholarly output.

Write on Site

Throughout her academic career, the first author also coordinated various faculty development activities modeled after the University of Illinois at Chicago's

'Write on Site' Group, facilitated by faculty developer Kerry Ann Rockquemore. As faculty development scholars, Robert Boice and Rockquemore note, such groups provide the accountability needed for prolific, regular writing. Boice (1992) found a significant difference between typical faculty members and faculty who wrote regularly, recorded writing progress, and were accountable to groups, which amounted to 17 versus 157 typewritten pages per year. Write on Site meets weekly for 2 hours. Participation is fluid resulting in sessions with as many as 12 to as few as 3 scholars in attendance. The focus of each meeting is writing output. However, the faculty leader also regularly shares writing strategies and mentors peers through writing barriers prior to writing sessions.

Write on Site may be implemented utilizing three models. With Model One, Rockquemore Style (which bears the last name of the scholar who shared this idea with the first author), scholars write and only write for 2 hours. Participants hold sparse knowledge of others' writing topics or progress beyond that shared during casual conversation prior to and following the meeting. Because of this, it may not be considered a formal accountability group. However, the act of meeting itself arguably may serve as a form of informal accountability. Writing sessions are held off campus.

With Model Two, or the Davis Hybrid Model, the first portion of the meeting consists of an optional 15 to 30 minute 'check in' where participants either report on their progress or share writing tips. The remaining 2 hours focuses on writing. This model includes both on and off campus components. However, the majority of sessions take place on campus in a conference room. Off campus sessions have taken place at informal, local venues or through organized group writing retreats.

Model Three combines both the Rockquemore and Davis formats in that it reflects Model Two the first and second weeks of the month. However, on the third and fourth weeks, writers move to Model One, writing continuously for 2 hours without check-in or accountability time. Table 29.1 summarizes the three aforementioned models.

Write on Site groups may also agree upon ground rules for sessions. For instance, academics may choose an open environment in terms of noise level versus collaborators meeting at other times of the week so as not to disturb non-collaborating group members. Writers often agree to other participation guide-lines, such as a drop-in policy versus participating for all or a determined portion

Table 29.1   Features of the three write on site models

Model type	Three Write on Site Models			
	Collective writing time	Verbal accountability	On campus	Off campus
Rockquemore style	✓			✓
Davis hybrid model	✓	✓	✓	✓
Davis and Rockquemore model	✓	✓	✓	✓

of a semester. Such agreements minimize the likelihood of unattended Write on Site sessions.

Peer mentoring in traditional writing and Write on Site groups

Peer mentoring occurred in both the traditional writing and Write on Site groups. Members of the traditional writing groups critiqued each other's manuscripts and grant applications. Participants with more experience on academe's tenure-track mentored junior members via offering additional suggestions on publishing strategies, funding options, and the tenure and promotion processes. The group also invited senior academics as guest speakers on such topics as grant writing and publication.

While review of others' materials did not occur outside of Write on Site meetings, mentoring with Write on Site focused on publication strategies, tenure and promotion, and learning strategies towards work–life balance. Given this leader's prior professional development and coaching, much of the mentoring conducted centered upon writing, particularly in regards to overcoming writing barriers. Fear of writing and writing block were common complaints from peers.

On inclusion and collegiality

In looking at writing groups as a strategy for research development, Lee and Boud's (2003) work suggests that mutuality, moving writing from the periphery to 'normal business' in work environments, identity, and desire are key to academic work. Mutuality moves beyond surface collegiality to peer reciprocity and genuine commitment and interest in 'developmental goals, the needs for change and development of its members in meeting those goals, [as well as] working to build collective strategies to meet … needs' (Lee and Boud, 2003: 194). Writing as normal business entails incorporating writing as central to practice in the workplace, while intellectual or professional desire and identity are noted as elements that sustain writing groups (ibid.). Similarly, Aitchison and Lee (2006) note that research writing pedagogy proves most effective when members hold common identification such as interests and life experiences, employ peer review as a group, and establish a sense of community.

In comparing two writing groups in terms of mutuality and collegiality, a difference was observed in the frequency in which the groups met and the degree to which members interacted outside of the writing group context. Group I consisting of the five African-American female academics met once every week for 2 to 4 hours per session. These were complemented by monthly fellowship gatherings off campus. Group II, a multiracial group of five women (two White, two Black, and one Asian), met monthly and never gathered outside of the campus environment.

On the surface, it appears that similarity in terms of race and socioeconomic background played a role in the more positive climate of Group I. The Black women appeared to have a strong genuine interest in each other's professional development and progress, demonstrating more traditional African, community-oriented ways of relating to each other. On the other hand, the majority of Group II members, while pleasant in demeanor, appeared to predominantly hold more individualistic motivations, not expressing interest in other members' development.

In the African-American group, or Group I, manuscripts were developed based upon collaboration born of common interests amongst group members or derived from a large joint project centered upon improving the university's community engagement. This common interest in minority research and community interaction comprised the core of mutuality present within the group. The originator of an idea for publication or a grant often acquired first authorship. Funding was sought to support professional activities for the group and members' interdisciplinary research or educational outreach initiatives. Research topics developed from the writing group reflected the expertise of members. Being diverse in terms of academic field, the effort yielded strong mixed-method, interdisciplinary research. Also, combining the unique skills and talents of group members, as well as having others to edit drafts, improved the quality of documents.

Participants of the African-American group reported a number of benefits. These include increased writing productivity, improved writing quality, expanded professional networks, a sense of community with group members, and writing accountability (Davis and King-Jupiter, 2007). Regular, output-based meetings resulted in the African-American group's increased outcomes. These benefits worked to improve the daily work lives of group members while serving as a continuous, long-term source of professional growth and development.

Group II, or the multiracial group, periodically scheduled speakers to lecture on topics related to research and writing. Computers were used to record notes or minutes for absent members, to email manuscripts for group review, and post manuscripts online via WEBCT. Participants held no prior relationships before joining the writing group and, despite the facilitators' efforts, expressed disinterest in collaboration. Overtime, the group met less frequently with fewer members participating. This lack of commitment and collaboration demonstrates the group's low degree of mutuality.

Another faculty leader's experience with a creative writing group

How can faculty writing groups serve as sites for mentoring or coaching? A group focused on creating time and space for writing and giving feedback can be likened to a cross-country team with the group leader as team coach or with all taking turns in the role of captain and coach, depending on how the group is structured. They work together, yet 'perform' individually – taking turns in the lead, pushing one another, coaching each other about pace and form, and celebrating individual victories.

The second author leads two groups, one inside and another outside Curry College. While some may not think of such writing groups as sites of mentoring, the group serves this purpose in many ways. The faculty creative writers' group is a site of inspiration, as well as a place where individual voices can be heard and valued in a holistic manner. The group challenges participants to think, to continue writing, and to get work out in the world beyond members' individual heads. It benefits them professionally by strengthening connections across different departments and disciplines, giving them the opportunity to get to know one another, while encouraging them to publish or present work. Finally, although pedagogy is not the focus of the group, teaching issues prompt peer mentoring through recommending texts and pedagogical resources.

Palmer (1998: x) writes that teaching well is a process of creating a 'reflective space where we can practice listening, being present, receiving others, and being truthful.' As a setting and structure that challenges academics to grow as scholars and supports that growth, the faculty creative writers' group at Curry serves as a site for collaborative mentoring and 'teaching' each other in the manner Palmer articulates.

Structure and format of the writing group

Upon arriving to Curry College, the faculty leader met several faculty members who were also creative writers. Through networking, she found five who wanted to join her in a creative writing group to support writing efforts and provide feedback on work. They met on campus once a month for an hour and a half to two hours. The group grew to eight members over four years. During 2010, they started meeting every two weeks for an hour per session. This allowed more continuity and opportunities for each individual member to receive feedback on writing. Before inviting new members, the group brainstormed expectations for participation, which were circulated to all members, revised and agreed upon (See the Appendix for an example). The group leader established a rotation and set meeting dates so individuals would know when to submit work for comments and ensured that everyone had equal feedback. Participants generally emailed several poems or a short prose piece (ten pages or fewer) a few days before meeting so others could read submissions ahead of time. During meetings, the writer reads the poem or an excerpt from prose followed by comments and discussion of the work. The writer tries to refrain from commenting or defending his or her work while the group gives feedback, though dialogue and discussion usually take place after initial comments. Sometimes the writer also receives written feedback from group members.

One benefit of the group is its diversity. The eight members represent full and part-time faculty, gay, straight, Black, White, married, single, those who are parents, as well as faculty new to Curry and those with many years at the institution. Two are men: one is a librarian at the college while another edits the college's arts and literary magazine, *The Curry Arts Journal*. The disciplines include education, English, history, as well as African-American, women's, gender, and honors studies. Members write poetry, fiction, memoirs, and scholarly works. The diversity of the group enhances its effectiveness as a site for mentoring.

New faculty members learn institutional culture and procedures from senior faculty, while experienced faculty learn new pedagogical approaches or resources from younger faculty. Professors from different disciplines share teaching strategies or knowledge from their fields. Listening to distinct viewpoints that arise from group members' varied experiences also encourages our practice of empathy and seeing issues from multiple perspectives.

BENEFITS OF MENTORING THROUGH FACULTY WRITING GROUPS

Currently in its fourth year, the faculty creative writers' group has benefitted all of its members professionally and personally. The group provides collegial mentorship in many ways. It strengthens our motivation to carve out writing time and affirms the value of the creative, social and emotional aspects of our being. The group also acts as a testing ground for work before it goes on to be published or presented publically; helps us solve teaching dilemmas within a supportive community of fellow educators; and strengthens our knowledge of other programs and departments at the college. One racial minority professor testified to how the group provided members with mentoring:

> [The group is] a place where colleagues can 'feed their souls' through creative writing. I cannot express how much this group means to me as someone who generally feels overwhelmed by the amount of non-teaching work required. This group provides a place where you can breathe and share your creative work with your peers and discuss it in supportive and substantive ways that are often impossible in the classroom. The group continues to provide support, boost self-confidence, and offer a sense of collegiality that is vital to helping faculty reach their full potential as scholars.

Another group member, a female associate professor who teaches English and Women's and Gender Studies, sums up the renewal that all benefitted from via participating in the writers' group when she commented that it has been 'one of my most rewarding and enjoyable experiences at Curry ... It inspires me and teaches me on many levels.'

An important aspect of mentoring that can happen in a faculty writing group concerns teaching and learning. A senior lecturer in English testifies to the educational mentoring that takes place in the group, praising the opportunities it provides 'to learn from ... colleagues' teaching in action' as they engage in thoughtful conversation about each other's work. All group members are educators, yet the group allows each to be on the receiving end of the kind of excellent teaching and coaching often extended to students. It functions like a stimulating class – one of those classes in college or graduate school that one looked forward to going to because the readings would be new and interesting and the discussion thought provoking with engaged and trusted classmates.

Even though the faculty leader directs the faculty writers' group by setting meeting dates and keeping members on task, each takes turns as 'master mentor' or 'master student.' As 'master mentors,' they listen to each other read work;

critique what others have written; ask questions that prompt clarification, reflection, insight, deeper thinking, and revision; and support and encourage each other as writers, scholars, and teachers. As 'master students,' they try to listen and learn from feedback and discussion. They continue to practice pushing back, asking questions, and articulating unique voices and visions. They follow through by revising and refining writing. In mentor roles they do for each other what they strive to do for students. In learner roles, they gain insight into and empathy for students' classroom experiences. The experience in the writer's group can give faculty the confidence and expertise to employ mentoring skills or peer mentoring in their classrooms, which can not only enhance students' learning, but also provide them with mentoring experiences they may draw upon in other settings.

In addition to the benefits previously described, the mentoring and work done through faculty writing groups resulted in publications and presentations. The faculty members' comments suggest the tension many faculty hold between the teaching, service, and publishing aspects of their professional lives. Participating in writing groups help faculty carve out time and mental space for scholarly, creative activity. Such groups can spur members on to further research and facilitate insight through writing, feedback, and critical discussion.

BENEFITS OF WRITING GROUPS AND THE THEORETICAL FRAMEWORK

The peer mentorship occurring within the featured writing groups yielded individual, interpersonal, collective, and extra-programmatic influences. The individual influence surfaced through participant interest in increased writing productivity, regular writing, and a desire to improve the writing craft. Through interactions with other women and minorities, these groups validated the presence of marginalized populations in academe, thereby promoting their inclusion.

The professional relationships nurtured via writing group participation and peer mentoring reflect interpersonal influences of mentorship. Informal face-to-face interaction with both leaders and other participants facilitated this. Group activities such as organized writing retreats, professional collaboration, and social interactions outside of the workplace fostered a strong sense of community among the groups.

Peer mentorship's collective influence took place through accountability in terms of expectations for participation, productivity, or feedback. Accepting responsibility for one another served as a key element in the African-American writing group's longevity. Accountability through the writing community prompted mutuality and inclusion of participants within the professoriate.

Peer mentoring yielded influences outside of the writing group context, or extraprogrammatically, at family, institutional, and social levels. Through both leaders' sharing their personal strategies in promoting work–life balance, peer mentoring positively influenced participants' personal lives by offering strategies to remain productive while spending more time with loved ones. Such strategies increase faculty satisfaction.

Increased scholarly productivity and knowledge of academic culture and expectations resulting from peer mentoring benefits postsecondary institutions by enhancing retention, promotion, and professional climate for participants. This outcome promotes the inclusion of underrepresented faculty in academe. Inclusion of underrepresented faculty in the professoriate works toward cultivation of a faculty reflecting the nation's racial demographics and strengthens student learning through diverse perspectives. Such structural and curricular diversity indirectly benefits society via an educated citizenry, prepared to contribute their skills and talents both nationally and globally.

SUGGESTIONS FOR PRACTICE

Mentoring within writing groups may influence policy outcomes by increasing retention and promotion rates of participating faculty. This is particularly critical for the inclusion of underrepresented academics. Though they make up over one fourth of the US population, underrepresented minorities comprise merely 9 percent of the professoriate, with Blacks comprising 5.5 percent and Hispanics representing 3.5 percent in tenure-track, tenured, and non-tenured lines. These groups represented 12.3 percent and 12.5 percent of the population during the 2000 Census (Cataldi, Bradburn, Fahimi, and Zimbler, 2006; Grieco and Cassidy, 2001).

Based upon our experiences and research, faculty writing groups are highly effective, rewarding and inexpensive vehicles for mentoring and fostering inclusive work climates within higher education. They enhance teaching through modeling sound pedagogical practices and reconnect faculty to ideas, writing strategies, and the process of intellectual discovery. Writing groups can also promote work–life balance and establish or strengthen professional relationships, often beyond the confines of a single department. Finally, the featured experiences demonstrate that faculty writing groups contribute to productivity through presentations and publications.

Institutions at the primary, secondary, and post-secondary levels may consider implementing similar initiatives to support occupational satisfaction and professional development. Universities and colleges can also share research with faculty on the benefits of writing groups. Formation of such groups can be facilitated by providing networking opportunities, valuing mentoring in promotion and tenure decisions, and offering resources such as space and funding for events where faculty present work developed through writing group participation. Some institutions have fostered collegial mentoring through supporting annual faculty writing retreats during semester breaks. These occur either on campus or off campus. Sending faculty to writing workshops together can also nurture writing output. Institutions may send faculty teams to conferences, with the expectation that the they meet afterwards to develop publications or presentations for the broader campus community. Further, institutions can enact policies rewarding and encouraging faculty mentoring initiatives centered on collaboration, writing and publication. Mentoring awards and course buyouts for both mentors and protégées exemplify such rewards.

For faculty writing groups to be successful, they should be voluntary and driven by goals that all members agree to, formally or informally. Some groups may find it helpful to set out written expectations or objectives (See the Appendix for an example). Ideally, faculty writing groups create a safe space for members to give and receive mentoring which can build collegiality, foster creative and intellectual growth, enhance pedagogical problem-solving, yield presentation or publication of scholarly work, and contribute to overall work–life balance.

APPENDIX

Writing group expectations for membership

Membership in the writing group is purely voluntary. In order to assure fairness and consistency, all members agree to the following:

1 Attendance
    a) Attendance at all meetings is expected.
    b) While we recognize that things come up, participants who regularly miss meetings will not be able to submit work and may ultimately be asked to reconsider their membership.
    c) If you are absent, please send your comments to the submitters by the day of the meeting.
2 Participation
    a) Participants are expected to come to each meeting having read all of the submitted work.
    b) As the intent of this group is to aid writers in improving their writing, we ask for substantive critical comments on all submitted work, either in writing or verbally during the meeting.
    c) Members who are absent can still participate by submitting their comments by email.
3 Submissions
    a) Membership in this group requires submission of work.
    b) Participants must submit work according to the published schedule.
    c) Work must be submitted no later than the Friday before a meeting, though it is preferred that work be submitted up to one week in advance.
    d) Work should be limited to no more than two poems, one short story, or less than ten double-spaced pages of other forms of work.
4 Reading
    a) Each member will have up to 30 minutes including reading and discussion.
    b) As work must be read before each meeting, you are limited to reading no more than a short excerpt of your submission.
    c) It is preferred that writers refrain from offering explanatory comments before reading to allow the work to speak for itself.

REFERENCES

Aitchison, C., & Lee, A. (2006). Research Writing: Problems and Pedagogies. *Teaching in Higher Education, 2*(3), 265–278.

Boice, R. (1992). *The new faculty member: Supporting and fostering professional development.* San Francisco: Jossey-Bass.

Cataldi, E. F., Bradburn, E. M., Fahimi, M., & Zimbler, L. (2006). *National study of postsecondary faculty (NSOPF: 04): Background characteristics, work activities, and compensation of instructional faculty and staff: Fall 2003* (NCES 2006-176). Washington, DC: US Department of Education/Institute of Education Sciences.

Davis, D. J. (2008). Mentorship and the socialization of underrepresented minorities into the professoriate: Examining various influences. *Mentoring & Tutoring: Partnership in Learning, 16*(3), 278–293.

Davis, D. J., & King-Jupiter, K. L. (2007). *The worldwide web: Scholars unite through the power of the pen and the Internet.* Paper presented at the meeting of the American Educational Research Association, April, Chicago, IL.

Fassinger, P. A., & Gilliland, N. (1992). Benefits of a faculty writing circle – better teaching. *College Teaching, 40*(2), 53–56.

Gillespie, D., Nivas, D., Kochis, B., Krabill, R., Lerum, K., Peterson, A., & Thomas, E. (2006). Research circles: Supporting the scholarship of junior faculty. *Innovative Higher Education, 30*(3), 149–162.

Grieco, E. M., & Cassidy, R. C. (2001). *Overview of race and Hispanic origin: Census 2000 brief. United States Census 2000.* Washington, DC: US Census Bureau.

Lee, A., & Boud, D. (2003). Writing groups, change and academic identity: Research development as local practice. *Studies in Higher Education, 28*(2), 187–200.

Little, D., & Palmer, M. (2011). A coaching-based framework for individual consultations. In J. Miller & J. Groccia (Eds.), *To improve the academy: resources for faculty, instructional, and organizational development* (pp. 102–115). San Francisco: Jossey-Bass.

Mullen, C. A. (2005). *Fire and ice: Igniting and channeling passion in new qualitative researchers.* New York: Peter Lang.

O'Malley, G. S., Bates, A., Latham, N., Lucey, T., Meyer, B., Spycher, E., & Wedwick, L. (2006). Promoting scholarship through writing groups. *Academic Exchange Quarterly, 10*(4), 171–175.

Palmer, P. (1998). Foreword. In M. R. O'Reilley (Ed.), *Radical Presence: Teaching as contemplative practice* (p. x). Portsmouth, NH: Boynton.

Pastemak, D., Longwell-Grice, H., Shea, K., & Hanson, L. K. (2009). Alien environments or supportive writing communities? Pursuing writing groups in academe. *Arts and Humanities in Higher Education, 8*(3), 355–367.

Wilson, R. (1997). Negative mentoring: An examination of the phenomenon as it affects minority students. *Diversity in Higher Education, 1*, 177–185.

Research Issues

30

E-mentoring and Educational Research Capacity Development: A Conceptual Perspective

Norbert Pachler and Ana Redondo

INTRODUCTION

Mentoring practices, however they are defined, evolve and change over time. One important driver for change in the last 15 years or so, which is in focus in this chapter, is the growth in online technologies for all aspects of our everyday and working lives, be they social or professional. Indeed, most people living and working in Western societies can be said to be leading digital lives to a greater or a lesser degree as technologies become increasingly embedded and integrated into work, commerce, entertainment, and so on.

As Ragins and Kram (2007: 3–4) rightly note, mentoring is an ancient archetype originating in Greek mythology. Its endurance as a form of teaching and learning must in part be attributed to it potentially addressing a persistent need in human socialisation and development: to bridge the gap between actual and potential levels of development through guidance from others. As such we deem it intimately linked to notions of capacity building.

Traditionally, mentoring has been seen as a developmental relationship embedded within the career context (Ragins and Kram, 2007: 5) involving a more experienced mentor and an often younger and normally less experienced mentee.

In their overview of key literature, Ragins and Kram (ibid.) distinguish between career functions and psychosocial functions, with the former focusing on professional learning and advancement, and the latter focusing on personal growth. In order to lead to successful outcomes, different mentoring functions rely on different mentoring behaviours and prerequisites such as status, knowledge, skills and attitudes of the mentor as well as on interpersonal factors, such as the 'chemistry' in the relationship, and contextual factors, such as the organisational context and the degree of formalisation and status of mentoring within the workplace.

In terms of the context in which mentoring takes place, literature on mentoring – as well as education more broadly – has increasingly focused on its embeddedness in developmental networks, so-called communities of practice (Lave and Wenger, 1991; Wenger, 1998), through a deepening process of participation and situated learning. That is, mentoring tends to be seen more and more as a multilateral activity which takes place between a number of often distributed actors, rather than as a bilateral activity between co-located actors. As a consequence, an important contextual factor for the purposes of this chapter is mode; that is, the question to what extent digital technologies can be, and are, being used as part of mentoring and how. The focus in this chapter is on 'e'-mentoring rather than mentoring *per se* and, given the relative dearth of literature on the topic, one of its purposes is to explore how e-mentoring best be understood by discussing key concepts and issues at a relatively high level of generality for their possible subsequent application to specific contexts; for example, as criteria for analysis of mentoring relationships or the planning of e-mentoring interventions.

Established distinctions between different functions of mentoring suggest the importance not only of behavioural and cognitive perspectives, but also of affective ones. It is interesting to note here that the literature on e-learning, in particular Garrison and Anderson (2003), makes a similar point stressing the importance of social presence, cognitive presence and teaching presence as prerequisites for a successful online educational experience.

One additional important variable to note briefly here is that of developmental phases of mentoring relationships. Kram's work (1983) shows that mentoring relationships evolve over time through phases that are characterised inter alia by different patterns of interaction between mentors and mentees. When talking about mentoring in general, and e-mentoring in particular, it might therefore be useful to distinguish mentoring episodes, behaviours and relationships (Ragins and Kram, 2007: 7) and explore what differences there might be in the use of online technologies in the different phases.

In short, mentoring – although the focus of an ever-growing body of research and scholarly literature – remains a concept which covers a number of purposes and which can be found across a wide range of contexts in a diverse form of articulations. E-mentoring is a rather new sub-domain which has evolved with the increasing availability of communication technologies. It is a field about which very few academic articles are in print to date and which, consequently, is arguably not very well understood as yet. As a consequence, this chapter first and foremost seeks to explore the terrain of e-mentoring with a view to establishing what concepts and issues are central in order to furnish interested researchers and practitioners with a frame of reference to talk about important aspects of the field. Given the overall focus of this section of the handbook, the chapter does so by locating the debate in the context of educational research capacity development.

TRANSFORMATIONS AND NEW PARADIGMS

Before we discuss e-mentoring in any detail, let us make some observations of a more general nature relating to technology. As is well documented, and ubiquitously evident, we are living at a time of social, cultural, economic and technological transformation (see, e.g., Pachler, Bachmair and Cook, 2010). This transformation has a tangible impact on the world of work; for example, in terms of the stability and requirements of the job market. For the individual this results in a requirement perpetually to acquire knew knowledge, skills and understandings as well as the need to continually update their 'technological literacy' in order to be able to do so (see also Brown and Adler, 2008: 18).

This transformation is accompanied by changes in paradigms of education and training away from a transmission-based model premised on the transfer of knowledge towards more participative models on the one hand, and more situated approaches on the other. Lave and Wenger (1991) and Wenger (1998), already mentioned above, coined the term 'communities of practice', which has found wide-spread adoption in the literature (albeit often rather uncritically), and alongside it the notion of 'legitimate peripheral participation' to describe how newcomers become experienced community members. In short, we have witnessed a move away in our understanding of learning from the primacy of knowledge and attendant processes of acquisition, such as, for example, memorisation, towards the understanding of learning as something that is also socially constructed and interactionally grounded (for a detailed discussion see Pachler and Daly, 2011). In order not to be misunderstood, this is not to argue the case for a decline in the significance and importance of knowledge and cognition, it is simply to acknowledge our growing recognition of the social and cultural dimension of learning.

Talk about knowledge economies abounds, as do discourse practices around knowledge workers; that is, the growing number of members of society regularly engaged *inter alia* in identifying, processing, analysing, categorising, managing, sharing and transmitting, enhancing and generating knowledge using research skills. What is changing, for example, is the volume, the speed of growth, its durability and longevity, the storage media as well as attendant processes and skills requirements and so on.

We consider education practitioners at all levels very much as knowledge workers involved in information-based transactions and interactions who need to be able to evaluate and analyse data to establish relationships, correlation and/or causality, make connections, identify and understand trends, think divergently and convergently and so on. The knowledge, skills and understanding involved need to be acquired through an ongoing process of development in which (e-) mentoring can be seen to play a legitimate, sometimes even an essential, role.

Alongside and intertwined with these developments, we have witnessed not only the advent of computer-mediated communication technologies but also a paradigm shift from content transmission and provision (Web 1.0) to collaborative and distributed content creation (Web 2.0, social networking).

It is against, and in relation to, this background, we posit, that e-mentoring needs to be considered. In order to excel in such an environment, Brown and Adler (2008: 20, 28) imply, learners need to have opportunities for what they call 'distributed cognitive apprenticeship' through memberships of communities of practice that enable what John Dewey called 'productive enquiry':

> We need to construct shared, distributed, reflective practicums in which experiences are collected, vetted, clustered, commented on, and tried out in new contexts. One might call this 'learning about learning,' a bootstrapping operation in which educators, along with students, are learning among and between themselves.
>
> Brown and Adler, 2008: 28

Mentoring and e-mentoring for us are closely linked to capacity building: not just in terms of enabling individual learners to cope with and thrive as individual members of the knowledge economy, but also in terms of making a systemic and systematic contribution to the management and exploitation of existing as well as the generation of new knowledge.

What, then, is educational research capacity and how is it best built? What body of research is to be built? Scientific? Applied, practice-based? Who are the researchers whose skills and methods are to be harnessed? Specialist researchers? Educators? Novice practitioners? And, who builds capacity? Scientists? Teacher educators? Fellow practitioners? Whose capacity is built? That of people, structures, systems? At what level? In what discipline(s)? And, importantly, to what end? To achieve sustainability, embeddedness, diversity, dispersion? For the purposes of this chapter the assumed focus is on the disciplines of education and social science at the level of the individual (practitioner) researcher rather than the system. The literature on capacity building is not really prolific and often appears to discuss medical/clinical contexts. For an overview of research capacity building in teacher education in the UK, see Murray, Campbell, Hextall, Hulme, Jones, Mahony et al. (2009).

The paradigm shifts touched on above have considerable implications for the types, role as well as functions of mentoring. Depending on the particular context, different variants of (e-)mentoring will be required. In a paper in *Teaching and Teacher Education*, Sundli (2007: 201), for example, argues for a new paradigm of mentoring taking account of the shift of focus away from individual cognitive processing towards situated cognition as well as the new and more complex competences, such as social reflexivity, the ability to deal with many choices and act in information over-rich and 'de-traditionalised' contexts demanded by post-modern society (2007: 204, 206). Clearly, digital technologies offer ample scope to address such an agenda for change. In the context of educational research capacity building, mentoring a teacher engaging in a piece of classroom-based practitioner research requires rather different skills and approaches than supporting a university-based researcher preparing his/her first Research Council bid.

Arguably, there is an ever-growing need for research in all walks of life, including educational practice – with research understood here as the search for knowledge through systematic investigation – in a world characterised by increasing complexity as well as international comparison and competition. A real challenge exists variously to ensuring high volume, high quality (rigorous, original, etc.), high impact, income-generating, leading-edge research for a wide range of reasons: to explore, describe and explain in order to understand (correlations and causalities in) the world in which we live (better), as well as to predict what might happen. This applies to the research function of universities as it does to the systematic enquries of education practitioners seeking to solve everyday problems occurring in their professional contexts, be they with individual learners, the ecosystem of their classrooms or the wider school setting. In a climate of perpetual (policy) change, competition, performativity, league tables and comparisons even in education, the ability of practitioners to implement national policy according to local requirements as well as to find solutions to local problems becomes paramount. One possible, and arguably potentially very effective way of impacting on quality of (service) provision and outcomes is local capacity building; that is, equipping professionals to be able to identify problems pertinent to their context, ask the right questions, know how to seek to answer them systematically, implementing tailored solutions to the problems they identified and disseminating findings to relevant colleagues as well as a wider audience. (e-)Mentoring, again, we deem to be key in developing local capacity.

In a recent paper, focusing on university-based research, Evans (2009) discusses the development needs of researchers in the context of a systemic capacity building agenda and coins the term 'developmentalism' by which she means 'the process whereby people's professionalism, or professionality, or professional practice may be considered to be enhanced, with a degree of permanence that exceeds transitoriness' (n.p.). She argues that many researchers seem to be lacking a commitment to – or perhaps simply an awareness of the necessity for – developing continually as a researcher. Referring to her own earlier work she defines professionality, which she views as a central prerequisite to capacity building, as 'an ideologically, attitudinally, intellectually, and epistemologically based stance on the part of an individual, in relation to the practice of the profession to which s/he belongs, and which influences her/his professional practice' (Evans, 2002: 6–7). Furthermore, Evans adopts Hoyle's distinction between *restricted* and *extended* professionality (1975: 318), which she proposes to be viewed as a continuum. She considers extended professionality to be an integral characteristic of a highly developed and well-functioning institutional research culture for which she offers the following working definition: 'shared values, assumptions, beliefs, rituals and other forms of behaviour whose central focus is the acceptance and recognition of research practice and output as valued, worthwhile and preeminent activity' (Evans, 2009: n.p.). We would see mentoring and (in view of the increasing importance and affordances of technological tools and resources in general and in research in particular as well as in view of the distributed nature of respective expertise) e-mentoring as an integral part of an effective research culture, itself best viewed as a sophisticated community of practice, with the purpose, in Evans' terms, of moving members on from restricted to extended professionality or, in Lave and Wenger's terms, from legitimate peripheral participation to reification through which common understandings are turned into meaningful artefacts (Binder, 1996). Evans sees the continuum from restricted to extended professionality to encompass *inter alia* a trajectory:

- from the use of established research methods to their adaptation and development;
- from low levels of methodological and analytical competence to a high level; and
- from a perception of research methods as tools and of methodology as a task-directed, utilitarian process to that of research methodology as a field of study in its own right (see Evans, 2009: n.p.).

(e-)Mentoring in the context of educational research capacity building, we would argue, can be viewed as a valuable process of scaffolding learning (Wood, Bruner and Ross, 1976) and of providing guidelines and explicit criteria of quality research.

Murray et al. (2009) offer the following definition for capacity from Desforges (cited in Davies and Salisbury, 2008: 9) whereby capacity equals expertise times motivation times opportunities. Again, (e-)mentoring arguably has a valuable contribution to make in all three respects: providing expertise, motivation as well as opportunities; for example, by identifying possible funding sources and the formulation of bids, advising on problem identification, the scoping of research, the formulation of research questions, the selection of relevant background literature, the structuring of the literature review, the identification of appropriate research methods and criteria for analysis, the formulation of recommendations, and so on.

THE BENEFITS AND COSTS, OPPORTUNITIES AND CHALLENGES OF ONLINE TECHNOLOGIES FOR MENTORING

Online technologies can be seen to be characterised by a wide range 'affordances'. In order to make judgements about their relative merits for mentoring, we first need to remind ourselves about some of the functions and types of mentoring. As has already been mentioned, the literature distinguishes career and psychosocial functions. The former – which for the purposes of this chapter we consider to comprise educational development as well – according to Ensher, Heun and Blanchard (2003: 267) includes the provision of vocational/instrumental support such as sponsorship, enhanced visibility, challenge and guidance as well as being a role model exemplifying desirable attitudes, values and behaviours. It also often includes modelling, skills transfer, watching in action, masterclasses, observation of practice, coaching and offering performance-related feedback. The latter is more pastoral, relates to self-esteem and is largely determined by the nature and quality of the relationship between both parties and the empathy shown by the mentor. Sometimes it involves counselling and/or friendship. These, and other functions can be performed as part of a formal mentoring scheme or informally. Allen, Eby, O'Brien and Lentz (2008: 352) distinguish the following types of mentoring relationships:

- informal (traditional);
- formal-company sponsored;
- supervisory–subordinate;
- faculty–student;
- formal-peer; and
- mixed.

Online technologies, and digital technologies more widely, can be seen to lend themselves variously to all these types of mentoring relationships: the abundance of social networking tools makes informal mentoring across temporal and geographical barriers much more easily possible. In teacher education and university tutoring contexts, tools such as e-mail, text messaging, Internet telephony, and synchronous chatting can all be seen to have had a profound impact on augmenting traditional mentoring relationships often with the effect of improving the communication flow between the parties involved.

With the rapid adoption of mobile devices and services a wider range of technological possibilities becomes available and we consider the prefix 'e' as inclusive in this respect; that is, as encompassing a wide range of new technologies, and not as specific to desktop or laptop-based computing devices.

Research suggests that 'informal mentoring relationships with frequent contact are better than formal relationships, although having any mentor is usually better than not having one at all' (Ensher et al., 2003: 267). The UK National Framework for Mentoring and Coaching (DCSF, 2005: n.p.) identifies nine mentoring activities:

1 identifying learning goals and supporting progression;
2 developing increasing learners' control over their learning;
3 active listening;
4 modelling, observing, articulating and discussing practice to raise awareness;
5 shared learning experiences e.g. via observation or video;
6 providing guidance, feedback and, when necessary, direction;
7 review and action planning;
8 assessing, appraising and accrediting practice; and
9 brokering a range of support.

According to the specific activities undertaken, we argue here, different technological tools can, and should be used. Active listening, for example, can be fostered by the use of (Internet-based) telephony; review and action planning by the use of e-portfolios and by e-mail; shared learning experiences through blogs and online resources.

Searching for the term 'e-mentoring' on the internet suggests that it is being extensively used for mentoring partnerships for young (and often disadvantaged) people by educational institutions, charitable organisations or employers for support with, and advice, guidance and feedback on learning projects. One example is Mentor which, according to its website, 'helps children by providing a public voice, developing and delivering resources to mentoring programs nationwide and promoting quality for mentoring through standards, cutting-edge research and state of the art tools'. A useful list of e-mentoring resources in this field is for example provided on the California Governor's Mentoring Partnership website at http://www.mentoring.ca.gov/e-mentoring.shtm. Such examples could also be interpreted as capacity building of sorts.

Few definitions of e-mentoring can be found in the literature. Ensher and Murphy's (2007: 300) appears to be the most recent; they define e-mentoring as 'a mutually beneficial relationship between a mentor and a protégé, which provides new learning as well as career and emotional support, primarily through e-mail as well as other electronic means'.

Metros and Yang (2006: 12–16) point out that there exist different phases of mentoring; they distinguish the following:

- identify;
- negotiate;
- facilitate; and
- graduate.

For each of these phases – with facilitation being the longest – they delineate a set of responsibilities for mentors and mentees (Table 30.1).

Not only do such lists represent a very useful description of some success criteria for mentoring relationships at different stages of the mentoring process but they also strike us as offering up a very helpful analytical frame for examining the potential role of online technologies. Questions to be asked include: do the technological tools used by mentors enable them to discharge the responsibilities outlined for the phase in question? Such lists also clearly show that e-mentoring requires much more than a working knowledge of relevant technologies, in particular how to adapt traditional mentoring skills to make the best use of the new modes available.

Depending on the specific (vocational/occupational) context, the roles and responsibilities of the mentor and mentee, their personal preferences and styles, the type of mentoring relationship and the phase of mentoring etc. there are different roles for the use of technology and different types of use are possible.

Table 30.1   Facilitate Phase Responsibilities

Mentor's responsibilities	Mentee's responsibilities
Advise, don't dictate	Actively listen and contribute to the conversations
Advise on what you know; admit what you don't know or refer to others	Understand your mentor will not have all of the answers – be willing to look them up
Provide relevant examples and resources	Access resources – do your homework
Recognize your mentee's weaknesses but build on his or her strengths	Acknowledge your weaknesses but build on your strengths
Give constructive criticism	Accept and reflect on constructive criticism
Don't shy away from difficult conversations	Don't shy away from difficult conversations
Periodically evaluate progress and reassess the relationship	Periodically evaluate progress and reassess the relationship
Celebrate successes	Celebrate successes
Be reliable	Be reliable

(*Source*: Metros and Young, 2006: 5.9)

Ensher et al. (2003: 272–6) propose the following types of technology use in mentoring:

- CMC-only;
- CMC-primary;
- CMC-supplemental; and
- FtF relationships.

According to this typology, the range available runs from face-to-face (FtF) only via different degrees of computer-mediated communication (CMC) supporting FtF communication to exclusive CMC use for mentoring. Our experience working on professional programmes in educational contexts very much suggests that a combination of CMC and FtF tends to work best. Whether or not CMC use is primary or supplemental depends on contextual factors such as, for example, how often mentor and mentee have the opportunity to meet depending on time, location and so on.

In the following, we will discuss some of the benefits and limitations of online technologies and social networking tools focusing on what their main strengths and weaknesses are in relation to the key functions, styles and phases of mentoring and what their impact is on the nature and quality of support provided.

One important point to be reiterated in the context of an examination of the possible benefits of online technologies is our perspective of mentoring as a learning-focused, communication-based activity. This is important, because it underlines the importance of language and communication in the mentoring process, an aspect of technology-enhanced and/or -based mentoring which, we argue, requires particular attention. Whilst one of the key strengths of online technologies is the ability to overcome barriers of geographical distance and time, these come at a cost, including miscommunication and misinterpretation, which can be particularly problematic in a context that is heavily reliant on effectiveness of communication as an inherent feature of trust; and we view trust as a fundamental pre-requisite for a successful mentoring relationship. Lee (2010) introduces the term 'perspective-taking' to describe attempts by a speaker to understand his/her interlocutor and to adapt his/her (linguistic) behaviour accordingly. For him, perspective-taking is more difficult for people who communicate using information and communication technologies because of the constraints of the technologies. Key questions, therefore, revolve around how conversations are shaped by the medium in which they take place.

The aspect of 'cost' appears central to us as the flipside of the potential benefits of (online) technologies which, in line with established discourse conventions in the field of technology-enhanced learning, we call 'affordances' in this chapter. They are an area Susan Brennan has explored in detail in a number of publications. All too often, it is the benefits of technology that get discussed at the expense of due consideration for possible limitations. We argue here that, in order to be able to use technology effectively for mentoring purposes, the possible pitfalls need to be borne in mind and, where possible, pre-empted.

Together with Herbert Clark (Clark and Brennan, 1991) Brennan puts forward the notion of 'communicative grounding' which problematises media constraints in terms of cost; that is, the paper examines the inherent characteristics of different communication media about which potential users make choices in relation to appropriateness for specific acts of communication (see also Lee, 2010). Clark and Brennan (1991: 142–5) list the following costs of grounding:

- formulation costs;
- production costs;
- understanding costs;
- start-up costs;
- delay costs;
- asynchronous costs;
- speaker change costs;
- display costs;
- fault costs; and
- repair costs.

This long list of potential limitations clearly shows how carefully mentors need to choose (online) technological tools for interactions with mentees. To pick out just one item from the above list: asynchronous costs. Whilst the ability to communicate in delayed time is a distinct advantage, in terms of promoting interaction between people who are not co-located in time and place, it is incumbent upon the mentor, for example, to ensure s/he responds to requests made by mentees in a timely manner to ensure the answer is perceived by the mentee as relevant and helpful. In order to be able to do so, mentors will need to go online regularly to make sure they know when requests have come in and to set aside time to respond to them. One important question for mentors, therefore, in choosing technological tools for communicating with their mentees is the costs associated with their use in relation to the assumed benefits.

In a piece written with Lockridge in 2006, Brennan describes the affordances of different media (shown in Box 30.1).

Box 30.1   Affordances of Media

1 *Physical co-presence*: Participants share a physical environment, including a view of what each is doing and looking at.
2 *Visibility*: One participant sees another, but not necessarily what the other is doing or looking at.
3 *Audibility*: One participant can hear another.
4 *Contemporality*: Messages are received without delay (close to the time that they are produced and directed at addressees), permitting fine-grained interactivity.
5 *Simultaneity*: Participants can send and receive messages at the same time, allowing communication in parallel.
6 *Sequentiality*: Participants take turns in an orderly fashion in a single conversation at a time; one turn's relevance to another is signaled by adjacency.
7 *Reviewability*: Messages do not fade over time.
8 *Revisability*: Messages can be revised before being sent.

(*Source*: Brennan and Lockridge, 2006: 778)

Physical co-presence may be considered highly desirable by the mentee in conversations about sensitive issues and the lack of it might be considered to be a distinct disadvantage. Reviewability is likely to be a particular advantage in the context of mentoring processes that are focused on supporting mentees working, for example, towards a particular set of academic or professional standards as they can use written comments as evidence towards having met such standards. Revisability comes into play, for example, when mentors and mentees have the opportunity to formulate their questions or responses very carefully to ensure a problem is fully captured or an answer comprehensive and clearly structured.

In Clark and Brennan (1991: 142) the above affordances are applied to seven specific communication media in terms of constraints (Table 30.2). This approach

Table 30.2   Seven communication media and their constraints

Medium	Constraints
Face-to-face	Co-presence, visibility, audibility, co-temporality, simultaneity, sequentiality
Telephone	Audibility, co-temporality, simulaneity, sequentiality
Video teleconference	Visibility, audibility, co-temporality, simulaneity, sequentiality
Terminal teleconference	Contemporality, sequentiality, reviewability
Answering machines	Audibility, reviewability
Electronic mail	Reviewability, revisability
Letters	Reviewability, revisability

(*Source*: Clark and Brennan 1991: 142)

is instructive for e-mentors in so far as it exemplifies the sort of cost-benefit analysis they should carry out in relation to any technology they intend to use.

Clearly, technology perpetually changes. For example, terminal teleconferencing and answering machines are less relevant today than blogging, micro-blogging, texting or instant messaging. Each of these new technologies also has certain benefits and costs: micro-blogging, for example, is instantaneous and can reach a large audience very quickly; it is limited to 140 characters and is arguably not particularly helpful beyond the sharing of URLs about web-based resources. The various tools might also lend themselves more or less well to particular types of mentoring delineated by Allen et al. (2008: 352).

FtF is clearly a very powerful medium enabling rich communication. E-mail, on the other hand, is characterised by considerable fewer affordances, albeit ones that are complementary to FtF interaction. This reinforces the need for a careful choice of communication technologies.

Brennan and Lockridge (2006: 775) also argue that contributions to conversations need to pass through two phases in order to 'count': a presentation and an acceptance phase. Only then can they become part of the 'common ground' shared between the speakers. In the context of e-mentoring in educational contexts, which will often revolve around sensitive topics, mutual trust is likely to be an important pre-requisite. Also, the notion of 'common ground' we consider to be very important in ensuring effective communication, and tends to be more difficult to establish in technologically mediated communication characterised by distributedness of interlocutors in time and/or place (see also Xin and Feenberg, 2006). Interlocutors need to provide evidence of implicit or explicit attention, understanding and uptake. Depending on the medium, as well as the nature of the utterance and the context in which it takes place, such evidence will vary and, importantly, will be more or less easy to ascertain by the speaker. Therefore, according to Brennan and Lockridge (2006), (technologically) mediated communication is a coordinated activity constrained by particular costs and affordances. They, rightly, point out that electronic communication can diminish the richness of face-to-face conversation whilst, at the same time, offer tangible benefits particularly in terms of overcoming inherent ephemerality of spoken utterances and enabling reviewing and editing (2006: 776). With reference to Whittaker (2002), Brennan and Lockridge remind us (2006: 776) that, whilst remote communication is much less efficient without speech, adding a video channel may not improve either communicative performance or efficiency. This is despite the fact, as Whittaker notes, that the visual mode affords feedback through facial expressions, nodding, gaze and gesture. Visual access to artefacts on the other hand is considered to be very useful in task-directed communication.

Lapadat (2002) explores the differences between synchronous and asynchronous communication. Interestingly, she argues that

> the interactive textual environment of asynchronous online conferences is particularly facilitative of both social and cognitive construction of meaning because the nature of online interactive writing itself bootstraps the construction of meaning. (2002: 1)

We interpret Lapadat's notion of 'bootstrapping' to refer to the way in which online, interactive writing engages interlocutors in processes of reflection through the writing process that the cognitive demands of speaking in real-time simply do not allow for.

The implications for effective e-mentoring for us are clear: it is important for mentor and mentee to establish 'common ground' and to develop the necessary techniques to do so depending on the technological tools used to mediate communication.

Furthermore, high communicative 'bandwidth' is critical to effective communication. By that we mean rich, preferably multimodal data. Technology as a mode of communication can provide this, for example in the form of access to shared visual artefacts. It is for this reason that we deem digital video artefacts depicting professional practice, such as short episodes from the classroom filmed with a video camera, to be of particular value in e-mentoring contexts. Task-orientated asynchronous online text-based discussions, preferably accompanied by relevant background reading, we also consider to be important.

As Brennan and Lockridge (2006: 777) rightly note, the establishment of common ground in technology-mediated communication does come at a 'cost' that needs to be factored in:

> Sub-tasks that incur grounding costs include getting a partner's attention in order to initiate communication (start up costs);producing a presentation by speaking or typing or in some other manner (production costs); timing the placement of feedback (asynchrony costs) or of a conversational turn (speaker-change costs); pointing, demonstrating, or gesturing in order to refer or clarify content (display costs); awaiting, reading, or listening to a partner's utterance (reception costs); monitoring the partner's focus of attention and, if the dialog is task-oriented, any relevant activities or tangible products that make up the task (monitoring costs),preventing misunderstandings or repairing errors caused by self or partner (repair costs), and maintaining politeness (face-management costs).

This enumeration of possible costs associated with technology-mediated communication serves as a poignant reminder to mentors concerning the potential complexity of establishing 'common ground' with the mentee when using CMC. E-mentoring clearly is not easy and a lot of effort needs to be expended on maintaining a productive (working) relationship with the mentee. For example, how can the sender know that the recipient has pperceived the salient points intended in an e-mail? How does s/he know how the message was received? Did the mentee interpret the meaning intended in the comments made particularly in a research supervision context where supervisors often deliberately refrain from giving deliberate instructions to ensure the final product remains that of the student and has not become theirs?

In online contexts, 'production costs' can be comparatively high owing to the fact that the written word tends to be used instead of the spoken word and that often trade-offs are necessary (although technological solutions exist which easily allow for audio and video messaging and conferencing (e.g. Skype [http://www.skype.com] or Google+ [http://plus.google.com/]. How easy is it, for example, to explain a complex ethical issue in asynchronous written interaction? How satisfactorily can the issue of unintentional plagiarism be discussed by e-mail? Or, how can independent and original thinking be fostered using CMC particularly when mentees come from cultural backgrounds which have socialised them into deferential attitudes towards established orthodoxy?

Production costs also impact on the granularity of utterances or exchanges. For example, asynchronous text-based media such as e-mails tend to operate at a much lower level of granularity than synchronous text-based chat potentially leading to misunderstandings and/or misinterpretations, yet with lower repair costs. In other words, given the time it takes to type and – given the comparative permanence of the written word – carefully formulate utterances, e-mails from mentors to mentees are likely to focus on the main points rather than on details and have less built-in redundancy and explication compared with oral feedback.

Ensher et al. (2003: 276–83) list the following additional challenges of e-mentoring:

- slower development of relationship online;
- requires competency in written communication and technical skills;
- computer malfunctions; and
- issues of privacy and confidentiality.

These challenges for us are particularly relevant in relation to establishing common ground and trust particularly if mentor and mentee enter into a relationship that goes beyond the episodic (see Ragins and Kram, 2007: 7).

Affordances of online technologies sometimes mentioned in the literature in relation to the inherent distance between interlocutors (even if synchronous technology-mediated communication may not feature any diminished immediacy) is a certain degree of anonymity and bias reduction around gender, age, nationality, appearance, and so on. Convenience and increased access are also mentioned as advantages. Conversely, the inherent distance can easily exacerbate potential problems in mentoring relations such as marginal mentoring, dysfunctional mentoring as well as negative mentoring; yet at the same time technology supports new forms of mentoring such as multiple mentoring, team mentoring and needs-driven mentoring (see Scandura and Pellegrini, 2007).

Facilitation of 'reflection' must be considered to be one of the key affordances of technology for mentoring: the distance afforded by asynchronous text-based technology-mediated communication, the archiving of previous conversations and discussions as well as engagement over a sustained period of time all support the process of knowledge construction through distributed cognition. One frequently used tool to systematise reflection are e-portfolios. The other key affordance is the multimodal nature of digital text enabling the production and reproduction, combination and recombination of speech, sound and (moving) image (see also Conole and Dyke, 2004, and Wong and Premkumar, 2007).

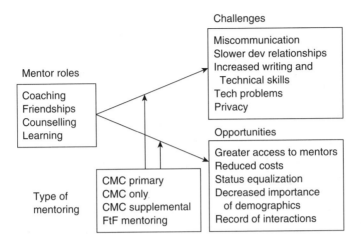

Figure 30.1   Research propositions for e-mentoring (*Source*: Ensher, Heun and Blanchard, 2003: 284)

Based on their discussion of online mentoring and computer-mediated communication, Ensher et al. (2003: 284) offer the summary of research propositions for the field of e-mentoring in Figure 30.1.

These research propositions, they argue (ibid. 283–284), can improve online mentoring by reducing negative aspects of the mentoring relationship with training and education. And, they advocate the use of multiple methods of contact and communication.

E-FACILITATION AS A CORE SKILL OF E-MENTORING

Despite frequent reminders in the mentoring literature about the mentor-centeredness of much of the debate (as opposed to mentee-centredness), we nevertheless – and in line with Ensher et al.'s (2003) recommendation about the importance of training – wish to make some observations here about what strikes us as a key 'pedagogical' skill for mentors, namely e-facilitation (for a detailed discussion see Salmon, 2003). The literature (see, e.g., Winograd, 2003) distinguishes different functions of e-facilitation, in particular organisational, social and intellectual functions. The intellectual functions seem particularly important here in relation to our understanding of e-mentoring, in particular if seen as a key strategy in research capacity building. According to Winograd (2003: 66–7) they comprise (amongst other things):

- modelling the intellectual tone;
- requiring contributions to be relevant and substantial;
- provoking, instigating and presenting conflicting opinions;
- contextualising;
- summarising; and
- presenting and weaving.

Whilst these pedagogical interventions are drawn from the field of e-facilitation of student learning, in our experience they are often equally important in individual e-mentoring in research supervision contexts.

Feenberg and Xin (n.d.) refer to the notions of 'absorption' and 'engrossment' which relate to the sharing of purpose. Clearly, mentors have a key 'leadership' role in terms of making the process an engaging and meaningful one that is based on a shared sense of purpose. If, in a supervision scenario, the research endeavour the mentee is embarking on is a medium- to long-term one, and if the mentee is at an early stage of their research 'career', the mentor has an important role to play in helping the mentee achieve a sustainable degree of engrossment through supporting him/her in identifying a topic that is worth researching and lends itself to be researched as well as to come up with a research question which has relevance and over which they feel ownership in order to foster and sustain the necessary degree of interest in and identification with the topic. Our own experience of mentoring students working on practitioner research projects in the course of mixed-mode and online professional development courses (see, e.g., Daly, Pachler, Pickering and Bezemer, 2007) strongly suggests that the need for an emphasis on 'recognition' is not at all misplaced. Feenberg and Xin argue that participants need frequent reassurance that their performance conforms to the expected norms – and we agree. Similarly, we recognise the role of online tutors and mentors in establishing a communication model and initiating and sustaining meta-communication.

In a paper on the pedagogy of online discussion, Xin and Feenberg (2006: 20) summarise the moderating functions of tutors (see Box 30.2). We argue here that the functions of e-mentoring are not at all dissimilar, particularly in the context of research capacity building: mentors working with novice research students require very similar pedagogical skills helping mentees conceptualise their research endeavor (functions 1–4) and then monitor their progress on carrying out their project through functions 5–10. Despite Xin and Feenberg's points being made in relation to tutor interventions in the context of academic multilateral discussions, they nevertheless seem equally apt in relation to ensuring bilateral mentoring exchanges add up to meaningful, learning-centred interaction.

Box 30.2   Summary of Moderating Functions.

Contextualizing functions

1   *Opening discussions.* The moderator must provide an opening comment that states the theme of the discussion and establishes a communication model. The moderator may periodically contribute 'topic raisers' or 'prompts' that open further discussions in the framework of the forum's general theme.

2   *Setting the norms.* The moderator suggests rules of procedure for the discussion. Some norms are modeled by the form and style of the moderator's opening comments. Others are explicitly formulated in comments that set the stage for the discussion.

3   *Setting the agenda*. The moderator manages the forum over time and selects a flow of themes and topics of discussion. The moderator generally shares part or all of the agenda with participants at the outset.

4   *Referring*. The conference may be contextualized by referring to materials available on the Internet, for example, by hyperlinking, or offline materials such as textbooks.

Monitoring functions

5   *Recognition*. The moderator refers explicitly to participants' comments to assure them that their contribution is valued and welcome, or to correct misapprehensions about the context of the discussion.

6   *Prompting*. The moderator addresses requests for comments to individuals or the group. Prompting includes asking questions and may be formalized as assignments or tasks. It may be carried out by private messages or through public requests in the forum.

7   *Assessing*. Participants' accomplishment may be assessed by tests, review sessions, or other formal procedures.

Meta functions

8   *Meta-commenting*. Meta-comments include remarks directed at such things as the context, norms, or agenda of the forum; or at solving problems such as lack of clarity, irrelevance, and information overload. Meta-comments play an important role in maintaining the conditions of successful communication.

9   *Weaving*. The moderator summarizes the state of the discussion and finds threads of unity in the comments of participants. Weaving recognizes the authors of the comments it weaves together and often implicitly prompts them to continue along lines that advance the conference agenda.

10 *Delegating*. Certain moderating functions such as weaving can be assigned to individual participants to perform for a shorter or longer period.

(*Source*: Xin and Feenberg, 2006: 20)

CONCLUSION

The literature shows that grounding is essential to communication. In this chapter we argued that in e-mentoring (understood as socially constructed, interaction-based, technologically-mediated, learning-orientated communication) there is a need to pay particular attention to the characteristics and challenges inherent in the technological tools chosen in order to ensure that the facilitation of learning experiences and reflective dialogue in relation to career functions and psychosocial support make best use of the affordances of technology and mitigate the inherent losses compared to face-to-face communication.

REFERENCES

Allen, T. D., Eby, L. T., O'Brien, K. E. and Lentz, E. (2008) The state of mentoring research: A qualitative review of current research methods and future research implications. *Journal of Vocational Behavior*, 73, 343–357.

Binder, T. (1996) Participation and reification in design of artefacts: An interview with Etienne Wenger. *AI & Society*, *10*(1), 101–106.

Brennan, S. E. and Lockridge, C. B. (2006) Computer-mediated communication: A cognitive science approach. In Brown, K. (ed.) *ELL2. Encyclopedia of Language and Linguistics* (2nd ed.; pp. 775–780). Oxford: Elsevier. Retrieved from: http://www.psychology.stonybrook.edu/sbrennan-/papers/BL_ELL2.pdf

Brown, J. S. and Adler, R. P. (2008) Minds on fire. Open Education, the Long Tail, and Learning 2.0. *EDUCAUSE Review*, *43*(1), 16–32. Retrieved from: http://net.educause.edu/ir/library/pdf/ERM0811.pdf

Clark, H. and Brennan, S. (1991) 'Grounding in communication.' In Resnick, L., Levine, J. and Teasley, S. (eds) *Perspectives on socially shared cognition*. Washington: American Psychological Association, pp. 127–149.

Conole, G. and Dyke, M. (2004) What are the affordances of information and communication technologies? *ALT-J*, *12*(2), 113–124. Retrieved from: http://repository.alt.ac.uk/596/

Daly, C., Pachler, N., Pickering, J. and Bezemer, J. (2007) Teachers as e-learners: exploring the experiences of teachers in an online professional master's programme. *Journal of In-Service Education*, *33*(4), 443–461.

Davies, S. and Salisbury, J. (2008) Researching and learning together: inter-institutional collaboration as a strategy for capacity building. Paper presented at the British Educational Research Conference (BERA), Edinburgh, September 2008.

DCSF (2005) *National Framework for Mentoring and Coaching*. Retrieved from: http://national strategies.standards.dcsf.gov.uk/downloader/77ca02adf778ec33962703c412632181.pdf

Ensher, E. A., Heun, C. and Blanchard, A. (2003) Online mentoring and computer-mediated communication: New directions in research. *Journal of Vocational Behavior*, *63*, 264–288.

Ensher, E. A. and Murphy, S. E. (2007) E-mentoring. Next-generation research strategies and suggestions. In Ragins, B. R. and Kram, K, E. (eds) *The Handbook of Mentoring at Work: Theory, Research and Practice* (pp. 299–322). Thousand Oaks, CA: Sage.

Evans, L. (2002). *Reflective Practice in Educational Research: Developing Advanced skills*. London: Continuum.

Evans, L. (2009) Developing research capacity in the social sciences: A professionality based model. *International Journal for Researcher Development*, *1*(2), 134–149.

Feenberg, A. and Xin, C. (n.d.) *A Teacher's Guide to Moderating Online Discussion Forums: From Theory to Practice*. Retrieved from: http://www.textweaver.org/modmanual4.htm

Garrison, D. R. and Anderson, T. (2003) *E–Learning in the 21st century: A Framework for Research and Practice*. London: Routledge/Falmer.

Kram, K. E. (1983) Phases of the mentoring relationship. *Academy of Management Journal*, *26*, 608–625.

Lapadat, J. (2002) Written interaction: A key component in online learning. *Journal of Computer Mediated Communication 7*(4). Retrieved from: http://jcmc.indiana.edu/vol7/issue4/lapadat.html

Lave, J. and Wenger, E. (1991) *Situated Learning: Legitimate Peripheral Participation*. Cambridge: Cambridge University Press.

Lee, C. S. (2010) Effects of ICT affordances on knowledge sharing: The role of perspective-taking. Paper presented at the Annual Meeting of the International Communication Association, Singapore, June 22. Retrieved from: http://www.snipurl.com/lee_2010

Metros, S. E. and Yang, C. (2006) The importance of mentors. In Golden, C. (ed.) *Cultivating Careers: Professional Development for Campus IT* (pp. 5.1–5.13). EDUCAUSE. Retrieved from: http://www.educause.edu/ir/library/pdf/PUB7201h.pdf

Murray, J., Campbell, A., Hextall, I., Hulme, M., Jones, M., Mahony, P., Menter, I., Procter, R. and Wall, K. (2009) Research and teacher education in the UK: building capacity. *Teaching and Teacher Education*, *25*(7), 944–950.

Pachler, N., Bachmair, B. and Cook, J. (2010) *Mobile Learning: Structures, Agency, Practices*. New York: Springer.

Pachler, N. and Daly, C. (2011) *Key Issues in e-Learning Research: Theory and Practice*. London: Continuum.

Ragins, B. R. and Kram, K. E. (2007) The roots and meaning of mentoring. In Ragins, B. R. and Kram, K, E. (eds) *The Handbook of Mentoring at Work: Theory, Research and Practice* (pp. 315). Thousand Oaks, CA: Sage. Retrieved from: http://www.sagepub.com/upm-data/17419_Chapter_1.pdf.

Salmon, G. (2003) *e-Moderating: The Key to Teaching and Learning Online* (2nd ed.). London: Taylor & Francis.

Scandura, T. A. and Pellegrini, E. K. (2007) Workplace mentoring: Theoretical approaches and methodological issues. In Allen, T. D. and Eby, L. T. (eds.) *Handbook of Mentoring: A Multiple Perspective Approach* (pp. 71–91). Malden, MA: Blackwell. Retrieved from: http://business.umsl.edu/faculty/mob/Articles/Blackwell_2007.pdf

Sundli, L. (2007) Mentoring – A new mantra for education? *Teaching and Teacher Education, 23*, 201–214.

Wenger, E. (1998) *Communities of Practice: Learning, Meaning and Identity.* Cambridge: Cambridge University Press. ·

Whittaker, S. (2002) Theories and methods in mediated communication. In Graesser, A., Gernsbacher, M. and Goldman, S (eds.) *The Handbook of Discourse Processes* (pp. 243–286). Hillsdale, NJ: Erlbaum. Retrieved from: http://citeseerx.ist.psu.edu/viewdoc/download?doi=10.1.1.18.7795&rep=rep1&type=pdf

Winograd, D. (2003) The roles, functions and skills of moderators of online educational computer conferences for distance education. *Computers in the Schools, 20*(3), 61–72. Retrieved from: http://jan.ucc.nau.edu/~etc-c/etc599DE/readings/Winograd,%20The%20roles,%20functions%20and%20skills%20of%20moderators.pdf

Wong, A. and Premkumar, K. (2007) *An Introduction to Mentoring Principles, Processes and Strategies for Facilitating Mentoring Relationships at a Distance*. Retrieved from: http://www.usask.ca/gmcte/mentoring/PDFPart2.pdf

Wood, D., Bruner, J. and Ross, G. (1976) The role of tutoring in problem solving. *Journal of Child Psychiatry and Psychology, 17*(2), 89–100.

Xin, C. and Feenberg, A. (2006) Pedagogy in Cyberspace: the dynamics of online discourse. *Journal of Distance Education, 21*(2), 1–25. Retrieved from: http://www.sfu.ca/~andrewf/books/xin%20and%20feenberg%20JDE_xin.pdf

31

Knowledge Base of Mentoring and Mentor Preparation

Sylvia Yee Fan Tang

INTRODUCTION

Mentoring is a major feature in various phases of teachers' professional development worldwide. Yet there is concern about the scant evidence of the codification of mentor knowledge (Jones and Straker, 2006). My goal here is to extend researchers' earlier work on literature review and map the knowledge base of mentoring. As background, I examine some major international literature reviews in mentoring. Hawkey's (1997) literature review presents the roles, responsibilities, and relationships in mentoring in initial teacher education (ITE). Roberts (2000) conducted a phenomenological review of the literature on mentoring and identified the essential and contingent attributes of mentoring. Wang and Odell (2002) worked on an extensive review of literature on mentoring support for preservice and beginning teachers in standards-based teaching. In a review of mentoring beginning teachers, Hobson, Ashby, Malderez, and Tomlinson (2009) acknowledge a range of potential benefits and costs associated with mentoring. They suggest that a key to maximizing the former and minimizing the latter lies in realizing contextual conditions for successful mentoring.

Findings of these major reviews show that the practical dimension of mentoring, with the subtle influence of conceptual issues and contextual factors, is a predominant theme of most literature in mentoring. As an extension of these reviews, I map the knowledge base of mentoring, with mentoring practices situated in multi-layered contexts and shaped by different conceptual influences (see Figure 31.1).

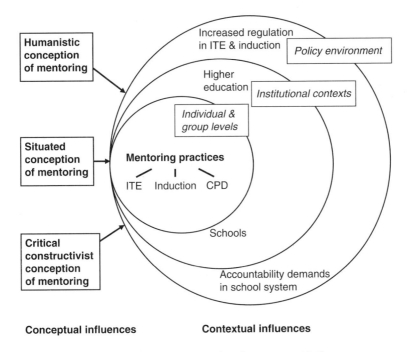

Figure 31.1   Mentoring practices: Contextual and conceptual influences

I also explore major components of this knowledge base and some implications for mentor preparation and development.

MENTORING IN CONTEXTS

Teacher development continuum

Mentoring can be examined in a teacher development continuum that covers ITE, teacher induction, and teachers' continuing professional development. In ITE, mentoring is regarded as a means of supporting student teachers' professional learning in bridging the theory–practice gap (Korthagen, 2010). Hawkey (1997) reviews the nature of interactions between mentor and student teacher in ITE. Wang, Odell, and Schwille (2008) view mentoring as widely used to support goals of teacher induction. Hargreaves and Fullan (2000) have argued that mentoring needs to go beyond supporting individual teachers' early professional learning. By contributing to building strong professional cultures among teachers in schools, mentoring can be a part of transforming teaching into a learning profession, and of broader improvement efforts to reculture schools and school systems. Mentoring carries the broad aim of enhancing teachers' professional development with visions of varied scope, ranging from facilitating teachers' early professional learning to mutuality in the professional development of teachers (e.g., student teachers, beginning teachers, veteran teachers) across experience levels.

Mentoring is practiced in a range of settings at the micro, meso, and macro levels. Britton, Paine, Pimm, and Raizen's study (2003) of teacher induction in Switzerland, Japan, France, New Zealand, and China (Shanghai) examined mentoring in teacher induction at various levels in its full complexity with regard to policies, programs, and practices. Taking Israel's example, Orland-Barak and Hasin (2010) identified mentoring settings ranging from individual to group mentoring, from internal school-based mentoring to external mentoring, and from regional mentoring to national mentoring. These examples suggest that mentoring is situated at different levels, including organizational context of schools, the dual context of ITE, as well as the education policy environment.

Mentoring in the organizational context of schools

At the organizational level, 'school culture and context have an enormous influence on how mentoring is enacted' (Carver and Feiman-Nemser, 2009: 324). Roberts (2000: 162) defines mentoring as

> a formalized process whereby a more knowledgeable and experienced person actuates a supportive role of overseeing and encouraging reflection and learning with a less experienced and knowledgeable person, so as to facilitate that person's career and personal development.

Howe's (2006) study of exemplary induction programs across eight countries suggests that the most successful teacher induction programs include opportunities for experts and neophytes to learn together in a supportive environment promoting time for collaboration, reflection, and acculturation into the teaching profession. Hellsten, Prytula, Ebanks, and Lai (2009) advocate the professional learning community approach to mentoring in which multiple mentors, consisting of new and experienced teachers, share experiences. Johnson and Kardos (2004) concur that an 'integrated professional culture' where there is ongoing professional exchange among all teachers across experience levels is highly prized for the development and renewal of teachers and schools.

Mentoring in the dual context of ITE

Mentoring is enacted in the field experience of ITE, which takes place in the dual context of higher education and teaching profession. Partnership arrangements and sharing of responsibilities between higher education and schools set the parameters for mentoring of student teachers. In England, school-based mentoring was introduced as a key strategy for supporting student teachers' professional learning in the university–school partnership programs in 1980s. Comparable development towards a more substantial involvement of schools with mentoring in ITE was also seen in North America (Tomlinson, Hobson, and Malderez, 2010) and some other parts of the world. ITE is not the exclusive province of higher education, and alternative routes for ITE have been growing in number internationally (Lai and Grossman, 2008). Mentoring is also a key strategy in supporting trainee teachers' early professional learning in these alternative routes to ITE.

Mentoring in the induction of beginning teachers

Teacher induction policy sets parameters within which mentoring is practiced. Carver and Feiman-Nemser (2009: 315) indicate that 'induction policy can set conditions that enable or constrain effective induction practices, specifically by how policy defines the problem of beginning teaching, sets policy boundaries, and provides policy-related tools and resources'. Kardos and Johnson (2010) drew attention to equity issues in mentoring support for beginning teachers in different schools in the US. Specifically, they found that beginning teachers in low-income schools are relatively not well-supported. Apart from resourcing, the relationship between mentoring and assessment of beginning teachers is a critical feature in teacher induction programs embedded in the induction policy context. Barrett, Solomon, Singer, Portelli, and Mujuwamariya (2009), Carver and Feiman-Nemser (2009), Harrison, Dymoke, and Pell (2006), as well as Piggot-Irvine, Aitken, Ritchie, Ferguson, and McGrath (2009) together present examples in Canada, the US, England, and New Zealand, respectively, where beginning teachers are assessed within a framework of professional standards with mandatory induction provision.

Neo-liberal influences on education policy

Researchers have identified the powerful influences of neo-liberal forces in the education policy environment that pose increasing accountability demands on teaching and teacher education by the turn of the twenty-first century (Furlong, McNamara, Campbell, Howson, and Lewis, 2008; Sleeter, 2008; Zeichner, 2010). Furlong, Cochran-Smith, and Brenan (2008) have argued that neo-liberal thinking drives governments in Australia, England, Singapore, the US, and elsewhere to aspire greater influence, if not control, over the form and content of ITE. England is an extreme example where a high level of regulation and accountability in ITE exists. On the one hand, there is the inspection of ITE by the Office for Standards in Education (OfSTED), with inspection outcomes used to determine future allocation of trainee numbers and funding (Whitehead and Fitzgerald, 2006). On the other hand, Professional Standards for Qualified Teacher Status (QTS) sets a statutory framework against which mentors are required to assess the competence of student teachers (Jones and Straker, 2006). In such a highly regulatory context, mentoring in ITE can be seen as a management tool (Hawkey, 2006).

In teacher induction, the tie-in of mentoring with the assessment of beginning teachers could be seen as being in line with the neo-liberal trend in education

(Fransson, 2010). This has been criticized as a bureaucratic–managerial approach that regards the beginning teacher as a technician conforming to externally defined standards and norms and encourages uncritical behavior in beginning teachers (Jones, 2009). Like ITE, teacher induction in England is governed by stringent government control and a centralized inspection program, with mentors as gatekeepers to the profession. Jones (2009) cautions that this assessment-driven mentoring model generates competing, potentially conflicting imperatives inherent in the mentoring role and thus would be a dangerous position to adopt.

The increasing accountability demands in some education systems call for the possible association of mentoring and pupil achievement. Orland-Barak and Klein (2005) caution that with standards and indicators of success becoming 'part and parcel' of the education process, the role of the mentor has shifted from a teacher development orientation towards a pupil achievement orientation. Jones and Straker (2006) argue that mentoring must not be exclusively perceived as a training device in relation to measurable outcomes. Devos (2010) echoes with a critical view that mentoring in Victoria, Australia is linked to school accountability and performativity agendas, embedded in new forms of managerialism characterizing public education. She criticizes the standardization of the mentoring process engendered in such policy context and questions whether beginning teachers are best equipped to meet the challenges of teaching in schools today.

CONCEPTIONS OF MENTORING

Apart from contextual influences, conceptual influences shape mentoring practices. Conceptions of mentoring refer to beliefs about the nature of teacher learning, purposes of mentoring, values and their promotion, the nature of mentoring relationships and practices, and knowledge needed in mentoring (Athanases, Abrams, Jack, Johnson, Kwock, McCurdy et al., 2008; Bradbury and Koballa, 2008). Basing on Wang and Odell's (2002) work, three major conceptions of mentoring – humanistic, situated, and critical–constructivist perspectives – are relevant. While each of them offers a unique conceptualization of mentoring, Wang et al. (2008) stress that none alone can fully address the complicated processes of teacher learning and expectations of teacher education reformers emerging in different countries.

Humanistic conception of mentoring

Central to the humanistic conception is that teacher learning is construed as a process of learning to understand, develop, and use oneself effectively. Mentoring then involves meeting beginning teachers' motivational and emotional needs. The humanistic conception views mentoring relationships as assisting 'beginning teachers' smooth transition into teaching by dealing with the reality shock and psychological stress' in induction (Wang and Odell, 2007: 475). Mentoring for developing the whole being (Sundli, 2007) and the counseling facet of mentoring relationships are emphasized. The humanistic conception, with stress on supporting beginning teachers' adaptation to the induction context, may likely result in transmitting knowledge and practice from mentors to mentees and hence maintaining the status quo.

Situated conception of mentoring

The situated conception is grounded in the situatedness of teacher learning for which knowledge is viewed as contextualized and as growing out of the context where it is used (Putnam and Borko, 2000). With the emphasis on the social and distributed nature of knowledge (Putnam and Borko, 1997), mentoring can take a one-to-one mentor–mentee form and/or assume a more equal relationship among teachers in a professional learning community. The situated conception, which stresses teachers' construction of knowledge in contexts of practice, may lead to transformation of knowledge and practice within existing institutional parameters.

In the induction context, mentors are experts with strong practical and contextualized knowledge who provide technical support and contextualized guidance to facilitate beginning teachers' construction of practical knowledge. While most literature focuses on pedagogical mentoring and construction of practical knowledge in teaching and learning, Rishel's (2006) work raises the importance of beginning teachers' interaction and connection with pupils. Jaipala's (2009) study informs the reciprocal development of professional knowledge of technology in mentoring relationships in ITE. Hellsten et al. (2009) point to a professional learning community approach to mentoring which goes beyond a one-to-one mentoring relationship. In the approach, teachers of different experience levels engage in collaborative inquiry within teaching and learning practices.

Critical–constructivist conception of mentoring

The critical–constructivist conception views learning as continuously deconstructing and reconstructing existing knowledge and practice towards emancipatory ends grounded on a progressive social vision (Wang and Odell, 2002). This mentoring conception views the purpose of mentoring as critiquing existing knowledge, structures, teaching, and schooling culture, while developing a strong commitment towards transforming knowledge and practice for social justice. Mentoring relationships put emphasis on concerns about social justice and equity, including persistent patterns of difference in educational opportunities and achievement among pupils in relation to race, ethnicity, language, and class. Equity-focused mentoring focuses beginning teachers on culturally and linguistically diverse pupils and on understanding diversity and equity issues as structural inequities that persist in larger societal contexts in which schools are situated (Achinstein and Athanases, 2005). Mentoring relationships aim at fostering more equitable and inclusive classrooms. In such classrooms, teachers differentiate instructional strategies to meet individuals' needs and use culturally appropriate pedagogy. Besides, mentors adopt a liberatory stance and take on moral and political challenges. Challenges include confronting possible taken-for-granted assumptions and resistance about culturally and linguistically diverse pupils, and critiquing current institutional arrangements in classrooms, school, and even society. The critical–constructivist conception of mentoring is likely to result in transforming knowledge and practice with interruptions to the status quo.

Achinstein and Athanases (2006) believe it is important for mentors to manage and negotiate tensions from a critical perspective while sustaining ties with schools, districts, and local communities. Achinstein (2006) emphasizes political literacy in reading, navigating, and transforming induction contexts in the mentoring relationships. On the one hand, mentors act as advocates for beginning teachers and support them in identifying the politics of their own identities, articulating their values, morals, and commitments. On the other hand, mentoring involves navigating the complex school–district power relations while strategizing advocacy of schooling that promotes equity. Mentoring relationships, characterized by mentors as mediators between newcomers to the profession and established communities of practice, likely reshape the teaching profession and contribute to broader improvement efforts to transform schools and school systems.

MENTORING PRACTICES

Mentoring practices grow out of the interface between contextual parameters and conceptual orientations I have discussed. Here I display practices in relation to the support and assessment functions of mentoring. Against the backdrop of practices that constitute the mentoring repertoire, I shall depict the professional artistry of mentoring in which strategies and approaches are adapted to meet the needs of learners (i.e., teachers) and specific mentoring settings. I start with a portrayal of the interactive nature of mentoring practices.

Interactive nature of mentoring practices

Researchers highlight the interactive nature of mentoring practices. Mentoring is 'a mutual affair, a co-constructed event' (Hamel and Jaasko-Fisher, 2011: 435) and is influenced by personal beliefs and perceptions as well as workplace features (Hennissen, Crasborn, Brouwer, Korthagen, and Bergen, 2008). Workplace features involve the availability and quality of contextual support, both structural and cultural, for mentoring practices in schools. Sundli (2007) views both mentor and mentee as agents bringing about effective mentoring. On the mentee side, openness to critiques and suggestions, as well as reflective and metacognitive skills are personal qualities that enable beginning teachers to benefit from mentoring (Roehrig, Bohn, Turner, and Pressley, 2008). On the mentor side, since it is unlikely that one person is able to fulfill all aspects of mentoring responsibilities, the distribution of mentoring function among multiple mentors may help fulfill the multifaceted, including educative, assessment, and counseling dimensions of mentoring (Harrison et al., 2006).

The interactive nature of mentoring practices is revealed in the compatibility of beliefs in mentoring relationships. Wang and Odell (2007) draw attention to the bi-level nature of teacher beliefs in the light of reform-minded teaching in mentoring relationships. In terms of compatibility of mentor–mentee beliefs in teaching and learning and learning to teach, they group mentoring relationships conceptually into 4 categories (and 16 variations) which are:

1   Mentoring relationships with consistent ideas about teaching and learning to teach.
2   Mentoring relationships with inconsistent ideas about teaching and learning to teach.
3   Mentoring relationships with inconsistent teaching but compatible learning to teach ideas.
4   Mentoring relationships with consistent teaching but incompatible learning to teach ideas.

Using this conceptual tool, Wang and Odell interpret that comfortable mentoring relationships, like those in categories (1) and (4), are grounded on mentor and mentee's shared beliefs in teaching and learning, and *vice versa*.

A versatile mentoring repertoire

Mentors need a repertoire with a wide range of mentoring strategies available for use in settings with varied contextual features. Crasborn, Hennissen, Brouwer, Korthagen, and Bergen (2008) argue for the importance of a versatile mentoring repertoire for adapting mentoring approaches to cater for the learning needs of participants in mentoring relationships. I next examine mentoring strategies and approaches that can constitute a rich as well as versatile mentoring repertoire.

Tomlinson et al. (2010) have identified from research some commonly used mentoring strategies in which mentors facilitate beginning teachers' professional learning. The strategies include provision of emotional and psychological support, lesson observation (both of and by the mentee) and lesson analysis, as well as dialogue in pre- and post-observation conferencing. Harrison, Lawson, and Wortley's (2005) work adds to the list reflective practice strategies in action research. Roehrig et al. (2008) suggest that mentors' highly effective teaching practices enable modeling effective practice for beginning teachers and may be used to evoke suggestions, examples, and problem-solving in mentoring dialogues. Tang and Chow (2007) maintain that 'learning-oriented assessment' feedback in post-observation conferences can sponsor beginning teachers' construction of professional knowledge and enhance self-regulated learning. Mentor's feedback in written lesson appraisals is a related mentoring strategy. Lock, Soares, and Foster's (2009) study draws attention to the content of mentor's written feedback in terms of professional knowledge categories, including topic-specific pedagogy, class management, and generic issues.

Studies on mentoring dialogue conducted by researchers from Netherlands (i.e., Crasborn, Hennissen, Brouwer, Korthagen, and Bergen, 2011) further illuminate our understanding of mentoring approaches. With the examination of mentoring dialogue, mentors' style and supervisory skills, the researchers developed a two-dimensional model with imperator, initiator, advisor, and 'encouragor' identified as mentor teacher roles. By mapping mentor teachers' role profiles, this model serves as a conceptual frame for understanding mentoring approaches and facilitating reflection on supervisory behavior.

In some mentoring settings, mutuality in the professional development of teachers of different experience levels is highlighted. Tomlinson et al. (2010) identified collaborative teaching, including planning and reflection, as a commonly used mentoring strategy to foster co-development in mentoring relationships. Whitehead and Fitzgerald (2006) report a generative, research-based approach to mentoring in ITE in a school–university partnership. Using video-recorded classroom practice as a tool and accessing voice, mentors and student teachers worked as co-learners engaged in reflection on teaching and learning, resulting in co-construction of situated professional knowledge in a learning community. In the professional learning community approach to mentoring that Lo (2004) advocated, teachers conduct Learning Study, a protocol-framed collaborative action research helping better learn particular objects of learning. Teachers across experience levels become researchers who generate knowledge about their own practice and hence enhance their own professional development.

Mentoring and teacher assessment

Earlier, I discussed issues related to mentoring and teacher assessment in a policy context with increasing accountability demands. Here I consider the debate about the assessment function of mentoring at the practice level. Hobson et al.'s view was that 'despite a wide range of literature on the question of whether the assessment and support functions of mentoring should be separated, the evidence base remains inconclusive' (2009: 213). Some researchers have argued that the assessment-driven mentoring model likely jeopardizes openness and trust required for meaningful support in beginning teachers' professional development (Harrison et al., 2006; Jones, 2009). Other researchers have found that support and assessment provide a clearer sense of direction for mentoring and can coexist in trustworthy mentoring relationships, though it sometimes makes that more challenging (Yusko and Feiman-Nemser, 2008). While acknowledging both sides of the argument, Fransson (2010) thinks that the social, cultural, philosophical, and political conditions of specific education contexts set the prerequisites for whether it is appropriate for mentors to be involved in assessing beginning teachers.

Tang's (2008) advocacy of the empowerment of the assessors and the assessed as agents striving for quality assessments sheds light on examination of assessment function as part of the mentoring repertoire. While this researcher states that the value of professional standards lies in its productive use as a conceptual reference for professional development, she cautions that professional standards can be counter-productive when used mechanistically as outcome measures in the assessment of beginning teachers. Athanases et al. (2008) echo that forms, scripts, and tools can serve as scaffolds for teacher learning yet may impede learning when they lose sensitivity to individuals and groups, and when they eclipse larger learning goals. In discussing how to strive for quality assessments, Tang's (2008) view suggests that 'assessment dialogue' occurs at two levels: (1) making explicit judgments about professional competence in teaching and sharing mentoring practices in the 'assessment dialogue' among mentors, and (2) engaging beginning teachers with assessment criteria that encourage taking an active role in this dialogue with mentors.

Professional artistry of mentoring

The professional artistry of mentoring draws on a rich and versatile mentoring repertoire in which mentoring practices are adapted to address beginning teachers' learning needs with contextual sensitivity to workplace features. Rather than undifferentiated use of mentoring strategies and skills, exemplary mentoring takes certain idiosyncratic forms subject to the characteristics of specific mentoring settings (Orland-Barak and Hasin, 2010). Mentors need to take advantage of teachable moments in mentoring relationships, vary mentoring approaches with suitable behavior that offer optimal learning opportunities for teachers, and engage in reflection on mentoring practices (Barrett et al., 2009). Besides, mentors should be cautious about power differentials in mentoring relationships and avoid as well as transform poor mentoring practices (Hobson et al., 2009; Parker-Katz and Bay, 2008).

The professional artistry of mentoring also entails the organizational dimension of mentoring. Achinstein (2006) discusses the importance of developing political literacy in mentors and beginning teachers. She argues that mentors need to work up, down, and across systems on behalf of beginning teachers, and supporting them in self-advocating. Gless (2006) stresses that mentoring in teacher induction needs to transform school culture via mentors who induct beginning teachers to see opportunities for ongoing professional learning in their own classrooms and schools, and mentors who help beginning teachers forge links with colleagues that feature collaboration and teacher learning.

MENTOR PREPARATION AND DEVELOPMENT

Building on the earlier discussion, here I examine mentor preparation and development. Gravey and Alred's (2000) view illuminates my interpretation of the substantive aspect of mentor preparation along two dimensions: (1) mentoring as a subject in its own right, which focuses on the knowledge base of mentoring; and (2) the preparation and development of mentors to perform mentoring in various contexts, which features mentoring practice.

Informed by Norman and Feiman-Nemser's (2005) notion of bifocal vision in mentoring and other researchers' work (Achinstein and Athanases, 2005; Jones and Straker, 2006), I offer a mapping of various aspects of mentoring examined earlier in a bilevel knowledge base of mentoring (see Figure 31.2). This knowledge base focuses on teachers in mentoring relationships and the ultimate goal of meaningful and effective learning for all pupils. At the level of knowledge which targets teachers, four domains are identified, namely learners and learning in mentoring relationships, mentoring practices, conceptions, and contexts of mentoring. At the level of knowledge which targets pupils, domains of teacher knowledge are included: content knowledge, general pedagogical knowledge, pedagogical content knowledge, curriculum knowledge, knowledge of learners (pupils) and their characteristics, knowledge of educational contexts, and

Targeting teachers	Learners and learning in mentoring relationships	Conceptions of mentoring	Mentoring practices	Mentoring in contexts
	Teachers as adult learners & their learning needs in the teacher development continuum	Humanistic conception Situated conception Critical constructivist conception	Mentoring strategies & approaches in ITE & induction Mentoring strategies & approaches in the professional learning community Mentoring & teacher assessment Organizational & political literacy	Mentoring in ITE Mentoring in teacher induction Mentoring in the organizational context of schools Mentoring in the larger education policy context

Targeting pupils	Domains of teacher knowledge (Shulman, 1986)
	Content knowledge; general pedagogical knowledge; pedagogical content knowledge; curriculum knowledge; knowledge of learners (pupils) and their characteristics; knowledge of educational contexts; and knowledge of educational ends, purposes, and values and their philosophical and historical grounds

Figure 31.2   A bilevel knowledge base of mentoring

knowledge of educational ends, purposes, and values and their philosophical and historical grounds (Shulman, 1987).

Wang and Odell (2002) identified three major models of preparing and developing teachers to perform the practice of mentoring: the knowledge transmission model, the theory-and-practice connection model, and the collaborative inquiry model. These models of mentor preparation hold different assumptions about learning-to-mentor and they have different potentiality for reaching mentors, require varying resources and time, as well as have different effects on mentors. In the knowledge transmission model, workshops are run to develop mentoring skills and knowledge about mentoring so that mentors can apply that knowledge in their own mentoring practices. In the theory–practice connection model, mentors develop competence in mentoring through integrating research-based knowledge and knowledge that grows out of their own mentoring experience (Tang and Choi, 2005). In the collaborative inquiry model, teacher educators work closely with mentors and beginning teachers in contexts of teaching and mentored learning-to-teach. Gardiner (2009) advocates a combination of comprehensive mentor preparation prior to the mentoring program and ongoing mentor development in practice settings. This helps mentors deepen their knowledge base, better conceptualize mentoring roles, and improve mentoring practices. Carver and Feiman-Nemser (2009) concur that the combination of formal training with ongoing support and development is a powerful professional development opportunity for experienced teachers and a chance to develop teacher leadership capacity.

Researchers point to various pedagogies in the preparation and ongoing development of teachers to perform the practice of mentoring while drawing on the knowledge base of mentoring. Some pedagogies involve training in observation skills and conferencing skills, as well as exposing mentors to various practices and situations, including observation of mentoring practices, analysis of mentoring dialogues, critical incident, and case-method pedagogy. Other pedagogies include analysis of and reflection on one's own mentoring practices and role profiles, as well as sharing and interrogating experiences in a community of practice for mentors (Orland-Barak, 2002).

Researchers' work on mentoring expertise and the development of reflectivity and versatility in mentoring further enriches our understanding of mentor development. Orland-Barak and Yinon (2005) present a dynamic, discontinuous, and interactionist view of the acquisition of expertise, highlighting the regressions and progressions that play out when teachers take on the mentoring role. Gordon and Borbeck (2010) argue for the development of a mentoring platform that facilitates deeper reflection on mentoring. Crasborn, Hennissen, Brouwer, Korthagen, and Bergen (2010) suggest that mentors' recognition of their own mentoring role and reflection on cognitions during mentoring dialogues help develop versatility in using strategies and skills for addressing beginning teachers' needs and for accommodating the specifics of mentoring practice settings.

CHANGING THE MENTORING KNOWLEDGE BASE AND MENTOR PREPARATION

In this writing, I have done some charting of the knowledge base of mentoring grounded on examining the contextual, conceptual, and practical dimensions of mentoring in the literature. Policy influences on mentoring is an emerging theme in the mentoring literature, which has predominantly focused on the practical dimension of mentoring. This changing landscape in mentoring literature coincides with the shift in studying teacher education as a learning problem from early 1980s to early 2000s and framing teacher education as a policy problem from the mid-1990s to the present day (Cochran-Smith and Fries, 2008). Some researchers caution that too much of the literature on mentoring has been celebratory and relatively uncritical in nature (e.g., Colley, 2002; Ling, 2009; Sundli, 2007). They consider mentoring research to be very much at the practical level without incorporating questions that interrogate the status quo.

Aligned with Sleeter's (2008) and Zeichner's (2010) advocacy of recognizing and confronting the neo-liberal pressures on policies and practices in teaching and teacher education, I would call for a new ideological space in which mentoring research is framed with a critical stance. This new ideological space is much needed in an era when mentoring practices are increasingly shaped by policies underpinned by neo-liberal values. Equally important, the critical stance provides an alternative ideological orientation in mentoring research at a time when neo-liberalism has framed the study of teacher education with a narrow focus on pupil achievement defined mainly in quantifiable measures (Cochran-Smith and Fries, 2008). Such intellectual inputs in research could bring vitality to the generation of knowledge in mentoring, both inform and interrogate policy and practice in mentoring, and provide new insights for mentor preparation and development.

REFERENCES

Achinstein, B. (2006). New teacher and mentor political literacy: Reading, navigating and transforming induction contexts. *Teachers and Teaching*, *12*(2), 123–138.

Achinstein, B., & Athanases, S. Z. (2005). Focusing new teachers on diversity and equity: Toward a knowledge base for mentors. *Teaching and Teacher Education*, *21*(7), 843–862.

Achinstein, B., & Athanases, S. Z. (2006). Towards effective mentoring: Future directions for theory and practice. In B. Achinstein & S. Z. Athanases (Eds.), *Mentors in the making: Developing new leaders for new teachers* (pp. 177–181). New York: Teachers College Press.

Athanases, S. Z., Abrams, J., Jack, G., Johnson, V., Kwock, S., McCurdy, J., Riley, S., & Totaro, S. (2008). Curriculum for mentor development: Problems and promise in the work of new teacher induction leaders. *Journal of Curriculum Studies*, *40*(6), 743–770.

Barrett, S. E., Solomon, R. P., Singer, J., Portelli, J. P., & Mujuwamariya, D. (2009). The hidden curriculum of a teacher induction program: Ontario teacher educators' perspectives. *Canadian Journal of Education*, *32*(4), 677–702.

Bradbury, L. U., & Koballa, T. R. (2008). Borders to cross: Identifying sources of tension in mentor–intern relationships. *Teaching and Teacher Education*, *24*(8), 2132–2145.

Britton, E., Paine, L., Pimm, D., & Raizen, S. (2003). *Comprehensive Teacher Induction: Systems for Early Career Learning.* Dordrecht: Kluwer.

Carver, C. L., & Feiman-Nemser, S. (2009). Using policy to improve teacher induction: Critical elements and missing pieces. *Educational Policy, 23*(2), 295–328.

Cochran-Smith, M., & Fries, K. (2008). Research on Teacher Education: Changing times, changing paradigms. In M. Cochran-Smith, S. Feiman-Nemser, D. J. McIntyre, & K. E. Demers (Eds.), *Handbook of research on teacher education: Enduring questions in changing contexts* (3rd ed., pp. 1050–1093). New York: Routledge.

Colley, H. (2002). A 'rough guide' to the history of mentoring from a Marxist Feminist perspective. *Journal of Education for Teaching, 28*(3), 257–274.

Crasborn, F., Hennissen, P., Brouwer, N., Korthagen, F., & Bergen, T. (2008). Promoting versatility in mentor teachers' use of supervisory skills. *Teaching and Teacher Education, 24*(3), 499–514.

Crasborn, F., Hennissen, P., Brouwer, N., Korthagen, F., & Bergen, T. (2010). Capturing mentor teachers' reflective moments during mentoring dialogues. *Teachers & Teaching, 16*(1), 7–29.

Crasborn, F., Hennissen, P., Brouwer, N., Korthagen, F., & Bergen, T. (2011). Exploring a two-dimensional model of mentor teacher roles in mentoring dialogues. *Teaching and Teacher Education, 27*(2), 320–331.

Devos, A. (2010). New teachers, mentoring and the discursive formation of professional identity. *Teaching and Teacher Education, 26*(5), 1219–1223.

Fransson, G. (2010). Mentors assessing mentees? An overview and analyses of the mentorship role concerning newly qualified teachers. *European Journal of Teacher Education, 33*(4), 375–390.

Furlong, J., Cochran-Smith, M., & Brennan, M. (2008). Editorial. *Teachers and Teaching: Theory and Practice, 14*(4), 265–269.

Furlong, J., McNamara, O., Campbell, A., Howson, J., & Lewis, S. (2008). Partnership, policy and politics: Initial teacher education in England under New Labour. *Teachers and Teaching: Theory and Practice, 14*(4), 307–318.

Gardiner, W. (2009). Rudderless as Mentors: The challenge of teachers as mentors. *Action in Teacher Education, 30*(4), 56–66.

Gless, J. (2006). Designing mentoring programs to transform school cultures. In B. Achinstein & S. Z. Athanases (Eds.), *Mentors in the making: Developing new leaders for new teachers* (pp. 165–176). New York: Teachers College Press.

Gordon, S. P., & Brobeck, S. R. (2010). Coaching the mentor: Facilitating reflection and change. *Mentoring & Tutoring: Partnership in Learning, 18*(4), 427–447.

Gravey, B., & Alred, G. (2000). Educating mentors. *Mentoring & Tutoring: Partnership in Learning, 8*(2), 113–126.

Hamel, F. L., & Jaasko-Fisher, H. A. (2011). Hidden labor in the mentoring of pre-service teachers: Notes from a mentor teacher advisory council. *Teaching and Teacher Education, 27*(2), 434–442.

Hargreaves, A., & Fullan, M. (2000). Mentoring in the new millennium. *Theory Into Practice, 39*(1), 49–56.

Harrison, J., Dymoke, S., & Pell, T. (2006). Mentoring beginning teachers in secondary schools: An analysis of practice. *Teaching and Teacher Education, 22*(8), 1055–1067.

Harrison, J., Lawson, T., & Wortley, A. (2005). Facilitating the professional learning of new teachers through critical reflection on practice during mentoring meetings. *European Journal of Teacher Education, 28*(3), 267–292.

Hawkey, K. (1997). Roles, responsibilities, and relationships in mentoring: A literature review and agenda for research. *Journal of Teacher Education, 48*(5), 325–335.

Hawkey, K. (2006). Emotional intelligence and mentoring in pre-service teacher education: A literature review. *Mentoring & Tutoring: Partnership in Learning, 14*(2), 137–147.

Hellsten, L. M., Prytula, M. P., Ebanks, A., & Lai, H. (2009). Teacher induction: Exploring beginning teacher mentorship. *Canadian Journal of Education, 32*(4), 703–733.

Hennissen, P., Crasborn, F., Brouwer, N., Korthagen, F., & Bergen, T. (2008). Mapping mentor teachers' roles in mentoring dialogues. *Educational Research Review, 3*(2), 168–186.

Hobson, A. J., Ashby, P., Malderez, A., & Tomlinson, P. D. (2009). Mentoring beginning teachers: What we know and what we don't. *Teaching and Teacher Education, 25*(1), 207–216.

Howe, E. R. (2006). Exemplary teacher induction: An international review. *Educational Philosophy and Theory, 38*(3), 287–297.

Jaipala, K. (2009). Re-envisioning mentorship: Pre-service teachers and associate teachers as co-learners. *Teaching Education, 20*(3), 257–276.

Johnson, S. M., & Kardos, S. M. (2004). Professional culture and the promise of colleagues. In S. M. Johnson, S. E. Birkeland, M. L. Donaldson, S. M. Kardos, E. Liu, & H. G. Peske (Eds.), *Finders and keepers: Helping new teachers survive and thrive in our schools* (pp. 139–166). San Francisco: Jossey-Bass.

Jones, M. (2009). Supporting the supporters of novice teachers: An analysis of mentors' needs from twelve European countries presented from an English perspective. *Research in Comparative and International Education, 4*(1), 4–21.

Jones, M., & Straker, K. (2006). What informs mentors' practice when working with trainees and newly qualified teachers? An investigation into mentors' professional knowledge base. *Journal of Education for Teaching, 32*(2), 165–184.

Kardos, S. M., & Johnson, S. M. (2010). New teachers' experiences of mentoring: The good, the bad, and the inequity. *Journal of Educational Change, 11*(1), 23–44.

Korthagen, F. A. (2010). The relationship between theory and practice in teacher education. In P. Peterson, E. Baker, & B. McGaw (Eds.), *International Encyclopedia of Education* (3rd ed., pp. 669–675). London: Elsevier.

Lai, K. C., & Grossman, D. (2008). Alternate routes in initial teacher education: A critical review of the research and policy implications for Hong Kong. *Journal of Education for Teaching, 34*(3), 261–276.

Ling, L. M. (2009). Induction: Making the leap. *Research in Comparative and International Education, 4*(1), 87–96.

Lo, M. L. (2004). Mentoring and teachers' professional development. Keynote speech presented at the Conference on the Development of Mentoring in Schools, The Hong Kong Institute of Education, Hong Kong, June.

Lock, R., Soares, A., & Foster, J. (2009). Mentors' written lesson appraisals: The impact of different mentoring regimes on the content of written lesson appraisals and the match with pre-service teachers' perceptions of content. *Journal of Education for Teaching, 35*(2), 133–143.

Norman, P. J., & Feiman-Nemser, S. (2005). Mind activity in teaching and mentoring. *Teaching and Teacher Education, 21*(6), 679–697.

Orland-Barak, L. (2002). What's in a case? What mentors' cases reveal about the practice of mentoring. *Journal of Curriculum Studies, 34*(4), 451–468.

Orland-Barak, L., & Hasin, R. (2010). Exemplary mentors' perspectives towards mentoring across mentoring contexts: Lessons from collective case studies. *Teaching and Teacher Education, 26*(3), 427–437.

Orland-Barak, L., & Klein, S. (2005). The expressed and the realized: Mentors' representations of a mentoring conversation and its realization in practice. *Teaching and Teacher Education, 21*(4), 379–402.

Orland-Barak, L., & Yinon, H. (2005). Sometimes a novice and sometimes an expert: Mentors' professional expertise as revealed through their stories of critical incidents. *Oxford Review of Education, 31*(4), 557–578.

Parker-Katz, M., & Bay, M. (2008). Conceptualizing mentor knowledge: Learning from the insiders. *Teaching and Teacher Education, 24*(5), 1239–1269.

Piggot-Irvine, E., Aitken, H., Ritchie, J., Ferguson, P. B., & McGrath, F. (2009). Induction of newly qualified teachers in New Zealand. *Asia-Pacific Journal of Teacher Education, 37*(2), 175–198.

Putnam, R. T., & Borko, H. (1997). Teacher learning: Implications of new views of cognition. In B. J. Biddle, T. L. Good, & I. Goodson (Eds.), *International handbook of teachers and teaching* (pp. 1223–1296). Dordrecht: Kluwer.

Putnam, R. T., & Borko, H. (2000). What do new views of knowledge and thinking have to say about research on teacher learning? *Educational Researcher, 29*(1), 4–15.

Rishel, T. J. (2006). Rethinking the roles of mentor and mentee in the context of student suicide. *Mentoring & Tutoring: Partnership in Learning, 14*(2), 207–226.

Roberts, A. (2000). Mentoring revisited: A phenomenological reading of the literature. *Mentoring & Tutoring: Partnership in Learning, 8*(2), 145–170.

Roehrig, A. D., Bohn, C. M., Turner, J. E., & Pressley, M. (2008). Mentoring beginning primary teachers for exemplary teaching practices. *Teaching and Teacher Education, 24*(3), 684–702.

Shulman, L. S. (1987). Knowledge and teaching: Foundations of the new reform. *Harvard Educational Review, 57*(1), 1–22.

Sleeter, C. (2008). Equity, democracy, and neoliberal assaults on teacher education. *Teaching and Teacher Education, 24*(8), 1947–1957.

Sundli, L. (2007). Mentoring: A new mantra for education? *Teaching and Teacher Education, 23*(2), 201–214.

Tang, S. Y. F. (2008). Issues in field experience assessment in teacher education in a standards-based context. *Journal of Education for Teaching, 34*(1), 17–32.

Tang, S. Y. F., & Choi, P. L. (2005). Connecting theory and practice in mentor preparation: Mentoring for the improvement of teaching and learning. *Mentoring & Tutoring: Partnership in Learning, 13*(3), 383–401.

Tang, S. Y. F., & Chow, A. W. K. (2007). Communicating feedback in teaching practice supervision in a Learning-oriented Field Experience Assessment Framework. *Teaching and Teacher Education, 23*(7), 1066–1085.

Tomlinson, P. D., Hobson, A. J., & Malderez, A. (2010). Mentoring in teacher education. In P. Peterson, E. Baker, & B. McGaw (Eds.), *International encyclopedia of education* (pp. 749–756). London: Elsevier.

Wang, J., & Odell, S. J. (2002). Mentored learning to teach according to standards-based reform: A critical review. *Review of Educational Research, 72*(3), 481–546.

Wang, J., & Odell, S. J. (2007). An alternative conception of mentor–novice relationships: Learning to teach in reform-minded ways as a context. *Teaching and Teacher Education, 23*(4), 473–489.

Wang, J., Odell, S. J., & Schwille, S. A. (2008). Effects of teacher induction on beginning teachers' teaching: A critical review of the literature. *Journal of Teacher Education, 59*(2), 132–152.

Whitehead, J., & Fitzgerald, B. (2006). Professional learning through a generative approach to mentoring: Lessons from a training school partnership and their wider implications. *Journal of Education for Teaching, 32*(1), 37–52.

Yusko, B., & Feiman-Nemser, S. (2008). Embracing contraries: Combining assistance and assessment in new teacher induction. *Teachers College Record, 110*(5), 923–953.

Zeichner, K. (2010). Competition, economic rationalization, increased surveillance, and attacks on diversity: Neo-liberalism and the transformation of teacher education in the U.S. *Teaching and Teacher Education, 26*(8), 1544–1552.

32

Mentoring Teacher Inquiry: Lessons in Lesson Study

Susan Groundwater-Smith

INTRODUCTION

Coaching and mentoring are well known in the business literature as strategies for induction and the development of the capacities of those engaged in learning organisations. More recently, those working in school education have turned to these powerful processes as a means of supporting practitioners at various pivotal points in their careers, whether as newly appointed teachers or as experienced school leaders (CUREE, 2005). The focus has been most often upon individual growth and development; however, my intention is to discuss a somewhat different orientation, that of working with a team of practitioners within a context of teacher inquiry. The process could be seen as a blend between coaching for individual development and mentoring for the support of a learning community. Effectively, the process that will be discussed is one where support is given to individual teachers who may be uncertain about the procedures that they might employ when they inquire into teaching and learning in their classrooms, while at the same time assisting a team of teachers in uncovering ways in which they plan for learning; developing, evaluating and enhancing those plans and their delivery.

Thus in this chapter I shall discuss my facilitation of a participatory action research project focused upon lesson study. I shall argue that the role of facilitator is a form of professional research coaching and mentoring with myself, as the academic partner, functioning as a 'knowledgeable other' as outlined by Watanabe and Wang-Iverson (2002). Clearly the role can be satisfied by a number of people such as content coaches, peer coaches and staff development officers and the like. However, in this case, because the process had an emphasis upon inquiry such as designing interventions, collecting and interpreting a range of data and reflecting upon practice, it was conceived that the 'knowledgeable other' for the project should be an academic partner who has had wide experience of teacher research undertaken in practice-based settings such as schools.

Over the years a number of models designed to enhance teacher professional learning have been proposed. Kennedy (2005: 236–7) identified nine such models: training, award bearing, deficit, cascade, standards-based, coaching/mentoring, community of practice, action research and transformative. I shall argue that the project was, in effect, a hybrid of the latter four models in that it worked with a group of teachers who identified themselves as a community of practice, it was supported by an academic partner, it was developed as participatory action research that involves teachers in worthwhile educational change 'through discursively opening up their practice to rational scrutiny by those who have a stake in its outcomes' (Elliott, 2007: 46). Its purpose was to transform practice, moving it from a teacher-centred model to one that gave young people greater agency and autonomy.

Before discussing the project in question and an argument that it was an embodiment of coaching and mentored participatory and transformative action research, it is important to first make a more explicit connection between being the 'knowledgeable other' and the function of these roles as facilitation. As has been indicated, much of the literature concerned with coaching and mentoring, in relation to workplace learning, constructs the activity as individualistic and fulfilling a nurturing function drawing upon the coach/mentor's experience and wisdom as one who can lead by example and provide confidential and secure advice. I would prefer to articulate a more interventionist and critical role. I believed that as a project coach and mentor I was interested in a form of professional community building that liberated participating teachers from the private nature of their classroom practices and developed a generative means for engaging in professional dialogue. Following Warren Little (2002: 918) I desired that the conditions be created that would permit the development of a professional community that would enable learning to result from 'the ongoing encounters that teachers have one with another' in the context of participatory action research and in association with myself as research mentor.

Supporting professional learning through participatory action research is a complex business. As Hoban, Ewing, Herrington, Smith, Kervin and Anderson (2010) have indicated, there are myriad, intersecting factors that are important for sustaining such learning, namely: the school's workplace conditions, the inquiry processes themselves, and the content and focus of the inquiry. Thus, the coaching and mentoring role required a sound understanding of school cultures, across a number of settings, experience in working with practitioners under conditions that may be challenging and unsettling and familiarity with the processes of lesson study and the ways in which these might be captured, reflected and acted upon.

PARTICIPATORY ACTION RESEARCH AND LESSON STUDY

Many who write of participatory action research emphasise its transformative and emancipatory nature; the work is seen to require conditions that will allow for genuine dialogue and for social outcomes that are just and equitable. In essence, it is informed by social relations whose intent is to fulfil a desire for

> doing the moral good – The emphasis is on the enhancement of ethically authentic action and the development of situated knowledge rather than on the accumulation of general (generalisable) theoretical knowledge.
>
> Ponte and Smit, 2007: 3

Those concerned with undertaking action research are familiar with the spiral of observation, reflection, theory building, planning and executing a study, followed by re-observation, further reflection, and so on. Participatory action research (PAR) has in addition a number of other key features identified by Kemmis and McTaggart (2005) as being: a social practice, participatory, practical and collaborative, emancipatory, critical, reflexive and transformative.

The conjunction between PAR and lesson study is seen by Perez, Encarnacion and Servan (2010: 77) as a 'specific form of cooperative or participatory action research specially designed for in-service teacher education' on the grounds that it achieves both change and understanding. In order to make this clear it is important to see lesson study as learning study. Shifting the focus from teachers' actions and planning, important as that focus is, to student learning is challenging and difficult. Wang-Iverson (2002) sees lesson study as a means of making teacher professional collaboration concrete by focusing on specific goals that examine not just teachers at work, but students at work, through the learning that is going on.

In this way teaching can itself become professional learning when the activity is collegial and where the learning arises, principally from the students' engagement and behaviours (Lewis, Perry, Hurd and O'Connell, 2006). In their advocacy for the study of teaching and learning through the study of lessons Fernandez and Yoshida (2004) place their greatest emphasis upon the culture of collegiality that brings teachers together to deeply consider their practice in the context of the classroom and the diverse needs of their students. Similarly, Chokshi and Fernandez (2004) argue for sustained lesson study work as a vehicle for helping teachers build a shared body of professional knowledge.

In essence, lesson study can be characterised as ways of seeing; that is observing how learners respond to a teaching episode that has been prepared collaboratively by a group of teachers with the intention of developing, refining and improving the lesson in the light of such feedback. Just as action research requires participants to engage in cycles of inquiry so too does lesson study as a 'system for building and sharing practitioner knowledge' (Lewis, Perry and Friedkin, 2009: 142). It is a particularly powerful process when the concepts to be taught are problematic for the students and where there is much scope for misunderstanding. Thus the process is based upon the concept of teachers as researchers – where the classroom practitioners are engaged in systematic inquiry regarding what it is that take place during the teaching episode, which can be characterised as a natural experiment.

Rock and Wilson (2005) see these 'research lessons' as being:

- focused on specific teacher-generated problems, goals or vision of pedagogical practice;
- carefully planned, in collaboration;
- observed by other teachers;
- recorded for analysis and reflection; and
- discussed by lesson study group members. (2005: 78)

They argue that lesson study is based upon principles of learning through social interaction rather than as a result of individual experience; that knowledge is acquired as an adaptive experience; and that knowledge is the result of active mental processing by the individual in a social environment. Much of this takes place in the classroom as the lesson itself is progressing. In effect, the classroom can be conceived of as a learning laboratory for the students as they come into contact with new ideas, principles and practices.

It is clear from the literature that there is no *one* formula for lesson study. As Lewis, Perry and Murata (2004: 3–4) have noted: 'Japanese lesson study is an extremely variable practice that has evolved over a century in tens of thousands of Japanese sites.' However, there are some overarching procedures among them the close observation of students as they engage in learning. Thus lesson study becomes a potent vehicle for teachers to systematically explore learning, on the basis of evidence, with an intention of improving it. It is a process that is described by Lewis (2002) as 'developing the eyes to see children'.

For many secondary school teachers the close observation of learning has not been a matter that has been uppermost in their minds. They are bedevilled by the detail of a crowded curriculum, high stakes assessment, and limited opportunities to know their students well (Ballet, Kelchtermans and Loughran, 2006). As well, they may not be familiar with the participatory action research cycle and may have a somewhat limited view of what constitutes 'research', equating it with a more positivistic set of procedures. In the case upon which this chapter is based, having a facilitator who could both coach and mentor them through the complexities of lesson study was seen as essential to the development of the project.

My role, then, was fourfold and clearly involved both coaching and mentoring by:

- preparing a discussion paper arguing for lesson study as an investigation of pedagogy;
- developing strategies for the collection and interpretation of data;
- acting as a critical friend in lesson study discussions; and
- drafting a final report that would meet the requirements of the funding body; and assisting practitioners in writing papers for professional associations.

The preparation of the discussion paper provided a resource that would create the basis for a dialogue between myself and the participating teachers and clarify the nature of lesson study. Inquiry methods similarly fulfilled a coaching function, by drawing attention to the many creative ways in which information can be gathered, discussed and interpreted, as well as some of the pitfalls and dangers associated with issues of validity and generalisability. Different teachers in the project had different needs and experience and it was often the case that individuals required personalised assistance in understanding processes and procedures.

The latter two practices, being a critical friend and supporting publication and dissemination, moved towards mentoring as the practitioners were encouraged to have greater collective agency, to learn from their shared experience and find ways of making these available to others.

THE PROJECT – DEEDS NOT WORDS

The project, *Deeds not Words*, involved four schools based in Sydney, New South Wales, and ten experienced teachers who taught two rounds of lessons in semester 1, 2007. The schools involved were diverse in socio-economic terms, gender, secular or religious nature and location.

School A was a comprehensive co-educational, government secondary school with a selective component to cater for students with exceptional ability in sport and was located in Sydney's west.

School B was a faith-based co-educational independent school K-12 to be found in the eastern suburbs.

School C was a faith-based school providing an education for girls, K-12 in the inner west.

School D was a comprehensive girls government secondary school located in Sydney's western suburbs.

The project focused upon planning for learning; observing learning and interpreting learning.

Planning

In their planning the participating teachers operated in teams of three to four that represented the mix of schools and their familiarity with the subject matter in the areas of commerce, economics and business studies being taught across the senior years. In each case the team met and discussed the framework of the lesson to be taught. Planning was based upon the principles of constructivism. This meant that the emphasis in planning was upon designing for learning; that is, focusing upon what the students would do and why. There was a number of elements that had to be considered when designing for learning. These were: problem setting, context, resources, connecting, questioning and explaining, demonstrating learning, and reflection.

Each of these elements needed to be considered in developing an overall unit plan and subsequent lesson plans. They were briefly discussed as a series of questions that had been posed by myself as the action research mentor.

The problem setting

What was the problem that the teachers wished for their students to understand? How did it fit into the overall curriculum in the key learning area?

The context

What was the nature of the context in which the students are learning? The school, the class and the dynamics of the group?

Resources

Along with the teacher, the most significant resource in the classroom was seen to be located in the students themselves: what had been their experiences? How much did they already know? How could they best share their knowledge? How would they evaluate each other's knowledge and understanding? Teachers would also be concerned with the kinds of material resources that could be used to support learning, such as models, graphics, narratives and the like. What media would they employ? What would be the impact of such tools as electronic whiteboards, computers and video?

Connecting

How could the teachers take account of ways to elicit students' prior knowledge and experience and how would they build a bridge between what they already know and what they need to do to achieve the learning goal?

Questioning and explaining

What kind of guiding questions would they formulate to stimulate student thinking and to maintain active learning? How would they accommodate student questions and provide the kinds of explanations that would support learning development?

Demonstration of learning

What processes would they employ that would enable students to demonstrate what they had learned? To what extent did they wish the learning to be individual or group based? How would these demonstrations be authentically assessed?

Reflection

How would they provide opportunities for students to reflect on their learning? What they learned from their teachers? What they learned from their peers? What they learned about themselves and their capabilities?

Observing learning in progress

In most cases in the *Deeds Not Words* study there were two observers in the classroom. It was seen as important that they have a specific brief that would be negotiated between them and the teacher of the day. A number of steps needed to be taken:

- Who would be observed?
- What would be the focus?
- How would the data be collected?
- How would the data be interpreted?

Additionally, it was argued that the learners themselves should be reflecting upon their learning experience. As research mentor I believed it important to outline ways in which these steps could be undertaken.

Who would be observed?

Being able to closely observe all learners in a dynamic and busy classroom was seen as a difficult task. One way to overcome this would be to videotape lessons so that the episode may be returned to at a later point and collectively analysed. Another way to deal with the challenge would be to deliberately select a small number of learners on the basis of contrasts. One might take three learners: one of whom is notably quiet, one who tends to be noisy and highly visible, and one somewhere in the middle. Or one might contrast the learners in terms of the teacher's perception of their motivation and engagement with the subject, or their level of achievement in the subject.

Such observation was seen to require a delicacy and willingness to note even the most obscure of detail – fidgeting, gossiping, turning in the seat, body language and the like; in addition to obvious signs of engagement with the lesson. The greater the detail the more that the account could be used in a subsequent interview with the student, offering him or her a stimulus for recalling the lesson and its impact.

What would be the focus?

Of course the focus of the observations was seen to relate to who is being observed and the purpose of the given lesson. It may be that the focus would be upon turning points in the lesson – when did it become more or less engaging? When did teacher explanations appear to overcome a particular 'roadblock' to learning? When did the insight of a student assist in the development of the lesson? Also, the observer needed to be responsive to unintended moments in the lesson and their consequence – what happened when a student introduces a digression or has clearly lost their way and what was the impact upon other students?

How will the data be collected?

Again, the processes for collecting data would be determined by the overall purpose of the observations. It may be that the observer would maintain a running record, using a time frame that accounted for the introduction to the session, its presentation and its closure. The observer might have some pre-determined categories such as:

- affiliation and rapport with teacher (smiling, nodding, how was attention secured, etc.);
- attitude (engagement – procedural or substantive, indifference, disengagement and distraction);
- approach to problem solving (seeking assistance, independence);
- connection to prior learning;
- curiosity and creativity (dealing with the unexpected); and
- monitoring both formal and informal aspects of the classroom; and so on.

The observer(s) could consider taking digital photographs at agreed intervals and use these to create a timeline of the lesson's development that could be discussed with the target students and later with the class teacher.

Student interviews

It was suggested that a powerful way to supplement observations would be to interview target students, perhaps starting with a general question regarding how they saw themselves as learners in this particular key learning area, what they found to be challenging and puzzling and how they coped with the pacing and sequencing of learning before turning to the specific lesson under observation.

Student reflections

A simple process for gathering student reflections would be for all students in the particular class to complete a minute paper where they could note:

- What went well for you in this lesson?
- What were the main points that you learned during this lesson?
- What puzzled or confused you?
- What would you like to change about this lesson if it could be taught again?

If the participating teacher chose to use the minute paper it was seen as important that it be kept brief and that students had the opportunity to respond anonymously.

Interpreting the data

Teachers saw that as they went about interpreting the data their main purpose would be to identify the strengths and weaknesses of the lesson and the ways in which it could be improved for the next cycle of teaching; always remembering, of course, that they were attempting to look at the lesson through the lens of the learners' experiences. I encouraged them to consider ways of clustering questions together. For example:

- How effective was the initial orientation? How clear were expectations?
- To what extent was attention paid to what the learners brought to the lesson?

- How were learners motivated? How was praise handled?
- How well was the lesson paced? How were digressions handled? Was there information overload?
- How were roadblocks to learning cleared?
- Who seemed to benefit most? Who seemed to benefit least?
- Was learning tailored to individual student needs?
- How helpful were the resources? How accessible were the resources?
- What features of the physical environment supported or impeded learning?
- Were there any specific contextual constraints – are they likely to arise during the next cycle?

LEARNING FROM THE PROJECT

So what could be learned from this project from the perspective of participating teachers and myself as the coach and mentor? Here I wished to address the following questions: Can an approach such as lesson study support collegial professional learning? What support is required to observe and analyse student learning *in situ*? Can a lesson study approach be seen as an opportunity for action learning?

Can an approach such as lesson study support collegial professional learning?

In spite of the logistical difficulties there was a strongly held view among the participants in this project that the processes opened up the classroom doors. The planning, observing and professional conversation following given lessons formed a powerful process of experiential learning. Teachers found themselves in discussions that were related, among other things, to matters of:

- precision and accuracy (how well have we defined the questions that we want the students to pursue?)
- connectedness (how do we use examples from our own and our students' lives such that the content is relevant for them?)
- metacognition (how will we familiarise our students with complex terms and their application?)
- managing impulsivity (how do we acknowledge a student's contribution, but create conditions whereby they are more reflective in providing answers?)

All of these matters and more besides were the basis of discussion and debate.

What support is required to observe and analyse student learning in situ?

This project drew attention to the difficulties experienced in closely observing student learning. The pressures that senior teachers face in meeting school requirements for results in a competitive educational market place meant that teachers have to closely attend to what is a demanding and crowded syllabus in economics, business and commerce classrooms. Nonetheless, the structure of the project allowed for several teachers to be present in the classroom at any one time. They brought to the practice different perspectives and teaching histories. They were able to make more problematic what was familiar to the regular class teacher who was not able to be too comfortable in his or her own 'home'.

Can a lesson study approach be seen as an opportunity for action learning?

In the context of the lesson study project, action learning is the approach that links the world of professional learning with the world of classroom action through reflective and dynamic processes across collegial groups.

In their investigation of the sustainability of professional learning through school based inquiry, Hoban et al. (2010) cited five conditions that can support action learning, these being:

- drawing on local resources and capacities;
- recognising the knowledge and wisdom of teachers;
- demonstrating that teachers are creative and knowledgeable about their environment;
- ensuring that all members of the inquiry team are part of the decision making process; and
- using academic team members (in this case the research mentor) who act as catalysts and who assist the school inquiry team(s) in asking key questions.

It is clear from the data that had been collected that each of these elements were present in the lesson study project. Additionally, the adoption of lesson study itself, as a vehicle, provided a framework for the investigation that gave it force and direction.

In spite of a number of challenges and difficulties and the short time that was available for the project it can be argued that it not only contributed significantly to the discussion regarding learning and teaching in the designated curriculum area and the performance of experienced teachers but also to the notions of coaching and mentored action learning in general and lesson study in particular.

CONCLUSION

Participatory action research is well recognised as a means for developing teacher professional learning. Its claim to professional knowledge building has been widely argued (Groundwater-Smith and Mockler, 2009). Less well theorised or understood is the manner in which an academic partner may function as a facilitator, coaching and mentoring practitioners in the field. Thus in Rosendahl and Ronnerman's (2006) study we find that there are very different expectations of facilitation arising from the cultural mores of the academics and the school-based practitioners; they argued that the former are looking to support careful and considered reflection, the latter for new ideas and techniques. Working within a collaborative framework itself can be seen to produce many dilemmas in relation to power and authority and the expectations and rewards that go with occupying different roles. Goldstein (2000: 523) in her revealing discussion regarding her project to work collaboratively with an early career classroom teacher observed: 'Any collaboration can be difficult. And when university researchers enter classrooms, some problems are bound to arise because of the issues of power and status inherent in these relations.'

However, I believe that such expectations can be transcended where there is a genuine coaching and mentoring orientation based upon trust and reciprocity, and where the moral intention is to improve teaching and learning practices for the consequential stakeholders, that is to say the young people in our schools. We are not wrestling for control or for status; instead we seek to work together as colleagues who hold each other in mutual regard. Coaching and mentoring the *Deeds Not Words* project certainly meant that I, as academic partner, was well positioned to facilitate the actual inquiry; but equally, I was a learner watching these dedicated teachers and their students struggle with concepts and ideas in ways that gave them agency and power. The opportunities were there for us all to grow and flourish.

REFERENCES

Ballet, K., Kelchtermans, G., & Loughran, J. (2006). Beyond intensification towards a scholarship of practice: analyzing changes in teachers' work lives. *Teachers and Teaching: Theory and Practice*, *12*(2), 209–229.

Chokshi, S., & Fernandez, C. (2004). Challenges to importing Japanese Lesson Study: concerns, misconceptions and nuances. *Phi Delta Kappan*, *85*(7), 520 525.

CUREE (2005). *Mentoring and Coaching CPD Capacity Building*. London: DfES.

Elliott, J. (2007). Reinstating social hope through participatory action research. In M. Todhunter (Ed.) *Action Research and Education in Contexts of Poverty: A Tribute to the Life and Work of Professor Orlando Fals Borda* (pp. 33–48). Bogota DC: Universidad de La Salle.

Fernandez, C., & Yoshida, M. (2004). *Lesson Study: A Japanese Approach to Improving Mathematics Teaching and Learning*. Mahwah NJ: Lawrence Erlbaum.

Goldstein, L. (2000). Ethical dilemmas in designing collaborative research: Lessons learned the hard way. *Qualitative Studies in Education*, *13*(5), 517–530.

Groundwater-Smith, S., & Mockler, N. (2009). *Teacher Professional Learning in an Age of Compliance: Mind the gap*. Rotterdam: Springer.

Hoban, G., Ewing, R., Herrington, T., Smith, D., Kervin, L., & Anderson, J. (2010). Evaluative inquiry into sustainability of professional learning through school based action learning. In A. Campbell & S. Groundwater-Smith (Eds.) *Action Research in Education: Volume Three* (pp. 103–120). London: Sage Publications.

Kemmis, S., & McTaggart, R. (2005). Participatory action research: Communicative action and the public sphere. In N. K. Denzin & Y. S. Lincoln (Eds.) *The Sage Handbook of Qualitative Research* (3rd ed.; pp. 559–603). Thousand Oaks: Sage Publications.

Kennedy, A. (2005). Models of continuing professional development: a framework for analysis. *Journal of In-service Education*, *32*(2), 235–250.

Lewis, C. (2002). *Lesson Study: A Handbook of Teacher-led Instructional Change*. Philadelphia: Research for Better Schools.

Lewis, C., Perry, R., & Friedken, S. (2009). Lesson study as action research. In S. Noffke & B. Somekh (Eds.) *The Sage Handbook of Educational Research* (pp. 142–154). London: Sage Publications.

Lewis, C., Perry, R., & Murata, A. (2004). What constitutes evidence of teachers' learning from lesson study. Paper presented to the Annual Conference of the American Educational Research Association (AERA), San Diego, April 16th.

Lewis, C., Perry, R., Hurd, J., & O'Connell, M. (2006). Lesson study comes of age in North America. *Phi Delta Kappan*, *88* (4) 273–281.

Perez, A., Encarnacion, S., & Servan, M. (2010). Participatory action research and the reconstruction of teachers' practical thinking: lesson studies and core reflection. *Educational Action Research*, *18*(1), 73–87.

Ponte, P., & Smit, B. (2007). Introduction: Doing research and being researched. In P. Ponte & B. Smit (Eds.) *The Quality of Practitioner Research* (pp. 1–8). Rotterdam: Sense Publishers.

Rock, T., & Wilson, C. (2005). Improving teaching through Lesson Study. *Teacher Education Quarterly*, *32*(1), 77–92.

Rosendahl, B., & Ronnerman, K. (2006). Facilitating school improvement. *Professional Development in Education*, *32*(4), 497–509.

Wang-Iverson, P. (2002). Why Lesson Study? Paper presented at the Lesson Study Conference. Chicago: November, 20–22.

Warren Little, J. (2002). Locating learning in teachers' communities of practice. *Teaching and Teacher Education*, *18*, 917–946.

Watanabe, T., & Wang-Iverson, P. (2002). The role of knowledgeable others. Paper presented at the Lesson Study Conference.

33

Research Mentoring in Higher Education

Jean Rath

INTRODUCTION

This chapter focuses on the need to develop research mentoring for academics within a framework of pursuing holistic understandings of academic practice that are informed by debates about the nature of authentic professional learning. Academic practice is generally understood to encompass inquiry (research in all its guises), teaching, and citizenship or service. This may be viewed across time (thus bringing in more personal issues about career and identity), and seen as occurring in the nested contextual spaces of the departmental context within an institutional context that is situated within the societal/supra-societal context (McAlpine and Norton, 2006). The disciplinary context both sits within and links between these nested elements. These overlapping contexts are dynamic; inter-acting to produce complementary and conflicting requirements, motivations and processes. Indeed, those committed to research mentoring in higher education (HE) are aware that within academic communities there are considerable pressures to privilege research skills. The majority of studies (e.g., Evans and Cokley, 2008) and academic career handbooks (see, e.g., in the US, Gray and Drew (2008) and in the UK, Grant and Sherrington (2006)) emphasize success in research and building a strong research profile as key objectives for an early career academic. Jawitz (2009) provides insights into the ways in which different disciplinary traditions incorporate research as key with their configurations of communities of practice. The study revealed complex ways to participate within configurations of teaching, professional and research communities, with Jawitz arguing that evidence of multiple identity trajectories indicates the key role played by individual agency within departmental and disciplinary cultures. Whilst Toews and Yazedjian (2007: 113) express the issue in more performative terms:

> The three-ring circus of academia is made up of research, teaching, and service. Research is similar to the high-wire acts and acrobats. It is a necessary 'act'. It is what draws many people to the circus and amazes them. Similarly, research is what brings prestige to the university.

This favoring of research often makes sense within the context of national research funding policies; however, it does not always sit comfortably with collegial relationships and can lead to unnecessary schisms between the practices of research, teaching and service (Robertson and Bond, 2001). As Clegg (2008) expresses it, academic identity becomes a 'vexed question', focused on the lived experience of exercising complex agency in a workplace that constantly applies pressures of performativity. These rapidly evolving workplace pressures expand research mentoring beyond the production of individually competent research practitioners.

There are strong traditions within the HE sector of early career academics recognizing, and drawing upon, the strengths and abilities of the senior professoriate. Conventionally, research mentorship has been perceived as a process through which novice researchers are acculturated into the norms of their disciplinary and institutional setting, and acquire the research skills and behaviors to develop into independent researchers. However, overall literature relating to the study of mentoring in HE contexts lags behind that related to school-based contexts. Teacher supervision, instructional leadership as well as mentoring pre-service and in-service teachers and working with pupils dominate the literature. Even within the HE sector most literature has focused on students, both undergraduate and graduate, with relatively little attention paid to the needs of academic staff. Although Johnson's (2006) book explores a variety of HE mentoring relationships, there remains a need to cover more comprehensively than present the range of requirements associated with research and researcher development. These include, amongst others:

- the diverse needs of early career academics;
- research capacity and capability building within a range of contexts, most notably within those disciplinary areas that have only recently migrated to the HE sector;
- reinvigorating mid-career researchers; and
- correcting historical imbalances regarding gender and ethnicity.

In addition, of the literature that does attend to this group there is sparse attention paid to the specific needs of research and researchers within the context of holistic academic practice. And it should be noted that self-selection bias is particularly significant in this area, as those with a strong aptitude and achievement orientation (aspects associated with mentee[1] success) are more likely to volunteer for non-mandatory research mentoring programs.

Although much mentoring in HE mimics approaches in the business sector, there are significant differences between the two contexts. Rix and Gold (2000) assert that academics have different goals and assumptions to those in business. Academic work has a different rhythm of production, the conceptualization of research products is always provisional and the HE sector is more skilled at maintaining internal control systems that resist the impact of broader societal shocks. Furthermore, researchers often identify with their disciplinary networks rather than with their university. As Quinlan (1999) suggests, this means that many important career relationships are formed with people who are not part of the daily work environment. Academics conduct research based in institutions, yet they build careers firmly within the context of their disciplinary area, where they are supported by national and international networks. Ramaswami and Dreher (2010) note a mentee may accrue the benefits of mentoring, whilst a detrimental outcome may be suffered by the organization. A clear example of this is when an employee uses a mentoring program to enhance their marketable workplace skills and thereby acquire the ability to leave the organization. Thus, within HE it is possible that mentoring may result in gains for the individual, or indeed the discipline, with little or no benefit to the employing institution. Additionally, as a senior researcher's loyalty may be primarily to the discipline it is possible that, when the two are in conflict, mentors may select mentees in order to enhance their field of study, rather than to support the institution. Such dynamics may contribute toward an apparent institutional ambivalence to supporting mentoring initiatives (Johnson, 2006, outlines many of the – outwardly, easily solvable – obstacles that institutions fail to tackle), such that many mentoring schemes in the US are funded by external bodies and even schemes reported in the literature as 'successful' seem unlikely to be sustainable in the medium to long term. This is evidenced by Zellers, Howard and Barcic's (2008) finding that many programs cited in the literature as successful are no longer in operation. Moreover, theory-informed practices tend to be rare, which results in a lack of clarity regarding terminology and practices. Mullen (2009: 12) notes that '*mentoring* is not only commonly used interchangeably with *advising* and *supervising* but also with *coaching, assisting, guiding, leading, teaching, learning, readiness, compensation, support,* and *socialization*'. Whilst it may be right to link these practices (as Mullen reminds us, mentoring is a multi-faceted set of activities), to do so with no regard to underlying understanding misses the opportunity to address the nuances of learning dynamics in relation to individual, institutional and disciplinary development.

THE HE ENVIRONMENT AND THE NEED FOR RESEARCH MENTORING

In recent years the HE sector has been driven by a range of rapidly evolving policies and practices that have been international in scope. For example, increasing internationalization and globalization of both staff and students (e.g., Teichler, 2004); burgeoning population of research-only staff with particular professional development needs (e.g., McAlpine, 2010); rapid growth of the HE sector including the escalating number, widening scope and increasing competitiveness of universities in a widening range of countries (e.g., Jones, Bailey and Lyytikäinen, 2007; Universities UK, 2007); the adoption of a range of quality assurance measures for both research and teaching (see Billing, 2004, for an international comparison); and alterations in national and international research funding regimes (e.g., Liefner, 2003). Furthermore, initiatives such as such as the UK's Researcher Development Statement (Vitae, 2010) have highlighted the complex knowledge, behaviors and attributes of effective researchers. Whilst national initiatives and mentoring consortia, often initiated at a disciplinary level, have come into existence in response to the rapidly changing HE context (see Girves, Zepeda and Gwathmey, 2005) this is not the focus of the chapter. Rather, the intention is to provide insights into the ways in which institutions and departments respond to the wider issues they face.

One prime instance of the way in which national and international policies have shaped the HE mentoring landscape has been the emergence in many countries of government funding policies based on research quality assessment. Institutions have been pressured to adopt research development strategies that focus on rewarding individuals who are successful at securing external funding, producing acceptable research outputs and generating measurable impacts. Such regimes improve accountability yet undermine the construction of authentic academic identities as performativity comes to the fore, undercutting nuanced longer-term research plans. Institutions devote considerable resources to compete in the research quality assessment arena, and the stress placed on individuals can be considerable (e.g., Sikes, 2006). One common response has been the adoption of *technical mentoring*, that is to say, 'a needs-based, short-term solution involving the transfer of know-how to apprentices within skills-building (advising and training) contexts' (Mullen, 2009: 15). Such approaches often rely on transmitting authoritative knowledge downwards within hierarchical organization systems, and may result in promoting managerial perspectives that reject holistic approaches to the development of academic practice. Roberts, Kavussanu and Sprague (2001) suggest that the internal and external pressures for institutions and researchers to demonstrate their research prowess may create research cultures that are antithetical to quality mentoring. They posit that departmental cultures controlled by highly driven, competitive academics focused on research productivity in the form of measurable outputs may have an adverse effect on mentoring and even on maintaining research ethics. Yet the promise of research mentoring is to facilitate not just the production of outputs or the acquisition of technical skills and knowledge, but also to foster critical awareness of how and why personal, institutional, and indeed disciplinary, assumptions have come to constrain the way we perceive, understand, and conduct research. Such transformative learning is capable of challenging and changing 'structures of habitual expectation to make possible a more inclusive, discriminating, and integrating perspective' (Mezirow, 1991: 167). Indeed, the ability to make choices and take action based upon new understandings is an attribute of creative research (Byron, 2009).

Entangled with the pressures to adjust research cultures to generate measurable outputs and generate income are the ongoing issues of diversity and equality, which still cause concern across the HE sector from undergraduate recruitment to professorial appointments. Significant gender (e.g., Blattel-Mink, 2001) and racial (e.g., Tillman, 2001) inequalities persist. Given the association between research success and academic career success, targeted research mentoring may be one way in which institutions and disciplines can address these issues. Whilst the statistics regarding lack of women in senior posts are clear, the mechanisms of discrimination are not overt, with commentators noting that gendered outcomes are the inevitable result of 'business as usual' rather than requiring a conscious motive to exclude women (Roos and Gatta, 2009). Sponsored career development remains important for all disadvantaged groups. There is evidence that mentoring can provide women with greater access to the kinds of status networks that will assist their careers. However, women may face personal and career issues that are outside men's experience (e.g., career breaks, expectations regarding parenting or other caring commitments) and thus mentoring relationships with senior male researchers may fail to address all of a mentee's circumstances, so she may not reap the same benefits as a male mentee with an identical mentor (Quinlan, 1999). Similarly, although there is evidence that cross-race mentoring dyads can foster professional networks and increase personal and career success, there is still a desire on the part of most members of minority groups to be mentored by a member of the same group. The literature supports this preference as psychosocial support is demonstrably improved in same-race mentoring (Tillman, 2001). Unfortunately, the existing inequalities within institutions often mean that cross-race mentoring may be the only available option. Johnson-Bailey and Cervero's (2004) account of their mentoring relationship provides an insight into the intricacies of cross-cultural mentoring and the opportunities for the process to be a positive learning experience. They recommend enhancing the cultural competency of senior, white, male academics, to ensure that they are more able to mentor across cultural differences (including the ability to address sensitive racial issues). They emphasize that proactive mentors need to recognize that their job does not end with building a relationship with a single mentee, but rather the situation calls for them to support broader initiatives to foster the upward career mobility of all people of color.

MENTORING MODELS *IN THE HE WORKPLACE*

As already noted, mentoring has traditionally been an integral part of the development of academic staff within HE. This often takes the shape of formal or informal dyadic mentoring pairs wherein the mentor holds a more senior position within the institution than the mentee and is a recognized researcher within the disciplinary area. Although traditionally these relationships have focused on early career academics, the HE workplace continues to evolve at a rapid pace and to widen the pool of potential mentees. For instance, alongside the increasing casualisation of research and teaching positions there is a rise in career instability, and mentoring is more likely to be relevant to researchers across the entirety of their working lives. As Darwin (2000) remarks, in the contemporary workplace, career age rather than chronological age is often more important in forming mentoring relationships.

Despite these issues, it is commonplace in many universities for departments to adopt a relaxed approach that assumes informal mentoring pairs will form 'naturally' and spontaneously, and/or assume that a person with a formal supervisory role over the mentee will act as mentor. There is agreement in the mentoring literature that in most cases there is a conflict of interest in being both evaluative supervisor and mentor, and that this situation should be avoided if possible (Zellers, Howard and Barcic, 2008). However, evidence shows that mentees in informal relationships (be they spontaneous or arranged) feel better supported, particularly with regard to career advocacy and psychological support (Johnson, 2002). Research focused on workplace mentoring indicates that formal mentoring is generally less effective than informal mentoring, as the kind of sustained, involved relationships associated with informal relationships have the best outcomes for mentees (e.g., Ramaswami and Dreher, 2010). Although this might be moderated by the design of formal programs to render them more akin to informal relationships, in many HE departments even formal mentoring programs are not consciously designed for maximum impact. As Quinlan (1999) observes with regard to the US (although also common elsewhere) it is a frequent practice that new members of faculty are allocated a mentor within their department, where a *laissez-faire* culture may mean that such relationships are not structured or nurtured and so tend to wither rapidly. As Tillman (2001: 317) states, '[T]he assignment of a mentor, in and of itself, may not always determine the success of the mentoring relationship.' In addition, some researchers have found experienced staff to be resistant to the introduction of formal mentoring programs. For example, Okurame (2008) reporting on experiences in a Nigerian university notes that the majority of respondents in his research disapproved of the establishment of a formal mentoring program. Instead, they focused on the need to encourage a culture of informal mentoring, supported by other professional development initiatives such as leadership training, external programs and targeted development for novices who display 'exceptional ability'. Such opinions are in line with literature that emphasizes the need to accept mentoring as a cultural value rather than a segregated practice (Lindenberger and Zachary, 1999), and with the position adopted by many in the field that formal programs should not be viewed as substitutes for informal mentoring, as they may serve as entryways to influential informal networks.

Boyle and Boice's (1998) criticism of universities' *laissez-faire* attitude to mentoring early career academics was focused on acquiring competency in the area of teaching and learning; however, they still have important points to make about the role of systematic mentoring programs in the HE context. They note that the expectation that positive relationships will appear spontaneously with little intervention from academic developers or others is overoptimistic. They argue that the approach results in the majority of early career academics receiving no mentoring, with women and members of minority groups particularly disadvantaged as they are least likely to receive informal support. In many North American and European institutions *laissez-faire* tends to translate to white, male, early career academics receiving informal mentoring with other groupings excluded. As in other contexts mentors (often senior, white men) favor mentees who are most like themselves. Boyle and Boice are clear that structured, formal programs are more likely to include mentors and mentees who are usually excluded from mentoring processes, and that mentors are more likely to learn from each other, and thus expand and enhance their roles. They go on to recommend a three-phase model of systematic mentoring: First, adequate planning is recommended, including clarity regarding expectations and options for inter- and intra-departmental pairing and early recruitment of program participants. Second, to impose a tight structure of mentoring meetings, they suggest brief, weekly meetings of dyads and monthly group meetings of scheme members. They emphasize the need to provide incentives for pairs to meet and recommend regular follow-ups by scheme organizers as a good way to monitor pairs and identify any difficulties early in the relationship. Finally, they propose rigorous assessment techniques to collect ongoing data about participation and involvement, bonding within pairs and context data (which they base on participants' records of meetings). This data is then fed back to inform planning the next mentoring cycle.

Notwithstanding such work to improve the inclusivity and depth of dyadic mentoring, many researchers and staff developers have sought to put in place creative collaborations and group-learning contexts in order to supplement, encourage and, in some cases, replace the evolution of traditional dyadic mentoring arrangements. These approaches recognize the structural limitations of the dyadic, hierarchical model and that nowadays it is rarely feasible for one mentor to assist in the holistic development of a mentee across the full range of skills, knowledge and attributes necessary to build a modern research career. Models are too diverse to iterate in full here; however, they have included expanding dyads to form consultative panels of mentors and various forms of group 'mosaic' mentoring schemes. Mullen (2009) urges proactive use of mentoring mosaics in order to model professional expectations and to support the success of previously disadvantaged groups. Such approaches offer mentees the ability to link with multiple people to gain mentoring across a wide range of personal learning needs. These programs emphasize the importance of building dynamic, co-operative, collegial cultures. As a technique to enlarge research capability and capacity this may build on the already strong team culture in some, mostly science and engineering, disciplinary areas and may provide enhanced opportunities for group research projects. Together, such programs encourage mentoring to be seen 'more as a process than as an activity' (Mullen, Fish and Hutinger, 2010: 181) and thus may address the dissatisfaction with traditional approaches and even develop sufficient momentum to change institutional, disciplinary or departmental cultures.

Panel-based mentoring groups bring together several mentors who can then be approached by mentees for consultation on individual issues. Here mentees and mentors are usually encouraged to interact according to mentee-identified needs; wherein mentees are provided with mentors' professional profiles and are required to be proactive, identifying the mentor with the appropriate expertise and seeking support according to immediate needs. As Mullen (2010) notes, such groups may provide relief to traditional mentors who might be at risk of burnout. This may be particularly significant when mentors experience the additional burdens of being a member of a group underrepresented at that level of seniority (see Quinlan, 1999, regarding the pressures experienced by overcommitted senior academic women). Recently, Cook, Bahn and Menaker (2010) have presented an interesting innovation to this type of scheme, which they call 'speed mentoring'. Their US-based scheme for early career academics in a college of medicine provided junior faculty members with a biosketch of each mentor and asked them to prepare key questions to ask during an event modeled on speed dating. The event was held in a large room with one mentor per table; each mentee was given a rotation schedule and allocated ten minutes with each mentor. Such 'fun' approaches can do much to improve access to mentors, as mentees are given permission to approach senior members of staff (a daunting objective for some) and the formal nature of the interactions mean that women and members of minority groups have access to appropriate mentors. This is key to righting historical inequalities, as women and minority groups, in particular, often experience difficulties accessing influential members of their academic disciplines both within and beyond their departments (e.g., senior academics who sit on grant committees, selection committees, promotion committees and who are journal editors). Indeed, even when adopting traditional dyadic pairings there is evidence that women and minorities paired with white male mentors can gain access to networks that are not otherwise available to them (Dreher and Chargois, 1998).

Mentoring groups bring together mentees usually at a similar career level or with a shared objective. Sometimes they include a mentor or facilitator, other times they are self-facilitating. Mentoring groups often draw on the expertise of a mentor, yet also rely on group conversations to share peer experiences and expertise in order to foster collaboration and reduce social and intellectual isolation. Darwin and Palmer (2009) report the successful implementation of an academic staff mentoring circles program at the University of Adelaide, Australia. Although not focused solely on research, their study demonstrates both how original mentee expectations regarding benefits are met and the way in which expectations can shift during a scheme to redefine the relative importance of different components. Thus pre-mentoring the mentees identified key expectations to be career progression and skills acquisition, whereas post-mentoring they focused on the significance of enhancing work–life balance and building new relationships. Darwin and Palmer were unable to identify clear benefits regarding career and skills development, whereas there were tangible benefits in the areas of networking and psychosocial support; in particular, participants reported reduced feelings of isolation. This latter aspect appears to be crucial in the acculturation and retention of graduate students (Mullen, 2010) and new members of academic staff (Gravett and Petersen, 2007). Such facilitated mentor-led groups have also proved helpful with the acquisition of research writing skills leading to successful publication (Lee and Boud, 2003) and writing successful funding applications. In a further expansion of the group concept, Gravett and Petersen (2007), based in South Africa's rapidly evolving and increasingly diversified HE system, describe how mentoring groups may be formed to assist the development of both mentors and mentees. They noted that newcomers often needed to modify their expectations of academic communities and were uncertain about academic culture. They were also concerned that mentors needed to hone their skills if they are to meet the needs of an increasingly diverse population of early career academics. Gravett and Petersen put forward a tiered, dialogic mentoring model consisting of a mentor-only learning group, mentee-only group, a small group of mentees with a single mentor and a combined learning group of all mentors and mentees. They note that such a system both supports newcomers and creates opportunities for mentors to critically examine their own and their institution's existing practices. Like many authors they explore the needs of mentors as well as mentees. As Ramaswami and Dreher (2010) indicate, the benefits of mentoring may accrue to mentees, mentors and the employing organization. It is perhaps worth noting that mentors in HE, as in other contexts, report their own psychosocial and career benefits. The former focus primarily on a sense of personal satisfaction, the latter include a revitalized interest in her or his own academic practice through exposure to fresh ideas and new perspectives (Zellers, Howard and Barcic, 2008).

It can be argued that all schemes relying on the seniority of mentors ultimately rest on what Darwin (2000: 203) calls 'recycled power relationships'. That is to say, the mentors' primary role is to provide mentees with a preview of what it means to have power, thereby initiating a mentee into the inevitability of the existing power hierarchy and reasserting a mentor's higher status. Peer mentoring groups, where all participants are at the same level of seniority but have differing experience, can subvert this hierarchy by being entirely self-facilitated. Such groups encourage peers to interact around an area of shared interest drawing on the strengths and qualities of partners; participants act as co-mentors shifting between roles as mentors and mentees to develop dynamic flexible structures that facilitate individual growth and the development of team-oriented projects. Even if they function simply at the level of supportive community network, they provide participants with access to peer knowledge resources and collegial friendships. Furthermore, since such groups lack formal hierarchies they may be more likely than formal, structured programs to have the flexibility to expand their remit to cover the wider brief of holistic academic practice, in which mentees are able to combine their learning of teaching, research and service in ways that contribute to more rounded expectations in relation to day-to-day working life within HE. Such flexibility may be particularly important in the development of practice-based researchers who are seeking to combine their professional and academic selves to create a coherent academic practice and identity (e.g., Cohen, Morgan, DiLillo and Flores, 2003). An expanded version of such schemes suggests the evolution of 'distributed' mentoring schemes which incorporate people outside the institution or indeed beyond academe altogether (Chesler and Chesler, 2002).

Inevitably, institutions often adopt mixed models of these approaches to research mentoring, and integrate these with other professional development strategies. For example, Rath (2009) reports a successful mentored internal research grant program. It was designed to give impetus to the research of early career academics and, in particular, to provide experience in completing successful grant applications. The program's hybrid nature included an orientation workshop, a written application for internal funding, committee review of the proposal, allocation of a mentor to provide expert feedback to help develop grant-writing skills and, once the mentor was satisfied with the amended application, the grant of research funding. This research-focused scheme was run in parallel with a university-wide, formal, dyadic mentoring program designed for academics at any career stage and including the full scope of academic practice career skills (Harper and Sawicka, 2001). McAlpine (2010) describes and advocates a multiple approach to working with research staff. First, dyadic, inter-institutional academic mentoring programs in which mentees are matched with alumni mentors employed by other universities; second, discipline-focused group learning events (akin to mentoring circles) to bring together doctoral students, researchers, new and experienced lecturers from different universities, in order to discuss the changing nature of academic practice and what it means for them in the workplace; and third, appropriate events (e.g., tailored induction and orientation) to encourage their participation in professional development activities. Indeed, models that integrate such mixed approaches to mentoring and other professional development practices, when customized to the local context, are more likely to produce effective personal and professional learning. Guskey's (1994) procedural guidelines for implementing effective professional development (developed for teachers, yet broadly applicable) still apply: change is an individual and organization process; approach in an incremental fashion; use team-based approaches; include procedures for feedback on results; provide continued follow-up, support and pressure; and integrate programs.

RESEARCH MENTORING AND AUTHENTIC PROFESSIONAL LEARNING

Effective professional learning is increasingly acknowledged as a long-term process, which must have direct relevance to practice and is best achieved within a context that recognizes learners as active and responsible participants (Webster-Wright, 2009). Whilst to some commentators, it appears evident that mentoring relationships of any type are about learning, as Darwin (2000) points out, the language of mentoring remains dominated by popular psychology and human resource development. She positions the mentoring relationship between adult learner (mentee) and teacher (mentor) as clearly within the sphere of adult education. She identifies much mentoring literature as written by authors who have no knowledge of adult education and sees this as impoverishing the understanding and practice of mentoring. In parallel professional developers, including academic developers, are starting to focus more astutely on the ways in which the very notion of 'professional development' itself can hinder productive personal learning and growth, and to self-consciously deploy adult learning theory to inform their practice. Webster-Wright (2009) argues that there is a need to refashion the delivery and evaluation of professional development programs as support for authentic professional learning. This encourages HE institutions to focus on *learning* academic practice rather than *developing* individual members of staff. Mentoring programs can act to disrupt assumptions about approaches to professional development practice. In particular, mentoring can encourage us to look closely at the project of supporting successful researchers and creating sustainable research practices in ways that take into account *learning* rather than *development*.

In this context, it is perhaps unsurprising that there has been a surge of awareness of mentoring for research within the HE sector, with mentoring at the forefront of strategies to improve learning in the academic workplace. Research mentoring is a welcome step away from the 'training' model of development and toward a more flexible, immediate and community-building understanding of ongoing, situated learning. This foregrounds mentorship as a 'complex and creative art' (Mullen, 2009: 16), and suggests that functionalist approaches should not be allowed to reduce mentoring to become merely supervising, advising and training – all of which oversimplify complex development issues and confine relationships to obey (and help reify) existing inequalities. The danger is that more creative solutions, such as greater reciprocity, group approaches and networked solutions, are excluded. Thereafter, mentoring becomes a mechanism to reinforce existing institutional power structures, restrict understandings and practice of research and thereby exclude or discriminate against certain groups. For example, indigenous Maori research in New Zealand has suffered the double blow of insufficient recognition in the national research funding assessment regime (Roa, Beggs, Williams and Moller, 2009) and a lack of appreciation for the specific cultural needs of mentoring within a Maori knowledge paradigm (Hook, Waaka and Raumati, 2007). As Darwin (2000: 198) warns we need to be alert to the dangers associated with implicit assumptions about knowledge, power and learning within our mentoring practices and move beyond practices 'framed in a language of paternalism and dependency' which stem from 'a power-dependent, hierarchical relationship, aimed at maintaining the status quo'. Nonetheless, technical mentoring may be appropriate and productive in certain circumstances, particularly in research contexts where there is a need to consolidate specific skills; for example, use of complex scientific or medical equipment. However, we need to be cautious about its use, and ensure that mentors and mentees are aware of the need to engage critically and reflectively with the approach in ways that facilitate significant interpersonal communication and holistic growth of academic practice.

The HE environment is driven nationally and internationally by a range of rapidly evolving policies and practices. There are opportunities for institutions and departments to respond to these developments by supporting programs that contextualize mentoring in ways that assist authentic professional learning sympathetic to the unique nested circumstances in which research activity is one element of academic practice. As Mullen (2009: 12) emphasizes, mentoring is 'a holistic form of teaching and learning that embraces the professional, personal, psychosocial, and career facets of a [mentee's] development'. Mentoring is capable of generating multiple and flexible responses to the evolving needs of individuals, institutions, disciplines and the wider community. As such it is perhaps the best way to encourage research and researchers in HE to develop as part of a holistic academic practice, which recognizes the interwoven career trajectories of inquiry, teaching and service in ways that complement each other within a dynamic culture of collaboration.

NOTE

1 This chapter is consistent in its use of the word 'mentee' rather than 'protégé' or 'protégée', as it is taken to indicate a more hopeful account of the mentoring relationship with greater reciprocity and fewer associations with hierarchical power play (Zellers, Howard and Barcic, 2008).

REFERENCES

Billing, D. (2004). International comparisons and trends in external quality assurance of higher education: Commonality or diversity? *Higher Education, 47*(1), 113–137.

Blattel-Mink, B. (2001). From bottom to top in higher education: Women's experiences and visions in different parts of the world. *The International Journal of Sociology and Social Policy, 21*(1/2), 3–19.

Boyle, P., & Boice, B. (1998). Systematic mentoring for new faculty teachers and graduate teaching assistants. *Innovative Higher Education, 22*(3), 157–179.

Byron, K. (2009). *The Creative Researcher (Vitae Researcher Booklet)*. Cambridge: Careers Research and Advisory Centre (CRAC) Limited.

Chesler, N. C., & Chesler, M. A. (2002). Gender-informed mentoring strategies for women engineering scholars: On establishing a caring community. *Journal of Engineering Education, 91*, 49–55.

Clegg, S. (2008). Academic identities under threat? *British Educational Research Journal*, *34*(3), 329–345.

Cohen, L. M., Morgan, R. D., DiLillo, D., & Flores, L. Y. (2003). Why was my major professor so busy? Establishing an academic career while pursing applied work. *Professional Psychology Research and Practice*, *34*, 88–94.

Cook, D. A., Bahn, R. S., & Menaker, R. (2010). Speed mentoring: An innovative method to facilitate mentoring relationships. *Medical Teacher*, *32*(8), 692–694.

Darwin, A. (2000). Critical reflections on mentoring in work settings. *Adult Education Quarterly*, *50*(3), 197–211.

Darwin, A., & Palmer, E. (2009). Mentoring circles in higher education. *Higher Education Research & Development*, *28*(2), 125–136.

Dreher, G. F., & Chargois, J. A. (1998). Gender, mentoring experiences, and salary attainment among graduates of an historically black university. *Journal of Vocational Behavior*, *53*(3), 401–416.

Evans, G. L., & Cokley, K. O. (2008). African American women and the academy: Using career mentoring to increase research productivity. *Training and Education in Professional Psychology*, *2*(1), 50–57.

Girves, J. E., Zepeda, Y., & Gwathmey, J. K. (2005). Mentoring in a post-affirmative action world. *Journal of Social Issues*, *61*(3), 449–479.

Grant, W., & Sherrington, P. (2006). *Managing Your Academic Career (Universities into the 21st Century)*. Basingstoke: Palgrave Macmillan.

Gravett, S., & Petersen, N. (2007). 'You just try to find your own way': The experience of newcomers to academia. *International Journal of Lifelong Education*, *26*(2), 193–207.

Gray, P., & Drew, D. E. (2008). *What They Didn't Teach You in Graduate School: 199 Helpful Hints for Success in Your Academic Career*. Sterling, VA: Stylus.

Guskey, T. R. (1994). Results-oriented professional development: In search of the optimal mix of effective practices. *Journal of Staff Development*, *15*(4), 42–50.

Harper, J., & Sawicka, T. (2001). *Academic Mentoring: A Pilot Success at Victoria University of Wellington.* Higher Education in New Zealand, Occasional Paper Series, Paper No. 5: Syndicate of Educational Development Centres of New Zealand Universities. Available at: http://www.utdc.vuw.ac.nz/research/OccasionalPapers/MentoringReport.pdf

Hook, G. R., Waaka, T., & Raumati, L. P. (2007). Mentoring Maori within a Pakeha framework. *MAI Review*, *3*, Target Article 2. Available at: http://ojs.review.mai.ac.nz/index.php/MR/article/viewFile/70/84

Jawitz, J. (2009). Academic identities and communities of practice in a professional discipline. *Teaching in Higher Education*, *14*(3), 241–251.

Johnson, W. B. (2002). The intentional mentor: strategies and guidelines for the practice of mentoring. *Professional Psychology: Research and Practice*, *33*(1), 88–96.

Johnson, W. B. (2006). *On being a mentor: A guide for higher education faculty*. Mahwah, NJ: Erlbaum.

Johnson-Bailey, J., & Cervero, R. M. (2004). Mentoring in black and white: the intricacies of cross-cultural mentoring. *Mentoring & Tutoring: Partnership in Learning*, *12*(1), 7–21.

Jones, N., Bailey, M., & Lyytikäinen, M. (2007). *Research Capacity Strengthening in Africa. Trends, Gaps and Opportunities: A Scoping Study Commissioned by DFID on behalf of IFORD*. London: Overseas Development Institute.

Lee, A., & Boud, D. (2003). Writing Groups, Change and Academic Identity: Research development as local practice. *Studies in Higher Education*, *28*(2), 187–200.

Liefner, I. (2003). Funding, resource allocation, and performance in higher education systems. *Higher Education*, *46*, 469–489.

Lindenberger, J. G., & Zachary, L. J. (1999). Play '20 questions' to develop a successful mentoring program. *Training & Development*, *53*(2), 12–14.

McAlpine, L. (2010). Fixed-term researchers in the social sciences: passionate investment, yet marginalizing experiences. *International Journal for Academic Development*, *15*(3), 229–240.

McAlpine, L., & Norton, J. (2006). Reframing our approach to doctoral programs: an integrative framework for action and research. *Higher Education Research & Development, 25*(1), 3–17.

Mezirow, J. (1991). *Transformative Dimensions of Adult Learning.* San Francisco, CA: Jossey-Bass.

Mullen, C. A. (2009). Re-imagining the human dimension of mentoring: a framework for research administration and the academy. *The Journal of Research Administration, XL*(1), 10–31.

Mullen, C. A. (2010). Naturally occurring student-faculty mentoring relationships: A literature review. In T. D. Allen & L. T. Eby (Eds.), *The Blackwell Handbook of mentoring: A multiple perspectives approach* (pp. 119–138). Oxford: Wiley-Blackwell.

Mullen, C. A., Fish, V. L., & Hutinger, J. L. (2010). Mentoring doctoral students through scholastic engagement: Adult learning principles in action. *Journal of Further and Higher Education, 34*(2), 179–197.

Okurame, D. E. (2008). Mentoring in the Nigerian academia: experiences and challenges. *International Journal of Evidence Based Coaching and Mentoring, 6*(2), 45–56.

Quinlan, K. M. (1999). Enhancing mentoring and networking of junior academic women: what, why, and how? *Journal of Higher Education Policy and Management, 21*(1), 31–42.

Ramaswami, A., & Dreher, G. F. (2010). The benefits associated with workplace mentoring relationships. In T. D. Allen & L. T. Eby (Eds.), *The Blackwell Handbook of mentoring: A multiple perspectives approach* (pp. 211–231). Oxford: Wiley-Blackwell.

Rath, J. (2009). A report of a New Zealand based funding initiative designed to improve a university's research culture. *The Journal of Research Administration, XL*(1), 88–98.

Rix, M., & Gold, J. (2000). 'With a little help from my academic friend': Mentoring change agents. *Mentoring & Tutoring: Partnership in Learning, 8*(1), 47–62.

Roa, T., Beggs, J. R., Williams, J., & Moller, H. (2009). New Zealand's Performance Based Research Funding (PBRF) model undermines Maori research. *Journal of the Royal Society of New Zealand, 39*(4), 233–238.

Roberts, G., Kavussanu, M., & Sprague, R. (2001). Mentoring and the impact of the research climate. *Science and Engineering Ethics, 7*(4), 525–537.

Robertson, J., & Bond, C. H. (2001). Experiences of the relation between teaching and research: What do academics value? *Higher Education Research & Development, 20*(1), 5–19.

Roos, P. A., & Gatta, M. L. (2009). Gender (in)equity in the academy: Subtle mechanisms and the production of inequality research in social stratification and mobility. *Research in Social Stratification and Mobility, 27*(3), 177–200.

Sikes, P. (2006). Working in a 'new' university: in the shadow of the Research Assessment Exercise? *Studies in Higher Education, 31*(5), 555–568.

Teichler, U. (2004). The changing debate on internationalisation of higher education. *Higher Education, 48*(1), 5–26.

Tillman, L. C. (2001). Mentoring African American faculty in predominantly white institutions. *Research in Higher Education, 42*(3), 295–325.

Toews, M. L., & Yazedjian, A. (2007). The three-ring circus of academia: How to become the ringmaster. *Innovative Higher Education, 32*, 113–122.

Universities UK (2007). *Talent Wars: The International Market for Academic Staff.* London: Universities UK.

Vitae. (2010). *Researcher Development Statement.* Cambridge: Careers Research and Advisory Centre (CRAC) Limited.

Webster-Wright, A. (2009). Reframing professional development through understanding authentic professional learning. *Review of Educational Research, 79*(2), 702–739.

Zellers, D. F., Howard, V. M., & Barcic, M. A. (2008). Faculty mentoring programs: reenvisioning rather than reinventing the wheel. *Review of Educational Research, 78*(3), 552–588.

Name Index

Subject Index